The Lives of Dalhousie University

VOLUME TWO

The Lives of Dalhousie University

VOLUME TWO, 1925–1980

The Old College Transformed

P.B. WAITE

P. B. Waite (signature)

McGILL-QUEEN'S UNIVERSITY PRESS

Montreal & Kingston • London • Buffalo

© The Governors of Dalhousie College and University 1998
ISBN 0-7735-1644-1
Legal deposit first quarter 1998
Bibliothèque nationale du Québec

Printed in Canada on acid-free paper

This book has been published with the help of a grant
from the Humanities and Social Sciences Federation of
Canada, using funds provided by the Social Sciences and
Humanities Research Council of Canada.

McGill-Queen's University Press acknowledges the support of
the Canada Council for the Arts for its publishing program.

Canadian Cataloguing in Publication Data

Waite, P.B. (Peter Busby), 1922-
  The lives of Dalhousie University
  Includes bibliographical references and index.
  Contents: v. 1. Lord Dalhousie's college – v. 2. 1925–1980,
  The old college transformed.
  ISBN 0-7735-1166-0 (v. 1)
  ISBN 0-7735-1644-1 (v. 2)
  1. Dalhousie University – History. I. Title.
  LE3.D32W34 1994   378.716'225   C94-900118-X

End papers: Aerial view of Dalhousie campus, 1967.
Dalhousie University Archives.

This book was typeset by Typo Litho Composition Inc.
in 11/13 Sabon.

Contents

List of Illustrations

Acknowledgments

The photographs in this book have been selected from a considerable collection in the Dalhousie University Archives. While some duplicate prints have surfaced, most of the photographs have been copied by Findlay Muir, of Dalhousie Audio-Visual Services, to whose skill and assiduity with some murky originals (the Tito one especially), I am most grateful. Karen Smith of Dalhousie Special Collections has made several thoughtful suggestions. Dr Donald Betts has lent two of the photographs, the rugby game and Hugh Bell's class in biology. Mrs Oriole Aitchison has lent the picture of J.H. Aitchison, and Mrs Nita Graham the picture of J.F. Graham.

Preface

Ten years ago W.A. MacKay, president of Dalhousie from 1980 to 1986, asked me to write its history. I thought it could be done in one volume and three years; it has taken two volumes and ten years, eleven by the time this book gets into print. Much of that time was needed for research; the Dalhousie Archives are comprehensive. Besides that, every so often a sudden and compelling richness of papers had to be exploited, and later would impose shifts in the balance of the narrative. Thus chapter 5 on the fall of President Carleton Stanley was made possible by the wealth of material in the Stanley Papers in the Dalhousie Archives; chapter 8 on C.D. Howe and Lady Dunn was enriched by correspondence in the C.D. Howe Papers in the National Archives in Ottawa.

This book is about lives, personal and institutional. There are many across this third half-century of Dalhousie's existence – students, professors, clerical staff, engineers, cleaners, deans, and presidents. One wishes there were more personal reminiscences. Many have had to be sought out. To do this systematically was never possible; the best one could do was to discuss Dalhousie lives and living with colleagues, students, widows, widowers, as opportunity served or necessity suggested. This becomes the more important in the period from 1960 to 1980 when Dalhousie's enrolment expands from two thousand to nine thousand students. There develops then a plethora of institutional evidence, and one has to make sure character and personalities do not become submerged.

Dalhousie had to have new buildings in those years, and for the first time it got massive help from the government of Nova Scotia. In those twenty years Dalhousie shifted habits, ideas, and philosophy, emerging by 1980 as a very different place. The "little college by the sea" of Archibald MacMechan's time, 1889 to 1931, had started to disappear by the end of the Second World War, though vestiges of it lingered on pleasantly into the 1950s. But the 1960s and 1970s brought a world of new dimensions and new challenges, and the old Dalhousie was finally transformed.

Thus the last four chapters, dealing with the presidency of Henry Hicks, soon become a horror of omissions. In one decade, 1960 to 1970, Dalhousie trebled its enrolment; by 1970 new problems, new buildings, new professors, new issues fill the campus. Thus what has been left out of this book could be as significant as what has been put in. Selection is a judgment call, always arbitrary; the historian can't include everything, he has to prevent his book from becoming an unreadable catalogue.

In this question of selection I have been greatly helped by advice from colleagues. There has been more than one delight in this long endeavour, but one has certainly been much support and comment, given graciously and without stint. Professor Murray Beck, professor emeritus of political science at Dalhousie, historian of Nova Scotia, who read all of volume 1 and all of this volume, chapter by chapter, offering encouraging comments but noting, in inexorable detail, aberrations of style, syntax, argument and errors of fact. He will know that I have taken up 95 per cent of his suggestions.

Dr Alan Wilson, Dalhousian, former professor of history at Acadia, Western Ontario, and Trent universities, was a searching critic, raising awkward questions based on his wealth of knowledge about Halifax, about Nova Scotia and the Atlantic provinces, to say nothing of his long experience of Trent. He has reviewed chapters 6 to 12. He was a student at Dalhousie in the later 1940s and knew its world far better than I. He has offered extended and critical comments on weaknesses of structure and faults of argument. I have listened, his advice made cogent by relevance.

Dr Guy MacLean, another Dalhousian, president emeritus of Mount Allison University, was at Dalhousie from the late 1940s to 1980 in ascending spheres of responsibility, from student to professor and eventually vice-president academic. That has given him a wealth of experience which he has brought to bear on the last five chapters of this book. Dr H.B.S. Cooke, dean of arts from 1963 to 1968, has read chapters 9 to 12 and offered valuable suggestions. So also D.H. McNeill, Dalhousie's business manager after 1948 and vice-president finance from 1969, who has saved me from making too much of a fool of myself with Dalhousie's finances. I have also been fortunate in persuading Dalhousie's architect, J.G. Sykes, to read the last four chapters about buildings in whose development he has played a conspicuous part.

Dr Rudolph Ozere has read and commented on all the sections that deal with the Faculty of Medicine. A former professor of pediatrics, he made suggestions about the men, women, and issues in Medicine that an historian, even one who knew medical professors from the small-campus days of the 1950s, would have hesitated to describe. In this state of ignorance, especially as medical events crowded up in the 1960s and 1970s, I am particularly grateful to my brother-in-law, Dr J.J. Sidorov, former professor of gastroenterology, for answering innumerable questions about the life and work of the faculty in which he played a significant role. In fact I have called upon numerous colleagues and friends for information and for critical readings of parts of this book. Their names I have set down in the notes, and they appear in the index. One of my most useful consultants was Professor A.J. Tingley of Mathematics, a historian of Dalhousie by avocation, who was Dalhousie registrar from 1973 to 1985, at the centre of a whole web of information.

William Allen White advised biographers, "First, kill the widow!" The widows whom I have consulted about their husband's careers were however both forbearing and forthcoming. But White's remark does point to a problem as history approaches the present. In a book ending in 1980 many of the men and women, and their children, are very much alive; the conscientious historian is caught between his duty to the truth as he sees it, and avoiding gratuitous offence to the living. Where there are doubts, one way out is suppression of hard truths; it is also a route one ought to avoid. The best answer to this dilemma is perhaps that of Philip Ziegler, one of the great contemporary British biographers; he wrote to Professor J.H. Aitchison (Political Science, Dalhousie) in 1986: "One will never get entirely right the balance between duty to the reader and respect for the privacy of others, but if at the end of the day one is satisfied that nothing has been left out which *had* to go in, and nothing put in just to shock and titillate, then I reckon one can sleep the sleep of the just." Despite that, it is harder than it looks.

This book may be a disappointment for scholars of university history, although they might enjoy it anyway. They may well object to lack of analysis of Dalhousie students, their family backgrounds, their later careers, why they came here and whither they went. I have been glad to use such studies, but have focused on narrative rather than analysis, trying to produce a readable life and times of Dalhousie.

The original manuscript was written by hand, then typed; eventually it was made over on the Department of History's word processor, first by Mary Wyman-LeBlanc, latterly by Dr Kathryn Brammall, a new Dalhousie PH.D., happily for the book between one fellowship and another. Both young women have been wonderful; Kathryn Brammall has coped brilliantly with the last five chapters and their revisions. Input from readers and author's second thoughts were trials she managed with deftness and aplomb. Mary Wyman-LeBlanc returned to work to encounter my not having used the McGill-Queen's house style; every date in every note had to be redone, a task she took on with singular good grace.

Diane Mew has edited the whole manuscript. Editing takes persistence, patience, perspicacity; besides that she is furnished with ranges of information from the Olduvai Gorge to Samarkand, from the Shetlands to the Falklands. She is a superb editor and I have accepted nearly all her suggestions.

Professor Denis Stairs of Political Science Department was vice-president academic from 1988 to 1993; through him this project has reported to Dalhousie's administration. It has been a happy arrangement that he has since continued his supervision, at once solicitous and enthusiastic.

Dr Charles Armour, Dalhousie University archivist, has put up with a presence haunting the back stretches of his domain on and off for the best part of a decade. He has dug out material selflessly and this book owes much to him and the institution he supervises. We have enjoyed swapping stories about Dalhousie's past and also about opera. There have been times, with parts of Dalhousie's history not always printable, when the one began to resemble the other!

My wife Masha has been arbiter of taste and form. I have relied on her discretion and good sense, needed the more as the narrative has come close to the present. There are many participants in this *Lives of Dalhousie* who still relish their own lives; I trust that this book is sufficiently frank to be interesting, honest enough to be challenging, and decent enough to hurt no one. Having set out that hope, it is time to get on with the story.

P.B.W.
Halifax, Nova Scotia
December 1996

The Old College Transformed

Introduction

Halifax in the 1920s. Dalhousie's résumé since 1818.

In July 1924 Professor Boris Petrovich Babkin and his wife were on a transatlantic liner en route from England to New York. A student and disciple of Pavlov's, Babkin was forty-seven years old and had been professor of physiology at the University of Odessa since 1915. During the upheavals after the Russian revolution he fled to England; but unable to find a suitable job, he was on his way to be an instructor in pharmacology at Washington University in St Louis, Missouri. It was the best he had been able to get. A steward came to him. "There is a cable for you, sir, in the wireless room." Babkin was astonished – who would cable him? It was from Dalhousie University, a place he had hardly heard of; would he come to Halifax to consider the professorship of physiology? After consulting in New York about where and what Dalhousie was, Babkin took the train through early August heat, surprised at the wooden buildings in Connecticut, Massachusetts, Maine, and thus not surprised at Canadian ones. At McAdam Junction, New Brunswick, the first stop in Canada, everyone got out for breakfast. It was cool and quiet; they were among spruce, pines, and birches that reminded him of Russia. When he got to Halifax that night, 7 August, the city was just concluding celebration of its 175th anniversary. The next morning the weather broke, rain streamed down, and Halifax's wooden buildings looked gloomy, even ugly. In the hotel lobby Babkin met President MacKenzie, "tall, dignified," who drove him to the president's office in the Macdonald Library. There they talked about the chair of physiology. Babkin liked MacKenzie at once; he liked still more the laboratory in the new Medical Sciences Building, where there would be five rooms and two assistants to go with them. This was followed by a Nova Scotian lunch at the Halifax Club: fish chowder (which he ate for the first time), fresh fish, and fresh blueberry pie. Asked if he knew that berry, he exclaimed, "Did I know blueberries!" He came from Novgorod in northwest

Russia; Babkins for the past four centuries had eaten blueberry pies! During a break in the afternoon he walked up to Barrington Street, came to St Paul's cemetery and found himself in front of the Crimean War monument. It was startling; his grandfather, Colonel Ivan Babkin, and his uncle, Lieutenant Alexander Babkin, had fought in the Crimean War on the Russian side. He had been brought up on memories of "perfidious Albion." These people's descendants now wanted him as professor. When President MacKenzie came to the hotel that evening to talk it over, Babkin's decision to come was already made.[1]

The Halifax of 1924 that Babkin saw was not a prepossessing city, though Dalhousie old timers such as Professor Archibald MacMechan liked its smallness, its intimacy, its closeness to woods and water, its golf and tennis. Halifax had only 58,000 people in the 1921 census and it showed. Outside of the Citadel and the parks, its public amenities were not extensive. For example, there was no decent public library, save for a cramped roomful of books tucked away in City Hall. There were still theatres with real stages and real actors, but as the 1920s went on they were slowly giving way to movie theatres that showed silent films. They came with sound after 1930. Halifax was still under prohibition rules, as was the rest of Nova Scotia, until 1930 when the creation of the Nova Scotia Liquor Commission allowed liquor stores in the few places that wanted them, of which Halifax was certainly the principal one.

Halifax was starting to resemble distantly the modern city; the changes that had started in the mid-nineteenth century were working their way through society, the way it lived, did its business, developed its institutions and its mores. It was only fifty years since an old lady in Antigonish, in 1878, fainted at her first sight of a railway train. In that time Halifax and Canada had been transformed industrially and commercially. In the process the old dominance of the learned professions, the church, law, and medicine, had given way to a much more diversified educated class. There were whole new ranges of professions, in business, engineering, public health, dentistry, pharmacy. Women dominated school teaching during most of that time; in 1901 78 per cent of Canada's school teachers were women and it was the same in 1931. In 1901 10 per cent of Canada's librarians were women; by 1931 it was 30 per cent. Women doubled their numbers as clerical workers from 21 per cent in 1901 to 45 per cent in 1931. They doubled their numbers as doctors, too, but that was only from 1 to 2 per cent, and slightly from 5.5 to 8.1 per cent as professors or school principals.[2]

Many of these new skills required secondary school, and not a few put an increasing emphasis upon a university degree. Professional employment was responding to a much more complex market economy. As the professions expanded their knowledge and techniques, so did the necessity of guaranteeing to the public that anyone who chose to carry the name doctor, dentist, lawyer, accountant, should be conversant with modern techniques. No one wanted their appendix removed by an unqualified horse doctor. What determined "qualified" was, increasingly, a university degree. Professional associations gradually developed criteria for evaluating even university degrees. Hence the delight at Dalhousie when in 1925 its MD was given an A1 rating by the American Medical Association, and when its Dental School was accredited in 1922. The professional associations watched the universities' training with close scrutiny. If the doctors, dentists, and engineers so accredited developed professional monopolies, that had the advantage of ensuring that certain standards had been attained. And new professions were gaining status. The creation of Dalhousie's W.A. Black Chair of Commerce marked that in 1921, although it took President MacKenzie seven years to find someone suitably qualified.[3]

Commerce permeated the pages of the Halifax papers and the *Dalhousie Gazette*. By 1920 comic strips had appeared in the populist Halifax *Herald*; "Bringing up Father" and "Mutt and Jeff" were early favourites; by 1929 even the more staid *Morning Chronicle* had a whole page of them, every day. Except Sunday, of course. Comic strips helped sell newspapers, and newspaper circulation helped sell advertising; with the cheap pulp paper readily available since the turn of the century, newspapers could increasingly exploit their double face, news and advertising; mayhem and murders on the one hand, make-up and manicure on the other. Advertisements extolling Bayer's Aspirin competed with tobacco offered in various forms, Old Chum, Macdonald's Cut Brier, at 80 cents a pound; Wilson's Bachelor cigars, "The National Smoke," at 10 cents. A new Nash car cost $2,150, a Maxwell coupe $1,415. Chevrolet (its logo the same as in 1997) boasted that its 1923 car had sixty-seven improvements over its 1922 model. A column in the *Chronicle* by "Trouble Shooter" offered advice on "When the Engine will not Start."

The changes in advertising were especially swift and dramatic between the end of the Great War and 1930. For example, in 1919 Listerine was soberly advertised as a safe antiseptic; by the early thirties, as advertised in the glossy magazines, its consistent use as a mouthwash could save young women from that awful fate, "Always a bridesmaid, but never a bride." In the Halifax *Chronicle* Aunt Madge consoled her niece, in tears over some social failure, delicately suggesting the transformation to be effected by the use of Lifebuoy soap.[4]

In the 1920s the *Chronicle* began to list the radio programs of the new and powerful American radio station WGY in Schenectady, New York. Halifax got its first radio station in May 1926 with CHNS, which operated out of the Lord Nelson Hotel. By the end of the 1920s radio was becoming almost a necessity to Halifax households, and it became a listening post to the suggestions of the world. Radio brought commercialism into the life of every family that owned one. Between 1924 and 1935 Canada produced one radio for every seven people in the country. Foster Hewitt brought the Saturday night hockey games of the Toronto Maple Leafs while carrying rather distantly tributes to the superior qualities of Imperial Oil; by the mid-thirties Jack Benny, the radio comic, was doing the same thing with Jell-o. Commerce thus permeated the very air; it was in the radio waves that caught every aerial, and steadily filled homes and their inhabitants with values they may not have wanted, desires they may never have heard of.

Nova Scotia and Halifax could escape only some of it. Nova Scotians being on a huge wharf in the Atlantic, as one might say, experienced these influences slowed and cooled, made less strident, by several hundred miles of forest or sea. That did not prevent local stations pumping out programs made in Toronto, New York, or Hollywood, but it helped Nova Scotians to weigh, and resist, the febrile fashions that emanated from the world outside. Thus they had benefits from their isolation and their distances. But there were disadvantages of which many Nova Scotians were not fully aware; they were apt to underestimate their cultural and intellectual isolation. Neither radio nor newspapers could quite overcome that. It was felt particularly by professors; they knew something of the world at large and fought to keep in touch with it. John Willis, then a young professor out of Oxford and Harvard at Dalhousie Law School, wrote about it years later: "No one [now] ... has any idea how isolated the teacher at Dalhousie was and felt he was – thirty hours at least by train, and with no money to get on the train ... from his colleagues in the rest of Canada."[5]

Plane travel was still very much an exciting novelty. Charles Lindbergh crossed the Atlantic in 1927 in his single-engine "Spirit of St. Louis," but that was a feat of great daring. Commercial plane travel in Canada was still a decade away. Halifax City did take over in 1930 a stretch of fields north of Chebucto Road, between Mumford Road and Connaught Avenue, as Halifax's airport, and laid down two short runways, but they were useful only for light planes. Anything bigger than a Tiger Moth was apt to have trouble.

Transport on the ground was by trains, trams, horses, and increasingly by cars. Jim Bennet ('53) writes of the 1930s:

> … When patient, plodding horses hauled the bread and milk and ice
> And postmen came six days a week, not once a day, but twice.
> When Boutilier's little ferry boat across the Arm would ply
> By oar in February and by motor in July …
> When Adams Transport lowbed wagons rumbled through the streets
> And honeymoons and hardhats were the penny-candy treats.
> The Black Ball on the Citadel told harbour ships the time,
> And kids could see Gene Autry at the Empire for a dime.
> Those tinker-toys of tramcars round the Belt Line used to buzz
> Past Hec MacLeod – the smartest traffic cop there ever was;
> When boys in capes and gaiters biked the telegrams around
> And Sis took in the tea-dance to the Gerry Naugler sound.
> The railway locomotives and road-rollers ran by steam
> And so did half the laundries in the city, it would seem …[6]

Jim Bennet grew up on South Street, just across from Dalhousie. His father, C.L. Bennet, a New Zealand veteran of the First World War, had come in the 1920s to help Professor Archibald MacMechan with the work of English 1. That Dalhousie of the 1920s was already a century old more or less. It had a strange history, told in volume 1, but a brief retrospect is offered here as background.

Lord Dalhousie's College, 1818–1925: A Résumé

George Ramsay, the ninth earl of Dalhousie (1770–1838) was born near Edinburgh, attending its high school and university. But when his father died in 1787, he abruptly took up a military career. After the Battle of Waterloo and peace in Europe in 1815, he looked for a colonial position and in 1816 received the lieutenant-governorship of Nova Scotia. He and his wife and youngest son came out on a British navy frigate that brought them into Halifax harbour on 24 October 1816.

Halifax with its substantial army garrisons and naval base was rough and boisterous. Alexander Croke, vice-admiralty judge, from his estate at Studley above the North-West Arm, noted that military and upper-class parties were anything but decorous;

> Great Harlots into honest Women made,
> And some who still profess that thriving Trade …

There was one college for the whole province, King's, founded in 1789 at Windsor, there out of reach of Halifax's wickedness. King's

College was however for Anglicans; students on graduation had to subscribe to the Thirty-Nine Articles of the Church of England. King's in 1817 had only fourteen students, not a high proportion of the estimated sixteen thousand Anglicans who were 20 per cent of Nova Scotia's population of eighty thousand.

Lord Dalhousie learned from his predecessor, Sir John Sherbrooke, that in the imperial treasury in Halifax there was a fund of some £11,596 (Halifax currency) called the Castine Fund.[7] It had been acquired by the British army during the occupation of eastern Maine in the War of 1812 from customs duties at Castine. What to do with that £12,000? Nova Scotia had no standing debt to pay off. Lord Dalhousie's Council had several suggestions: road and bridges, an almshouse, the Shubenacadie Canal. R.J. Uniacke, the attorney general, mentioned a college. Lord Dalhousie decided that a non-denominational college in Halifax, open to all comers in the way Edinburgh University was, would be much the best use of the money. His Council approved, and early in 1818 so did Lord Bathurst, the colonial secretary. So the Dalhousie building was started, right in the middle of Halifax, on the Grand Parade where City Hall now is. On 22 May 1820 Lord Dalhousie laid the cornerstone. Then almost at once he left for Quebec to take up his new position as governor general of British North America.

The difficulties now started. Lord Dalhousie's enthusiasm and foresight was shared by very few others; his Council, despite their initial approval, were sceptical and the Legislative Assembly almost recalcitrant. The truth was that in an age of strong religious attachments and rivalries, a non-denominational college seemed an idea altogether utopian. In London, England, unlike Edinburgh, there was no non-denominational college until 1828. The Dalhousie College building was finished in 1824, but it was a building without college life; there were no professors and no students. Instead the Dalhousie board rented out the premises to secular realities such as a brewery and a bakeshop.

Dalhousie College was brought into being in 1838 under Thomas McCulloch, its first president, but inept management by its board, outside rivalries, and the death of McCulloch in 1843, put Dalhousie into twenty years of limbo as a Halifax high school. In 1863, however, Joseph Howe and Charles Tupper, rivals in politics and so much else, cooperated to put Dalhousie College on its feet with a new charter and six professors. Dalhousie kept its non-denominational character in its board but the spirit and energy driving it was Presbyterian and Presbyterian passion for education. Dalhousie was given a tremendous lift in the 1880s by George Munro's endowment of several new chairs and by 1912 it had over four hundred students and three professional faculties, Law (1883), Medicine (1912), and Dentistry (1912). All were crowded within the brick building on Robie Street that had become by 1887 Dalhousie College. The city had taken over Dalhousie's space on the Grand Parade.

Mercifully, the Dalhousie Board of Governors of 1911 rose to the new challenges and bought the whole forty-three-acre block of the Studley campus. As the First World War came, the first new buildings began to appear, first the Science Building and then the Macdonald Memorial Library, both looking a little stiff and very isolated amid the stretches of grass, the willows along the creek, and the white pines that crowned the hill above the Arm. Space there was!

Dalhousie had a difficult time during the First World War; although the Halifax explosion of 6 December 1917 did some damage, the real loss was income from student fees, for Dalhousie's enrolment in two years of war shrank by 35 per cent, with shoals of its male students joining the Canadian army. By 1919 they were coming back and Dalhousie's enrolment in 1920–1 was double what it was in 1916–17.

Then came the university federation movement in 1921, so far-reaching and so involving Dalhousie and its campus that it seemed to absorb all its energies for the next three years. King's College, Windsor, had a devastating fire on 5 February 1920. There was talk of rebuilding in Windsor, talk of an appeal to the Carnegie Foundation of New York to fund it. That great philanthropic institution had been supporting aspects of Maritime college education for some years, but it now decided it needed an inquiry into the state of higher education in the Maritime provinces. K.C.M. Sills, president of Bowdoin College, Maine, and Dr W.S. Learned of the Foundation conducted it in October and November 1921, and their report was published in 1922. It was not very cheerful. Dalhousie generally got high marks, but not for its library; Acadia's was better. But all the colleges, Dalhousie included, were underfunded, undermanned, under-equipped, carrying on somehow with old staff sustained by old loyalties. The Nova Scotian colleges were the worst off, for they had no funding at all from the Nova Scotian government; that government had bailed out of it completely in 1881.

The solution that Learned and Sills recommended was federation of all the colleges, especially Nova Scotian ones, using Carnegie funds to move Acadia, King's, St Francis Xavier, Mount Allison to the Dalhousie campus. There they would become constituent colleges in a federated university. Dalhousie supported the idea, at least its board, president, scientists, and doctors did; they assumed that such a new federated university would at last be able to get the Nova Scotian government to fund badly needed laboratories and equipment; Dalhousie's Arts professors were much less happy with what to them seemed an expensive and wrenching experiment. Archibald MacMechan, professor of literature since 1889, grumbled that Dalhousie was being invited to commit hara-kiri all in the name of a dubious standard of higher education. He and some others thought Dalhousie would be better off by itself.[8]

In the end it came to that. After extensive negotiations through the last six months of 1922, the Acadia Board of Governors declared on 16 February 1923 that it did not want to enter such a federation. Acadia's withdrawal took the life out of the project. Mount Allison was doubtful. St Francis Xavier had been doubtful from the start. The only college that now had any interest was King's and that was because of necessity. Carnegie offered money for King's to rebuild provided it did so on the Dalhousie campus. That was agreed to between King's and Dalhousie on 1 September 1923. But by 1925 the rest of the university federation was virtually dead, and it would not be revived soon. Dalhousie would now go on with its own life, on its own campus, with King's College buildings going up on the northwest corner, the only reminder of the three years of work Dalhousie had put into university federation.

· I ·

Dalhousie in the 1920s

The Board of Governors in the 1920s. George Campbell, G.F. Pearson, and President MacKenzie. Murray Macneill, Dalhousie's registrar. The style and idiosyncrasies of Archibald MacMechan. Founding the *Dalhousie Review*. H.B. Atlee and Obstetrics. The Dental Faculty. Completing Shirreff Hall. The President's house. The Dalhousie Student Council and the *Gazette*.

The charter of Dalhousie University in the 1920s was still the act of 1863, with an 1881 addition to comprehend the new Law Faculty and another in 1912 to bring in the Halifax Medical College and the Maritime Dental College. The Board of Governors consisted of twenty-three gentlemen and one lady, the alumnae representative, Dr Eliza Ritchie. All were appointed by the lieutenant-governor-in-council (the provincial cabinet) on the nomination of the board. Close ties with the government made that process effortless. The board included George H. Murray (1861–1929), the premier since 1896. Most board members lived in or near Halifax; R.B. Bennett ('93) was one of the few not normally resident in Nova Scotia. He was MP in Calgary, leader of the opposition in the House of Commons after 1927 and from 1930 to 1935 the prime minister of Canada. W.S. Fielding, another important board member, was a Nova Scotian, former premier, but until 1925 mostly in Ottawa as Mackenzie King's minister of finance. The board of that time was powerful and vigorous, representing both sides of politics, federal and provincial, and with many ties, personal and business, to the life and work of downtown Halifax. The board can be described as conservative. It could hardly be otherwise. Dalhousie University was paid for by student fees and endowments, and the only source of endowment came from rich men and women within and outside the province. Scrounging money was the board's job and to some extent the president's. So far, certainly since 1908 when George S. Campbell became chairman, Dalhousie's board had made a fair fist of that.

Campbell was influential in persuading the Dalhousie board to take over the Halifax Medical College after the disaster of the Flexner Report. In 1909 Abraham Flexner, a classicist from Johns Hopkins, was commissioned by the Carnegie Foundation to survey 147 medical schools in the United States and the eight in Canada. Flexner savaged most of them, and nearly half the American ones were forced to close down. The Halifax Medical College, distantly affiliated with Dalhousie, was not too well thought of either. But there had to be a medical school east of Montreal and in 1910 Dalhousie stepped in and the result was the creation of Dalhousie's Medical Faculty in 1911. Campbell it was too who brought the board to buy the Studley estate early in 1911. Campbell had also done much to forge links between Dalhousie and the city. And his presence as such an active working chairman attracted others.[1]

The Dalhousie men who conceived and brought Studley into being liked and respected each other, especially the triumvirate of Campbell, G.F. Pearson, and President MacKenzie. Pearson took a Dalhousie LL.B. in 1900 and on the death of his father in 1912, succeeded him as the owner of the Halifax *Morning Chronicle*. As much as Campbell, Pearson brought Dalhousie into the Halifax business community. He used to stress the value of Dalhousie in plain business terms, likening it to a great enterprise with a capital of over $2 million, a plant estimated conservatively at $3 million, and contributing $1 million annually to the city's business. As president of the Alumni Society he galvanized that sleepy organization into life. When the new buildings were going up at Studley during and after the war, Pearson watched them almost stone by stone. He seemed more often at Studley than he was at his desk at the *Chronicle* building on Granville Street. Pearson's recognition of the desperate shortage of student accommodation in Halifax after the war brought the purchase of the Birchdale Hotel on the North-West Arm in June 1920.[2]

President Arthur Stanley MacKenzie (1865–1938) had been since 1911 the executive head of Dalhousie upon whose shoulders had fallen the weight of responsibility, correspondence, and supervision, together with the unending and thankless work for the federation movement. Much of the tone and character of the university, for good or ill, depended upon what sort of man the president was. Having been a widower since his wife's death in 1897 (after barely more than a year of marriage), himself bringing up their infant daughter, MacKenzie's life had a different centre to it than had other Dalhousie presidents. He never remarried, and there is not a scrap of evidence that he ever cared to. After he came as Munro professor of physics in 1905 MacKenzie established a powerful reputation; as a teacher he had a commanding presence and was a positive artist with chalk and blackboard. He was the first Dalhousie graduate to become its president, and from then on Dalhousie became the core of his life. Loyal, patient, far-sighted, generous, MacKenzie was a rare president, blessed with dignity and common sense, who seemed to be able to mix Scotch and fishing with his many Dalhousie responsibilities.

One illustration of MacKenzie's style, his feeling for Dalhousie and her traditions, was his reply to Professor Archibald MacMechan who in 1923 wanted out of invigilating examinations. Most professors hated that chore, and MacMechan at age sixty-one felt he was entitled to look for an easing of that unrewarding burden. MacKenzie was both kind and firm, reading MacMechan a lesson in old Dalhousie democracy:

I was surprised and pained to receive your written complaint this morning about the work of invigilating. You have mentioned it to me verbally once or twice, and I took it in the only spirit in which it should be taken. Have you forgotten the good old adage "noblesse oblige", which in this case might be read "vieillesse oblige"? I do not see how any distinction can be drawn between one member of the staff and another, unless decrepitude sets in, and have that democratic spirit retained through the whole faculty which is an essential of our Dalhousie mode of life. Personally, I hope the time will never come in my stay at Dalhousie when I shall feel superior to attending to the miserable, petty, time-consuming little details and jobs that come before me every day.[3]

Of course Dalhousie asked much of its professors. Some had to earn, some chose to earn, extra income. MacMechan worked many of his summers, teaching at Columbia, Harvard, or elsewhere, in the heat of big cities. In winter he wrote a weekly book column for the Montreal *Standard*, "The Dean's Window." Salaries were not unreasonable for the standards of the time, but after 1917 inflation made life more difficult on a fixed income.

Murray Macneill, Archibald MacMechan, and others
After the president, the most important university official was the registrar, Murray Macneill, professor of mathematics. He was a power in the university. Registrars had to be exigent to prevent the world, professors, and students, from making end runs around rules and regulations. Murray Macneill had come to Dalhousie in 1892 out of Pictou Academy at the age of fifteen, a brilliant student and still growing up.

He graduated in 1896 at the age of nineteen with the Sir William Young medal in mathematics. He made a lasting impression on a number of people, not least Lucy Maud Montgomery who was at Dalhousie for a year in 1895–6. There is a Macneill family tradition that the character of Gilbert Blythe in *Anne of Green Gables* (published in 1908) was modelled after Murray Macneill. He was not enthusiastic about the alleged resemblance. He went on to do graduate work at Cornell, Harvard, and Paris. When Professor Charles Macdonald died in 1901 Macneill was a candidate to succeed him. But he was only twenty-three years old and the professorship went to Daniel Alexander Murray ('84), a PH.D. from Johns Hopkins. Macneill was too young then, but when the mathematics chair again became vacant in 1907, Macneill was appointed. He came back to Dalhousie from McGill and stayed for the next thirty-five years.[4]

He became Arts and Science registrar in 1908 and in 1920 registrar of the university. The same year he was given an associate to help him in teaching mathematics, while he took over the correspondence with students and getting out the calendar – for all of which he was given an additional $500 a year. It was a taxing job. He would see each student at registration, and would consider in the light of their matriculation marks, their own wishes, and Dalhousie's rules what best they ought to do. More than one student found not only hopes for dodging hard courses thwarted, but ended up the better because Murray Macneill found some combination of classes that suited the student's talents, knowledge, and experience. Frank Covert, who walked up to Dalhousie in 1924 at the age of sixteen, had reason to be grateful to Macneill not only as registrar but for his luminous teaching in mathematics. Covert said he was "one of the greatest teachers I'd ever known." Macneill's specialty was analytical geometry. John Fisher, not as able as Covert, entered a few years later; his matriculation marks in French and Latin were abominable and, heading for Commerce, he wanted to avoid Latin at all costs. Could he not take another language instead? Macneill's massive head with the fuzzy fringe made a slow and deliberate negative sweep. "Well thanks, Mr. Macneill," said young Fisher. Then he played a desperate card put into his hands only minutes before. Macneill was an avid and successful curler; Fisher asked if he could come and watch Macneill curl sometime. The registrar pricked up his ears. "Come and see me next week when I'm not so busy," he said. Fisher duly came back, expecting to get out of taking Latin. It was not even mentioned; they discussed curling. Fisher never did escape Latin. Perhaps it was good for him. He reflected later, "After all, his [Macneill's] first love was Dalhousie University. He had helped to guard her high standards."[5]

The oldest of these guardians of standards in Arts and Science was Howard Murray, McLeod professor of classics since 1894, dean of the college since 1901. He was sixty-six in 1925, happy in his work, and would not hear of retirement. Murray was a careful, solid, and for some students too stolid, lecturer; but he was much in demand as after-dinner speaker, for he had wit, with mordant sarcasm and cryptic apothegms thrown in for savour. Once a year in Latin 2 he would relax and read slangy versions of Horace's odes, including one that began, "Who was the guy I seen you with last night?" After one of those he would double up with laughter.[6]

Archibald MacMechan, Munro professor of English since 1889, was three years younger than Murray and quite a different character. He was often the first professor the first-year students encountered, for he did English 1 himself. There he would stand in the big Chemistry theatre, well-proportioned, elegantly dressed, with gown, handkerchief in his left sleeve, his squarish face made less so by a well-groomed, pointed beard. He expected his students to comport themselves as gentlemen and ladies. He much disapproved of chewing gum, and it was not tolerated in his classes. He also had a horror of sweaters, so much so that he would not even use the name, calling them, with disgust, "perspirers." Any student who was misguided enough to wear a perspirer would be politely asked to leave the lecture.

MacMechan was proud of Dalhousie, proud of her traditions, proud of what he sometimes called "that pastry cook's shop," proud of his students. His lectures were not flashy; they were, rather, carefully crafted and they covered a great deal of ground. He commended Ruskin's definition of poetry: "the suggestion, by the imagination, of noble grounds for the noble emotions." That says something, also, of MacMechan. He touched other literatures besides English; G.G. Sedgewick ('03) later professor of English at the University of British Columbia, first learned of Goethe's magical "Kennst du das Land" and Beethoven's music for it from Archie MacMechan.

MacMechan worked hard. He read and marked all of the twenty themes each student in English 1 had to write, until in 1922–3 he got an assistant, C.L. Bennet, a New Zealander, to help him. His comments he would put on the themes in red ink; beside something he particularly liked he would put a wavy red line, what he called "a wriggle of delight." MacMechan's own writing was like him, fastidious not forceful, full of grace and delicate elaborations. Yet he liked blood-and-thunder history and could render it, writing majestically of ships and the sea. And he could rise to occasions. He gave a speech to a football pep rally once, though it could not have had that name or

Professor Archibald MacMechan's book plate, showing the Winged Victory of Samothrace and the lamp of learning. The German under MacMechan's name reads "Ich bin Dein," "I am yours."

Archie would never have come to it; he knew the game of rugby, although he was lame and could not play. He gathered the Dalhousians around him, and spoke. It was grave, quiet, almost solemn. One felt more in a chapel than in a pep rally. He made the Dalhousie students feel as if they were the privileged citizens of a great and wondrous city. "No one will ever persuade me," wrote one of the students present, "that Archie did not turn the trick of victory (it was a near thing) on the next afternoon."[7]

There were the younger men; Howard Bronson, Munro professor of physics who had come in 1910 out of Yale and McGill. A fine teacher with a knack for asking seriously inconvenient questions on examinations, he was becoming preoccupied now with the Student Christian Movement and was losing his grasp of research in physics. His younger rival was J.H.L. Johnstone, short, strong, and with a robust practical edge to his physics. George Wilson in history, and R. MacGregor Dawson, a political scientist who taught economics, roomed at 93 Coburg Road with Sidney Smith, the new lecturer in law. They were three young bachelors and could kick up a precious row now and then, like overgrown schoolboys. Dawson was from Bridgewater via the London School of Economics, and as Wilson once said was "noisy as hell and straight as a tree"; Dalhousie would not be able to hold him. George Wilson loved the place, admired MacKenzie, and had no urge to move. He migrated to Ontario each summer to the family farm in Perth or to the Ottawa Archives to finish off his Harvard PH.D. Sidney Smith it was, newly appointed in law, who chased Beatrice Smith, the eighteen-year-old secretary of Dean MacRae, down the hall of the Forrest Building on his bicycle. She escaped and the new lecturer ran into President MacKenzie instead. Dawson and Smith were Nova Scotians who ended in the University of Toronto; Wilson was an Ontarian who ended in Nova Scotia. All were unusually bright and vigorous teachers.[8]

H.L. Stewart and the Dalhousie Review

Among the Europeans at Dalhousie was H.L. Stewart (1882–1953), Munro professor of philosophy since 1913, hired from the University of Belfast. Writing was Stewart's forte and he had a sharp eye for the contemporary scene. With good reason he was appointed the founding editor of Dalhousie's first venture into academic publishing, the *Dalhousie Review*, which appeared in 1921.

The *Dalhousie Review* was a successor journal to the *University Review* which, before it faded after the war, had been a quarterly based on contributions from McGill, Queen's, Toronto, and Dalhousie. The proposal to begin a literary and scientific quarterly at Dal-

C. L. BENNET, M. A., A. M.

A New Zealand veteran of the First World War, Bennet came to Dalhousie via Cambridge in 1922 and stayed for the rest of his life: George Munro Professor of English, 1931–58; Dean of Graduate Studies, 1956–61; Vice-President, 1958–61.

housie was discussed at MacKenzie's house just before Christmas 1920, with the board executive, Dugald MacGillivray of the Canadian Bank of Commerce, Clarence Mackinnon, two other board members, and a group from the Dalhousie Senate – Dean MacRae, Archie MacMechan, Howard Murray, H.L. Stewart, together with Alumni and Alumnae representatives. The journal was announced to the three thousand or so Dalhousie alumni in March 1921, and promptly produced fifty subscribers. Despite that thin start, the Review Publishing Company was formed and the shares were taken by board members and alumni; thus its board of directors was a subset of the board itself.

The early years of the *Dalhousie Review* was a savoury feast, a deft blending of old and new, popular and academic, eminently readable. Stewart would run it for twenty-five years. He endeavoured, with some success, to render untrue a limerick he received in the mail in 1937:

> There was a young man from Peru
> Who'd a cure for insomnia, new,
> Let the insomniac
> Just lie on his back
> And read the *Dalhousie Review*.

It was the first of the important university quarterlies – critical, independent, and crossing a wide spectrum of interests. H.L. Stewart's work on it meant, however, that his attention to his philosophy classes was thinner than before. When he first came he was an able teacher; by the 1920s there were suspicions that he was easing up on the oars. That was the view of the registrar, Murray Macneill. In 1919 only one student registered for Philosophy 4. Dalhousie practice was to give a course even if there were only one student. The student withdrew; Macneill believed the student had been "persuaded," although Stewart denied it. With good students Stewart was generous, inviting them to his house for tea and talk; but generally by the mid-1920s it was known privately that Dalhousie philosophy teaching was a far cry from the great days of Schurman, Seth, or Walter Murray. Stewart's publications and research, his work of editing the *Review*, and by the 1930s his work in radio, would take their toll on his undergraduate lectures, upon which Dalhousie set such store.[9]

H.B. Atlee and Obstetrics

In 1922 a Dalhousie professor was hired who would become just as well-known as Stewart at publication and a good deal better at his lectures, a young gynaecologist and obstetrician, Harold Benge Atlee.

Herbert Leslie Stewart, Professor of Philosophy, 1913–47, founding editor of the *Dalhousie Review*. An able writer and well-known CBC radio commentator, by the 1930s his philosophy lectures were a disaster.

He had graduated from the old Halifax Medical College in 1911 on the eve of its metamorphosis into the Dalhousie Medical Faculty. Atlee (1890–1978) was born in Pictou County, brought up in Annapolis Royal; he carried off school prizes, tied for a prize at medical graduation, and went overseas for postgraduate study after two years of private practice in rural Nova Scotia. He took up surgery, came to specialize in female surgery, and was in charge of that division at St Mary's Hospital, London, when the 1914 war broke out. He joined the Royal Army Medical Corps, served at Gallipoli, Salonika, and in Egypt, emerging a major with a Military Cross and twice mentioned in the despatches. He took his FRCS (Fellow of the Royal College of Surgeons) in Edinburgh in 1920. He then sat down and wrote President MacKenzie.

It was not exactly a modest letter, but Atlee had never been modest. He said there were few Halifax doctors who had given more time to postgraduate study than he had. He was planning on returning to Halifax, and he hoped the president would keep him in mind should an opening develop at Dalhousie in Obstetrics and Diseases of Women. MacKenzie encouraged him, saying that Dalhousie was confidently expecting Rockefeller money to help finish the new maternity hospital. As Atlee doubtless knew already, the professor of obstetrics and gynaecology, Dr M.A. Curry, performed no surgery at all, and was close to retirement. The Grace Maternity hospital would open soon. Part of the agreement between the Salvation Army and Dalhousie (with the Rockefeller Foundation as the benign and rich uncle in the background) was that there would be public beds in the Grace to which Dalhousie would have the nomination of medical staff. Five were duly nominated, active in obstetrics, one of them expecting to be named professor when Curry retired. None was. The reason was the Victoria General and Dalhousie had concluded that drastic action was needed to improve the teaching and clinical work in obstetrics and gynaecology. It meant the appointment of a new professor and a department that would combine the Obstetrics at the Grace and the Gynaecology at the Victoria General. In September 1922 the dean of medicine, Dr John Stewart, and President MacKenzie recommended, as professor and chairman of the first combined Department of Obstetrics and Gynaecology, as chief of service at the Victoria General, the thirty-two-year-old Harold Benge Atlee.[10]

The appointment of Atlee created an almighty row. The obstetricians resented the young outsider. The surgeons at the hospital took the view that their level of competence required fifteen to twenty years of practical experience. Moreover, they had substantial gynaecological work; any appointment that aimed to separate them from their gynaecological surgery would be resented, indeed resisted. What made this one worse was that this young man, from out of town, seemed to think he could do it, and he would have control over such patients in the general wards. The Halifax *Mail* called the appointment "a quite extraordinary one." At this stage Atlee was technically on leave, still working in specialist hospitals in London, where he was earning the highest praise from eminent surgeons. In Halifax the Hospital Commission met the outrage of the four surgeons most affected with the rejoinder that the recommendation for the appointment belonged to Dalhousie and Dalhousie alone, and it would not be undone. Nevertheless, President MacKenzie suggested to Atlee that he continue to work in England until June 1923 to let the furor cool down. That would take some time; on 12 April 1923 there was an evening's debate about it, with criticism of the government, in the House of Assembly. Atlee, who was then at the Royal Chelsea Hospital for Women, took it all as free advertising, confident that by the time he returned to Halifax reports by senior colleagues in London would abundantly justify Dalhousie's decision. "The impression we have all got," wrote Dr Comyns Berkeley, FRCS, senior surgeon at the Royal Chelsea Hospital, "is that Professor Atlee is a very able man, both in judgment, diagnosis, operative dexterity and the after care of patients ..."[11]

That and other recommendations from England stopped public criticism, as Atlee and MacKenzie believed they would. But it would take years before the bitter resentment of hospital colleagues would dissipate. Even the nursing staff were against him at first. One result was that he got very few specialist referrals in Halifax. It was not really until his own students were established in practice that Atlee received a sufficient number of referrals.

So he had to do something else: he wrote stories for the pulp magazines and for *Maclean's*. One morning in the middle of his class, the professor of pathology came in to say that Atlee's wife was on the telephone and had to speak to him. As he excused himself from class, Atlee wondered what new financial catastrophe was in store. What Margaret Atlee had to tell him was that the mail had just come and three of his stories had been sold! For a number of years Atlee would write a seven-to-eight-thousand-word story almost every weekend, some of them published under the *nom de plume* of Ian Hope. By 1928 he was earning more than $5,000 a year from magazines.[12]

Between 1922 and 1925 Atlee also wrote a weekly column in the *Chronicle*, "As I Was Saying," under the initials P.D.L. Atlee was often outspoken and rough, the opposite of Archie MacMechan. There were hardly a dozen buildings in Halifax, he said, that were not architectural atrocities; not for Atlee the joy of the late nineteenth-century porches on Tower Road and South Park Street. He called those houses "clapboard monstrosities." He was opinionated and he delighted in it. He would tell his students in obstetrics, via mimeographed notes (for he came to distrust student capacities for taking accurate notes), on symptoms of pregnancy, that as a rule their patients would be respectable married women; but it would "fall to your lot occasionally to be called upon by a venturesome virgin, or an incautious widow ..." Atlee came to have opportunities to move elsewhere, but he never took them. He liked life where he was, feuds and all, architectural monstrosities or not. He eventually even lived in one, on South Park Street.[13]

Two years after Atlee's arrival on staff, with the Grace Maternity Hospital going up, the Pathology Laboratory extended, the Medical Sciences Building completed, and the Public Health and Out-Patient Clinic at full service to the Halifax community, the council of the American Medical Association voted Dalhousie's Medical School the coveted class "A" certificate. Dr A.P. Colwell, the secretary, had visited Dalhousie in the summer of 1924, and now sent this happy news to MacKenzie, adding, "I know of no institution in which this higher rating is more richly deserved." That was especially sweet to Dalhousie ears, for Colwell had helped Flexner do his 1910 survey of the old Halifax Medical College, and the devastating report that followed. The *Dalhousie Gazette*, the student paper, put out a special eight-page medical issue in November 1925 to celebrate the good news. The State Medical Boards of New York and Pennsylvania now gave recognition to Dalhousie Medical School degrees.[14]

The Faculty of Dentistry
Dalhousie's newest faculty, Dentistry, had received outside recognition in 1922, ten years after it had been incorporated in Dalhousie. Nova Scotia had got its first Dental Act in 1891, and the Nova Scotia Dental Association was formed the same year. A board was established by which dentists were approved and registered. That did not mean they had degrees; in 1909 there were 114 dentists registered in Nova Scotia and nineteen of them had no degree at all. The other ninety-five had degrees, mostly from Philadelphia or Baltimore. The basis for the proper development of dentistry as a profession had to be a dental college in the Maritimes, and in 1907 a new Dental Act allowed the Dental Association of Nova Scotia to set up a College of Dentistry in Halifax. The following year Dalhousie Senate struck a committee to meet with Dr Frank Woodbury, the dean of the Maritime Dental College, to establish an affiliated Faculty of Dentistry. It was an arrangement similar to the one Dalhousie had made with the

Halifax Medical College: the Dental College gave the tuition and Dalhousie the degrees. Dalhousie also provided the Dental College with lecture rooms and clinical facilities tucked in at the southwest end of the main floor of the Forrest Building, where the library was, adjacent to where the present Dental Building now stands. The Maritime Dental College was owned and operated largely by the dentists themselves – a practitioners' school, but better than most, for the dentists had been conscientious in designing its program. In 1911–12 there were seventeen students in the college; eight were in the first year of a four-year program, for which entrance was the same matriculation standards as the Faculty of Arts and Science.[15]

The Flexner Report, which forced the Halifax Medical College into abandoning its name and becoming Dalhousie's Faculty of Medicine, had consequences for the Maritime Dental College as well. In 1912 Dalhousie took it over as it had taken over the Medical College. Thus the first class to register in the newly created Maritime Dental College in 1908 graduated in 1912 as Dalhousie's first class in the Faculty of Dentistry.

The moving spirit behind this rapid development, as rapid it was between 1891 and 1912, was Dr Frank Woodbury. He was born near Middleton in 1853, graduated from Mount Allison, and took his dentistry degree at Philadelphia in 1878. He eventually established a practice with his brother in Halifax. His great work was the incorporation of the Maritime Dental College into Dalhousie's Faculty of Dentistry in 1912. Woodbury was one of those selfless men, sometimes from a Methodist background, with an uncompromising devotion to civil, provincial, and national work. Dean of the old Maritime Dental College, he became dean of the Dalhousie Faculty of Dentistry and it was Woodbury, as much as anyone, who helped to give Dalhousie Dentistry its standing. At the end of January 1922 Dr W.J. Gies and four colleagues from the Carnegie Foundation (and the American Dental Association) visited Dalhousie's Faculty of Dentistry and gave it a glowing report. All that was inhibiting further development was financial need. Shortly after the assessment team departed, Dean Woodbury died suddenly of heart failure. It was a sad blow, for there was almost no one among the volunteer dentists whom MacKenzie could fall back on. His successor was Dr F.W. Ryan and after Ryan's death two years later, Dr D.K. Thomson, who would be dean until 1935.[16]

Curriculum and Students of the 1920s
The Dalhousie of the 1920s was crowded by all previous standards. In 1922 it had the largest enrolment so far, 753 students, of whom 60 per cent were in arts and science, the remainder divided between med-

icine, law, and dentistry. Women students comprehended 36 per cent of the arts and science programs as against 23 per cent in 1902. Some 45 per cent of arts and science students now came from Halifax, up substantially from twenty years before when only 30 per cent did. Overall, 35 per cent of Dalhousie's students were Haligonians. Noticeable shifts occurred in regional representation. Pictou County, which in 1902–3 contributed 13.5 per cent of Dalhousie's students, now gave only 8 per cent; Colchester County's representation halved, as did Prince Edward Island's; Cape Breton doubled.[17]

Admission to Dalhousie was by matriculation, sometimes called junior; students deficient in some subjects could make them up. In that case they were allowed to take only four classes in the first year. If they were weak in Latin or French, often the case with those whose matriculation was deficient, they were allowed to take only three classes. If students failed more than four classes at Christmas, they had to withdraw from Dalhousie, for at least a year. Class attendance of 90 per cent was required, and records were kept.

The big classes were in those old Dalhousie fundamentals, classics and mathematics, though modern languages were now required along with the classical ones. In effect some of the old mathematical core had been shifted over to modern languages. The twenty classes for the BA were the following:

2 classes in Latin or in Greek
2 classes in French, German, or Spanish
2 classes in English
History 1
Philosophy 1
Mathematics 1
1 Science: physics, chemistry, biology, or geology
1 3rd-year language class, or Economics 1, or Government 1
8 other classes chosen so that at least four classes must be in one subject, and three classes in each of two others.

In 1922–3 some 220 students took Latin at various levels, divided roughly evenly between elementary Latin (an important make-up class) and Latin 1 and 2. Some 208 took French, mainly in French 1 and 2. There were 342 students in various levels of English, nearly half of those in the first year. First-year physics, history, and economics had about one hundred students each, chemistry's first year had 141 students, with biology not far behind with 129.

The classes in the first year were each three hours a week with science classes requiring an additional two- or three-hour laboratory per week. Elementary Latin was offered to students whose Latin was rocky or non-existent, every Tuesday, Thursday, and Saturday at 11 AM with a fourth hour added after the class was formed and time-tables worked out. Latin 1 required Cicero's *Oration against Cataline*, Virgil's *Aeneid Book VI*, and exercises in sight translation. Latin 2 went on to Livy and Horace.

There was talk in Senate of changing the attendance rule from 90 to 100 per cent. One-third of the students met on 5 November 1922 to protest such a change, and the proposal was withdrawn. At Christmas 1922 another rule came into question. Fourteen arts and science students, having failed more than four subjects, were asked to leave. It got into the local papers, and the press thought it too severe. President MacKenzie reported to Senate that the fourteen were in three groups: five students were "hopeless. They were idlers who took no interest in their work and showed no likelihood of possible improvement." The second group "did not lack the diligence, but could not stand up to the work because of inferior ability." A third group pleaded extenuating circumstances. The Senate decided that the first group would still be asked to leave Dalhousie, while the remaining nine were put on probation for four weeks.[18]

That occasioned some student comment. Was it true, the *Gazette* asked, that "Idlers, Drones, Social Climbers" were being ruthlessly weeded out? Who ought to be? Max MacOdrum ('23) took this up. A few months before, the president of Dartmouth College, New Hampshire, had raised similar questions, and came up with fairly stern answers. University was not a place, said President Hopkins, for "dainty idling, social climbing." The only way to preserve Dartmouth College standards was to eliminate the deadwood. An "aristocracy of brains" existed, and the duty of the university was to discover it. Max MacOdrum's answer did not question those assumptions so much as to ask what was the best means to eliminate deadwood. He was not at all sure that written examinations for first-year students were a good test. Two weeks later the *Gazette* offered the aphorism, reminiscent of old Charlie Macdonald's 1892 address, that "following lines of least resistance makes rivers and men crooked." With all the physical changes of the 1920s, so obvious to students, President MacKenzie reminded them that the university "is the same old Dalhousie, with the same old Scottish ideals of the steep, lonely path of learning. You go out from its halls with the feeling that you have earned what you have won."

The first day of lectures of the session of 1922–3 was on Wednesday, 4 October. The length of the university year was cause for an extended debate in Senate that took up most of that autumn. The

Canadian average was twenty-six weeks, shorter by several weeks than in the United States. The committee making recommendations wanted twenty-nine weeks, but it was divided and its divisions reappeared in Senate. President MacKenzie wanted the twenty-nine weeks, the length of the medical and dental years, conditions for those being quasi-statutory. Since arts and science classes ended three weeks earlier, conditions in some classes became, as MacKenzie put it, "demoralized." At the end of a wrenching debate, medicine and dentistry continued with their twenty-nine week sessions, law was extended to thirty weeks, and Senate approved the idea of lengthening the arts and science session, though it could not yet say by how much. By the autumn of 1923 all that happened was that arts and science began on the first Monday instead of the first Wednesday in October.[19]

In January 1923 once more Senate tackled the lively issue of student dances. Students could not seem to get enough of them: Senate thought they were taking up entirely too much time and energy not only of the students but of Senate, which had to debate permissions to hold them. A dance policy was duly laid down: there would be a dance officer of Senate; Dalhousie dances were to be on Dalhousie premises; only students would be allowed to go (unless otherwise authorized); dances would end at midnight except the dance at Convocation which was allowed the luxury of 12:30; they could be on any day but Sunday; there were to be seven in all, three in the autumn, three in the spring, and the Convocation Ball. At each dance two members of staff had to be present. Smoking at dances was allowed but only in special rooms. Women students were not allowed to smoke.[20]

An advertisement in the *Gazette* for Rex cigarettes was social comment. The cigarette was consolation; a man in white tie and tails – Dalhousie dances were formal and tails were *de rigueur* – was sitting out a dance by himself, reflecting that the dance may be a bore, "the lady of one's choice may be dancing with another – and yet there's still a morsel of satisfaction in the dreariest of festivities for the man who says, NEVER MIND – SMOKE A REX!"

The *Gazette*'s joke column, both original jokes and those culled from other university papers, illustrated something of the 1920s too:

Ray – Let's kiss and make up.
May – Well, if you are careful I won't have to.

That was the first *Gazette* of the 1922–3 session. Also announced was the first Freshie-Soph debate, for Thursday evening, 19 October: "Resolved that a Dirty, Good-Natured Wife is Better than a Clean, Bad-

Humoured One." Freshmen were to argue the negative, in favour of cleanliness and querulousness. It was a decidedly male theme. Jokes allowed other perspectives, including delightful ambivalence:

"What shall we do?" she asked, bored to the verge of tears.
"Whatever you wish," he replied gallantly.
"If you do, I'll scream," she said coyly ... [21]

Shirreff Hall and its World

Jennie Shirreff Eddy's ambitions, and Frank Darling's translation of them into architecture, aimed rather higher than all that. Dalhousie's women students were to be introduced in Shirreff Hall to a social ambience in keeping with Dalhousie's intellectual ambitions. Shirreff Hall opened in the autumn of 1923 under its new warden, Margaret Lowe, the former national secretary of the Student Christian Movement in Toronto. She was paid $1,500 a year with her room and board, and she would remain warden until 1930. Shirreff Hall was a special world and was so intended. It was to foster in young women modes of civilized living that not all of them had had opportunity to develop yet. Indeed, Shirreff Hall struck one girl, Florence MacKinnon of Sydney, as being too rich for her blood, that unless she were to marry a millionaire, she did not anticipate living in a millionaire's house seven months of the year. Mrs Eddy aimed to provide a home life that would have the effect, as she put it, of "rounding out the university's training." Frank Darling of Toronto was greatly intrigued with Shirreff Hall – it was his last major work – and thus Mrs Eddy's and President MacKenzie's concerns, and Darling's ingenuity at translating them, showed. And still does.[22]

The *Morning Chronicle* of 3 October 1923 praised it as a building of imposing beauty, inside and out. The stone was MacKenzie's discovery. The local Halifax stone, ironstone, a metamorphosed slate, had been creating problems, mostly because it was so hard that mortar did not properly bond to it. The Macdonald Library and the Science Building had both revealed such problems, though none as bad as the new Anglican Cathedral was currently demonstrating. MacKenzie found a pinkish quartzite from New Minas, used successfully at Acadia. At Shirreff Hall it was mixed with triprock of a greenish hue. He was also particular about the slate for the roofs; that of the other Dalhousie buildings had been a sea-green slate from the north of England.

The interior fittings were done with love and attention, not least by a much travelled R.B. Bennett who found the firm in Minneapolis that manufactured doors that Bennett had seen and liked. A few months later, on his way to England, Bennett sent MacKenzie note-

A group of Dalhousie students and alumnae in the late 1920s. Note the cloche hats and short skirts.

paper with the Shirreff crest. It was a rearing horse holding an olive branch, the motto being the well-tried, "Esse Quam Videri" (To be rather than to seem). That was for the china Bennett was proposing to order for Shirreff Hall in England.[23]

Shirreff Hall pleased nearly everyone. "I have never known," MacKenzie told Bennett, "any building receive greater admiration and praise ... I never look at it but I think how entirely pleased Mrs. Eddy would have been." She had died in August 1921, and Frank Darling never lived to see the opening of Shirreff Hall; he died in May 1923. MacKenzie expected sixty-five girls for Shirreff Hall; there were, however, far more applicants than spaces, and that first year, 1923–4, there were eighty-five girls in Shirreff Hall, every corner occupied.

Fire drill in a late evening in March 1924 created a special stir. Fire captains found it hard to convince early sleepers that it was not morning although thoughts of breakfast stirred some. It brought forth some interesting specimens; as the *Gazette*'s Shirreff Hall reporter observed, one young lady "in curl-papers whose short jacket over a draped dressing gown was charmingly set off by a pair of rubber boots." One student was missing from the roll-call, and Miss Margaret Lowe was much worried that had there been a real fire, the young woman would have been burned. But Miss Lowe's fears were "calmed by the assurance that in the event she [the student] would only have boiled."[24]

The long love affair between Shirreff Hall and Pine Hill now got under way. Pine Hill was the Presbyterian Divinity College on a lovely site on the North-West Arm, built in 1899. Pine Hill became United Church in 1926 and there were often more rooms than theological students to fill them. Dalhousie had never had male residences; the Birchdale Hotel that Campbell and Pearson had bought in 1920 for that purpose Dalhousie had had (reluctantly) to lease to King's in 1923, pending completion of King's own buildings in 1930. Thus Dalhousie male students lived everywhere in Halifax, although the university kept track of them and, from time to time, of the condition of the houses they lived in. Dalhousie men had always liked to board at Pine Hill when they could, just a half a mile's pretty walk from Dalhousie (and Shirreff Hall in 1923). The *Gazette* noted it in January 1925, with a sprightly cartoon of Pine Hill, his arm around Shirreff Hall, she with her bobbed hair and silk stockings (with seam),

The Faculty may shake their heads
    With ominous disdain
But what care we when we can be
    Together once again!

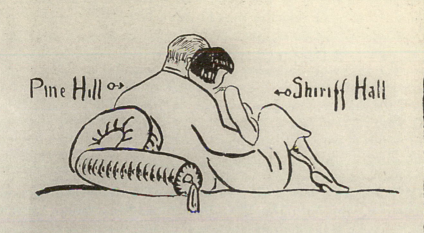

Pine Hill →   ← Sheriff Hall

O now exams have rolled away
    And we are free once more
With storm and rapids put behind
    And luring bends before
The faculty may shake their heads
    With ominous disdain
But what care we when we can be
    Together once again!

                                    H·A·D

At Shirreff Hall bobbed hair was by that time very much in fashion: "the army of the unbobbed diminishes daily. Sometimes the shorn lambs do not much resemble their former selves."[25]

A House for the President

R.B. Bennett, who had been mainly instrumental in bringing Mrs Eddy and Dalhousie's need for a women's residence together, also effected the change of the president's home from 14 Hollis Street. It was MacKenzie's own house, bought before the new railway station at Cornwallis Square had been built, but handy to welcome presidents who came by train for federation meetings. Its access to Dalhousie was not so convenient. In 1924 G.S. Campbell was in the West on bank business but also looking at university buildings at Saskatoon, Edmonton, and Vancouver. Some of them made his mouth water, he said, "but for style, appropriateness, Dalhousie need not take second place to any of them." In Calgary he met H.A. Allison, a partner in Bennett's law firm, who asked advice about selling the property of his late brother, E.P. Allison, at 24 Oxford Street in Halifax. Campbell said Dalhousie would have loved to buy it but didn't have the money. Bennett and Campbell met in London, England, in May 1925 and Campbell raised the question. Bennett had already left a substantial gift for Dalhousie in his will, but seized the opportunity to do something here and now. Early in June 1925 he telegraphed Campbell asking him to find the lowest price for which the Allison property could be bought. By that time the field behind it had been sold to a speculator, but there was still the big house and its grounds, 214 feet along Oxford Street and 326 feet deep, in all an acre and a half. Assessed at $14,000, it was bought by Dalhousie for $20,000, assessments being old and prices new. Bennett promptly donated the money. "I am really gratified," he said, "to send this gift to the university to which I owe so much." Campbell wired MacKenzie in Ottawa the good news. "Bennett donates twenty thousand to buy Allison house[.] prepare for an elaborate and juicy house warming." Dalhousie spent another $8,000 fixing up the Allison house, and MacKenzie moved into it, as his official residence, late in 1925, with his daughter and her husband.[26]

Campbell convened an informal meeting at his house on 9 September 1926 to consider ways of developing better relations between students, staff, and alumni. Dalhousie's big student body in the 1920s developed momentum of its own; the familiar staff-student relations of old did not seem to work as well. Since 1919 Dalhousie's administration, especially President MacKenzie, had been heavily preoccupied with building and with university federation. Campbell's informal meeting was the origin of the Committee of Nine – three students, three members of Senate, and three alumni – struck to work out relations between the students and Senate.[27]

Dalhousie Student Council and the Gazette

The Dalhousie Student Council had been established in its 1920s form in 1912, and for eight or nine years had worked well, dealing with student discipline and the administration of funds for student clubs. But beginning about 1920, and especially by 1925–6, the system began to break down on both those functions. Dean Howard Murray thought the Student Council had gradually abdicated its responsibility for student discipline, that its attitude appeared to be "that the Council's function was neither to maintain order itself nor to assist the Senate in maintaining it, but to be oblivious of all infractions of discipline; that members of Senate must do the detective work, and that, when students are to be disciplined, the Council should interfere as far as possible to secure mitigation of the punishment." L.W. Fraser, for the Student Council, explained to Senate that accusations about slack administration of student finances, particularly the lack of audit of club moneys, was true. As to discipline, students differed. Many of them felt they did not have a sufficient voice in establishing the rules. President MacKenzie noted that the Student Council had approved the original rules of 1912, and subsequent changes were made in consultation between the council and Senate. The Council of Nine may not have had, as the Gazette suggested, "plenary power to regulate University affairs" but it was an important body where the students could ventilate grievances. The Dalhousie Gazette was fairly blunt:

In the past the relation of the student towards the university has been, no matter how loyal, servile. He has had consciously or unconsciously a fear of the university administrators, because the latter have in their hands all authority ... Take for example the shameless way university authorities use that old gag: "Remember that your presence at the university costs society every year so many hundreds of dollars. It is up to you to justify the investment." No student has ever felt free to say to the university authorities: "Remember that society has entrusted to you – in addition to millions of dollars – the lives of its most promising youth. If you betray that trust, society is undone."

Students had several complaints. One was against professors who kept their classes after the first bell and thus forced students to be late for one immediately afterwards, at which they would usually be marked as absent. Students objected to the library closing at 4:30 PM and in March 1926 a number petitioned for a closing time of 6 PM. They got 5 PM, and returned to the issue in November 1926:

The University Library is like a sponge of vinegar to a thirsty man. The books are not available. The Library opens at nine o'clock in the morning and closes at five in the afternoon. On Saturdays it closes at one o'clock; on Sundays it is not open at all ... The stacks should be open to the student. Though hide and seek is all right in its place, there seems no reason why we should play this game with the university books ... Wake up, University Authorities! Dalhousie has given you for the time being the job of running the university; we will not put up with any nonsense.

It was probably these last two sentences that occasioned a message for the editor, Andrew Hebb, to talk to the chairman of the board, G.S. Campbell. They met at the Halifax Club. Hebb apologized to Campbell and to the board in an editorial, and the library *was* opened in the evenings from 7:30 to 10 PM, beginning Monday, 6 December – an experiment on which future library hours would depend.[28]

In general the *Gazette*'s relations with the university were rarely so brusque. Andrew Hebb ('25, '28) had been sub-editor the previous year when he roused the ire of David Soloan ('88) the principal of the Normal School in Truro, for having praised short skirts. Soloan complained to Hebb, who replied that the principal needed special glasses that would prevent him from seeing the lower half of any woman he met! That was not well received in Truro, and the issue ended up on President MacKenzie's desk. MacKenzie was patient and sensible to Soloan's protests. He was sorry the *Gazette* went in for that sort of thing, but it was the students' paper and the Senate did not control it. Dalhousie did not interfere with the editors unless they did something

which is subversive of discipline or print anything which is disgraceful or discreditable, or directly runs counter to the best interests and good name of the University. Outside of that we find experience of a couple of generations has proved that it is much wiser to leave the students fairly free in their carrying on of their paper. This gives them a chance to blow off steam, and we have found that, with this spirit of arrangement between us, they seldom over-step the bounds set for them.[29]

Hebb probably knew nothing of this defence, but when he became editor in 1926 there was a definite effort to improve the *Gazette*'s style and vigour, to make it more a student newspaper and less a student literary magazine. There were newspaper connections as well;

one sub-editor, a dental student, had worked for the Sydney *Post*, another on the Saint John *Telegraph-Journal*. Hebb's adventures with Campbell in November 1926 did not prevent him some two months later from ascribing the large number of failures at the Christmas exams as faults, not only of students, but of professors. Students were usually aware of their weaknesses; professors were not, and they failed students right and left, not always being aware of their own failings as teachers. And there was sage advice in the *Gazette* in January of 1927. Dalhousie and Halifax were starting in on "the gray days" of winter, and even if they were monotonous as weather – there had been very little snow – they should not be allowed to drift by:

... for all that, the gray days have a charm, which is entirely lacking in those earlier, more interesting ones. There is practically nothing worthwhile doing in them but working and thinking ... Let us try and get the most of these gray days. They are solid gray rocks, on which foundations may be built.

They were also occasional literary touches, one of them a poetic echo of gray days:

> I love quiet things
> Grey birds on grey wings
> Night with the wind still
> And grey fog upon the hill,
> Rolling mist along the shore,
> Lamplight through the open door
> I love quiet things
> Grey birds on grey wings.[30]

A New Chairman of the Board and Dalhousie's Finances

George Campbell's opening the library in the evening was one of his last contributions to Dalhousie. He had been ill in April 1927 but the doctors were hopeful he had recovered. In Montreal on business, he died suddenly of a heart attack on 21 November at the age of seventy-six, still president of the Bank of Nova Scotia, still chairman of the Dalhousie board. His greatest gift to Dalhousie had been his twenty years as its chairman. As President MacKenzie said, "Steadily, if slowly, he brought his colleagues ... to see that his dreams were practicable ... [As to his purchase of Studley], the effect was almost electrical." MacKenzie's and Campbell's personal relations across those twenty years had been unusually harmonious and fruitful. For the loss of the strength, the mettle, of George Campbell there was no easy substitute.[31]

Convocation procession, May 1931, Murray Macneill, the registrar, leading. Note the segregation, the women graduates coming first.

Nevertheless, his successor, Fred Pearson, had vigour of mind and fecundity of ideas. If he was more volatile than Campbell, he had tremendous energy and enthusiasm, which he gave readily to Dalhousie. It was Fred Pearson who had led the greatly successful Million Dollar Campaign of 1920, which had earned $2 million.

MacKenzie had told the board in 1922 that Dalhousie needed new endowment; by 1928 Dalhousie's needs and ambitions had grown. Early in October 1929 MacKenzie urged the board to consider a new campaign for 1930–1. Dalhousie needed $5 million, but he anticipated $2 million in bequests over the next few years, and a campaign could aim at $3 million. MacKenzie and Pearson between them decided that they needed technical assistance, and they consulted John Price Jones, Inc., an American firm that specialized in university campaigns. It had recently delivered satisfactory results to Ohio State, Wellesley, Harvard, and Temple.

By American standards, Dalhousie was not well geared for an extensive campaign. The questionnaire prepared by John Price Jones asked, among many questions, "How many staff in the alumni office?" Dalhousie's answer, "There is no staff in the alumni office." Asked about an alumni secretary, Dalhousie replied there was none, nor had there ever been one. The last *Alumni Directory* was fairly recent, published in 1925, and a card catalogue of alumni had been a legacy from that. Dalhousie did have active alumni associations in Vancouver, Toronto, Montreal, and New York as well as in Halifax. On this basis the American firm prepared an organizational plan of campaign. This initial assessment cost $3,000, but the campaign was estimated to cost $100,000. If the campaign realized $3 million the cost would amount to only 3.3 per cent.[32]

Dalhousie's current balance sheet for 1928–9 was as follows: income, $257,753; expenses, $254,953. Of its income, tuition fees represented 49 per cent, investments 36 per cent. Its expenditure broke down as follows: professors' salaries, 59 per cent; building and maintenance, 18 per cent; administration expenses, 14 per cent; laboratories, 5 per cent; and libraries, 5 per cent.

Dalhousie's total endowment had grown from $650,000 in 1919 to over $2 million in 1929. It was a portfolio not ill designed to absorb some of the shocks of the stock market crash of October 1929. Its investments were highly conservative, exemplified by cautious investments in stocks. Only 24 per cent of Dalhousie's portfolio was in common stocks, two-thirds of which were bank stocks (mostly Bank of Nova Scotia), the rest in railways and utilities. The great staple of Dalhousie's portfolio was bonds, some 62 per cent, of which almost two-thirds were in government bonds (mostly Dominion of Canada), and the rest in industrial bonds and trust debentures. By 1930 only 7 per cent of Dalhousie's portfolio was in mortgages. The average rate of return across the whole of Dalhousie's portfolio, as of 30 June 1930, was 5.68 per cent.[33]

But the effect of the October 1929 crash and the world financial crisis that followed meant that hopes for a great 1930 Dalhousie campaign that would exceed the 1920 one had to be reluctantly given up. Nevertheless, Pearson moved into the chairmanship with some confidence, demonstrated in his handling of the Gowanloch affair early in 1930, and Dalhousie's change of presidents a year later.

· 2 ·

Changing the Guard
1929–1933

The Gowanloch affair, 1930. MacMechan and MacKenzie retire. Dalhousie and dances. King's establishes itself on campus. The new Dalhousie president, Carleton Stanley. R.B. Bennett is unhappy with R.A. MacKay. Stanley defeats the chairman of the board, G.F. Pearson. Death of MacMechan.

Gowan is the Scottish word for daisy, and James Nelson Gowanloch was one – a poet, a stamp collector, a considerable researcher, and a splendid teacher. Born in 1896, he took degrees at the University of Manitoba and went on to do his doctorate at Chicago. He finished all the work but, for some reason, never his final orals. He was teaching at Wabash College in Indiana when President MacKenzie hired him in August 1923, on strong recommendations from the University of Chicago and the Wood's Hole Oceanographic Institute. A specialist in marine biology, he organized the Dalhousie Biology Club which celebrated its success with a splendid banquet in November 1928, the guests of which included not only Gowanloch's senior students but the lieutenant-governor and other local luminaries. His work was both concentrated and eclectic; in 1928 he broadcast a series of fascinating lectures on biology over CHNS; he published an essay in the *Dalhousie Gazette*, "The Unicorn, and the Childhood of Biology," a clever blend of myth, history, and science, shot through with Gowanloch's ideas of life as process of becoming. "Living as we must," he said, "in an instant present ... a paradox – an instant present that has no beginning and no end. Nothing is being, all is becoming."

Gowanloch had lost a leg when he was young, pulled under the wheels of a carriage; other than that he looked like a shorter edition of Bertrand Russell, with the same aquiline features and some of Russell's other qualities as well. He was a vivacious lecturer, a delightful raconteur, and he mixed well with students of both sexes. One morn-

39

ing after a dance when he did not arrive for his class, some students went over to his house at 93 Le Marchant Street, and found him asleep in full evening clothes. Nothing loath, he came to class and gave the lecture as he was. He had other casual habits, including those with money; dunning letters found their way to Dalhousie's bursar, to President MacKenzie and others, demanding payment for books, biology supplies, and stamps (he specialized in airmail covers). In 1929 he published in the *Dalhousie Review* a presentable sonnet, "Absence," of which the sextet was

> So long I, O Beloved, with thee again
> To watch the moon's broad silver on the hills
> Or see her slenderest seaward crescent stand
> Sharp in the azure, while the slow surf fills
> Our pause of speech, and from the darkening land
> Comes, slow re-echoing, the sea's refrain.

The beloved might have been his wife, Louise Ross, whom he was supporting while she finished her MD in New York. She visited Halifax from time to time. But since she was considering divorce in 1928, probably her husband was thinking of someone else.[1]

The possibility of finding a co-respondent for a divorce was opportunely presented to Louise Gowanloch after her return to Halifax. In March 1930, in the hallway of Gowanloch's flat on Barrington Street, she encountered Eleanor, a Dalhousie senior in biology living at Shirreff Hall. Under Mrs Gowanloch's badgering, she confessed her relations with Professor Gowanloch and the fact that she wished to marry him. Eleanor was not exactly a beauty; one contemporary described her as a "picked chicken" – short, blonde, and scraggly; nevertheless, there she was. Nor was it the first time scandal had been bruited in Gowanloch's relations with his female students. None of it might have got out had not Mrs Gowanloch wanted to use Eleanor as co-respondent in her divorce action.[2]

Under some pressure, Eleanor went home to Hantsport on 13 March to get academic work done. Whatever she told her parents, it is certain that, frightened of her father, she ran away to the Gowanlochs on Monday, 17 March. Her father, so it was said, came to town with a gun looking for Gowanloch, but was successfully headed off by the dean of law, Sidney Smith, and Margaret Lowe, the warden of Shirreff Hall. By this time Eleanor was in hiding with friends of Gowanloch's on Morris Street. That same day Mrs Gowanloch came to G.F. Pearson (President MacKenzie was in Montreal for medical reasons) and said she was launching her divorce.[3]

There were certainly doubts as to what Eleanor's relations with Gowanloch actually were; her father believed his daughter innocent, and so did others, including Margaret Lowe and Murray Macneill. But Gowanloch told Pearson that life without Eleanor was impossible. It was difficult to know whom to believe; Murray Macneill reported that after Gowanloch had given details of his adventures with Eleanor, he had then retracted it all.

The Board of Governors met on 20 March and agreed that Gowanloch and his wife, employed as assistant, should be instantly suspended. Gowanloch submitted his resignation the next day. He was not allowed to do even that: he was, instead, dismissed, as of 2 May 1930. Mrs Gowanloch was on contract and her contract was allowed to expire. In the meantime the Gowanloch divorce took place quietly in late April with Eleanor as co-respondent.[4]

Unlike the Norman Symons affair at King's in 1929, where a professor of psychology was unobtrusively dismissed for teaching Freud, the Gowanloch scandal was soon known at Dalhousie. Everyone was shaken by it. Then Eleanor's mother approached Senate to ask that her daughter be allowed to sit her final examinations at Supplementals in September 1930. That request occasioned an anguished debate in Senate in April, over the proper course to pursue. Some of the younger spirits, George Wilson of History and Hugh Bell of Biology, admired the girl's courage in wanting to return – some thought she might be pregnant – to finish her year. Others in Senate disliked very much allowing this young woman, even for ten days in September, to publish her adventures amid the virgins of Shirreff Hall. A majority of Senate were inclined, as Mac-Mechan put it, "to mercy on the girl." Debate could not be concluded and had to be put off until the May meeting. Wilson and Bell moved that Eleanor be allowed to write supplemental exams; a motion to have her write her examinations clandestinely at home was defeated by 10 to 9 and the Wilson motion passed. President MacKenzie had opposed leniency. His view seemed to be that as a senior student Eleanor had behaved irresponsibly, not to say wickedly; nevertheless the younger men in Senate defeated him. Not only that, but Eleanor wrote and passed her examinations in September and was awarded her B.SC. in October 1930.[5] As to her pregnancy, there never was any. However her affair with Gowanloch started, there is reason to suspect collusion between wife and husband, with Eleanor, plain, naive, and willing, caught in the middle. Gowanloch left Halifax, with debts and a bad name trailing after him; his talents, however, earned him a good position as chief biologist in the Louisiana Department of Conservation.

One member of Senate whose good sense was missing in that long and difficult debate was the university's dean, Howard Murray. He had been ill with gallstones for some time. Being "cut for the stone," as the saying went, was a very old operation; a good *inciseur* in Louis XIV's time could do it in under ten minutes, which, in the absence of any anaesthetic other than brandy, was fortunate. In the 1920s it had become as routine as an operation for appendicitis, but Murray resisted having it. MacMechan went to visit him at his home in May 1930 and found him "sitting in a chair by the fire with Pain & Apprehension for companions. He suffers from the slightest movement, a cough, a sneeze, laughing. 'To each his suffering,' as Gray says. May I have fortitude when my time comes."[6] Murray did not improve. By the time he agreed to the operation on 9 September it was too late. He died the same afternoon.[7]

Archibald MacMechan Retires

Murray's death set MacMechan thinking. A month later he saw MacKenzie about his retirement. MacMechan was sixty-eight years old, and would have to retire anyway in 1932 at age seventy, the Carnegie rule for pensions. He was still in good form, enjoying his world, his work, his golf. "A good world!" he exclaimed at New Year's in 1930, "a pity to leave it so soon!" He had been walking along South Park Street in the late afternoon and caught "a beautiful lemon-gold sunset." He had been out at a conference in Edmonton on English in November 1927, and came home, as MacKenzie wrote Walter Murray in Saskatoon,

quite walking on air. You must have had him at a garage and turned on the air under quite high pressure. It is a question as to whether his old tires will stand it. It is a great thing for a cold-blooded being like myself to see how others can get surcharged with satisfaction and enthusiasm in minor matters of life.

That gets the apposition between the two old friends and colleagues about right.[8]

So MacMechan laid out his position and hopes with President MacKenzie. He had had forty-two years of service at Dalhousie, and for the latter half of that time his salary was inadequate; he had always had to supplement it with journalism or teaching summer schools. The board had twice made him loans, all repaid. He had never had leave. He now asked for a year's leave with pay, and since his Carnegie pension would be $1,765, he asked if Dalhousie could bring it up to his current salary, $3,500. The board did that, and went one better; half of their addition, $1,735, would go to his wife, after his death, during her lifetime. MacMechan was grateful, especially about the provision for his wife; it seemed to him, towards the end of his long Dalhousie career, that "my forty-two years at Dalhousie have been full of happiness. As I look back the way seems all sunshine, un-clouded to the end."[9] So indeed it was. "The last of the old guard is leaving us," said the *Alumni News* in March 1931:

To a whole generation of Dalhousians the thought of the Little College with-out its historian will be like the *Tempest* without Ariel, or *A Midsummer Night's Dream* without Puck. For there is something of Ariel, something of Puck, in the twinkle of that lively eye; there is a lightness, a gaiety … in him … He was an Ontarian who out-Nova Scotiaed Nova Scotians. He came a stranger, was faced with the suspicion a stranger inevitably involves, but what son of Ultima Thule has done for it and for its story, what he has done?

MacMechan did not escape the effects of the stock market crash of October 1929. Like many another paterfamilias, he had to set to and support one of his married daughters with $1,000, when he was al-ready paying off a bank loan himself. Nevertheless by 1931 Mac-Mechan and his wife were able to go abroad to England for a year and Dalhousie English was taken over by a young tall New Zealander from Jesus College, Cambridge, C.L. Bennet, who had come in 1923 with King's. He now transferred to Dalhousie and became Mac-Mechan's successor as head of the English Department for the next thirty years.[10]

The Resignation of President MacKenzie
President MacKenzie, three years younger than MacMechan, had found MacMechan's kindness and directness had made his own work tolerable. It was true of MacKenzie's relations with most members of his staff. As he said, it "has been a happiness to me, and I must admit I shall find it hard to leave them." For MacKenzie, too, was going to re-tire. In 1929 when the new campaign for funds was being considered, MacKenzie thought he would wait until it had been completed. But with the campaign postponed, the lull in building and other activity seemed to him a good time to allow Dalhousie to look for a new presi-dent, different from himself, with different ideas. "It is also a time," MacKenzie told the board in December 1930, "when the whole orga-nization of the University should be looked into. This University is very different, with its many sides, from the University of 1911 which I undertook to preside over." So saying, he placed his resignation, effec-tive 1 July 1931, with the secretary and walked out of the room. The

whole board stood up as he left. The board were sad and grateful at the same time. "Never has a man given more unselfishly of himself to any cause," they agreed, "than has Dr. MacKenzie given of himself to Dalhousie." The board adjourned to the president's house, now just five minutes' walk away on Oxford Street, for Scotch, reminiscences, and mutual commiseration over age, time, and change. MacKenzie's going would leave a huge gap, difficult to fill. The staff were uneasy too. George Wilson wrote how much affection and respect he had for MacKenzie, hoping "with all my heart that you may see your way clear to remain President for a few more years." So did the young dean of law, Sidney Smith, on behalf of his faculty.[11]

But MacKenzie did not change his mind. He replied to Smith that he had thought about it for over a year. A new president had to come sometime; when things were running smoothly was a good time for him "to *learn* Dalhousie." MacKenzie did not want to wait until his retirement was "considered a relief. I'm afraid that would finish me." He was not displeased at what he had accomplished; his own view, given to MacMechan three years later, was that he had made a college into a university, and given it a businesslike administration. That was as accurate as it was realistic. He also recognized that Dalhousie had been heavily preoccupied with building Studley, with the war, with working up the Medical Faculty, and with university federation. Dalhousie had never done much with student and alumni relations, as MacKenzie admitted in 1928 at a reunion to honour R.B. Bennett. Dalhousie, being dependent upon private support, said MacKenzie, should honour those who made possible her progress, "indeed, at times, her very existence." Bennett was there that day to launch, with $25,000 of his own money, a campaign for $100,000 to endow a Dean Weldon Professorship of Law (Weldon had died in 1925), plus another $100,000 for a library and scholarships. Bennett talked about the Dalhousie traditions of work, adding "not Heaven itself can change the past if it is wasted opportunity." MacKenzie too would have subscribed to that; he trusted the old steep, lonely paths to learning.[12]

That had worked well enough in the old days when Pictou County and the Presbyterians looked towards, and came to, Dalhousie. But even before the 1925 union of Presbyterians and Methodists in the United Church, those Pictou County loyalties had been decaying; after 1925 Presbyterian loyalty was sending some Presbyterian students to Mount Allison.

Dances and Pep Rallies
By the end of the 1920s Dalhousie seemed less a place of learning than it used to be. The old Dalhousie standards still held, but new

mores around dances, cars, and cards were gathering force; against old rocks new waves produced turmoil and undercurrents. In her final report in June 1930, before leaving to become principal of Bishop Strachan School in Toronto, Margaret Lowe pointed out that the lack of an adequate social life at Shirreff Hall was a growing problem and the remedy difficult to prescribe. Since dancing was almost the only form of social entertainment, the out-of-town girls had difficulty developing a social life; those from Halifax who had come through the school system together had already established their acquaintances. "A girl from outside," said Miss Lowe, "has to be exceptionally attractive to men to be able to break into [it]." This was especially because of "the modern custom of 'pairing off' for all social affairs. The girl without a steady partner feels awkward about going [out] unattended." Nor did the system work well with some men students; "there is a tacit understanding that at the beginning of the year a man selects his partner for the year, and the less affluent men hesitate to bespeak a girl when his means of entertainment are limited." Hence the very ones, female and male, who needed social experience, were apt to miss out on it.[13]

There were complaints that girls' success at Dalhousie was too apt to be measured in social terms. "Alice" reported in the *Gazette*, on 3 December 1930:

I once heard a Dalhousie co-ed questioned as to how another girl was "getting on" at college.

"Oh – uh – not very well, I'm afraid" was the answer.

"Really – I always thought she was clever."

"Oh, she made five first classes, but I mean she didn't get to many of the dances." ...

This year a Freshette came up to me at Registration Day and said, "Write down five things for me to take – anything at all but Algebra or Latin. I don't care."

The irony was the freshette could not avoid taking both, unless she preferred Greek to Latin.

At Christmas 1930 Dalhousie was, said the *Gazette*, on the verge of going dance crazy. For although the Senate could control official Dalhousie dances, it could not, at any rate did not, control student club dances. They had academic and social consequences. Some romantic ones were charmingly metamorphosed into poetry:

> A dream I think it was so fair, so fleeting,
> Moonlight through a sudden blur of tears:

O Dear Heart, thy golden, golden laughter
Echoing down the garden, down the years.

Academic results were sometimes the price too. In January 1931 came the Christmas examination marks in arts and science: 58 per cent passed all examinations, 18 per cent failed in one, 10 per cent failed in two, 14 per cent failed in three or more subjects. Those who failed in four or more were subject to the rule that they might be asked to leave Dalhousie.

In May 1930 the list of failures had seemed "catastrophic" to Mac-Mechan. Because they were partly owing to declining Nova Scotia school standards in Latin and mathematics, they raised the perennial question of what to do about Dalhousie's compulsory two years of Latin or Greek. Dalhousie taught them as languages; the *Gazette* implied what was significant was not *how* the ancient Greeks and Roman wrote, but *what* they wrote. The news a year later that Yale had given up Latin for its BA encouraged such attitudes.[14]

American examples had other effects. There was the new habit of organized cheering, imported, said the *Gazette* disapproving, from American universities. To be entreated to yell oneself hoarse "under the direction of a wildly gesticulating figure" was ridiculous. Pep rallies and other such activities put "undue emphasis on winning a game at the expense of real sportsmanship ... absurd manifestations of immaturity." There were complaints about the *Gazette* itself from C.F. Fraser (Arts '31), who said its 1930 tone – silly, shrill, and sophomoric was a disgrace "to the intellectual abilities of Dalhousians."[15]

That same intellectual character concerned President MacKenzie in finding a new warden for Shirreff Hall. Miss Lowe had been a part-time lecturer in English and French; he always wanted a warden of high academic ability, provided she had the talent for running a women's residence. To that end he hoped to appoint a young biologist, Dixie Pelluet, a PH.D. just out of Bryn Mawr, a university where MacKenzie himself had taught. She had already accepted an appointment at Rockford College, Illinois, but an exchange of telegrams in June indicated she much preferred Dalhousie. When interviewed in Halifax, she seemed ideal; but when MacKenzie wrote W.A. Maddox of Rockford College asking, president to president, if Dr Pelluet could be released from her contract, he got "a curt if courteous refusal." So Dalhousie took the next-best candidate, Anna MacKeen, a Nova Scotian graduate of McGill.[16]

King's College was an added dimension to the problems of Dalhousie in the late 1920s. King's gradually discovered that the rules it had agreed to in 1923 to qualify for the Carnegie grant were inconvenient and constraining. President Boyle resigned in 1924 and was succeeded by the Reverend Arthur H. Moore, editor of the *Montreal Churchman*, an experienced writer and speaker, with some knowledge of business. As president he took a hard look at the terms of the 1923 agreement to see if there were any useful niches to be exploited. In particular, Moore sought amelioration of section 11 ("King's shall hold in abeyance its power of granting degrees except in Divinity"). W.E. Thompson, secretary of the Dalhousie board, replied firmly that section 11 was one of the cardinal conditions for the Carnegie grant. Moore laboured hard and long to raise the $400,000 required to obtain Carnegie's $600,000, and succeeded in the nick of time. Dalhousie had to remind him, however, in October 1928, that the $400,000 was not King's own to use for Divinity, but to be used conjointly with Dalhousie and the $600,000 to establish university instruction for both King's and Dalhousie students.[17]

The cornerstone for the new King's College was laid on 9 May 1929. The buildings were unofficially opened with a three-day King's Alumni reunion in August 1930, and officially, on 2 October. That meant that Dalhousie was free to resume its possession of Birchdale, though too late in 1930 to be of any use to Dalhousie for 1930–1. Birchdale was the handsome seven-acre property on the North-West Arm that Dalhousie had bought in 1920 as a men's residence. It had been leased reluctantly to King's in 1923. The old hotel had not been improved by its seven-year occupation by fifty to seventy King's students. The Buildings and Grounds Committee of the Dalhousie board thought it would require $45,000 just to restore and refurnish it, which was more than the entire building was worth. In December 1930 it was decided to raze the building, deferring for the moment construction of a new one. Birchdale (Dalhousie called it University Hall) carried a mortgage of $100,000, and it was decided to pay off $30,000 of that and take advantage of the offer of a contractor to raze Birchdale for nothing, if allowed to take what he wanted.[18]

As Birchdale was coming down, another building was going up on the Dalhousie campus, invited there by Dalhousie, but rather apart from it: the Public Archives of Nova Scotia. Nova Scotia did not have an archives until an anonymous Nova Scotian offered to provide it if the provincial government would support it. MacKenzie and the Dalhousie board liked the idea of having it on the campus, and offered land. Andrew Cobb designed the handsome building. It is still there, still elegant, now occupied by the Dalhousie Mathematics Department. The Nova Scotia government, under Conservative Premier Edgar Rhodes, made an unusual arrangement – the Archives would be run by "a responsible Board which would have direct supervision of the design, construction and maintenance ... which would function in perpetuity free from political or other adverse influences."

The Archives of Nova Scotia was formally opened on 14 January 1931 with the unknown donor present. It was W.H. Chase, from the Annapolis Valley, on the Dalhousie board since 1916. The first archivist was Daniel Cobb Harvey (1886–1966), a Dalhousie Rhodes Scholar of 1910, brought from the University of Manitoba. He had been wanting to return to Dalhousie for many years, and as well as his duties in the Archives, became lecturer in history. D.C. Harvey was a fine scholar, commanding a terse, elegant prose that carried authority. He sometimes wore a sad air, as if he felt he had not got from the world what he thought he deserved. But he had a saving sense of humour; after a colleague's paper on whaling in the South Seas, Harvey remarked to a young woman, "Pretty dull stuff, wasn't it? Not even the rustle of a grass skirt!"[19]

The Archives building was first used by Dalhousie for the 1931 convocation. Early on 7 May 1931 the Dalhousie gymnasium, built in 1921, burned down in a spectacular fire. Dalhousie examinations, convocations, had all been held there. The loss amounted to $51,000, covered half by insurance; but the replacement, begun at once under MacKenzie's urging, would cost $150,000. There were rumours that the fire was arson, set by a disgruntled student, and there were even a few who claimed to know who the culprit was, though no charge was ever made.[20]

Appointing a New President

By May 1931 the search for a new president was well under way. That January the board sent Pearson and MacKenzie to New York, Montreal, and Ottawa to look for presidential possibilities. They discussed them with the prime minister, R.B. Bennett. They had already circulated other university presidents for information and suggestions. By March they had a list of fifty candidates with profiles of twenty of them. Twelve names were selected; who the candidates actually were was a secret, well kept as it happened.[21]

From the beginning the board seemed to have been thinking more of external candidates, as there were no obvious internal ones. Murray Macneill had nursed the idea in 1911 that, had MacKenzie been unwilling to return to Dalhousie, the board might well have risked asking him, the thirty-five-year-old registrar, to be president. He would then have accepted. Mrs Macneill, one of Dalhousie's more delightful hostesses, thought in 1931 her husband should have been asked. Macneill said, however, that in 1931 "nothing could have induced" him to be president. The new dean of law, Sidney Smith, appointed in 1929, was a possibility. C.J. Burchell, a powerful downtown lawyer, urged Smith's appointment as strongly as he could with friends on the board. But Smith was young, only thirty-four, a vivid and flamboyant lecturer; his law examinations not infrequently featured a Halifax law firm, Stickem, Good and Proper; the board's other lawyers were not adventurous. Three years later Smith accepted the presidency of the University of Manitoba.[22]

Of external candidates, there was a short list of three, of whom two names are known: A.L. Burt, recently appointed professor of history at the University of Minnesota, and Carleton Stanley, assistant to the president of McGill and professor of Greek. Letters went out in late April inviting them to Halifax to see and be seen. A.L. Burt (1888–1970), two years younger than Stanley, was an Ontario Rhodes Scholar who had been head of history at the University of Alberta before migrating to Minnesota in 1930. Of Burt's Halifax visit little is known; in any case he was not Dalhousie's first choice. On Carleton Stanley there is much more, not least because his own personal papers are extensive.

Carleton Stanley in April 1931 was the heir apparent to the principalship of McGill. Sir Arthur Currie, the principal, had taken leave for six months while he attended the opening of the new Indian Parliament in New Delhi as official representative of Canada. Stanley, a friend of the chancellor, Edward Beatty, would be Currie's replacement during his absence. Named assistant to the principal, he hated the title; he wanted to be acting principal, or vice-principal. But he was in command at McGill, and he got to like it. Many began to find him a very different animal from Currie, the unobtrusive old warrior.[23]

When Sir Arthur Currie returned in April 1931 he knew of Dalhousie's offer, which Stanley had been mulling over for a week. Halifax was tempting: better schools for his children; an excellent house, as opposed to the one he had in Mount Royal which his father-in-law, Professor W.J. Alexander, thought limited and shabby; affordable domestic help for his wife Isabel and their two children. Moreover, Isabel Stanley had been born in Halifax and her mother was a Haligonian. Stanley's immediate ambition, however, was to be principal of McGill and he did not want to compromise that possibility. But Currie was only fifty-six years old, and it might be a few years before the McGill principalship became open. These were the balances in Stanley's mind when he went to see Currie on 1 May.[24]

Whether from Currie or from Beatty, Stanley got enough encouragement about his prospects at McGill to send a refusal to Pearson. But Pearson was anxious that Stanley visit Halifax before coming to any decision. "I think it is of greater importance that a prospective

President of Dalhousie should fall in love with the opportunity for hard work presented than that we should, at first sight, select him because we like the colour of his hair or are impressed with his stature." Stanley decided to come to Halifax for a visit, Pearson making it clear that he was still entirely at liberty to turn the offer down. Stanley was at Dalhousie for four days in May 1930, and he was impressed:

What did amaze me was the sheer pub.[lic] spirit of every single Gov.[ernor] I met. A good committee man could use that team to do an endless good for the whole country. Hx [sic] always has been the friendliest place in the world, I enjoyed myself; but through all the hospitality I cd. feel the hardheaded determ[inatio]n. to get the best man poss. and to have Dal. get on.[25]

Dalhousie was sufficiently hard-headed that in the middle of Stanley's visit MacKenzie wrote to an old friend and former colleague, Daniel Murray, newly retired as professor of mathematics at McGill, about him. MacKenzie knew of Stanley's scholarly reputation, but what of his other side? Some McGill men were saying he was unpopular, "very opinionative [sic] and for that reason makes a poor executive." Murray replied that he knew Stanley only from the McGill Faculty Club, that he was "frank, straight-forward and outspoken." What his reserves of executive tact and patience were, Murray had no way of knowing.[26]

Stanley was tempted. Though his relations with Currie were friendly, Currie was not an academic, and "with the best will in the world [Currie] can hardly realize the needs." Stanley believed *he* did. On 16 June Pearson wired R.B. Bennett; would he talk to W.A. Black (MP for Halifax, 1923–34), and William Herridge (Bennett's brother-in-law) about Stanley? Murray Macneill, in Montreal on his way overseas, was astonished to find, after all the favourable information, a number of people who at the mention of Stanley as president "threw up their hands in horror and cry 'impossible', 'ruin', 'a quarter century of stagnation'." One person at McGill in whom Macneill had great confidence was D.A. Murray, and he favoured Stanley. When Macneill's letter reached Halifax, MacKenzie sent a radio message to the *Doric*, asking Macneill whose opinions he had been reporting, but Macneill could not divulge that. The board met on 23 June; that evening, sweetening its salary offer to $10,000 (MacKenzie's salary was $7,500), it moved that Stanley be appointed. He accepted, resigning from McGill on 10 July 1931.[27]

Shipping his household effects, Stanley and his family set out for Halifax. He arrived on a rainy day in late July, his car with a broken spring, a flat tire where the spare was, his wife with a ulcerated tooth, to discover that the CNR freight car containing his household goods had been broken into. Pearson wrote that he was entitled to some sympathy, but he would be all right. "Don't forget 'there is only one God (Dalhousie) and Stanley is his prophet.' "[28] That may not have been the best advice; Stanley was ready to be both God and prophet.

President Carleton Stanley

The president Dalhousie got was exceptional. Born in 1886 in Rhode Island, his father from Derbyshire and his mother Irish, he was brought up in Canada. After two boys and two girls, the father left, surfacing only every so often. Young Carleton worked from the age of eleven, as church janitor and driving a milk delivery truck, managing to put himself through school and the University of Toronto, where in 1911 he took the Rhodes and two gold medals. His discipline was classics. At New College, Oxford, in 1913 he took first class in Greats (classics), the only colonial, his tutor told him, who had ever been given a clear first in Greek and Latin prose composition.[29]

Stanley spent some time in Germany, touring it by train and bicycle with Frank Underhill, some of whose ideas he shared and whose life-long friend he remained. Stanley was comfortable with German; he was good enough to be an External Affairs examiner in German translation during the Second World War. Indeed, Stanley's linguistic accomplishments were formidable: Latin and Greek, of course; French and German; enough Spanish for business dealings. And his classical disciplines had tempered and sharpened his English. The rich vocabulary of English in weasel words, forms of hypocrisy built into the language, Carleton Stanley would have none of: his English was trenchant, forceful, at times almost vehement. He said what he meant. Vivacity is the impression left by his letters: a well-read mind, a versatile intelligence, deployed with energy. A good example is a 1931 letter to a member of the board whom he liked, Dugald Macgillivray, general manager of Eastern Trust, in which he registered surprise at learning from President Moore of King's that neither Greek nor Hebrew were compulsory for the King's degree in divinity. Stanley was indignant:

We can and must wake up to the fact that this and other things of the kind – notably a similar dearth of Mathematics – means simply a lapse from civilisation. Filling up our schools and colleges with alleged economics, alleged psychology, alleged sociology, in place of these fundamental studies is nothing less than the American "primrose path" to barbarism.

No man is a hero to his valet, it is sometimes said, but Stanley was a hero to his secretary, Lola Henry, with whom he worked rapidly and skilfully on his own and Dalhousie's correspondence. She found it a joy to work for such a president.[30]

His social sympathies were with the underdog; he had come up the hard way himself. He knew and liked many of the socialist intellectuals of his day, including Laski in England, Frank Underhill, Frank Scott, King Gordon, and others in Canada; but he associated easily with businessmen, having been one, and he came to know Edward Beatty, chairman of the board of the CPR, William Herridge, and through Herridge, R.B. Bennett. It was part of the ease with which he met and greeted men and women of the great world outside universities.

Stanley was apt to make his own decisions on his own strong premises; he was not a man who found consultation natural. Nor was it easy for him to accept advice that went contrary to his own instincts. He was a man not easily persuaded; he could be stubborn, determined, wilful. His own thinking could change, but mainly from his own internal processes, and he was not always aware of them. Stanley sometimes reminded people of Humpty Dumpty in *Through the Looking Glass*: " 'When I use a word,' Humpty Dumpty said in a rather scornful tone, 'it means just what I choose it to mean, – neither more nor less.' " Many years later his wife said much the same.

Stanley met Isabel Alexander while in Toronto, teaching classics at Victoria College. His eyesight kept him out of the army, but he found teaching rather thin going financially and in 1916 he went into the cloth-importing business in Montreal. He seems to have been successful enough at it, but in 1925 the McGill professorship of Greek opened up, so Stanley applied and was appointed. Ambitious, he wanted a substantial honours program in classics and mathematics and at the same time a strengthening of those subjects in the Quebec high schools. These efforts, and his spirited defence of academic values, brought him to the attention of important members of the McGill community, especially Edward Beatty.

Now he had come to Dalhousie, brilliant, used to acting on his own, driven by a strong sense of duty, and not altogether aware of his limitations. One wise friend told him in October 1931 that all will be well if you let Dalhousie "flower to its own ethos." It was percipient advice, for both Stanley and Dalhousie. Stanley could not guarantee "in this fluctuating and distracting age" that that could be done. In 1936, five years later, he would quote Molière,

C'est une folie à nulle autre seconde
Vouloir se mêler de corriger le monde

but believing it only partly true. A translation of it might be rendered,

It's the worst of follies being hurled
At trying to reform the world.[31]

Stanley threw himself into his work, armed with ideas, reforms, penchants, upon a university community that was slow to change. It was willing to listen, but was not used to being instructed in crisp language what best it ought to do, and by a man from Toronto and McGill at that. To masses of good advice from Pearson, Stanley paid only a modicum of attention. He might well have benefited from reflecting on the Nova Scotian definition of an expert: "an s.o.b. from out of town." Stanley did little to meet this innate uneasiness. When he first came to work Monday, 3 August he was introduced to Murray Macneill, the registrar, by Beatrice Smith, secretary in the office. "Mr. Macneill knows everything," said Miss Smith with a smile. That did not endear him to Stanley. To Macneill, who offered help and information, Stanley made it clear that he would not need much of either, and certainly not from Murray Macneill. The two men took an instant dislike to each other.[32]

The Senate was more tolerant and patient. Pearson went to some pains to educate Stanley about Senate. He was at Stanley's office several times a week the first six months, at Stanley's request, to give him advice; he also suggested his should be balanced with advice from others. Pearson was particular about Senate, notably its power under the Statute of 1863, Dalhousie's fundamental charter: section 7 committed the internal regulation of the university to the Senate, subject to the approval of the board, not the president. Whatever the president did, in the long run he could only function properly by and with cooperation from Senate. A Senate with its heels dug in was to be avoided. It had, after all, defeated even as well-liked a president as MacKenzie on the Gowanloch affair just a few months before.[33]

Stanley found it difficult to take that in, or at least to absorb fully its implications. He was the more disposed to take his own line when he found that a number of members of Senate were not particularly brilliant, many with reputations that did not reach beyond the three-mile limit. He was too poor a hypocrite to prevent his views from showing even at his first meeting with Senate on 15 October 1931. The next meeting he did not attend, after which there was no Senate meeting until January 1932. He succeeded in giving Senate the impression he was going to run Dalhousie as he thought best.

Stanley's official inauguration on 9 October 1931, at the Capitol Theatre on Barrington Street, was a considerable affair. In 1911

MacKenzie said he had no time for an inauguration, but that would not have been Stanley's way. The board tried hard to get R.B. Bennett to come, rescheduling the ceremony in that hope. But the business of being prime minister was too pressing even for Bennett's energies; what the board did do was arrange to have Bennett's ten-minute speech relayed from Ottawa by telephone, then broadcast directly through loudspeakers to the assembled throng. It was pronounced a great success both as engineering and speech.

Stanley then followed, setting out his basic philosophy. Standards of scholarship at Dalhousie needed raising in those foundation subjects, mathematics and classics, and also the level of its graduates. It was not entirely Dalhousie's fault; schools in Canada were failing the students and the universities were failing the high school teachers in not providing training adequate for effective teaching of mathematics and classics. Moreover, boys after a certain age needed to be taught by men teachers, not women. In Canada the universities were probably getting the best brains from the schools, but they were not giving them back as teachers, especially what Stanley called "the very best male brains." These were disappearing into the professions, and thus, for teaching the next generation, their skills were lost.

Dr H.B. Atlee added comments of his own a year later. It was hopeless, he wrote Stanley, to expect much improvement in the secondary schools. Nova Scotian colleges would have to improve themselves first. "If my study of human history is correct it is from the top that improvement comes and not from the bottom." Atlee had been brought up in Annapolis Royal and was under no illusions about virtues inherent in rural Nova Scotia. He exaggerated, as usual, but there was experience in what he said. Rural Nova Scotia "is reactionary and timid; fearful and parsimonious; ... and cannot be moved by any other force than an actual demonstration of what can be done."

With something of his own philosophy in mind, Stanley persuaded the Board of Governors to establish four entrance scholarships for male students, two each in mathematics and classics. The board even found a donor to produce the money. So far, so good. The terms on which such scholarships were to be won were, however, Senate's to lay down. The first Senate knew of it was the announcement in the newspapers, terms and all. But Senate did not repine; much could be forgiven a president who was on the right side of standards, even if he did seem to be taking short cuts.[34]

The Prime Minister Quarrels with R.A. MacKay
Working with President Stanley was not Fred Pearson's only difficulty that autumn. On 15 October there appeared in *Maclean's* an article

by Professor R.A. MacKay, "After Beauharnois – what?" It was on the implications of the Beauharnois scandal for Canadian political parties, especially for their campaign funds. MacKay was thirty-eight years old and had been Dalhousie's Eric Dennis professor of political science since 1927. The article was not shrill or vituperative; but it had not taken full account of the latest evidence from parliamentary committees. MacKay concluded that the Beauharnois scandal showed that both political parties had "become pensioners of selfish interests," and that election laws needed changing to protect the public.

What really annoyed the prime minister was the Conservative party being lumped in with the Liberal party. The Beauharnois promoters had given some $700,000 to the Liberal party for the federal election of 1930, and though they offered money to the Conservatives, on Bennett's instructions, it was presumed, his party refused to touch it. Not only that, but on Mackenzie King's urgent request, Bennett had agreed to suppress evidence of King's Bermuda hotel being paid by Senator McDougald, a Beauharnois promoter. (It got out because a Progressive MP refused to accept the suppression.) Thus the prime minister, a governor of Dalhousie University, took umbrage at MacKay's article. In December 1931 Bennett made it known that he might resign from the board, or not allow himself to be re-elected (his second six-year term was up in 1932), because R.A. MacKay had not been fired. Pearson and Stanley both attributed that to temporary petulance, but thought Bennett's remarks ought to be kept quiet. Stanley liked critical journalism; and he was right in believing that "it would be almost disastrous for the P.M.'s reputation if it got abroad that he was potting at a rather obscure young professor. Just think," he wrote to W.D. Herridge, "of the damage done to himself if someone like J.S. [John Stevenson] in Ottawa got hold of this." Stanley also pointed out that Mackenzie King, the leader of the opposition, had been in Halifax in November, met a student club, and encountering Professor MacKay, promptly pitched into him for the *Maclean's* article. There were cogent reasons for trying to cool Bennett down.

Pearson, too, wanted very much to keep Bennett on the board and wrote directly to him, explaining how the article had come out as it did. MacKay, said Pearson, was something of an idealist, at times of the Don Quixote kind, who felt it his duty to draw the moral from Beauharnois for students and public. When *Maclean's* told him his article was accepted, he read over his draft copy and decided he had gone further than the evidence warranted and asked that certain statements be deleted. It was too late; *Maclean's* had already gone to press.

Bennett was not altogether mollified. No one had the right to say that he was in the pay of any interests. Surely Professor MacKay had not forgotten that in 1927, when Bennett become leader of the Conservative party, he had stated he no longer had commitments to any business firm, that he had resigned all his directorships and sold a good deal of his stock. MacKay "may be an idealist," Bennett grumbled, "but I am sure you will agree that untruthfulness and idealism are not synonymous, and that idealism is not usually expressed in slanderous or libellous words." That was heavy-handed, for there was little of either; still, in April 1932 Bennett postponed the question of his membership on the board for subsequent discussion. Pearson was grateful, for, as he wrote Bennett, "We are going through a most difficult period at the moment and if ever we needed friends and supporters it is now." That difficulty was the rift, rancorous and widening, between himself and President Stanley.[35]

Pearson Is Brought Down

None of the contentious issues were of much importance in themselves, but by March 1932, they had cumulated suddenly into a fearful realization by Pearson that Stanley was the wrong man as president. Pearson had grown up with Dalhousie, graduating in 1900 in law, and had been living with its ways of working since he had first come on the board in 1916. Charming and brilliant, Pearson can also be judged by his friends, G.E. Wilson, J.L. Ilsley, Maynard Archibald (later of the Supreme Court of Nova Scotia). Pearson was not just a loyal Dalhousian but a passionate one, a bonding established across thirty years and more. Now he saw Senate being bypassed by a new (and imported) president, and surely deliberately, for Stanley had been instructed by Pearson repeatedly about the importance of Senate. Stanley ignored Senate over the Armistice Day service; after Christmas he sent home thirty students who had failed four or more classes, of whom, according to Pearson, at least eight or ten should not have been dismissed; on 3 March 1932 a quarrel arose over the *Dalhousie Review* and H.L. Stewart's editorship, when Pearson told Stanley "he was a God-damned fool." The culmination was a row with the students over a post-Glee Club dance, proposed for Friday, 18 March, which for some years past Senate had permitted the students to hold. The president prohibited it. The *Gazette* protested; it was true, the *Gazette* said, that Dalhousie students may have had too many dances, but the president's action was not the way to solve it.

Pearson brought the current state of affairs before the board executive on 24 March, with the strong suggestion that President Stanley's actions should be reviewed after convocation. The executive asked Stanley to call a Senate meeting forthwith, at which, so it was said, he told them what "a mutinous crew" they were. Stanley seems to have concluded, however, that Senate's alleged unhappiness was a teapot tempest brewed in Pearson's mind.[36]

On a trip to New York together later that month, the two men had the torture of occupying the same drawing-room on the train. After their return, over a period of ten days in early April, Stanley told eleven professors individually that he had had a miserable winter fighting the board to prevent cuts in salaries, and that members of the board had encouraged students over the dance issue. Both assertions, according to Pearson, were untrue; certainly the board had not proposed any reductions in salary. It seemed to Pearson that Stanley was working to ingratiate himself with Senate against the board. Pearson then saw four of the eleven – Dean Smith of Law, Professors R.J. Bean of Medicine, Howard Bronson of Science, and George Wilson of History, who confirmed what Stanley had said. When the executive committee of the board put this to him, Stanley denied most of it. The four however repeated their evidence at an executive meeting on 4 May. Pearson summed up his long indictment of Stanley to the board on 21 May 1932:

A year ago we were a happy family at Dalhousie. The Board, the President, members of the Staff, and the student body were pulling together ... That is not so today. The Board is the same, the members of the staff are the same, and the student body is practically the same. Only the President has changed and it is significant that conditions changed with him.

Stanley's reply on 6 June was an attack on Pearson personally rather than an answer to the points Pearson raised. On that day, at a meeting of the full board, which heard Pearson's charges and Stanley's defence, Pearson asked, as chairman, if anyone wished to present a motion. No one did. Pearson proposed his own, that a committee of three be appointed to investigate the administration of President Stanley, to take evidence, and to report as soon as possible. No one supported it. Pearson resigned at once, stunned and bitter.

There were headlines in the *Halifax Chronicle* the next day: "Dalhousie Chairman Resigns When Board Declines Probe." But no information was available. "Governors are Mute," said the *Chronicle*. Governors, Stanley, and Pearson were in damage control mode; they simply closed ranks. Pearson's parting shot was a long letter refuting Stanley's defence. By then the board was weary of the issue and wished to put it behind them. All it would say to Pearson was that its duty was to give the new president a chance to get properly into the saddle, to familiarize himself with Dalhousie and Nova Scotia. "It was in the best interest of the University that the matters referred to in your letter had better not be re-opened." But it did publish, anonymously, a severely limited edition of the correspondence.[37]

Carleton Stanley had won. He had learned something from the episode; but in the process several professors who had tried to adjudicate between Senate and Stanley, between Pearson and Stanley found that Stanley did not forget. He could not get rid of them but he did not have to forgive them.

In that strange conflict there was no clear and unequivocal truth. Stanley was capable of twisting truth, for the perverse reason that he set great store by it, and would do his utmost to have it on his side, even if it meant suppressing inconvenient facts. Pearson had a temper and was sometimes capable of making mountains out of molehills. In the absence of any substantial collection of documents about Stanley's appointment, one can only surmise: Pearson may have been more ready to appoint Stanley than was President MacKenzie, and Pearson's subsequent animus may have been owing to feeling betrayed by Stanley and by his own judgment.

Friends of Dalhousie and Pearson, who knew Stanley, were baffled by the quarrel and its bitterness; but few believed the fault was all Pearson's. In August 1932 Stanley was told by a friend and admirer, J.M. Macdonnell of the National Trust, Toronto, that the criticism he had heard of Stanley's administration at Dalhousie was that he was in too much of a hurry; he had taken "too little time to come to an understanding of the conditions ... and have not been considerate enough of your colleagues." You've been driving them, not leading them, said Macdonnell.[38]

Stanley's reply was to admit that Macdonnell was 55 per cent correct. His most effective defence was over the Christmas examinations rule that required students to discontinue their year if they failed four classes. Some in Senate believed that if the rule were to be continued at all, it ought to be enforced. It may be recalled that in 1922 the local newspapers put pressure on the application of that rule, and since that time it had been largely disregarded. "The students," said Stanley, "have laughed ever since." Stanley told Senate that if anything more drastic than usual were done at Christmas 1931 about enforcing the rule, that he, as the new president, would be blamed. Stanley never minded taking blame; if Senate wanted to restore the rule's function, then he would back Senate to the hilt. Thirty students, 3 per cent of the university, were thus asked to discontinue after Christmas. The one dissenting voice to this process, according to Stanley, was the registrar, Murray Macneill, who, I was warned by Pearson & every one else, was the great troublemaker of the University, & of whom I heard my predecessor complain as far back as 1927. Not only was he impossible in meetings – he talked sympathetically to suspended students & their parents.

Another of Stanley's criticisms to Macdonnell was the Dalhousie order of classes. Dalhousie's twenty classes, with a few obvious exceptions in the case of languages and mathematics, could be taken in whatever sequence fitted the students' timetables. This was, Stanley asserted, "a barbarous, or American innovation of my predecessor. The only person on the Arts staff who defended it was the aforesaid prof. of maths., registrar and trouble maker." The reason for it was timetable exigencies of professors, and to Stanley those were caused by insufficient staff.

But the real reason why Macdonnell was 55 per cent right, Stanley said, was because he knew himself to be, almost unconsciously, a taker of short cuts. Further, he and his wife both were

unconventional, unworldly, and unrespectable. What I know is that this is a highly and deeply conservative, conventional, worldly and respectable community. I feel they have conserved more things worth conserving than any conservatives I know of on this continent, and that their respectability cloaks fewer vices and less offensive vices than troubled me elsewhere in the last twelve years of my life. Yet I am just beginning to discover now that head-shaking has gone over my taking my exercise, as I did at Toronto and McGill, by walking with students (male students, I hasten to add). What an undignified thing for a University President to do!

But, Jim, I can only be myself, pedestrian, persevering, and an endless embarrassment to the unstraightforward. Gott helfe mir, as Luther said, ich kann nicht anders.[39]

That is as fair a defence of Stanley as can be found. It gets him, and perhaps the Halifax of the 1930s, about right.

Stanley's predecessor, President Emeritus A.S. MacKenzie, believed that Pearson had handled his side of the affair badly; but he also thought the board should have backed him and investigated his charges against Stanley. MacMechan thought that Pearson's charges amounted to very little, certainly not enough to unseat an incumbent president; but "Pearson's position is tragic none the less." Indeed it was. There was some irony in Pearson's advice to Stanley, in happier days in July 1931, about Joyce Harris, bursar and president's secretary. She was difficult to get along with, Pearson said, but she had great capacity for work and she was loyal, almost too much so. She staunchly believed the president needed protecting, that "her chief was a much put upon individual and that he should not be harassed and distressed by the inconsequential difficulties of the impractical professors who adorn the staff of the University." You might not want to begin by firing her; leave it to me, Pearson suggested. "I'll give it careful thought ... I do not wish to come back 'from the ride / With the Chairman inside / And a smile on the face of the tiger.'

The tiger Pearson meant was Joyce Harris; the real tiger was Carleton Stanley. Dr H.B. Atlee, who knew and respected Pearson, claimed it was Pearson who persuaded the Murray government in 1910 to establish the commission management of the Victoria General Hospital, and thus take the running of the hospital out of politics. Pearson was also the driving force behind the Public Health Clinic established in 1924. "During the 1920s," said Atlee, "he was the beating heart of Dalhousie." When his colleagues failed him in June 1932, Pearson was a broken man. After sixteen years as an unselfish and devoted member of the board, all his connections with Dalhousie were severed. He was only fifty-five years old, but he lived only another five years.[40]

In all of this the former president kept his distance, keeping out of it as much as possible. One thing that upset MacKenzie and brought him out of retirement was President Stanley's dismissal in 1933 of Zaidee Harris, the assistant librarian, which MacKenzie believed was a gross injustice. She was knowledgeable, but was also deaf and, like her sister Joyce, sometimes difficult to work with. He rallied MacMechan around and the two old colleagues went to the new chairman of the board, Hector McInnes (LL.B. '88), to see if they could get her reinstated. McInnes said Zaidee Harris had refused to do extra work, and C.L. Bennet, chairman of the Library Committee, agreed she should be dismissed.[41]

MacMechan was teaching summer school in 1933, as he always had had to do. He was reading new books for "The Dean's Window," his column in the Montreal *Standard*. From time to time MacMechan's leg would become painful with swelling in the ankle or calf. He knew his heart was weak; suddenly, on Monday evening, 7 August, it just gave out. His funeral was at Fort Massey, his church from the beginning; he was buried in Camp Hill cemetery, where he would have liked it, amid the trees and sunsets of Nova Scotia, that he had so often celebrated.

MacMechan was a teacher as much as a writer. He always said a teacher was made not by tricks of method but by the transparent love of his subject and his desire to impart it to students. MacMechan's classes, as the *Gazette* noted, exemplified Edward Thring's definition of education, "the transmission of life from the living, through the living, to the living." He had his whims and prejudices; one might not agree with his estimate of Sir Walter Scott, Kipling, or Jane Austen; but, said the *Gazette*, "he made them gloriously alive." MacMechan was a happy man who had had a good life, and his dignity, courtesy, gentleness, and generosity was its outward expression.[42]

Coming back from MacMechan's funeral, Carleton Stanley could survey his Dalhousie with some complacency. He had had a rough introduction, but he had triumphed over his opposition. A vigorous chairman of board, rival in a potential dyarchy that threatened to divide his rule as president, had been driven from the field in disorder. Pearson's replacement, Hector McInnes, was seventy-two, and if wiser much less active. Stanley's other enemies were subdued and brooding. Only the fact that there had been a row had got abroad; the printed version was hard to find, seemingly being kept within the close circle of the Dalhousie governors. Stanley admitted that the row had been bad for the university; it would take him a while to pick up the pieces. But notwithstanding that, as he wrote a St James Club friend in Montreal after Pearson's defeat, "it has been a most interesting year, and we have got a great deal done. The University has endless possibilities because there is such excellent human stuff in it. Also, the whole family likes Halifax exceedingly."[43] By 1933 Stanley was fairly launched upon his Dalhousie presidency.

· 3 ·

Carleton Stanley's Kingdom
Dalhousie 1933–1938

Business, the professions, influence the universities. Stanley's standards. The Medical Faculty and the Public Health Clinic. Angus L. Macdonald, Dalhousie law professor, premier of Nova Scotia. The 1935 Dalhousie Act. Stanley deposes the registrar. Dalhousie students as middle-class survivors. European affairs impinge on Dalhousie. Death of MacKenzie.

The Commercial Undermining of Liberal Education

By the mid-1930s every college and university, in or out of Nova Scotia, was at grips with a problem that bore in upon them with pressure inexorable: the increasingly commercial test of old and tried intellectual values. Commerce cared little for Coleridge or Kant, and what was irrelevant to commerce and business began, increasingly, to seem to be so elsewhere. Thus the intellectual values of western culture came under attack, and in an insidious form, by being made to seem unimportant to life, living, and progress.

The old core of the university was Arts and Science and the universities had accommodated professional schools with some reluctance. At Dalhousie the Law Faculty was started with a Munro professorship in 1883, and then in 1911 came the duty, as it seemed to Dalhousie, of having to take on Medicine and Dentistry, because there was no one else to do it. Robert Hutchins, president of the University of Chicago from 1928 to 1945, in *The Higher Learning in America* maintained that the only reason for including professional schools in a university was the influences that Arts and Science might bring to the dreariness of the professional disciplines:

Vocationalism leads, then, to triviality and isolation; it debases the course of study and the staff. It deprives the university of its only excuse for existence, which is to provide a haven where the search for truth may go on unhampered by utility or pressure for "results."[1]

Archibald MacMechan would have agreed. He pointed out in the midst of Dalhousie's Million Dollar campaign of 1920 that the university's growth was owing to the accretion of professional schools; while these were important even essential acquisitions, there had been "no corresponding growth in the original Arts departments, which gave Dalhousie her standards and her reputation." A university of seven hundred students in 1920 with one solitary professor of history, one of modern languages, and one in mathematics, was starved.[2] There was some improvement in the 1920s with modest reinforcement from King's in 1923, but the point was more relevant in 1930, with Dalhousie's registration running high (838 in 1928–9) and going higher (902 in 1929–30).

President MacKenzie, scientist that he was, effortlessly made room at Dalhousie for Medicine and Dentistry, and found no intellectual difficulties in doing so. His problems were financial, and institutional, in getting Dalhousie's research criteria accepted by a conservative medical community. Atlee's appointment was a good example. Some of MacKenzie's fellow scientists thought the new sciences in medicine were not very good science, and were being built up at the cost of more worthy research. Humanities professors such as Carleton Stanley would find it still more difficult to appreciate the needs of medicine. Stanley was interested in science, especially biology. One of his more quixotic academic adventures was trying to establish an honours course in Greek and biology; the students would read Aristotle's science in Greek, and slowly work their way to the present day. The biologists managed to defeat it. A proper science course could not be built around the history of science; it had to be done around modern research, techniques, apparatus, and outlook.[3] MacKenzie, who had in his time been well out on the cutting edge of physics research, knew that; Carleton Stanley didn't. Stanley aimed in other directions. His outlook, with a big intellectual range, is set out in his annual report for 1940–1, from his 1941 convocation address:

But I do call university graduates illiterate who have not read, and who show no likelihood of reading later ... at least some of the books which on one side or another give a man some inkling of the fabric of European civilisation. On the side of history, politics, law, for example, a man is illiterate who has not read Thucydides' *History*, Aristotle's *Politics*, Hugo de Groot's *Law of Nations*, Guizot's *History of Civilization in Europe*, Bryce's *Holy Roman*

Empire, and at least some of the work of Maitland or Vinogradoff on juris-prudence.[4]

Carleton Stanley's own major work was on Matthew Arnold, published by the University of Toronto Press in 1938. In *Culture and Anarchy* (1869), Arnold described the middle class as Philistines, honest doers but not thinkers, with no real appreciation of arts and letters. Stanley, like Arnold, was trying to re-establish the authority of older disciplines which he now felt were in jeopardy. In some ways Stanley resembled Arnold's description of Oxford, a university Stanley knew well, "whispering from her towers the last enchantments of the middle Age[s] ... Home of lost causes, and forsaken beliefs, and unpopular names, and impossible loyalties!"[5]

Struggling to Raise Standards

Stanley set out to reform some Dalhousie practices that he regarded as pernicious. The first was admitting students with incomplete matriculation, which they would make up during the next years. He discovered that one-quarter of Dalhousie's undergraduates had not completed matriculation, and many of them had been at Dalhousie three, four, or even five years. At his first meeting with the Arts Faculty in September 1931, he appointed a committee to study Dalhousie's curriculum. They reported in February 1932, recommending that students take all of Dalhousie's required classes, including make-up matriculation ones, before being allowed to take any electives. The committee's second recommendation, with more serious implications, was that the forthcoming 1932–3 calendar carry the prescription that English and five others of the eight matriculation subjects be required for admission to Dalhousie. "It is hoped," the committee added, "that in the near future complete matriculation required in eight subjects will be adhered to." But on motion of the registrar, Murray Macneill, that was deleted.[6]

Here lay a developing quarrel between the president and the registrar. Stanley did not know Nova Scotia; Murray Macneill did. Of the thirty-five members of the Arts Faculty, assistant professor rank and above, twenty-six were from outside Nova Scotia. That had many advantages, in the style, knowledge, and experience of the professors; but it did have some disadvantages. Murray Macneill was a Maritimer, born in Maitland, Nova Scotia, brought up in St John's, Newfoundland, and in Saint John, New Brunswick. He recognized what some others did not, that there were good reasons for students to come to Dalhousie with incomplete matriculation. It was not just students finding an easy back door into university, though there were

Carleton Stanley about 1936, President of Dalhousie, 1931–45: "a well-read mind, a versatile intelligence, deployed with energy."

some of those; it was because relatively few high schools in Nova Scotia, New Brunswick, Newfoundland, or Prince Edward Island could properly prepare students in Grade 11 to pass provincial matriculation examinations. Macneill's was the position of George Trueman, president of Mount Allison (1923–45), who as a boy had been the victim of just such a school system. Trueman had grown up in Point de Bute, New Brunswick, near the Nova Scotia border, within sight of the Tantramar marshes. Trueman told Stanley in March 1934, "in this sparsely settled country, any system that denies opportunity to those who have not been able to attend good high schools ... is wrong." Outside of Halifax, the Dalhousie Faculty of Arts and Science recognized only a few good high schools in Nova Scotia capable of solid matriculation work.[7]

Nevertheless, in 1933 the faculty agreed that beginning in September 1934 the Dalhousie minimum entrance requirement would be English, Algebra, a foreign language, plus four other matriculation subjects. These new rules would be sent to all Maritime provinces high schools and to Newfoundland schools. In this tightening of rules, Dalhousie wanted to carry the other colleges with her; but although there was talk of doing so, only St Francis Xavier followed Dalhousie's lead. Stanley complained bitterly that some colleges, notably Acadia, were pouring graduates out into the school system as teachers without requiring either Latin or mathematics or a foreign language of any kind for a BA. What kind of teachers would such students make?[8]

Dalhousie's restrictions on admission had an effect on enrolment, which dropped from 1,015 in 1931–2 to 846 in 1934–5. Mount Allison's enrolment stayed fairly consistent at about 400 between 1930 and 1935. That was owing, according to Stanley, to blatant recruiting; Mount Allison hired six young women as canvassers, who each had a car and were given five dollars for every student they secured. Acadia was alleged to have matched that with six dollars. The president of the University of New Brunswick, C.C. Jones, grumbled to Stanley in October 1934 about both colleges; one student had telegraphed President Jones, "Am offered $100 by Mt. Allison, and $100 by Acadia. What do you offer?" Jones replied, "If you are fully matriculated, we offer you the best education we can give you." That was not always good enough. UNB's registration was down 15 per cent in 1934–5, and according to Jones, there were many at both Acadia and Mount Allison whom UNB would not have admitted. Jones congratulated Dalhousie on doing what it had done, refurbishing standards, risking enrolment.[9]

Privately Stanley had much fault to find with Dalhousie. The university had no economics professor; Stanley did not consider

W.R. Maxwell at King's, with a Harvard MA, up to standard. Dalhousie had no professor of Greek, nor of German, although both subjects were taught; he thought the staff in mathematics weak (the head of the department was Murray Macneill); J.G. Adshead, with a first-class degree from Cambridge, was appointed in 1927 (King's), and Charles Walmsley also from Cambridge in 1929. Both were good lecturers, Adshead in particular. But neither were research-minded; distant frontiers had little appeal for them, and they swung easily into teaching routines under Murray Macneill. Stanley thought the Department of English, now that MacMechan was gone, no better.[10]

However, as the result of submissions made by MacKenzie and Pearson in 1931, the Carnegie Foundation gave $125,000 in 1933 to endow a chair in geology. In 1932 Stanley appointed George Vibert Douglas, aged forty, a big, vibrant bear of a man, noisy, open-hearted and energetic, a Canadian from McGill, who had taught at Harvard, and had been on Shackleton's last Antarctic expedition in 1921. Douglas had been geologist for the Rio Tinto copper mine when the depression closed it down. "It would be hard to find," wrote L.C. Graton of Harvard recommending Douglas, "a man more charged with dynamic energy, constructive ideas, absolute loyalty and concentrated sunshine." Douglas was Stanley's man from the day of his appointment to Dalhousie. Douglas stirred up the campus. One student recalled his first lecture in Geology 1 in 1932; Douglas could be heard coming, clumping down the hall in his walking boots, starting to lecture as he came through the door. He liked to throw open a window, fall or winter. He smoked a gnarled pipe, loaded with a Canadian tobacco called "Old Chum," which he lit with long Eddy matches that were carried in a long waterproof cylinder. He was a character, knew it, and revelled in it. He was also a one-man department, giving eight separate courses. He was a good lecturer; if his science was occasionally rusty, the students liked him for his forthrightness and generosity, his ebullient air of imperturbable cheerfulness.

Stanley wanted to appoint new men in whom he could rejoice; with him every new Dalhousie vacancy was a golden opportunity to find the best man available. Stanley saw Dalhousie, and many another Canadian university, cursed with the results of appointments made in a hurry: "the landscape is littered with misfits and experiments that never flowered or even burgeoned." He was not going to make that mistake. Moreover, he said, "I must get people to reinforce my own plans." Those included trying to raise Dalhousie's standards. He was persuaded by his own experience, and perhaps that of his father-in-law, W.J. Alexander, that the Dalhousie graduates of 1885 to 1905 were far above the current crop. "Not only were these men and women well educated," said Stanley, "but they nearly all had some nobility of soul. At least one could say that they formed a little nucleus of public conscience in the communities in which they lived."[11]

Stanley's most outspoken public criticism was against the Nova Scotian (and Canadian) public schools, against weak teachers and bad textbooks, against the spurious pedagogy that in his view encouraged both. He sent his own son to Rothesay Collegiate, a private school in New Brunswick, in 1934. The printed annual reports of Dalhousie presidents are not noted for their charm or intellectual vigour; some, like President MacKenzie's, seem almost to have been deliberately pedestrian and low-key, as if the secret of successful development was understatement. Stanley's annual reports were quite the reverse – vigorous, trenchant, forthright; they called spades spades. He would quote Lucretius, *De Rerum Natura*, to explain why,

> ... Medio de fonte leporum
> Surgit amari aliquid quod in ipsis floribus angat.

> ... In the midst of a fountain of delights
> Comes up bitterness that chokes their very beauties.

His annual report for 1933–4 is a case in point, condemning public school education and all its works, and not sparing universities either:

But if so many teachers in the secondary schools are illiterate, and have to be spoonfed by pretentious editors, whose fault is that? Are the universities forever to be permitted to rail at the schools for sending them students who are dunces ...? If the teachers of French in our secondary schools cannot read a sentence of French so that a Frenchman would recognise the words, whose fault is that? Has it to do with the vicious importation [from the United States] of a certain kind of pedagogy which says openly, blatantly and continuously, "it matters not whether teachers know what they teach, so long as they know how to teach it"? This is equivalent to claiming that it does not matter whether you know *what* to feed a baby so long as you know *how* to feed it. Get the proper bottle and the proper nipple, and it does not matter whether you fill the bottle with cow's milk or arsenic, especially if you have taken a course in nutritional psychology.

That was hard-hitting, but he won approval in New York at the Carnegie Foundation. James Bertram congratulated Stanley on his courage and force, and showed the address to one of the Carnegie trustees who said, "This is a fine blast, and I'm sure President Stanley is right." Stanley sent Bertram's comment to F.B. McCurdy, chairman of the board's Finance Committee, to counter criticisms the report had, not surprisingly, earned for Stanley and Dalhousie. McCurdy wrote back, "Am glad to read the above comment, though regretful that his important approval could be purchased only at the cost of so much local good will." Stanley was confident there was not much ill will. "I don't believe it exists," he told McCurdy confidently, "outside the minds of a few. And I have strong evidence that the few grow fewer." But he was wrong. By 1938 and a few more blasts, Stanley himself admitted that Dalhousie's only friend among the secondary schools of Nova Scotia was the Halifax Ladies College. There were times when Stanley could usefully have remembered Sir John A. Macdonald's old saw, that one caught more flies with honey than with vinegar.[12]

By 1934 Dalhousie's financial position was better than many colleges, though it was serious enough. The depression had cut dividend and bond income, but Dalhousie's investments had been so well placed that losses on capital were slight compared to others. That was the good side. The bad side was current debt. The new gymnasium, built in 1931–2, cost $150,000, much of it borrowed, and it added substantially to Dalhousie's existing debt. As of 30 June 1938 the accumulated deficit was $201,170. How was one to prevent it rising further? McGill University had reduced its academic salaries by 10 per cent. Stanley had opposed that, and neither Pearson nor his successor Hector McInnes had suggested it. McInnes thought it could not be done without the consent of the professors. There was talk in 1936 of a campaign, but no real spirit for it. J.L. Hetherington, a member of the board, told R.B. Bennett:

The immediate Dalhousie constituency is somewhat lukewarm and suffering perhaps a bit from divided enthusiasm and an inferiority complex ... it may be apparent to yourself that the staff is without personalities such as it had in former days. The Board, as well, unfortunately, is not conspicuous in leadership among its members, many of whom are now elderly men who have served their day.

Hector McInnes, chairman since 1932, was seventy-six and there were several other prominent members in their seventies. But to Bennett it was not so much a question of age as impossibility. "I know of no means," he told Hetherington, "by which you can raise half a million dollars within the next few years."[13]

The crunch was at the Medical Faculty. Its 1929–30 income was $90,611, but its expenses were $20,000 more. Of that deficit, $15,000 was incurred by the Public Health Clinic, which had been running annual deficits on almost the same scale for the past few years. The endowment needed to give $20,000 additional annual income was, at 4.5 per cent, $444,444. New money like that was nowhere in sight.[14]

The head of the Public Health Clinic was the assistant dean of medicine, W.H. Hattie, who really functioned as dean. The dean himself, Dr John Stewart, CBE, had been in the office since 1912 and had had an honourable career: assistant under Lister in Edinburgh, an able surgeon in Halifax, then head of Canadian Stationary Hospital No. 7 in the Great War. But by the end of the 1920s he was old and tired; Hattie was doing all the work, Stewart just signed the forms. Hattie was loyal, modest, and generous; his specialty was mental illness. He used to tell fourth-year medical students, many interested in surgery, that it might be ten years before they would see a patient needing a gall bladder operation, but they would see a psychiatric patient in their first hour of practice. In December 1931 Hattie died in harness; Stewart resigned six months later.[15]

Dean H.G. "Pat" Grant and the Medical Faculty

A new and active dean of medicine was now imperative. In November 1931 there was even consideration given to shutting down the Schools of Medicine and Dentistry altogether. President Stanley's position was straightforward. New as he was to the scene, having acquired as yet little authority with the board, he nevertheless took this position:

You can't cut limbs off the community like that without taking the community into your counsels. Since 1868, by something like a succession of miracles, you have maintained a Medical School here, and for many years a Dental School. You say the public is indifferent and has never offered you support. Have you let the public know that you need support?

Perhaps, said Stanley, Nova Scotians think that the private endowments of Carnegie and Rockefeller, so talked about in the early 1920s, signified that Dalhousie did not need public money. Stanley concluded that through drift and the absence of any strong dean, the Public Health Clinic had been allowed to go on haemorrhaging the university.[16]

The board girded itself up and faced the future, carrying its Medicine and its Dentistry burdens as best it could. And they found a new dean – a Nova Scotian, Harry Goudge Grant, forty-three years old, who had taken his MD from Dalhousie in 1912. He and Atlee had done postgraduate work in London together. Grant's specialty was preventive medicine, and he had become director of county health work in Virginia where he was epidemiologist since 1926. Grant would stay as dean for the next twenty-two years.

Harry Grant (he was always called "Pat") was very different from Stewart or Hattie. He had little of their paternalism. One of Grant's younger colleagues, Dr H.L. Scammell, remembered being in Fredericton with him, interviewing UNB students for Dalhousie Medical School. Scammell was much struck by the obliquity of Grant's questions. How did they spend their summers? What did they work at? What games did they like to play? Grant was trying to elucidate their character. He was a great ideas man; he rather liked leaping at suggestions. As this was combined with a generous and incurable optimism, Grant would often promise more than he could deliver. But he would try anyway. He persuaded the faculty, rather against its will, to make the fourth year of medicine a clinical year.[17]

Of the income of the Medical Faculty for 1929–30, 41 per cent came from class fees. The cost of the whole faculty, per student, was $642. Income per Canadian student was about $180, American $320. It was not good arithmetic. Grant's first major exercise in December 1932 was to cut the 1933–4 budget of $71,000. He managed a 6 per cent cut, pointing out he did not think the faculty should be charged with a share of the cost of Shirreff Hall. He also reminded the board – it was neither the first nor the last time that a dean of medicine would find this threat useful – that "Our Medical School is at present a class A medical school, and drastic economies within our various departments will undoubtedly result in our losing that status."

Fundamentally, Stanley was angry with the whole medical question. McGill thought it had the best medical school in Canada, but it had been overtaken by Toronto, where politicians understood what Montreal millionaires did not, "that a medical school requires a mint of money." Dalhousie's undertakings in medicine were not the "gallant and courageous endeavours" Stanley had heard them called. "They were blunders by ignorant and stupid people who wanted to make a show. On top of that we undertook a Public Health Centre."[18]

The clinic was the sore point with Stanley. President MacKenzie had warned the city in 1928 that Dalhousie would have to close it down if help were not forthcoming, but nothing was done about implementing the threat. In 1929 Hattie pointed out to the city what the clinic was and how important were its functions. The city opted for the happy thought that Dalhousie would not carry out its threat, that the clinic was needed for Dalhousie's own medical students. In part that surmise was correct.

The clinic's purpose was simple, its functions many. None of the Halifax hospitals had out-patient departments. Rich and middle-class patients could find and pay their own doctors; but the only place the poor could go had been, for nearly a century, the Halifax Visiting Dispensary. In 1924 the dispensary accepted Dalhousie's invitation to take space in the new Public Health Clinic, with out-patient doctors supplied by Dalhousie. The Public Health Clinic also provided free accommodation to the Halifax Welfare Bureau and a VD clinic for the provincial Department of Health. Opening on 1 November 1924, the clinic handled nearly seven thousand cases in its first year, and by 1930 that had more than doubled.

Great assistance in running the Public Health Clinic had come from the thirteen full-time nurses and one doctor of the Massachusetts-Halifax Health Commission. The commission, chaired by G.F. Pearson, had been an outgrowth of the Halifax explosion, but such outside philanthropy could not go on for ever. The commission announced that its work would end on 31 May 1928. From the thirteen full-time nurses the staff at the Public Health Clinic was reduced by 75 per cent.[19]

The running of the Public Health Clinic was now wholly in Dalhousie's lap. President MacKenzie was worried about what responsibilities Dalhousie should retain, and there was uncertainty in the minds of some of the Dalhousie governors. The Public Health Clinic, said Dugald Macgillivray, "was always draped with a good deal of mystery and individual possession by both Pearson and MacKenzie, and what it meant or was to mean in cost to Dalhousie never gripped us." That suggests some deliberate obfuscation by Pearson, a strong public health man, confident doubtless that in time the City of Halifax would be willing to shoulder its proper responsibilities.[20]

There was no doubt that the teaching value of the clinic was considerable, with its great variety of out-patient cases. Hattie had devised a follow-up arrangement whereby the medical students would visit out-patients in their homes and thus see the environments that had nurtured TB, infant mortality, and other public health problems. Those visits were a revelation to many students. Nevertheless, Dalhousie was now paying for the clinic from its own money, and Hattie's efforts to get the city to pay for any of it were unavailing.

Halifax for its part was struggling to get back on its own feet. After the explosion of 6 December 1917 the task of rebuilding the city was taken over by governmental and philanthropic boards. The Halifax Relief Commission was established by the Dominion government early in 1918 to provide permanent care for the injured and crippled, and to rebuild the shattered north end of Halifax and parts of Dartmouth. The city was going to be hard up for some time yet; its tax base had shrunk, some of it permanently, and swaths of property belonging to two governments, the armed services, educational institutions, churches, and cemeteries were wholly exempt from taxes. Thus

Dalhousie's request to have the city fund the Public Health Clinic was put off as long as possible.[21]

This problem of the Public Health Clinic was the first thing Carleton Stanley encountered in September 1931. The Board of Governors recognized the importance of the clinic's work, but where could it find the money without adding to Dalhousie's burgeoning debt? Over the years Dalhousie had already contributed more than $100,000 to the clinic. It had done much to bring medical students face to face with health and preventive medicine as a social question. But as Dean Grant pointed out in a letter to the papers two years later, "It can be said without fear of contradiction that in no other place in the world is it [the medical care of the sick poor] done by a University." Carleton Stanley claimed that the knowledge so gained from the clinic had not done much public good, for "the slums that send us patients ... are allowed to remain."[22]

The president and the new dean of medicine went to New York in the autumn of 1932 to make an appeal to the Rockefeller Foundation for funding for a Department of Preventive Medicine. The City of Halifax was approached for $10,000 annually for the clinic; the best it could manage was $2,500. The Nova Scotia government was asked for $5,000 per annum, and it proved more generous. It happened that Dalhousie's professor of clinical surgery, Dr G.H. Murphy, was elected in a 1929 by-election for Halifax County, and became minister of health in August 1930 in the Conservative government of Premier G.S. Harrington. That gave Dalhousie an entrée. In February 1933, being finally persuaded of the importance to the province of public health, the Nova Scotia government offered $5,000 a year on condition that Dalhousie raise a like amount somewhere else. As Stanley told Dr Murphy, "the help comes in the very *nick* of time." It allowed Dalhousie to show local support to Rockefeller. Dr Alan Gregg of the Rockefeller Foundation came to Halifax in May 1933, and the upshot was that the Foundation offered a matching grant, up to $8,800 a year, for five years, to support a Department of Preventive Medicine, built around the work of the Public Health Clinic.[23]

That was how the Public Health Clinic grew in the 1930s. This noble ambition, as Stanley put it in 1937, was supported by large gifts by Carnegie and Rockefeller, by the public conscience of Dalhousie, and, not least, by the generosity of the city's doctors, dozens of whom served the clinic for many years without reward. However, the new arrangements merely eased Dalhousie's financial problems with the clinic; the City of Halifax's $2,500 was a woeful example of underfunding.[24]

When Angus L. Macdonald and the Liberals defeated the Harrington government in the provincial election of August 1933, Dean

Grant, adroit and assiduous, made sure that the new minister of health, Dr Frank Davis of Bridgewater, saw something of public health practices. Davis was a country doctor and "had his eyes opened very wide," Stanley said, to see what other cities like Toronto did.[25]

Angus L. Macdonald (1890–1954), the new premier, was born in Cape Breton, the gold medallist at St Francis Xavier in 1914, and joined the Canadian army. After the war he took his LL.B. at Dalhousie in 1921, worked for the attorney general, and came to Dalhousie in 1924 as professor of law, teaching statutes and rules of their interpretation. He found $2,500 a year thin going for a man newly married, and resigned in 1930 to go into private practice, becoming leader of the opposition Liberal party that year. He was elected for Halifax South in the Liberal sweep of August 1933.[26]

Angus L. was not Nova Scotia's first Roman Catholic premier, but he was the longest lived politically. With brains, vigour, and not a little fighting skill in the Assembly, he was soon unassailable. He needed it, for he had had a feud with Bishop Morrison of Antigonish over university federation. Angus L. explained it confidentially to Carleton Stanley in 1937. The Antigonish *Casket* in 1922 had argued that St Francis Xavier should not join university federation. It was impossible to get anyone in the Antigonish diocese to answer the *Casket* articles, so Angus L. wrote a dozen pro-federation articles from his desk at the Dalhousie Law School. The *Casket* refused to publish them, so Angus L. sent them to the Sydney *Post*. The bishop did not forgive what he viewed as reckless freedom. Angus L. wanted to get rid of the Maritime degree-granting colleges in favour of one first-class university in Halifax, with a college for Catholics, one for Baptists, and so on. He still did in 1937; a university could have been created, he told Stanley, like a Canadian Princeton, instead of what the Maritimes ended up with in 1937 – thirteen colleges each with their graduates going forth into the world believing they were university-trained. What they had, said Angus L., was "only about equivalent to a first-rate high school."[27]

The 1935 Dalhousie Act

The connections between Dalhousie and the government allowed it to seek a new act to bring its charter up to date. Opening up an institutional act is never entirely without risk. If the government is strong, or there is good will on both sides of the House, there is usually no difficulty. It had been discovered that the members of the Board of Governors had not been properly appointed. The reason was the power, given in the 1863 act, to the person or body endowing a chair to nominate a governor and name the professor. The board also nominated governors, and the two principles had become confused. This was briefly patched up in 1934, pursuant to a new act to be passed in 1935. A joint committee of board and Senate began meetings in October 1934. Hector McInnes, chairman of the board, decided simply to correct mistakes and bring the 1863 act up to date. The new act was not intended to provide a new constitution for the university, nor to alter the powers of board or president; it would merely regularize existing appointments, and "eliminate the antiquated right of nomination of donors" of either governors or professors. The old right of the Church of Scotland to nominate a governor and appoint a professor lingered, now converted to the right of the United Church to nominate a governor.[28]

Senate members liked the idea of a wholly new act. Hugh Bell noted that for many years past Senate and board had been drawing apart; now was a good opportunity to pull them together again. Senate on the whole liked Bell's argument, but Senate did not get its way. The board wanted to end appointments to its board by the provincial cabinet, but it did not get its way either.[29]

The board constituted by the 1935 act consisted of twenty-two governors appointed by governor-in-council, six Alumni representatives, three Alumnae, two representatives from King's College, the United Church governor, and the mayor of Halifax, *ex officio* – thirty-five in all. There were three new departures: an executive committee of the board was formally constituted; full-time professors were excluded from membership on the board; and as *quid pro quo* for that, a formal attempt was made to bring board and Senate together on major issues of university policy. This last was Senate's idea. It had in mind the creation of a court, modelled on the University of Edinburgh, that would deal with such matters as annual expenditures, university policy, buildings, and the development of new departments. The board preferred ad hoc joint committees when necessary, but Senate stuck to its guns, and thus the compromise emerged creating what came to be called "The Six and Six." The wording is interesting:

3. (1) The Board shall from time to time when any new department, building, project or policy arises for consideration, appoint a committee of its members to meet with a like committee of the Senate, which joint committee shall investigate the same and recommend to the Board its findings thereon.

The act required a statutory meeting of the Six and Six every October, at which anything pertaining to the welfare of the university could be discussed, and there could be ad hoc meetings at any time. Stanley claimed that the Six and Six clause was a result of the backstairs influence of G.F. Pearson. Indeed, said Stanley, the whole 1935 revision had been set going by that "arch-imp" downtown. Certainly the 1935 act absorbed a great deal of Stanley's energies over the winter of 1934–5.[30]

What did not get into the 1935 act was a clause about the duties of the president. Stanley thought there was need for it. No one would know, he said, from the brief allusion to the president in the 1863 act that the president had what Stanley called "undisputed prerogatives": to recommend all teaching appointments to the board; to busy himself with university finance; to preside at all faculty meetings if he wished; to represent Dalhousie before the public; and to oversee grounds, buildings, curricula, and discipline. Stanley also wanted a clause on academic tenure. "It is part of the unwritten law about Canadian Universities that anyone who secures a post as high as Associate Professor is appointed for life or on good behaviour."[31] Stanley got neither of these clauses. Common law lawyers resist setting down more than they have to. The powers of the president would remain undefined, and the tenure of professors the same. Stanley hated the Dalhousie charter. Five years later, out of temper both with board and Senate, Stanley told the chairman that what Dalhousie needed was "the abolition of the fatuous charter under which we operate."[32]

Dismissing Murray Macneill

In 1936 Stanley managed to depose his *bête noire*, the registrar, Murray Macneill. Macneill would remain only United Church professor of mathematics. Probably no one will get to the bottom of that feud. That Macneill was devoted to Dalhousie and its reputation is patent; that he was difficult at times to get along with is true. There were minor incidents; Angus L. asked Macneill if he would act as Nova Scotia's civil service commissioner in his spare time. To Macneill's request for permission Stanley offered two months leave without pay. That was not what Macneill asked for, and Angus L. had to intervene. In 1936, having had no holiday for five years, Macneill asked permission to go to England for a few weeks to see his daughter, Janet Macneill Aitken. She had married Lord Beaverbrook's son, Peter Aitken, and had a new baby. The baby was fine: the marriage wasn't. There was an Imperial Universities' Conference on that summer, and it would save Macneill money if he could be one of Dalhousie's four delegates. To his request, Stanley replied crisply that Macneill could go but "as to the representation of Dalhousie at the Conference of Imperial Universities, I have made other arrangements."[33]

The immediate issue between Stanley and Macneill was Dalhousie's standards of admission. Stanley had changed from 1931–3 when he

M. M. MACNEIL, M. A.

Murray Macneill, Professor of Mathematics, 1907–42; Registrar, Arts and Science, 1908–36; University Registrar, 1921–36. A student at Dalhousie during Lucy Maud Montgomery's year, 1895–6, he was said to be the model for Gilbert Blythe in *Anne of Green Gables* and was not pleased.

wanted to tighten them, to 1936 when he was willing to make them more flexible. One reason was Dalhousie's declining enrolment, down 24 per cent in Arts and Science between 1931–2 and 1935–6. There were many reasons for it, the depression not least, but one was the notorious competition for students between colleges in Nova Scotia and New Brunswick. Macneill for his part seems to have gone the other way, finding reasons for tightening Dalhousie's admission standards. Stanley and Macneill each seem to have been using the issue to get at the other.

Stanley had a list of some fifty-five students from Dalhousie and King's, the correspondence with whom proved to Stanley that they were being discouraged from coming to Dalhousie. There were complaints from A.H. Moore, president of King's, of Macneill's rigidity. King's was losing students, said Moore, and Macneill should not to be so choosy. Remember, he warned Stanley,

that the majority of these principals and teachers is made up of Acadia graduates, and I would not put it by some of them that they would welcome more active requirements on our part in order that they might say to their students: "To enter Dalhousie or King's you will have to have all these, but with a smaller list of qualifications it will be possible for you to go to Acadia."[34]

In view of "the intensive and persistent campaign that other schools are making for students," Stanley wrote, Macneill's attitude was "simply madness ... If we paid someone to keep students away, how could the salary be better earned?" Thus he charged Murray Macneill with lack of support and cooperation, and asked the board to dismiss him as registrar.

In mid-May 1936 the executive of the board sat through two meetings and four hours listening to Stanley's complaints against Macneill. Some were not serious, some were explained, but most charges Macneill thought so ridiculous he would not answer them. What troubled the executive most was the bitter enmity between the two men. Nor would Macneill accept the board's offer to resign. He was in England when the board relieved him of his duties as registrar, on 30 May, effective the next day, notifying him by cable. His office staff were much upset at what they felt was very shabby treatment. Macneill, bitter and aggrieved, wrote the chairman of the board:

My whole life has been devoted to Dalhousie University. My own feeling is that I have been charged with disloyalty without reason, and with very evident malice. The executive have apparently seen fit to agree to charges which

I consider ridiculous and untrue ... All I can ask now is to be allowed, for the few years that remain of my active life, to be of what service I can to the college I have always loved.

That meant his work as professor of mathematics, a position which of course he retained until his retirement in 1942. His family believed his dismissal as registrar quite broke his spirit. He was the second person thus broken by Dalhousie's philosopher-president. Dalhousie had been Macneill's whole life. Since 1907 the Macneill home at 83 Inglis Street had been a Dalhousie social centre. Every Sunday afternoon in term there would be a tea party, or in winter snowshoe or skating parties.[35]

An immediate consequence of Macneill's dethronement was Stanley's discovery that he would need a dean of arts and science. Hitherto he had not had one, preferring to run his own show in that faculty. Professors Bennet and Johnston would be part-time co-registrars, and a dean would organize the faculty, by which Stanley meant setting agendas for meetings and preventing a waste of time in them. In June 1936 he persuaded Professor C.B. Nickerson of the Chemistry Department to accept the deanship for three years, at $1,000 a year extra pay. Nickerson had been at Dalhousie since 1918, was well connected, being married to Agnes Harrington, sister of the Gordon Harrington, the premier from 1930 to 1933. He was well liked by the staff, popular with students, ever ready with a genial comment or timely anecdote. He and his wife, with no children, were often chaperones at the many Dalhousie dances.

Profile of Dalhousie Students

In 1933 it was said that Dalhousie had "a dance a day." Stanley explained it to C.F. Crandall, president of British United Press, Montreal, who thought his daughter Ruth at Shirreff Hall had too much social life. College life, said Stanley, had changed much since our time. What students called "activities" bulked large. "A dance a day" was a slander on most students, but near the truth if one counted them up. "It's notorious that it is a small fraction of our students that keep all these dances going." Stanley asserted that of the nearly one hundred students who failed in three or more subjects in the spring of 1933, most were not the weaker students but those who went to all the dances.

By the time Ruth Crandall graduated in 1935, students had begun to realize something of the sacrifices it was taking to get them to university and keep them there. They were survivors rather than radicals. The typical Dalhousie student of the later 1930s came from a besieged but surviving family. Some parents borrowed money to send a daughter or a son to university because they passionately believed in higher education. There were a few students from wealthy families on Young Avenue, and a few others from blue-collar families, students who had managed to hang on by wits and determination beyond Grade 8. Students in general worked at their studies; law students worked harder at Dalhousie than they did at Toronto according to John Willis, who taught at both. But he also claimed that the law students of the 1930s were not as good as in former years. He attributed it partly to Dalhousie Law School accepting students they should have rejected, needing the fees. Willis also claimed that too many of his law students of the later 1930s were there because well-to-do fathers could afford to send them, there being so few jobs available.[36]

So far as fathers' occupations can be traced, of 2,271 fathers of Dalhousie students during the 1930s, 28 per cent were professionals, 31 per cent businessmen. That was perhaps to be expected. But 21 per cent of Dalhousie students had fathers who were artisans, farmers, fishermen, skilled or semi-skilled workmen. The great majority of Dalhousie students were from backgrounds that can be described as middle class, for whom a university education was a major expense, especially where fathers were school teachers or clergymen. As to defining what middle class was, one easy (but treacherous) definition from the 1930s was that it was those families who used napkin rings. Upper-class families had fresh napkins every meal; lower-class families neither knew nor cared about napkins; middle-class families had napkins, cared very much, and washed those symbols of their respectability once a week. Middle-class students, once graduated, tended to move upwards within the middle class. But of the male graduates of Dalhousie between 1931 and 1940, 25 per cent cannot be traced, whereas of the group between 1921 and 1926, 92 per cent can be. That suggests that a group of Dalhousie graduates in the 1930s remained unemployed or worked at jobs they did not care to report on. Or perhaps they were killed in the Second World War.[37]

Women graduates improved their positions, but it was less through professional work as teachers, librarians, nurses and more by marriage. Tracing Dalhousie alumnae through the *Alumni Magazine*, as Paul Axelrod has done, suggests that only seventeen of the fifty-nine women who graduated in 1936 found professional work. Thus women who aspired to professional careers in the 1930s probably had a decidedly chancy time of it.

Women were 28 per cent of Dalhousie students in 1930, that figure going to 23.5 per cent in 1939. The reason was simple: as money got tighter, families opted for educating sons who could better anticipate a working career. Sons also found summer work more readily than daughters, and thus were less of a drain on family funds. Nevertheless it is noteworthy that 22 per cent of Dalhousie students in 1935 were women.

For the quarter of Dalhousie students that were women, Lucy Maud Montgomery, writing in a special co-ed issue of the *Gazette* in February 1939, had some shrewd advice. An old lady once told her, "Don't marry as long as you can help it because when the right man comes along you can't help it." It was, said the author of *Anne of Green Gables*, the same with writing. And, she added, don't try to hit the public taste: "The public taste does not really like being hit. It prefers to be allured into some fresh pasture surprised." Finally, she said, write about what you know: "tragedy is being enacted in the next yard. Comedy is playing across the street." That was advice the other 75 per cent of Dalhousie students could well profit from too.

Male and female, Dalhousie students of the 1930s, based on averages for 1930–1, 1935–6, and 1939–40, were 67 per cent Nova Scotians. Students from the United States were prominent in medicine and dentistry. Jewish students, especially, found it difficult to crack the unvoiced principles of exclusion at American medical schools, so they came north. Dalhousie's Medical School, being class A, allowed Jewish students to graduate from Dalhousie and return to the United States and get state licences to practise.

Dalhousie students' religious affiliations in the 1930s had changed somewhat from the decade before. The new element was Jewish students – now 11 per cent of enrolment, up from almost nothing in the 1920s. Roman Catholic students were up slightly from 13 to 15 per cent. Anglicans increased from 14 to 23 per cent, the result of the addition of King's. Presbyterian students were the most serious concern. In the early 1920s they were 51 per cent of Dalhousie students. After the creation of the United Church in 1925, one should have expected an increase with former Methodist students added. Instead, the United Church students at Dalhousie were only 34 per cent, plus some students whose old Presbyterian families refused to accept the 1925 union, another 6 per cent.[38]

The decrease in the number of Pictou County students at Dalhousie worried President MacKenzie, who first made it public in his annual report for 1911–12, when Pictonians in arts and science had fallen from 18 per cent in 1891 to 13 per cent in 1911. By 1931 the figure was 8 per cent. The New Glasgow *Eastern Chronicle* commented on it, attributing it to parents being happier with the sterner oversight of students at Antigonish, Wolfville, and Sackville. And less metropolitan temptations: F.B. Squire in the *Dalhousie Gazette* suggested that

Senate's attempts to ban student renting of hotel rooms at the Nova Scotian Hotel's Saturday night dances was not done for morality but to calm uneasy parents. It was also true, as the *Eastern Chronicle* noted, that Dalhousie, a little like UNB, had no longer a distinct denominational background. Since "Dalhousie is one of Pictou's gifts to the welfare of Nova Scotia," more work was needed to recruit students in Pictou County. This and other pressures caused the chairman of the board, Hector McInnes, born and raised in Pictou County, to make three visits to Pictou to stir up relations, friends, and alumni in 1936 and early 1937.[39]

There were not enough scholarships. The Munro exhibitions and bursaries had gone with Munro's death in 1896, and nothing quite like their scale had been substituted since. The bursaries and scholarships that did exist were also less rich than before because of a diminution of dividends and bond interest. There was even a suggestion from the president that those who won scholarships and did not need the money return it to the university. By the end of the 1930s 11.6 per cent of Maritime students had entrance or undergraduate scholarships which averaged $113 a year. That was better than in the West but slightly below that in Ontario.[40]

Student tuition costs in 1930 were about $112 a year in arts, rising to $125 in 1932 over President Stanley's objections. Arts classes were $25 each, sciences classes $40. A student needed about $300 for room and board in Halifax. Thus a year at Dalhousie, including books and personal expenses, would come to about $600. Henry Hicks was given a $500 prize when he graduated from Mount Allison in 1936, and used it to come to Dalhousie in 1936–7. It just about covered his expenses, which were "five hundred and forty-six dollars to attend Dalhousie then, and pay for my residence at Pine Hill Divinity Hall where I lived and even to take a girl to the supper dances at the Nova Scotian Hotel every other week or so." The sum of $546 may seem modest, but it has to be set against salaries then current. In 1937 a beginning bank clerk was paid $400 a year, an experienced typist $700.[41]

Henry Hicks lived at Pine Hill; so had Larry MacKenzie, fifteen years before, as there were no men's residences. Male students were not expected to make their own way completely in the untender world of Halifax boarding houses; Dalhousie kept an avuncular eye on boarding and rooming houses used by its students. The dean of medicine reported in February 1935 on 214 houses for male students: ninety-one offered room and board, sixty-eight were rooms only, thirty-nine offered room with breakfast. For sleeping accommodation the dean reported that half provided double beds. There was nothing strange in the 1930s about men sleeping together; indeed, that was the way many of them had grown up. Three-quarters of the houses had what Dalhousie designated as good washing and toilet facilities – that is, bath, washbasin, and toilet for every six students. Stanley was not satisfied and kept hoping for $750,000 that would enable Dalhousie to build a men's residence; but it did not come.[42]

For that reason a few modest branches of American fraternities appeared at Dalhousie in the 1930s. President MacKenzie had seen them coming and wondered how best to deal with them. Robert Falconer's advice from the University of Toronto was to ward them off, if possible, "but unless you can get residences for men, or keep the college small, they'll come." Sidney Smith told Stanley much the same in 1932, but Smith was positive, seeing fraternities' useful function as residences for men. They were self-governing largely, communal boarding houses run by the occupants, and usually owned by a small clutch of benevolent alumni. At first Stanley did not like them, but within a couple of years he had begun to find them useful. Dalhousie never recognized them, but neither did it ban them. By the end of the 1930s there were seven fraternities and two sororities. They tended to be anti-Jewish, the law fraternity specifically so; but there is no evidence that in Nova Scotia they were what they sometimes were in the United States, anti-Catholic. The *Gazette*, in October 1934, gave an opinion that while fraternities raised hell now and then, and tended to play student power politics, on the other hand they were pleasant houses for men of like interests. President Stanley preferred them kept under control.[43]

The president ran afoul of student opinion in the great badminton crisis of 1934. Mixed badminton Stanley himself suggested as a useful antidote to the erotic temptations of dancing, but he wanted the game taken seriously, with proper clothes, which meant white flannels for men and white skirts for women. One day he found a young woman playing badminton in shorts, and a ban on mixed badminton issued forthwith from the president's office. To the *Gazette* it was irresistible:

> The boys and girls must play alone,
> They cannot play together –
> Your father wouldn't sanction it,
> And neither would your mother.

The Halifax *Citizen*, a leftish local weekly, chimed in with an editorial; Hitler decreed what the German woman should wear, but "President Stanley's dictatorial rule" says what Dalhousie girls shouldn't wear. The *Citizen* wondered what would happen about bathing suits should Dalhousie ever have a summer session! But Dalhousie students never liked downtown interference; they told the *Citizen* to leave well alone, that it understood nothing of campus conditions.

However, Dalhousie could not be kept out of the Halifax papers. During the League of Nations crisis of October 1935 over the issue of sanctions against Italy for its invasion of Abyssinia, the students conducted a poll, the results of which were illuminating. Of 850 students, 464 voted as follows:

	Yes	No
For economic sanctions against Italy	444	16
For military sanctions against Italy	205	235
Support of military measures for League	175	277
For participation in war	157	289

That made headlines in local papers, which concluded, rightly, that Dalhousie students wanted to punish Italy but did not want to have any part in the punishing. This was reinforced a few months later when the *Gazette* insisted that Dalhousie students be neutral in any European conflict. "We have close sentimental ties binding us to Great Britain," said the *Gazette*, "but that is no reason why we should fight the battles of British Capitalism and Imperialism in all parts of the world."[44]

That was something President Stanley approved of: students being students should be outspoken, revolutionary if need be. His concern, he told the students in October 1935, was if they were *not* revolutionary:

My young friends, you should be. There is no other hope for the world. There are many things always to revolt and rebel against. Somewhere or other stupidity is always enthroned. Somewhere or other there are always wrongs to right. Sooner or later there is going to be a wholesale revolt on the part of the youth in North America against what is offered them, by selfish, commercial interests, in the name of amusement and entertainment. Suppose that you began a revolt here and now against the so-called music that I have been listening to for the last four years at Dalhousie, and against what I have for four years heard called in the name of dancing.

But Stanley would not be able to call out the students on that issue. Perhaps not on any issue. He found them ill informed and not well read. He interviewed personally all new students; many of the new men, for law, medicine and dentistry, from other colleges, had never read a book in their lives but the textbooks they had been obliged to read, or "detective stories and trashy novels." But Stanley's utterances on such an issue were not always to be trusted. A year later he was

At the Convocation Ball, May 1939. L. to r., President Carleton Stanley, Miss Muriel Woodbury, Mrs H.A. MacDonald (a member of the board in the 1970s), Mrs Isabel Stanley, T.H. Coffin (a current member of the board), and Dr W.W. Woodbury, Dean of Dentistry, 1935–47.

saying how solid Dalhousie students were, how they read books and debated serious questions. The difference was not, probably, that between the students of December 1937 and those of October 1938; it was, rather, the correspondent he was writing to. But it is true the world had become a more serious place after Munich.[45]

A German Refugee Founds the Institute of Public Affairs, 1936
Stanley defended and supported the cause of German refugees, whether Jewish or not. The day in January 1933 that Hindenburg asked Hitler to be chancellor, Dr Lothar Richter and his wife decided to leave Germany with their young son. Born in 1894 in Silesia, Richter obtained two doctorates, in political science and in law. He was a senior official in the Ministry of Labour of the Weimar Republic, drafting its labour legislation; but with the Nazi party winning a plurality of seats in the 1933 elections, he correctly predicted future events and left for Britain. Through the Archbishop of Canterbury, Richter obtained a temporary post at Leeds University. Carleton Stanley heard about him from the archbishop. Since Dalhousie had no professor of German, when the Rockefeller committee in New York offered to pay his salary as a German refugee for several years, Stanley, impressed with Richter's qualifications, hired him sight unseen as professor of German. He and his family arrived in Halifax in August 1934.

Richter was one of the best of his kind, a highly educated, hardworking, purposeful German civil servant. With all that, he was modest and he never ceased to be grateful to England for taking him in, and to Dalhousie and Canada for giving him a permanent home. He became a Canadian citizen as soon as he could. Before 1934 was out, Richter in his quiet way pointed out to Stanley the Rockefeller Foundation's support in several American universities for departments of public affairs, and that there was no such institution in Canada at all. Richter thought such a department could be organized at Dalhousie, not as a new department but by pooling the resources of existing ones – Political Science, Economics, History, Education, and Law. By that means, said Richter, Dalhousie could prepare students for the civil service, municipal politics, journalism; it could train civil servants already in harness. It could sponsor fact-finding studies that would help Nova Scotian municipalities.

In 1935 the Rockefeller Foundation's Department of Social Science sent its director, Dr Stacy May, to Halifax. He met Richter and others from the modest band of social scientists at Dalhousie and was impressed. The upshot was that the Rockefeller Foundation offered $60,000 ($15,000 a year for the first three years, then in diminishing amounts with Dalhousie contributing). It would begin on 1 September 1936, end on 31 August 1941.[46]

Dalhousie's Institute of Public Affairs owed its inception, its versatility, and its success to Lothar Richter himself. He was ingenious at bringing groups and interests together. It was his idea to get Sir Robert Borden to be honorary chairman of the institute. Borden met President Stanley in 1935 and was impressed with what Borden called his "broad outlook and splendid erudition." Thus Borden, now aged eighty-three, who had been declining similar invitations for the past few years, wrote Stanley: "Your invitation, however, relates to a subject in which I am profoundly interested; and for that reason I have given it serious consideration." He hinted he could accept if the duties were nominal. They were. Richter also persuaded colleagues in other departments to work with him; he brought municipal officials, labour unions, and provincial governments on side; he tried to bring other universities to the institute. He got prominent civil servants to give lectures. Whatever Richter touched seemed to turn, magically, to sensible use and function. He started *Public Affairs*, the second quarterly published by Dalhousie, in 1937.

Some board members in 1937 were uneasy about this new venture in publishing. Why not merge the *Dalhousie Review* and *Public Affairs*? asked Senator W.H. Dennis. Stanley replied that part of the Rockefeller grant was for *Public Affairs*. The reason why two other members of the board executive had asked the same question was that "there have been so many changes in the Executive of the Board that it is hard for that body to have a continuous memory."[47]

He did indeed have a point. In 1937 the board had suffered a number of changes from death and retirement. H.E. Mahon, manager of the Montreal Trust, had died in April; Dugald Macgillivray of the Canadian Bank of Commerce, Carleton Stanley's favourite board member, who had supported the *Dalhousie Review* in both a literary and financial sense since its inception, died suddenly in August. The bronze bust of Lord Dalhousie is his gift to the university. The chairman, Hector McInnes, died of a heart attack in June at the age of seventy-seven. He had graduated from Dalhousie Law School in 1888, was nominated secretary to the board in 1892, treasurer in 1898, appointed to the board in 1900, and succeeded Pearson as chairman in 1932. He had been a Dalhousian most of his adult life.

The board appointed as the new chairman a less judicious, more vigorous, younger lawyer-businessman, another Pictonian, James McGregor Stewart, who had come on the board in September 1929. Forty-eight years old, crippled by polio when young, Stewart had ability and ambition, those two essential elements of success. He had been gold medallist at Pictou Academy and went to Dalhousie, taking the University Medal in Law in 1914. A director of the Royal Bank of Canada since 1931, his erudition, legal and otherwise, was known nationally; he was reputed one of the best lawyers in the country. Stewart walked with crutches, and had an immensely powerful upper body; he smoked three packs of menthol cigarettes a day and drank Scotch in the same proportion. He was a marvellous poker player, his bluffing notorious. But he was a worker. "If you went out with the boys," he used to say, "you must get up with the men." He was a strong Conservative but his home was open to all parties. "Many an evening," wrote his nephew, "Angus L. Macdonald lustily roared out Scottish songs at J. McG.'s piano." This was the man who would be chairman of the Dalhousie board for the next six years – tough, abrupt, capable.[48]

As J. McGregor Stewart took over, two other men died, partners in the pre-1931 Dalhousie. G.F. Pearson died in September 1938, his wife still bitter over what had happened in 1932. Eleven days later President MacKenzie, in hospital for a minor operation, succumbed to a stroke and died shortly afterward, on 2 October. Dalhousie went into mourning for MacKenzie; the *Gazette* devoted a whole issue to him. Beneath his cool exterior MacKenzie was a loyal Dalhousian whose devotion was the more impressive because it was never paraded. R.J. Bean recalled an August day in 1923 when he and his wife first met MacKenzie in the Copley Plaza Hotel in Boston. Bean was so impressed with MacKenzie that, when invited to come and see Dalhousie, he said it was unnecessary – he was coming anyway. More personal notes came to MacKenzie's daughter Marjorie. An old friend from Bryn Mawr days wrote: "He was such fun! ... I went to see you the day he brought you back from Indianapolis to Bryn Mawr [in 1897]. I know his gallant effort to keep his sorrow in the background ... and to make your childhood a happy one." And it seems to have been just that. Another friend wrote about her Halifax childhood and Marjorie MacKenzie's, "such a happy time in my life when your Father, my Father, and Mr. Barnstead were such important, loved grown-ups and gave us the feeling everything was all right and would go on forever." Such indeed is the happy child's kingdom.[49]

But in the wicked world outside there were increasingly few hopes for that. The war that came in 1939 would test Dalhousie more sternly even than the 1914 war, and its classicist president. One can imagine Carleton Stanley, tall, slim, curly haired, coming out of his office in the Macdonald Library with bowler hat and umbrella, his black Newfoundland dog Pontus waiting for him on the steps, ready for a walk. At such times he would survey his campus a little absently, as if he could not quite have said whence he had come or whither he was going.[50] That was an illusion: for Stanley was strong, stubborn, and determined. He would demonstrate those qualities over the next six years.

· 4 ·

Dalhousie, the Second World War, and the Philosopher-King 1939–1943

Affairs external: the coming of the war. Atlantic provinces cajoled for support for Medicine and Dentistry. Selling the Birchdale property on the North-West Arm. Dalhousie crippled by wartime demands. The 1943 R.B. Bennett gift. A new board chairman, K.C. Laurie.

In 1938 the Royal Commission on Dominion-Provincial Relations took as one of its five commissioners R.A. MacKay, Dalhousie's Eric Dennis professor of political science. His substitute at Dalhousie during 1938 and 1939 was Arthur R.M. Lower, an articulate, liberal-minded historian on leave from United College, Winnipeg. United College was a tense and riven institution; Lower found Dalhousie relaxed and pleasant. As MacKay told him, the professors at Dalhousie live "in a condition of genial anarchy." What MacKay meant was that every professor, old and young, taught in ways that seemed to him best. It was the duty of the head of the department to determine what courses were to be taught, but their mode, their style, their essays, marking, examinations, were the professor's to choose and to exact. Lower found the results, stemming from half a century and more of this tradition, good. But he found Dalhousie uneasy about its president. Seven years of Carleton Stanley had divided the faculty, and there was a substantial section with whom "he was extremely unpopular." Others, such as G.V. Douglas and H.L. Stewart, supported him. Stewart's view was: "Some say this about Stanley, some say that. But I say he is on the side of education which is more than can be said about many a university president."

In that sense Stewart was right. Lower, Stewart, and President Walker of King's were on the CBC on New Year's Day of 1939, in a radio debate about Canadian foreign policy, with Walker the imperialist, Stewart the League of Nations collectivist, and Lower the Canadian nationalist. Lower and Walker certainly suited their roles. Lower said to Walker: "The difference between you and me is that when you say 'we' you mean Lancashire, and when I say 'we' I mean Canadians." That brought a telegram to Stanley from H.P. Robinson of the board of New Brunswick Telephones in Saint John. Did that represent what was being taught at Dalhousie? Stanley not only supported Lower's words, but even more his right to speak them.[1]

Munich had sharpened the debate within Canada. The shock of it, in September 1938, and even more Hitler's flagrant repudiation of it by his march into Prague on 15 March 1939, shifted a significant block of Canadian opinion away from isolationism. Canada's Department of External Affairs was still strongly isolationist, as were most French Canadians; but English Canadians and Dalhousians were coming to the grim conclusion that if a major war broke out between Britain and Germany, Canada would have to be in it in some form. On 29 March Neville Chamberlain, the British prime minister, gave the surprising guarantee to support Poland if she were attacked by Germany. That was Chamberlain's violent reaction, shared by many in Britain and Canada, to having been humiliated a fortnight before by the German march into Prague.

The British guarantee to Poland had consequences very different from what Chamberlain intended. It stiffened the Poles, already resistant to giving back any territory that Poland had acquired in 1919 from Germany. Hitler could not believe Britain intended to honour her quixotic commitment to support Poland, but when she made that clear, Hitler acted. Early on Friday, 1 September 1939, the German tanks rolled, and the German air force bombed Polish cities. The British government reluctantly declared war two days later.[2]

The Halifax and Dalhousie Views of the War
Unlike the outbreak of the Great War, Canada did not at once follow Britain into the conflict. O.D. Skelton, under-secretary of state for external affairs, wrote a bitter memorandum for the prime minister on 26 August:

The first casualty in this war has been Canada's claim to independent control of her own destinies ... we have thus far been relegated to the role of a Crown Colony. We are drifting into a war resulting ... from policies and diplomatic actions initiated months ago without our knowledge or expectation ... the foreign policy of Canada is in the hands of the Prime Minister of Great Britain ... The British Government with bland arrogance has assumed that whatever its policy, whether it be appeasement or challenge, we could be counted on to trot behind, blindly and dumbly, to chaos.

That was not what the Halifax *Herald* said. Its headline read, "Empire Stands with Britain." Two days later, on 28 August, Bob Chambers, the cartoonist the *Herald* had bribed away from the *Chronicle* in a 1937 cloak-and-dagger operation, put out a cartoon, "The Call Goes Forth," which showed a bugler under the Union Jack sounding a call to arms to bring Nova Scotians, rifle in hand, from the mine, desk, farm, factory, and fishing vessel.[3] On 4 September, came the news that the *Athenia* had been sunk with the loss of 112 lives by a German submarine. Canada was not at war, not yet, but the sinking of the *Athenia* brought it closer.[3]

The position of most English Canadians was between O.D. Skelton and the Halifax *Herald*, perhaps closer to the latter than the former. English Canadians, and Dalhousians, in September 1939 were really of three groups: first, imperialists such as the Halifax *Herald*, Britain right or wrong. Second, a large group that believed that a major war in Europe was a dreadful commentary on European politics, but with so many friends, relations, and the monarchy, in England, if bombs were falling on London, how could Canada stay out? Nevertheless, Canadians should determine the degree of their commitment to any war. Third, a group that believed that bombs or no bombs, it was not Canada's war. Geography and luck made it virtually impossible that Canada need be involved in any war. The United States had renounced the conquest of Canada; the Monroe Doctrine would protect Canada from any outside power. Senator Raoul Dandurand put the doctrine in a celebrated speech at Geneva in 1924: "Nous habitons une maison à l'épreuve du feu ... Un vaste océan nous sépare de l'Europe." That would have been the position, indeed, of many French Canadians and a small and well-entrenched group of English-Canadian intellectuals, of whom O.D. Skelton was one.[4]

Carleton Stanley was a Canadian with the range of a Britisher, well capable of distrusting his own or any other government. He was proud of British traditions, but he was close to the Labour party and, like it, unhappy with the conduct of British foreign policy since 1933. He told one New Brunswick imperialist that it was a mistake to think that whatever the British government of the day did was right and everyone else wrong. Some Canadians certainly had doubts, and there were plenty of newspapers and MPs in England that had also. Stanley's annual report for 1938–9 seemed to sum up his own experience: "Has any period in history been more difficult for any sort of assertion than the period, 1931–1939?"

So many things, the world over, are going by the board, so much of our political faith, so much of ethical belief, so many indeed of our first principles.

But year after year the thing goes on, and we are forced to realise that civilisation is breaking up; that the great discoveries of science are being manipulated by the Devil; that individual human greed is careless of general human happiness.

Stanley quoted a late Thomas Hardy sonnet, that glowed like the portent it was:

> And that when nations set them to lay waste
> Their neighbours' heritage by foot and horse
> And hack their pleasant plains in festering seams, ...
> Yes. We are getting to the end of dreams![5]

In the period of the "phoney war," when it was phoney in the West and very real in Poland, Dalhousie's life went on much as before, though the Canadian Officers' Training Corps, which had barely survived as a committee in the mid-1930s, was more vigorous. It would become much more important, as would manpower in general by June 1940.

Trying to Support Medicine and Dentistry

Stanley in the meantime was fighting other battles on the home front, ones that he did not always relish. An American Medical Association visit in 1936 pointed out, tactfully as was their wont, serious deficiencies in the Medical and Dental Library. Dalhousie's collections of medical and dental books and periodicals were housed in odd ways, often inaccessible, and reading-room space was on the same casual scale. The AMA suggestions carried considerable clout; Stanley was convinced that if the Medical School lost its A rating it might just as well go out of business. The Rockefeller Foundation offered to support the visit of Eileen Cunningham, medical librarian at Vanderbilt University, Nashville, Tennessee, to advise Dalhousie. She came in June 1937. Stanley thus had expert advice to go on, and he spent a hard week in New York in September 1937 doing the rounds trying to collect $100,000 for a new medical library. In December Carnegie came through with $50,000 if Dalhousie could find another $50,000 to match it. The board dug into their private pockets and found only $8,500. Stanley much disliked the whole process. "It's not the president's proper job," he told one important New York alumnus in January 1938, "to go about cap-in-hand like this." But in March 1938 J.C. Tory (1862–1944) offered one hundred shares of Sun Life Assurance (of which he had been a senior official). That did it.[6]

The cornerstone of the new Medical-Dental Library was laid on 18 August 1938 amid a large and singularly happy alumni reunion celebrating the centennial of Dalhousie's first university teaching. On that occasion Dalhousie outdid itself and gave thirteen LL.D.'s, including one to the oldest Dalhousie graduate, Alexander Ross ('67). At a Dalhousie dinner at the Nova Scotian Hotel the evening before, another new LL.D., Sir Walter Langdon-Brown, a Cambridge physicist, evoked the *gaudeamus igitur* of student life past and present:

Being at a university is like falling in love; no one can ever have had such an experience before ... What is it about one's university that colours the whole of the rest of life? ... Is it not ... the discovery of oneself in relation to the general scheme of things, which was there before us and will outlast us?

He quoted Augustine Birrell, also a Cambridge man:

Which of us who is clad in the sober russet of middle life can gaze without emotion upon the old breakneck staircase in the corner of an ancient quadrangle ... where were housed for a too brief season the bright-coloured, long since abandoned garments of youth, a youth apparently endless, and of hopes that knew no bounds?[7]

Among the thirteen LL.D.'s that sunny August were the three provincial premiers of the Maritime provinces: Thane Campbell of Prince Edward Island, A.A. Dysart of New Brunswick, and Angus L. Macdonald of Nova Scotia. Campbell and Dysart had graduated from Dalhousie, Macdonald had been a Dalhousie law professor; so the gift of those honorary degrees was based on some hope for government support. On the other hand the Dalhousie Board of Governors was profoundly sceptical; very few believed that anything would come of approaches to any of the Maritime governments. They denigrated it as "just Stanley's idea." Stanley stoutly believed that all Dalhousie had to do was to say to all three governments, "Well, gentlemen, if at long last, you decline to support medical training as other Canadian premiers do, we *must* close down."[8]

The Nova Scotian government had consistently refused because of political pressure exerted by the other universities, who would insist on a *quid pro quo* for every grant to Dalhousie. The first break was the $5,000 public health grant of 1935, and it was conditional on Dalhousie establishing a Department of Preventive Medicine. That could be justified on the ground of public health. But an outright grant to

Dalhousie Medical School? When J.C. Tory made his gift for the Medical Library he was, in effect, saying to Stanley, "You are dead right, the governments must give you money, and Nova Scotia must take the lead." It was his way of underlining what he believed was the clear and unmistakable duty of the other Maritime governments. Moreover, the foundations were becoming less accessible. When Stanley approached Rockefeller in March 1939 for a grant of $60,000 per annum to meet current deficits, they replied promptly that they doubted if any further support along such lines was possible.[9]

By 1939 Dalhousie could make other arguments for funding from Maritime governments. When Dalhousie's medical and dental students were largely Americans, governments could resist. By 1938 there were more Newfoundlanders and New Brunswickers than Americans in first-year medicine, and by 1943 first-year medicine had no Americans at all. In fact that year showed something of the proportions of Atlantic provinces' population: of forty-nine first-year students, twenty were Nova Scotians, eleven New Brunswickers, nine Prince Edward Islanders, and eight Newfoundlanders. That change was effected mostly by Dean Grant's going around the Atlantic provinces, largely on his own money, and meeting prospective medical students and encouraging them to come to Dalhousie.

The Carnegie Corporation had not given up its interest in Maritime education; in 1934 it commissioned H.L. Stewart of Dalhousie to make a survey and in November 1935 their representative warned that, compared with a decade before, college standards were slipping, as the number of colleges slowly increased. That view was echoed by Carleton Stanley; the Central Advisory committee on Education in the Maritime Provinces and Newfoundland, a group of college presidents which reported to the Carnegie Corporation, struck a sub-committee to discuss it. At the annual meeting of the advisory committee in Moncton on 29–30 December 1936 they unanimously agreed,

that since none of the colleges was prepared to accept the responsibility of establishing [professional] schools that they were under a real debt to Dalhousie and that they should take advantage of any opportunity occurring to bring home to the governments their responsibility for the support of the professional schools and especially of the medical and dental colleges.

It was understood that if the Nova Scotian government decided to support Dalhousie's medical and dental facilities, the other colleges would not ask for a *quid pro quo*. Here was a mighty first step.[10]

In the autumn of 1937 the Dalhousie governors finally agreed that the time had come to approach the provincial governments for support for medicine and dentistry. In 1938 a memorandum went to all the Atlantic province governments on the subject. It received a friendly enough reception; Newfoundland's Commission government said it would help if it could; Prince Edward Island said it would help too, but it could not take the lead. New Brunswick was cordial in the visits that Stanley and Dean Grant made, following up their memorandum. But none of the other governments would, or could, move without some fundamental beginning by the government of Nova Scotia.

Stanley's account of his and Grant's interview with Angus L. Macdonald on 21 March 1939 is of some interest. The premier began by making objections; notwithstanding the Moncton resolution, the other colleges would be after him if he gave any money to Dalhousie. Stanley showed him the text to prove that was not so.

GRANT: You cannot deny, Mr. Premier, that the medical and dental schools are a great boon to these provinces; nor that they should be supported by these provinces as other professional schools are elsewhere.

ANGUS L.: Well, it cannot be maintained that they enter into the picture of education. They are technical schools rather –

STANLEY (interrupting): Yes, Mr. Premier, they are technical schools for medicos and dentists just as the Nova Scotia Technical College is a technical college for engineers. To that you give $150,000 annually.

Angus L. seemed to give ground a little. He was not, he said, fighting against Dalhousie; the arguments he had been using were those that other people would put up. Stanley then pointed out how Rockefeller refused to give any more money as long as the Nova Scotian community did not. Finally Angus L. said, "Well, we are in debt ourselves this year but I guess we will have to do something for you. I suppose it affects Nova Scotia more than the other provinces." Stanley did not hesitate to remind him that the majority of students in both dentistry and medicine were Nova Scotians. Dalhousie had to have $60,000 a year to keep the Medical and Dental schools going; he pointed out, with examples, "how we had stripped the Arts and Science School to maintain decent professional schools." Angus L. made yet another objection. Dalhousie had allowed experts to bully them, and was "attempting to do things on the scale of New York City." But Stanley gave him no quarter about that, and "he looked as though he wished he had not said it. Then [he] grew very friendly, and drove us home."

That did not mean Dalhousie had won. It had simply taken the first round. Angus L. did not believe the Maritime colleges could be so high-minded about giving Dalhousie free access to the government of

Nova Scotia. He wrote each of the college presidents, asking if they had voted on the 1936 Moncton resolution, and how they felt about the question now, in March 1939. The replies Angus L. elicited not only supported Dalhousie's position; they re-emphasized its necessity. With Stanley's willing acceptance Angus L. sent an accountant to examine Dalhousie's books to see if it were true that it actually needed the $60,000 a year. Finally, in June 1939 Angus L. indicated that his cabinet had no objection to an annual grant to Dalhousie of $25,000. Stanley said that was less than two-thirds of what Nova Scotia should be paying. Angus L. replied, "You can tell Dysart or any one else that we shall assume our share."[11]

Stanley had his work cut out when he visited Dysart in Fredericton, in April. Dysart said New Brunswick could not offer any support to Dalhousie, for it had UNB to look after. Stanley did not accept that. He pointed out how the Saint John General Hospital was a Dalhousie teaching hospital and "no hospital is up to scratch unless it is a teaching hospital, connected with a university, as your Saint John hospital is connected with us. It is notorious among professional men how slackness creeps into a hospital unless it has graduating internes in it who, in the very nature of things, have eyes like hawks." There was good sense in that. Many of the best doctors, said Dr Allan Gregg of the Rockefeller Foundation, "welcome the responsibility of teaching, since it keeps them up to date and at 'concert pitch.'" Stanley also suggested useful analogies from the two schools for the blind and for the deaf in Halifax, to which all three Maritime provinces contributed. "You are a gallant warrior," said Dysart on 26 May 1939, "returning to the fray with such vigor." But Dysart was not giving anything, despite arguments. The blind and the deaf were wards of the state; medical and dental students were not.[12]

In April 1940, despite earlier suggestions of $25,000, Nova Scotia produced only $10,000, with a statement that Dalhousie was not to count on it for 1941 or 1942. The Dalhousie board, stung by that, decided in April 1940 not to cash that cheque, but held two meetings to determine if they would shut down the Medical and Dental schools. Dalhousie went back to the Nova Scotian government and was promised more. The board hung on, hoping that the Atlantic provinces governments would somehow, sometime, awaken to what seemed to Dalhousie as their legitimate responsibilities. Moreover, as Stanley explained to C.H. Blakeny, New Brunswick's minister of education, to make an announcement that Dalhousie was shutting down her professional schools would make it virtually impossible ever to get staff and students together again. But in July 1940 Angus L. Macdonald left for Ottawa as minister of defence for naval services, and the issue dropped.

In January 1941 the government promised $20,000 and would lean on the City of Halifax to put up $5,000 for the Public Health Clinic. That was better, but it was a continuing struggle. Dalhousie still needed not $20,000, but $60,000 a year to keep the schools and the clinic going, and the board had again to go to the government in April 1942. This time it brought evidence that the Rockefeller Foundation had just given $150,000 to develop and improve medical teaching facilities in the new expansion of the Victoria General Hospital the government was undertaking. Not only that; in 1941 Dalhousie was awarded $5,000 a year to establish a Department of Psychiatry. Dr R.O. Jones was soon winning golden opinions in both Halifax and New York. Despite that, in 1943 the government reverted to $10,000, saying that the $20,000 of 1942 was a special grant. Stanley went after the government about that, and three months later it added $10,000. But, as this turgid tale reveals, it was stiff, difficult going.[13]

Dalhousie had, however, received some additional support from outside the province, from Newfoundland. Dalhousie had long been a friendly home for Newfoundlanders; it had strongly supported the creation of Memorial College in 1925 and had sent J.H.L. Johnstone, professor of physics, and a colleague to St John's in May 1925 to advise. The idea of Memorial College had not been received with much enthusiasm by Newfoundlanders; Johnstone thought a great deal had been accomplished by the Memorial group, against heavy odds of apathy and ignorance; "every sympathy and consideration should be shown them." President A.S. MacKenzie thoroughly agreed. Thus Dalhousie followed up Professor Johnstone's visit with advice about registration, curriculum; the Memorial Student Council was based upon Dalhousie's. When planning scholarships for students leaving Grade 11, Dalhousie wanted to include Newfoundland; Stanley feared that Dalhousie might be accused of raiding Memorial's students. He need not have worried; the president of Memorial replied, sensibly enough, that he was delighted for Newfoundland students to get any financial support possible.[14]

Stanley was the first Dalhousie president to actually go to Newfoundland. He had long wanted to broaden the Dalhousie board to include governors from Newfoundland and New Brunswick, and he was able to announce at a luncheon in St John's in 1934 the appointment of the Honourable F.C. Alderdice of St John's to the Dalhousie board. Alderdice was succeeded by Raymond Gushue, Newfoundlander and Dalhousie graduate (LL.B. '25), who became Dalhousie's unofficial ambassador to the Court of St John's, and at one point a member of two boards of governors, Dalhousie's and Memorial's. In 1942 Stanley and Dean Grant, war or no war, again went to New-

foundland, a journey not without risk. Two months later, on
14 October 1942, the s.s. *Caribou*, the passenger ferry between Sydney and Port aux Basques, was torpedoed by a German submarine,
taking 137 people down with her. Grant and Stanley put Dalhousie's
case before the Commission government. Between 1923 and 1938 an
average of ten Newfoundlanders annually were in Dalhousie Medical
and Dental schools; in 1942 it had risen to twenty-two. Could the
government endow a Newfoundland chair of, say, public health, or,
failing that, make an annual grant? It was not all business, as Gushue
reported, making amends for a too-abrupt departure from a Newfoundland party for Stanley and Grant:

These talk-fests have a bad effect on me, but they always take place when the
Judge [William Higgins] and the Mayor [Andrew Carnell] get together. They
are both as good as gold, but the combination of a goodly company and a
little hospitality is too much for them. It hurts me a little to watch the Judge,
splashing about unconcernedly in a whirlpool of circumlocution, and neither
emerging nor submerging, or to see the Mayor who has a heart of gold, mas-
ticating with drooling relish the cud of half-digested clichés. When I left I
feared that they were just getting around to "one standing up" with a speech
or two to finish up the evening. So – if you thought I was rude, I probably
was.

The upshot was the Commission government's offer in October 1942,
of $5,000 a year for five years for Dalhousie's medical and dental
schools.[15]

As for the New Brunswickers, they were friendly enough when
Stanley and Grant met the cabinet in March 1943, but neither the example of Nova Scotia nor Newfoundland made any difference, not
even in 1946 when the minister of education was deeply appreciative
"of the splendid work done by the Dalhousie Medical and Dental
Schools." In 1946 the demands of the New Brunswick school system,
so ministers alleged, made any grant impossible. In March 1947
Prince Edward Island included $3,000 for Dalhousie in its estimates,
and it may have been that that finally tipped the balance at Fredericton in Dalhousie's favour. The New Brunswick cabinet authorized
$20,000 in May 1947.[16] But the process, over a whole decade, 1937
to 1947, had been like pulling teeth.

The initiative in this struggle was Stanley's. Most of the Dalhousie
board not only doubted the feasibility of getting any money out of
Maritime governments; they were sceptical even of the wisdom of trying. Stanley stuck to his guns. When the first money from the government of Nova Scotia was about to come in 1940, J. McGregor

Stewart ("Jim" as everyone called him) wrote Stanley an appreciative letter. "I am sure," he said, "the Board will be unanimous in their thanks to you, for the idea was yours and the patiently worked campaign was yours."[17]

The Birchdale Affair

But there was a problem between Stanley and Stewart waiting in the wings, that came on a year later: the Birchdale affair. Dalhousie's financial difficulties in the early 1940s were patent enough; one consequence, regarded by many in the Dalhousie community as unfortunate, not to put a stronger word on it, was the sale of the Birchdale property in September 1941. It was unusual for a university corporation to let property go once it owned it. Not for nothing did medieval monarchs fear mortmain, the dead hand; the church, once it acquired property, kept it until, presumably, the Day of Judgment. The universities in this respect were apt to be the church's modern successors. Dalhousie did indeed give up the Parade in the 1880s, after long negotiations with the city, but it clung to whatever else it had acquired. It bought Birchdale in 1920 for $160,000 as a men's residence at a time when student housing in Halifax, more than two years after the explosion, was difficult to find. Birchdale was a spacious old hotel on the Arm, with some 600 feet of water frontage, and one good deep landing place, the land running back some 550 feet. It was the only large area vacant on the Halifax side of the Arm. Birchdale was not, however, contiguous with any other part of Dalhousie, being about a quarter-mile distant from the president's house on Oxford Street and the campus on the opposite side. Students going back and forth from 1920 to 1923 did not seem to mind the distance, and they loved the Arm.[18]

In September 1923, and loath to do it, Dalhousie leased Birchdale to King's until King's could put up their new stone buildings on the Dalhousie campus. Seven years as a King's residence was too much for the old hotel. In 1930, when Dalhousie got Birchdale back again, the decision was made to raze the building rather than repair it. Birchdale was subsequently written down on Dalhousie's books from $160,927 to $34,317. In October 1932, F.B. McCurdy, chairman of the Finance Committee, recommended immediate sale of the property to help reduce the burgeoning deficit. But both the Executive Committee and the full board concluded that this was no time to sell. Nevertheless, in November 1933 the Building Committee had two requests about Birchdale: one from Dean Grant asking if the board would grant permission to professors to build their houses on the property, and another from Dugald Macgillivray asking for an option to purchase all of it for an unnamed principal. It was agreed that the board did not want to lease lots to professors, but that if Macgillivray wanted an option he could have one for three months, on the understanding that the minimum price would be $40,000. The interest of J. McGregor Stewart, vice-chairman of the board, and his wife Emily, was piqued. Their property, Braemar, was at the southern end of Birchdale, and the only road access to their Arm garden was the shore road through Birchdale. If Birchdale were sold, that access was ended. Hence they wanted a strip along the south side of Birchdale that would give them access through property they owned.

The Macgillivray option expired without its being taken up. Several board members questioned whether any of Birchdale should be sold, and the issue went back to the Building Committee for recommendation. Professor H.R. Theakston, Dalhousie's engineer in charge of buildings and grounds, recommended sale of the strip for $3,500 to Mrs Stewart. But at that point Mrs Stewart's interest seems to have lapsed; perhaps the board's resistance to sale may have suggested to her husband the virtue of postponement.

There the matter rested for five years. During that time Dalhousie could not get the land exempted from city taxes, even though it was used to teach engineers surveying. The taxes averaged about $700 a year. In February 1941 J. McGregor Stewart, now the chairman, reported that Eastern Trust had received written offers to buy lots on the Birchdale property. That summer the seven acres were surveyed and divided into nine lots, each about three-quarters of an acre. Lot 9 was different from the others; it was a strip on the south side, 60 feet wide and 490 feet deep. The other eight were the conventional rectangles. In September 1941, under financial pressure, the board agreed to sell the whole of Birchdale to the Eastern Trust for $30,500, the Trust's 5 per cent commission to be deducted from the sale price. The resulting $28,700, after some other expenses were deducted, would be applied to the $43,000 5 per cent mortgage on the whole of Studley. That would produce a saving to the university of $1,425 per year, which, with the taxes saved, amounted to $2,100 annually.[19]

That is as cool a gloss on the transaction as can be given. There were, on the other hand, disturbing aspects to the sale: the price itself, which seemed to some too low; more important, the fact that the wife of the chairman of the board got lot 9, the 490-foot strip, with water frontage that included one of the best landing places on that side of the Arm.[20] Mrs Stewart's prospective purchase was only known at the last stage when it was before the full board on 18 September 1941. While the Stewart strip might have been regarded by some as an innocent acquisition, not only did it not look right, it was not right. It was alleged that Stewart's friends bought several of the lots. President Stanley opposed the sale or the break-up of Birchdale at every stage, and later claimed to have acquired some obloquy in so doing. A more extreme view of the Birchdale sale was taken by Miss Lola Henry, Stanley's percipient secretary. Miss Henry was a staunch defender of Dalhousie's (and President Stanley's) interests; she claimed that Dalhousie's need for the money was only a pretext, that Stewart became chairman of the board in 1937 mainly because he intended to get that piece of Birchdale. And, asserted Miss Henry, he stayed until he got it; then, a year and a half later, in 1943, he resigned as chairman. Dr Beecher Weld, the new professor of physiology, thoroughly disliked the whole business.[21] The transaction slowly became public knowledge. Among Dalhousians it left a bad taste; it was a conflict of interest on the part of the chairman of the board. He did not vote on the issue in September 1941, but if he wanted a piece of Birchdale that badly, he might have resigned from the board before the issue of sale came up in February 1941. Still, it is right to suggest that it was an age when conflict of interest was not looked upon as severely as now. It was a smaller world, and in downtown Halifax one might have conceded that the Stewarts were only looking after their property.

Thus did Dalhousie lose its hold on six hundred choice feet of the North-West Arm. Stanley's hopes for a biological station were never realistic, for the Arm was already insufficiently clean; but his idea of a Dalhousie rowing and canoe club was a real possibility. It was from this time that Stanley and Stewart, president and chairman, began to move apart. Once when Stanley was in New York talking to Dr F.P. Keppel of the Carnegie Foundation, perhaps in 1941, he complained that someone upon whom he had built hopes had broken in his hands. Keppel replied, "You didn't make a mistake. The man was capable of doing what you hoped, but he couldn't stand the strain of finding that you trusted him." Was it J. McG. Stewart of whom they were speaking? Stanley continued to value Stewart's strength, vigour, and financial capacity, but seeds of distrust had been sown.[22]

Stanley and the Board Begin to Draw Apart
Stanley's disillusionment with the board seems to have begun not long after the death of Hector McInnes in 1937. In November 1937 Stewart fell and broke his leg; the vice-chairman, Dr J.C. Webster, the New Brunswicker whom Stanley had been instrumental in having appointed, was seventy-four years old and lived two hundred miles distant in Shediac; the board secretary was a decent old fellow, W.E. Thompson (LL.B. '93), now virtually an invalid. Much of the work

fell on Stanley's shoulders. What began to make him angry was the way the board members seemed to disappear when anything substantial had to be done. Especially was this so after the outbreak of war, when Ottawa cheerfully requisitioned whomever and whatever it wanted. On 26 April 1940 the board, meeting at Stewart's house, agreed to send a small delegation to see the Nova Scotian premier, and to have Stanley arrange an appointment for 30 April. Just before the delegation was to go downtown Stanley discovered that Stewart had gone off to Ottawa without a word. "A second-hand junk shop could not prosper if handled in such a way!" Stanley complained in 1940 to K.C. Laurie, newly on the board.[23]

The financial campaign of 1939 had gone to ground in the same fashion, so it seemed to Stanley. In 1938 the board decided it would launch a substantial campaign for $4.4 million in 1939, to be called the Loyalty Campaign. Dalhousie's 1939 needs were estimated as follows:

Cancellation of present debt	$ 400,000
Endowment to maintain present faculties	2,310,000
Men's residence	1,000,000
Biology and Geology Building	500,000
Anatomy Building	200,000
	$4,410,000

As early as April 1939 the campaign was hanging fire badly, Stanley said, with almost the whole board out of town, and for weeks. A circular letter went out from John S. Roper, campaign secretary, in June 1939, written from "Lord John's office in the little red college," evoking memories of the happy alumni reunion of August 1938. But by August 1939 Stanley complained that those who should have been in the forefront of the campaign had gone to sleep. By the spring of 1940 several board members, including the chairman, thought the campaign should be put off until after the war. Some money was coming in; Stanley was impressed with "the generosity of school teachers and preachers on low salaries"; many of Dalhousie's professors had been very generous, some subscribing as much as 10 per cent of their year's salary. But impetus was lacking. S.R. Balcom of the local drugstore chain, who was chairing the campaign, discovered the board chairman wanted it to close down; the secretary, when he discovered the same thing, resigned. Balcom went to Ottawa, later becoming the chief medical stores inspection officer in 1944. Thus did the Loyalty Campaign come slowly to a stop, not without recriminations.[24]

By 1940 Stanley himself found academic meetings multiplied, too many of them "unnecessarily and irrelevantly long." At Senate on

28 November when, as he put it, he could not get the Senate to see reason, he lost his temper and walked out, with the remark, "I will not have my time wasted any further today." Stanley was worn out, so much so that by April 1941 he was in bed with pleurisy. The rest of the university struggled as best it could, enrolment falling steeply. It was 908 in 1939–40; by 1942–3 it was down to 676, a drop of 26 per cent in three years.[25]

There was a developing backlog of unanswered problems, including some with King's, which was trying to break some of the 1923 terms. "King's is chilling," Stanley told McGregor Stewart in December 1940; "Can it be that they want to advertise to the world that they have flouted the federation we thought we had? Is not the time approaching when the Carnegie Corporation will have to be advised of what is going on?" Nor was Stanley's attitude improved by an ill-advised article by President Walker in the Halifax *Chronicle* two months later, a tactless and graceless comment on what Carnegie had done for King's in 1923, giving it $600,000 on condition that it find a further $400,000. That King's managed to do by 1927. A further condition of the Carnegie grant was that the combined $1 million be applied to support instruction at both King's and Dalhousie. Dalhousie had the strong suspicion that some of that income was being used to support King's program in divinity, something specifically prohibited in the terms of agreement. In December 1941 Stanley was in New York and saw the Carnegie people. R.M. Lester was familiar with King's violation of the agreement; Keppel, the president, wished to have King's sued to enforce the terms of 1923, but Stanley claimed that he had persuaded Keppel not to sue. But King's would have to wait; neither Stanley nor Stewart had the time for it. Two years later Stanley referred to the useful Latin principle, *Solvitur ambulando* – let time resolve the King's issue, as time resolved many things.[26]

The Effects of the War on Dalhousie

The war devastated Dalhousie, not by bombs or explosions, but by the tremendous weight of government manpower needs in a vital seaport city, and by the concomitant haemorrhage of staff, of students, of energies. Within three years C.L. Bennet, registrar and professor of English, himself a veteran of the First World War, could say, "You couldn't form even a platoon of able-bodied men at Dalhousie right now. There aren't any."[27]

It helped that the universities now had a collective voice. The National Conference of Canadian Universities (NCCU) had its origins in 1911, but developed in the early months of the First World War, especially through the efforts of Principal Peterson of McGill, supported warmly by President MacKenzie. After the war it continued, usually meeting annually, with presidents taking turns at presiding. Stanley was president of the NCCU in 1935–6. After the Second World War began, the government found the conference increasingly useful as a liaison body with the universities of Canada. J.S. Thomson, president of the University of Saskatchewan and NCCU president at the time, praised the enlightened attitude of Ottawa, especially its acceptance of the principle that the best contribution by students to the war was to finish their courses.[28]

The conference had hitherto been what its name suggested; but by July 1940 it had become the vehicle for the development of man-power policies as they affected the universities. In 1941 more mina-tory actions by the government made themselves felt. The Wartime Bureau of Technical Personnel was set up by order-in-council in Feb-ruary 1941, and it had dictatorial powers. At the June 1942 NCCU conference severe shortages of engineers and scientists were reported. Some presidents were ready to make their universities into the work-ing instruments of government needs; in November 1942 Cyril James of McGill and R.C. Wallace of Queen's devised a scheme, the nub of which was that university teaching in law, the humanities, and the so-cial sciences could usefully be shut down for the duration of the war. There was some talk in the *Financial Post* and the *Globe and Mail* during the latter part of 1942 that supported such a position. Presi-dent Stanley was furious with James, "an extremely crude mischief maker," he told Sidney Smith of Manitoba. Stanley had another rea-son for his dislike; James had suggested in April 1942 that Dalhousie students finishing third year, by going to McGill for ten weeks, could get a McGill degree at the end of that summer. Stanley replied indig-nantly that it was a gross attempt to steal students from other univer-sities, and he would have nothing to do with it. He stirred up Cody of Toronto. So the James proposal about abandoning arts came from a president whom others thought a maverick. Cody of Toronto, Smith of Manitoba, Larry MacKenzie of British Columbia, and several oth-ers joined Stanley in agreeing that the James-Wallace proposal was thoroughly bad.

Stanley did not much like Sidney Smith, at Dalhousie or anywhere else, but that feud was patched up for the sake of the emergency. Smith was president of the NCCU that year, and wrote Stanley from Winnipeg: "Frankly we wondered – to use a slang expression – whether the two men in question, who are frequently in Ottawa and who are close to governmental authorities, are 'selling us down the river.' " A special meeting of the NCCU was called for Ottawa in Janu-ary 1943, the university communities very much on the *qui vive*, and ready to take up arms. There the whole proposal was shot down; its only supporters were Wallace and James. Not even the government wanted it. The agreement that emerged did what Arthur MacNamara, the sensible deputy minister of labour and director of national selective service, suggested: weed out incompetent students of whatever kind. James had his fingers burnt and was bitter. But in fact the thinking of the prime minister at that point was that the expansion of the military had gone quite far enough.[29]

In 1942 Dr Lothar Richter, the director of Dalhousie's Institute of Public Affairs, claimed Dalhousie was the greatest war casualty of any of the Canadian universities. He was not far off that himself; he and his family had to lie low because anti-German prejudice was rife in Halifax. Stanley was angry at the bigoted and unthinking attitudes of Nova Scotians against the Richters, who had after all fled Germany because of Hitler.

And the war brought into prominence sometimes officious and unintelligent people in wrong places. A young Dalhousie law professor, Allan Findlay, got into trouble in 1939 for sending a letter to Denmark that had a crude sketch of Halifax harbour in it, to show his Danish fiancée the geography. Dark rumours circulated in Ottawa about Findlay's revelations such as aiding German bombing runs over strategic points in Halifax harbour; Scotland Yard in London allegedly affirmed that the address in Denmark housed a Nazi spy centre. Censors never could be brought to realize that the Germans had whole charts of Halifax harbour and its approaches. Findlay mailed the letter on 29 October 1939; on 2 December he was charged under the Defence of Canada Act with having sent a treasonable letter. J. McG. Stewart, chairman of the board, thought Findlay should be fired. Stanley resisted. Stanley had friends in high places, not least the governor general, Lord Tweedsmuir, who saw the letter at External Affairs and told Stanley the young man was innocent. So it virtually proved to be; in the trial before Magistrate Inglis on 28 December, Inglis said that although Findlay was technically guilty, a romantic impulse did not constitute treason. Inglis found him guilty as charged; the fine was $1 plus costs. They were $6![30]

Dalhousie found itself being steadily crimped and crippled by government demands, especially for the loan of staff for technical projects. J.H.L. Johnstone and George Henderson in the Department of Physics were seconded to the National Research Council in 1940 on part-time leave for naval research, as soon as magnetic mines made their appearance. The huge cables that were wound around corvettes just inside the bulwarks resulted partly from the work of Johnstone and Henderson on the principle of degaussing. As of 31 August 1942 both Dalhousie physicists were gone for the duration of the war. Four senior members of Senate and two members of Arts and Science, Vincent Macdonald, dean of law, and some thirteen members of the Medical Faculty, are recorded in the 1944–5 calendar as on leave for the duration.

In December 1940 the Red Cross cheerfully announced that in the event of any real emergency in Halifax the first building they would requisition would be Shirreff Hall. The board even accepted that. Whole sections of the Dalhousie campus were sequestered. The corner of Coburg and Oxford streets became the site by 1943 of a barracks for the Women's Royal Canadian Naval Service (WRCNS). In September 1941, at government request, King's leased its whole building to the navy. It informed Dalhousie only when it was a *fait accompli* and it did not bother informing the Carnegie Corporation at all. Both Lester and Keppel of the corporation told Stanley in December 1941 that, legally and morally, they should at least have been consulted. King's students went to Pine Hill. The navy arranged to build a mess hall for its officers in training at HMCS *King's* on the foundation of the old Dalhousie gym, opposite the Physics Building. The new 1932 gym was used heavily by navy, airforce and army personnel; by 1944 HMCS *King's* was taking twenty-four hours a week of the Dalhousie gym. The Canadian Women's Army Corps wanted accommodation; they took over Shirreff Hall for the summer of 1942, and to Dalhousie's surprise left it cleaner than it had ever been seen before. Eventually the government would develop a site for a CWAC barracks just off Dalhousie land on Morris Street.[31]

Dalhousie's financial loss from the war was considerable. By the autumn of 1942 attendance was down 25.5 per cent from that in 1939. Stanley claimed that Dalhousie's loss of students, male students especially, was much the highest in Canada. Average yearly loss from the shrinkage of student fees alone was $50,000. Dalhousie's Medical and Dental facilities were being used by the armed services during the early stages of the war; the Public Health Clinic had to cope with VD in the navy and on the merchant ships. Aside from the loss of student fees, Dalhousie calculated in 1943 that it had spent some $124,000 in staff time and overhead, and thought that some compensation from Ottawa was both appropriate and essential:

A – Degaussing ships (Physics) $42,250
B – Precision instrument course (Physics)   12,750
C – National Research Council projects (Chemistry)   700
D – Medical Research, NRC, National Defence, Department of
    Pensions, Royal Canadian Navy   3,000

E – Medical; Diphtheria immunizations	46,316
F – VD treatment for merchant seamen	2,000
G – Work for armed services by Dalhousie's Pathology Department	10,310
H – Rent for university buildings	6,000
	$124,326

This went to C.J. Mackenzie of the National Research Council on 13 March 1943. A similar request had gone forward in 1942, supported by C.D. Howe and Angus L. Macdonald. J.L. Ilsley, the minister of finance, Nova Scotian though he was (BA Acadia, 1913, LL.B. Dalhousie, 1918), was obdurate to both requests. Not even the cost of drugs spent on VD and diphtheria was allowed. Only one minor claim was accepted. When Angus L. Macdonald, minister of naval defence, wrote to Dalhousie on 8 March 1943 asking for permission to build a drill shed, 160 feet by 86 feet, on the campus, Stanley noted an earlier 1942 request of the navy for something similar. The board therefore decided that no further negotiations with any government department for facilities would take place until some settlement had been reached about Dalhousie facilities already granted. In 1944 Stanley told R.B. Hanson, the leader of the opposition in Ottawa, that "the letters we received from the Finance Minister about these matters have to be seen to be believed."[32]

By 1943, however, Dalhousie's pressing financial difficulties, while still real, were helped by new and considerable gleams of hope. Fortuitously money began to appear. Alex Ross, Dalhousie's oldest graduate, whom Dugald Macgillivray had once whiskeyed and nourished, gave via his estate $102,500 for libraries; the George S. Campbell estate gave $108,000 to found a chair in biology; most important of all, in April 1943 there came a personal visit from R.B. Bennett's secretary, Alice Millar, and R.B.'s brother, Captain Ronald Bennett. They presented Stanley with a missive from R.B. Bennett. "Your letter," wrote Miss Millar to her employer in England, "shook him to his roots for he had no warning." It was a gift of $725,000 with the promise of another $250,000 to come. Bennett, then living at his country estate at Mickleham in Surrey, decided at the age of seventy-three to distribute some of his Canadian assets, not being able to get any money out of England. Stanley had once told Bennett of Harvard President Conant's remark that the value of a university lay not in its buildings but its professors. Bennett listened. Thus the $725,000, with $25,000 that Bennett had earlier given to begin endowment of a Dean Weldon chair of law, would be established to endow at least four professorships, any balance to go to Dalhousie's endowment:

- a Mrs E.B. Eddy professorship in Medicine, preferably connected with Nursing (it came to be in Public Health and Nursing)
- a Harry Shirreff professorship in Science, preferably connected with pulp and paper manufacture (it came to be in Chemical Research)
- a law school professorship, the Dean Weldon chair
- a second law school professorship, the Viscount Bennett chair.

There was to be no publicity for the present; Alice Millar stressed the point, no talk at all. Stanley took her so much at her word that he did not even tell his chairman of the board. It was not until five months later that the Royal Bank, needing signatures in connection with $725,000 of Dominion of Canada bonds, forced Stanley to ask Ronald Bennett if Dalhousie's good fortune could not be made known to the board. That was done, and the board at once struck an R.B. Bennett gift committee.[33]

The two chairs in medicine and science were new specialties, and thus did not relieve Dalhousie of existing financial commitments; but with the two Law School chairs there followed a tug-of-war with the Law School, which wanted the full weight of the Bennett bequest to come to them. The Law School's old regimen, "Three men and a boy and a stenographer," would now be, they hoped, four full-time teachers at $5,000, plus a full-time librarian and a stenographer. At this point, the Law School was actually down to two full-time professors, since Dean Vincent MacDonald was also assistant deputy minister of labour in Ottawa. John Willis, acting dean, solicited MacDonald's support to help the Law School argue its case with the Board of Governors. Stanley, on the other hand, asserted that the Law School had for some years, along with the Medical School, eaten up money that should have gone to Arts and Science. Stanley's position was reinforced by McGregor Stewart who would, he said, "definitely oppose the continuing withdrawal of general University funds in order that the activities of the Law School may be extended beyond the present facilities. The Law School has been a great drain on the general funds." In the end Stewart and the board won their holding action.

Stewart also believed that parts of Dalhousie could be altogether closed for the duration of the war; indeed, sometimes he said all of it. That had arisen, Stanley claimed, several times since 1939; in fact, there was "no part of the University which he has not at one time or other urged me to close down." Stanley resisted, but it had never come to a quarrel. Stewart was suave; if Stanley objected, that was all right with Stewart, who was too preoccupied with the war labours to fight the issue.[34]

Colonel K.C. Laurie, Chairman of the Board, 1943–55: "bluff, affable, kindly … a decent proud squire."

A New Chairman of the Board, 1943

In April 1943 Stewart was no longer chairman of the board. He had to give that up, having too much to do in Ottawa and in Halifax. Stanley regretted losing the leadership of such an able man: "one could hardly imagine a person better qualified." Stewart was like a great strong horse; even if Stanley no longer fully trusted him, Stewart had tremendous pulling power. But he had been so busy that board meetings had become sporadic and his board colleagues restive. There were two possible successors. One was F.B. McCurdy (1875–1952), appointed to the board in 1928, its leading financial expert, and now its treasurer. He had been a Conservative MP, and a minister in the 1920–1 Meighen government. He also had Liberal connections, married to Florence Pearson, G.F. Pearson's sister, and in fact took over the running of the Halifax *Morning Chronicle*, the Liberal standard-bearer, from Pearson in 1926. McCurdy was sixty-eight years old and comfortably rich; McCurdy's paper was less tolerant of the CCF and socialism than was the Conservative *Herald*. According to Stanley, his appointment as chairman of the board at Dalhousie would have been a shock to the community and to its conscience.

The other candidate was Lieutenant-Colonel K.C. Laurie, "a fine gentleman and public-spirited citizen," as Stanley wrote Webster in Shediac, "conscious of his own limitations as compared with the man he would have to succeed." Opinion on the board was divided; at first there was more support for McCurdy, but by May 1943, perhaps with encouragement from Stanley, opinion began to swing rapidly toward the colonel. J.C. Webster thought it would help if he (Webster) resigned, having always felt his appointment as vice-chairman was a mistake. It would give the board more room for change. Stanley begged the eighty-year-old Webster to stay on; Webster was an ally. On 27 May K.C. Laurie was confirmed as chairman.[35] A soldier born and bred, he looked the part; but he was not chosen for that reason. Why he was chosen in 1943 may have been more a comment on the board and the busyness of the other men and women who composed it. Whatever his strengths and weaknesses, K.C. Laurie would be chairman for the next twelve years.

· 5 ·

Firing Carleton Stanley
1943–1945

The Dalhousie of 1943. K.C. Laurie of Oakfield. President
Stanley's strengths and weaknesses. The 1944 issues with
Laurie and McGregor Stewart. Trying to force Stanley's resignation. The battle begins, November 1944. And ends, February 1945. Publicity good and bad.

The Dalhousie that Colonel K.C. Laurie now superintended in 1943
was heavily permeated with war. King's College had one hundred
young naval officers in training, trooping across the campus past the
Murray Homestead to the dining hall (where the old gym was), doing
their early morning exercises in front of King's, and practising their
signals the rest of the time in semaphore and Morse. There were uni-
forms everywhere one went. Halifax was thronged with people: line-
ups at all the downtown restaurants, especially good ones like the
Green Lantern; taxis difficult to find; the city and its institutions bursting at the seams. The sheer grimness and griminess of Halifax in that
wartime had to be seen and experienced to be understood. One rather
starchy New Englander, John Marshall, from the Rockefeller Foundation, found Halifax in April 1942 the dirtiest city he had ever visited,
and the public amenities virtually non-existent. Halifax's public library
was housed in one small and dingy room in City Hall, and operated on
a budget of under $6,000 a year. Perhaps Marshall might have remem-
bered that Halifax had been the centre of the Atlantic coast war operations for three years, and for every service, navy, army, airforce, and
whole fleets of merchant ships; the strain of it was showing.

The students were no better off than anyone else. The usual student
boarding houses were expensive and tended to be crowded out by
wives and families of servicemen. Wherever one went on campus,
there were stories of harsh treatment of students by Halifax landlords
and landladies; you would hear the stories in classes or at Roy At-

wood's gym store. The latter was the nearest approach to a student common room on the whole campus. Atwood started it in 1930 by arrangement with President MacKenzie in the old gym, and after it burned down in 1931, he moved to the basement of the Arts Building, then in 1933 to the new gym. Much talk and philosophy was dispensed there. One student remarked that talk with his fellow students was the most valuable part of his Dalhousie years, "time to sit around and see where we were going and what to do about it." Roy's was the one place on campus you could do it.[1]

Campus Life

War or no war, students were students. Life and dances, work and flirtations went on. In the same 1941 issue of the *Gazette* that condemned three provincial premiers (Pattullo of British Columbia, Hepburn of Ontario, and Aberhart of Alberta) for refusing to discuss the Rowell-Sirois recommendations, an advertisement for Cousins Dry Cleaning suggested other interests than political or academic:

> In whispering taffeta, velvet, sheer,
> In net or rustling satin,
> The Tech Ball finds her more at ease
> Than does a class in Latin.
>
> Ah, she'll not decorate the walls,
> Nor "sit them out" in dozens,
> She's learned that to be really chic
> Her dress must go to Cousins.

At Shirreff Hall formals it was still *de rigueur* for men to wear tuxedos, and there were even occasional flashes of white tie and tails, reminiscent of older days when they were the only formal clothes a gentleman could wear to a ball. By 1942 the favourite dance band was that of Glenn Miller, who specialized in a svelte trombone sound; but he was closely followed by the Canadian band, Mart Kenney and his Western Gentlemen, whose theme song, "The West, a Nest and You, Dear," emanated from the Royal York, Toronto. Shirreff Hall girls were told to hang on to their medical students; lawyers were too clever, taught to see through strategies, even female ones, "whereas doctors are so beautifully simple." Servicemen were preferred by Shirreff Hall girls to the callow, less well-mannered students. They were more interesting and they treated you like a lady; when you came into a room, they rose to their feet, as gentlemen should. If you went out with them, they had planned their evenings; true, they might take the

A sunny convocation committee in 1942 on the steps of Shirreff Hall. Standing, l. to r., Kenneth Bate, Louise Bishop, Penny Patchett, Andrew Dunn; seated, Edward Rettie, Catherine Hicks.

odd drink now and then, but a girl never had to worry about how she would get home.[2]

The first Dalhousie sweater queen was announced in November 1941. Oh, shades of Archie MacMechan! Any co-ed was eligible who had ever worn a sweater, any type of sweater. Women could vote as well as men. There were striking differences in male and female attitudes to sweaters; most co-eds preferred loose-fitting ones, several sizes too big; male students, not surprisingly, preferred sweaters (on women, that is), two sizes too small. The 1941 sweater queen at Dalhousie was Susan Morse ('45). As to those indispensable items of female clothing, silk stockings, they had become nylons in 1939, both stronger and better. As nylon came to be used for parachutes and many other war functions, nylon stockings became harder to get, and there was a wartime propensity to opt for lisle. Some 60 per cent of Shirreff Hall girls tolerated them, and 40 per cent hated them. Said one negative Shirreff Hall girl, "The same thing happens to girls that wear lisle stockings as it does to girls who wear black woollen stockings – NOTHING!"[3]

The favourite campus comic strip in 1941 was Blondie, closely followed by Li'l Abner, though student opinion reversed itself by 1942 with Li'l Abner ahead. Sadie Hawkins day, in February, had been going since before the war.[4]

A longstanding grievance on campus was the sexual segregation of the reading room in the Macdonald Library, men at the east end, women at the west end. Some girls liked the segregation for they could flirt with impunity behind the stern enforcement and occasional cautions of Miss Ivy Prikler, the librarian. Most students wanted the system changed but it remained until after the war. Worse than that, the stacks were hallowed ground; the gate was guarded by vestal virgins of steely eyes and unbending hearts; the only students who were allowed in were honour and graduate students. Undergraduates were allowed only two books out at a time.[5]

By Christmas 1942 failure at examinations began to have more serious consequences. A federal order-in-council of 21 October 1942 made it clear that failure at Christmas meant for male students being made immediately eligible for military service, though President Stanley explained that it was Dalhousie that determined whether a student was in good academic standing or not. In both 1942 and 1943 the Christmas casualties were light.[6]

The New Chairman of the Board

The students' first meeting with their new chairman of the board was something of a social disaster. At a fall convocation, probably 1943,

Colonel Laurie, very new to addressing students or any other academic gathering, was tackling his prepared text. Just as he was getting into his stride a dog wandered onto the stage. Titters from the students; Laurie raised his voice. Then there were two dogs, then three. No one was doing anything about them; Colonel Laurie ploughed inexorably on, speaking louder and louder to a totally distracted audience. It was more than Dixie Pelluet, associate professor of biology, could stand. She marched into the middle of the centre aisle and called out in her strident, clipped voice, "Grab the *bitch*!" Someone did and the dogs disappeared. All this time Colonel Laurie never stopped. It was a sort of military triumph.[7]

Laurie had been appointed to the board in 1939, a tall, spruce, fifty-eight-year-old man with a military bearing. Although born in London, England, he was brought up on his father's estate at Oakfield, on Grand Lake, twenty miles north of Halifax. His first memories were of being taken by his father, Major-General J. Wimburn Laurie, to the Intercolonial railway line, which ran near the estate, to cheer the Halifax militia going west to the Northwest Rebellion of 1885. Laurie was schooled in Nova Scotia and in London, ending, as his father had done, at the Royal Military College at Sandhurst, serving in the Boer War and the Great War; in the meantime he had married Violet Boardman, the daughter of an admiral of the Royal Navy. They retired to Oakfield in 1922 and became the country squire and the chatelaine of the district.[8]

Laurie's familiarity with universities was thin, to say the least. A Sandhurst education, admirable no doubt for its purposes, was not adequate for a position that required familiarity with finance, with universities, and with the ways of the world in both. Laurie would have to be taught perhaps by the former chairman, J. McGregor Stewart, perhaps by Carleton Stanley, especially since Dalhousie lacked a resident vice-chairman. When Laurie first visited his vice-chairman at Shediac, probably in the summer of 1943, he impressed Dr Webster with his "marked humility" in the face of his lack of academic experience.[9]

Unlike other members of the board who were businessmen or lawyers with a great deal else to do, Laurie had the advantage of being a gentleman of leisure, or as much as running a large estate with a herd of prize cattle (and other animals) would allow. Laurie was not brilliant: he was bluff, affable, kindly, in some ways intellectually naive. His spelling and syntax were precarious. Nor was he a hard-drinking, hard-riding army officer; he and his wife were Anglican teetotallers. If you were invited to the Lauries to dinner (and he believed in inviting professors to dinner, especially younger ones), you received not wine but quantities of sweet, purple grape juice, made from Concord grapes. Laurie took his duty as governor earnestly; it was his form of *noblesse oblige*, what one owed to the Nova Scotian community. Laurie was a decent, proud squire, doing the best he could, though with military penchants.

In November 1943, six months after becoming chairman, Laurie felt inspection of his command was in order – that is, to attend some Dalhousie lectures and see how the professors managed their classes. When Stanley heard about that idea, he drove out to Oakfield to dissuade Laurie. He had talked about it before, but Stanley did not believe he was serious. Now he was. Laurie said, "I am now the Colonel of the Regiment: it is my duty to find out what the subalterns are doing with the privates." Stanley pointed out that Dalhousie was not the military, that Colonel Laurie knew little of academic procedure, and he would do his standing in the university great harm. Stanley claimed Laurie promised he would not do it.

Then Laurie wanted two King's professors promoted to full professor, S.H. Prince in Sociology and W.R. Maxwell in Economics. The Dalhousie board, by clause 15 of the Dalhousie-King's agreement, had to approve such promotions as it had to approve all King's academic appointments. Neither McGregor Stewart nor Stanley thought much of either professor, and the promotions had been turned down. President Walker, now that an Anglican was chairman of the Dalhousie board, had thoughtfully opened the question up again. Laurie argued that he knew more about King's than Stanley and Stewart, and went on to ask if Stanley would have any objection if the two promotions were rushed through a meeting? Stanley said:

Why rush that, or anything, through a meeting? If you want to bring it up, I have no objection; but why not, in bringing it up, admit that the request was previously over-ridden, and give your reason for re-opening the matter? Then give the Board a month or two to think it over?

Whatever the mode, Stanley agreed that the two professors could not do Dalhousie much more harm as full professors than as associates. A revealing exchange then developed over Stanley's hard-working secretary, Lola Henry. She had been underpaid for years, doing virtually the work of three, and thought she should have a raise; she even talked of resigning at the end of 1943. Laurie broke in with vehemence, "You leave her to me. I'll give her a damned good talking to." Stanley replied quietly, "Colonel Laurie, if you do that Dalhousie will lose her." Laurie said there were plenty of others to take her place. Stanley was not having that:

Colonel Laurie, please! Will you not ask others, if you cannot see it yourself, that it would take years and years to train up another person ... to take Miss Henry's place. After fifteen years of filing Miss Henry knows, in many ways, more about the University than any one living. You have always said you wanted to help me. Don't you see that I cannot possibly go on bearing all the burdens I bear if Miss Henry gets ill even – to say nothing of having her leave.

Stanley followed that with a note. No one knew how hard he had driven Lola Henry. "I am blessed, or cursed, with an ability to work quickly. And she, up till lately, has wonderfully kept pace ... The business pace in Halifax is the most leisurely in the world I know. And these men presume to tell me that I am no more over-worked than they, & that consequently the lady is no more over-worked than other helpers!" At the board meeting three days later, the two promotions were rushed through. Miss Henry did get her increase (to $2,100 per annum as of 1 December 1943), some board members even suggesting that she should have someone to help her.[10]

Whatever Colonel Laurie had promised about not "inspecting" classes, John Willis at the Law School found him at the back of his class one day. After the lecture Laurie said to Willis apropos one student's questions, "Why, that student's a socialist!" "So," said Willis, "am I." Willis probably was not. The colonel's next encounter was with J.G. Adshead's class in mathematics. That day Adshead was dealing with the parabola. "Ladies and gentlemen," said Adshead, "we are singularly fortunate today in having with us Colonel Laurie, who has specialized in artillery and has considerable experience in the practical applications of the parabola. Perhaps, Colonel Laurie, you would like to explain how you handle the mathematics of it?" Laurie thought his mathematics too rusty. Both Willis and Adshead were furious. Had Laurie asked the professors first, his attendance might possibly have been tolerated at least once; as it was, abrupt and unexpected, it wore the face of an inquisitory exercise. Nor was Laurie just trying on his innocence; while that mode of surveying his new command came to an end, it did not prevent Laurie from making comments to Stanley on the teaching he had encountered during his ill-advised progress.

Laurie had other weaknesses. While it was an advantage to have a chairman who could devote time to his job, Laurie knew only a little of university business and not much more of the ways and thinking of businessmen. And a fund-raiser he was not. Not only did he not speak their language, but he was too decent. He told Stanley, "I think I am a hopelessly bad beggar! I can be put off far too easily!!"[11]

The Style and Character of President Stanley

Stanley, on the other hand, believed himself to be both businessman and philosopher. He had in his time been fairly successful in business. He claimed he had spent more time in business than in universities. He left school when he was thirteen, finally as he thought. His education had been peculiar. An older sister taught him Latin; he could already speak German. Eventually he got more languages and a great deal of theoretical mathematics. Together they helped him, he said, as nothing else could have done, to meet the practical world he encountered as a businessman in Montreal. He thought it was inevitable that in North America young people would be drawn to practical pursuits. He was certainly not against business on principle, but by the late 1930s he had become a philosopher first. He was close to the CCF in many ways, especially in his sharp criticism of the business establishment, not as business but as unthinking establishment, too cocooned in its own comfort. The economic injustices of the 1930s bothered him terribly. He told Senator W.H. Dennis, in response to Dennis's pamphlet on a bill of rights for Nova Scotia, how justice and equity once won, never stayed won. They had always to be fought for again. As for economic injustice, the late 1930s reeked of it: "The neglect of public health; the folly with which we destroy forest lands; the unscientific and unsocial way in which we use all land; the planlessness of our cities."[12]

Stanley hated other kinds of injustice as well. In August 1942 three Austrian Jewish refugee medical students in Canada applied for admission to fourth-year medicine. Stanley, having consulted Ottawa and the dean of medicine, promised them admission. When the three applications came before the Medical Faculty, said Stanley, "Hell broke loose." Seventy per cent of the faculty were part-time, in effect downtown practitioners and members of the Medical Society of Nova Scotia, and the fourth and fifth year examinations were conducted jointly by Dalhousie and the Medical Society. The members of the society threatened to plow those three students, no matter how well prepared they were. Stanley chaired the meeting and tried to get an explanation. All he got was bogus patriotism, but then one old doctor shouted, "You are taking the bread out of our mouths!" The downtown practitioners won. It was not Dalhousie, nor its dean, nor its full-time professors who effected that nasty exclusion. Stanley roundly told the part-time faculty and the Medical Society of Nova Scotia that they were fighting the very cause of the enemy. It was, he said, the first struggle for academic freedom that he had ever lost, and he did not like it. He quoted Goethe's play *Torquato Tasso*, to William Inglis Morse, as if it were a description of himself,

Es bildet ein Talent sich in der Stille,
Sich ein Charakter in dem Strom der Welt.[13]

He and his old friend, Professor Frank Underhill of the University of Toronto, had many things in common, including leftish political ideas and a willingness to speak out. In August 1940 Underhill made some fairly innocuous remarks about the effects of the recent Ogdensburg Agreement between Roosevelt and Mackenzie King; we in Canada, said Underhill, "can no longer put all our eggs in the British basket." Underhill had already irritated newspapers and governors; now it was almost as if they were waiting to get him. Pulled out of context, Underhill's remarks created a storm that lasted six months and more. President H.J. Cody of the University of Toronto was fed up with Underhill and recommended his dismissal. Stanley had known Underhill a long time, since they were students in Oxford and travelled England and Germany together. Stanley wrote to Cody:

I know how trying Underhill can be ... I know how irresistible he finds it to say a thing which is clever though it may wound his friends. I, too, have professors who do not please certain sections of the community and who, time and again, write or say things which give me endless trouble ...

Now, what I have to say is this. If there is any more talk of Underhill being asked to resign, or being forcibly dismissed, I shall resign both my university degrees from Toronto, and I shall do so in the most public way possible.

Something like that, he assured Cody, will strengthen your hand in helping Underhill. Underhill escaped in the end, thanks to similar kinds of pressure brought to bear; although a majority of Cody's board still wanted Underhill's head, Cody backed away.[14]

Stanley's defence of Underhill was not just that due to an old friend and colleague of thirty years' standing. It was fundamental to his perception of academic freedom and independence. In the struggle to save R.A. MacKay from R.B. Bennett's wrath over the 1931 Beauharnois article, the real leader had been the chairman of the board, G.F. Pearson; but Stanley had his own role. J.McG. Stewart, then just two years on the board, suggested that Stanley consider dismissing MacKay, otherwise Dalhousie might lose a great deal of future Bennett money. Stanley was not having that. He replied that if the board were called for that purpose, it would have his resignation also. "I have read the article the professor wrote, and I see nothing wrong in it, and quite a lot that is right." And he added to himself, "While I am head, Dalhousie University is not for sale." A few months later, when Wilson, Bean, Smith, and Bronson were involved in the Pearson affair,

Stewart thought they might be dismissed. Since Dean Smith of Law was the principal offender, Stewart delicately suggested that as the University of Manitoba was known to be looking for a president, and since he, Stewart, had powerful connections in Winnipeg, if Stanley really wanted to get rid of Smith, there was no better way than giving Smith an enthusiastic letter of recommendation. Stanley asked, was it fair (he thought of using the word "honourable") to recommend as president for the University of Manitoba a man whom he wanted to be rid of as dean of law at Dalhousie? It was, replied Stewart apparently unabashed, "a great opportunity." It was not done. Smith did go to Manitoba as president in 1934, but on his own merits. Nor were the three other professors dismissed.[15]

Stanley believed that the Board of Governors had little to do with the hiring (or firing) of professors. That was the president's job. The real function of the board was to find money, and nothing else. Before he came to Dalhousie as president, he had been assured by Pearson and MacKenzie that he would never have to worry about finance. At his first board meeting he was given the same assurance. The staff of a university, he said, can help the president in many ways, as can the students: "But the Board of Governors can help him in only one way ... that is, to find the money to maintain the institution ... if this is not the Board's chief and supreme function, what function have they?" Other university presidents, such as F.W. Patterson of Acadia, were not as scornful of fund-raising; probably it was something Stanley did not do well and knew it, and so relegated it to the board. It was a function hardly more than alluded to in the 1863 act. Certainly section 4 indicated that the board had a great deal more to do than raise money: the approval of appointments, of buildings, of monies, of, in short, the superintendence of the university.[16]

Dalhousie's Board of Governors of 1944–5 was a mixture: old and pious well-wishers, Alumnae and Alumni, women and men with varied and rich experience of business or academic life. There were thirty-three in all (Stanley included), with two governors absent representing King's college whom the college had not nominated. Some of the most useful members of the board could not always be there. S.R. Balcom was busy in Ottawa on war work, as were others such as Stewart, who was federal coal controller until July 1943. Judge G.G. Patterson of Pictou and J.C. Webster of Shediac were octogenarians who disliked travel and the strain of meetings; Raymond Gushue was in Newfoundland, H.P. Duchemin ran the Sydney *Post*; both were in Halifax infrequently. Two men on the board were in the Medical Faculty, Dr J.G. MacDougall, professor of surgery, and Dr J.R. Corston, associate professor of medicine. Two others were part-time in the Arts and Science Faculty, D.C. Harvey, Nova Scotia archivist and lecturer in Canadian history, and J.W. Logan, lecturer in classics. Dr Roberta Nichols, widow of Professor E.W. Nichols who died in September 1939, was an Alumnae representative. Three Alumnae and six Alumni representatives leavened, one might say, the Halifax businessmen who carried much of the weight of the board's work.

All of the governors were unpaid and had other jobs. Dalhousie got their spare time and energy. They were governors from a sense of public duty and educational obligation. Most of the businessmen were on other corporation boards, though it is doubtful if they behaved any differently around Dalhousie's boardroom table. Governors were the organization's conscience some of the time, fund-raisers at others, and provided ultimate control over the functioning of the president. They were not so much running the university as auditing it and its president.[17]

Stanley, then, was powerful, and he had influenced the appointment of a number of governors, including Duchemin, Gushue, and Webster. He had inherited others, important governors such as Mitchell, McCurdy, and Stewart. Colonel Laurie had been suggested by Dugald Macgillivray. Where the initiative lay in appointing governors was unclear, but it was probably between the president and the chairman of the board – a rapport so essential to the ongoing work of the institution. After J. McGregor Stewart took up war work, and Laurie became chairman in May 1943, Stanley found his role enhanced and his power increased. Laurie lived twenty miles distant; he knew just enough of Dalhousie to get into trouble if he ignored Stanley's advice. By that time Stanley was used to getting his own way, with methods and ideas of his own. He had been right so often! Those who had opposed him had been broken or silenced: Pearson broken, Macneill silenced, the board executive proved wrong on the appeals to Maritime governments for the Medical and Dental schools. There are presidents who handle their boards with some contumely. One president was reported to have said, "You treat the board like mushrooms – keep them in the dark and feed them a little manure now and then!" That *grossièreté* exaggerates Stanley's position, for in a small university he had to carry his board with him; but, quick, sharp and determined, he had considerable independence, and he exercised it.[18]

With students he was kind and generous. He took trouble to meet the new students; he was cordial, gracious, and he listened; when he met them on campus afterwards, he remembered. He loved walking and the situation of Dalhousie that made walking so pleasant. He would take students, usually one on one, for his favourite walk, down to the little ferry at the foot of Oakland Road and across the

Arm (for 10 cents) to the Dingle, for half an hour and then back again. There was some early disapproval of Stanley's practice – the president with a *student*! – but Stanley simply faced it down. One student remembers being asked to go walking with the president and found the experience, far from being intimidating, agreeable. Stanley talked vivaciously and well. One graduate student from UNB, J.R. Mallory, who came to Dalhousie in 1940 to study under R.A. MacKay in political science, remembered "the civil and charming presence of Carleton Stanley, whom I much admired." Stanley met all new students personally, and freshmen students would often be invited by Mrs Stanley to tea, shy socially though she was. "They were always so hungry," Stanley's daughter Laura remembered. He made great efforts to help needy students. Once in Lunenburg he met a promising lad of humble origin and encouraged him to come to Dalhousie. Some weeks later the young man arrived at the door of 24 Oxford Street, suitcase in hand, expecting to stay there. Stanley found lodging for him. Within his own family, however, Carleton Stanley was an uncertain quantity, gentle with his daughter, peremptory and demanding with his son.[19]

With some of his staff he was respected as a thorough academic, as ready to defend professors as to denigrate those who were, in his judgment, incompetent. One day, probably in 1938, a new lecturer arrived to teach French; Stanley spoke to him in French, and discovered the lecturer could not speak it. Stanley revoked the hiring on the spot. But by 1943 even those of the staff who had hitherto supported him were gradually finding, in countless little ways, that he could not be trusted. His word was not necessarily his bond. Stanley undoubtedly thought it was; but he could bend facts to suit his subjective thinking. He had always set great store by the truth; his children were brought up with that constantly before them. The difficulty was, what truth? Whose? Stanley's came from the confidence of a first-class mind at ease with itself. It also betrayed a supreme egotist. In 1943 W.J. Archibald met Stanley in the Chateau Laurier in Ottawa for a job interview in the Physics Department. Archibald primed himself nervously for it, but he need not have bothered. Stanley asked Archibald not a question; he spent the hour talking about himself. Archibald accepted the job at Dalhousie; he thought its president decidedly self-centred.[20]

Dr Beecher Weld, an able physiologist from UBC and Toronto, was hired by Stanley in 1936 on the recommendation of C.H. Best of the Connaught Laboratories, in the teeth of Medical Faculty resistance. It was not easy for Weld; Murray Macneill never would speak to him, assuming Weld was a Stanley creature. Yet Weld was not a Stanley

R.A. MacKay, Professor of Political Science, 1927–47, is on the left; his son, W.A. MacKay ('50) was appointed to the Law School in 1957.

loyalist. By 1943 he had come reluctantly to the conclusion that Stanley was "a continuous and incorrigible liar." That was increasingly the opinion among the faculty. Stanley seemed incapable of dispassionate assessment. If you opposed his arguments, you were opposed to him. And he could distort. He said in 1944 that Stewart ordered him to fire the four offending professors in 1932; what Stewart actually said was, "Why don't you consider recommending dismissals?" Stanley had properly countered with the argument of academic freedom, said Stewart; they then discussed how far that went. Stewart was sensible and listened. "If I had been pressing for dismissals I assure you I would have brought the matter before the Board. But I was satisfied with the decision and I dropped it." Working with Stanley, Stewart told the board in 1945, was not easy and it was not getting easier. And what was the problem?

I will tell you. And I will tell you in a nutshell – this is from my own experience. The President cannot treat seriously any opinion that differs from his own. He resents and ascribes wrong motives for it in every case. If two or more agree to differ with him, then they are in a foul plot against him ... Not only that, he cannot conceal his contempt for those who disagree. And by this unfortunate attitude, he has built up hostility and enmity that is mounting as the years go by. Dr. Stanley has not had an easy row to hoe at Dalhousie. Things were difficult for him from the start ... and yet, gentlemen, we have had twelve years since in which he might have made his adjustments. Twelve years is a long time ... yet I have the temerity to assert that never has there been less cooperation and less confidence than there is right now.

Stewart went so far as to claim that Stanley aimed at reducing both Senate and board to rubber stamps for his own ideas, and by 1944 it had begun to appear to Stewart as if Stanley were succeeding.[21]

Stanley did not have a dean of arts and science any more. C.B. Nickerson had died suddenly of coronary thrombosis in December 1940. Thereafter no dean was appointed. The probability is that Stanley could not find a professor whom he trusted and who would have been acceptable to the faculty. It is a comment on Stanley that in 1941 he reverted once more to being his own dean of arts and science. Faculty did not like it and tried to push Stanley into having a dean. Stanley would not be pushed.

Many in faculty and not a few on the board felt Stanley's stiffness. He had few close friends. The secretary of Senate, George Curtis, said he had no Halifax friends at all. He could not reach out to people. One of his closest friends, his father-in-law, W.J. Alexander, died during a visit to Halifax in the summer of 1944. As one sympathetic board member, the secretary, C.F. MacKenzie, remarked one day, "President Stanley is a lonely man."[22]

The lonely man had a strong social conscience. Though never ostensibly a member of any political party, he was closer to Bennett than King – that is, to the Bennett of the CBC, Bank of Canada, and "New Deal" legislation of 1935. He may well have been closer to the CCF than to Liberals or Conservatives as such. Canada's social safety net was meagre; old age pensions for the needy were introduced in 1927, but that was all until unemployment insurance in 1940. Family allowances (called the baby bonus) came in July 1944, a Liberal attempt to steal votes and platform from the CCF. Stanley had long been upset by the living conditions in Halifax, especially in the North End, and he was fiercely critical of a social system that could produce slums and poverty so degrading. In his twelve years he had spoken out against the Nova Scotian educational system, and against fascism whether Spanish, Italian, or German. Some of that he published anonymously in local papers under the name "Sam Slick," at other times in addresses to students and to convocations. He might even have agreed with Arthur Morgan, the principal of McGill from 1935 to 1937, that the aim of universities was to "produce great societies, not great men." Stanley would at least have argued for both.[23]

This restiveness with the social system grew; two months before Mackenzie King launched family allowances, Stanley pointed out to the graduating class of 1944 that "a university city which is largely a slum is not merely a contradiction in terms; it is an unexploited human dynamic." That statement in the presence of governors, parents, alumni, was Stanley the social reformer, speaking words made more imperious by his sincerity. It was alleged by his daughter, and others, that from that time onward governors began to ask themselves privately about the suitability of Stanley for his role. Such speeches may have helped to draw needed attention to Halifax's slums, but it did not do much for a university 90 per cent dependent on endowment and fees. Dalhousie was still, and would be for many a year yet, virtually a private university, needing private money.[24]

A Stanley speech a month later in Ottawa also caused trouble. The chairman of the Ottawa Dalhousie Alumni was John E. Read, former dean of law and now a powerful figure in the Department of External Affairs. He was Dalhousie's Rhodes scholar of 1911 and took an Oxford double first, BA in 1912, and BCL in 1913. After entering practice in Halifax, he joined the Canadian Artillery in the First World War, and was lucky to escape with wounds, being invalided home in 1918 with the rank of acting major. He returned to the Halifax law firm he had started in, and in 1921 became full-time professor of law at Dalhousie at the age of thirty-three. He became dean of law in 1924, and in 1929 O.D. Skelton, under-secretary of state for external affairs, told President MacKenzie that he had to have Read in Ottawa for several important international cases. MacKenzie reluctantly let Read go and brought Sidney Smith back from Toronto as dean.[25]

The basis of the enmity between Read and Stanley is not clear. John Read said many years later that Stanley wanted "to drive out of the Law School any Harvard influence there might be." Read was not from Harvard, though he had had a year at Columbia and was close to Harvard influences in Sidney Smith. Stanley attributed to John Read the federal government's determination to have Allan Findlay prosecuted late in 1939. Whatever Stanley said to the Ottawa alumni in June 1944 – the speech was off the record – Read took considerable exception to it. Stanley had criticized, Read said, the work of his predecessors, though not by name, saying that Dalhousie's financial affairs had been badly mismanaged during the presidency of A.S. MacKenzie and the chairmanship of G.S. Campbell. The second point Stanley made, again by inference, was that low standards of admission prevailed during the Forrest and MacKenzie regimes, that Dalhousie had much improved its standards since those wicked days. The answer of Halifax-educated Read was that many of Dalhousie's best students came from country schools, even though they could not obtain full matriculation. Stanley claimed such students lowered the standard of their classes. S.R. Balcom, a board member and Stanley supporter, said Read's attitude was "unwarranted prejudice." Stanley's secretary, Lola Henry, thought Read had a persecution complex; he had been in her father's law firm, where her father thought him an "awful lemon." But as legal scholar and professor Read was a tremendous success in that intimate, intense little group at the Dalhousie Law School. Donald McInnes (LL.B. '26) remarked fifty years on that "John Read was altogether a darling soul." Read's power at External Affairs and with Dalhousie alumni explains why his allegations worried Stanley and why he went to some trouble to refute them.[26]

That was followed in August 1944 by Laurie's insistence that Miss Anna MacKeen, warden of Shirreff Hall, be fired. Just prior to the board meeting of 22 August, Laurie asked Stanley to telegraph her to that effect. There had been criticism of Miss MacKeen; there was a row in 1939 when the *Gazette* attacked her for refusing to allow a Delta Gamma dance. The *Gazette*'s argument was that Shirreff Hall was the nearest place Dalhousie had to a social centre; Miss MacKeen said there had been quite enough dances at Shirreff Hall without adding one more. In July 1944 Donald A. Cameron, an official with Sun Life and an important alumnus, presented criticisms of Miss Mac-

Keen's regime at Shirreff Hall, raised by eight ex-residents, not one of whom had a good word to say about her. Stanley refused to be coerced by what he felt was a small minority of carpers, on very slim grounds. He reminded Colonel Laurie that the Board of Governors had, a few months since, established a Shirreff Hall committee, chaired by Mrs F.H. Pond, and that such a matter should go to that committee. It reported that Miss MacKeen was a particularly good warden, and in fact she would remain until 1947.[27]

There followed the question of appointing the new Bennett professor of epidemiology and public health. J. McG. Stewart and Laurie wanted to appoint their favourite, an able Halifax doctor, H.L. Scammell. Stanley did not want Scammell, whom he associated with the Medical Society's refusal to admit the Austrian Jewish refugees to the Medical School in 1942. Dean Grant and Stanley had been working for some time to find the best man possible, and it was not J. McG. Stewart's candidate. It was Chester B. Stewart, no relation.

Chester Stewart was a Prince Edward Islander, from Prince of Wales College, who came to the Medical School via a B.SC. from Dalhousie. An incident at the Medical School in 1936–7 reveals something both of young Chester Stewart and President Stanley. The medical students that year became exercised over a course called Materia Medica, taught by George Burbidge, dean of the Maritime College of Pharmacy, a Dalhousie affiliate. Two hours a week in second-year medicine were devoted to pharmacy work and prescriptions. The course was severely practical, required a test a week, and seemed to absorb half the students' time. They questioned the relevance of so much effort in studying the making of pills, the proper position of the arm when using a mortar and pestle, or the scientific definition of cotton wool! The students wrote a letter to Burbidge about the course. A week later he failed to come to class. Chester Stewart thought the letter was a poor piece of work, but that the students were right about the issue. He was designated their spokesman when the students were summoned to the dean of medicine's office. They half expected the summons; they did not expect to find President Stanley in the dean's chair. Stanley proceeded to berate them without mercy. Chester Stewart, both angry and scared, replied. The next day he was called to Stanley's office. Stanley would not admit he had been in the wrong, but he was solicitous about the students' workload in Materia Medica. The course was eased off and changed the following year.

Chester Stewart took his MD in 1938, having distinctions in thirty-one of thirty-three subjects, unprecedented in Dean Grant's experience. He was a doctor for the RCAF in Toronto when Dalhousie began to look for a good man for the Bennett chair. Chester Stewart was interested. One Toronto colleague told him: "If I were offered a chair of anything I would take it!" However good Dr Stewart was, Stanley believed in seeing him first, especially after the nasty surprise of the lecturer in French. Appointing professors without seeing them, as Principal Fyfe of Aberdeen (late of Queen's) told Stanley, was perilous, seldom ventured without regret. So in the summer of 1944 Chester Stewart came down to see Stanley at his summer place at Seabright on St Margaret's Bay. Stanley clearly approved.[28]

The Quarrel between Stanley and the Board

On the morning prior to the board executive meeting of 15 September 1944 J. McG. Stewart and Colonel Laurie came to see Stanley and Dean Grant. For an hour Stewart sternly urged the appointment of Dr H.L. Scammell. Dean Grant replied that he thought the appointment of Scammell would be improper and gave reasons. Stanley concurred. As Stewart and Laurie were leaving, Stewart turned and said, "If you don't make the appointment, you will live to regret it." At first Stanley thought that Stewart meant to suggest that Dean Grant and Stanley would live to see they had made a mistake; but, he reflected to himself later, "perhaps it was a threat." Dr Chester Stewart was appointed at the board executive meeting that day. He was an excellent choice, but it was the last victory Stanley won. The forces moving against him were already marshalling.[29]

That same evening, the full board met to discuss the future financial campaign. It would go forward, the board agreed, but there were great practical difficulties. A small committee of five was to make recommendations on organization, needs, and personnel; it would be chaired by Colonel Laurie, who was given power to choose the other four members. These were: Mr Justice John Doull, J. McGregor Stewart, C.F. MacKenzie (nephew of the late president and board secretary), and George Farquhar. It met a fortnight later and came to the unusual conclusion that a financial campaign was much needed but impossible: it could not proceed given "the antagonism which – rightly or wrongly – exists in the constituency to the present President."[30]

The slant, the wording, was meant as an offer, not unkind in the circumstances, for Stanley quietly to resign the Dalhousie presidency, without fuss, publicity or loss of face. McGill got rid of a president in the 1930s that way, Arthur Morgan, an English mistake, in twenty months. President Loudon of the University of Toronto was fired in 1907 when he was replaced by Robert Falconer of Pine Hill; there a royal commission eased the change, though it was public enough. Stanley however believed that he was fighting only a cabal of his board that wanted him out; although it was powerful, he believed that with support from Senate, Alumni, other governors, he could send the cabal packing. He had fought the chairman of the board in 1932 and won; who was to say he could not do the same thing again in 1944?

Thus when Laurie and McGregor Stewart came to see him on 24 October, and read the letter embodying the committee's conclusion, Stanley had no hesitations. When he was asked for a statement for the Pre-Campaign Committee, he replied tersely that he would give no statement; instead, he wanted to know what specific charges the committee was pressing. Outside of the sweeping but general allegation of antagonism, all Laurie and Stewart could specify was the Read letter from Ottawa and that Professor G.V. Douglas sending his two daughters to Mount Allison was the greatest scandal in Dalhousie's history. The latter was easily refuted; Douglas's daughters wanted to do music and drama, not available at Dalhousie. The following dialogue then ensued:

STANLEY: Till now you have said nothing definite, either of you, except about Prof. D.
STEWART: Nothing except that you have no friends but many enemies.
STANLEY: A tub of lard has no enemies; but a man who does things, or even tried to do them has enemies.
STEWART: And the same goes for the University: it has too few friends, and too many enemies.
STANLEY: Because of me?

As to what he would do, Stanley gave no hint or answer.[31]

Colonel Laurie then went to Shediac to see the vice-chairman, J.C. Webster. A day later, Stanley arrived at Shediac and Webster laid before him Laurie's arguments and got explanations. Webster took the position that Dalhousie was more important than any single person connected with it; certainly charges that any person in authority was creating enemies should be fairly and fully investigated. But, Webster wrote Laurie, the charges made by the Pre-Campaign Committee had nothing to do with Stanley's ability, morals, scholarship, or success in bringing in money. The main allegation against him, said Webster, seemed to be, "dictatorial manner, obstinacy, egotism and self-glorification." For *that* you want his resignation? There was no justification for such action; certainly it ought not to have been proceeded with without first having consulted the entire board. The catalogue of the president's alleged sins was wholly inadequate; some were ridiculous. John Read's Ottawa account was biased and unfair. The whole thing, said Webster, came from the animus of a few individuals; if you continue this misguided attempt to force Stanley's resignation, you will open up a sharp, even violent debate that can do no good to anyone. For my part, Webster concluded, "I stand by the President. If this attack on him continues I shall communicate with prominent alumni, including Lord Bennett. I shall, also, feel it my duty to give full information to the Carnegie and Rockefeller people … If the attack should succeed, I shall resign from the Board and make my reasons known to as wide an audience as can be reached."[32]

That was laying it down in earnest. Those who saw things in a cooler light thought Webster's threats deleterious to his cause. Behind Webster's strong words, however, was Stanley's determination to fight it out. He was not going to be pushed from his presidency of Dalhousie by a cabal, by a gang (he used both words); he believed he could win such a fight. With support from the rest of the governors he could face down and vanquish the "Gang of Five."

Stanley did not have a contract with Dalhousie. He had not had one at Toronto, nor at McGill; he doubted whether there was a president in Canada who had one. His tenure as president of Dalhousie was without term; he could work until such time as he chose to retire or until the board chose to retire him. At fifty-eight years of age, in vigorous health, he was some distance yet from retirement.[33]

Stanley said that the real reason for the attack was not himself or enemies he may have made. It was because he refused to appoint incompetent people, such as to the Bennett chair in epidemiology, and because he refused to dismiss professors and staff unjustly charged, among them the four professors of 1932 and Miss Anna MacKeen in 1944. Friends of Dalhousie, he told Viscount Bennett in Mickleham, think that "the whole future is threatened if I give in." Webster told Stanley that he "must fight with bare fists if necessary. You cannot lie down before their attack." Stanley made one effort to heal the breach. After his weekend visit to Webster, the following Tuesday morning he arranged a visit to J. McG. Stewart downtown,

to see whether he and I could not do something in Dalhousie's interest despite all the beans that had been spilt. I told him that it had been my idea entirely to see him, but that one or two honourable gentlemen with whom I had discussed matters, after they had heard things from the other side, had concurred with me in the belief that he, Mr. Stewart, was able to do much, even at this late hour, to prevent a widening out of the scandal – though these gentlemen had urged me also, for the good of Canadian affairs, as well as Dalhousie's, not to let the game go by default.

Stewart was not unfriendly, and said he would be in touch very soon.[34]

What happened next seems to have been a decision by the five colleagues, "the Gang of Five" as Stanley now called them, that they needed broader support if they were going to succeed in ousting Stanley. On 8 November Colonel Laurie telegraphed board members for a meeting on the 10th. It was a meeting of "the majority members of the Board." The call amazed H.P. Duchemin of Sydney; he had never heard of a meeting called that way. There were nineteen governors present at the meeting. The vote in favour of the Pre-Campaign Committee's recommendation to get Stanley to resign would appear to have been ten; the others did not vote. Ten of thirty-three members was not overwhelming support for pressing Stanley's resignation; but the Gang of Five were sufficiently confident to send an envoy to Stanley to persuade him to resign.[35] The envoy was Dr D.C. Harvey, Nova Scotia archivist, part-time lecturer in history, and an Alumni representative on the board. Harvey, civilized, earnest, and scholarly, hated the confrontation he was now facing. He met Stanley on Monday, 13 November, agitated, unhappy, but wanting the whole issue to be settled quietly as gentlemen should. He said how sorry he was for Stanley, how he hoped Stanley would not do anything to hurt Dalhousie, how often Stanley had come to him in the past for advice; all of that Stanley in his cool, assured way referred to as "irrelevant personal stuff."

HARVEY: ... on Dalhousie's behalf, I make this suggestion to you: What are you going to do if the Board draws up a resolution against you? Are you still going to try to run Dalhousie without a Board? I know that the Board will make a most generous arrangement with you, if you will back down and go away ... Don't you think you ought to do this to save Dalhousie? ...
STANLEY: Harvey ... I am only beginning.

Stanley's last word was that any possibility of negotiations had been taken out of his hands by the abruptness of the attack against him.[36] A main battle therefore would be at the next meeting of the full board, a fortnight hence, on 28 November.

To avoid such a battle cooler heads now suggested caution. Donald A. Cameron was a former Alumni governor who had been called in during 1944 to look at Dalhousie's finances, preliminary to the campaign. Stanley sent him a report, with some paranoia embedded in it. "You speak of 'intrigue'," replied Cameron, "Dr. Webster of 'animus' ... Perhaps I am dumb, but I never discovered either." Webster had in any case nullified whatever he might have said in your defence, Cameron went on, by the threats at the end. Stanley answered that many things at Dalhousie recently were hard to believe. As for the board,

Stanley said, only three of the thirty-three were knaves, but those three had great influence, notably J. McGregor Stewart. Nevertheless Stanley thought their influence would reach only ten or eleven governors. Cameron was incredulous; to think that any of the board was impelled by motives inimical to Dalhousie "is beyond me." But, he said, whether you win or lose, the result of any contest would be bad. Your best course would be to say to the board: for thirteen long and trying years I have served you faithfully. "If that's not good enough, good-bye and God bless you."[37]

Cameron's cool counsel counted for little. One of Stanley's rules of conduct was, so he said, "when in any doubt about *a course of action don't take it*." Obviously he had no doubts and by now he had the bit between his teeth. He now began looking for even proxy votes. At least three of his supporters – Webster, G.G. Patterson, and S.R. Balcom – could not attend a board meeting. Lola Henry reported that proxy votes looked very doubtful; Stanley claimed however that at the last board meeting of the Pearson era, in June 1932, R.B. Bennett had telegraphed his vote. That was simply not true. Either Stanley had forgotten details of events a decade before, which was possible, or he was able to twist the truth even when communicating with his trusted friend, Clarence Webster. The strain of events was now starting to show, more on Mrs Stanley than on her husband. On 19 November they flew to Montreal for a few days' rest.[38]

The board met at 8 PM on Tuesday, 28 November in the Dalhousie Library. Some twenty-five of the thirty-three governors were present: all the Alumni governors; of the three Alumnae governors, only Georgene Faulkner was missing and she was anti-Stanley; Gushue came from Newfoundland, Duchemin from Sydney, both Stanley supporters. After routine business there came the report of the Pre-Campaign Committee, introduced by J. McGregor Stewart, that the campaign could not begin so long as President Stanley remained. Stanley had great qualities, but hostility to him was now strong in Senate, in government, in the board, in the Alumni, in King's, in the Halifax and Nova Scotian community. "I have spent," said Stewart, "ten years of my life defending Dr. Stanley, but there is a wall of hostility, and we are losing the constituency to which we must appeal." There were questions. What was the purpose of such a motion, asked one governor, to "get money or get Stanley?" Was Stanley's resignation being asked for? No, said Stewart; passing the resolution meant postponement of the campaign. Everyone there knew, and no one said, that it was an open, pointed invitation for Stanley to resign.[39]

Stanley had no such intention. He gave a thirty-minute fighting speech. One of the handsomest men on campus, he stood like an

Apollo, as one Alumnae governor felt, giving crisp, spirited, and sometimes convoluted and tortured answers to questions. Then, holding up two letters of Colonel Laurie's, his arms flung wide, Stanley asked him, "Are these letters in your handwriting?"

COL. LAURIE: Yes, they are.
STANLEY: And in your spelling too. [Speech is not spelled] s-p-e-a-c-h.

Stanley could not then resist a further cutting remark on Laurie's grammar. It was a tactical blunder. Stanley had always been privately contemptuous of his chairman's syntax and spelling; here he ridiculed him in open meeting. It revealed to board members hitherto disposed to be neutral that the things that Stewart and others were saying about Stanley's arrogance might possibly be right.

After three hours, it was clear Stanley's supporters were struggling. The debate was heated; they wanted the meeting cooled off and urged postponement of the vote. Mayor Lloyd, a Stanley supporter, moved an amendment that the board meet again the next evening; meanwhile let all governors sleep on it. The amendment was defeated, twelve to eleven. The main motion, approving the Pre-Campaign Committee's resolution, passed, sixteen to six. The atmosphere of the meeting Stanley described as "mephitic," poisonous. The six Stanley loyalists were Gushue, Duchemin, Mayor Lloyd, Chesley Allan, Major Logan, and T. C. Coffin, the only Alumni governor to vote for him. None of the women supported him, not even Mrs Pond of whom Stanley had been fairly confident three weeks before. All had different reasons. Dr Roberta Nichols hated Stanley, a quarrel of some years over her children's fees; Margaret Pond worshipped him, but felt the pressure against him; Eileen Burns was taken aback by the crudeness of Stanley's attack on Colonel Laurie, whom many regarded as decent and amiable, if slightly bumbling.[40]

For there was decency in Colonel Laurie all through; he may have been possessed of no blazing intelligence, he may have been unread, used the King's English in ways more suited to the army than the university, but he was honest. There is a ring of truth in his letter to Stanley a month earlier:

I hope that you can realise, and believe how miserable I have felt about this whole matter. Having a great admiration for your abilities and the tireless way in which you have worked your hardest year in, year out, for the University ...

I stand to lose the companionship and contact with my greatest friend at Dalhousie ... and I can assure you I would have evaded this had I seen any way of doing so consistent with what I believe to be my duty.[41]

The morning after the board meeting Raymond Gushue called on Stanley; he begged him, for his own happiness, to resign. Stanley would have no part of it. He was off to New York to look for money, meetings that had been in train for some time. While in New York he saw Alan Gregg of the Rockefeller Foundation, R.M. Lester of the Carnegie, as well as the John and Mary Markle Foundation who had contributed $6,000 to equip Dalhousie's Anatomy Department. All three foundations, according to Stanley, agreed not to contribute a sou to Dalhousie as long as "the reptiles" were running things. At the urging of all three Stanley went to Washington and talked to the American Association of University Professors. Their chief interest was academic freedom; for their six investigators they wanted six sets of Dalhousie documents, which Stanley had prepared in the offices of the Carnegie Foundation. Stanley went on to Ottawa to see the cabinet ministers whom he was alleged by Stewart to have offended.[42]

Thus did he gird himself for the next battle, a full board meeting now called for 23 January 1945. Several friends suggested he call off the war. G.G. Patterson of New Glasgow, on the board but too old to travel, recommended Stanley not wait until the board carried a resolution demanding his resignation. From Toronto J.M. Macdonnell said the same, for good reason:

I would not make this suggestion if I felt that in a struggle with the Board you would have overwhelming or even substantial support from the Staff or the Graduates. Though I say it with great regret, such information as I have would make me doubt you have this ... if you embark on a struggle without such support the result will be disastrous.

Stanley measured things differently. He had his supporters, notably Major J.W. Logan, who went around to governors individually and argued vociferously in favour of Stanley. One Alumnae governor remembers Logan going at it for two hours, during which the major was not always being able to control his temper. Stanley solicited support from Viscount Bennett in England, who weighed in with a 365-word cable to K.C. Laurie. It was almost incredible, said Bennett, that "sixteen adult Maritimers" could put on record such a resolution as that of 28 November. Bennett had also sensible advice: if you fire Stanley, where are you going to find your next president? "No really competent man will accept presidency" where his position would be dependent on such allegations, not upon his capacity.[43]

The board had been looking for new grounds for its attack. In December it had sought the records connected with Stanley's appointment in 1931 and found nothing. The resolutions proposed by the board in mid-January 1945 were still general but were put on a different basis; they noted the necessity of confidence between board, president, and staff – confidence that had deteriorated under Stanley and which had "imperilled" relations between Dalhousie and its constituency. If Stanley resigned by 7 February and agreed to leave the president's house by 30 June 1945, he would receive his salary to 30 June 1946. These terms were presented to the board meeting of 23 January, with twenty-four governors present. Letters supporting Stanley were read; Bennett's cable was read – twice. To Bennett's criticisms, Stewart replied he did not see how the board could have done other than it did.

I know I have tried, and the Chairman has tried, to make this whole incident as easy as possible ... On October 24, we tried to put it on a basis that would not hurt him in the first instance. By his continuous failure to realise the situation as it exists, he is making it more difficult as time goes on. Lord Bennett has not seen that side of him.

Laurie enlarged on this last point in a letter to Bennett:

Those who have not had to work closely with Dr. Stanley naturally know best his attractive qualities. That was my own experience until a couple of years ago. There is, however, another side that is far from attractive or admirable, and this is the side so frequently presented to those whose duty it is to try to work with him.

As George Farquhar pointed out, either the president or the board had to go. Farquhar claimed that the teaching staff did not trust President Stanley: "When they have an interview with him they go out and make a memo of it for their own protection." The board voted eighteen to five in favour of Stanley's resignation. The last words recorded in the minutes were Stanley's: "The matter is simple. I am not resigning."[44]

That position was fundamentally untenable. The initiative now lay with lawyers, but Stanley had also consulted a Dalhousie alumnus lawyer in New York, who suggested using Dalhousie's necessity to extract better terms. The original terms had not been very generous. Dalhousie needed not only Stanley's resignation but especially his silence; publicity was not that far off. So there were lawyers' negotiations and new terms. It was agreed that if Stanley resigned he would hold office until 30 June 1945 and his house to 31 August 1945. Dalhousie would pay him a monthly, retiring allowance, on the basis of $5,000 a year until he was sixty-five (that is, until 1951) or his death, whichever came first; if the latter, half his income would go to his wife. The condition attached to these terms, not spelled out in the board minutes, was that as long as Stanley remained president, or received his Dalhousie pension, he would not attempt to "prejudice or impair" the work of the board or its dealings with staff, students, or alumni. He was to shut up; the board feared what he might yet do in a convocation address, in his presidential report, or through his many newspaper connections.[45]

Publicity was now in the wind. One of Stanley's old friends from the 1920s, when Stanley was Canadian correspondent for the *Manchester Guardian*, was John Stevenson, editorial writer at the Toronto *Globe and Mail*. Stanley had kept him informed. Stevenson showed the papers to George McCullagh, president of the *Globe and Mail*. McCullagh took great interest, and Stevenson was sure he would be allowed to write a fine, smashing editorial. But on 31 January McCullagh decided he would not touch it. Stevenson thought this was owing to Sidney Smith, president-designate of the University of Toronto, of which McCullagh was a governor. Stevenson put it with an old Scots proverb, "corbies [ravens] don't pick out other corbies' eyes."[46] Stanley believed that his ouster was an attack on academic freedom and he sought to establish it. He was fired, he said, because he had refused to promote, to appoint, or dismiss professors on improper grounds. The American Association of University Professors was doubtful this point could be established; in any case the Dalhousie Board of Governors refused them permission to attend the board meeting of 23 January on Stanley's behalf. The board simply said academic freedom was not the issue. *Saturday Night* carried an editorial on Dalhousie on 24 February 1945, but neither the board nor Stanley (now reluctantly silent) were giving anything away. The reasons given publicly were simply that differences between Stanley and the board were based on temperament, not on academic questions. An editorial in the Sydney *Post-Record*, on 1 March 1945 said much the same, adding that Stanley's "erudition, integrity of purpose, unflagging industry and passion for service" would be difficult to replace.

So they would be. For although board members might say (as many did) that Stanley was becoming increasingly impossible to work with, Dalhousie would not so soon again have a president who read and spoke German and French with ease, who could (and would) give the students Pericles' funeral oration in Greek just for the sound of it, who quoted Lucretius or Goethe at will, whose friends sent him papers on G.E. Moore (the philosopher) and who had published a book on the writings and life of Matthew Arnold. Stanley was a lively and vigorous scholar, with a scholar's sense of superiority over the petty minds around him, and with his own arrogance towards the grubbiness of businessmen and politicians. His private estimate of Angus L. Macdonald was venomous.[47]

Judith Robinson, a Toronto freelance reporter, writing in the New York *Nation*, admitted Stanley lacked tact. "He is difficult, exacting, inclined to be high-handed with his staff. But he has resolutely defended the integrity of his university from outside interference." She made a political issue of Stanley's being fired. So did J.V. McAree in the *Globe and Mail*, who claimed that the issue at Dalhousie was whether "a group of moneybags shall direct the fortune of one of the most honourable seats of learning in the country." Every Canadian university, he said, should be concerned about what had happened at Dalhousie. McAree said it was Stanley's remarks about "the slums of Halifax" that cost him his Dalhousie presidency. That of course was only one part of a much more complex truth.[48]

There is a postscript to this strange story. After the board meeting of 23 January that demanded Stanley's resignation, an Alumnae board member, Eileen Burns, one of the eighteen who voted for it, telephoned the news to Mrs Fred Pearson.[49] At the other end of the line, in the house on Francklyn Street with its stretch of snowy garden down to the Arm, Agnes Pearson, gracious and graceful as always, allowed herself an audible sigh of satisfaction. "Ah," said she, "at long last, after thirteen years, my husband is vindicated!"

· 6 ·

A.E. Kerr and the Veterans
1945–1951

Finding a new president, 1945. Dean of arts and science, George E. Wilson. Second World War veterans and their influence. Dalhousie's space problems. Erecting the Arts and Administration Building. Trying to get and keep good professors. Board and president, powers and boundaries. A Faculty of Graduate Studies, 1949.

If the papers surrounding the appointment of Carleton Stanley in 1931 are thin, those on the appointment of his successor in 1945 are almost non-existent. The board struck a small committee in February 1945 to gather information about a new president. Then there is silence. That may have been owing to a dearth of candidates. Was R.B. Bennett's prediction right: how will you find a competent man to be Dalhousie president? Warren Publicover, past president of the Dalhousie Club of New York, asked, "What kind of a spineless boot-licker do they expect to put in the office – I can only think of someone like — who is Heepish enough to take the job." The Uriah Heep candidate was not identified. Stanley had said the same to the board on 23 January: "What sort of a rubber stamp do they think the President of a University should be?" The board was not looking for a rubber stamp; nevertheless, a university that fires its president cannot avoid a consequent reputation. The Stanley affair was known far and wide, and it did Dalhousie no good. It was also expensive. It cost the Board $5,000 a year, the income for a professorship, just for Stanley's pension.[1]

Stanley and his family moved slowly out of the big presidential house, selling pictures, furniture, rugs, chunks of his vast library as they went. He had no idea where they were going other than to their cottage on St Margaret's Bay. He had been offered a temporary appointment at United College, Winnipeg, to replace Arthur Phelps in English, on sabbatical, but it carried a mighty teaching load of sixteen to eighteen hours a week. Stanley declined that in May 1945, but he accepted another offer a few months later. He was to be a professor at United College until he retired to Uxbridge, Ontario in 1953.[2]

While it searched for a president, the Dalhousie Board of Governors was in a mode now called damage control. The full board was given little information; thirty-three people (together with wives or husbands) do not easily keep secrets. The nominating committee and the executive kept close the names of candidates. A meeting of the full board was called for May, it was presumed to meet a candidate, and then abruptly cancelled. This candidate was one the board was serious about, and whom it brought to Halifax: Dr James Doull (BA '11, MD '14), director of preventive medicine and public health at Western Reserve University, Cleveland. According to McGregor Stewart, Doull was much the best candidate available, though Stewart regretted that he was a little old for the job. He was the younger brother of Mr Justice John Doull of the Dalhousie board. He came in May 1945 to see and discuss; then he backed off, though not definitely. Colonel Laurie telegraphed him in July, asking if the board should consider him for the presidency. Though Dr Doull now turned down Dalhousie's offer, he seemed well disposed, believing President Stanley's opinions "rather extreme," and the board not amiss in resenting his methods. At Laurie's request Doull wrote both the Rockefeller and Carnegie foundations to explain that Dalhousie was now on track again, and that it had given Stanley "very handsome treatment" after his resignation.[3]

Alexander Enoch Kerr, 1898–1974

The new president was Alexander Enoch Kerr (BA '20), the forty-seven-year-old principal of Pine Hill Divinity School. His elevation to the Dalhousie presidency came as a surprise to many, not least to himself. Shortly after Doull's refusal in July 1945, Laurie phoned Principal Kerr to say he was coming to see him at Pine Hill. Kerr's wife asked what Laurie could want, and her husband's reply was that Dalhousie had probably found its new president and Laurie, as a courtesy, was coming to tell him who it was. Kerr was stunned when Laurie broached the prospect of none other than himself becoming Dalhousie's president. Kerr had few social or academic connections with members of the Dalhousie board. He would face a huge shift in scale: Pine Hill had perhaps forty students in 1945, plus King's students sharing residence; Dalhousie had 650 and would double that in September 1945. But intrigued by the offer, Kerr talked to his board; then, with uncertainty about the wisdom of what he was doing, he accepted.

Of the four Dalhousie presidents from 1911 to 1980, A.E. Kerr is the least accessible to the historian. He seems to have left no personal papers or letters beyond those found in the files of his office. There is nothing, either, to indicate why the board chose him. He had a reputation at Pine Hill for economy and rectitude; given the circumstances of 1945 that may have been recommendation enough. As Beecher Weld wryly observed, "a clergyman couldn't be a liar."[4]

Other Dalhousie presidents stand on their own several merits; their papers allow them to be seen more in the round. A.E. Kerr can best be described by drawing the world from which he came. He was born in Louisburg, Cape Breton, in 1898. His father, Rory Kerr, had been raised on a farm at St Ann's, having only a few months' schooling. Rory Kerr's life was fishing, sailing, farming, building boats and barns, that clutch of skills so frequently met with in the Maritimes of the nineteenth century. He married, took up a little farm, and built a small schooner to deliver pit props to Sydney coal mines, and bring potatoes and turnips to Cape Breton from Prince Edward Island. The family, three children already, moved to Louisburg in 1895, when the little port (ice-free, unlike Sydney) was booming with coal exports. There on Ellwood Street, Alexander Enoch was born into a household of hard work and piety, surrounded with echoes of the Gaelic from grandparents on both sides. Family worship on Sunday nights was conducted by both mother and father. The Bible was sometimes read in Gaelic, and prayers always. It was well known to Presbyterians that God understood the Gaelic better than any other language.[5]

In that Louisburg society, education was the hope of the common people. Two of Kerr's sisters became school teachers; a brother became a locomotive engineer then railway official; Alex and a brother ended at university. Alex was a pugnacious little debater. A visitor at the Kerr dinner table undertook to prove the world was flat by drawing the inference from the Lord's Prayer. "Thy will be done *in* earth," not *on* earth. Alex, in Grade 10 in Glace Bay at the time, said there was nothing to that argument; in Greek, from which the text came, both "in" and "on" were the same. Rory Kerr laughed delightedly at this.[6]

Alex took his senior school grades in Glace Bay, getting the highest marks in Grade 12 in the school. That was the summer of 1914, when his father died at the age of sixty. Alex worked for two years at the cable station; in 1916 he had enough money to go to Dalhousie for two years, before joining the Royal Air Force in 1918. He was overseas when the war ended, and came back to Dalhousie for his BA in 1920.[7]

Kerr took theology at Pine Hill and at Union Seminary, New York. Ordained a Presbyterian minister, he was assistant minister at

St Andrew's, Sydney when he met and married Nessie Beaton. She was a jewel. A lady to her finger tips, she had social skills her husband never commanded. With a word or a gesture, Nessie Kerr could make the most bashful visitor feel at ease. She sincerely wanted to please people, and she succeeded. Kerr's ministerial career went very well: whether in Montreal, Vancouver, or Winnipeg, he was a popular preacher wherever he went. In 1939 Pine Hill brought him to Halifax as its principal and teacher of systematic theology. His reputation as principal was as a narrow administrator, not spending any more money than he could help. His youth in Louisburg and pastoral work in north-end Winnipeg had shaped that. He was not bookish. He seems not to have much liked libraries or understood them. They may have intimidated him. As for librarians, they were hired hands who ordered books, catalogued, tidied, and dusted them.[8]

Kerr was a teetotaller and a strong one. Although there had been whisky in his Louisburg home, it was medicinal whisky, to be taken as such and not enjoyed. Kerr's dislike for alcohol was so intense as to suggest something deeply engrained from childhood experience, beyond his control, a compound of loathing and fear. That did not mean that he castigated drunkards; his Christianity triumphed over his instincts. No lush need fear Alex Kerr; what they got was sympathy. There is a singular example of the difference between those two teetotallers, Kerr and Laurie. A Dalhousie rink manager of the 1950s was a drunkard; Kerr, who could not stand drinking, was charitable; Laurie, who did not mind people having a drink (though a teetotaller himself), would not have an alcoholic on the staff.

Another curious example of the contrast between chairman and president was the case of A.K. Griffin, professor of classics. He had become a widower and after the war wanted to marry his graduate student, Julia Swanburg. Laurie was appalled; professors ought not to marry students, especially one thirty years the professor's junior. The president, however, was sympathetic, saying that Griffin was a lonely man. "But," spluttered Laurie with vehemence, "the man's got a radio, hasn't he?" Griffin and Julia Swanburg were married and proceeded to have four children.[9]

Despite these social sympathies of the president, those Dalhousie faculty who knew Kerr at Pine Hill were shocked by his appointment as president. Stewart Bates, the William Black professor of commerce, had been called to Ottawa in 1942, Stanley resenting the way the Canadian government "picked off man after man that we had appointed to accounting." In April 1945 Bates told Laurie he was returning to Dalhousie. The day he arrived in Halifax he learned of Kerr's appointment to the Dalhousie presidency. That night he phoned his

A.E. Kerr, President, 1945–63, in his office in the Macdonald Library. A popular
Presbyterian (later United Church) minister, he was a hard-working but not popular
president of Dalhousie. He would encounter some intransigence from faculty in the
1950s.

Ottawa chief, the deputy minister of finance, W.A. Mackintosh, and said he wanted any job going in Ottawa that Mackintosh could find; he was not going to stay at Dalhousie under Alex Kerr. G.V. Douglas, Carnegie professor of geology, a Stanley loyalist, tried to move to McGill in 1945, but found that impossible to effect, so remained at Dalhousie, an irritant to the new president.[10]

A Dean for Arts and Science, 1945

Adjudicating between Professor Douglas and President Kerr was George Wilson of History, the new dean of arts and science. It was an office with an old name but a new purpose, its history not a little curious. The first dean of Dalhousie College was Howard Murray, appointed by Senate in 1901 to save an aging President Forrest from having to track down and not infrequently capture Dalhousie students bent on mischief. A burly, genial professor of classics, Dean Murray was in charge of student discipline, helped after 1912 by Senate's delegating to the Dalhousie Student Council responsibility for minor infractions. Eventually Murray was called the dean of the university, his authority and function different from the other deans of law, medicine, and dentistry. He died in September 1930 and no new dean was appointed until after Carleton Stanley fired Murray Macneill, the registrar, in 1936. He then needed an arts and science supervisor, not for student discipline but to run meetings of Arts and Science professors, and decide domestic details of curriculum and examinations. Such was the work of Dean C.B. Nickerson who died in 1940; after that Stanley was his own dean of arts and science. The last meeting of the Arts and Science Faculty that Stanley attended was partly taken up with the questions of a dean. Wilson proposed that faculty nominate its own dean, or at least elect someone to act as chairman. Stanley, his own man to the end, insisted there was nothing for a dean or chairman to do in the coming months, and so persuaded the faculty to agree to exactly that, nothing.

But in September 1945 came a new president much less sure of himself than Stanley, lacking Stanley's brilliance, and needing to learn almost everything about running a university, its Faculty of Arts and Science especially. He needed someone to organize its meetings, deal with its academic concerns, find and recommend staff. On 10 September 1945, at his family farm in Perth, Ontario, Wilson received a telegram from Kerr: "Am taking you up on promise to help make Dalhousie Arts best in Canada. Will you accept deanship?" Wilson accepted on two conditions: that there be "perfect candour and confidence between us" and that the Arts and Science Faculty be consulted before he was appointed. "The morale of the Arts faculty is very low," said Wilson. "It is not necessary to explain why. If the faculty is consulted about the new dean it will have a most satisfactory effect." Nine days later the faculty voted unanimous concurrence. Thus began Wilson's ten years as Dalhousie's dean of arts and science.[11]

Low morale was due in part to the war, but more to a steady decline in appointments and funding across the previous twenty years. Wilson pointed this out to President MacKenzie in 1930, but the penury of the 1930s, the stresses created by the war and by Carleton Stanley, made it difficult to revive the spirit of the faculty. The new dean in 1945 was to be part of that process. Wilson, although not a great reformer, was a considerable humanist and teacher. At Dalhousie since 1919, he had become fond of the place and its people.

Wilson had grown up on the "Scotch Line" in Perth, Ontario, and went to Queen's. He did history slowly, as if it were to be his life's work, which indeed it was. A big man, over six feet, and strongly built, he spent the long summers working on his parents' farm. He was a farmer who looked like a Roman senator; his Dalhousie lectures were carved with dignity and authority, and he wore his black academic gown like a toga. As for research, it was to him mostly self-glorification. "Produce and advertise instead of digest and live" was his contrast between research and teaching. He aimed to make his knowledge as comprehensive as possible, not only to distill it for students but to climb farther up Parnassus. As he told President MacKenzie in 1930, "I do not care who was the first white child born in Halifax. What I want to do with students is to make them historically minded, and show them that history is really a subject for the mind and not for the memory."[12]

Wilson tramped Europe with friends and with Baedeker. Every three or four years, he fell upon Europe "like a thirsty man who has to get enough to drink to carry him through." In May 1934 he spent a marvellous day at Fountains Abbey in Yorkshire, one of the great Cistercian abbeys destroyed by Henry VIII in 1529. As he walked Wilson tried to reconstruct the world of the abbey as it was before Henry VIII's spoliation. The more he tried, the more he felt his ignorance. "I have become more and more sceptical," he wrote Carleton Stanley, "about our real knowledge of history. I feel how true is Faust's remark ... that history is a book sealed with seven seals."

He tried to open it, by any means available. He would sit on the Acropolis of Athens, looking across towards Thebes, and reflect about the eighty generations since Socrates. Religious power fascinated him, hence his appreciation of Napoleon's remark that religion was a marvellous policeman. Chartres Cathedral he would visit with the utmost reverence, not only for the church's God but for the

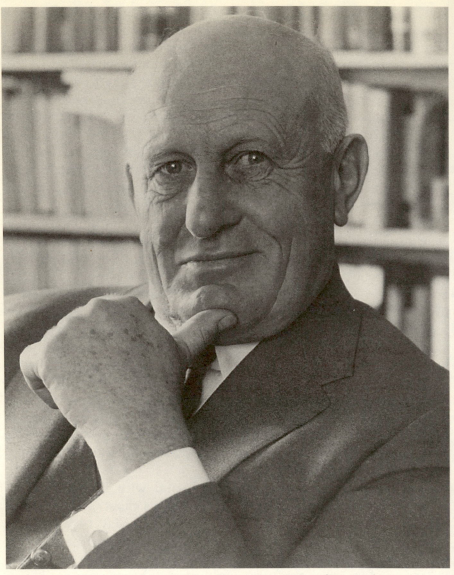

George Earle Wilson, Professor of History, 1919–69, Dean of Arts and Science, 1945–55. This fine portrait was taken by an admiring alumnus, R.H. Campbell (MA '39) and dates from the mid-1950s.

majesty, the beauty with which the church was wrought and the power it represented. He would sigh deeply; Chartres consoled him for the wickedness of history. Like Gibbon, Wilson believed history to be the record of the crimes, follies, and lusts of mankind; but the instinct to create beauty was mankind's form of redemption. His own character was shot through with these alternations: delight in the world and sadness at what too often went on in it; sentiment and scepticism, both deepening as he became older. He was in many ways a monk, and gave his life to absorbing knowledge and giving it back to students. He had enormous influence, and more than one student worshipped at his feet. He never forgot that history really happened, and that men and women made it happen. History was never an abstraction, always a reality.[13]

This was the man who was Dalhousie's dean of arts and science just as the big wave of veterans was returning to campuses all across Canada. Canada's population in 1945 was 12 million. Of that, almost 10 per cent were abroad, a million men and fifty thousand women. After the surrender of Germany in May 1945, and before the atomic bomb on Hiroshima in August 1945, most of the veterans were already on their way home. The great majority returned to former employment or used re-establishment credits to start new businesses; but about 15 per cent applied for training at university or elsewhere, many of them in university for the first time.

The Coming of the Veterans

The federal government announced its policy early in the war, by order-in-council in October 1941, subsequently incorporated in the Veterans' Rehabilitation Act. It provided $60 a month to support veterans who wished to attend university or do other training, $80 a month for married veterans, with additional modest provision for dependants. The government also paid fees. Both grants and fees lasted for the length of the veterans' overseas service. It was a system that compared favourably with those in other Commonwealth countries and the United States, better in fact than most.

It was an idea that the National Conference of Canadian Universities (NCCU), established in 1911, had tried to persuade the Borden government to accept in 1918. The government then said it could not afford it. But in the 1940s both government and Parliament were more generously disposed, and Canadian casualties overseas, although heavy, were not so high proportionate to Canada's population as in the First World War.

The force behind the veterans' grants for university education was the NCCU's Committee on Post-War Problems, created in 1942 and chaired by Larry MacKenzie, then president of the University of New Brunswick. MacKenzie had returned to Dalhousie as a student in 1919 to discover he would have to pay for his own education. That he did; but he felt the government could have been more generous. He got back at them in the Second World War.[14] Of the 15 per cent of veterans who sought further training under the act, about half, some fifty thousand, decided to go to university. Some wanted to complete work already started, but most veterans were beginning university for the first time, some with only junior matriculation. The Ontario universities, where senior matriculation was the rule for admission, usually waived that for veterans if they had junior matriculation.

The veterans surprised nearly everyone. Although university administrators had much to do with getting the government committed to university grants to veterans, some were uneasy at the prospect of Canadian warriors, battle-hardened in manners and morals, transferring their war experience to essays, examinations, and academe. There were fears that lazy servicemen might live at taxpayers' expense, doing the minimum to keep a college nirvana going. Those fears were a chimera. It was true that veterans familiar with English pubs or continental bars found their absence in Canada old-fashioned. But that was the way Canada was. University residences were also still governed by rules established on the principle of *in loco parentis*; most of the veterans had been away from home for years and were well past needing or wanting parental control. One member of the Mount Allison Board of Regents was dismayed to be offered a beer when visiting a veteran in residence at Sackville; on the other hand, Larry MacKenzie, president of the University British Columbia by 1944, went the other way, and would actually ask for a beer when visiting veterans at Acadia Camp.[15] But for the great majority of veterans their real thirst was for knowledge and training. Books on reserve at Dalhousie's Macdonald Library for English 2 or History 1 were more precious than Oland's beer, and harder to get. In class veterans asked questions, respectfully enough but persistently – questions driven by intense curiosity and with a wealth of experience and maturity informing them.

In the years from 1945 to 1950 the veterans made the going. Dean Wilson, pacifist on principle, was not always comfortable with them. He suspected their aims were as much acquisitive as academic, professionals on the make at government expense. So indeed some were, but there was more to it than that. Most veterans were acutely conscious of the meagre income and lack of independence they had had before the war; for many from rural and small-town Nova Scotia, it was the chance of a lifetime to break out of a recurring circle of low education

Professor Burns Martin's class in English about 1947, mostly veterans and apparently all male, reacting to Martin's wit in replying to a student's question. Note the jackets and ties (with one exception) and the polished shoes.

and poverty. Veterans sought a new life on a new basis, and that fierce search could be for them, and for the professors who taught them, a moving and wonderful experience. Every week they were conscious of how the plane of their intellectual horizons reached out farther. Moffatt Hancock, professor at the Law School from 1945 to 1949, remarked of the veterans, "They had a sense of humour and a sense of scepticism, they were delightful, keen, sharp, hard working." For students and professors, it was a time without equal.[16]

C.L. Bennet, George Munro professor of English, was supervisor of Dalhousie's veterans' programs, and a New Zealand veteran from the First World War. He recalled a compulsory English class composed mostly of long-serving veterans, conducted under every possible disadvantage of accommodation, part of a professional program; their marks were mostly solid middle ground, but the questions and classroom contributions came from everyone as from a group of selected honour students. One student under the pen name "Omhpos," wrote a summary of Milton's life and thought in heroic couplets. "City after Rain" in the *Dalhousie Gazette* was Halifax in modern poetry:

> Hushed lies the city
> After the rain.
> Blurred lights slide down the wet streets ...
> Then comes the fog – creeping –
> Up from the harbour.
> Gently it blows out the lights ...

The veterans' ability was frequently revealed where least expected: in the cultural subjects, literature, history, political science. Veterans found that great writers were great because they had something powerful and permanent to say. Nor was Latin excluded. The high school students' objection to Latin at Dalhousie was, "Why?" The veterans did not ask why. Years of military discipline had perhaps expunged such fundamental questions about regimens, military or academic. They asked, "How do I learn it?" As Bennet said,

[The veteran] has found out not only how to learn and to think but also how to judge and decide for himself ... What he has lost in the ability to memorize, he has gained in understanding; what he may lack in dexterity, he makes up for in grasp ... he knows what he knows, and wastes little time in betraying what he doesn't know.

If a veteran failed two of his classes his government subsidy stopped until the failure was redeemed, at his expense of course. In all of this

Bennet was patient, understanding, and generous. The veterans liked him so well they presented him with a gold watch at the veterans' annual smoker in February 1948, at the officers' mess of the Halifax Rifles. The prohibition writ of Dalhousie's president did not run there. It was a rare evening, war stories and songs from two wars, "Tipperary" (and others) from the First, and the best one from the Second, the German "Lili Marlene." Translated long since, troops on both sides of the war had marched to it. It spoke to longings in all soldiers. Bennet was admirable on occasions like this.[17]

If the veterans were influenced by Bennet and other Dalhousie professors, they in turn profoundly affected Dalhousie, especially young Dalhousie students. The contrast between the Dalhousie of 1944–5 and 1945–6 was, as one student put it, "electric." Dalhousie's enrolment in 1943–4 was 654, the lowest it had been since 1919–20, when it was 621. In 1944–5 it rose by 9 per cent, but in 1945–6 the increase was a huge 62 per cent. Some 1,153 students registered in the fall of 1945, of whom the veterans were nearly half. They were still 40 per cent of the student body as late as 1950. Veterans transformed the place; discussions and bull sessions in Roy Atwood's "gym store," as it was called, became as important as lectures. Essays, lab projects, lectures were discussed, hashed out there. Dalhousie was not exactly a hotbed of socialism, but more articulate and committed veterans talked about it, discussing aspects of the welfare state that they had observed abroad, sometimes translated into ambitions at home for the CCF. Canada's socialist party came second in the Ontario provincial election of 1943 and took power in Saskatchewan in 1944. In the 1945 general election the CCF polled almost 16 per cent of the Canadian popular vote, despite the King government's appeal, "Vote Liberal and keep building a New Social Order in Canada." Many veterans were after just that; some had no great love for the King government other than as the purveyor of their education.[18]

Dalhousie's Space Problems
Dalhousie's big increases in enrolment posed tremendous problems of space. In 1944, anticipating such difficulties, the NCCU got the federal government to accept direct dealings between the universities and the Crown Assets Allocation Committee of War Assets Corporation. Each university set about scrounging wartime buildings as fast as it could. At UBC whole west-coast army camps were transferred to the campus. Dalhousie's requirements did not require such drastic solutions. Brooke Claxton, minister of national health and welfare, asked Colonel Laurie in August 1945 if Dalhousie might want to acquire buildings from HMCS *Cornwallis*, the naval base on Annapolis Basin;

An afternoon lecture in biology, probably by Professor Hugh Bell in 1948. Note the segregation of the women students, and at the front of the class.

but Dalhousie had access to other buildings nearer at hand. On 1 June it got buildings built by the navy during the war on Dalhousie land as barracks for the Women's Royal Canadian Naval Service, at the corner of Oxford and Coburg streets. A typical wartime H-shaped building, it would be used for Geology and Engineering. Dalhousie also got the building the navy had put up on the site of the pre-1931 gymnasium, used as a mess hall by naval officers in training at HMCS *Kings*. For single veterans' housing Dalhousie wanted part or all of Cathedral Barracks, built by the federal government on land donated by the city, the Sacred Heart Convent, and the Anglican Cathedral, for the Canadian Women's Army Corps. When it was vacated in the spring of 1946 it was turned over to the federal Department of Public Works to administer. Dalhousie hoped to lease certain buildings; the Nova Scotia Department of Public Health wanted the same ones, especially the officers' and sergeants' mess. The Nova Scotia government got what it wanted, for its nurses in training; Dalhousie got four barrack blocks, a mess building, and an administration building, for some 165 single veterans.

These facilities did not come for nothing. The Department of Public Works thought Dalhousie should pay $15,000 per annum rent, which, together with costs of operation, came to $21,000 a year. Student fees would cover only $7,500 of this. President Kerr complained to Ottawa, via Senator Gordon Isnor, that Dalhousie should not be expected to pay $13,500 of its own money for veterans' housing. That was apart from the fact that students' tuition covered only a proportion of the university's costs – 68 per cent in arts and science, 35 to 40 per cent in medicine and dentistry. The answer of the Department of Veterans' Affairs to both those questions was to allow to all universities the percentage of any university deficit that the numbers of veterans bore to total student enrolment. There was a maximum, however: $150 per student. By 1948–9 the Department of Veterans' Affairs was providing 11 per cent of Dalhousie's income, nearly as much as the Atlantic provinces' provincial grants to medicine and dentistry. Endowment added 23.4 per cent. Fees still made up 46.3 per cent of Dalhousie's income.[19]

Cathedral Barracks was not without its problems, but C.L. Bennet reported a fairly good first year in 1946–7, despite some incidents over the Easter weekend in April 1947. The Dalhousie Student Veterans' Association promised Bennet that such incidents would not be repeated, that future breaches of residence discipline would be dealt with "swiftly and summarily." That reflected not only military experience, but the determination, characteristic of student veterans, not to allow anything to get in the way of the remaking of their lives. A loud radio, too much hilarity, was apt to get short shrift in the form of peremptory knocks on thin walls with instructions to "Cut it out!" Veterans may not have been strong on the "pray" in Dalhousie's motto, but the "work" they took at full stride. As accommodation Cathedral Barracks left something to be desired, but it was evidence of real need that Dalhousie retained one building of that complex as late as December 1951.[20]

If housing for single veterans was in short supply in Halifax, it was much worse for married ones, especially those with families, who needed more than just a room and a cafeteria. Kerr went to Ottawa to see C.D. Howe, minister of reconstruction, about what to do. Howe said it would cost more to move buildings than they were worth. Kerr asked, "What would you do, Mr. Howe, in our place?" Howe said, "I would get Mulgrave Park in the north end. Those apartments are for married workers at the shipyard, whose work is now largely at an end." Early in the war three buildings had been put up as emergency accommodation for shipyard workers, on north Barrington Street, just across from the shipyard. In 1946 Central Mortgage and Housing Corporation subsidized the conversion of Mulgrave Park into married veterans' apartments, some sixty units in all. What was convenient for shipyard workers in 1943 was not quite so for student veterans in 1947, who had to live beyond the end of the Barrington tramline, a long way from Dalhousie. The university originally took a three-year lease on Mulgrave Park; despite the distance, student demand was such that Dalhousie had to keep its lease going for nine years. By 1957 none of the Dalhousie students and their families in Mulgrave Park were veterans, but as late as February 1958 the Dalhousie Student Council appealed to the city (to whom the buildings finally reverted) to allow some students in Mulgrave Park to finish their year.[21]

In March 1946 the *Dalhousie Gazette* ran a poll on student veterans' cost of living at Dalhousie. Of 485, some 40 per cent responded:

	single	married	married with 1 child
No. students answering	149	26	22
current monthly expenses	$57	$99	$110
additional expenses per month	$33	$51	$51
	$90	$150	$161
less DVA allowance	-60	-86	-101

To the question, "Have financial difficulties seriously hindered your studies so far?" only 8 per cent of single veterans so indicated. The percentage was higher among married ones: 15 per cent, and for

The *Dalhousie Gazette* office and staff, February 1947: l. to r., back row,
A.W. Moreira, Kenneth Boyce, R.C. Tuck; front row, William Kelly, J.D. Lusher,
A.A. Lomas, J.R. MacCormack (who has identified those named here). Note the
pin-ups from *Esquire*.

those with one child, 18 per cent. For those few with two or more children, the percentage was between 27 and 33. Clearly in 1946 the great majority of Dalhousie veterans were managing well enough on what the government was providing for their university education.[22]

King's Repossesses its Buildings

By the fall of 1945 HMCS *Kings* had become King's College once more. From 1923 to 1939 King's had held, fairly consistently, 7.5 per cent of the total of Dalhousie students, 12 per cent of those in arts and science. During the war, this dropped to 3 per cent. During the years 1946 to 1950 it averaged 7 per cent, declining slightly in the years to 1955.[23]

All King's students paid their fees to Dalhousie, which in turn remitted them to King's less a proportion kept back by Dalhousie for the heavy cost of science classes. The veteran students enrolled at King's had their fees paid to Dalhousie by Ottawa, and the same principle applied. Although Dalhousie kept back 16 per cent of the fees for science classes in 1946–7, it still calculated it lost money with King's students. In 1946–7 the average cost of an arts and science student to Dalhousie was $229; since King's students that year totalled 126, they cost Dalhousie $29,000, less $4,000 in fees held back for science classes. Thus the net cost to Dalhousie of educating King's students was about $25,000. This Dalhousie calculation, made in 1949, did not take into account the cost to King's of educating Dalhousie students, but with only a modest array of staff and classes, the cost to King's was a good deal smaller.[24]

These worrying calculations might not have been made at all had President Walker of King's been mild and cooperative. He was neither; he was tough and intransigent. What particularly aggravated President Kerr was his insistence on what came to be called the DVA supplementary grants. These were grants paid by Ottawa to the universities to supplement the extra costs, over and above fees, that they were forced to incur for educating veterans. This came to be $150 per student. Thus the supplementary grant for 1947–8 for the twenty-four veterans at King's was $3,600. But King's had not incurred supplementary costs; Dalhousie had. King's in 1944–5 contributed nine members to the common Arts and Science pool of staff, and in 1947–8 only eight. Dalhousie, on the other hand, went from fifty-one in 1944–5 to 108 in 1947–8. Dalhousie also provided all the veterans' advisory personnel and administrative staff, and not improperly claimed the $3,600 for itself. President Walker said that money belonged to King's. The twenty-four veterans took 120 classes, of which seventy-nine were given by Dalhousie and forty-one by King's; Kerr therefore, in order to make peace with President Walker, offered a *pro rata* split of the $3,600 – $2,600 to Dalhousie and $1,000 to King's. In the light of all the facts, said Kerr, this was generous. Dr Walker replied tartly that if he were to make such a recommendation to the King's board, "he would be laughed out of court." Kerr discussed this impasse with Milton Gregg, minister for veterans' affairs in Ottawa. Gregg knew something of both veterans and universities; he was a VC from the First World War, a Dalhousie student, then president of UNB from 1944 to 1947. He made it painfully clear that Dalhousie and King's would have to sort out their own quarrel. Finally, in July 1950 Dalhousie agreed to accept a 50/50 split of the DVA supplementary grant insofar as it affected veterans at King's. It had taken three years to come to this solution.[25]

Behind Walker's bitterness was his belief, shared by others at King's, that Dalhousie had been surreptitiously working for twenty-five years to "absorb her [King's] and her funds." Outspoken on the subject, he declared publicly that the Dalhousie-King's Association was "the fag-end of an experiment that failed." There may have been truth in that summary conclusion, but it did little good to say so. Walker's relations with President Stanley had been unfriendly, sometimes poisonous. When something had been concluded not to Walker's liking he was apt to say he had not received the correspondence. Stanley told McGregor Stewart in 1941, "Yes, King's is chilling." Probably King's enjoyed greater advantages from its association with Dalhousie than vice versa, but King's resentment of the 1923 terms overshadowed proper appreciation of the benefits. King's really wanted a form of equality with Dalhousie and it was unrealizable. That may have been at the bottom of the many demands of, and complaints against, Dalhousie. King's could not be satisfied.

Dalhousie's policy was appeasement, even if contrary to the 1923 terms. Its concessions over twenty-five years were considerable. If the 1923 Association was failing, it was because one institution carrying 10 per cent of the load wanted recognition of equality with the other carrying the 90 per cent. President Walker was on leave in the year 1952–3, and died suddenly in December. During that time Dalhousie and King's agreed to more flexible rules, set up in the new Terms of Association of November 1954. But problems would arise even under this new agreement, suggesting that the difficulty was not just President Walker, but endemic in the union of two bodies with such disparity of resources.[26]

In all of this President Kerr seems to have played a constructive role, relying on the advice of Colonel Laurie, who was not only chairman of the Dalhousie board, but as a wealthy Anglican was associated with King's as well. Kerr's administration of Dalhousie was apt to be close-fisted; money did not grow on trees in Louisburg, and the best rule for administering anything was to be canny about the use of its money. A curious example of Kerr's canniness with money was when his old car needed a new tire. Not wanting to pay the regular price, he got Dalhousie's business manager, D.H. McNeill, to phone Imperial Oil's tire section to ask for a "fleet" price. "You can phone from my office," said Kerr helpfully, never one to underestimate the value of secrecy. "How many tires do you want?" Imperial Oil asked McNeill. He was forced to admit that President Kerr wanted only one. Imperial Oil refused point blank. Kerr was upset at having to pay full price; McNeill was so embarrassed he called Imperial Oil later to explain the pressure he was under.

Guarding Dalhousie's finances as if they were Kerr's own was not such a bad rule; certainly the board liked it. In March 1949, in appreciation of the president's work, and now receiving increased financial support from governments, they offered him a new Pontiac. Ten months later they raised his salary from $10,000 to $12,000 per year, as of 1 January 1950.[27]

In financial matters Kerr was apt to believe that he was translating his experience (and success) at Pine Hill over to Dalhousie. But Dalhousie was a very much bigger operation and it took some time to grasp the magnitude of the shift. McNeill suspected that he never did altogether. Nor could he quite escape the narrow, pinched views of men and money he had grown up with. But he learned something as he went. If he was very much his own man in many things, he worked well with the financial men of the board, and learned from them.[28]

But if he learned finance from board members, he found it difficult to improve his social skills. Kerr was kind in his stiff, ministerial way, helpful to those in trouble, as if coming from a well-disciplined professional sense of duty. But generosity of spirit he had not, nor did he learn much from his wife, who was splendidly endowed with it. Nessie Kerr loved life, enjoyed social occasions, warmed and nourished her family (and others), gave freely of herself, her time and energy. Veterans and veterans' wives thought the world of her. She was Kerr's better half in every sense of the expression; those who knew her believed her possessed of tremendous strength and resilience.

The 1947 Expansion Campaign and
the new Arts and Administration Building, 1949–51
The expansion campaign of 1947 was not Kerr's doing. It was a re-energizing of the one launched in the spring of 1939 which had been halted by the war. It had been due for revival in 1945, but had never

started, for the board believed Carleton Stanley an impossible president for a financial campaign. Finally it was launched in January 1947 under the chairmanship of J. McGregor Stewart, the driving force behind the ousting of Stanley. It was to run for five years and was for $3 million, the largest sum Dalhousie had ever undertaken to raise.

It had several aims. An Arts and Administration Building was the first. The Law (Temporary Arts) Building that housed Arts was bursting at the seams and would become the home of the Law Faculty as soon as a place could be found for the Arts Faculty. That new Arts Building would also be what President MacKenzie and Frank Darling had planned, thirty years before, as the centrepiece of the Studley campus. A men's residence was another desideratum. There was one of a sort: the mess hall built by the navy for officers in training on the site of the old gym. As the *Gazette* remarked, men lived there and ate there; there was nothing further to be said. By 1950 half the $3 million had been raised, and by 1954 most of the balance, although not in ways the board had anticipated.

To design the new Arts and Administration Building the board wanted the best architects possible. In February 1948 its Building Committee reported that their unanimous choice was Mathers and Haldenby of Toronto, who had designed several successful University of Toronto buildings. Their fees would be 6 per cent of overall cost. They came to Halifax in May 1949 and declared that Dalhousie had "the one unspoiled campus in Canada." That hyperbole ignored UBC but it implicitly acknowledged the new building's commanding presence. Plans available by September 1948 estimated the cost at $1,568,029. That was a nasty surprise. In November 1946 Senate had allotted $750,000 of the $3 million campaign money for the A. and A. Building, as it was called. G.V. Douglas, Carnegie professor of geology, protested that the new estimate was more than double Senate's allocation and threatened a motion in Senate against spending such an inordinate sum. Dean Wilson pointed out to President Kerr in May 1949 that such a motion would also be supported by those who wanted a new building, but feared that capital cost and upkeep would be such a drain on Dalhousie's resources that a first-class faculty, adequately paid and staffed, would be impossible. Although Wilson himself believed that staff was more important than buildings, he dissuaded Douglas from pressing his motion. The board took the view that the building ought to be proceeded with anyway, that Dalhousie's policy "could not be guided with pessimism as to the future."[29]

The chairman of the board's Building Committee was a veteran of the two wars, Brigadier H.V.D. Laing, CBE, Dalhousie's 1921 Rhodes

The Law (Temporary Arts) Building about 1950. The Cobb-Darling combination at its most harmonious, it was built in 1921 and used by Arts until 1952. Law then occupied it until the completion of the Weldon Building in 1967. It afterwards became, as it still is, the University Club.

scholar, and now vice-president of National Sea Products. He was adamant that no local architect should design such an important building, though he had to accept a local supervisory architect, Leslie Fairn. Fairn was not perfect, and there would be strains with him; but as Laing put it later, having gone through the mill with him, one was at least "prepared for his deviltry."[30]

The A. and A. Building was a large four-storey building (counting the ground-level basement), with the main storey reached from the east by two broad flights of stairs. There were two substantial wings, with a tall tower standing above the centre. The board liked the design very much, although the central tower was of some concern since it added $30,000 to the cost. The whole building was an attempt to create a colonial-style edifice in keeping with the rest of the campus, but on a much larger scale. Here was missing the poetic sweep of Frank Darling, the ingenuity of Andrew Cobb; it was a large building for a large purpose, but it topped the hill at Studley without being its crown. The tower seemed either too long or too short, its proportions unsatisfying. There were rude remarks about it from the moment it was finished in 1951. Inside, however, the building was spacious, with wide halls and good rooms, and the view from the faculty room at the top (the southwest corner), or any of the third-floor faculty offices on the south side, was one of the best in the city, out to the sea horizon beyond Mauger's Beach Lighthouse and York Redoubt.

It was the view that Dean Wilson's office took in, some two floors and a long corridor away from the president's office. It was so chosen for its distance, physical and intellectual. Nevertheless, theirs had been a fruitful relationship. In the beginning President Kerr had a lot to learn about Dalhousie and knew it. He had the good sense to lean on his dean of arts and science as his main support until his own legs were stronger. He learned to be generous with younger staff. When David Farr, a young lecturer in history in 1946–7, found himself needing a summer job in 1947, Kerr found him work clearing up odds and ends at the bottom of the library stacks, and at pay 10 per cent higher than he had been earning as lecturer. Farr was on his way to Carleton University; Kerr was willing to match Carleton's salary, but he couldn't match Carleton's promise of permanency.

A very hard worker, Kerr used that talent to conceal other weaknesses. Several times in the spring of 1947 he looked all in. He and his dean of arts spent much time together, and in 1948 Wilson introduced Kerr to the history of Paris by spending a few days walking it with him. In the long summers Wilson would write reflective letters from his farm in Perth, revealing his and Dalhousie's concerns in the late 1940s.[31]

One of Wilson's pet abominations was any form of military training included as part of a liberal education. Some believed, he said, that anything could be stuck into an arts program. "What would Vince [MacDonald, dean of law] say if we suggested Psychological warfare instead of torts or what would Grant [dean of medicine] say if we suggested Propaganda instead of anatomy?" But apart from resisting such hideous innovations, Wilson impressed upon the president how important it was to get and keep good professors. A case in point was Wilson's friend J.G. Adshead, professor of mathematics at King's. Some of Adshead's recent graduates were being paid much more than the $3,000 King's paid him. Adshead had a first-class honours from Cambridge, was an excellent teacher, and had administrative talent to boot. If President Walker of King's could not pay him more, he should transfer to Dalhousie. He did, in 1947.

Staff, Old and New

Wilson felt, as President Stanley had, that the Department of Mathematics had been unsatisfactory for some years. Part of the difficulty may have been with Murray Macneill's preoccupation, until 1936, with being registrar; but the fact was that not enough good professors had been appointed. It was a general difficulty across the whole Faculty of Arts and Science. In Medicine and Law, it was facts and knowledge that came first, and such professors were paid as outside competition in those professions required. But in Arts, said Wilson, what mattered was spirit and energy. He wanted Dalhousie to recover the reputation it had once had for great teaching. Perhaps, he suggested, it never quite deserved that reputation, but whatever it was, he wanted it back. Three things were necessary in new staff: that a professor be master of his subject; that he be a scholar outside his subject – universities in Canada were full of illiterate specialists; and that a professor have character.

The last was the hardest of all to find. President MacKenzie used to say, said Wilson, the search was hopeless, that Dalhousie would have "to be satisfied with respectability." Wilson sought more; he wanted professors who had their own inner light. "What you are speaks so loudly that I can't hear what you say," was one of his favourite quotations. Nevertheless, he recognized that Dalhousie would be lucky to get and hold good younger men. Hire good ones, he would say, but don't count on their staying more than a few years. Get the best you can from them while they are young and energetic; if then they go to Toronto, McGill, or UBC, recognize that Dalhousie was a good jumping-off point. By and by Dalhousie will look good on their c.v. too.[32]

By the late 1940s the demands on Dalhousie's staff in Arts and Science was punishing; with so much teaching, correcting exercises, there was no time for anything else. Dalhousie needed to lessen teaching loads and increase academic salaries. To Wilson that was more important than a new Arts Building. Some of these problems were subsumed in discussions with R.A. MacKay, Eric Dennis professor of political science. Wilson had been listening to MacKay's plans for a Social Sciences division for twenty years. He liked MacKay but distrusted his judgment, for he was never realistic enough. He wanted time for research and money to go with it. MacKay hated being what he called "a drudge undergraduate teacher." But to do what MacKay wanted meant hiring another professor in political science, unpopular with other departments which needed new men more than Political Science did.

In that debate between Dalhousie and MacKay lay a gap in educational philosophy. MacKay was only four years younger than Wilson, but in wanting a Social Sciences division he was a decade ahead, well aware that American granting agencies liked the concept and that it promised funds and scholarships. The value, present and future, of MacKay's approach eluded Wilson and in the end eluded Dalhousie too. The truth was that a Social Sciences division was simply beyond Dalhousie's reach, financial as well as philosophical. MacKay exhausted Wilson's patience, got an offer from the Department of External Affairs, and left in August 1947.[33]

It was difficult to replace him. The Department of Political Science staggered on with special lecturers for two years, while Wilson searched for a good man, with help from his old friend, R. MacGregor Dawson, now professor at the University of Toronto. Dawson recommended J.H. Aitchison, nearly finishing his PH.D. at Toronto, at thirty-nine years of age, an exceptional teacher and a very hard worker. Dalhousie would be lucky to get him. McMaster wanted him too, and badly, Dawson said. Don't delay. And be sure to offer him $4,000 with a promise of going soon to $5,000. Aitchison came in 1949, perhaps on Dawson's private urging, and was everything Dawson said he was. Best of all he stayed, and came to be a tower of strength in Arts and Science.[34]

Philosophy had not been a tower of strength. Herbert Leslie Stewart had come in 1913 at the age of thirty-one, a first-class mind, with a book and several articles already to his credit. He commanded a considerable range of information, assimilated with awesome ease. He had a quick and versatile pen, and enormous energy and dedication to writing and publication. He was the founding editor of the *Dalhousie Review* and carried it on his shoulders for twenty-five years, from

J.H. Aitchison, Eric Dennis Professor of Political Science, 1949–74.

1921 to 1946. Released from that, his publications went up even further. He had lectured weekly on CBC radio on world affairs in the 1930s, and was a popular lecturer at luncheons in downtown Halifax. His reputation inside and outside Nova Scotia was considerable. If an informed radio listener in Toronto were asked in the 1930s to name a Dalhousie professor, it would have been H.L. Stewart.

All that came at a heavy price, both for his family (he was always at his typewriter), and for the Department of Philosophy at Dalhousie. In senior classes his skills could be deployed among small groups of good students, though even there his philosophy was old-fashioned, dealing with issues popular at Oxford forty years before. But in first-year philosophy, from which everything really started, his reputation was terrible. He was a tough marker; but unlike many such, who repaid their students with stimulating lectures, Stewart gave his first-year students only the bare minimum. He would arrive at Dalhousie with minutes to spare, rush into his office, grab the relevant lecture from a drawer and proceed to class, where he simply read it. Even his jokes were predictable; if a student had the previous year's notes, or as some alleged, the previous generation's, she or he had no need to come to Stewart's lectures. They could be read at home. As Dean Wilson put it to President Kerr, philosophy at Dalhousie had had a "forced exile of at least thirty years."[35]

In 1947 Stewart was sixty-five and thinking of retiring. Dalhousie wanted a first-class philosopher to replace him. Wilson sounded out a Dalhousie graduate whom he had long been in touch with, T.A. Goudge ('31), teaching at the University of Toronto, but Goudge preferred staying where he was. So Dalhousie fell back upon their second choice, a young Rhodes scholar from Queen's, George Parkin Grant.

Grant came from a well-known Canadian family. His grandfather, George Monro Grant, had done much to re-establish Dalhousie in 1863 and in 1877 became principal of Queen's, well-loved and vigorous, until his death in 1902. G.P. Grant's father was W.L. Grant, principal of Upper Canada College from 1917 to 1935; his maternal aunt was Alice Parkin Massey. G.P. Grant duly graduated from Queen's in history in 1939 with a Rhodes scholarship. In 1947 he was not yet an accomplished scholar – he was only thirty years old – but in Dalhousie's view, which meant that of Dean Wilson and his old friend in Toronto, President Sidney Smith, Grant had the ability to become one. He was not even a philosopher, but was working on a theology PH.D. at Oxford. Nevertheless, based on Sidney Smith's recommendations, Dalhousie was confident that Grant would be an excellent teacher and would restore philosophy at Dalhousie to its rightful place as in the great days of Lyall and Seth. Grant was offered an assistant professorship at $3,000 and took it.[36]

Grant came to Dalhousie as a huge breath of fresh air. His tremendous vitality fuelled his intellectual enthusiasms at centrifugal velocity. His first-year philosophy classes had no set texts; his lectures were open and searching discussions. He also liked to meet students on their own ground, so there was after-class talk in the gym store, over Atwood's thin coffee and watery soup. He raised as many questions as he answered, and soon had a large and devoted following.

Dr Lothar Richter also had a following at the Institute of Public Affairs. It had been established in 1937 with Rockefeller money; by the time that ran out in 1943, Richter, who had carefully husbanded his grants, had generated local support. A Bureau of Industrial Relations, made up of Maritime business leaders, was established in 1943 with an annual budget that carried the overhead of the institute. *Public Affairs*, a quarterly established in 1937–8, was by 1943 self-supporting with 1,600 subscribers and 1,100 further copies purchased by the Union of Nova Scotia Municipalities, the Department of Education, and others. Cooperation with Maritime governments, provincial and municipal, was effected by two further step-children, the Maritime Labour Institute and the Municipal Bureau of Nova Scotia.

Richter was one of the few Dalhousie professors who deliberately reached out to the community around him, and he had a powerful influence on veterans, many of whom attended his noon-hour lunch-and-learn talks on public affairs. The idea that learning could be usefully put to work in the Nova Scotian community was immensely attractive; the institute's philosophy was essentially that private enterprise could profitably work with state enterprise.

The Institute of Public Affairs was on the Dalhousie campus and used the Dalhousie name, but it functioned as a quasi-independent organization. Richter and Stanley had been quite content to have it that way. Richter regarded it, as President Kerr noted disapprovingly, "as an autonomous department within the University." Kerr wanted it brought directly under Dalhousie's control. What irked him was Richter's habit of calling conferences, inviting speakers, without first consulting the president. Although Richter professed never to "ignore the interests of the President of the University ... he persistently does so," said Kerr. J. McG. Stewart, who had helped to set up the institute in the first place, resisted too heavy a hand with it, especially since he liked Richter and appreciated what he was trying to do. Before anything had been decided, Richter died. Riding his bicycle from Dalhousie one morning in November 1948, he drove into the side of a truck, and died three days later of a brain haemorrhage.[37]

There was, literally, no one to replace him, no one who could match his talents, knowledge, his tremendous range of Maritime contacts, and the respect he enjoyed. After reorganizing the institute after his death and putting it more directly under the university, Dalhousie struggled valiantly to keep Richter's principles and practice going. But there was only one Richter, and many years in the future, after a succession of hard-working heads, it would become Henson College.

President Kerr's desire for more central control, illustrated by his relations with Richter, seem also to have inclined him towards cultivating the board more than the Senate. Wilson had done what he could to bring President Kerr into the world of scholarship and learning; but apart from acquiring expertise in finance, Kerr remained largely as he was, not growing greatly in sagacity or knowledge, and increasingly wanting to be his own man.

Powers and Boundaries of the President

The board may have contributed to strengthening the president's role by attempting, in May 1946, to define it. Carleton Stanley had exploited the president's undefined power; a year after the contretemps with Stanley, the board felt it was time to set down the president's functions as nearly as possible in black and white. The president was responsible for the general supervision of the university, which comprehended its teaching and administrative staff, as well as the student body and extra-curricular activities. He was a member of each faculty and entitled to act as its chairman, though he usually delegated that function to the dean. The president had the power to delay any action by Senate or faculty or committee thereof that he believed injurious to the university, pending a decision by the Board of Governors.

The board usually, but not always, backed the president. In 1950 President Kerr was nominated moderator of the General Council of the United Church to Canada. Colonel Laurie seems to have found nothing wrong with it, and the matter was handled at a board meeting on 29 May 1950 as if requiring no discussion. The president was not even asked to leave the meeting. But George Farquhar, Alumni member of the board, was not having it. He thought President Kerr ought long ago to have intimated to the United Church that he could not accept such a nomination. Kerr dearly wanted it, however, and had even discussed arrangements for his replacement at Dalhousie while away on moderator's duties. The president claimed that when he accepted the presidency in 1945 the first condition was that he retain his rights as a minister of the United Church, and that that assurance had been given. Farquhar denied, however, that the "headship of one of the great ecclesiastical bodies of Canada was even remotely contemplated." Six weeks later the president announced he would not accept the nomination.[38]

Thus there were limits to what the board would allow the president to do outside the university; inside, the Senate was the main curb on the president's authority, and while there had been rumblings in 1949 over the cost of the new A. and A. Building, Senate was still tractable. The president had been heavy-handed about alcohol on campus. He had hardly arrived in 1945 when he learned with horror that on Friday and Saturday nights in an upstairs room in the gym the faculty played poker and drank beer. Kerr phoned the president of the Faculty Union and asked if it were true. "Yes, it is," said Professor Murchy McPhail of Pharmacology. "Then you have to stop it right now," said President Kerr. "It can't continue any more." It continued of course, but off-campus. When the *Dalhousie Gazette* approached the president in 1950 about opening the newly built skating rink for Sunday skating, Kerr, after consulting two members of the board and some senators, refused categorically to allow it. The board backed the president. Kerr also took umbrage at the *Gazette*'s "The Diary of Sam Peeps." This came to climax in October 1948:

Lord's Day. I to King's Abbey, stepping over sleeping scholars I did find a pew. Here Dr. Runner [A. Stanley Walker] did begin to nibble at the Common Prayer, by saying "Glory to the Father etc." after he had read two psalms ...

Thence to the Lady Hamilton [Lord Nelson Hotel], gaining entrance by a back door, where I drank several bottles of Hall ale. Much company I found to come to the innkeeper, she being very pretty and wanton ...

Went a-walking to the college on the hill, called jokingly by the scholars Dullhousie. Here I was much surprised to see that pretty maids of the nobility, and some not so noble, are to be scholars, they having lodging in a mighty fine house and large, called Marmalade Hovel [Shirreff Hall].

Dr Kerr had the sobriquet Dr Hound, until it was discovered that he pronounced his name "Carr," not "cur," and then he became President Otto.[39]

"Peeps" was Jack D. Lusher ('49), a Canadian army veteran, dedicated to shaking Dalhousie up a little. One of his achievements in 1947 was to bring Canadian football into prominence on campus by reporting it heavily, and deliberately downplaying English rugby, the traditional Maritime game. The issue that got him into the most trouble was a parody of the *Halifax Mail*, the *Halifax Wail*; it was ill received downtown at the *Mail*, especially by its owner, Senator W.H. Dennis, after whose brother Eric the political science professorship

Rugby on a wet day in 1948, Arts and Science versus Commerce. Arts won, 18-0.
D.D. Betts ('50) is running with the ball. He was later Dean of Arts and Science,
1980–8, and Dean of Science, 1988–90. Struan Robertson ('53), who is trying to stop
Betts, was, forty years on, to be Chairman of the Board.

had been endowed in 1921. Lusher's forced resignation from the *Gazette* provoked a student protest; the Student Council majority supported him and he was reinstated. The president then went to the Senate and got it to strike a committee on the *Gazette*. The committee reported unanimously on 22 January 1949 that some things in the *Gazette* were apt to bring Dalhousie into disrepute; but there the unanimity ended. As to action, none was recommended, other than to strike a further committee to consider relations with the Student Council. A year later Senate simply reiterated its traditional power over the internal discipline of the university, and continued to delegate relevant authority to the Student Council, so long as that appeared "to be managed with due regard to the interests of the student body and the position of the University in the community."[40]

The Creation of the Faculty of Graduate Studies, 1948–9

The creation of the Faculty of Graduate Studies also met a mixed reception in Senate. It was an initiative especially from the Science side of the faculty, and there was a disposition in Arts to think the time not yet opportune. Dean Wilson tended to see graduate studies as a means for science professors to acquire assistants to help run laboratories. Wilson did not like, either, the MA theses that D.C. Harvey of the Nova Scotia Archives supervised, on what Wilson regarded as the minutiae of Nova Scotia history. The truth was that, whether Dalhousie was ready for it or not, it was being forced into graduate work. Between 1930 and 1950 it had awarded three hundred masters degrees, and they amounted to 60 per cent of all such degrees awarded in Maritime province universities. In 1948–9 some seventy-five students registered for the MA or M.Sc. On 19 October 1948 Senate agreed that the question of a Faculty of Graduate Studies be studied by a joint board-Senate committee. It was duly recommended. Since the push came from the science departments, it was no accident that J.H.L. Johnstone of Physics was appointed the first dean in 1949.

As to financial support for Graduate Studies, Dalhousie took the view that it should be supported by the Nova Scotia government on the same lines as it did Dentistry and Medicine. President Kerr asked for $36,500. He had already taken the precaution of sounding out the presidents of Acadia and St Francis Xavier to see if they had objections. Ostensibly they had not, saying that a government grant to Graduate Studies at Dalhousie would not produce a commensurate request from them. Nevertheless, Watson Kirkconnell of Acadia found it impossible to resist writing Premier Angus L. Macdonald privately, suggesting that Acadia did do graduate work, including some twenty-two students for the B.Ed., at that time a graduate degree.

Kirkconnell hoped that the Nova Scotia legislature would show "equal sympathy towards provincial assistance to Acadia University in other areas of its work."

The premier was ready to give Dalhousie's request serious consideration, but wanted it reviewed by some outside body, as the Carnegie Corporation used to do in the 1920s and 1930s. But that time had gone by. Carnegie told President Kerr and Dean Johnstone that they did not do that sort of thing any more. The premier (and the president) then appealed to Sidney Smith, now president of the University of Toronto. Apart from the cost, asked Macdonald, can Dalhousie with its present staff do "real Post Graduate work?" Smith came back unequivocally; there should be a School of Graduate Studies east of McGill, and Dalhousie should have it; but it was not paying salaries adequate to attract first-class scholars. Kerr's aim was not pitched high enough.[41]

The Nova Scotia government was beginning to yield on another front as well. In 1948 as a result of discussions between the two Macdonalds, Dean Vince and Premier Angus L., the Nova Scotia government announced it would fund a chair at Dalhousie in public law, to supplement the Law Faculty's complement of "four men and a boy." W.R. Lederman, the first Province of Nova Scotia professor of law, was appointed in 1949. Behind these positive developments on the part of the Nova Scotian government lay Angus L.'s fear of federal encroachment into Nova Scotia's jurisdiction in health and education. Naturally, so he told Dr P.J. Nicholson, president of St Francis Xavier, he wanted what was best for Canada as a whole. "But I do not wish to see Federalism destroyed in a left-handed way by the Federal Government's taking over bit by bit provincial fields." In the coming session of 1950, he hoped, Nova Scotia might be able to grant $500,000 to the Nova Scotian universities. This on a per capita basis would give St Francis Xavier about $100,000. Having won in the June 1949 election twenty-eight seats in the thirty-seven seat legislature, Angus L. could well make good on what he suggested if he wanted to.[42]

Four months earlier, however, the federal government of Louis St Laurent had appointed the Royal Commission on the Arts, Letters and Sciences in Canada. One of the members of that commission was Larry MacKenzie, a Dalhousian who was president of UBC. While the report was being drafted, the prime minister, in a speech at the University of Toronto, hinted strongly that some means had to be found to support universities. Not least in this argument was the fact that the federal government itself was the largest customer in Canada for university graduates of all kinds. The report of the Massey Commission, as it was now called, was on St Laurent's desk by 1 June 1951. It would effect substantial changes in the hopes and prospects for development of Dalhousie and its sister universities. Those changes would not come all at once; but in fact Angus L.'s move was being upstaged by Ottawa, and the old world of Dalhousie's dependence on endowment and fees was slowly to change.

· 7 ·

The Ways of the Fifties
1951–1957

Curriculum and enrolment. Style and manners of students. Lives of professors. Distrust of publication in Arts. Science departments, strengths and weaknesses. The Massey Commission and its effects. The 1953–4 row between president and Medical Faculty. The Law Faculty. Dentistry and its new building. Changes in the Board of Governors.

The *Gazette*'s 1951 recipe for creating a Dalhousie graduate was as follows:

1. Take One Student Body
2. Soak Thoroughly
3. Add Exams Freely
4. Pluck Well
5. Keep Steaming for 8 ½ Months
6. Cool for a Summer
7. Repeat Several Times

Dalhousie's BA in the early 1950s was much the same as it had been for the past half-century. It retained its old emphasis on classics; two of the twenty classes had to be either Greek or Latin. Also required was one class in a modern language, two classes in English, one each in mathematics, science, and history 1, European civilization. The other twelve classes represented a creative curriculum designed to give the student a major subject, while offering three electives that allowed some rudimentary versatility.

It had not been all that different in 1904–5. The Dalhousie student of the 1950s had a few more options, one year less of compulsory Latin or Greek, one year less of German or French. Many freshmen were now admitted to a three-year program with Grade 12, and an important course became English 2, C.L. Bennet's Shakespeare and Milton, the campus common denominator. Even B.SC. students could not escape that. Altogether it reflected an attitude that Principal W.A. Mackintosh of Queen's described in 1951: "One cannot master knowledge in general. One must master it in particular ... It is well to know something about many things but only in mastery is higher education attained." One difference between Queen's and Dalhousie in these years was that the principal of Queen's understood what first-class meant; President Kerr of Dalhousie really did not. Fortunately the professors at Dalhousie who did helped the university get past the sirens who sang of secretarial science and home economics, the dangers of which Kerr, with his love of numbers and enrolment, never really understood.

The curriculum of the early 1950s that had stood virtually unaltered for so long began to change in 1956. In April that year there was a general debate in the Faculty of Arts and Science about curriculum. Dean Wilson was concerned with strengthening standards, in English, French, history and other humanities disciplines. But what caused the most debate was a proposal from classics that, some said, went the other way: the abolition of compulsory Latin 2. (Latin 1 was senior matriculation Latin.) The substitute for Latin 2 was now to be classical literature in translation. Some spirits in faculty fought this change, but as one professor noted, a student's having completed Latin 2 did not mean that he or she was able to have any substantial skill in Latin literature, or much appreciation of it. That view was endorsed by the Classics Department, somewhat uncomfortable but resolute. Faculty approved the change, and so Dalhousie's longstanding requirement of two years of Latin (or Greek) came to an end.

That was not necessarily bad. Classical Latin was difficult to teach and no easier to learn. Classical literature in translation allowed the rounding out of the discipline into its many diversities – history, culture, society, architecture – without the severe concentration on grammar and philology. While some regretted the loss, for English, of Latin's terseness, turns of phrase, its grammatical sure-footedness, for many classicists it was "a blessing in disguise."[1]

By 1953–4 Dalhousie's enrolment had declined to 1,409 and not until 1956–7 did it reach what it had been in 1950–1, 1,553. The enrolment percentages in 1953–4 were consistent for most of that period:

Arts and Science	61 per cent
Medicine	19 per cent
Law	10 per cent
Dentistry	4 per cent
Graduate Studies	4 per cent
Public Health Nursing	2 per cent

The religious affiliations of students were:

United Church	33 per cent
Anglican	26 per cent
Roman Catholic	15 per cent
Baptist	9 per cent
Presbyterian	7 per cent
Jewish	5 per cent
Lutheran	1 per cent
Others	4 per cent

Three-quarters of Dalhousie students were men, and they lived all over the city. Their eating places were few; there was the Lord Nelson Tavern, Diana Sweets on Coburg Road, and on campus Roy Atwood's gym shop, now being called the Canteen, as it moved from the gym to the unlovely Arts Annex.

In arts and science 31 per cent of the students were women, with the proportion in law, medicine, and dentistry being about 5 per cent. Of the 335 women students at Dalhousie, one hundred lived at Shirreff Hall, which tended to function as Dalhousie's social centre though only for special occasions. Shirreff Hall functions had style; that had been Jennie Shirreff's intention from the beginning. Its dances, for example, had a certain gala quality that she would have liked. Shirreff Hall was also indispensable for certain state events such as convocation teas.

The warden of Shirreff Hall from 1947 to 1955 was Miss Mary Mowat, whose salary was $2,000 a year with a small suite for her use. She was a lady in her mid-fifties of poise and of a charm faintly sad; in years gone by she had been disappointed in love and remained single ever since. She looked more tractable than she was, and she could be offended easily, not least by President Kerr. She expected Shirreff Hall rules to be followed, and she ran the Hall with aplomb, though some of her views were old-fashioned. Late one Saturday evening she observed one of her charges in one of the stone alcoves (the tales those stones could tell!) in a too ardent embrace with a young man. On Sunday morning Miss Mowat called the young woman up on the carpet. "But, Miss Mowat," she protested, "I *love* him!" "I should *certainly* hope you do," was Miss Mowat's unrelenting reply. Shirreff Hall girls told this story with some amusement, recognizing that Miss Mowat's attitudes from the 1930s were not the ways of the 1950s.

The fact was, as related by Helen Reynolds, Mary Mowat's successor, that girls in residence did rather better on examinations that those that lived outside. She told faculty that at Christmas 1958, 13 per cent of Shirreff Hall girls made averages over 80; 17 per cent had failing averages. For those who lived outside, the figures were 2 per cent and 27 per cent respectively. That marked difference bespeaks something of the character of life at Shirreff Hall.[2]

Although enrolment in the 1950s was about 50 per cent higher than in the 1930s, apart from the new A. and A. Building and a few wartime shacks, Dalhousie was not all that different. It still dealt with the familiar problem: developing in students love of learning, hunger for research, appreciation of the world's knowledge, its sciences, languages, and literatures. Many students came from backgrounds that had little pretence to learning; how could the professors get them to value those things, instill in them something of the wonder and excitement of intellectual life? On the other hand, brilliant students would sometimes let the professor know, by a distant sign, if the lecture did not come up to their high standards. It was from those rare students that professors learned. Most professors could discern the glazing over of the minds of ordinary students and would try to counter it with some fresh explanation, some invented metaphor, to explain the point; but it was vital to meet the high standards, almost always unspoken, that radiated from the brilliant student. One Dalhousie student put into poetry what Bishop Berkeley had set down as philosophy, *esse est percipi* (to be is to be perceived), about colour:

> Colour is not real; it seems to shine
> And hover like a butterfly; above
> The flower, the book, the gown, whatever things
> Would like to claim the colour as its own.
> The green of grass could thin like morning mist
> And vanish in the trembling heat of noon;
> A pitcher is inside its veil of blue,
> Its halo.[3]

The minds of most Dalhousie students of the 1950s came in conservative guises. The veterans had been vigorous and outspoken, but they were leaving, and their influence had largely passed. Dalhousie undergraduates were unused to the questioning of assumptions, unused indeed to questions, apt to be unclamorous; they were ready to soak up ideas and information if conveyed in the right way. That meant some performance by the professor, thespian as well as intellectual, to arouse interest. Some Dalhousie professors could take a class through municipal finance and keep the students fascinated; some could not. Students could usually recognize a good lecture, even though they could not always determine a bad one. It was too easy to assume a dull lecture meant a weak professor with unsatisfactory material. Students had their own names for the idiosyncrasies they met up with – for example, "Whispering Willie" for W.R. Maxwell, head of Economics, whose too soft voice and calm manner disguised, too easily, an able mind and a progressive thinker.

Students tended to dress conservatively. With the men, jackets and ties predominated, though after the veterans left sweaters slowly came to be accepted. In January 1957 there was a letter in the *Gazette* complaining that some students did not dress properly; collar and no necktie was "sloppiness and laziness." The *Gazette* commented that Dalhousie had no rules about dress and hoped it would continue. But the pictures in the *Gazette* tell the story: neckties were generally the rule.

Although female dress appeared casual, it usually was not, being a casualness carefully studied, elegantly sweatered, and almost always with skirts. Slacks were rarely seen at classes. Some young women were dressed in a fashion quite breathtaking, and almost certainly so intended. One young professor of English had in one of his classes a beautiful Canadian princess who came nearly always three minutes late, usually clad in a fur coat, the rest of her ensemble to match. When she arrived, all communication between the professor and his class stopped. Some senior professors were less susceptible. Burns Martin of King's (English), a fierce but talented grammarian, preferred brilliant women in his classes; they seemed to tolerate his occasional frankness. Engineers loved him. Martin delighted in such novels as Hawthorne's *Scarlet Letter*, Flaubert's *Madame Bovary*, Tolstoy's *Anna Karenina*, all on fallen women. On the other hand, most Dalhousie professors were careful not to strain recognized conventions too far.[4]

From time to time, there were laments about what some perceived as lack of college spirit. Dalhousie was a city university and its student life inevitably reflected the diversities, disparities, and distances of Halifax. Dalhousie was also different from the other universities – Acadia, Mount Allison and St Francis Xavier; they were residential colleges; virtually everyone in them was from out of town. They had few cliques, nothing to compare, for example, to the Queen Elizabeth High School clique at Dalhousie. Moreover, at Dalhousie the professional schools tended to segregate themselves, with their own functions and *esprit de corps*; those professional students that came from Acadia or St Francis Xavier were not so much part of Dalhousie as belonging to a tightly knit group in the Law School or Medical School. These were distances and separations at Dalhousie as much mental as physical.

Dalhousie was also older in tone and attitude. As H.L. Scammell, out of Pictou County and Dalhousie registrar from 1947 to 1952, remarked, "Students who came here from high schools, or colleges like high schools, felt that the atmosphere at Dalhousie was by comparison, cool, restrained and stuffy. It was difficult for us to realize that we were to act like adults and be treated like adults." To C.L. Bennet, the spirit of a college revealed itself by the absence of obtrusive display of college spirit. In the 1920s, he recalled, two student leaders called a well-advertised meeting to discuss "What's wrong with Dalhousie?" and drew a total attendance of five. Dalhousie students had enough common sense, said Bennet, to realize that "little good has ever been done by mass meetings, vigilance committees and pep rallies." Dalhousie's students were "quiet and restrained, self-contained and self-sufficient." It was not a bad description.[5]

Nevertheless Dalhousie students, like most, loved to poke fun, needle academic government, occasionally test tolerances. A *Gazette* offering, "The Miracle of Sunova Beach," in January 1953 set the university on its ear. Written by "S.O.S.," it was a burlesque on the Miracle of Fatima, the Portuguese village north of Lisbon where a new basilica, dedicated to the Virgin Mary, was being consecrated that year. The "Sunova Beach" story was about a drunk who saw two suns and persuaded others in a similar condition that they were seeing a miracle. Since 15 per cent of Dalhousie students were Catholics, and Halifax had two Catholic universities and a considerable Catholic population, the repercussions can be imagined. One young lady in second-year law remarked that "S.O.S." was something you cleaned pots with, and recommended the author do the same. The pages of the *Gazette* for the next three weeks rang with similar messages. President Kerr wrote complaining not only of the article but of the time he had had to devote to people whom the article had offended. On 3 February, with almost the whole *Gazette* devoted to letters, the editor closed the correspondence down. The Senate Discipline Committee met and reminded the editor of the *Gazette* of his duty to consult the Student Advisory Committee if any article promised to be controversial. The editor replied, too ingenuously, that he had not thought "Sunova Beach" was. There it ended.[6]

In the autumn of 1953 there was a row over initiation. George Grant, chairman of the Student Advisory Committee, had succeeded in establishing a rule that "hazing that inflicts personal indignity upon any student is not in accordance with the true conception of the university." Grant banned such goings on, leaving only the wearing of beanies optional, aiming at an initiation without indignities and without compulsion. Students did not take kindly to his rules. The real indignities were probably few, although at an open forum on 13 October 1953, Grant cited from other universities a litany of broken ribs, mental anguish, cold water baths, cod liver oil hair rubs, and such. Although conceding the importance of student opinion, he held the freedom and dignity of the individual student had priority. Senate's action, the *Gazette* admitted a year later, came as the result of some personal indignities. Nevertheless in February 1955 it urged the return of initiation, promising the absence of oil, molasses, flour, or other noxious substances. Professor John Graham of Economics claimed that it had not been Senate's intention to ban initiation but simply to stop hazing, that is, "all elements of compulsion." So in the autumn of 1955 initiation returned, largely shorn of excesses, although these would resurface from time to time as they had for the past ninety years.[7]

Professors and Their Lives

Between the years 1951 and 1957 Dalhousie had a full-time staff of about fifty in Arts and Science, eighteen in Medicine, seven in Law, and one lone full-time professor in Dentistry, the professions relying heavily on part-time lecturers from downtown, who were also paid a pittance. Most Dalhousie professors were also paid very modestly and lacked outside income. The younger ones looked forward to a spartan life of genteel poverty; as the *Mail-Star* pointed out in 1957, "some lecturers get less than [the] janitor who sweeps out the classroom, assistant professors less than plumbers." Older professors assessed their pensions ruefully, hoping that they might somehow, against all the evidence, meet the costs rising up around them. The preoccupations of the 1920s and the years of penury since 1930 had exacted their toll, not only on salaries, but also on the library, breaking its runs of periodicals, squeezing its purchases of books. The sciences, pure, applied, and medical, had to get along with antiquated equipment; a professor of biochemistry had to apply to his dean even to get a new beaker. The amount of money and time available for research was meagre.

The new Arts Building, opened in the autumn of 1951, demonstrated to faculty and students the priorities of president and board. The building was needed as accommodation, but every stone seemed to carry its price, as if each were holding down some part of the faculty's thin budget for salaries. It seemed to bear out J. McG. Stewart's remarks when he laid the cornerstone on 15 November 1949: "Poverty is a badge of every good college ... It forces us to prefer simplicity to profusion." Stewart made a virtue of necessity, but Alistair Fraser, on the board since 1952, regretted that the carrying charges for the $600,000 necessary to finish paying for the building precluded "doing anything for raising staff salaries." Even professors' cars parked behind the big new building were an ironic juxtaposition. They were

Princess Elizabeth signing Dalhousie's guest book, November 1951. In three months she would be Queen. From l. to r., Miss Lola Henry (the president's secretary), Princess Elizabeth, the Duke of Edinburgh, and Colonel K.C. Laurie, Chairman of the Board.

usually ancient ones that limped through the world trailing the smell of burnt oil and ancient seat covers. New cars seemed to belong either to the president or to a student who had temporarily sequestered the family car.[8]

Dalhousie was a small university by Canadian standards, with fourteen hundred students, about two-thirds of the enrolment at Queen's. There were limitations to smallness; it was certainly possible to be, as Principal Mackintosh of Queen's put it, "cosy but second-class." Most Dalhousie professors fought hard to make Dalhousie better than cosy, trying to keep it abreast of the great world of learning and science, but the facilities available were nearly always inadequate.

Dalhousie had always allowed its professors, even younger ones, considerable room to follow their bent. A junior professor would be assigned the classes the department wanted taught, but told little about how or what to teach in it. Lectures, examinations, essays, were given, set, marked, according to the professor's lights. Freshman classes were normally taught by experienced senior professors, their character and traditions gradually made manifest to junior staff. Failure rates were heavy enough in first-year classes, especially at Christmas. The students' most salutary day of reckoning was the first day of classes in January, when the Christmas marks went up, as Sam Peeps put it, on the "Great Weeping Wall" in the Arts Building. One could note the following passing rates in freshman classes at Christmas, 1954:

Class	No. of students	Passing rate (%)
English 1	137	65
English 1A	50	38
History 1	96	70
Latin 1	38	42
French 1	88	49
Psychology 1	84	85
Economics 1	69	64
Mathematics 1	202	52
Biology 1	153	55
Chemistry 1	191	57
Geology 1	53	43
Physics 1	185	53

There was only one soft option (Psychology) in that list! A too generous passing ratio was apt to be considered a reflection of a too great naiveté or too low standards. Fundamentally the young professor was thrown upon his or her own resources and made to feel the weight of responsibility.[9]

That had been a long tradition, the independence of the professor, old and young. Various professors in ancient days had commented on it, MacGregor, Seth, MacMechan; some professors had exploited it, such as H.L. Stewart, and had gradually brought philosophy low in consequence; the contumely of his colleagues was the price he paid for radio and publication fame. This tradition of academic independence probably came from the Senate's role in the university's academic life. The board provided the money and overall legal sanction for everything that was done: the academic authority was worn by the professors in Senate. Senate was not easily aroused and a wise president usually went to some pains to take it into his confidence. Carleton Stanley had never really learned that. It remained to be seen if his successor was skilful enough to manage it. Though formally composed of all full professors and heads of departments, about fifty in all, it was in fact a working group of about twenty-five members, meeting once a month from October until May. In the early 1950s it developed a stronger bond as its distrust slowly grew of the ways and means of President Kerr.

Although Dalhousie had increased in size since the 1930s, the smallness and the essential kindliness of the place lingered. For new assistant professors, breathless from a long, hard run at a single discipline, the collegiality of Dalhousie could be exhilarating. Young professors could explore other disciplines, other faculties, go to each others' lectures, watch experiments. Over the winters, they could skate in the new Dalhousie rink, except on Sunday when it was severely closed; there was also skating out-of-doors at Chocolate Lake, Frog Pond, Williams Lake, or the marvellous reaches of the Dartmouth Lakes. Dinner parties allowed young faculty to meet old. Faculty wives were often good cooks, and faculty bachelors watched and imitated. Dinner parties could be punctuated with periodic hunts in the *Britannica* (eleventh edition, of course) to settle some point of learning, or to a row of Baedekers.

Through it all the younger men, especially those on the arts side of Arts and Science, were taught to distrust publication. The Arts professors at Dalhousie who had published could be numbered on the fingers of one hand: Lyall, Schurman, MacMechan, H.L. Stewart, three of them philosophers. Stewart had brought publishing into disrepute. At Dalhousie one read one's subject. Publication was the refuge of drones; German academics had started it, and American ones had taken it up with enthusiasm. So they chiselled their cherry stones, and published their little pieces in the academic journals. What mattered in Arts at Dalhousie was not adding a meagre drop to the ocean of truth, but to measure its depths and distances. In the

The first Senate meeting, January 1952, in its new A. and A. home. Front row seated, l. to r., Dixie Pelluet, Dean Horace Read (Law), Dean J.H.L. Johnstone (Graduate Studies), C.L. Bennet, President A.E. Kerr, Dean George Wilson (Arts and Science), Dean J.S. Bagnall (Dentistry), Dr H.L. Scammell (Registrar), Dean H.G. Grant (Medicine). Back row, standing, l. to r., H.P. Bell, C.B. Weld, D.J. Tonning, C.H. Mercer, W.J. Chute, H.R. Theakston, W.R. Lederman, R.S. Cumming, J.H. Aitchison, John A. Aldous, George Grant, A.S. Mowat, G.V. Douglas, R.S. Hayes, C. Lamberston, Burns Martin, A.K. Griffin, J.A. McCarter, Charles Walmsley.

1950s what a professor wrote did not matter all that much; it was his or her reading, the weight of knowledge that counted. In Arts it could be said that all generations in the past were equidistant from the present, that Plato, Dante, Shakespeare, Descartes, Goethe, Tolstoy were each severally relevant to the world of learning, their value measured by their substance, not by their distance from a too obtrusive present.

The Dalhousie Sciences

Science was fundamentally different, cumulative in essence. Truth was what the latest research said it was. Archimedes, Newton, Faraday, Pasteur, Osler, Fleming were of historical interest, but they counted only as history. Good Dalhousie science was research science and so measured. J.G. MacGregor, Dalhousie's first Munro professor of physics, was elected Fellow of the Royal Society, London, on the basis of his research; A.S. MacKenzie crossed over from research to administration probably because he could not command the money, apparatus, or time at Dalhousie. J.H.L. Johnstone made his reputation in experimental physics that developed into practical naval research. W.J. Archibald (BA '33, MA '35), brought to Dalhousie in 1943 to underpin physics while Johnstone and Henderson were on war research, believed the physics he had learned in the 1930s was well out of date; Dalhousie was still teaching Niels Bohr's atomic theory that dated from the First World War. Archibald believed that it was probably impossible to build a great research department in Nova Scotia, simply because Dalhousie lacked the critical mass.[10]

Dalhousie's Department of Chemistry also had good men, beginning with George Lawson and Ebenezer Mackay; its first research professor, Douglas McIntosh, was a considerable scientist, who left to direct research at Shawinigan Chemicals. His successor, more teacher than researcher, was C.B. Nickerson, head of the department from 1930 to 1940, and dean of arts and science from 1936 to 1940, who had published one good paper on inorganic analysis. He spent his summers at Boothbay Harbour in Maine, and was known as the "Rural Dean." But his successor, Carl Coffin (BA '24), was an experimentalist, ingenious and efficient. Elected a member of the Royal Society of Canada at the age of thirty-two, he became Harry Shirreff professor of chemical research. The main bent of his work was the application of radioactive tracers to chemical processes. By 1945 he was wholly preoccupied with the flood of veterans which saturated Chemistry with the biggest classes of any in Arts and Science, taking up, it was said, every broom closet and lavatory. Though well liked both as a chemist and a person, Coffin had what Henry Fielding used to call "an amiable weakness," that could produce domestic consequences not so amiable. One night in 1948, working in the laboratory, he drank methyl alcohol mistaking it for ethyl. By the morning in hospital he was blind. He continued to work and to publish, but died in 1954 at the age of fifty-one.[11]

Another Dalhousie professor with such problems was Professor Raymond Bean, appointed in 1923 to be a one-man department of Histology and Embryology in the Medical Faculty, his PH.D. incomplete. His wife Elizabeth, in the same field, had hers and had several publications to her credit. After producing a daughter, she went to work as Bean's assistant in 1927, with the full approval of President MacKenzie. By the end of the 1930s Bean's research had largely stopped because of his alcoholism, the burden of his teaching supported by his talented and devoted wife. That arrangement came to an end in 1951; Laurie and Kerr had had enough of his binges and he was retired with his wife.[12]

The Department of Geology was eccentric. G.V. Douglas, the Carnegie professor whom Carleton Stanley hired in 1935, liked tramping the hills and rocks of Nova Scotia and Labrador. The female student taking Geology 1 as her compulsory science course was advised to buy the tallest-lacing boots she could find and wear them every day of the week including Sunday. Douglas's science was rudimentary and his geology too close to handbooks. He once found some strange blue rocks in Labrador and sent them to Toronto for analysis, to be told that the seagulls had been eating lots of blueberries that summer![13]

A stronger science department was Biology, headed after 1930 by Hugh Bell, a botanist appointed in 1920. Genial, noisy, and well-liked, he was a good researcher. Dalhousie was fortunate in replacing the talented and notorious Gowanloch, fired in 1930, with Ronald Hayes, a terse, able, demanding, fishery zoologist. When Bell retired in 1954, Hayes became head of the department. His specialty was comparative vertebrate anatomy, one of the toughest of the science courses, and required of all prospective medical students. If a student were very good, Hayes would try to persuade him to go on in zoology, though often his best students ended up as doctors of medicine. He was also death on illiteracy. At an oral examination on the anatomy of a cat, Hayes pointed to something and asked his student, "What is it?" "That," said the student from Guysborough County, "is your renal artery." A nerve was pointed out. "That is your sciatic nerve." The answers were correct, but the student failed. He asked why. Hayes said, brutally, "They were not mine; they were the cat's." It was understood that doctors should be literate.[14]

Women Faculty Members

In 1934 Ronald Hayes married Dixie Pelluet, the assistant professor of biology, an able specialist in cell biology. They became a husband-and-wife team of substance and reputation. She had been appointed in 1931 on her own merits by President MacKenzie, who had formed a well-developed respect for women academics while professor at Bryn Mawr. The couple had no children and worked as professional academics. In 1941 Dixie Pelluet was made associate professor by Carleton Stanley, a promotion he said was both deserved and belated, though without an increase in salary. Not only could Dalhousie not afford it, but there was a general view in society, stemming from the depression, that two jobs in one family was taking more from the economy than it should decently stand. Thus the attitude to hiring and keeping married female professors was based on what was perceived as a double taxing of the limited job market.

President Kerr feared women on the faculty, especially clever and articulate ones like Dixie Pelluet; she was never deterred by social niceties from speaking her mind with startling clarity. In 1949 Dalhousie adopted as future policy not to employ both husband and wife on permanent staff above the rank of lecturer. While this did not apply to Dixie, she felt the burden of the attitude. In 1949 at the age of fifty-three, doing excellent work both in teaching and research, she felt her promotion to full professor long overdue. Both Dr Kerr and Colonel Laurie went to see her in December 1949 to explain that a new pay scale, effective 1 January 1950, by which associate professors would get $4,000 a year, would not apply to her. Not only did she not get promoted, she would not even get the new salary for her old rank. What she got was $250 raise in pay. She was not pleased. "You should feel," she told them, "that I have been kind to you in not becoming very angry." Three years later she reiterated that she was being unjustly penalized for being a woman, "which I cannot help," and by being married to another Dalhousie professor, "which is my private concern and does not interfere with the fulfilling of my academic duties." The board had also added an anti-feminist rule in 1946, which decreed that retirement for women was to be at sixty years of age, though in exceptional circumstances they might continue until sixty-five. As it turned out, under a different president, Dixie Pelluet retired when she was almost sixty-eight.[15]

Kerr did not like husband-and-wife combinations. When Dean Wilson thought of hiring a young woman to teach English, he told the president, "Do not be frightened. She is not married to a member of the staff and she was a remarkably fine student." But even with single women professors, President Kerr feared difficulties might arise.

Dr Louise Thompson, formerly head of psychology at the University of New Brunswick, was hired in 1949 as a clinical psychologist under a federal health grant. She did not stay single. At Christmas 1951 she married a Halifax businessman and in June 1953 presented Dalhousie with its first case of a pregnant professor. The baby was due in October and Dr Louise Thompson Welch (as she now was) wanted to go on three-fifths time and three-fifths salary after the baby was born, continuing her classes and supervising research. President Kerr and Colonel Laurie reacted to this proposal in old-fashioned ways. They were aghast that any "woman teacher, in an advanced state of pregnancy" would appear before innocent students at Dalhousie. Dean Wilson thought in ordinary circumstances having a baby ought to end a woman's appointment. "She can't eat her cake and have it too," was his metaphor for it. But Dr Welch's circumstances were not ordinary; she was a full professor with tenure, in a government-supported position. Wilson therefore suggested they leave well enough alone; change might invite attention from the government and "our rivals might even take advantage from the fact." Let Dr Welch have her baby and start her classes two weeks late; they were mostly for advanced students anyway. That was the way it worked out. Dr Welch took three-fifths time for 1953–4 and had two advanced classes. With the support of Hilton Page, head of psychology, she did exactly what she said she would do. But after discussion in 1956 between Senate and board the president got what he wanted – that marriage by a woman faculty member was deemed to terminate her appointment, though the university might propose continuance under special contract. Thus the old ethos continued to prevail. Married women ought to be at home; if they thought and did otherwise they had to make their way as best they could. It was not easy.[16]

The Evolution of Federal Support for Universities

Although federal health grants were added to Dalhousie's strength and diversity after 1949, it was still dependent on endowment; in 1953–4 endowment, with a book value of $5 million and a market value of $7.5 million, gave Dalhousie 22 per cent of its income. The AUCC estimated the norm for Canadian universities was 8 per cent. Provincial grants, nearly all of it for medicine and dentistry, accounted for 16 per cent as against the AUCC norm of 33 per cent. Fees accounted for 44 per cent of Dalhousie's income. Income from veterans' fees and support grants had been 10 per cent in 1951, but fell rapidly as veterans completed their degrees, though there was a slight bulge in medicine and dentistry into 1952 and 1953. By 1953–4 Dalhousie's income from veterans' fees was down to 2 per cent.[17]

This era of declining numbers and increasing costs squeezed the universities badly and as early as 1948 the AUCC began putting pressure on the federal government. The initiative for the Royal Commission on the Arts, Letters and Sciences came from student Liberals, who proposed it to the Liberal leadership convention of August 1948 that chose Louis St Laurent as successor to Mackenzie King. Brooke Claxton, minister of national defence, took it up and so did Jack Pickersgill, the prime minister's influential secretary. The Massey Commission reported in June 1951. It was a remarkable survey, perhaps the most remarkable of the many royal commissions sponsored by the federal government since Confederation. Donald Creighton described its view of Canadian cultural life, past and present, in his opulent prose: "The Massey Commission surveyed this dismal [cultural] scene with panoramic amplitude and pitiless detail." The recommendation it brought forward with the greatest reluctance was the one the St Laurent government first seized upon. "I think many of us recognize increasingly," he said to the University of Toronto in October 1950, "that some means must be found to ensure to our universities the financial capacity to perform the many services which are required in the interest of the whole nation." Within the Massey Commission Larry MacKenzie of UBC pushed that policy hard; two others, Hilda Neatby, professor of history at the University of Saskatchewan, and Georges-Henri Lévésque, dean of social sciences at Laval, came round to the same way of thinking, and in the end Massey accepted it.[18]

On 19 June 1951, St Laurent announced that for the academic year 1951–2 each province would be given 50 cents per head of population for its universities. That formula severely penalized Nova Scotia, which had more university students per capita than any other province. By this formula in 1953–4 Newfoundland received $477.56 per student, Ontario $144.55, and Nova Scotia $89.70, the lowest in the country. Dalhousie's share came to $109,572.40. For a principle that was national in concept, this formula created ten different rates for ten different provinces. Nova Scotia MPs protested, especially Colonel S.R. Balcom, MP for Halifax and a member of the Dalhousie board, and George Nowlan, MP for King's, on the Acadia board. But constitutional impediments to revising the formula proved insurmountable.

Thus did the Nova Scotian universities get federal funding. And though it was in a highly unsatisfactory form, compared to what other Atlantic provinces universities received, it was a great deal better than nothing. It did not, however, cure Dalhousie's chronic annual deficit, nor the accumulated shortfalls from building projects. As of 30 June 1954, Dalhousie's total accumulated deficit was $852,668.

The cost of running the Medical Faculty was especially burdensome. In 1953–4 the four Atlantic provinces together contributed 23 per cent of its total cost of $525,786 but with gross disproportions, Nova Scotia paying almost three-quarters, New Brunswick only one-sixth. Federal health grants, channelled through the provinces, had begun in 1949–50, and contributed 20 per cent; Halifax chipped in $20,000, or 4 per cent, for the Public Health Clinic. That left Dalhousie somehow having to supply the remaining 53 per cent.

President Kerr and the Medical Faculty, 1953–4

Every university president whose jurisdiction comprehends a medical faculty tends to fear it; the scale, costs, necessities (real or alleged), habits of working and thinking, are all very different from arts, and they require experience, intelligence, and patience to understand and weigh. Doctors are used to wielding authority and turf wars among them are not infrequent, aggravated by being about money as well as status. The dean of medicine since 1932, H.G. "Pat" Grant, was genial and easy-going, apt to embrace new projects, taking on more than circumstances warranted. But he had a perceptive eye for good people. Dalhousie could not always import able doctors, and where possible it liked to grow its own. Grant kept track of exceptional students, encouraged them to go abroad for specialized training, and trusted that their Nova Scotian roots would bring them back.

Robert Orville Jones was quintessential Nova Scotian, out of Bridgetown High School, who worked in the summers at Digby Pines, which his father managed. While there in the summer of 1930 he took a young waitress for a walk to Point Prim; as they were sitting on a lobster pot admiring the view, he kissed her and promptly announced that he was going to medical school and couldn't marry her for six years! They were married in 1937. Encouraged by Dean Grant and Benge Atlee, Jones went to London for postgraduate training in psychiatry. He and his wife were back in Canada in the summer of 1939, planning to return to London in late August in the *Athenia*, when he was told he had been awarded a two-year fellowship at Johns Hopkins. So they called off their return to London. It was as well they did, for the *Athenia* was sunk on 3 September by a German submarine, with the loss of 112 lives. At Johns Hopkins Jones studied under Adolf Meyer, a Swiss who was much influenced by the Harvard psychologist William James.

With the help of the Nova Scotia Department of Health, Jones was brought back to Halifax as assistant professor of psychiatry in 1941. He wore doctrines pragmatically, as William James had done. He liked to remind medical students of Dr Hattie's philosophy that one-third of the patients coming into their offices in future would suffer from no organic illness at all. By 1948 he managed to establish the Dalhousie Department of Psychiatry, and from there developed community psychiatry in eastern Canada. In 1951–2 he became the first president of the Canadian Psychiatric Association. That was when he was offered a professorship at the University of Colorado, where the increase in financial rewards would be considerable; but he had built up a strong department at Dalhousie and wanted to stay with it. A decade later, in 1966, he would refuse the University of Toronto on the same grounds. It was a good indication of Jones's character that he used neither the Colorado offer nor the Toronto one as a bargaining counter for more money, only for better facilities for psychiatry at the Victoria General. He was the only psychiatrist ever to be made president of the Canadian Medical Association in 1965–6.

Another Grant appointment of the Carleton Stanley years was Dr Richard Lorraine de Chasteney Holbourne Saunders (1908–1995), a young South African. Born in Grahamstown of Scottish parents (his father was a doctor) Saunders ended at Edinburgh, where he studied medicine and became lecturer in anatomy from 1933 to 1937. Dalhousie needed a new man in anatomy, and the Campbell professor since 1930, Dr Donald Mainland, was in Britain in 1937 and found Saunders. He came in January 1938.

Saunders set up the Medical Museum that same year. In 1948 he was made professor of pathological anatomy and director of medical museums, an appointment that may have owed something to developing strains between Saunders and Mainland. Saunders was ambitious and was never prone to underestimate his own talents; he also liked to make sure that others didn't either. At times he could be a terrible curmudgeon. Mainland gradually found that he couldn't stand Saunders, and in 1950 left to take an appointment at the Bellevue Centre in New York. Beecher Weld (1899–1991), professor of physiology, remarked that it was the only occasion where he had seen a junior man drive out the senior one. Saunders in 1950 took over Mainland's job as Campbell professor of anatomy, and celebrated the occasion by carving the Dalhousie mace, for he was a man of many talents. He would be professor of anatomy for the next twenty-three years.

Saunders was a consummate stylist; he fascinated students not only with his lectures but with his anatomical drawings, using both hands at once. His anatomy teaching was well ahead of its time, ranging well into physiology. He was European in manner, and expected much from his students, often more than they could deliver. Authoritarian he was. Professors of anatomy, observed Dr Rudolph Ozere, have tended to be that way for several centuries. Who can dispute their

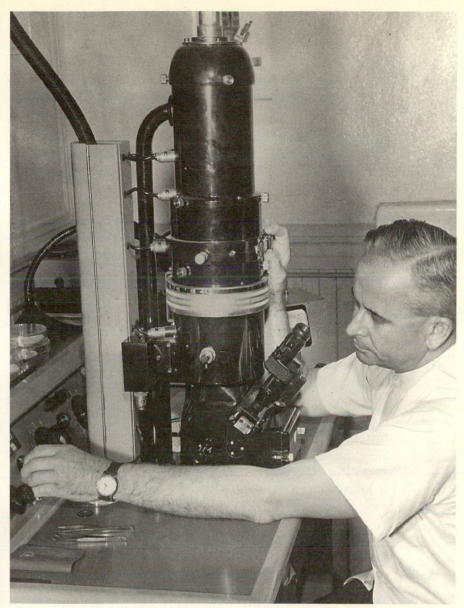

R.L. deC.H. Saunders, Professor of Anatomy, 1937–74, with the new electron micro-
scope.

expertise in their dissections of the human cadaver? As Saunders grew older, his authoritarian style became more pronounced; but to the end of his long Dalhousie career he was an exceptional and forward-looking anatomist.

President Carleton Stanley had left Dean Grant to do his own thing down at the Forrest Building, not much liking medicine, doctors, or the financial burden they imposed on Dalhousie. But President Kerr from the beginning set about establishing control over the Faculty of Medicine. As Dean Grant grew older he grew more casual, and when President Kerr started to interfere in many matters that might well have been considered within the dean's compass, Grant let him. When R.O. Jones requested a part-time secretary, Kerr met him on the street, told him the board had approved it, and added, "Let me know when you have candidates to interview." Kerr wanted to be there; Jones could not even select his own secretary. Some doctors said that Kerr would insist on interviewing cleaners and support staff.

Kerr also wanted to give prior approval to medical research grant applications. One of a list of topics discussed with Dean Grant in 1951 was whether a medical professor could initiate research grant applications without the president's (and the dean's) approval. Grant did not mind, but the president did. Kerr could also be picayune. One day in 1951 he summoned heads of all medical departments to an emergency meeting. "Gentlemen," said he portentously, "I have called you here today to discuss an emergency … the Faculty has a $7,000 deficit!" (It was 1 per cent of the total faculty budget.) Dr Benge Atlee, head of obstetrics and gynaecology, blew up. "J-J-Jesus Christ, Dr. Kerr, did you call us all up here to talk about measly $7,000? I'm a busy man, Dr. Kerr – We're all busy men. Call us when you have something serious to talk about!"[19]

Kerr irritated people by meanness in little things. Dean Grant, due to retire in 1954, applied in December 1953 for a $250 travel grant to attend, as he always had done, the meeting of the Association of American Medical Colleges, the last time he would go as dean. The president refused. He said that with Grant's retirement so near at hand the $250 expenditure could not be justified.[20]

Early in 1953 both faculty and president agreed to look for a new dean of medicine. An advisory committee to president and dean was struck for that and other questions. Composed of seven respected senior and junior members, it wanted a good deal of input about the new dean. An inside candidate was Dr Chester Stewart, professor of epidemiology; the leading outside one came to be Dr O.H. Warwick, a New Brunswick Rhodes scholar, then on the medical faculty of the University of Toronto. Warwick visited Halifax not only as a possible dean of medicine but also as possible head of the Victoria General's Department of Medicine, and thus of Dalhousie's Department of Medicine.[21]

The Department of Medicine – as distinct from the faculty – dealt with human diseases and their cure by non-surgical means, in many ways the centre of any medical faculty. The head of medicine at Dalhousie and at the Victoria General Hospital was Dr Clyde Holland (BA '21, MDCM '23), by 1945 the J.C. Tory professor of medicine, its first "geographic full-time" member. That meant the doctor accepted severe restriction on his private practice, limited generally to two afternoons a week. Dr Holland was a fine clinician but no administrator, and failed to share his clinical knowledge in ward work. Dean Grant was considering replacing him when in 1952 Holland had a heart attack and resigned, leaving the headship of the Department of Medicine in the hands of an interim committee. The departmental problem was made worse by the resignation of one of its only research men, Dr Martin Hoffman, who despite strenuous efforts to retain him, resigned in 1952 to go to McGill. Rumour was that Hoffman found disagreeable the anti-semitism in some of the older doctors he had to work with.[22]

Dr Warwick came to Halifax in October 1953 to survey the ground. He wanted to be both head of the department and dean of the faculty; without both combined he would not accept. By that time the faculty's advisory committee had concluded that the two positions together created a load impossible for one man, that combining them meant inefficiency in one or the other. When President Kerr visited Dr Warwick in Toronto in late November he discovered his persistence in wanting both positions. Kerr decided he would have to approach the local candidate for dean, Dr Chester Stewart.[23]

Stewart's candidacy arose from his competence, perceptiveness, and patience. Like most able men he had had opportunities to move: Ottawa wanted him at the Department of National Health, and Saskatchewan wanted him to stand as candidate for its dean of medicine. But he liked Halifax and his candidacy was supported by friends, well represented on the medical advisory committee. At the core of Stewart's support was an informal social world, centred in drinks and talk in each others' kitchens and dining rooms, but represented more openly by the Izaak Walton Club of Dalhousie. It was an informal group that went every May, after examinations and convocations, to the woods and lakes for fishing. Old Dean Grant was the moving spirit; he, John Aldous of Pharmacology, Beecher Weld of Physiology, and Chester Stewart of Preventive Medicine, had started the club in 1948 and it lasted with subsequent additions until 1976.

The only rule was that there be absolutely no mention of Dalhousie, the medical school, or medicine. Fishing mornings began with Grant's "Eye-Opener": a good jigger of gin, a quarter lemon in a quarter glass of water, with a heaping teaspoon of Eno's Fruit Salts added for fizz. It fizzed all right inside and out. Delivered to club members still in their sleeping bags, the CO_2 in the Eno's speeded mightily the distribution of alcohol. In a few minutes all were warm from head to toe. The club says much about Dean Grant's way with younger members of his faculty, of whom Stewart was one, though it may have had only indirect influence on Stewart's actual appointment as dean.[24]

All that was pending when the revolt of the Faculty of Medicine, brewing for several months, broke into the open in January 1954. A number of issues faced the faculty, of which the deanship was only one: the low salaries of full-time professors, the lack of research policy, and, not least, a woeful lack of physical space. Research in the medical sciences was choking for lack of space. In a blistering report in 1953, J.A. McCarter of Biochemistry pointed out that while Dalhousie got 97 per cent of the research funds it asked for from the National Research Council (as against Queen's 66 per cent), it was last of thirteen Canadian universities in the average value of its grants. Researchers could not request bigger grants because they could not use them.

But what drove the revolt was the insistent, narrow perspectives of President Kerr. Fundamentally the faculty wanted more autonomy for its dean and its professors, especially in a faculty so specialized, so different as medicine. Too many matters about salaries, appointments, technical personnel were being held up in the president's office at Studley – matters that could have been settled quickly by a good dean. What especially irked the faculty was the president's regular visitations to its meetings. Indeed, Dr Kerr insisted that without him no faculty meeting could properly take place. That kept him in touch with medical issues, about which, as a theologian, he had much to learn. Perhaps he learned too confidently; by the 1950s he would not infrequently pre-empt Dean Grant's function as chairman of faculty.[25]

The meeting called for 26 January promised to be rough. Dean Grant had three scotches before he came. President Kerr was scotchless, pale, but stood his ground. Whatever else he was, Kerr was not craven. Many of the medical professors were angry, Dr Atlee not least. The coolest but most resolute was Dr Norman Gosse, who told the president he would do well to remember the fate of Charles I of England. The resolutions, passed unanimously by faculty, comprehended wide changes. The president and Board of Governors should function like the governor general of Canada, with the dean and his council as the effective cabinet government, taking the lead in policy, projects, curriculum, appointments, salaries, budgets. All Medical School resources unallocated should be under the control of dean and council. A statutory meeting with the Board of Governors should be held once a year.[26]

The board clearly could not concede such sweeping powers, which would have meant virtual independence for the Medical Faculty; but it had to give something. At a joint meeting of a special board committee and representatives of the Medical Faculty on 18 February 1954, the medical representatives may have pulled back a little; having presented their arguments, they retired and waited while the board group discussed them. At that point, Alistair Fraser, recently appointed to the board, now also lieutenant-governor of Nova Scotia, came out to talk to the medical committee. Fraser had no love for President Kerr: "You people had that slippery bastard in your sights, and the Board were waiting for you to shoot, but all you had in your gun was bird-shot!"[27]

The majority of the board however supported the president, as they probably had to do. Indeed, six months later they raised his salary by 25 per cent. Chester Stewart for his part was not interested, as he said, in being dean of a grade B medical school, nor even of a grade A one holding its rating by a thread, which he believed Dalhousie's was. It had to be strengthened and merely appointing a new dean would not do it. There were meetings of sub-committees from both sides at Government House under Lieutenant-Governor Fraser's auspices. Kerr gave ground with the greatest reluctance. Stewart fought a long battle over Kerr's insistence that the president have "unfettered freedom" in administering the Medical Faculty. Stewart argued that if such freedom were to exist, there was no point in having any arrangements at all. The phrase was eventually omitted. Negotiations led to compromises – some twenty-eight clauses – that had emerged by March 1954. These included devolution of authority and initiatives to the dean of medicine, which the board believed gave away little as a "constitution" to the Medical Faculty; in fact, the basic system was not changed. What was changed was the way things were done. President Kerr was instructed by Colonel Laurie that "once the new dean is installed, he is to be given a *very* free hand, even at the cost of some mistakes so as to let the present turmoil settle down." He was, and it did.

Dean Stewart was appointed in May 1954, and would remain in office for the next seventeen years. His relations with President Kerr from that time on were excellent. They travelled together occasionally and talked freely across many subjects except one – what had happened in January to March of 1954. As Stewart remarked, "that was buried and stayed buried." But the new working arrangements stood, the first serious check on the president's power.

In 1954 it had been seven years since Dean Grant had been trying, with indifferent success, to have each of the Atlantic provinces pay an annual operating grant to Dalhousie based upon the average enrolment from each province in medicine and dentistry. Newfoundland and Nova Scotia somehow managed this; New Brunswick and Prince Edward Island, which took its lead from Fredericton, dragged their feet. One of Dean Stewart's first duties was to persuade the four governments to raise the annual operating grant. Stewart and Dean McLean of Dentistry set off on their rounds, having to deal with a different (and usually indifferent) department in each government, until they got to Newfoundland. There they were shown into the office of the premier, Joey Smallwood. He sat behind a huge desk stacked high with papers, journals, merchandise, and one hip-length fisherman's rubber boot. They gave him a brief statement of Dalhousie's position and their needs. Then came Joey's turn; he fired questions like a machine-gun. He must have liked their answers, for he picked up the phone and got his deputy minister of education on the line. "I have Dr. McLean and Dr. Stewart in my office, and they are coming down to ask you for money for Dentistry and Medicine at Dalhousie. Give them what they are asking for." He then turned to the two deans and said, "We are a proud people in Newfoundland, we pay our bills. You are providing service to our students which we cannot give here, and we will pay our way." Replies from the other three provinces had been that Dalhousie had a case but cabinet would have to be consulted, and Dalhousie would have to wait. Not in Newfoundland! Old Dean Grant would have rejoiced.[28]

There was a curious and sad postscript to Dean Grant's career. His pension on retirement would be all of $100 a month, not enough to live on even in Halifax. Dalhousie pensions had originally been established through the Carnegie Corporation. When Carnegie set up the Teachers Insurance and Annuity Association (TIAA) in 1918 Dalhousie followed; but by the 1930s these pensions had failed to provide sufficient income. The board then put them into Dominion government annuities, which had not done all that well either. The board felt Dean Grant's $1,200 a year was too thin, and gave him an additional $1,300 a year as an *ex gratia* pension until his death. Before the Izaak Walton Club could go on its May 1954 expedition, before Grant had drawn a cent of retirement income, he died suddenly of a heart attack on 8 May.

Dean Stewart's best acquisition was a new head for the Department of Medicine, Robert Clark Dickson (1908–84). Negotiations were worked out in the summer of 1955, mainly concerned with the outside income to be allowed him and how much time he could devote to earning it. In the end it was agreed that the best way of limiting outside work was not by money earned but by time spent. Dickson was allowed two half days a week for that purpose, soon standard for what was designated as "geographical full-time."

In Dickson Dalhousie got an exceptional doctor and administrator, a rare combination. Dickson came from small-town Ontario, St Mary's, west of Stratford, and via good Ottawa schools had ended at the University of Toronto where he graduated with MD in 1934. For the next five years he specialized in gastroenterology. He joined the Royal Canadian Army Medical Corps in 1939, going overseas with the 48th Highlanders of Toronto, and most of the next six years he spent in North Africa and Italy, ending as head of medicine in No. 15 General Hospital, with the rank of lieutenant-colonel. At the end of the war Britain gave him an OBE. He was on staff at the University of Toronto and physician in charge of medical services at the Wellesley Hospital when the Dalhousie offer came.

Robert Dickson was a big man in more ways than one; heavy-set, hearty, generous, he enjoyed life and work, food and drink. He and his brother-in-law, J. Tuzo Wilson, sailed his yacht from Toronto to Halifax. He drove with delight his sporty red MG convertible on his hospital visits. There was nothing abstemious about Bob Dickson – not about his enthusiasms, his care for his patients, or his belief that if competence and knowledge were a doctor's most important attributes, a close third was compassion. There was no substitute, he said once, for "a hand on the shoulder, a turn in the doorway ... with a smile and a word of encouragement." That applied to staff as well as patients. Medical students named him affectionately, "Daddy" Dickson. The most striking thing about Dickson was his percipience, at judging people, needs, situations; he seemed always able to look forward a few years. He and his wife came to love Nova Scotia and his Dalhousie life; parties at the Dicksons were legendary, Dickson carving the roast and with no dearth of wine and conviviality.

Before Dickson came, the Department of Medicine was a poor cousin to surgeons and surgery, who had rather ruled the roost for the best part of a century. But remedies for human ailments by non-surgical means, which was what medicine was about, had developed remarkably. The first break was with insulin for diabetes in the 1920s. Other drugs followed at the time of the Second World War. Sulfonamides brought in medicines with a great range of curative powers. Up until then pneumonia in Canada killed 30 per cent of those who got it, including robust young adults. Sulfapyridine brought mortality from pneumonia down to 5 per cent. Penicillin and the whole spectrum of antibiotics followed and changed medicine for good. By the 1950s the Department of Medicine was potentially the most significant in the faculty. Much of that was owing to the new drugs, but not a little of what Medicine at Dalhousie became was owing to R.C. Dickson.[29]

Clyde Holland had started the practice of guaranteeing an able bright resident a Dalhousie appointment when he had completed his sub-specialty training and passed the difficult examinations of the Royal College of Physicians and Surgeons of Canada (FRCPC). Dickson selected his specialists carefully. About seven o'clock one morning a senior resident doing a pulmonary resuscitation was surprised to find the head of the department at his side. "Let me help you, Joe," said Dickson. Dr Joseph Sidorov could hardly believe Dickson even knew his name. After a successful conclusion, Dickson urged Sidorov to consider doing specialist training in gastroenterology. After weighing it up, that's what he did. Dickson also extended Holland's principle; he wanted his newly qualified specialists to do further training, abroad if necessary, his recommendations backing them up for research positions and money. Dickson would appoint them lecturers at Dalhousie with leave of absence for the time they needed, usually a year. Thus did the strong shoulders of Medicine develop in the subspecialties, among which gastroenterology, cardiology, neurology, haemotology, and nephrology that would help the Department of Medicine sustain the tremendous load of new responsibilities in the 1960s.

Relations Between Senate and Board

The quarrel between the Medical Faculty and the president had concomitants elsewhere in the university. Colonel Laurie's view of the university was simple and hierarchical; the deans reported to the president, and the president to the board. To Laurie's mind that was quite satisfactory. By this perception, the president was the critical isthmus of communication between the university and its Board of Governors. Meetings of the Six and Six, a statutory annual meeting brought in by the 1935 act, might have brought opinions to the board other than the president's; but Six and Six meetings had become pro forma or omitted altogether; they were potentially dangerous to Laurie and Kerr because Senate could thus bypass the president's control of planning, policies, problems, and balance sheets. As it was, the Senate was woefully handicapped in not knowing the financial background of buildings, endowments, or bequests. In 1949 Professor Beecher Weld asked for a joint board-Senate committee on research bequests, but Laurie replied that it was not the board's policy to have joint committees.

The July 1952 meeting of the Six and Six revealed some restiveness by the Senate members. The following dialogue ensued:

BRIGADIER LAING: The real residuum of power is in the Board. Board is the overriding authority over Senate. It has an absolute right to veto.

PROFESSOR J.H. AITCHISON: The Board could not take away the power of internal government from the Senate.

PROFESSOR BEECHER WELD: "Subject to the approval of the Board" is the natural safeguard for the Board; but Board and Senate are almost equal partners in the government of the University.

BRIGADIER LAING: The Board is supreme to the Senate.

DEAN HORACE READ: Senate is responsible for initiating policies ... Equality is subject to the overriding of the Board.

BRIGADIER LAING: Senate wants to control finances.

PROFESSOR WELD: There is no official information re finances available to members of Senate. There is not enough freedom of information. To do our duty properly in regulating the university we should know more about finances.

BRIGADIER LAING: The Board of Governors take the responsibility to say whether the university can afford anything or not.

PROFESSOR WELD: Let us record the thought that this type of meeting gives pleasure to Senate and Board. Senate can learn facts and dispel rumours that may come along regarding policies of the Board of the University.[30]

Six months later, in January 1953, Senate established a committee to study the responsibility of president, deans, and heads of departments in faculty appointments, promotions, and tenure. The committee reported to Senate in March 1954, and asked for a joint Senate-board ad hoc committee. That request aroused the opposition of some of the governors, notably J. McG. Stewart, who was "amazed that the Board would even consent to the appointment of such a committee to discuss such matters with the Senate. They have no possible right to make such a demand." He was himself unwell, but he wanted the strongest men on the board for that kind of work – men such as Laing, Gordon Cowan, Alistair Fraser, not weaker men, too close to the professors, too apt to lean in the direction of the Glasgow-Edinburgh, Oxford-Cambridge forms of university government.

Nevertheless, the regulations that emerged, approved by the board on 2 February 1956, while they revealed the board's stiffness about established systems of authority, recognized that academic freedom was "the essence of a university" and required "reasonable security of tenure for scholars." Rules for tenure were established, as well as something the board had refused in 1949: a system of sabbatical leaves every eighth year, with half pay for twelve months, or full pay for six months, on an approved research program.[31]

That such rules were established reflected changes in the board. The redoubtable J. McG. Stewart died in February 1955, leaving half his estate to his wife, and upon her death 90 per cent of the remainder to Dalhousie. Colonel Laurie, seventy-four years old and feeling it, first resigned as chairman of the board in March 1955 and, although dissuaded briefly, resigned definitely in August, though he continued on the board. The new chairman was Brigadier Horace Vivian Darrell Laing (BA '20), Dalhousie's Rhodes scholar of 1921. He had served in the two wars, earned a CBE, and had long been a power in National Sea Products. On the board since 1947, he was chairman of the board's New Construction Committee, 1947–52, and of Buildings and Grounds since that time. He was an authoritarian, but an able one, and armed with a knack for mastering complicated issues. He had a much better mind than Laurie and was a sophisticated financier. When D.H. McNeill, Dalhousie's business manager, worried aloud about Dalhousie's debt in a Board of Governors meeting, Laing remarked, "You pay attention to the books and we'll find the money."[32]

The 1954 Dalhousie-King's Agreement

One problem Laing had largely mastered was Dalhousie's relations with King's, and it was Laing, more than anyone, who was instrumental in drawing up for Dalhousie the revised agreement of association in 1954. King's, in its constant search for a raison d'être, was finding the Carnegie 1923 terms difficult to live with. On the other hand during recent years, to Dalhousie's expenditures on its new Arts Building, gymnasium, and rink, which totalled $2 million, King's had contributed exactly nothing. President Kerr had begun charitably enough disposed to King's, but when its complaints became a constant litany, his attitude hardened. In March 1952 special committees of both boards met to consider the possibilities. One was to dissolve the 1923 Dalhousie-King's federation, each university taking half of the Carnegie funds, a procedure close to illegality. King's thought the two committees should concentrate on revising the 1923 agreement, realizing that King's would gain nothing by breaking up with Dalhousie. Laing put his finger on three main points: King's recognition of Dalhousie as the central university; the status of the Carnegie grant, the income from which was to be used to the benefit of both institutions; and the payment by King's of its fair share of Dalhousie's cost of educating King's students. Dalhousie felt that King's had done nothing to increase its Carnegie endowment, and that whatever new monies it had acquired had been channelled into funding King's Department of Divinity.

The revised agreement was duly signed on 5 November 1954 and passed both boards. Dalhousie would apply for the government grants, remitting to King's its portion after deducting Dalhousie's costs. An accountant was charged with assessing Dalhousie's costs of educating King's students. King's could grant degrees in fields not occupied by Dalhousie, not precluding Dalhousie's future entry to them. It could also grant honorary degrees, and not just in Divinity. While the 1954 agreement did not end tensions between King's and Dalhousie, it did provide a more ample framework to resolve them. King's was never satisfied, but the reason was its age (founded in 1789, with an 1802 royal charter), its pride, and its thirst for a status remotely consonant with both. But at least there was also a new and more tractable Anglican as King's new president, Canon H.L. Puxley.[33]

The Law Faculty: Juxtaposition of Appearance and Reality

The Law School's normal capacity was seventy-five in all years; when the veterans came there were two hundred. The old practice had been to let in anyone who had the minimum qualifications, relying upon slashing numbers for quality at the end of the first year. In 1945 when A.E. Kerr first came, his dean of law, Vince MacDonald, had to confess he was the only member left of the Law School staff. Three others, all young, were hastily appointed that summer, J.B. Milner, Moffatt Hancock, and a newly graduated student, Thomas Feeney. Milner "lived in a world of balanced probabilities." His first lecture opened with the word "Suppose," then followed seventeen questions for which there were no answers. His aim was to make his students think. The most theatrical of the law professors, Moffatt Hancock, managed to dramatize even lectures in Property 1. One student wrote, "You never knew what to expect except that from each dazzling hour would come some vivid and unforgettable impression."[34]

In 1949–50 the Law School went through another of its periodic disintegrations of staff. Its history had been punctuated with similar disasters, stemming from lack of money, as in 1945, or 1934 when Sidney Smith and Horace Read both left. In 1949 Hancock left to go to California, ending up at Stanford; Milner went to Harvard for graduate work; and early in 1950 the dean himself was appointed to the Supreme Court of Nova Scotia. One unhappy concomitant of the comings and goings of staff was the constant reassignment of classes. In W.R. Lederman's nine years at Dalhousie Law School from 1949 to

1958, he taught ten different classes in both private and public law. That prevented his too early specialization and opened up new horizons, but it was hard on the professor, harder on the students, and played havoc with research. As the Law School's historian remarked, "How fragile was the base upon which Dalhousie's Little Law School's 'solid reputation' rested!"[35]

In 1949 Premier Angus L. Macdonald, knowing the parlous condition of the Law School, had provided public money for a chair in public law to which W.R. Lederman was appointed. Then Sir James Dunn, part of the Dalhousie Law School family network, as Professor Willis has called it, gave an Algoma Steel professorship in law, and money to begin a graduate program in law, whenever staff and library resources permitted it. In 1950 Dalhousie needed most of all a new dean of law; it got Horace Read.

He was the first dean of law at Dalhousie who could properly claim to be a professional law teacher. His predecessors had been co-opted as law teachers from the ranks of professional lawyers. Read came from Cumberland County, and took his BA at Acadia. There he had swept the board, but in his first year at Dalhousie, Judge W.B. Wallace failed him in torts. Read thought his career ruined; it was anything but. Within a year of graduation in 1924, he was appointed lecturer in law. Associate professor in 1933, he was awarded a research fellowship at Harvard. Though intending to return, he could not resist an offer in 1934 to go as full professor to Minnesota, one of the best law schools in the United States. President Carleton Stanley could not match that. Dalhousie was lucky to get him back in 1950; he was earning about $11,000 at Minnesota, and the best Dalhousie could offer was $7,000. But Premier Angus L. Macdonald offered a mighty sweetener – chairmanship of the Nova Scotia Labour Relations Board at $3,500. Read would remain dean, and chairman, until 1964.[36]

He came to ancient premises that he knew all too well; the Law School had occupied old rooms in the north wing of the Forrest Building ever since it had first moved there in 1888. As one student noted, they reeked of the 1880s, literally; the softwood benches, with their low backs, not at all comfortable, were seamed and gnarled with students having distracted their discomfort by carving initials. Both great and lowly were so represented.[37]

Read was shrewd, cool, knowledgeable, proud of his achievements at Minnesota, and especially proud of his Dalhousie Law School. There was not much to be proud of in 1950, but he saw it *couleur de rose*. He was never short of words either. In the *President's Report, 1950–1954*, Dean Wilson's report on Arts and Science took two pages, Dean Read's on Law twenty-two. Nor did he ignore what he

Horace Read, Dean of Law, 1950–64, Vice-President, 1946–9.

himself had been doing. Thus all was best in the best of all possible worlds as the Law School moved in 1952, at last, out of the Forrest Building to its new-old building on the Studley campus. Built in 1921, and originally intended for Law, it had just been vacated by Arts and Science in 1951. It was probably the handsomest building on campus, the Darling-Cobb architecture at its most harmonious.

A New Dean and New Building for Dentistry

Dalhousie needed a third new dean in the early 1950s, in Dentistry. Dentistry had no endowment whatever, nor any full-time professors except the dean. With Carleton Stanley's help it scrounged money from Nova Scotia in 1939, Newfoundland in 1943, and shamed Prince Edward Island and New Brunswick into it in 1947. Dean J.S. Bagnall had somehow managed to keep the faculty going, but its facilities in the Forrest Building were worse than unsatisfactory. The Canadian Dental Association, which had recently begun accreditation, visited Dalhousie in 1951 and had been severely unimpressed. Dean Bagnall much resented its unwillingness recognize Dalhousie's difficulties, but President Kerr thought Bagnall's resentment too strong, and asked him to draft a more judicious reply. In effect the Canadian Dental Association asked Dalhousie to put more money and effort into Dentistry or risk losing their status altogether.[38]

Bagnall was due to retire in 1954 and in 1952 Kerr sought help from the Canadian Dental Association for a successor. Its nominee was James D. McLean, a part-time professor at the University of Alberta, Edmonton, with a practice on Jasper Avenue. McLean was inclined, said one supporter, "to be very outspoken, a little cocky" and he did not suffer fools easily; but he had energy, determination, and talent. In July 1952 McLean came to look things over. Not that there was much, with twelve students admitted a year, a one full-time faculty member (the dean), and many dedicated part-timers. Dentistry also imperatively needed new quarters. The key members of the board, Laurie, Stewart, and Laing, accepted that and agreed to look for $500,000. Senate was extremely uneasy at this proposal, remembering the doubling of the cost of the Arts and Administration Building; they were assured, during Six and Six meetings, that the dental building would be built with "new money." McLean also wanted some time for private practice, claiming that even after a few weeks of disuse a dentist's hand loses some of its cunning. Dalhousie compromised and offered him $1,000 not to set up a practice in the first year, while he kept his hand in with clinical patients that came to the school. He came on staff in 1953, and took over when Dean Bagnall retired in 1954. The new dean's relations with president and board

The Studley campus, August 1957. Note the flag: Dalhousie flew the Union Jack, not the Red Ensign, until 15 February 1965 when the new Canadian maple leaf flag was proclaimed.

were good. The president had finally learned the necessity of letting the professional faculties do their own work with as little interference as possible.[39]

Teaching dentistry was, and is, expensive, requiring equipment and machinery of a high order. There were no teaching hospitals; Dalhousie had in effect to create its own, the Dental Clinic. Buildings compounded all of it. Yet it was extremely difficult to get government granting agencies to grasp that fact. Without the Kellogg Foundation, and increases in federal grants, the dental building could not have been built, whatever the Board of Governors might have said about "new money." Heroic efforts by the dentists themselves produced only $34,000. The cornerstone was laid in November 1956, and the building was completed and occupied in 1958. It had been projected to cost $500,000; it was double that. The best that two Maritime governments, Nova Scotia and Newfoundland, could provide was less than a quarter of that cost. New Brunswick and Prince Edward Island contributed nothing. The W.K. Kellogg Foundation of Michigan put up a full 10 per cent of the cost. But even so, Dalhousie board was still left holding the bag for 62 per cent of the building's costs.[40] So much for "new money"!

The fourth new dean was in Arts and Science. Dean Wilson, sixty-five years old in 1955, believed it was time to step down, a bit rueful that such was the way of the world. The board wanted to keep him as head of history, however, and gave him a contract to September 1958. For his successor as dean he recommended C.L. Bennet, or W.J. Archibald, or as third choice, Hayes of Zoology. Archibald took the job, hoping to reinvigorate the faculty's research orientation, get rid of dead wood, and bring in strong new staff. It was easier said than done. President Kerr was ready to accept a famous professor or two on staff but unwilling to provide the salary. In Arts and Science Dalhousie had ambitions but neither the wherewithal nor the capacity to realize them. Even outsiders recognized that somehow Dalhousie's priorities had got into stones and mortar. Archibald would find this increasingly frustrating; that fact measured the changes since 1951. The results of the medical revolt, and the slowly increasing weight of Senate, had begun to shift the balance of power against the president. New vigour in the board was generally welcomed by Senate.[41]

Sir James Dunn and Dalhousie

In August 1952 Colonel Laurie had proposed for board membership Sir James Hamet Dunn. Dunn had always taken an substantial interest in Dalhousie. He had graduated from Law School in 1898, his marks getting lower year by year, as he discovered the necessity of outside work to keep him going. His mother was a widow and a guardian uncle had squandered whatever money they had had. Once graduated, he moved into finance and made money rapidly. By 1908 Murray Macneill was soliciting him for help to bring in a professor of biology. Dunn put up $1,000 for new microscopes in 1910 and with $25,000 in 1911 helped launch the Dalhousie Forward Movement. When in 1928 R.B. Bennett started an endowment for a Weldon chair of law with $25,000, Dunn added $5,000; the stock market crash stopped the fund at $40,000 but the Bennett gift of 1943 established the Weldon chair properly. In 1949 and 1950 Dunn established two professorships in law, the Algoma Steel and the Sir James Dunn, Bart. Thus of all the many contributors to Dalhousie, Dunn was the longest serving, the most loyal, and one of the most generous. Dunn himself – irascible, headlong, harsh, sentimental, determined, and fastidious – was loyal to the end, loyal to the memory of Dean Weldon and the Law School that had nurtured him. He came on the Dalhousie board in November 1953, being assured that he was not duty-bound to be in active attendance.[42]

Sir James had had three wives. In 1901 he married Gertrude Price, who bore him five children. Divorced in 1925, he married Irene Clarice, the former Marchioness of Queensberry, in 1926, who bore him a daughter. The third Lady Dunn came in by the office door. Marcia Christoforides was hired as his secretary in June 1930 when she was twenty years old and Dunn was fifty-six. Daughter of a Greek Cypriot tobacco merchant, educated at Roedean, she was a high-mettled, handsome young woman, soon indispensable to his business and eventually his bed. In 1941 she and the second Lady Dunn worked out between them which woman was the more important to Sir James; Christofor (as she was known) won. She and Sir James were married in 1942 and were inseparable.[43] He died in St Andrews, New Brunswick, on New Year's Day, 1956, at the age of eighty-one, Christofor beside him. His estate was probated at $66 million, half of which went to her. Within three months she was in touch with Dalhousie about the records of her husband's career and his gifts. There was much more to come, and changes would follow in rapid succession.

· 8 ·

In the Fast Lane:
C.D. Howe, Lady Dunn, and Others
1957–1963

C.D. Howe becomes Dalhousie's first chancellor, 1957. Lady Dunn and the Sir James Dunn Building. Changes in the Law School. Howe's dissatisfactions with A.E. Kerr. Lady Dunn's legacy. Mrs Dorothy Killam. Howe's contributions to shaking up Dalhousie. Henry Hicks as dean of arts and science, 1960. Kerr's resignation, 1962–3.

On Monday, 10 June 1957, to his own chagrin and others' surprise, Prime Minister Louis St Laurent and his Liberal government were defeated in the federal election. It broke a Liberal regime in place since 1935. The architect of that débâcle more than anyone else was the cabinet minister who had been there since 1935, Clarence Decatur Howe. Nine Liberal ministers lost their own ridings; Howe lost his in Port Arthur, ousted by an NDP school teacher, Douglas Fisher. Howe had thought about getting out of politics in 1955 while the going was good; now he was kicked out. Still active at seventy-two years of age, he did not like it. The new Conservative government of John Diefenbaker was sworn in on 21 June, and it had an ineradicable belief that after twenty-two years of Liberal rule the public service, especially its senior ranks, were badly diseased with incurable Liberalism. For Howe, Ottawa was now insufferable and lonely, his public service friends keeping him at a discreet distance.

In July 1957 Howe gloomed his way down to his summer home in St Andrews, New Brunswick. St Andrews was not unlike Nova Scotia's Chester, Maine's Bar Harbor, Quebec's Murray Bay – a summer refuge of the rich, its social life a round of sailing, golf, bridge, and cocktails. There had long been a clutch of acquaintances in St Andrews, richer than himself, Isaac Walton Killam and Sir James

Dunn among others. The relations of Dunn and Howe had been frosty during the first years of the war, but by 1947 they had warmed to each other, and in 1953 travelled to the coronation of Elizabeth II together. There is a striking photograph of the Howes and the Dunns at a coronation reception, the ladies in tiaras, Lady Dunn looking quite as beautiful as when she married Sir James a decade before, Alice Worcester Howe the solid Yankee she had always been. In 1915 she had been startled by Howe's abrupt proposal of marriage, thought it over for four months, and agreed. The date of their 1916 wedding had been determined by Howe's priorities, a Saskatchewan provincial election and deadlines for grain elevator tenders, but Alice's strong intelligence accepted them. Behind the garden gate, Alice Howe ruled her home, five children, and a monster Port Arthur furnace.

In 1953, the year of the coronation, Dunn invited Howe to become president of Algoma Steel, an offer repeated in vain in 1955. Dunn lived at St Andrews in a large house that he called "Dayspring," with a nine-foot wall around it; it was his main Canadian home. His work was at Algoma Steel in Sault Ste Marie, but the company supplied two planes and four cars, and there was a small airport at Pennfield Ridge, thirty kilometres away from St Andrews. Thus St Andrews and the Soo came within commuting distance. Sir James died of thrombosis at "Dayspring" in January 1956, but Lady Dunn continued to live there. Howe had become part of the St Andrews summer community, joining the rich regulars in the back room at Cockburn's drugstore to gossip over the morning papers before a round of golf.

To this world Howe retreated, vast space looming in front of him. He confessed to Lady Dunn that he'd suffered a terrible blow, that he was now nothing more than a discarded politician, a gentleman of unwanted and unwonted leisure. Lady Dunn was a very rich widow, now fifty-seven years old. The death of her husband had been devastating to her; Lord Beaverbrook said she had wanted to go to a convent. He commented that she would have disliked the food and she "would certainly quarrel with the Mother Superior." Her Greek ancestry showed in her quick temper and readiness to speak her mind. She was no fool at business either, and willing to take gambles. She was well aware that she could use Howe's tremendous grip of finance and of the way things were done. She needed him. It is also fair to say that in some ways Howe needed her. No one had asked him to do anything; a company or financial institution that might have thought of him weighed up the 1956 pipeline debate and the obloquy he had acquired. Howe had been dropped out of his old world suddenly and completely.[1]

Howe Becomes Dalhousie's First Chancellor

Without much apparent warning, on 8 August 1957, Dalhousie University invited Howe to join its Board of Governors. It was the first such invitation he had received since his defeat and he was thrilled with it, and with what followed. A week later, as the result of discussions at St Andrews between Lady Dunn and President Kerr, the executive committee of the board agreed to create for Howe the office of chancellor. Howe was to be invited to assume the office "forthwith." On 29 August the full board unanimously ratified this new departure. Howe was more than willing, not only from his circumstances in August 1957, but also because he owed much to Dalhousie and its men of 1908–12, "for my introduction to Canadian life," as he put it to Archie MacMechan's widow in Chester. "Perhaps I will now be able to pay a part of the debt that I owe to Dalhousie."

Who prompted Dalhousie to act in this matter is not certain; Darrell Laing, chairman of the board, had never met Howe, but Howe's name turns up as early as 28 June 1957 in correspondence between Laing and President Kerr. It is possible that Lady Dunn suggested Howe. It is certain that once Dalhousie had resolved upon Howe for its Board of Governors, she wanted him made chancellor. Howe thanked her; he said that his appointment was

due wholly to your intervention ... I do believe that, between us, we can do much to make Dalhousie outstanding among Canadian universities. Fortunately, Dalhousie has a surprisingly high standing throughout Canada and many former students will be happy to see new life being injected into their Alma Mater.

I hope that our discussions with Dr. Kerr and Brigadier Haldenby will be productive.[2]

For C.D. Howe and Lady Dunn talked about more than Howe's becoming chancellor. He had said to her: "You should do something for Dalhousie yourself. After all your husband wanted to. Why not build the Physics building?" Thus the St Andrews discussions were also about buildings and Lady Dunn's role in funding them. The two official priorities of the board were, first, a men's residence, for which federal money was available; and second, a new science building for Physics, Engineering, and Geology. To Lady Dunn, a men's residence had little appeal; unlike Jennie Shirreff, who delighted in the prospect of imbuing young women with ideas of gracious living, Lady Dunn wanted a memorial to her husband more substantially academic. A new Law building was not yet in the cards; Law had moved into its new/old building on the Studley campus just four years before. Lady

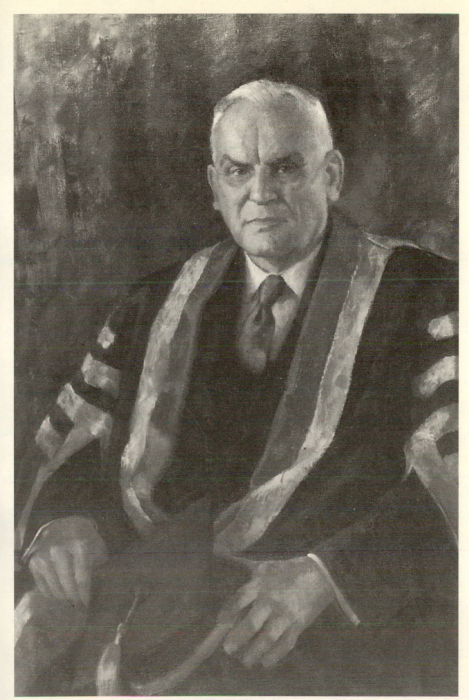

Dalhousie's official portrait of C.D. Howe as its first chancellor.

Dunn's and Howe's priority was Science and she offered substantial money, the whole cost of the building in fact. The public announcement was made within forty-eight hours of Howe's acceptance of the offer of chancellor.

Thus Howe, Lady Dunn, and the Physics building – now to be called the Sir James Dunn Science Building – all came to Dalhousie at the same time. The science building would cost $1,750,000. The architects were to be Mathers and Haldenby of Toronto, neither Howe's choice nor Lady Dunn's. They had done the Arts and Administration Building, and although it had proved lamentably leaky, a report in 1956 on its defects attributed this to the contractors rather than the architects. Early in 1957, before Lady Dunn had invested the scene with her ideas and presence, Mathers and Haldenby had prepared a model of the campus showing old buildings and proposed new ones; it was not unreasonable that Dalhousie should turn to the same firm. Dalhousie's priorities were now, however, abruptly reversed, in line with Lady Dunn's, though planning on both buildings would be started at once.[3]

Creating the Sir James Dunn Science Building
Lady Dunn, Howe, and the board came to the official sod-turning ceremony for the Dunn building on Sir James's birthday, 29 October 1957. That was fast work! Lady Dunn intended to have her memorial to her husband built and running as soon as possible, consistent, that is, with her demands for quality in materials and in construction. There was to be nothing slipshod in anything. She drove the enterprise and all connected with it hard – architects, engineers, contractors, university officials, and C.D. Howe. It was all they could do to keep up with her. She claimed her aggressiveness was apt to show when she was trying to shake off "an overwhelming depression." If so, Howe endeavoured to combat it, especially relating to her finances. The steep succession duties made her feel she was gobbling up her capital too rapidly. Then there was her income; Howe patiently explained that the Sir James Dunn Foundation, being a charitable trust, had to spend 90 per cent of its income on charity each year. For now, the bulk of that would be going to Dalhousie for the Sir James Dunn Science Building. He assured her she was doing well financially and would do better. She had sold her Algoma Steel shares at what would be for a long time the top of the market, and her future problems would come not from having too little income but from too much. At Dalhousie, Howe said, she was already thought of as the "Guardian Angel" of the university, and she would derive great satisfaction from her association with it.[4]

C.D. Howe laying the cornerstone of the men's residence, October 1959.

But despite Howe, it was not smooth going. It became a parallelo-
gram of forces: Lady Dunn (and her Montreal lawyer W.H. Howard),
President Kerr, Mathers and Haldenby, J.H.L. Johnstone of Dalhousie
Physics Department, with Howe trying to keep it all in strained balance. Mercifully for Dalhousie, Howe was neither by inclination nor
talent just a figurehead; his energy and experience he applied vigorously to Dalhousie's problems.

Lord Beaverbrook took notice of what was going on between Dalhousie and the widow of Jimmy Dunn, his old friend. He was always
on the look-out for the chance to improve the interests of the University of New Brunswick; he had been its chancellor since 1947, and life
chancellor since 1954. In September 1957 he invited Howe to Fredericton, showed him proudly around *his* university. Nor was Beaverbrook without designs on redirecting Lady Dunn's interest from
Dalhousie to UNB; he was constantly sending her what she called "interesting" letters. And she was not the only rich widow Beaverbrook
was looking to. He and Mrs Dorothy Killam both wintered regularly
in Nassau. One night Beaverbrook arranged for a number of male
guests to dine, telling them ahead of time that the object was to get
some of Dorothy Killam's money for UNB. She would be the only
woman there and she would like that. The men were as charming as
possible; Dorothy Killam was likewise, aided by her consummate
knowledge of men and finance. It was a delightful evening, but
Mrs Killam left without giving anyone anything other than thanks to
her host. Beaverbrook said afterward, "She beat us all." Howe met
Mrs Killam in New York in September 1957 about the use of monies
that her husband had given Dalhousie years before under the rubric of
"Anonymous Donor." Howe knew enough about the ways of the
very rich not to push his luck until time and occasion offered. For if
Dorothy Killam could say no with grace, as with Beaverbrook's
crowd, she could also be cuttingly abrupt.[5]

Howe himself, that autumn of 1957, was being solicited to join
boards. Far from dropping out of public life, his view in August and
September, by December he had been accepting a directorship every
three weeks: National Trust, Atlas Steels, Federal Grain, Bank of
Montreal, Domtar (an E.P. Taylor paper company), to say nothing of
the board of the Massachusetts Institute of Technology, where he had
graduated fifty years before.

In the meantime Dalhousie collected ideas about what chancellors
actually did, from McGill, Toronto, and Western. The duties were
laid down in board minutes in December 1957. The chancellor was
elected by the board for a term of five years. If present, he or she presided at convocation. The chancellor was a member of the board but

not the chairman. In effect, the office was what the chancellor chose to do with it. Frank Covert likened it to the role of the crown in Parliament. He was delighted with Howe's appointment, "probably the most outstanding man in Canada today," and wanted him kept au fait with Dalhousie business from month to month, for he "grasps things quickly and has an extraordinary talent for overcoming difficulties in the quickest, simplest and most effective manner." The appointment of a chancellor did require changing the Dalhousie Act of 1863, which was now to be thoroughly revised and brought up to date. Opening up the act was not too risky, as Robert Stanfield ('36), premier since 1956, was well disposed to Dalhousie. The revision was actually done in the spring session of 1958.[6]

None of Howe's new interests got in the way of his primary occupation: building up Dalhousie University. It was just as well, for Lady Dunn's relations with Dalhousie officials and the architects required constant attention. Brigadier Laing wrote her in November 1957 with the sensible suggestion that Dalhousie would save money by tendering for both the Sir James Dunn Building and the men's residence at the same time. She was indignant. Mathers and Haldenby should not have their attention thus diverted. "Now Clarence dear," she wrote Howe, "do not be vexed but I wrote a sharp retort to Brigadier Laing." The residence could be dealt with by local architects in Halifax, but let Mathers and Haldenby concentrate upon her building. "I do not want a POOLED JOB I want a PRIORITY JOB." She suspected Laing and the Dalhousie board of trying to wheedle money – Dalhousie needed a further quarter-million for the men's residence – and that pooling tenders for the two buildings might be one way of disguising it. Howe reassured her. There would be no double tendering. Laing was, Howe said, a first-class man and had no ulterior motive. Howe would himself keep a close watch on the Dunn building, go over the tenders himself, a business in which, he said, "I have had a good deal of experience ... If we do not get a first-class job I will admit that I know nothing about the construction business." Lady Dunn was mollified, but noted, shrewdly enough, "as you see, things wander around a bit unless the reins are tightly held – I am so glad you have all the reins in hand now."[7]

At this point President Kerr interposed a completely new suggestion: would Lady Dunn like to broaden her support by establishing a chair in divinity? Howe wasn't having it. A most unwise move, he said, not only because it distracted her, but it threatened to disturb the hitherto harmonious relations between Dalhousie and Pine Hill Divinity School. At New Year's 1958 Kerr suggested that Dalhousie should use Lady Dunn's support to found a chair in Gaelic. Howe was cool to that suggestion too: "My advice is that we move slowly in widening the range of education at Dalhousie. The expansion in science will require two or three new professorships, and no doubt reinforcement of your existing staff is required in other directions." Clearly he was developing a dislike of Dalhousie's president.

Howe was officially installed as chancellor on 29 March 1958. By some egregious error on Dalhousie's part, Lady Dunn was not invited. She was angry as much at the "casual impromptu flavour [of the ceremony] which I deplore" as at not being invited. She soon learned that after the ceremony Dalhousie gave only a buffet lunch and in the basement of the Arts Building at that. The drink was water. *Think* of it! she wrote Howe. When Beaverbrook installed himself (as she put it) as the chancellor of UNB there was "one week of revelry and merriment, with BANQUETS & BALLS ... I find it hard to take that this truly HISTORICAL OCCASION should be given only a Buffet Luncheon with *water*."[8]

That was not the end of Lady Dunn's unhappiness. In mid-April 1958, when the contract had been awarded for the basement and foundations of the Dunn building, out of the blue the architects' estimate of the total cost rose suddenly by $350,000, (that is, 20 per cent) to $2.1 million. This time Howe was indignant; there should have been some warning of a change of such magnitude. "Why Dalhousie wished to use a Toronto architect," he grumbled, "is beyond me." The 20 per cent hoist only came to light because W.H. Howard, Lady Dunn's Montreal lawyer, required specifics before the 1 May payment from the Dunn Foundation was made. Lady Dunn was anything but pleased. She paid up, protesting to Howe that this new figure was going to be the absolute limit. It was.[9]

In May 1958 Howe presided at Dalhousie convocation and the graduation ball at the Nova Scotian Hotel where, he added, there was no alcohol but the students enjoyed themselves anyway. He found convocation tedious and the tea party afterwards at Shirreff Hall no compensation. Lady Dunn was already planning a big party and ball for the students on 29 October, when the cornerstone of the Dunn building was to be laid, and was prepared to do it in style. President Kerr was adamant that there be no beer, wine, or any form of alcohol. Lord Beaverbrook told Lady Dunn that at such a function to do without beer or wine would be "bloody." Better not have a party at all! She echoed Beaverbrook's sentiments. She had been looking forward, she told Howe, to "a gay, gladsome, gala affair and NOT just an ordinary HOP with POP." She wrote Kerr severely that "one could not celebrate a Birthday (especially this one) in tap water." She would await his views. Kerr still insisted that it was contrary to university regulations. Lady Dunn could, if she wished, give a birthday ball privately. "In my thirteen years at Dalhousie we have never served liquor of any kind at university functions, and I hope it will continue that way." It was left to the chairman of the board and Howe to sort out.[10]

The next shock – in mid-August 1958 – was the postponement of the official completion of the building from 1959 to 1960. That too was treated casually and without explanation. Lady Dunn and her lawyer were grievously annoyed. Why was she not told and some reasons given? Off went a blistering letter from W.H. Howard to Brigadier Laing; Dalhousie's treatment of Lady Dunn was quite inexcusable. And, the lawyer added in a sinister turn of phrase, "It may well prove to be most unwise." Laing did not like receiving such missives, not from lawyers, not from anyone. He suggested with some terseness that Howard control his language or his letters would not be answered at all. Howe tackled Haldenby in Toronto, accusing the architects of neglecting supervision of the Halifax work, in particular the expediting and management of materials. This effected some shaking up there and in Halifax. William Wickwire was made chairman of the board's Building Committee, and Howe got Professor J.H.L. Johnstone of Physics to act as Wickwire's deputy.

Johnstone and Howe were on first-name terms. They had known each other since Howe's days at Dalhousie; Johnstone had graduated in 1912, Howe's last year as professor of engineering. A specific example of their cooperation occurred in early October 1958 when a major hold-up occurred in getting cut sandstone from Phillipsburg, Quebec. The contractors seemed powerless; Johnstone phoned Howe. Howe leaned on the quarry management; the stone was shipped by truck and was in Halifax in five days. Johnstone also was hard on the contractors. At the beginning Howe and Johnstone had to read them the riot act more than once; Johnstone's refusal to let defective material get by was unpopular with them, but as Howe put it later, it was "very popular with me."[11]

On 29 October 1958, the day of laying the cornerstone, the university declared a half-holiday. At a special convocation Beaverbrook gave the principal speech, about his old friend Sir James Dunn. By this time Lady Dunn had backed away from giving a party, reserving that for the completion and opening of the building. Instead, Howe gave a dinner at the Nova Scotian for 150 guests and a ball for the graduating students in Arts and Science, Law, and Engineering. He would demonstrate that Halifax could do things in style! Beer, wine, and liquor were to be served at both, in the teeth of Kerr's resistance. It came up at the board meeting just before Howe's party. The president said he assumed no drinks would be served, as this was not the Dalhousie custom. Howe smiled and said nothing. Towards the end of the meeting he repeated his invitation, saying that he would see everyone at the Nova Scotian at 7:00 PM that evening. Kerr spoke again; he would wish to remind the new chancellor about the Dalhousie restriction on alcohol. At this Howe bridled. "See heah Doctah Kahr," said he with his flattened Massachusetts "r"s, "this is my pahty, not yours. Just remember that and if I plan to have wine served, wine will be served. You don't have to come if you don't want to." Thus had Howe and Laing solved the impasse between the president and Lady Dunn.[12]

Brigadier Laing, tough, exigent, able, was one of Dalhousie's most effective board chairmen. But on 1 September 1958, at the age of fifty-nine he died suddenly of a heart attack. Howe took on the task of finding a new chairman of the board. He tried to persuade his former cabinet colleague J.L. Ilsley, the chief justice of Nova Scotia since 1950, to take it, but failed. The next best prospect was Donald McInnes (BA '24, LL.B. '26), whose father, Hector McInnes, had served on the Dalhousie board for over forty years. McInnes accepted. William N. Wickwire was named vice-chairman. They were both busy Halifax lawyers, and the danger existed that neither would spend enough time at Dalhousie affairs; both together, Howe reasoned, might get results. It was just as well, Howe told Lady Dunn, for "there is a job to be done that cannot be too long delayed."

Strengthening the Law School

That job in November 1958 was strengthening Dalhousie's staff with new appointments, better salaries, an end to the quasi-starved condition that had prevailed under Kerr's aegis through the 1950s. The Law School was one of the first of these concerns. In 1957 changes initiated by Osgoode Hall made Dalhousie Law School graduates more exportable than ever before. The Dalhousie LL.B. had won partial outside recognition in 1952, and complete, in all the Canadian common-law provinces, in 1957. Thus an Ontario student wanting to practise in Ontario no longer had to go to an Ontario law school. For the Dalhousie Law School which had always, as its historian John Willis put it, to export or die, it was a considerable step forward, and the first of three substantial changes in 1957.

The second was raising the standard for Law School admission. Dean MacRae in 1921 (effective in 1924) raised the requirement to two years of arts, and persuaded the Canadian Bar Association that it should be the standard in all the Canadian common-law provinces. Dalhousie had in effect imposed a new national standard. In 1957 a three-year arts prerequisite became the national rule, and perforce adopted by Dalhousie; this time a Canadian rule was imposed on Dalhousie.

A third 1957 innovation was the arrival of G.V.V. Nicholls, who had been editor of the *Canadian Bar Review* for ten years, trained in civil law in Quebec and France. Nicholls had a formidable mind; experienced, tough, he was ready to question traditional Law School ways of doing things. He established a compulsory first-year course in legal research and writing, which required every student to present in writing a reasoned solution to a legal problem. As a method of training law students it was far more effective than the prevalent case method, in which the student had to do no more than to take part – or not – in class discussion. Prior to Nicholls's course, some students had never submitted anything to anyone until they wrote examinations. Nicholls gave supervision on an individual basis and hard work it was for him and his students.

Nicholls's course in turn compelled a long overdue development of the law library. Nicholls was shocked by it: no catalogue, no full-time librarian. The runs of old law reports probably sufficed for case method courses, but were wholly inadequate for legal research and writing. Dean Read, armed with a savage report from Nicholls, now sought a full-time librarian. But he had little money and no success until Lady Dunn came to the rescue.[13]

Her interest was aroused by a letter from W.R. Lederman, the Sir James Dunn professor of law, a chair established by Sir James in 1950. Lederman had found it impossible to resist the invitation of Queen's to become the founding dean of its new law school, but he felt it his duty in July 1958 to acquaint Lady Dunn with his concerns at Dalhousie:

In the field of legal education, the most striking advances in Canada's history are now rather suddenly developing in other places. This means that exceptional and sustained efforts are necessary if Dalhousie Law School is to hold the position it has always had in the very front rank of Canadian law faculties. I fear that the urgency of this situation is not at present appreciated, except among the members of the Dalhousie Law Faculty itself.

When he pointed out that the Law School was not being given its fair share of the university's resources, Lady Dunn took it up at once, and made sure that Howe knew. "Please tell me," said she to Lederman in effect, "the wisest course to follow." Lederman replied that four things needed attention: salary levels, more staff, a well-qualified law librarian and money for books, and scholarships for good students.

Howe arranged to see Dean Read. Within three months in October 1958, answers to Lederman's questions were announced at the symposium and convocation to celebrate the Law School's seventy-fifth anniversary: Lady Dunn would give $16,500 a year to hire a good law librarian and assistants, with the proviso that Dalhousie would give $10,000 a year for books, and $10,500 a year to provide seven Sir James Dunn law scholarships at $1,500 a year each. The scholarships were unique; no other law school in Canada had anything like them.

Dean Read found working with Lady Dunn no easier than Jack Johnstone had. When he asked the foundation to help make public the scholarships, Lady Dunn bridled. An *agent* of the Law School! She thought the scholarships could and should stand on their own. Read then made the mistake of asking for advice on getting out an announcement. Lady Dunn wanted decision. It was, she thought, "a most discouraging beginning." She did not even want to see Read. Howe got Read to draw up the pamphlet on the Dunn scholarships, which turned out to be exactly what Lady Dunn wanted.[14]

Howe hoped for much from Donald McInnes, the new chairman of the board. The first issue he seems to have tackled was raising Law School salaries, something Kerr had long resisted. McInnes locked horns with him in December on that and won. Lady Dunn was delighted, but told Howe that Dalhousie would need Howe's continued pressure. The most serious problem was the salaries and conditions of the Faculty of Arts and Science.

Lady Dunn believed in first-class staff, a lesson she had absorbed from her husband's experience with Algoma Steel. He had gone to Sault Ste Marie knowing nothing about making steel but hired the best men he could get to make it. Lady Dunn took the position that it was money wasted to have a first-class Physics building without first-class professors to run it. Both she and Howe had been making this point with increasing insistence. From the faculty side it was Dean Archibald who brought it to a head, and he made sure his protests got past the president's office to McInnes and Howe. His term was three years, and in September 1958 he handed in his resignation, telling the board the reason he did not want to continue was President Kerr's complete disregard of his recommendations for the improvement of salaries, especially in science. Lady Dunn backed Archibald. She liked him personally, and thought Archibald's own salary was well below what it should be. Indeed, she felt, all the Arts and Science professors were underpaid. After negotiations, Archibald agreed to carry on. A new salary scale brought in by the board, as of 1 September 1958 no doubt helped, but Archibald insisted that adjustment in a clutch of a

Donald McInnes, Chairman of the Board, 1958–80.

dozen individual cases was necessary, indeed urgent, since they affected the best women and men in Arts and Science. To do otherwise was to risk losing them.[15]

Lady Dunn and Howe versus President Kerr

Other problems with Dr Kerr annoyed Lady Dunn. When Dalhousie did not publish Beaverbrook's tribute to Sir James Dunn at the laying of the cornerstone, she had it printed herself. She did not complain about paying the cost; what upset her was that Dalhousie had not thought of it. Apparently no one, except Howe, had any flair for handling such matters of state. Indeed, Beaverbrook's speech would not have even been reported had not the Saint John *Telegraph-Journal* arranged for it. It was symptomatic of a whole range of issues from large to petty. The gifts to Dalhousie that ought to have given Lady Dunn pleasurable challenges had produced mainly irritating ones. She complained that with Kerr as president she had lost her enthusiasm. "I expected to be quite active and interested but I certainly have been disappointed, frustrated and irritated." Probably few presidents could have avoided offending such a formidable lady, but Kerr did not help. Dalhousie's gratitude offered her "an abundance of superficiality" but was "sadly lacking in *tangible* appreciation." Kerr was unquestionably appreciative of all she had done; he did not know how to translate it either in letters or in action. His letters were prosy, flat, and unconvincing.[16]

Howe entirely understood. It shook him that Lady Dunn had to pay for the publication of Beaverbrook's speech.

The whole trouble at Dalhousie is Dr. Kerr. He is a mean spirited man. Everyone agrees he should go, but no one seems to do anything about it. I hope I can stir things up while I am in Halifax ...

Bringing the standards of Dalhousie, both in business and in education, up to those of the Dalhousie of my day, is a real challenge, but I believe that it can be accomplished. I am going to do my best to that end. The Dalhousie tradition is worth restoring ... There seems to have been a complete lack of leadership since Kerr became President. I still have hopes of Donald McInnes.

One task he had in hand was to join with Ray Milner, the chancellor of King's, to promote better understanding between Dalhousie and King's. Here again Kerr was the main obstacle, and his fighting "vigorously against any concession by Dalhousie ... did not help." Nevertheless a new Dalhousie-King's convention was signed a few months later, in November 1959.[17]

According to Lady Dunn, Kerr was trying to carry two roles, that of a United Church minister and president of Dalhousie. She was perturbed that in a period of expansion Dalhousie should be saddled with a part-time president. "I do not intend to be meddlesome," she told Howe, "but since I have had Dalhousie very much to the fore in future planning, I do intend to know – what now?" There were strong intimations that, while she disclaimed any intention of being presumptuous, she expected to be consulted before a new Dalhousie president was appointed. Howe agreed. "I have made it clear to all concerned that you must be consulted about all matters associated with the change in the Presidency."[18]

Among Howe's grievances with Kerr, one was uppermost: he was not listening to his deans or sufficiently consulting his board. He was apt to make important decisions and commitments without consulting anyone, referring less important ones to the board. Howe had more confidence in the management of Dalhousie when Kerr was away than when he was there. Steadily he and McInnes worked to increase the authority of the deans. In any case, Howe confided to Lady Dunn, Dalhousie should get rid of its president as soon as possible. Howe pushed McInnes, reminding him that Kerr's standing in the Canadian university world was small credit to Dalhousie, that as long as Kerr was there it would be difficult to attract men of high calibre to the staff or keep good professors. But McInnes was made of rather soft metal, and getting rid of an incumbent president who had no intention of going was difficult. McInnes disliked contretemps; if President Kerr would not resign on his own, McInnes was not yet ready to force him. And there was another reason: Dalhousie had fired its president in 1945, only fourteen years before, and its board now had a natural reluctance to fire another one. Thus while Howe could talk, suggest, even lead at times, he had only one vote on the board the same as the others, and he did not always get his way. Indeed, "some of the Board regarded him as an interfering bustle from Ottawa not a real Nova Scotian."

Howe explained it all to A.T. Stewart, professor of physics, who was leaving Dalhousie in September 1960 to go to the University of North Carolina, mostly because of Kerr. Howe had tried to persuade the board to buy Kerr off, but they wouldn't move. Changing the president of a university, Howe confessed to Lady Dunn, was "almost as difficult as changing the leader of a political party." Howe did solicit nominations for a new Dalhousie president in September 1960, from his old friend Larry MacKenzie of UBC, but until President Kerr actually intimated resignation it was bootless to go further.

Howe told Kerr that Dalhousie's obsession with buildings had allowed its staff to deteriorate. The building program had been extravagant and Dalhousie salaries showed much evidence of penny pinching. Fifty years ago, Howe reminded the alumni, Dalhousie was one of the four great English-speaking universities in Canada even though it had only one building. Not only that, but fifty years ago, too, Howe's salary as a young professor of engineering, $2,000, was a great deal more than the $5,000 that Dalhousie professors of similar age were earning currently.[19]

These were the shadows in the background when the Sir James Dunn Science building was finally opened in October 1960 with considerable fanfare, Howe giving another splendid dinner party at the Nova Scotian, flaunting the occasion to show Lord Beaverbrook what he and Dalhousie could do. As he told President Kerr,

I was annoyed at the invasion from New Brunswick, and also fed up with reports from Fredericton on the wonderful dinners given by Lord Beaverbrook on a similar occasions. My purpose was to show New Brunswick that we in Nova Scotia could also arrange a dinner. I think that Beaverbrook got the point.

I was not in the least perturbed about the cost.

Lady Dunn was finally thrilled both with the building and the way it was celebrated. The weather of late October was perfect.

By this time, however, Lady Dunn's frustrations with Dalhousie during the three-year process from sod-turning to opening had turned her towards Beaverbrook. In 1959 she asked him to write a life of Sir James Dunn; he asked for and got her help and the papers she had. She spent some weeks early in 1960 at Beaverbrook's place, La Capponcina, in the Riviera, and her correspondence with Howe gradually dried up. Howe warned McInnes that Beaverbrook was making a tremendous play for Lady Dunn, that they were spending most of their time together. Ostensibly this was because of the biography of Sir James; but Beaverbrook had a darker purpose, to redirect Lady Dunn's money from Dalhousie to UNB. Howe cautioned her with shrewd advice: whatever money she gave Dalhousie would glorify her husband; anything she might give UNB would simply glorify Beaverbrook. She paid attention to that. Still, it did not prevent her from marrying Beaverbrook in June 1963. He died a year later, having failed to divert any of his new wife's money to UNB although she did build the Sir James Dunn Playhouse in downtown Fredericton.[20]

She left a considerable legacy at Dalhousie. No one had ever given it so much money nor created more problems in its giving. She was a strange figure, descending upon Halifax out of St Andrews; some suggested aerial conveyance other than aeroplanes. She worked her will

Lady Dunn presenting the key of the Sir James Dunn Science Building to Donald McInnes, October 1960.

with outrageous ruthlessness. Her poetic effusion about her husband she required every Dalhousie graduate student to sign for. *Remembrance* was as risible in content as in process, studded like her letters with block capitals, radiating her delight in her husband. Her memory of him also included his lessons, that "IGNORANCE was a calamity," that "there is no substitute for CONCENTRATION – it is a MAGIC FORMULA." After this sermon there followed an eight-page poem, "The Ballad of a Bathurst Boy, 1874–1956," perilously close to doggerel most of the time, in it at others:

> His fighting heart had won for him
> A ten dollar boxing prize –
> Intrigued by "Memory Lectures"
> Proclaimed by posters of great size.

(Sir James had spent his $10 prize going to a lecture on "assimilative Memory.") But she left an imposing building, and splendid Sir James Dunn scholarships in law. She had strong views of what Dalhousie ought to be, and she wanted it soon. It was not an easy prescription for a university with fractured and complex governance to translate into action. It was C.D. Howe who was the main Dalhousie stand-by and through whom her demands and complaints were channelled. She had one aim: to make the Sir James Dunn Building as handsome as possible within the money, $2,175,000, and the time various exigencies had forced her to accept. She aimed high and kept Dalhousie's best interests to the forefront; but she was quick to take offence and often got her exercise jumping to conclusions. She wanted everything just right, and if it wasn't right she wanted it done again. She did *not* want the tops of the elevator shafts protruding from the top of the building; a $250,000 parapet was put on to conceal them. She did *not* like the marble in the lobby; it was replaced. The door handles were all wrong; they were changed. The details were interminable. And through it all ran her fear of, as she put it, "being soaked" unless she were vigilant, or as it turned out, she persuaded Howe to be.

Howe found her difficult. Very early he complained to the architects that he and they were "victims of too many bosses, including especially Lady Dunn and Dr. Kerr." But as Howe put it two years later, with some exaggeration, "Lady Dunn's benefactions ... constitute the most exciting development in the history of Dalhousie. It has put new life into the university, and is attracting interest, both from students and potential staff." Jack Johnstone, upon whom rested much of the local supervision for the Dunn building, was in hospital in September 1960 as the building was completed, his work much appreciated by

Howe "in keeping everything first class." That Dalhousie was able to close accounts on the Dunn building with a $27,000 credit balance was, said Howe, due largely to Johnstone. As for Johnstone himself, by 1959 he had had all he could stand of Lady Dunn. At one point a colleague asked him jocularly, how much would he kiss someone's a ... for? Johnstone replied with a rueful grin, "I can tell you that exactly: $2.1 million."[21]

Dorothy Johnston Killam, LL.D.

Howe also had in mind the care and cultivation of Mrs Dorothy Killam, an exquisitely sensitive operation. Beaverbrook had failed. So also had Ralph Pickard Bell, who chaired Mount Allison's fund-raising committee in 1959 and became chancellor in 1960. On hearing that the Reverend W.S. Godfrey, a well-known Mount Allison alumnus, was going to the Bahamas to see Mrs Killam, Ralph Bell told him to back off, that he would go. Bell, not famous for subtlety, got nowhere and angered Mrs Killam. "He told me how to spend *my* money!" "There was," said her lawyer, Donald Byers, "a certain delicacy required." Watson Kirkconnell, president of Acadia University from 1948 to 1964, knowing Mrs Killam was fond of baseball, especially of the Brooklyn Dodgers, spent hours studying both before going to the Bahamas. "Oh, yes," he said, "and it didn't do Acadia or me one darn bit of good." Dalhousie's credentials were better, however. Isaac Walton Killam was a Dalhousie graduate, and his Halifax lawyer had been J. McG. Stewart. The "Anonymous Donor Fund" was started by Killam, and Howe was hoping to get another half-million to add to the $50,000 already there. If so, Howe noted, it would be the first gift Dorothy Killam had made since Killam's death in August 1955. But she told Howe at that point that she proposed to give no money except in her will.[22]

That did not prevent Dalhousie from offering her an honorary degree in 1958; she could not accept it then, but when the offer was renewed in the spring of 1959, she did. Howe told Kerr that Mrs Killam was unpredictable, that even if she accepted it did not mean that she would come. Mrs Killam's possible arrival in Halifax posed awkward questions. She very much liked centre stage, and her entourage would be certain to make a considerable splash. Lady Dunn was well capable of being jealous; she had been offered the degree and had declined it because the Dunn building was to commemorate her husband, not herself. Nevertheless, she would not enjoy seeing Mrs Killam getting one. What seems to have happened – it is an hypothesis – was that Howe persuaded Mrs Killam not to come, that the accommodation she wanted at the Nova Scotian Hotel was not available, and that no amount of pressure from McInnes and himself could change that. Why not, he said, plead illness, and he would undertake to persuade the Dalhousie Senate to give Mrs Killam her degree *in absentia* in spite of tradition to the contrary. C.L. Bennet, the vice-president, was sure that Senate would accept this breach of its rules, if some responsible person would assure Senate of Mrs Killam's inability to be present. Senate did so accept. Thus did Mrs Killam get her Dalhousie LL.D.; thus did Howe manage to keep Dalhousie's two queen bees separated.[23]

In due course Mrs Killam's lawyer authorized the use of the $50,000 for the improvement of Dalhousie salaries. No part of it, said he sternly, was "to be used for capital expenditure." In December 1959 Dalhousie received $100,000 as a tangible expression of Mrs Killam's ongoing interest, and no doubt gratitude for the honorary degree. Howe told McInnes not to tell Kerr or anyone else about the latest gift, that when the cheque arrived to let him (Howe) know, and he would send a proper letter of thanks. Another $100,000 came a year later. Mrs Killam assured Howe on 19 December 1960 that handsome provision for Dalhousie was being set out in her will.[24]

Howe seems to have urged the appointment of Frank Covert as chairman of the board's new committee on the pension fund. The pension initiative had come from Senate, raised in a joint meeting with the board in April 1959. The whole question of Dalhousie pensions badly needed further study, and a joint committee was struck chaired by the ablest financial expert on the board, Frank Covert (BA '27, LL.B. '29). He was fifty-two years old, and RCAF veteran with Distinguished Flying Cross, a friend of Howe's from late in the war when he worked for the Ministry of Munitions and Supply. Now a director of the Royal Bank, Montreal Trust, National Sea Products, and on the Dalhousie board since 1955, Covert had energy and determination. A comprehensive report on Dalhousie's existing scheme prepared by J.S.M. Wason showed its inadequacy, and a new plan was developed, to go into place on 1 January 1960 (later backdated to 1 September 1959) replacing the antediluvian one based upon Dominion annuities. The most ingenious aspect of the new Dalhousie pension was the decision to take up a trusteed plan rather than an insured one. This meant that Dalhousie would now administer its own pension fund on terms it itself decided on. Much depended on judicious, systematic, progressive administration of the fund. That, it is proper to say, is what it got.[25]

Covert wanted restrictions on the portability of the new Dalhousie pension. The Canadian Association of University Teachers had been urging portability upon Canadian university presidents. So had Dean

W.J. Waines, of the University of Manitoba. Covert had worked with Waines on the Royal Commission on Transportation; "a nice fellow," Covert said, "but 'all sail and no rudder.' " For a small university, portability of pensions was impossible, but big universities such as British Columbia, Manitoba, and Toronto liked it. As soon as a better offer came, the professor at the small university left, taking his whole pension with him. It "makes me boil," Covert said, "when people slavishly say somebody recommends it, someone does it, and therefore we ought to, and I think I have made it clear, insofar as Dalhousie is concerned, that we should have nothing to do with portable pensions." If a professor wished to move he could take with him his own pension contributions, but Dalhousie's contributions only on a sliding scale: after eight years' continual service, one received 8 per cent of the board's contributions, which increased at 8 per cent per annum until, after twenty-one years' service, full portability was achieved. That, of course, was the best part of a working lifetime. Still, the new 1959 pension plan was a vast improvement on what had gone before.

The problem remained of older professors, with substantial years under the old plan, but with few additional benefits from the new one. Some professors who retired in the 1960s found the financial going difficult. A few could not even afford to live in Halifax any longer, but migrated to the countryside around, or to a less expensive university town such as Wolfville. Covert had some sympathy for such professors; when G.V. Douglas complained in 1957 that his pension was only $1,721 a year, the board supplemented it with $700. But Covert reminded President Kerr of an old perspective: the great majority of people still did not get pensions from their place of work. Covert noted that Douglas, as full professor from 1932 to 1957, had a salary far higher than anything Covert got as a lawyer until well after the war, and Covert said he had to work harder for what he got. Furthermore, he had to fund his own pension. In those days, before the Canada Pension Plan of 1966, people had to save and plan for their retirement. That was Beecher Weld's rejoinder to griping by retired colleagues. Still, a modest pension in a time of steadily rising prices too often produced income woefully inadequate.[26]

Dalhousie's endowment was entirely separate from its pension funds. It, too, needed systematic and hard-headed administration. Dalhousie's endowments, Howe suggested to D.H. McNeill, the business manager, were scattered to such an extent that it was impossible to watch them all. Now would be a good time to consolidate. Furthermore, Dalhousie "should not be operating with a substantial surplus at a time when faculty salaries are substandard." Any appeal for funds could hardly go forward on the basis of Dalhousie's financial position. It ought not to be having surpluses. Two years later Frank Covert, now chairman of the board's Finance Committee, was asked to prepare a report on Dalhousie investments. The result was a stern indictment of the work of the Finance Committee. Covert criticized too slack control, too many easy-going investments such as municipal bonds, and not enough concentration on growth stocks. "We as the Finance Committee," he told McInnes, "have done a poor job." He also called for new blood; Dalhousie's endowment was now too big, with a market value of $14.5 million, "to leave it in the hands of amateurs."[27]

One of the last changes Howe presided over was the appointment of a new dean of arts and science. Archibald had agreed to stay on in 1958 on condition that there would be some improvement of staff salaries, a subject on which Kerr gave ground unwillingly but which Howe and Lady Dunn fully approved. By 1960 Archibald was finding it impossible to work with the president. There were numerous examples. Archibald badly wanted to keep Professor Peter Michelsen in German. Kerr dragged his feet, and when he was finally badgered into making a decent offer, Michelsen had accepted a post in Braunschweig. D.J. Heasman of Political Science was invited to the University of Saskatchewan for a year as visiting professor. Archibald had the sensible view that this was good for Heasman and good for Dalhousie, and told Aitchison, the head of the department, that it was an excellent idea. Kerr was not pleased. Archibald should have discussed the whole matter with him first. Crowning it all in the summer of 1960 was Kerr's meanness over J.H.L. Johnstone's salary. Johnstone had done tremendous work for the Dunn building, and almost died from a duodenal ulcer that summer. He would return to work that autumn and he thought a salary of $10,200 would be fair. Archibald thought so too. Kerr accepted the salary minus Johnstone's annuity entitlement of $1,620. It took another round of negotiations before Johnstone's salary was finally established at $10,000 without any deductions.[28]

As those disagreements suggested, the president was at the core of the decision-making in Arts and Science, and he proposed to stay there. It was by far his most immediate interest. But his ideas were increasingly out of tune with faculty's. Dean Archibald spent hours trying to hold off Kerr's pressure for new programs such as secretarial science or home economics, that aimed at accessibility at the expense of Dalhousie standards. Archibald needed a faculty council to help him "keep Kerr on the rails," as he put it. In a stern letter addressed to Kerr, C.D. Howe, and McInnes in April 1960, Archibald insisted that dean and faculty be given freedom of decision about appointments and salaries within an approved budget. Three days later, the faculty passed without a dissenting voice a bluntly worded resolution:

The Faculty is now in the precarious state reached by the Medical School six years ago when Dr. C.B. Stewart wrote of it … "only a strong and concerted effort … can bring it to safety, let alone to the position of eminence that it should occupy." As the situation now is, members of the Faculty cannot convince, or even honestly advise, desirable staff members that they should come to Dalhousie … it is essential that the Faculty be given the degree of autonomy and machinery of administration and consultation possessed by the Medical School.

Kerr said he was in agreement, though he may not have had much choice. A faculty council of eight members was struck within a week.[29]

Resignations were the most obvious evidence of disaffection. In the summer of 1960 D.G. Lochhead, the university librarian, left for York University, the new university in Toronto, after seven years of fighting Kerr. He said that Kerr did not like libraries or librarians, so niggardly had been his treatment of them. Lochhead concluded that the board had been tight-fisted because its chief executive officer was. A.T. Stewart of Physics was amazed not only that his $100 travel voucher had to be signed by the president, but that the president would give him a lecture on how George Grant's departure would benefit Dalhousie.

George Grant left Dalhousie in 1960 for the same reasons, and like Lochhead for York. Kerr had once liked and approved of Grant but now found his philosophical and theological opinions too unsettling. King's used to require their divinity students to take Grant's Philosophy 1, but now discontinued the practice. Grant raised doubts about their faith, President Puxley said, giving them nothing in return but scepticism. Roman Catholic students were cautioned against attending Grant's lectures. Grant resigned in December 1959, effective the following August, but he was out of his York job when he left Halifax in August 1960, having quarrelled with President Murray Ross over the terms of his York appointment. Grant might have been persuaded to stay; Kerr would not have it.[30]

Thus it was not surprising that in the fall of 1960 the *Gazette* under Denis Stairs, editor-in-chief asked, "Why Did the Professors Go?" He suspected friction between professors and president, but suspicions were not reasons. He waited. When there was no answer the following week, he noted the fact. By that time the *Gazette* had been encour-

George Grant, Professor of Philosophy, 1947–60, and of Religion, Classics and Polit-ical Science, 1980–4.

aged privately with information from good sources: Professors J.G. Kaplan, of the Department of Physiology, of the Dalhousie Faculty Association, and Allan Bevan, head of English. Most interesting of all, Stairs was urged to press on by a board member who complained that between the executive committee and the president, ordinary members of the board were kept in the dark and had little idea of what was going on. A week later, "Why Did the Professors Go?" was in still bigger type, the *Gazette* saying that Dalhousie's "teaching and research conditions are stifling." On 27 October "WHY DID THE PROFESSORS GO?" took the whole top of the page. The *Gazette* suggested that the conditions in Arts and Science resembled those that produced the 1954 Medical revolt. It urged the new Faculty Council of Arts and Science to take up the torch. The Dental Faculty was, however, angry at the *Gazette*; the big headline came during an important dental conference in Halifax. J.D. McLean, dean of dentistry, wrote the president:

The impropriety of this exceedingly ill-timed editorial, however, has caused great alarm. Regardless of any semblance of fact that it may contain, the advertisement to our distinguished guests of this week from so many parts of the world, could do our university untold harm which may take years to correct.

In Senate there was talk of the editor's suspension, choked off by the sensible argument that it would be counter-productive. The editor, Denis Stairs, in his final year in honours history, was then approached by one of his professors who said the *Gazette* had made its point, and the president could not properly reply owing to the confidentiality of his information. Still, the fact that the president said nothing at all suggests that he simply did not deign to answer. The following week, the *Gazette* shut itself up on the subject, its case already made.

All that autumn of 1960, C.D. Howe had been busy. One day in Halifax, Gordon Archibald of the board was driving him to the airport bus, mentioning that he worked for the Heart Fund. Howe, jocular, said, "Well, heart disease solves a lot of problems." During one three-day period in mid-December Howe attended meetings, in New York, Welland, and Quebec City. His acquaintances noted his exhaustion. At Christmas he had a cold and stayed home. On 29 December he went to his office to deal with correspondence, then wrapped himself up at home again. On New Year's Eve he started to watch the Saturday night hockey game on television, but went to bed feeling unwell. There Alice Howe found him a short while later, dead of a heart attack.[31]

Howe's Achievements at Dalhousie

Howe had been Dalhousie's new chancellor for just three and a half years, but the changes he effected were considerable. The whole board was shaken up and invigorated, and in some important respects that applied to the whole university. Howe was a mover and shaker almost by instinct. He was not a lawyer trying to keep the status quo in balance but an engineer who aimed to make things work, improve them, make more efficient the world he moved in. For Howe, the means were less important than the end to be achieved, provided it was. He had little difficulty juggling several things at once. In the midst of working with Lady Dunn over her building, tenders were called for the new men's residence at the end of March 1959. The lowest came in at $1,470,000; the building was to be in stone like the rest of the campus, though in Lake Echo shale, a more tractable stone than the ironstone prevalent elsewhere, and less expensive. Howe laid the cornerstone in October. He did not christen the building Howe Hall; a grateful board did after his death. New energy, new direction, new tone; "Daddy Atwood's" canteen, after years of agitation, would at last be made over. The "Coffee House Revolution" went even further: the students were now encouraged to develop plans for a student union; that movement had started in 1957 when students voted $20,000 to establish the Student Union Building fund. The letter from Donald McInnes to Dave Matheson and Murray Fraser, co-chairmen of the building committee of the Student Council, on 27 November 1959, was positive: Dalhousie would provide the land; while the board could not help with the SUB immediately, having the Sir James Dunn Building and the men's residence on hand, nevertheless the board would like to encourage the Student Council to proceed with the planning for it. This new positiveness by the board cannot be attributed wholly to Howe, but the vigorous responses to longstanding student concerns probably owed much to him. As the *Gazette* put it, "The Old Order Changeth." In February 1960 the students voted 1,124 to 124 for a $10 fee increase to help pay for the SUB.

Howe's positions at Dalhousie were academically sound, though politically to the right. He disliked the Canadian Association of University Teachers (CAUT) and told Kerr to have as little as possible to do with it. He thought professors should keep out of politics, especially CCF politics. He did not appreciate J.H. Aitchison's connections with CAUT or the Nova Scotia CCF. The growing muscle of the Dalhousie Faculty Association he seems not to have objected to; he knew doubtless that its rhetoric was justified by Dalhousie's long delays in dealing with salaries.[32]

Some university chancellors are wealthy figureheads, but Howe was never that. He was more active than the Dalhousie board had quite bargained for; some thought of him in terms of the Nova Scotian definition of an expert: an s.o.b. from out of town. But he had played the important role of broker between Lady Dunn and Dalhousie, and he had helped in bringing Dalhousie to Mrs Killam's attention and interest. He knew the ways of the very rich. Altogether Howe's vigour, realism, quickness, his protean range of interests and responsibilities, his ready knowledge of how the world worked, had all been deployed to Dalhousie's great benefit. Even the appointment of Dalhousie's new dean of arts and science in October 1960 had had Howe's imprimatur and interest.

Dean Archibald had resigned on 18 October 1960, pleading ill health, though the real reasons were the frustrations of his office. G.E. Wilson was made acting dean, but it was clear that a new dean would be needed and at once. The president did not invite nominations; rather he resisted them. A number of senior men were possibilities, but Kerr sought out a much younger man, an historian, aged thirty-one, who had a decided knack for administration, Guy MacLean. MacLean was taken completely by surprise by the president's suggestion that he consider being dean of arts and science; he asked for twenty-four hours to think it over. After discussing it with Wilson, MacLean had decided to accept the challenge. But when he came back to Kerr's office, the president said that an important candidate downtown had come to his attention. Thus the suggestion was withdrawn.[33]

Henry Hicks Becomes Dean of Arts and Science

The downtown candidate was Henry Davies Hicks. Howe may have had a considerable hand in the choice; certainly he approved it. Hicks himself believed, however, that when President Kerr approached him about the deanship, the moving spirit in the nomination had been Frank Covert. Hicks, leader of the Nova Scotia Liberals, had just been defeated for a second time in the June 1960 provincial election by the incumbent Conservative premier, Robert Stanfield, losing his own seat in Annapolis East in the process. It was time, Hicks thought, to get out of politics and make some money in law practice. He approached two law firms in Halifax, one of which was glad to make room for him, Stewart, MacKeen, Covert, et al. But Frank Covert believed that Dalhousie needed new blood more than his law firm did, and thought of the recurring problem of the deanship of arts and science. Hicks would be an interesting possibility.

Hicks himself was not sure that he wanted it, but his younger brother urged him to take it. "Who remembers the governors of Massachusetts?" asked Duff Hicks, "but everyone remembers the presidents of Harvard." What Dalhousie offered was not the presidency, certainly; but it was the deanship of arts and science, and the vice-presidency when C.L. Bennet retired in 1962. The vice-presidency was not important as long as Kerr was president, but for Hicks it was a foot in the door. The board would probably not have promised, informally or otherwise, the presidency of Dalhousie. What was being offered was opportunity; if Hicks should develop well as dean of arts and science, then he would certainly be a real possibility for president. Lady Dunn did not like what she had seen of Hicks, but Howe trusted the judgment of his board colleagues. Nevertheless he took the precaution of talking to Robert Stanfield, the premier, to ascertain that he would have no objections to the leader of the opposition being appointed dean of arts and science at Dalhousie. Stanfield said he had none at all.[34]

Hicks was a better candidate than he looked at first sight. Although he had only bachelor degrees, still there were four of them: Mount Allison (BA '36), Dalhousie (B.SC. '37), Oxford (BA [Juris.] '39, and BCL '40). He had been minister of education under Angus L. Macdonald from 1949 to 1954, and in his own government when he was premier from 1954 to 1956. He had urged President Kerr in 1951 to insist on proper entrance qualifications for Dalhousie students, in order to remedy Dalhousie complaints about the quality of high school education. On the Board of Regents of Mount Allison since 1948, Hicks had been saying that Mount Allison needed to set higher standards, and any expansion of enrolment ought to take second place to that fundamental.

Dalhousie professors, especially those in Arts and Science, were rather taken aback by the choice of Hicks. They knew him mainly as a twice-defeated Liberal leader, having few academic credentials. While many in the faculty were willing to suspend judgment and risk the experiment, others were sceptical. Some were offended, if not outraged, by President Kerr's procedure, by the very limited consultation the president had used. Kerr played his cards close to his chest but did talk privately to President Puxley of King's on 19 October about his choices, saying none of the senior Dalhousie professors was qualified to be dean. Puxley urged Kerr to take faculty into his confidence, if only for morale:

If the Faculty sees that you do not care at all for their views or whether they have any confidence or not in your new appointee, you are bound to forfeit forever what remains of their interest in and loyalty to the University ...

A succession of physicists, taken about 1960. L. to r., Howard Bronson, 1910–43; E.W. Guptill, 1947–76; W.J. Archibald, 1943–77; J.H.L. Johnstone, 1914–60. Both Johnstone and Archibald were students of Bronson's.

My fear is that by appointing a complete outsider [Hicks] and/or one of the youngest and most junior members in the Faculty [MacLean], you will be "chastising them with scorpions", will finally stifle the loyalty of your older men ... and will hasten the decline of the University.

A.S. Mowat, secretary of the Faculty Association, urged the president to consult senior men, suggesting J.H. Aitchison (Political Science), J.F. Graham (Economics), R.S. Cumming (Commerce), and F.R. Hayes (Biology). Kerr consulted Hayes, who did not say yes to Hicks but, according to Kerr, did so by implication. Two of those not consulted, Aitchison and Graham, plus James Doull of Classics, arranged to meet Hicks downtown to discuss the question. The three explained that they did not like the manner of Hicks's appointment, and that while most of the faculty were probably willing to accept him, a minority, perhaps strong, opposed the mode and possibly the man that came with it. Hicks owed it to the faculty, and to himself, to ascertain their wishes. Hicks agreed to meet with faculty. There were others, former Dean Archibald among them, who urged Hicks to come anyway, that he would be accepted.[35]

Hicks was used to criticism. Politics requires a carapace, and Hicks was not seriously upset by the visitation of what he sometimes later called Dalhousie's three wise men. But he paid attention to what they said about consultation. It is also fair to add that they did not attempt to frustrate his work, and they remained on friendly terms with him long afterwards. If there was some unease and coolness in the faculty, it gradually dissipated. In later years Hicks was not above teasing the three; on the other hand Hicks, who had been led by President Kerr to hope he might be allowed to lecture in political science, was resolutely prohibited from doing so by Professor Aitchison, the head of the department. The reason was not animus but academic credentials. Mere experience was not enough.

Hicks knew sufficiently little about the inner workings of his faculty that he relied on his Faculty Council for advice and consultation, and used them rather as he had his cabinet when he was premier. The faculty grew to like it. He also had a different view of money from the president; although his room for manoeuvre was restricted, he was more progressive, open, and generous. Moreover, having been minister of education for eight years, he knew something of education in the province, and he brought to bear on Dalhousie's problems a range of knowledge informed by experience of Mount Allison and some of Acadia. This showed almost at once, when, ten weeks after he assumed office, he submitted his first report to President Kerr on the state of his faculty.

Before he came he had heard rumours that Arts and Science had fallen behind; what he had seen since confirmed it. In the departments of English, Mathematics, and Biology, staff/student ratios were double what they had been twenty years before. Hicks reported he would need thirty additional professors, and as soon as possible, and over the next five years Arts and Science would need to double its staff. Hicks offered the following table to the president of total faculty budgets against student numbers, showing expenditure per student by faculty and compared to Yale:

Dalhousie	A & S	Law	Medicine	Dentistry
1938–9	$ 259	$ 233	$ 432	$ 362
1948–9	265	251	873	922
1958–9	712	1,069	2,408	2,604
1960–1	696	1,720	3,100	3,410
Yale				
1959–60	1,825	1,825	3,800	–

Hicks rubbed it in by comparing Dalhousie's 1958–9 per capita expenditure on Arts and Science with Acadia's and Mount Allison's, $908 and $900 respectively. In 1960–1 Dalhousie would spend less for its 1,425 students in Arts and Science than did Mount Allison for its 1,061. Hicks concluded:

It seems quite evident that with its necessary and commendable concern for the reputation and quality of work in its professional faculties in the postwar years, Dalhousie has allowed its undergraduate Faculty of Arts and Science to become neglected. Today this Faculty, with more than two-thirds of the students in the University, expends about one-third of its budget, and this I understand includes the whole cost of carrying the University Library.

Hicks hoped to discuss his report as soon as possible, and enclosed extra copies in case Kerr should wish to submit it to the executive committee of the board. It would have been unlike Kerr to do so, and therein lay the fundamental problem. Kerr guarded that isthmus between the board and the rest of the university, and saw to it that such criticisms went no further. He did not like it at all when attempts were made to bypass him.

Three weeks later at Senate, the president said he had had no submission from Arts and Science. Hicks was surprised and pained at the president's remarks, and wrote the next day a chiding letter. "May I suggest, with the greatest respect, Mr. President, that I doubt if you fully appreciate the low morale in the Faculty of Arts and Science."

Old Howard Bronson of Physics, who had donated his property at LeMarchant Street and University Avenue to Dalhousie in 1950, wrote Kerr in much the same vein. When he came in 1910 Dalhousie was thought of by the Rockefeller and Carnegie people as the possible Johns Hopkins of Canada. Now, in spite of the new research facilities in the Dunn Building, physics lacked the professors to do good research. "Really good men ... want to be proud to represent their University ... I think the men in Law, Medicine and Dentistry now feel this way ... but it certainly is not true of most of the members of the Arts and Science Faculty."[36]

By this time the movement to define, regulate, and strengthen faculty and Senate influence in Dalhousie's governance had gathered force. The most powerful expression of faculty restlessness was the appointment by Senate, on 8 December 1960, of its Committee on University Government, with a sweeping mandate to "review the present structure and practice of government at all levels within the University and to make recommendations thereon." This was followed in 1961 by the creation of Senate Council, a working cabinet of Senate, which became operational in December 1961. In the late spring of 1962, as the Senate Committee on University Government gathered its documents, strength, reach, and determination, the president suffered a slight stroke. Dean Hicks took over as acting president until September 1962.

President Kerr Resigns
The board now decided it was time for Kerr to retire. When Donald McInnes told him so, it came as a shock. Although he was sixty-five years old, Kerr did not have to resign; his term was open-ended. But the fact was that he could no longer cope with the pressures and problems rising up around him. Unlike his predecessor in 1945, Kerr would go peacefully, and late in November he announced his resignation, effective 31 August 1963. The board expressed the regrets usual to such occasions, and singled out Nessie Kerr for special mention. She deserved it. She it was who had made Kerr's presidency tolerable. Everyone liked her; she had gaiety and delight. She reminded one of Browning's "My Last Duchess":

> ... She had a heart – how shall I say? – too soon made glad,
> Too easily impressed; she liked whate'er
> She looked on, and her looks went everywhere.

Her life was not easy. At dinners Kerr would not only turn down his own wine glass but hers, when she would not have minded a glass of

A low temperature physics experiment in the Sir James Dunn Building.

wine. He was angry when his son Donald married a charming Jewish girl, Lucille Calp of Saint John, and Kerr's attitude was not temporary. Nessie Kerr also knew too well her husband's standing in the Dalhousie community; the only dean who spoke well of him was another authoritarian, McLean of Dentistry. At a student concert given by the "Limelighters," Kerr stood up and objected to the lyrics of one song, about a lady whose dress was up to the neck in front, "but so low in the back that it revealed a new cleavage." Another president might well have ignored it. The students did not appreciate Kerr's intervention and booed. He, of course, left. It is difficult to avoid feeling sorry for A.E. Kerr; he could not help his constricted Louisburg background that he never quite seemed to rise above. Though sufficiently endowed with intelligence, he lacked taste, style, manners. A devoted servant of the university, he conceived his duty within a hard, tight focus. Even the board had come to realize by the late 1950s that he was increasingly a liability. In short, the job grew but he did not, or not sufficiently.[37]

His talent lay in saving money, but it was often brutal or *mesquin*, pinching librarians' salaries, or refusing the British Museum catalogue to the library. "Too rich for our blood," he had said. Douglas Lochhead left Dalhousie because of a whole litany of such meanness. Kerr's joy was in seeing buildings emerge from his economies; but in the end economies were his worst enemy as staff morale slowly crumbled around him.

Nor was he ever sufficiently seized of the autonomy of the university. There was an interesting incident in 1961. John Diefenbaker, the prime minister, came to speak at Dalhousie mainly about Canada's role in world affairs. The crowd of students were polite but thought he neglected national issues. On the front page five days later the *Gazette* reported, "Mr. Diefenbaker said: ..." and followed that with three inches of blank column. The Halifax *Herald* noted it and reproduced it on its front page a few weeks later. Diefenbaker saw it and he was furious. He promptly phoned Donald McInnes, who besides being chairman of the board was a leading Nova Scotia Conservative. McInnes phoned president Kerr, who summoned the president of the Student Council, and got Henry Hicks, the new dean of arts and science, to talk sternly to the editor, Michael Kirby. But Hicks relished the *Gazette*'s jibe, and his reprimand to Kirby had no weight in it. All he insisted on was a promise not to do it again.

A year later the *Gazette* came out with a comic edition; under the rubric, "John Causes Fall of Hall," a front-page article, with a photograph of a urinal, suggested that the fixture had got installed in Shirreff Hall by mistake. The *Gazette*'s editor was Ian MacKenzie, son of

Dr Ian MacKenzie, professor of surgery. The father thought the *Gazette* issue tasteless, which it was; but the president was outraged and wanted MacKenzie expelled. The father was on the Senate Discipline Committee, and naturally stepped down when it heard his son's case. But Senate refused to do anything.

In fighting the *Gazette*, Kerr usually lost. He had rows with three successive and able *Gazette* editors – Denis Stairs, Mike Kirby, and Ian MacKenzie. All three were trying to get a rise out of him and all three succeeded. A wiser man might have left well enough alone, and let Senate, or student opinion, take on the *Gazette*. The difficulty for the president was that the *Gazette* was read off-campus, and he invariably got the brunt of outside reactions, as with the Diefenbaker non-speech. But, unlike President Stanley MacKenzie or Carleton Stanley, Kerr's attitudes came from wrong premises.[38]

The Board of Governors kept Kerr as long as they did owing to the enormous weight and momentum carried by a full-time president. Members of the board were always unpaid volunteers who, outside of board committees, rarely met more than once a month, sometimes less; under Darrell Laing, board meetings were apt to be dispatched in an hour. As Gordon Archibald remembered, Dr Kerr would raise a subject and Laing would say something like, "Well that's all settled, isn't it, Dr. Kerr," who would say "Yes" and the board would move to the next item. Meetings convened at 7:00 P.M. were often over by 8:00. Donald McInnes was a more phlegmatic and patient chairman, but he too liked to see the board agendas got through with celerity and without rancour.

McInnes also knew and liked Henry Hicks. It was not surprising that as early as December 1960, in reflecting about a new president for Dalhousie, old Jack Johnstone could say with his usual shrewdness,[39] "The rails are greased for Henry H."

· 9 ·

Dalhousie Being Transformed:
The First Years of Henry Hicks
1963–1968

Henry Hicks, president and presence. Stanfield intervenes with government support. University Grants Committee, 1963. Changes in federal funding. Proposal to unite Nova Scotia Technical College and Dalhousie. Capital grants for buildings. Dorothy Johnston Killam and her will. Graduate Studies. The Tupper Medical Building. Faculty of Health Professions, 1962. The Weldon Law Building. H.B.S. Cooke of Arts and Science. Grade 12 admission, 1966. A Student Union building, at last.

He's a bon vivant and scholar whose white locks curl past his collar
And on whose nose there sits a pair of gold-rimmed semi-specs,
'Tween town and gown a catalyst, politico, philatelist,
Part pragmatist, part poet, part Tyrannosaurus Rex.
In Oxford days a rowing Blue, a middling hockey player too,
An advocate in later years who reached the Premier's chair
Now Senator and President and alternating resident
Of gracious South End Halifax and Ottawa so fair.
He knows the vintages of wines from labels to the very vines,
He knows his jazz recordings and he knows his Oscar Wilde;
He even knows a thing or two about the TV interview
And how to leave a viewer half-annoyed and half-beguiled.
He loves the limelight, loves the chair, loves gallivanting here and there
Loves pontifical perks and all prerogatives of rank.
In fact, to sum up everything, it might be well to crown him King …
He'd likely be the best one since the days of Louis Cinq.

That 1979 sketch of Henry Davies Hicks by Jim Bennet ('53), introduces the man who moved into the president's office on 1 September

244

1963. Hicks was neither tall nor especially dignified; he was slim and energetic, mercurial and quick-witted, not strong on patience or persistence; he gave the impression of being ready to jump at fences before he had quite got to them. But he had considerable talents. He had a politician's tolerance of critics and criticism; he was not thin-skinned. He also had style, a happy amalgam of Nova Scotia and Oxford, a knack for making celebratory occasions memorable, a rich and engaging blend of black tie formality and earthy humour. Delicacy was not his strong point, and some could be offended by his abrupt and salty shafts. Nor was he subtle; if his bowler hats were from St James Square, London, his humour was from Hicks' Ferry, Nova Scotia.

The Hicks family were Yankee stock out of Rhode Island who had come in 1759 to take up old Acadian land in the Annapolis valley. John Hicks, JP, was a member of the Assembly from 1768 to 1770. Originally Quakers, the Hicks men married Anglican and Methodist women and by the time Henry was born in 1915, the eldest of four children, the family at Hicks' Ferry were Methodist. Motor cars forced the building of a bridge over the Annapolis River and the name Hicks' Ferry was given up for Bridgetown. Hicks's father ran a woodworking and lumber business; when a local undertaker, who owed a great deal of money, went bankrupt, Hicks's father became a funeral director and licensed embalmer. Young Hicks finished high school in Bridgetown in 1932 with the highest graduation marks of any in the provincial examinations. His parents thought him young at seventeen for the rigours and temptations of college, so he taught a one-room school for a year. His bent was chemistry and physics; with several scholarships on offer, Hicks chose not the nearest college (Acadia) but Mount Allison over in Sackville, New Brunswick, with its Methodist connection. By the time he graduated from Mount Allison in 1936 his interest in chemistry and physics had begun to wane and he wanted courses about the world, its history, and the way it worked. So he came to Dalhousie and took a fat roster of classes in the social sciences. There was also a story, not ill-founded, that he came to Dalhousie to polish possibilities for getting a Rhodes scholarship. That he did in 1937.

By that time Hicks had decided to study law. In Exeter College, Oxford, his Nova Scotia Latin saved him, for two of the five final law papers were in Latin, though they could be answered in English. Hicks had come to Oxford a Methodist teetotaller, but he rapidly developed a palate for wines, and within two years he was one of the more knowledgeable members of his college about Rhine wines. Hicks learned rapidly. Within one year, knowing nothing about rowing, he was coxswain of his college crew, being too light to row. He acquired fame in a bold and definitely unorthodox manoeuvre on the Thames at Oxford, and in the spring of 1940 was coxswain of the Oxford crew in the annual Oxford and Cambridge boat race. Oxford lost by five lengths, rather a lot, though probably not owing to their coxswain.[1]

In 1941 he joined the Canadian army, became a specialist in radar, and had risen to captain when he was discharged in 1945. He ran in the Nova Scotia provincial election of October 1945 as a Liberal for Annapolis County, the same year as his marriage to Paulene Banks, daughter of a newspaper editor in Caledonia, Queens County. They had four children.

Hicks had flair, elegance, and self-confidence. Careful, calculating, cool judgments were not for him. He was impatient of fools and rarely hesitated to show it, hypocrisy not coming naturally to him. He was frank and open, almost to a fault, and thought Dalhousie should be too. "If I can't show Dalhousie's books to anyone – and still get away with what I want to do – I shouldn't be president," he told a colleague once. He enjoyed being outspoken. He liked to excel at whatever he chose to do, carpentry, stamps, wine, indulging his literary tastes for authors such as Edgar Allen Poe and Oscar Wilde. His intellectual agility was considerable. More than one observer noted how quickly Hicks would get at the nub of a problem, even after hearing only part of the evidence; businessmen liked him for that. He could recognize talent in others, and was attracted to brilliant, off-centre people, "odd-balls" as one friend remarked, and would bring them into Dalhousie's service. This worked, though there was occasionally a disastrous misjudgement. It was clear that Hicks would be a president very different from his predecessor.[2]

By the end of 1962 Senate's Committee on University Government had considered the appointment of a president, proposing a joint committee of four each from Senate and Board of Governors, all the proceedings to be confidential. The proposal had not yet been accepted by the board. At Senate's request, four members, Dickson, Edwards, Guptill, and Read, met with McInnes before Christmas 1962, suggesting they would like a joint meeting with the board executive on the appointment of a president, that while it was not their purpose to transgress upon the power and function of the board, they would like an interchange of information. McInnes agreed to try to arrange it. But the board did not wait. On 4 February the executive committee reviewed the names of several possibilities and agreed that Henry Hicks was their man, and so recommended to the full board that very day. By this time Hicks really wanted to be president and would have been disappointed had he not been asked.[3]

The board was uneasy about Hicks's political connections and asked him to pledge not to take an active role in politics or express political opinions. They produced a letter to that effect for him to sign. Hicks refused. "Gentlemen," said Hicks to the board committee, "you've made a mistake. First of all, you've made a mistake in offering the presidency of the university to someone who[m] you think you have to tie by a commitment like this, but secondly, you've made a mistake if you think I would ever sign such a letter." In the past three years, he said, his minor political activities had been quite harmless and they would so continue. But he refused to be bound. The committee picked up the letter and the matter was never heard of again. Hicks believed that members of the university should be allowed to become MPs, MLAs or whatever, and later persuaded the board to make it as convenient as possible for staff members to run in elections. That was a tradition that went back eighty years to Weldon's election to the Canadian House of Commons in 1887.[4]

The question of the president's house on Oxford Street was more awkward. The official residence, given by R.B. Bennett in 1925, actually abutted part of Hicks's lot, which faced Coburg Road. Hicks's house was a big comfortable place, in good repair, and he had no wish to move his whole household a distance of a mere two hundred feet. Moreover, he was convinced the board would not spend the money needed to bring the old place, built about 1890, up to scratch. Thus he preferred to stay where he was; to that end in 1964 he sold his house to Dalhousie for about $40,000, a fair market price. Dalhousie would thus pay upkeep and taxes. On Hicks's retirement he would have the option of buying it back. The regular president's house on Oxford Street would now be vacant. But nothing around Dalhousie in those days was vacant for long. There was talk about using the house for space desperately needed for the Psychology Department. R.B. Cameron, chairman of the board's Building Committee, took "rather violent exception" to that idea, but he was eventually overruled by necessities.[5]

Thus was Hicks appointed, effective 1 September 1963. He was forty-eight years old. His appointment was officially until the 31 August after his sixty-fifth birthday – that is, until 1980. His salary would be $18,000 a year, with a car allowance of $1,000 a year and a similar entertainment allowance.

As Hicks was being installed as president on 31 January 1964, his wife Paulene was dying of leukemia. She was diagnosed with it in December; the drugs given her to conquer the disease broke down her immune system, and she died of pneumonia in February. The last time she was out of hospital was to attend her husband's installation. Hicks was left to cope with his house and four children, ages ten to sixteen, growing up and needing attention. His domestic life under some strain, a year later Hicks would marry a lady he had first known when he was at Dalhousie in 1936–7, Margaret Gene Morison. They had also faced each other in the 1950s when he was minister of education and she the negotiator for the Nova Scotia Teachers' Union. They were both fifty years old.

Hicks was fortunate also in another partnership, his vice-president, Horace Read, dean of law from 1950 to 1964, who would remain vice-president until 1969. Read was a good choice, well respected downtown in legal circles, cool, unflappable, knowledgeable. In Hicks's absences from Dalhousie for weeks at UNESCO conferences in Paris in the autumns of 1964 and 1966, to say nothing of university business outside Halifax, Read was the solid back-up; if conservative, he was so in the best sense, wanting what was best of the old, while ready to adopt what was useful in the new. He was also good at smoothing academic feathers ruffled by Hicks's abrupt ways.

While in important respects Dalhousie and Hicks were lucky to find each other, it was also true that both benefited by the turn of federal politics. The Diefenbaker administration was defeated in the general election of April 1963 and the Liberal government which succeeded it would last until 1979, through nearly all of Hicks's presidency. With fifteen years' experience as a Liberal politician in Nova Scotia, Hicks could count on friends and political colleagues in Ottawa, and he was never averse to using them. It also happened that the Nova Scotian government, under Robert Stanfield, was for Dalhousie a benign presence. Stanfield was fair-minded, intelligent, judicious, a Dalhousie alumnus ('36), who had long been a friend of Dalhousie. As both Conservative premier and minister of education, within the limits of being seen to be fair to other universities, he would continue his support, even if at times he would find Hicks headlong and demanding.

Nova Scotia Decides to Support its Universities
In 1958 Stanfield had decided that the Nova Scotian universities needed some modest financial support, and provided a grant of $250,000 for all the Nova Scotian universities to strengthen Arts and Science. Of that Dalhousie got 27 per cent. The sharing was not derived from a formula but represented Stanfield's judgment of what each university should get. It would stay the same for the next four years, while Dalhousie and other Nova Scotian universities wrestled

with increasing expenses and stationary revenue, with serious and potentially overwhelming increases in student numbers looming portentously on the horizon.[6]

In 1955 Edward Sheffield, former registrar at Carleton, then with the Dominion Bureau of Statistics, launched a blockbuster paper at the annual meeting of the Association of Universities and Colleges of Canada (AUCC); he predicted drastic increases in student numbers over the next decade. How right he was! The university-age population in Canada almost doubled, from 860,000 in 1950 to one and a half million in 1970. More significantly, the percentage of that population attending university increased markedly, from 7 per cent in 1950 to 20 per cent in 1970. Those figures meant formidable changes. McGill would more than double its student numbers from 1950 to 1970, and Dalhousie would more than quadruple, from 1,553 in 1950 to 6,616 in 1970, some 426 per cent.[7]

What had created this crisis – for crisis it was – was the weight of demography. The war veterans came home in 1945 and 1946 and it showed at once in the rise of the birth rate. Dalhousie registration changed little in the 1950s, but by 1958–9 it started to climb; the big increases were between 1962–3 and 1965–6, when enrolment rose at an annual average of 13 per cent. In one year, 1964–5, enrolment jumped over 19 per cent above the year before. Thus the Dalhousie of 1,496 students in 1957–8 had become 2,613 six years later. Dalhousie was not unique; every university in the country, in varying degrees, was going through similar trauma. "Our university crisis far worse this fall," said the *Financial Post* in October 1963, "as students jam in." The Halifax *Herald* in February 1964 accepted "wholeheartedly" the need for a major increase in provincial spending on universities. The $250,000 a year for all the Nova Scotian universities was only the first drop in a huge bucket of necessities. Drastic and immediate increases were now required.

On 17 December 1962 a delegation of university presidents went to see Stanfield on just that mission. They wanted the $250,000 increased to $1 million, and even agreed about its distribution. Stanfield forestalled that; he created a University Grants Committee. He needed specific, detailed, and informed advice about what Nova Scotia should do, not only about the private universities but about public institutions such as the Nova Scotia Technical College, the Nova Scotia College of Art, and the Nova Scotia Agricultural College in Truro. He also needed advice about facilities and standards, how to avoid duplication and increase cooperation between all the institutions. The committee he struck was a small but powerful engine. Chairing it was Larry MacKenzie, just retired from the UBC presidency; with him was Dr Arthur Murphy ('30), a well-read and respected Halifax surgeon, associated with Saint Mary's; the third member of the panel was E.L. Goodfellow, deputy minister of finance of Nova Scotia. Stanfield set it up formally on 7 January 1963 by order-in-council, and made it statutory in the Universities Assistance Act of 1965.[8]

Stanfield wanted his new University Grants Committee to give him an interim report by the spring of 1963 and a much fuller one in the autumn. It soon became obvious when the Committee met the Nova Scotian university presidents on 23 February, that MacKenzie *was* the committee, bringing to bear a range of experience of both universities and committees that quite eclipsed the others. The policy of the committee was to make recommendations to the Nova Scotian government sufficiently strong that they could not be refused. The course MacKenzie had pursued with the British Columbian government he was determined to follow with the Nova Scotian: get the government to respect his recommendations. Hence his remark to his colleagues, "The day the Government reduces our funds by one penny we can call it quits."[9]

Hicks bluntly told the University Grants Committee how far Nova Scotia had to go to catch up to Ontario and British Columbia. In 1962–3 Dalhousie's income was $3.9 million, the main sources of which were:

	%
Students fees	27
Endowment	15
Federal grants (general)	12
Federal grants (research)	20
N.S. support (health and medical, dental, law)	13
Gifts and bequests	7
	94

Over and above that Nova Scotia contributed to Dalhousie general funds only what might be called the Stanfield money, $67,520, 1.74 per cent of Dalhousie's total income. As Hicks pointed out in 1963, Nova Scotia may have excelled in the past, but since 1945 it had fallen steadily and cumulatively behind other provinces. There was some irony in his saying this, for Hicks himself, as minister of education and as premier, had done nothing for the universities. Of course, in the 1960s circumstances had changed. Even the following year, 1963–4, when Nova Scotia had substantially increased its grants – Dalhousie's was now 9 per cent of its income – the comparative grants per full-time student were startling:

	$
British Columbia	949
Alberta	1,053
Saskatchewan	1,267
Manitoba	706
Ontario	1,193
Quebec	614*
New Brunswick	575
Prince Edward Island	425
Newfoundland	678
Nova Scotia	180

*The Quebec figure was difficult to calculate for it involved three different departments.

Hicks did not feel that Larry MacKenzie was sufficiently seized of the urgency of Dalhousie's position: its professional faculties were under enormous pressure, and its graduate studies had trebled registration between 1960–1 and 1963–4. Hicks and MacKenzie met to discuss this and other questions in November. A year later the University Grants Committee suggested that Dalhousie discuss with King's, Saint Mary's, and the Nova Scotia Technical College the prospect of a major university library, a common athletic centre, with Dalhousie assuming the bulk of the expensive scientific and pre-engineering programs. Hicks knew very well the jealousies and the difficulties implied in those suggestions. "I am sure you realize the delicacy of Dalhousie's position," he told the committee. But, he added, the new Association of Atlantic Universities had improved cooperation and such new departures might just be possible.[10]

The Association of Atlantic Universities (AAU) came from a suggestion by the Grants Committee in December 1963. Two earlier forums had been the Central Advisory Committee on Education in the Maritime provinces, set up in 1924, and more recently the APICS, Atlantic Provinces Inter-University Committee on the Sciences, founded in 1958 by W.R. Trost, who became Dalhousie's dean of graduate studies in 1961. The purposes of these groups were narrowly focused. The AAU developed a broader mandate. It was started at Dalhousie in January 1964, at a meeting presided over by Hicks, where his warmth and verve were especially effective. It would be administered through an executive committee and an advisory board, its first executive director being Monsignor H.J. Somers of St Francis Xavier. The early meetings went extremely well, so much so that Colin McKay, president of UNB, wished they had created the AAU ten years ago.

The business of the AAU soon ramified. One of its many advantages as a forum for common policies was that it could operate at different

Henry Hicks was known for off-the-cuff remarks, sometimes barbed, but nearly always driven by a rich sense of humour. Not all his targets were amused.

levels, involving presidents, vice-presidents, and others. In July 1964 the business officers of ten universities met to discuss common problems. Even physical plant supervisors had meetings. In 1966 the deans of residences, male and female, debated current issues such as, for example, the question of liquor on campuses. In general, the Atlantic universities did not permit liquor on campuses, a convention impossible to enforce. The deans agreed to recommend that drinking by students of legal age should be permitted on campuses at controlled outlets, subject to provincial liquor acts.[11]

A New Mode of Federal Subsidy

In the autumn of 1964 the AAU convened a special meeting at the Halifax Club to meet the Bladen Commission. Dean Vincent Bladen of the University of Toronto had been appointed in 1964 by the AUCC, at the request of the Pearson government, to recommend a new mode of administering the federal grants to universities in ways more consistent with constitutional propriety. The federal grants which it had administered since 1951–2 had started on the basis of 50 cents per head of population in each province. The amount was doubled in 1956–7 and by 1962–3 was $2. The Bladen Commission noted that the level of capital expenditures in the Atlantic provinces' universities might have to be tripled or even quadrupled to bring them up to standards in the rest of Canada. The Pearson government did not like these recommendations and rejected them at a federal-provincial conference in October 1966. Instead, with the acceptance of the provincial governments, it adopted a new scheme: the unconditional transfer to the provinces of four percentage points of income tax, one of corporation tax, topped up by whatever was necessary to give each province one of two options, either 50 per cent of its expenditure on all post-secondary education, or $15 per capita of population, whichever was the greater.

The problem for the universities was that the money so transferred went to the provinces directly. Instead of getting a fat cheque from the AUCC, it would come from the provincial government. Nor was there any control over how the provinces would spend the federal money; if they chose, they could spend it on highways. They could also decide which option they preferred. Nova Scotia preferred the 50 per cent principle; thus future federal transfers would depend upon the level of provincial post-secondary spending. The more Nova Scotia spent on universities, the more it got.[12]

Since Ottawa had been giving $5 per capita in 1966–7, the increase for 1967–8 would, in effect, treble Ottawa's contribution. The new arrangements offered some difficulties – Ottawa had not yet defined what operating costs would comprehend – but the new system was finally put in place in the 1967 Federal-Provincial Fiscal Arrangements Act.

One effect of the government's new mode of handling university grants was to force the AAU universities to deal more directly with the provincial governments; as Colin McKay put it to Hicks, "We should be content to work out with our provincial governments the securing of a fair share of the federal revenues paid over to the provinces." That was not going to be easy. In a speech at the installation of Monsignor MacLellan as president of St Francis Xavier in January 1965, Stanfield reflected about university autonomy when the province was now going to foot such a substantial proportion of the bill:

The public will not recognize the right of any university to do what it likes at the expense of the taxpayer. If Dalhousie should wish to maintain a graduate school in Egyptology the people of Nova Scotia are surely not compelled to finance it ... In other words, academic freedom cannot mean freedom to use public money for objectives which the Legislature does not accept ...

A university may of course decide what its objectives are, and may raise money to achieve those objectives; but it cannot decide the objectives for which the taxpayer's money may be spent.

That speech certainly fluttered the dovecotes and upset the presidents and the *Chronicle-Herald*. But Dalhousie's president was not upset. As a former politician he understood what Stanfield meant, and indeed congratulated him on being so forthright. Stanfield for his part remarked that he intended no restrictions on academic planning, only that the legislature had to have authority to deal with universities.

An example of such efforts occurred later in 1965. A row developed over the University Grants Committee's effort to streamline engineering education in Nova Scotia. Dalhousie and the Nova Scotia Technical College (NSTC) liked the proposals, but in the other universities they met so much resistance that Stanfield commissioned a report on the whole subject of engineering education from R.R. McLaughlin, dean of engineering at the University of Toronto. McLaughlin bluntly recommended the union of NSTC with Dalhousie, with NSTC becoming the Dalhousie Faculty of Applied Science and Engineering. All the universities would continue to offer pre-engineering as before. This sensible recommendation was bolstered privately by C.J. Mackenzie a Dalhousie engineering graduate of 1909 (the last engineering class before the NSTC was started), and head of the National Research Council from 1944 to 1952. He told Hicks (the letter being passed on to Stanfield and to George Holbrook, president of the NSTC), that "The ideal solution for Nova Scotia is, in my opinion, crystal clear. The NSTC should become a Faculty of Dalhousie and be built into a strong applied science centre."

That idea got short shrift from the other universities. Hicks was un-usually cautious. He knew how tender a subject it was. He told C.J. Mackenzie that he doubted "how useful or effective it would be for me, as President of Dalhousie, to become an active protagonist of the views you have expressed." Stanfield, in the face of the political power wielded by Acadia, St Francis Xavier, and Saint Mary's, was very guarded in his comment to Hicks:

There may be very rigid and widespread views on this subject. Consequently I do not know that we are likely to see any change or not. I think all we can do is see what happens to the recommendations made by Dean McLaughlin. My guess is that not very much will happen unless the government is pre-pared to push people around pretty fiercely, and this might have unfortunate repercussions.

Other universities feared Dalhousie; Acadia, for example, resented Dalhousie getting control over the entrance process to yet one more profession. It had Law, Dentistry, and Medicine: was that not, surely, enough, without adding engineering? It was an attitude analogous to that which had led the universities in 1907 to establish NSTC in the first place. Thus, except for the sharing of a few classes between Dal-housie and NSTC, nothing was done.

All the universities, Dalhousie included, could at times be greedy and noisy. In March 1965 the presidents of the Nova Scotia universi-ties sent Stanfield a minatory letter about funding increases which he answered with some heat:

The time seems to have arrived for a very frank exchange of views. I would like to see you at your earliest convenience ... I wish to say immediately, however, that I find ... [part] of your letter [of March 5, 1965] together with its implications deeply offensive ... It had seemed to me and to my associates in the government that this increased assistance to our universities [for 1965–6] would be very significant. If it does not appear so to you, one in my position is tempted to conclude that we might very well use this money for some other significant purpose, and we have many available.

Stanfield was not going to be pushed around.[13]

Provincial Capital Loans: The Lever for Building
Stanfield did mention, however, that there would be significant in-creases in capital grants. This was Nova Scotia's other major contri-

bution to universities, especially to Dalhousie. Hitherto capital grants to universities in Nova Scotia had been negligible. Dalhousie was given $150,000 in 1956 toward the new Dental building; other than that until 1964 the only capital grants had been to the Nova Scotia Technical College and to Dalhousie for the Sir Charles Tupper Medical Building. In 1965 the Universities Assistance Act authorized capital grants. An ingenious practice developed of funding new university buildings: Dalhousie (or other university) would apply to the University Grants Committee for a provincial loan up to 90 per cent of the cost of construction of a proposed building and would find 10 per cent of the construction costs itself and pay for the land and the interior furnishings. Residences, being subject to funding by Central Mortgage and Housing Corporation, were not eligible. The loan would be interest-free, and a separate accounting would be established for each building. The loan would be repaid by the university at 3 per cent per year; the government would set up a sinking fund to which it would contribute 2 per cent a year. At the end of twenty years the loan would be paid off, the 3 per cent annual contribution being part of the university's operating expenses.

These two things – operating costs split between Ottawa and Halifax, and capital project loans arranged through the Grants Committee and the provincial government – were the base that allowed Dalhousie to build so rapidly in the 1960s, and enabled it to accommodate the trebling of student enrolment between 1960–1 and 1970–1. The Central Mortgage and Housing Corporation loaned money for residence extensions, up to 95 per cent of cost, the repayment period not to exceed the useful life of the building, in any case not more than fifty years. On this basis, Shirreff Hall's east wing was finished in 1963, and the two extensions to Howe Hall, the northeast wing in 1964 and the southeast in 1967.

As those big numbers of students began to loom on the horizon in 1960, campus planning at Dalhousie began to take shape. On 15 December 1960 Senate moved that each faculty should submit proposals for a five-year plan, to be submitted by 28 February 1961 and discussed in Senate a year later. Out of this came, jointly with the board, the extension to Shirreff Hall, as well as the extensions to Howe Hall. Hicks had not given much thought to the physical planning of the campus. His instinct seemed to be that Dalhousie could put up a building wherever it liked. H.B.S. Cooke, dean of arts and science, uneasy with that cavalier attitude, told Hicks that campus planning needed priority, and soon. In November 1963 Cooke calculated that by 1970–1 his faculty would need nearly three times as much physical space as it then had available. Brought up short by that

President Henry Hicks breaking ground for the new Law Building.

kind of analysis, Hicks recognized its urgency and so the Montreal firm of Marshall and Merrett was consulted. They reported in 1964. Campbell Merrett told the Board of Governors in July 1964 that Dalhousie would need 65 per cent more land than it had at present, at a cost of between $5 and $7 million. He recommended that most of the area between Coburg Road and South Street, between Oxford and Robie streets, should be slated for park and industrial zoning and that Dalhousie should get powers of expropriation to take what it really needed. Merrett even talked of Dalhousie going south of South Street and north of College Street.

Planners and presidents seemed not, or not yet, to have realized the fundamental disruption the expansion of Dalhousie would create for lives and property in Halifax's south end; or, if they had, Dalhousie's necessity was thought sufficient justification. Larry MacKenzie of the Grants Committee pointed out in November 1964 the need for high-rise thinking on the Halifax peninsula, that the delights of horizontal development would soon have to end. City staff were more conscious of local opinion; they saw the way the tentacles of Dalhousie's growth were choking out well-established local housing, local life, to say nothing of depletion of local taxes. Thus they recommended against rezoning College Street, and would cut the Dalhousie request to as small an area as possible along University Avenue – that is, to one hundred feet deep on either side, which was only half of what Dalhousie had asked for. One Marshall and Merrett recommendation Hicks adopted immediately: the joining of the Macdonald Library with the Chemistry Building. That gave some 40,000 square feet of new floor space. Hicks believed that suggestion alone justified the expense of the report.

The new School of Architecture at NSTC, under Professor Douglas Shadbolt, graduated its first class of five students in May 1965. Their final-year project was to produce a development plan for the Dalhousie campus, using Marshall and Merrett data and with Dean Cooke as the "client." They introduced the platform concept of indoor circulation areas between the major buildings at the basement level. They also suggested purchasing properties in the open market for departmental use between Studley and Forrest.

The architectural students' plan appealed more to city staff than the Marshall and Merrett one, for it helped to resist Dalhousie's plans for rezoning. Hicks suggested that Shadbolt's students' plan had helped to weaken Dalhousie's case at City Hall, and that in turn produced a temporary sharpness between Shadbolt and Hicks. Hicks apologized graciously – he was good at that – but he was not above firing a few parting shots, offering his own comments on the Tech proposals. Nevertheless, both plans had merits. The Technical College plan assumed that Dalhousie's departmental office needs could be met by ordinary purchase of properties in the open market, a sensible suggestion that Dalhousie had already begun to adopt, rather than by building a new departmental Arts and Science extension west of the existing Arts and Administration Building, as Marshall and Merrett wanted. On the other hand, the latter thought that official university buildings, between the Studley and Forrest campuses on University Avenue, would help tie the two campuses together. Thus the Law School, then the Student Union Building, and later the Arts Centre, were a product of this line of thinking.[14]

Few planners mentioned Dalhousie's power needs, but the university engineer did. In February 1965 Professor Arthur Chisholm told the president that Dalhousie's power use had grown so much that it really needed a sub-station. He described the existing complex of transformers, some owned by Dalhousie, some owned by Nova Scotia Light and Power, with assorted meters in different sections of the campus. The breaking point was the amperage that could be supplied on a 4,160-volt line. Dalhousie's needs would soon exceed that. Then the supply would have to jump to 23,000 volts. It seemed to Chisholm that Dalhousie should take over complete responsibility for electrical distribution on both campuses, build its own transformer station to take the 23,000 volts, and put it all on one meter. There would be 4,000-volt feeders for the Forrest and Studley campuses. Hicks had been a radar officer in the Canadian army during the war and knew what Chisholm was talking about; accordingly the transformer station – the new central services building between Seymour and Henry streets – was begun in 1968. The location was Hicks's idea, away from the main campus axis but sufficiently accessible. The 23,000-volt electrical distribution would be effected via utility tunnels connecting the major Studley buildings. These would carry not only high-voltage electricity, but telephone cables, steam (for heating), chilled water (for air conditioning where essential), with step-down transformers in several localities.[15]

In February 1965, as the Chisholm-Hicks correspondence developed about Dalhousie's needs for electrical power, Hicks was being made aware of huge new increases to Dalhousie's financial potential from quite another source. There had appeared on the scene a very rich widow, wealthier than Lady Beaverbrook, with a more civilized intelligence, but apt to be almost as ruthless: Dorothy Johnston Killam.

Dorothy Johnston Killam Comes to Town
Izaak Walton Killam died on 5 August 1955 from a heart attack while on a fishing trip in Gaspé. After paying substantial estate duties

President Henry Hicks addressing convocation, 1968.

(which the government used to establish the Canada Council) Dorothy Johnston Killam inherited over $40 million. Within ten years she had made that into $93 million. Born in 1899 in St Louis, Missouri, she was well educated, spoke passable French, and thanks to a long visit in Germany, German. She had wanted to be an Olympic swimmer, but her father had refused to countenance it. In 1921 she went to a party in Montreal and saw, as Douglas How relates it, "this tall, shy, withdrawn man with the eyes of an owl, and promptly announced to a friend her intention to marry him." She did just what she said she'd do. She was twenty-two years old, he was thirty-six. When she married and moved to Montreal, she mastered golf and tennis with the same determination that had won her medals in swimming. She had no children; she had one miscarriage and no babies came after that. Her husband had especially wanted to fund research in science, medicine, and engineering. But he did not like donating money for bricks and mortar; if people wanted money for a project, they should at least be able to put up the building for it. Dorothy Killam wanted what her husband wanted: that the Killam money stay in Canada, that it should enhance Canadian higher education, that it should strengthen Nova Scotia. She wanted to arrest the export of Canadian researchers to the United States. Dalhousie combined higher education, research in medicine, science, and engineering (via physics), and was Nova Scotian. Moreover, Dalhousie gave Killam an honorary degree in 1946, and herself one in 1959.[16]

Her will was years in the making, and the influences in its process were partly Nova Scotian. About 1962 she invited Stanfield, apparently at Henry Hicks's suggestion, to go to the World Series in New York. Mary Stanfield was not invited. Stanfield braved his wife's anger and went. One night in the Plaza Hotel they talked until 3 AM; Stanfield's impression was that she wanted to talk to someone whom she could trust. On the way to the New York airport the next day she outlined to him what she would like to do for Nova Scotia and Dalhousie.[17]

In January 1963 Dorothy Killam gave Dalhousie, under conditions of strict anonymity, 4,353,607 preferred shares in Canelco Services Limited, the income to be used to fund graduate scholarships in science, medicine, and engineering towards work leading to or subsequent to a doctor's degree. There were as yet no dividends, but each share could be redeemed for $1; the university was cautious and only cashed one million shares, to produce an income of about $130,000 a year. (After Quebec launched the James Bay hydroelectric project in 1971 the value of the shares rose steeply to about $12 a share.) Dorothy Killam used the gift as a test run to see how Dalhousie handled it, and for a few years it was known as the Anonymous Donor's Fund, its income being split between the Faculty of Graduate Studies (75 per cent) and Medicine (25 per cent). She clearly liked what she saw.[18]

In 1964 she had decided to change her domicile from Montreal to Halifax; she and her entourage (thirteen people plus dogs) descended on Halifax in April 1965. Her Halifax lawyer was Donald McInnes; at a McInnes dinner party in Dorothy Killam's honour, Gene Morison Hicks, the president's new wife, was appalled to hear her husband indicate that the Hickses would like to entertain Mrs Killam. That dinner party, the final touches that would finally bring Dalhousie $30 million, cost Gene Hicks $35; she was still teaching and had to take the day off, so the Education Department duly docked her a day's pay.[19]

In May Dorothy Killam asked Hicks to give another dinner party so that she could meet the Dalhousie deans; there were to be no ladies present but herself and Gene Hicks. It went well. She expected to leave the party at 10 PM and stayed till midnight. She sat by the window in the Hickses' house quizzing each of the deans in turn, Cooke of Arts and Science, Stewart of Medicine, McLean of Dentistry, Mac-Donald of Health Professions (the newest faculty), MacKay of Law, Trost of Graduate Studies. She liked the young deans, especially McLean, who had a brilliance and a presence that appealed to women, as Hicks conceded enviously. Blonde, petite, Dorothy Killam liked to wear a black dress and diamonds; diamonds suited her and she never believed that they should be locked away. Dean Cooke, South African and a geologist, fascinated by both diamonds and lady, estimated she was carrying close to $1 million worth. Despite her flair for clothes, jewelry, and drama, she liked good taste and good manners and hated vulgarity, rough talk, noisy or drunken guests. She loved music and had a sophisticated taste; she was on the board of the Metropolitan Opera and launched a new production of Richard Strauss's *Die Frau ohne Schatten* and others.[20]

Dorothy Killam was sufficiently impressed with the Dalhousie men, board chairman, president, and deans, that she began to think she should make further revisions to her much-revised will. These changes would give Dalhousie all her uncommitted money, without being split (as at that point it was in the residue section of her will) between Dalhousie, UBC, the University of Alberta, and the Montreal Neurological Institute. On 22 July 1965 she phoned Hicks from her Riviera villa, "La Leopolda," a place she had bought two years before. (The flight of steps leading up to it was made famous by a scene in the movie "The Red Shoes.") She told Hicks that she now wanted to leave to Dalhousie all her uncommitted funds. She also wanted to leave in Halifax a second memorial building to her husband's name, one on the Dalhousie campus to match the Children's Hospital to which she was already committed. She was thinking of a centre for post-graduate education; Hicks, knowing that Dalhousie's crying need was for a good library, suggested that it could also house a post-graduate centre. Dorothy Killam asked where such a library would go, for she knew Dalhousie geography by this time. Hicks told her at the corner of University and LeMarchant. "How much?" she asked. Hicks said he thought about $5 to $6 million. She thought it would cost at least that. (It would end costing $7.3 million.) Donald Byers, her Montreal lawyer, was already in France; he found her ready to redo her will, but also very weak from internal bleeding. She had had arthritis for years, but more seriously cancer, which was now either inoperable or which she refused to have treated further. She died peacefully at "La Leopolda" on 27 July 1965, five days after her last talk with Hicks, without the final changes being made.[21]

Nevertheless her will, carefully wrought, gave much to Dalhousie. She left $93 million, so designed that only a small portion of it was taxable through estate duties on personal bequests. The rest went to institutions: Dalhousie $30 million, UBC $14 million, the universities of Alberta and Calgary dividing $16 million, and $4 million going to the Montreal Neurological Institute.

The Dalhousie gift was complex, tied to Dorothy Killam's vision of what she wanted Dalhousie to be. It had three parts:

- $2 million, the income to be used for two Killam Memorial chairs in the sciences, to attract professors "of the highest distinction."
- $8 million, known as the Killam Memorial Salary fund, separate from all other funds, and to be used to help pay salaries for professors other than those in arts, by which she meant, the fine arts.
- The residue section was complicated but Dalhousie emerged with a considerable share of it, just over 30 per cent, or about $20 million.

This residue or reserve fund was to be used to provide fellowships, known as the Killam scholarships. She described what she expected: "A Killam scholar should not be a one-sided person and each scholar's special distinction of intellect should be founded upon sound character and good manners. No person should be qualified or disqualified as a Killam scholar on account of his or her race or religious opinions." The scholarships were tenable for two years, subject to review (and possible termination) after one, and renewable for as many years as deemed appropriate. They were to be available to Canadians or foreigners; Canadians could hold their scholarships anywhere in the world suitable to their purpose; those scholars from outside

Dorothy Killam married Izaak Walton Killam in April 1922. After her husband's death in 1955 she more than doubled the fortune he had left her. Of that, some 32 per cent came to Dalhousie, the largest gift it ever received.

Canada had to prosecute their study and research in Canada. The aim of the scholarships was clearly graduate study and research.[22]

There was a danger in those big legacies to Dalhousie which Hicks was well aware of, and pointed out to Colin McKay of UNB. McKay wanted to use the Killam gifts to Dalhousie as an argument for the New Brunswick Grants Committee to raise its grants to UNB. The danger to Dalhousie, as Hicks said, was that the Killam income might be deducted by the government from its grants. That had happened at McGill, where private money it had collected was deducted by the Quebec government from McGill's grant. The effect of such action, Hicks asserted, would be "to dry up completely the sources of donations to the universities in the future."[23]

The Killam money did for Dalhousie what government grants towards operating expenses and capital projects had not done: it gave Dalhousie funds it could call its own, which it could use to promote graduate work and research, and to attract scholars from across Canada, especially to its sciences but also to the new PH.D. programs in the humanities and social sciences, English, history, and political science.

Developing Graduate Studies

The major legatee of the Killam money was Dalhousie's Faculty of Graduate Studies. It had been created in 1948 as an umbrella to handle the MA students who had crowded into several departments of Arts and Science after the war. Its first dean was a scientist and researcher, J.H.L. Johnstone; in 1956 he was succeeded by C.L. Bennet of English. In the Dalhousie of the 1950s, graduate studies had an easy-going, slightly ramshackle quality; that began to change when a PH.D. was started in biology in 1955. Within ten years the major science departments all had PH.D. programs, and graduate work became decidedly more earnest and purposeful. What drove this development was the steep rise in graduate work experienced by all Canadian universities in the 1960s, and in this Dalhousie exceeded the national average. When Hicks was told in 1961 that graduate studies would treble within four years, he thought it was gross exaggeration by an ambitious dean. It wasn't an exaggeration. In 1960–1 Dalhousie had seventy-eight graduate students, in 1963–4 nearly 244, enrolment jumping by 66 per cent and 40 per cent in two successive years, with a further 35 per cent increase predicted for 1964–5. In fact Dalhousie was only able to accept one-fifth of those who applied, and those who were accepted soon exceeded Dalhousie's capacity to fund them, since they far outstripped professors' external grants. Dalhousie's graduate enrolment was drawn from four roughly equal sources: Dalhousie itself, other Atlantic universities, other Canadian universities, and foreign universities, about half of which were British or American. The Killam money was the glitter that caught the attention of external students.[24]

The dean who encouraged this development in the 1960s was Walter Trost, a chemist, who had come to Dalhousie in 1948 with a McGill PH.D. and an Oxford post-doctoral fellowship. On 1959 he had started the Atlantic Provinces Inter-University Committee of the Sciences (APICS), the first academic attempt by Dalhousie to reach out to the other universities to coordinate and develop post-graduate work in the sciences. Thanks to Trost's energy and standing, it got full encouragement from the National Research Council in Ottawa, which in 1962 gave him a three-year enabling grant. Stanfield also helped. It went well; Trost, who was ready enough to build an empire within Dalhousie, was shrewd enough to be much more careful with other empires. When the Association of Atlantic Universities was founded in 1964, APICS became its committee on the sciences. Trost was appointed dean of graduate studies in 1961, almost certainly in recognition of his work in creating APICS. In 1965, when Mrs Killam met the deans *seriatim*, she quizzed Trost perceptively about what graduate studies needed, with such questions as "How would you use the money? What other sources do you have?" She liked his answers. She liked him.[25]

Trost also pushed for the PH.D. in the social sciences and humanities. There was more resistance here, for those disciplines required substantial library collections, which were difficult and slow to build, to say nothing of new staff. Nevertheless English began PH.D. work in 1965, History and Economics in 1967, Political Science in 1968.

Trost is a German word meaning comfort or solace, but he was often unlike his name. With colleagues who published, who did research, who did not mind him taking turf space, he could be inventive and helpful; but with those whom he did not respect, for whatever reason, or who threatened the growing hegemony of Graduate Studies, he was persistent, cantankerous and occasionally brutal. Alex McCarter of Biochemistry, one of the most valuable members of the Medical Faculty and in Senate, left Dalhousie in 1965 to be director of the Cancer Research Institute at the University of Western Ontario. "I feel bound to say to you as I leave Dalhousie," he wrote Hicks, "that I have found the relationships of this department with the Faculty of Graduate Studies and particular with Dean Trost, a source of frustration and irritation." Trost was not the main reason McCarter left, but as he put it, it contributed to "tripping the balance." Even with the president Trost could be blunt. "I must totally oppose," he told Hicks in March 1965, "any further cuts in the budget of the Faculty of Graduate Studies and of the Library." Hicks did not like him the less for that. Nine months later when Trost said he had invitations from Queen's and from Tufts (in Medford, Massachusetts) to give papers on his specialty, molecular orbital calculations in metallic systems, Hicks not only approved but was delighted. Be sure, Hicks said, "you take sufficient time to do a first-class job ... I know the dangers of administrative duties making such inroads on the time of scientists like yourself."[26]

Perhaps that was Hicks's effort to redirect some of Trost's energies away from his empire of graduate studies, for there had been nine months of wrangling over its role and function. Every Canadian university had had to come to terms with graduate studies in its own fashion. Trost believed that the dean of graduate studies had to have a lively interest in professors' appointments, in departmental budgets, in research programs, even in reporting publications, and in all departments, in all faculties, that did post-graduate work. The dean of medicine believed that most of that, in his faculty, was *his* concern and no one else's but the president's. The Faculty of Medicine, he said, "is not prepared to accept any precedent which places responsibility for research programmes of Dalhousie University in the hands of the Faculty of Graduate Studies." Trost was never strong on tact, and it has to be said that the medical professors on the Forrest campus had long been used to doing their own thing in their own way; they were under a dean, Chester Stewart, who delighted in controlling his bailiwick and who was not ready to tolerate interference of a new and aggressive dean of graduate studies. One dean, H.B.S. Cooke of Arts and Science, found it possible to work with Trost, though even his tractable good sense was tried sorely that summer of 1965. President Hicks finally took the view that Dalhousie departments, those in Arts and Science not least, must have one departmental head, and that departmental budgets applied to all activities both graduate and undergraduate, and that these would go "through one dean only." Hicks was not having departmental budgets carved up between two deans.[27]

Trost and Dean Stewart fought their war on into 1966. Trost praised Stewart as an able and intelligent dean of medicine, but quoted another administrator's opinion that Stewart was "the toughest and meanest in-fighter" that he had ever known. Part of the difficulty was a personality clash, part the distance between Studley and Forrest and the absence of understanding and communication. Stewart said most graduate students were "research assistants to a Professor, paid from his grant-in-aid, and chosen by him because of their research interests." That was undoubtedly true in medicine, and in some science departments, but it was not true in the humanities and social sciences. A 1966 outside adjudication by President James Beveridge of Acadia, at Hicks's request, solved little; what did it was Trost's departure. He accepted the position of vice-president of the new (1966) University of Calgary. A new and more sensible dean of graduate studies, Guy MacLean, a historian, succeeded in cooling things down. As MacLean wrote in February 1967 about Studley professors' joint membership in the two faculties, it "has not been a source of personal torment ... Those who have been interested in graduate work have been active in the Faculty of Graduate Studies; those who have not been interested have ignored it." It was a good Dalhousie recipe.[28]

Chester Stewart and the Tupper Medical Building

Dean Stewart had presided over the Medical Faculty since 1954 and had won golden opinions. Alex McCarter of Biochemistry, who had been with him since 1948, remarked, "One could not wish for a better man to deal with." Shrewd, perceptive, courageous, Stewart was a realist who enjoyed the dean's office and its power. He was also a dean who preferred decision to discussion. An interesting example was the row that developed in Physiology over the successor to its head, Beecher Weld, due to retire in 1965. Weld wanted as his successor an able, flamboyant, outspoken, bilingual American, J. Gordin Kaplan, on the staff since 1950. To Stewart's mind, Kaplan was too argumentative by half and he did not want him as head of Physiology; he wanted his own nominee. After consulting his Faculty Council and a small committee created by himself and Hicks, Dean Stewart invited John Szerb, the European-trained professor of pharmacology, to become head of Physiology, a subject in which Szerb would prove to be well qualified. Szerb accepted; he had an offer to move to the University of Ottawa in his old discipline, but he liked Dalhousie and the prospect of teaching physiology. His appointment was announced in February 1965 while Kaplan was on sabbatical leave in France. Kaplan was furious. He claimed the procedure dictatorial, blamed the dean for doing it, Szerb for accepting it, and returned in due course to wreak what havoc he could. He resigned a few months later to go to the University of Ottawa. Hicks was sorry to see him go but understood that Kaplan's violent opposition to the new head made his staying at Dalhousie difficult. A year or two later, a Dalhousie colleague whom Kaplan knew and respected, John Aldous, met him in Ottawa and got a big bear hug from Kaplan – that, too, was Kaplan's style. Kaplan promptly said, "I was a damn fool, wasn't I, for leaving Dalhousie?" Aldous looked at him. "Yes, you were."[29]

Sometimes Stewart had to be unrelenting. In 1964 the New Brunswick government said it would pay Dalhousie $60,000 for support of the Medical and Dental schools; Dalhousie estimated that the sixty-two New Brunswick students in those faculties cost $4,000 each annually – about $250,000. It had always been difficult to get Fredericton to pay its fair share of Medical and Dental school costs; that was partly out of old New Brunswick jealousy of Nova Scotia, and partly an instinct for not letting haughty Halifax take good New Brunswick money. Early in 1965 it came to a showdown between Stewart and Hicks on the one side, and Premier Robichaud of New Brunswick on the other. Neither side was giving an inch. Dalhousie threatened to cut New Brunswick's usual number of entering medical students, about twenty, down to four. The Robichaud government was warned, the New Brunswick Medical Association was advised, and the reasons explained. It got into the papers at the end of March and stirred up a hornet's nest. Hicks went to Fredericton, but only got a promise of $100,000, when at least double that was needed. Dalhousie still wasn't giving in. An exchange of telegrams in May brought another $50,000, at which point Hicks and Stewart agreed "to try to find places for as many deserving New Brunswick students as possible." Early in 1966 Robichaud promised $225,000 for 1966–7, and added another $50,000 backdated for 1965–6. As the row developed, there was talk of building a Medical School in Saint John, and a New Brunswick Medical Schools survey committee was struck in October 1966, to which Dalhousie submitted a strong brief, arguing against another medical school. Newfoundland was planning to open a medical school within five years and a third in the region was unnecessary. The New Brunswick proposal was in fact given up. Robichaud then helped Dalhousie get a big federal grant for its new medical building, and that year, 1967–8, the New Brunswick grant was $397,000.[30]

Dean Stewart's major contribution was the creation of the Sir Charles Tupper Medical Building. The Forrest Building was impossibly crowded and antiquated, and the Medical Sciences Building, put up with Rockefeller money in 1920–1 on College Street, was much the same; periodic review committees from the American Medical Association had noted it all pointedly. Dalhousie had made do, somehow, in the years since the war, but its A rating was probably dependent on getting substantial new headquarters.

The idea of naming a Dalhousie building after Sir Charles Tupper had occurred to G.F. Pearson half a century before. As premier of Nova Scotia in 1863 Tupper, with the help of the leader of the opposition, Joseph Howe, had brought Dalhousie into its new existence.

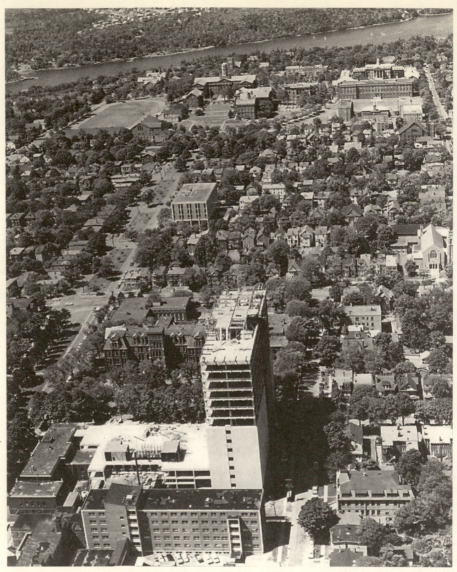

A good view of the Dalhousie complex as of 1966 looking west towards the North-West Arm, with the partly completed Sir Charles Tupper Building immediately in front.

Both men remained on the Dalhousie board until they died, Howe in 1873, Tupper in 1915. In May 1916 Pearson had suggested the possibility of naming a building after Tupper to President Stanley MacKenzie. But the suggestion disappeared and when it surfaced again it seems to have come independently to the fertile and expedient mind of Chester Stewart. One day in 1962 he was seeing President Kerr; Stewart had seen an announcement by Diefenbaker of $100 million to help celebrate Canada's centennial in 1967. Stewart wondered aloud if that might be tapped for a new medical building. Kerr was sceptical about such money for a private university. A fortnight later the light came on in the dean's mind: a new medical building could be named after Sir Charles Tupper, a Father of Confederation, a medical doctor who was the founding president of the Canadian Medical Assocation, and the principal founder of the Dalhousie University of 1863. "Think of the advantages of *that*!" Stewart said as he phoned Kerr with the idea. Kerr thought well enough of it to pass it to Donald McInnes. Thus a letter went to the Canadian Centenary Council on 29 November 1962, suggesting good reasons for a substantial grant towards the cost of a new Dalhousie medical building, to be named after one of the Fathers of Confederation, also one of the longstanding governors of Dalhousie. It so happened that the president of the council was none other than Larry MacKenzie, who had retired as president of UBC just five months before. He took an immediate interest in the project and pushed it. So too did the *Chronicle-Herald*.[31]

Within a week of Hicks becoming president in the fall of 1963 he was plunged into the work for the new medical building. The board appointed J. Philip Dumaresq architect two days later. The site for it had been debated all summer by the Medical Faculty's building committee. The chairman of the board building committee, R.B. Cameron, believed that the dean, the architect, and the university engineer should visit selected medical schools in Canada and the United States. First, however, they had to resolve the question of whether the new building should develop horizontally or vertically.[32]

The estimated cost of the building at that point was $5 million, which was what Dalhousie asked for. After the Pearson government took power in April 1963, the centennial grant to Dalhousie took on a specific form, $2.5 million, which was matched by the province early in 1964. By September 1964 the space requirements had risen by over 50 per cent and the total cost likewise, to $7.5 million.

Philip Dumaresq turned much of the architectural work over to Michael Byrne, who consulted professors about space requirements. Byrne found the most useful medical authority to be Dr Richard Saunders, Campbell professor of anatomy. During the planning stages

Saunders was sceptical of closed-circuit TV terminals in his area of the building; yet when everything was done his two floors for Anatomy had more terminals than any other two in the building. He and Dean Stewart were more than once at odds; both were authoritarian and both liked to defend, occasionally to extend, their own turf. It helped that in the dean's office much of the work for the new medical building devolved upon the assistant dean, Lloyd Macpherson, likeable, hard-working, sensible, who would himself become dean when Stewart retired in 1971.

The architects failed on some technical points, since they had not included furnishings needed for laboratories; and a Montreal firm, Affleck, Desbarats, had to redo some of the electrical and ventilation systems. Thus, by 1966, the cost was $10.5 million, with equipment estimated at a further $1.5 million. Fortuitously, the federal government's Health Resources Fund was in place, providing $500 million across Canada for the cost of facilities for research and for training health professionals. An application to that fund by Stewart in January 1967 produced $9.5 million. By that time, the reinforced concrete frame of the fifteen-storey building had been completed, the outside skin and windows were on, furniture was at hand, and the building was on schedule.

It was not the only new Dalhousie building going up at that time. There were also the Weldon Law Building, Shirreff Hall and Howe Hall extensions, and the Student Union Building, all of which were under way at various stages. Hicks threw himself into it with tremendous energy. In 1964 he also spent six weeks in Paris as head of the Canadian delegation to UNESCO. In January 1965 he went to hospital with a severe viral infection, from which he did not emerge until March. His colleague, President Cragg of Mount Allison, was not surprised. "You have been going at a fearful pace." A visitor in 1966, surveying Dalhousie's administrative structures at Hicks's request, remarked on the difference between the Dalhousie of 1961 and 1966. "I am impressed," Earl McGrath of Columbia wrote, "with the enormous vitality you have poured into the place." The fifteen-storey tower that now dwarfed the old 1886 Forrest Building was a symbol not just of Chester Stewart's percipience, Lloyd Macpherson's energy, but also of Hicks's readiness to take on responsibilities and his deft use of his many connections in Ottawa.[33]

Hicks had in hand a proposal for the Queen Mother to open the Medical Building as part of the centennial celebrations in July 1967. By Christmas, Prime Minister Pearson had agreed to come, and also the sixteenth Earl of Dalhousie, with the proviso that he could go salmon fishing on the Miramichi afterward with Hicks. There was hope that the grandson of Sir Charles Tupper, Sir James Macdonald Tupper of Vancouver, might attend, but he was old and ill and died as the building opened.[34]

The Sir Charles Tupper Medical Building was opened on Friday, 14 July 1967, by the Queen Mother. The ceremony was planned for outdoors; but there was rain that morning and at 7 AM Dean Stewart and Arthur Chisholm, the university engineer, decided it would have to be held in the rink. A hot and muggy place it was, that foggy July afternoon; but everything else went well, in Hicks's best style, grace, good humour, sufficient dignity but little stiff formality. The Tupper Medical Building was Nova Scotia's biggest centennial project; it symbolized Nova Scotia's contribution to medicare which was already in train and would begin on 1 April 1969. With Stanfield, Pearson, and other political dignitaries, Hicks and his wife dined that night with the Queen Mother on the *Britannia* in Halifax harbour. Then he went off salmon fishing with the sixteenth earl.[35]

The final bill for the building was $13 million and the equipment cost $5 million. The Kellogg Foundation gave money, Dalhousie alumni chipped in, so that the total received from federal, provincial, and other sources totalled $15,250,000. But Dalhousie still had to find the additional $2.75 million from somewhere. It was not the first nor the last time that it was left holding substantial and inconvenient remnants of big bills, and it would be a source of cumulative expense and frustration to Hicks and the Dalhousie board in the future.

The old Medical Sciences Building would now become the home of the College of Pharmacy. Pharmacy in Nova Scotia had received its first formal recognition in 1875 with the formation of the Nova Scotia Pharmaceutical Society, and a College of Pharmacy followed, affiliated with Dalhousie in 1912. In 1917 it was called the Maritime College of Pharmacy. George Arnold Burbidge, the Newfoundlander who had taught there since 1908, became its dean in 1925 and remained so until his death in 1943. In 1959 a survey by the Canadian Association for the Advancement of Pharmacy recommended that it be incorporated into the university. That was done by the board in February 1961 and Dalhousie courses leading to the bachelor of pharmacy were set up, under its first director, J.G. Duff, brought from the University of Saskatchewan.

The idea for an umbrella faculty for all the paramedical groups came from the Medical Faculty Council in 1959 and was finally put in place in 1962 as the Faculty of Health Professions. The other main element in the new faculty was the School of Nursing. In 1949 the old hospital-based program, the RN, required admission levels of high school that sometimes depended upon the community. Windsor

The Queen Mother at the convocation for the opening of the Sir Charles Tupper Medical Building, 14 July 1967. L. to r., the sixteenth Earl of Dalhousie, Premier Robert Stanfield, the Queen Mother, President Henry Hicks.

Hospital admitted to the RN girls with Grade 9; Halifax hospitals wanted junior matriculation. The RN program was described in one Dalhousie argument as the "poor girls' university." There was nothing wrong with that; but it explains why Dalhousie and the nursing profession sought in 1949 to upgrade the standards and training of nurses. Its first director was Electa McLennan, who did the hard pioneering work for twenty years. Her steely determination was masked by a lively sense of humour. She was a good person to have around in a crisis, and it was she who really built the Dalhousie bachelor of nursing. By 1963, when nursing joined the new faculty, it had ninety-five students, of whom 35 per cent were in the degree program. In that year, through the energy of Dr Arthur Shears of Physical Medicine, the School of Physiotherapy was put together and added. Thus was the Faculty of Health Professions created. It got an exceptional dean, Dr R.M. MacDonald, quiet, determined, unflappable; one's instinct was to trust him with anything.[36]

The Weldon Law Building

Law, too, got a new home. The building that had originally been designed and built for it in 1921–2, the faculty only got into in 1952. By then it was inadequate. In 1962–3 there were eight full-time professors (all but one of them, incidentally, Dalhousie graduates) and seventy-six students. That was expected to double in the next four years. New capital funding available from the province made planning of a new building both possible and desirable. After some difficulty in getting property (Dalhousie did not have, and would not have, powers of expropriation), a site was chosen on the north side of University Avenue, between Henry and Edward streets. Eastern Contracting was the low bidder on a contract for $1,385,166. The final cost was $1,809,801.

Dalhousie did for the new Weldon Law Building what it had never done before: it hired an interior decorator, an idea suggested by M.H.F. Harrington, the architect, and accepted without enthusiasm by Hicks, who suspected a frill Dalhousie could do without. However Beecher Weld, chairman of Senate's Cultural Activities Committee, noted in May 1965 "the stark, uninviting character" of Dalhousie buildings, especially the interiors, and recommended using 1 per cent of the contract price to embellish them. Of all the new buildings at Dalhousie, the Weldon showed a sense of style, a feel for elegance, not always found in the interior of others.[37]

The convocation to open the Weldon Law Building was held on 18 March 1967, with seven honorary degrees, among them one to Lady Beaverbrook. She was, for once, thoroughly pleased. Dalhousie

The first graduates of the new four-year bachelor of nursing program, July 1967, with Director Electa MacLennan in the centre and Assistant Director Jean Church upper right.

had a president who knew how such occasions should be handled. She said to her secretary, R.A. Tweedie, on their return to New Brunswick, "This has been a day that I won't soon forget." She seemed to revise her opinion of Henry Hicks and the Dalhousie people generally; it was probably owing to that success that in 1968 she accepted Dalhousie's invitation to become its second chancellor.[38]

In these years the Law School tended to dominate student politics. In the 1967 election for Student Council president, Wayne Hankey ('65) of classics lost to Dennis Ashworth ('64, '68) a second-year law student, by 1,103 votes to 332, a lopsided victory made possible, said the *Gazette*, by Law School's political machine. The Law School–Student Council connection encouraged Senate, in January 1968, to invite the Student Council president, and two colleagues chosen by the council, to become full members of Senate. They were welcomed to their first meeting on 12 February 1968. It was the result of work by the Senate Committee on University Government. But the person who was steadily behind bringing students into the governance of the university was the dean of arts and science, Herbert Basil Sutton Cooke.[39]

Linch-pin: Basil Cooke, Dean of Arts and Science

Basil Cooke was a South African geologist and palaeontologist, whom Dalhousie had brought to Halifax in 1961 from the University of Witwatersrand in Johannesburg. Educated at Cambridge and in South Africa, Cooke was forty-six years old on his arrival in Halifax. He already had a solid reputation in African paleontology, and would develop his pioneering work until well into the 1970s. Within two years Hicks asked him to be the new dean of arts and science. When he accepted, he told Hicks: "I'll be making decisions when you are not here." Hicks did not mind people making decisions. Cooke's decisions had the weight of perceptiveness and patience behind them, a combination of virtues useful for a dean. The contrast between Hicks and his most important dean could not have been more marked: a president who couldn't wait and a dean who could. Cooke was not a procrastinator; he had a forward mind, as his push for student senators illustrates, but he moved around obstacles rather than at them. Cooke knew well enough that academics tended to resist anything that looked as if it was being imposed from above. Thus when he wanted his faculty to do something that they might resist, he would get a few leading spirits to bring it up at a faculty meeting. Then from the chair he would proceed to pitch into it, why it should not be done. That would induce certain refractory elements in the faculty (there are always those) to prick up their ears and support the proposal. In this back-handed fashion, the dean would often get his way. Not always

Lady Dunn (Lady Beaverbrook after 1963), pleased with Dalhousie at last, opening the Sir James Dunn Law Library, March 1967.

however. There was a move in 1967 to persuade Arts and Science to establish a Department of Geography, one with which Cooke sympathized. A small committee was struck and so recommended. But it was shot down by Economics and by Sociology, on the ground that Geography's methodology was naive, its techniques descriptive, its purview already covered by other disciplines. The rest of the faculty was either indifferent or unfavourable, despite strong letters from outside authorities. Ultimately, Saint Mary's would take it up.

One difficulty Dalhousie was not able to avoid was stress between pure and applied mathematics. Applied mathematics in some respects included theoretical physics, and the issue can be summed up in the experience of Alex MacDonald, a Cape Bretonner who graduated in 1945, returning in 1949 to Dalhousie to teach theoretical physics. In 1960 MacDonald went to Palo Alto, but did not like California; President Kerr, after the 1960s departures, was pleased to get him back in 1962 as professor of applied mathematics and head of a new division within the Department of Mathematics. With National Research Council money, MacDonald brought to Dalhousie its first big computer, an IBM 1620, so big and ponderous that it had to be hoisted with a huge crane into the upper floor of the Dunn Building via the roof. The IBM 1620 had hundreds of vacuum tubes and they all had to work, and the more the machine was used the hotter it got. Still, it did the work of twenty men in minutes. A modern desk-top computer is fifty thousand times faster and about that much smaller; that revolution got under way with micro-processors in the early 1980s.

Alex MacDonald was ambitious and in late 1964 he set out a roster of classes for 1965–6 that in effect pointed to the creation of a Department of Applied Mathematics. Dalhousie decided that this was not the way to go. It was amiable enough, but MacDonald resigned and went back to California. Hicks was philosophical, thanking MacDonald for getting the computer centre started, but observing that pure and applied mathematics usually developed "only with some friction."[40]

Cooke worked hard to bring in new staff, his wife Dorette doing much to help them socially when they came. The student-staff ratios in 1964 were bad: Biology was 99 to 1, and Economics needed a new appointment to bring its ratio down from 114 to 100. English was worse, new staff being urgently needed to prevent its ratio from going to 138. History got a new assistant professor, but Mathematics needed three. French had too many poorly qualified teachers, all overloaded with work. Political Science brought K.A. Heard from Durban, a South African liberal fed up with the regime, who became a tower of strength. Psychology was expanding so rapidly under Henry James that it was almost off the scale, and had a huge graduate

Hoisting the new IBM 1620 into place at the top of the Dunn Building, March 1964.

program. Cooke did not panic; he rarely did. He urged Hicks and Hicks listened, though there was a crisis in April 1968 when the new premier, G.I. Smith, insisted that notification of university monies had to await formal Assembly approval of the budget. For over a month Hicks had to temporarily suspend all new appointments.

As for salaries, they were a growing problem by 1968. Dalhousie was unlikely to get new PH.D.s in English, Philosophy, or Political Science for less than $9,000. The Physics Department wanted to hire one of its own PH.D.s but Acadia and St Francis Xavier were offering nearly $10,000, and Dalhousie had at least to match that. The problem was even worse, said Cooke, because five of the junior staff in Physics were not yet making $10,000! Several department heads besides Physics were making this same point: upward revision of salaries was essential, for "it would be impossible to make new appointments without grave injustice to loyal members of the departments of some standing."

Overall, in Arts and Science full-time staff would go from 110 in 1963–4 to 315 in 1973–4, in the long run roughly equal to the increase in student enrolment. By 1973 the pattern of the origins of Dalhousie teaching staff was 65 per cent Canadian, 15 per cent Commonwealth, 20 per cent other countries. Of this last 20 per cent, about three-quarters were American. These proportions varied from faculty to faculty, and in Arts and Science from department to department. Sociology had many American (as did sociology departments in many Canadian universities), but that was slowly changing as new Canadian PH.D.s became available. History, Political Science, and English tried to strike a balance between Canadian, British, American, and other professors. But for the most part Dalhousie, Hicks in particular, was looking for talent; the nationality it came with was less important. That had been a Dalhousie characteristic from the beginning. The 1973–4 statistics for full-time faculty are of some interest:

	Total	Canadian	US	Commonwealth	Other
Arts and Science	315	167 (53%)	69 (22%)	53 (17%)	26 (8%)
Law	30	20 (67%)	1 (3%)	8 (27%)	1 (3%)
Medicine	181	147 (81%)	11 (6%)	18 (10%)	5 (3%)
Dentistry	28	24 (86%)	1 (4%)	2 (7%)	1 (4%)
Health Professions	65	43 (66%)	10 (16%)	11 (12%)	1 (2%)
Graduate Studies	33	24 (73%)	5 (15%)	4 (12%)	0
	652	425 (65%)	97 (15%)	96 (15%)	34 (5%)

Cooke was flexible. There was none of the hard edge to his dominion as there was in Medicine. Dean Trost of Graduate Studies asked early in 1964 if Cooke would agree that all future recommendations for new staff in Arts and Science be co-signed by Trost. Cooke recognized and conceded the point without jealousy or demur. Hicks thought Cooke might, in his honesty, be giving away too much. Hicks did not mind the departure, he told Cooke, "but I *do not* concede that it is necessary for the Dean of Arts and Science to so bind himself for the future."[41]

One of Cooke's major changes was getting his faculty to accept senior matriculation for admission to Dalhousie. Since 1963 the Nova Scotia Department of Education had been urging this upon all Nova Scotian universities, and in 1965 Dalhousie approved it, effective in the autumn of 1966. It was a bold move, resisted by some, for 36 per cent of Dalhousie's entering students came with junior matriculation and only 16 per cent with full senior. The rest were in between. It gave Dalhousie one year's respite form the rising tide of student numbers; freshman students would be one blessed year more mature. The proposal was accepted in principle by all the Nova Scotian universities, but only Dalhousie actually implemented it. The others, fearing for their enrolment and money, backed out. Some Dalhousie people were uneasy too; Dalhousie had always felt its first year much better than Grade 12, as doubtless other universities did. But Cooke and a strong majority in Arts and Science believed that on balance Grade 12 admission was better, and while second thoughts about it would surface from time to time, it stood.[42]

Dalhousie had worried about the first-year failure rate under the old junior matriculation system. The downtown papers in November 1961 publicized the 46 per cent failure rate in English 1, suggesting that Grade 12 admission would obviate such a costly process. A.E. Kerr got Allan Bevan, head of English, to find comparative figures for first-year English. They were: UNB, 38 per cent; Mount Allison, 51 per cent; Saint Mary's, 37 per cent; Acadia, 13 per cent. Dalhousie failure rates at Christmas 1964 showed figures similar to English 1 in other disciplines:

Chemistry 1	45.6 per cent
Geology 1	40.8
Mathematics	47.1
Physics 1	47.8

Some of the social sciences had less horrendous figures:

Economics 1	35.2 per cent
History 1	30.9
Political Science 1	24.8
Philosophy 1	25.3

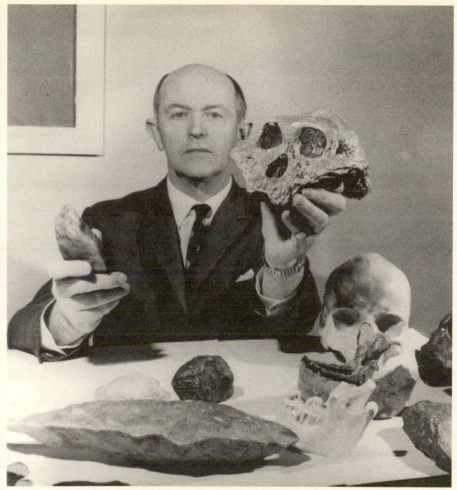

H.B.S. Cooke in 1971, having returned to paleontology after his deanship of Arts and Science, 1963–8.

Failures in sociology 1 (15.2 per cent) and Spanish 1 (15.7 per cent) looked to some in the faculty as suspiciously low. The sociology failure rate dropped even further in April 1966 to 5.2 per cent. Students added that everyone passed Spanish 1. In general, failure rates eased between 1964 and 1966, even before Grade 12 admission was introduced; it was owing, said Dean Cooke, to more rigorous selection of students for admission, better instruction, and tutorials.[43]

Arts and Science was expanding so rapidly that old Dalhousie traditions were being weakened almost without one being aware of it. Graduate Studies acquired a new emphasis from the Killam money and government research grants would follow. Left unsung, even unrewarded, was good undergraduate teaching. A number of departments in Arts and Science still held to the old tradition where senior professors taught and marked first-year classes, on the assumption that old hands were more skilled. But teaching styles were difficult to quantify; it was easier to reward research, tangible, assessable, and delivered across the desk in print. Gradually that became important; good teaching was all very well, but it became apparent that publication was the new way forward at Dalhousie by the end of the 1960s.

Student life and a Student Union

Dean Cooke told the students in March 1966: "All education is really self-education"; that required self-discipline. "All play and no work makes Jack a quick drop-out," he added. As the *Gazette* reported in 1967, if a student were at the Sorbonne, he would have no external discipline of any kind, none but those exigent orals at the end of the process; it did not matter whether one went to lectures or not, or even whether one stayed in Paris. Joan Hennessey, a graduate student in French, gave a supplementary class in French twice a week for those who needed it. She had the stern view that the vast majority of students who failed in any subject did so simply because they did not work. Of 250 students in French 1 (failure rate 36 per cent) ten came fairly often to her class, though most days she had only five students, and probably not the five that needed help the most.[44] A 1959 poem, in the style of A.E. Housman, touched the issue of self-discipline:

> When I was once a Freshman
> I heard a wise man say,
> "Give hours from your leisure,
> Not lecture time away.
> Spend your spare time chatting,
> But keep your classes free."

But I was once a Freshman
No use to talk to me.

Now I am a Sophomore –
I heard him say again,
"The lectures that one misses
Are never missed in vain;
One pays by flunking finals
And with nights of endless rue.
Now I am a Sophomore,
And oh, 'tis true, 'tis true.[45]

A more ruthless comment on the same subject came in a February 1964 interview with "Joe P.", a procuror of girls for any and every occasion, of whom, he said, there were about two hundred free-lancing in Halifax. Had Joe anything to say to university students? Yes, Joe had, and it was pungent enough:

Most of you come from sheltered homes. You've never had to wonder where your next meal was coming from; never had to hope you'll find a homosexual in a generous mood, or, if you're a girl had to walk the streets or starve. When I hear you complaining about how hard your professors are on you with work, it makes me sick. And I've heard it ... Take it from someone who knows. You're getting an education that will make you somebody, and you're getting it pretty damn easily. You don't know how lucky you are.[46]

Other forms of self-discipline were required, at least of male students, in the era of the mini-skirt that began in 1959. The young cavalier who wanted to make the right impression had to be decorous and controlled. The *Gazette*'s 12 November 1959 article, "The Art of Dating, 20th Century Style," closed with this delightful exercise, hypocrisy perhaps rewarded:

When opening the car door [for her], especially when the fashions are on short skirts, avoid looking at your date's legs. She will appreciate your good manners, enjoy your feigned discomfort, and accept your modesty as a challenge. The sacrifice on your part is sure to be temporary.

Students for years had suffered from a lack of breathing space on campus. There had long been Atwood's, crowded, noisy, confusing, unrelenting Atwood's, with its mugs of hot, thin, watery coffee, steam looking for caffeine. For residents of Shirreff Hall and Howe Hall, there was space, but in 1967–8, 55 per cent of Dalhousie's students were from metropolitan Halifax. During the day over two thousand students needed a *pied-à-terre*, to eat, talk, work, or even – this a new development of the late 1960s – have a glass of beer.

A Student Union building was one of Hicks's early priorities. The students had been collecting money for it for years, and as of 30 April 1964 they had $118,294.97 on deposit at Eastern Trust, though the cost of construction was rising faster than the fund. By that time, the board had given Hicks authority to put together a suitable parcel of land. It was awkward, for Dalhousie needed power of expropriation and could not get it. As late as 1966 the project was being held up by Miss C.G.M. Musgrave's property at 1247 LeMarchant Street; Dalhousie needed if not the whole property at least some few feet at the eastern end for the Student Union. The letter to Miss Musgrave showed Hicks both benign and forceful. "Believe me," he wrote, "I know that this is difficult for you, and can only say that I am charged with the responsibility of directing the growth of a great university." But Miss Musgrave was adamant and the building was redesigned without using any of the Musgrave lot. At one point the building was without the site of the present front entrance. The owner did not want to sell; however he was nagged by his wife about the virtues of having a fine apartment in the new Park Victoria. "God dammit," he told her, "we'll move there." According to Arthur Chisholm, the university engineer, the papers were signed the next day. C.D. Davison again redesigned the building. Davison was a good architect for that building, careful, painstaking, level-headed, a useful balance against the gusts of enthusiastic suggestions that came from students.[47]

Senate's Building and Campus Development Committee, chaired by J.H. Aitchison of Political Science, received suggestions for the Student Union Building; one of them, from Dean Cooke, was acted on. The new building, Cooke said, should have a room large enough to seat at least a thousand students, preferably twelve hundred, with a floor suitable for dancing, with a simple stage for a dance band. There was no place on campus "with a congenial atmosphere where mass meetings of students can be held."

In April 1967 ten firms were invited to tender and in July the work was given to MacDonald Construction for $2,673,000. Dennis Ashworth, president of the Student Council, wrote to Hicks on 7 July 1967: "I must also thank you, Sir, for the time and energy that you have expended into the planning of this building over the past few years. I am sure that without your enthusiasm the construction of this building would not be commencing as early as this summer."

But there was more to it than that. The Student Union had as administrator, since the mid-1960s, a retired naval officer, John G. Graham,

An authority of deans, 1967. L. to r., W.A. MacKay, Law; G.R. MacLean, Graduate Studies; C.B. Stewart, Medicine; J.D. McLean, Dentistry; R.M. MacDonald, Health Professions; H.B.S. Cooke, Arts and Science.

who had come to Dalhousie to do an MA in economics. The students appointed him to help run Student Council business. He was manager and coordinator, working in the background and letting the students run their own show. He functioned as a template against which they would try out their ideas. He also provided year-round continuity. He had much to do with the planning of the building; it would turn out to be, indeed, a very good building. It was a little too good for the *Chronicle-Herald*. Under the heading "Gracious College Life," it praised the design but had reservations about "the luxury of its appointments, furniture and equipment." Randall Smith, of the Student Council, reminded the *Chronicle-Herald* that they should get their facts right; the students paid for the cost of the furnishings, and there was little enough luxury.

The major clue to good working relations between the Student Council and the president's office was not only the Student Council presidents themselves, but also the rapport between John Graham and Eric Mercer, assistant to the president. Informally, they would try out ideas on each other, Graham representing the Student Council and Mercer the president and the administration. It was sufficiently successful that in the autumn of 1968 UNB made tactful inquiries about how it was done.[48]

By that time the western end of University Avenue was a busy and messy place: not only was the Student Union Building up, but the Dalhousie Arts Centre, the Killam Library, the central heating plant and the tunnels and services relevant thereto, were all under construction. Dalhousie's building program and its jocose and spirited director-general were still at full throttle.

· 10 ·

Testing Limits: The Cohn, the Killam, the Life Sciences, the Radicals 1968–1972

Rebecca Cohn's world and her building. Tito's LL.D., 1971. The Killam Library. Duff-Berdahl Report and after. The rise and fall of Dean Henry James, 1968–9. The Life Sciences Complex. Student unrest, 1968–70. Sociology's adventures. President's office occupied, April 1970. Transition year program. Maritime School of Social Work joins Dalhousie. The Fenwick Tower, 1971. Hicks becomes senator, 1972.

Rebecca Cohn was born in 1870 in Galicia, in what is now Poland but then was Austria-Hungary. She was brought up speaking German and was probably convent-educated. She married Moses Cohen and in 1906 they emigrated to Canada, part of the considerable exodus of Austrian Jews to North America at the turn of the century. The Cohens had a difficult time at first. Rumour was that they got their start selling goods from a handcart in Halifax streets. They were childless, they worked hard, and they prospered. She was the brains of the team. They lived in Jacob Street, at the corner of Brunswick Street, north of what is now Scotia Square, their prosperity exemplified by gradual purchases of property around them which they renovated and rented. Moses Cohen became an invalid and died in 1921, but Rebecca went from strength to strength. She was clever, tough, reclusive, with snow-white hair and piercing pale blue eyes that seemed to see everything. She came up to one of her workmen one day. "You're stayin' here, Mrs Cohen?" he asked. "I'm staying here until you finish," she replied. "In that case," he rejoined, "I'm finished *now*!" She told this with some amusement. She was also good at law and by herself could draw up a working document for the sale or conveyancing of property. She died in the Victoria General in October 1942 at the age of seventy-two, referred to obliquely in the Halifax *Daily Star* as a business woman, "well known in real estate circles."[1]

Her will made some specific gifts, but her executors were instructed to sell her properties after twenty years and use the money for "such charitable purposes as they see fit and proper." She seems to have had in mind an old age home for Jewish people in her native Rzeszow (pronounced "Zheshú"); but after the war the trustees came to consider a Halifax project. How the bequest came to Dalhousie and for an auditorium is mysterious; but it seems to have been through the friendship between Rebecca Cohn's nieces, Marian and Louise Keshen, and the wife of Professor John Aldous of Pharmacology. Eileen Aldous was a splendid creature, who charmed everyone she met; she seems to have suggested to the Keshen ladies that Dalhousie would be a good place for their money and what Dalhousie needed more than anything else was a proper auditorium.

In November 1962 the board announced that the estate of Rebecca Cohn (the name had been somewhere shortened and made less obviously Jewish) would donate $400,000 to enable Dalhousie to build an auditorium. In April 1963 a deed of gift conveyed that money plus any interest arising, on condition that the building be ready within five years. It was the largest gift Dalhousie had received since Lady Dunn gave the Physics Building in 1957. In September 1963 the board appointed C.A.E. Fowler as architect. But the university did not yet know quite what it wanted to do. Dalhousie's previous contributions to the Halifax cultural life had consisted mostly of public lectures given by enterprising members of faculty. In the days before television these were usually well attended. Once a year the students mounted a Gilbert and Sullivan production, ranging from very good to mediocre; they produced plays that could come off with startling *éclat*. Basically Dalhousie thought of itself as an academic centre, not a cultural one.[2]

In 1961, after prodding from Arts and Science, the Senate struck a committee to manage Dalhousie's collections of paintings; in due course it was widened to the Senate Committee on Cultural Activities, under the vigorous chairmanship of G.V.V. Nicholls of Law. By that time Senate concluded that an art gallery, and cultural events generally, should come under the university, not any one faculty or department. But this was all slow and cumbersome, and Hicks was already uneasy over the timetable. He appointed Dean Cooke to plan what should be done with a Cohn building. What departments, if any, should it house? Who should control the building's operations? Might there be a conflict between an arts centre's public functions and its academic ones? It was not easy. In March 1967, with ground not even broken, Hicks had to ask the Cohn trustees for an extension until June 1969.[3]

Another underlying reason for the slow start was that Hicks had developed big ideas of what he might do. Half a million dollars (with interest, that's what the Cohn bequest became) was just seed money, though vital for that very reason. By now Lady Dunn (now Lady Beaverbrook), installed as chancellor in May 1968, had been persuaded to give half a million herself for a theatre named after Sir James, and the Nova Scotia government had been induced to give $2 million for a cultural centre in Nova Scotia's capital that had been notably bereft of any such thing since 1749. At last in May 1968 the first sod was turned; by some unfortunate oversight the two surviving nieces of Rebecca Cohn, Marion and Louise Keshen, were not invited. They were most displeased. They had also heard that the design of their auditorium was such that it would be useless as a concert hall. They got the architect on the phone and told him plainly they were fed up and were calling their lawyer to see if they could get their half million back. Fowler calmed them down. A month or so later they wanted the Cohn expanded; it had been designed to seat eight hundred; the Keshen ladies wanted one thousand. Mercifully, without too much extra trouble and only modest extra expense, the Cohn auditorium was expanded to seat 1,075. It was in fact better that way.[4]

The contract was finally let in May 1969. It was massive: $3,827,581, to Kenny Construction of Yarmouth, the building to be called the Dalhousie Arts Centre, the Cohn Auditorium to be its the most important part. Then the construction company ran into financial trouble and the contract had to be assigned to R.A. MacCulloch. The construction itself was by no means what it should have been, beginning with a leaky roof on the Dunn Theatre. As late as March 1971 Hicks was much concerned about the shortage of money to finish and equip the Arts Centre. The Molson Fund contributed $100,000, but the arithmetic gave the board no pleasure, though the auditorium did. The total contributions were $3.1 million; the total cost was $5.2 million. Dalhousie's own contribution to the Arts Centre was 40 per cent of its total cost.[5]

What sort of place would it be? What kind of programs would appear there? Hicks wanted it as a lighthouse in the Halifax community, attracting all sorts and tastes. As Malcolm Ross of English told the Halifax Rotary Club in January 1971, it was not merely a centre to serve the high-minded in Dalhousie and south-end Halifax. John Cripton, its first director of operations, wanted not just concerts and quartets but folk groups and rock bands. The raunchy, the rough, and the popular would help pay for ballet and symphonies.

It was opened officially in November 1971 with two major events. The main scenario was a week of cultural events launched by a convocation on 20 November 1971, with honorary degrees to stars in the Canadian cultural scene: Leon Major, director of the Neptune Theatre from 1963 to 1970; Elmer Iseler of the Toronto Festival Singers; Lawren P. Harris, the painter; and Jean Sutherland Boggs, director of the National Gallery from 1966 to 1976. The program went extremely well. The acoustics in the Cohn were a delight.[6]

It was upstaged, however, by a development that came to maturity two weeks before: the arrival of, and convocation for, Marshall Josip Broz Tito of Yugoslavia, and Sir Fitzroy Maclean, a British officer who had been parachuted in to meet him during the Second World War. It is a curious story. One of the wilder officers of the Canadian army was Major Bill Jones ('23) a veteran of the First World War who got himself parachuted into Yugoslavia in the Second. He created a considerable reputation for himself among the partisans in Slovenia. Guy MacLean, historian, and dean of graduate studies, pursuing research on the war in Yugoslavia, met Jones in Ontario in 1968. The original idea to bring Tito to Dalhousie seems to have come from MacLean; Jones added his weight by writing to Hicks. There were representations in other quarters; Mitchell Sharp, then the minister of external affairs, surprised Hicks by phoning to ask, "What's all this about an honorary degree to Tito?" Hicks enjoyed that. MacLean was going to London to interview Sir Fitzroy Maclean about his wartime mission to Yugoslavia, and Tito was added to the agenda. At lunch MacLean asked Sir Fitzroy if he could make inquiries. At first Sir Fitzroy was bleak and uninterested, but soon warmed to it.[7]

It was a bold idea. Tito was not exactly *persona grata* in North America, and in Canada there was a forest of Yugoslav exiles who had some reason to hate him and the Communist regime he represented. The Jones and Fitzroy Maclean connections worked. Tito was interested, though it turned out that there would have to be a state visit, even if only to Halifax, and External Affairs and the Yugoslav embassy in Ottawa had to be involved. It was also thought desirable for security reasons to keep the news quiet for as long as possible. It was all settled through the Yugoslav embassy by early October 1971, and announced two weeks later. There were plenty of protests, from within Canada and from the United States, but Hicks did not mind these. Security in Halifax was tight. The Mounted Police were out in force, both as national police and as secret police.[8]

On Saturday, 6 November 1971, the day of Tito's convocation, there were security men everywhere, on the roof of the Cohn Auditorium, on the roofs of houses across the street; there were fifty in the Arts Centre itself. And armed. But there was no incident. All went well, almost too well. Tito and Sir Fitzroy got their degrees; as his

The Tito convocation, November 1971; from l. to r.: Sir Fitzroy Maclean; Dr Harold Uhlman, Dalhousie Registrar; Marshall Tito; Lieutenant-Governor Victor Oland; President Henry Hicks.

convocation address Tito proceeded to give a Slavic policy speech, a good forty-five-minute run at Yugoslav gross domestic product, exports, imports, and other such important things, all in his Serbo-Croat language. It was translated, sparingly, into English. Afterwards there was a reception; Dalhousie supplied sherry and slivovitz, the latter ordered from Montreal and in quantity. It is made from plums, distilled into a white, fiery spirit. In the countryside of Yugoslavia it can be rough; what Dalhousie supplied was smooth as silk. Tito never drank the stuff if he could help it. He liked Scotch, and so in haste Dalhousie supplied bottles of Johnnie Walker Black Label. The party went on for some time. The government of Nova Scotia gave a dinner that evening for Tito at the Nova Scotian Hotel, where Premier Regan promised an annual scholarship to Dalhousie to a deserving Yugoslav student. Tito ended up at the lieutenant-governor's and was still going strong at 3 AM. Thus did Tito get his only North American honorary degree, and thus did the Cohn Auditorium begin. Eileen Burns told Hicks the next day that he had presided magnificently. "Never was I so proud of my University nor of its President." The Yugoslavs were proud and pleased too. Sir Fitzroy Maclean went back to London in Tito's jet, for both he and Tito were lunching on Monday at Buckingham Palace. Prince Philip teased the two new Dalhousie doctors of law. "Dalhousie could not have picked," he told them, "two more *illegal* people ... !"[9]

In later years Hicks said the Arts Centre was one of his great achievements: "With this gift of half a million dollars, I undertook the construction of the Arts Centre, costing ultimately between six and seven million dollars. But that gave me a great satisfaction to be able to manipulate that nice [Cohn] donation into something that was at least fifteen times ... the original." Note "manipulate"; that says it all for Hicks's methods.[10]

The Killam Library

The last thing Dorothy Killam and Hicks had talked about before her death was giving Dalhousie a new library. Thus the name Killam attached to the big Dalhousie library represented intentions, not reality. As to need there was no doubt. J.P. Wilkinson, the librarian from 1960 to 1966, did the best he could inside the skin of the Macdonald Memorial Library, but it was clear even before he came that Dalhousie needed a new building. There were two things wrong with the library: its collection was too big for its building; and more dangerously, its collection was not growing nearly fast enough. In 1960–1 it had 175,000 volumes, ninth among university libraries in Canada. But it was falling steadily behind, its accessions only 60 per cent of McMaster's which ranked tenth, and only 41 per cent of Saskatchewan's which ranked eight.

Dalhousie departmental libraries had also become desperately crowded. Dean Cooke looked at the whole library position in December 1964; the Chemistry library needed space; Biology could be accommodated only by moving out old issues of journals to accessible storage. But, he concluded, "The whole fact of the matter is that there is no solution other than the construction as soon as possible of a substantial new Library Building."[11]

Wilkinson resigned in 1965 to take up teaching at the University of Toronto Library School. Dalhousie now needed a first-class librarian, and they were not easy to find. Hicks did not want just a librarian; he wanted someone first-class; he was "loath to settle quickly for anyone who does not fall in this category." He also preferred a North American. In December 1965 a meeting of librarians and deans discussed possibilities, including the founding of a School of Library Science. H.P. Moffatt, deputy minister of education, had urged a library school as early as 1960 and a joint Senate-board committee was struck. Wilkinson reported it would cost $47,000 per annum for a library school that could meet accreditation standards. That cooled Kerr's ardour, and in 1963 Moffatt called it off temporarily to await the findings of the new University Grants Committee. One thing was clear: Hicks would not have a library school that was not accredited.[12]

In 1966, after a year's search, Dalhousie got its librarian. The Library Planning Committee was chaired by S.E. Sprott, a Milton scholar from Australia, who worked tirelessly on the new library. The committee decided that Laird Fairn, the architect, Art Chisholm, and Guy MacLean should visit some recently built libraries in New England. At Brown University (seven thousand students) in Providence, Rhode Island, a fine library had just been completed, some 1.5 million volumes. MacLean noticed that all Dalhousie's questions were being answered by the associate librarian, a lively Greek, Louis Vagianos. It was learned that he would be interested in considering a move. Hicks was told, and within days Vagianos was visiting Halifax. He and Hicks hit it off from the start, and Vagianos was hired virtually on the spot. He came officially on 1 May 1966. After that the Library Planning Committee sat back and watched Vagianos run with library planning.

His background was philosophy, history, and library science, but he was a systems man who saw things broadly. His parents were Greek and that origin showed. He was ebullient, sharp, and spoke his mind with refreshing, occasionally disconcerting candour; there were few weasel words in Vagianos's vocabulary. His brisk and brusque ways created opposition at first which surfaced in Senate in a motion of want of confidence in the new librarian. Vagianos won it, by one vote. He came to Hicks despondent. "Don't be unnerved by it," said Hicks, "You won, 39 votes to 38. You won big. But don't let the opposition get consolidated."[13]

Vagianos's philosophy was that students mattered more than librarians or professors. Make the library serve the students. Make xeroxing as cheap as possible; it will help save library books from being mutilated or stolen. In place of earlier restrictions on book borrowing, Vagianos believed in letting students take out as many books as they pleased. Books did no good sitting on library shelves. If they were needed they could always be recalled.

Dalhousie needed to spend much more money on its libraries and Vagianos worked hard to convince the board. Libraries, he said, were the only Dalhousie investment that rose in value all the time. He re-emphasized that Dalhousie's acquisitions had not been growing in proportion to students and staff. In the Canadian hierarchy of university libraries, Dalhousie's was going down:

I do not wish to underestimate the value of administrators, faculty or librarians but, ultimately, it will be the quality of the book collection that will determine Dalhousie's greatness. It is not a coincidence that every good or great university is supported by a good or great library. *There is no exception to this.*

Hicks ran into some scepticism among board members and fought it. Dalhousie, he told the board, had already been bypassed by McMaster, and in 1968 would be by Windsor, and in 1969 by Victoria, unless things changed. The problem was made more urgent, he said, because Dalhousie was trying to establish a reputation as a graduate school; it had to add at least thirty thousand volumes a year for some years to bring the library up to scratch. Hicks and Vagianos aimed at a major referral library of one million volumes, big enough for the whole Atlantic region, by the end of the 1970s. It would have to begin with staff. When Vagianos came to Dalhousie, libraries had a staff of fifty-four of whom only nine were professional librarians. Within a year it was eighty-five, of whom twenty-three were professionals.[14]

Although Laird Fairn was the overall architect, the real design of the Killam Library was done by Ojars Biskaps, professor of architecture at NSTC, with Vagianos directing the library's input. The design was approved by the board in October 1966. There was a debate over the outside finish; Fairn recommended Indiana limestone which, he claimed, had a mellowness not characteristic of pre-cast concrete. Dissenting was A.G. Archibald, who wanted something resembling what

L.G. Vagianos in 1974, University Librarian, 1966–9; Vice-President University Services, 1975–9; Vice-President Administration, 1977–80.

was proposed for the Arts Centre – that is, pre-cast concrete with local stone impregnated in it. Archibald got his way; at the next meeting of the board in February 1967, the Indiana limestone decision was discussed at length, then overturned in favour of pre-cast concrete with local stone in it. Hicks managed to get rosewood installed in parts of the interior, his knowledge and skill as cabinet-maker showing; Basil Cooke recommended, as geologist, the micaceous slates for floors and stair treads, and even in the elevators. The computer centre in the basement was included in the overall design. The call for tenders was issued in November, the lowest being from Fraser-Brace Maritimes, at $6,098,700. Completion date was to be 31 July 1969. The Macdonald would become the central science library when the Killam was ready. That would not be until 1971, however, for labour shortages held up completion of the Killam. The final cost was $7,280,000.[15]

Remaking Structures

Since the early 1960s Dalhousie, especially the Faculty of Arts and Science, had been struggling with growing pains, staff, students, structures, curriculum. It is almost an axiom that linear increases in numbers produce strains that have consequences of geometric proportions. Infrastructures break down from sheer weight; committee systems and established procedures become overburdened. Thus, as new buildings were going up, old structures of university governance were being changed. The debate about the place of academics on boards of governors had been going since the late 1950s, urged on by the Canadian Association of University Teachers (CAUT, founded in 1951), which urged that professors should be on boards of governors. Some thought they should even be in a majority. Anyone, however, who has read C.P. Snow's *The Masters* will know the infighting academics are capable of when an important decision (in that case the headship of a college) rests in their hands. W.P. Thompson, retired president of the University of Saskatchewan, observed shrewdly in 1960:

Faculty members do their best to avoid decisions which may injure particular interests or persons ... And for the welfare of the institution such decisions must be made. It is better to leave such decisions to experienced, thick-skinned administrators who expect to have to make them.[16]

As this debate was under way, the AUCC and CAUT together commissioned a report on the working of Canadian universities. The two commissioners were Sir James Duff, retired principal of the University of Durham, and Robert Berdahl, a political scientist from San Francisco State College who had published an authoritative book on university-government relations in Great Britain. They began work in 1964 and reported in 1966. They concluded that Canadian universities needed reform. The major problem was that too many of their senates were ineffective, too large, too divorced from the academic side, too filled with administrators and alumni representatives. Dalhousie's Senate did not have all those problems, but it was large and cumbersome, including as members all full professors and heads of departments. Duff-Berdahl also urged that faculty should have a major role in the selection of university administrators, chairmen and deans in particular, whose terms of office should be limited and short.

Canadian universities listened, and acted with astonishing speed. By the end of 1966 a dozen universities had begun extensive revisions of their charters and procedures. So much so that a year later Sir James Duff remarked in Toronto, "The Walls of Jericho appear to have fallen with but one blast of the Duff-Berdahl trumpet."[17]

Dalhousie had reacted to these structural tensions five years before the publication of the Duff-Berdahl Report. Appointed in December 1960, Senate's Committee on University Government was given a sweeping mandate "to review the present structure and practice of government at all levels within the University." It first created Senate Council in December 1961, a working cabinet of Senate, and went on from there. As to the Duff-Berdahl Report, the Dalhousie Faculty Association liked it; on the other hand some members of the Board of Governors bridled at some of its assumptions. Frank Covert did not think faculty needed any more power than they already had, and student demands, he thought, were ridiculous. But authoritarian though he was, Covert had a clear idea of the limits to the board's decision-making power. His view also throws a telling light on the power of Dalhousie's president for action and decision:

... they [Duff-Berdahl] suggest discussion and decision by the Board; actually this is not the way a board of a Company operates ... nor is it the way a board of a university should. If anyone really believes that a board makes decisions, I think they ought to have their heads examined. Very frankly, administration of a university ... make the recommendations and they should be so well made that they convince a board; while a board may not be a rubber stamp, by and large if the decisions of the administration are not correct and adopted by the board, then there should be either a new administration or a new board.[18]

In 1967 the Dalhousie Senate recommended that "heads" of departments should be replaced by "chairmen." "Head" savoured much of authority, and many heads, in Medicine not least, revelled in it. More-over, once appointed head, it was not easy for the incumbent to step down. That was, too often, owing to delight in the power the headship represented; but, as the Senate report noted, it was more complicated than that:

... it has been difficult to make a change [in the headship] without very con-siderable embarrassment. If a retirement has been involuntary, it has been re-garded as a public declaration of "no confidence" ... if it has been voluntary, it has usually been taken as a confession of failure.

The appointment of chairmen was now to be made by the dean on the recommendation of a three-person committee chosen wholly from outside the department concerned. The appointment would be for three years. The process began in June 1968 with committees ap-pointed for History, Psychology, and Sociology, the last a new depart-ment split off from Economics in 1966. Not all faculties found chairmanship to their taste; Medicine continued in its old ways; there were still heads of departments on the Forrest campus.[19]

As to the appointment of deans, that was also being discussed by the Senate committee. It was something that the president took a lively interest in, because he wanted deans in whom he had confi-dence. But there was faculty's interest also. Hitherto the choice of a dean had been largely the president's prerogative, though he usually consulted members of faculty. The appointment of Hicks as dean of arts and science in 1960 showed how limited that consultation could be. Hicks as president recognized the value of faculty consultation; his inclination was to turn as much of the process as possible over to fac-ulty councils, provided they could get on with it (never easy for a large committee), and provided also that he was involved in the pro-cess. An interesting and instructive example was the appointment in 1968 of a dean of arts and science to succeed Basil Cooke.

A New Dean of Arts and Science, 1968
Cooke had tried to retire at the end of his three-year term in 1966, but no one wanted him to go and good candidates were scarce. A three-year stint as dean played havoc with one's research and ability to keep up with one's subject. The honour and the glory were all very well, but where was one at the end of three years? In 1966 Sydney Wise, a historian at Queen's, was offered the deanship, but he turned it down in favour of a better offer in Ottawa. By October 1967 it had become urgent; Cooke announced that he would not continue as dean beyond June 1968. Faculty Council gathered nominations, six from within the

Four doctors in 1978. L. to r., R.C. Dickson, retired Head of Department of Medicine; C.B. Weld, retired Head of Physiology; Sir Peter Medawar, honorary degree recipient; Chester Stewart, former Dean of Medicine.

faculty and three from outside. One outside candidate, Professor Hickman, a biologist from Western Ontario, was invited to accept, but negotiations broke down over salary, Hicks not being able or willing to offer enough to entice him to leave London, Ontario. Perhaps Hicks preferred one of the internal candidates. Most had fallen by the wayside, but Faculty Council was "very favourably" disposed to one whom it interviewed in March 1968. Hicks thought highly of him and he was appointed dean as of 1 July 1968, at the substantial salary of $21,000. He was P.H.R. James, head of Psychology.[20]

Percival Henry Rowland James was English, brilliant, gifted, confident. He was born in 1924 in Bath, the old Roman town whose most celebrated buildings were either second-century Roman or eighteenth-century English. There was indeed an eighteenth-century character about James, versatile, stylish, not easily contained within the petty cloisters of academia. He was first-class in nearly everything he took on: first class in the Classics Tripos at Magdalene College, Cambridge; first class in the Moral Sciences Tripos. He then joined the Royal Navy in 1942 and became Japanese translator in Intelligence. Research fellow in psychology at Cambridge in 1948–50, instructor at Harvard in 1950–1, he was lecturer in psychology at the University of London, when Queen's found him and brought him over in 1957 as associate professor of psychology. He came to Dalhousie in September 1962, as professor and head of psychology.

Dalhousie Psychology had been philosophical and clinical. F.H. Page had been the department since 1928, one of the best-read men in the university, though he wore it quietly. In 1959 the department had four members, mostly in clinical psychology and this was where its modest graduate work centred. Then came Henry James. He changed everything. An instinctive driver, smooth, aggressive, he effected a massive metamorphosis in the old department, and in one direction: towards experimental psychology. He recruited widely, and the best people he could get. Within four years Dalhousie Psychology had the largest graduate enrolment in the university except for English, and by 1966 his department was considered one of the four leading departments in the country. As Silver Donald Cameron puts it, his staff "ran sophisticated experiments, gave papers at important conferences, and reeled in foundation grants like so many mackerel. Other departments trembled as Henry James smoothly appropriated budgets, space, equipment and influence. His highrolling young cohorts admired him, abetted him, and nicknamed him, 'Prince Henry the Navigator.'"

It was all in experimental psychology. In most departments of psychology the fissure between experimental and clinical is inherent. In some departments bridges are built; in others the split is so bitter that two departments have to be created. James was not concerned with the value to Halifax society and medicine of clinical and social psychology; much of that research he despised as dross, unscientific, utilitarian. He wanted research that would open up real science, that aimed outward at horizons of knowledge. He expected his staff to get research grants, and they had to get them within two or three years, or else. They did. James built empires; some colleagues thought him ruthless. Some thought him a genius; but geniuses can be ruthless too. Cameron, who observed him admiringly from the English Department, remarked: "James had a way of projecting what a university could be, what it *should* be, and of making a young academic feel part of a breathlessly exciting and invigorating enterprise."[21]

Thus as head of Psychology James achieved astonishing results. Dalhousie found it difficult at times to rein him in; the only person that could do that was Henry Hicks, and he admired James. The Psychology Department soon moved from its old quarters in the A. and A. Building to something much bigger, the unoccupied president's house on Oxford Street; there the old gardens were soon filled with temporary shacks and the basement given over to animals, mazes, and the paraphernalia of experimental psychology.

As vigorous and sweeping as James was, so seemed also his imperviousness to argument. He was not a good listener; driven by his own ideas he could not seem to stop to absorb those of others, especially if they ran counter to his. He also tended to say what he thought, as if not fully cognizant of the effect of his words. He thought the English Department was filled with uncreative, unimaginative professors, and said so, even to candidates who proposed to come to English. He made no secret of his views.

What may be effective in a head or chairman of a department may not translate well at another level of administration. A brilliant head does not necessarily make a brilliant dean. James's techniques for building Psychology elicited different responses when he became dean of the faculty. Those who produced research, wrote papers, or got grants were on his side and were rewarded by his approval; those who just taught and produced little research were the objects of his contempt. He rode hard his penchant for brilliant, creative people; they would gather in his living room at a crowded party, acolytes at his feet swapping ideas on what made a department, a faculty, a university great. James's wife Jenny, vivacious, handsome, intelligent, helped make the Jameses parties seem like an intellectual adventure, which indeed some of them were. It was heady stuff.[22]

The trouble was really with those who were not there, who did not or could not imbibe James's vision of what Arts and Science should be. Thus, five months under his deanship, his faculty had grown uneasy and restive; over Christmas 1968 the beginnings of a split could be seen, notably between the science departments (including Psychology) on the one hand, and the Humanities, Classics, English, and some of the social sciences, on the other. History was divided. So was Philosophy. There were younger and yeastier members of many departments that liked what James was trying to do. Even older ones applauded some things.

Arts and Science was a big unwieldy faculty, with some 150 full-time staff and two thousand students. In January 1968 when there had been talk of splitting it into two, only one-third of the faculty supported the idea. The humanities and social sciences feared the split, believing their support and their access to research funds might be weakened. Many professed the belief that the mix of arts and science was good for everyone. One report to faculty in January 1968 began, "Strong medicines can produce remarkable cures, but they can also kill the patient." This was the majority view when James took over as dean.[23]

Into this state of unease came James's radical proposals for reform of curriculum, to break down departmental boundaries, put accountability into departmental budgets, and get them to concentrate their work in fields where they had solid expertise; they would be the driving force to real excellence both at the undergraduate and graduate level.

There was not much wrong with most of those suggestions, but with them came rumours and distortions derived from James's style and public utterances that made his proposals mutate into fearsome engines of tyranny. James told a meeting of high school administrators that Latin grammar was dull, and though useful to make students think, it was not very helpful in a modern arts curriculum. Was this an attempt to demote classics? James liked some social science departments; those he did not name became uneasy. There were allegations that the new chairmen of Physics, and of Chemistry, were put there because James manipulated the committees to put in men he wanted. Nearly all of these miasmas were later disclaimed by an investigating committee, but in the meantime the rumour mill flourished.

The tensions boiled up at a faculty meeting on 11 February 1969. James was held up by weather in Montreal and the chair was taken by his associate dean, Dr D.E. Coates, a systems analyst whom James had brought in a few months before. The meeting did not go well and Coates lost control of it. A motion for adjournment came from the floor; Coates tried to deflect it, but it was not debatable. It passed overwhelmingly and the meeting broke up in a buzz of elation and confusion.[24]

In the meantime several heads of departments had visited Hicks and told him sternly that James would have to go. As A.R. Bevan, head of English, remarked, at a 25 February faculty meeting, "although the Dean's ideas were admirable, his methods were deplorable." After several meetings faculty decided that its council would discuss the dean's proposals for change, and a special investigating committee would discuss the dean. Both were to make recommendations. On the first, council recommended that a vice-president academic was needed whether Arts and Science were split or not and that a faculty club was now a matter of urgent importance. With so many departments outside the A. and A. Building, there was no common place to meet and talk. Other proposals would be dealt with in due course. As for the dean, the investigating committee, headed by Horace Read, former dean of law, concluded that James, while not intending to do so, had "alienated a substantial proportion of the members of the Faculty," that he "tended to devote excessive energy to the pursuit of what he believes to be objectives of urgent importance," excessive because the energy had come at a considerable cost to the dean's vital function, maintaining morale and harmony.[25]

Dean James announced his resignation on 15 April 1969, though he would continue in office until a successor was appointed. At the faculty meeting in May he was thanked by F.H. Page, former head of Psychology, for his efforts, Page expressing sympathy with James's difficult task of "guiding a Faculty composed of many diverse points of view." There was a round of applause; in this civilized way, the James affair was over. The most civilized was Page himself; his work had been largely ignored, pushed aside by the new head; clinical and social psychology were barely surviving. Yet Page's essence, Christian sweetness of spirit, came through on that occasion. Page could resist, however; if he might bend, he would not be intimidated. He reminded one of Sir Thomas More, a man for all seasons; there was time for firmness, not very often indeed, but somewhere there had to be a stopping point. He was a marvellous man, too little noticed, not that he would have minded. Henry James would return to teaching psychology after giving up the deanship at the end of August 1969, and was then appointed Killam professor of psychology.

The new dean of arts and science was Guy MacLean, an historian who had been dean of graduate studies, an academic very different from James. Where James was hot, MacLean was cool. MacLean was a natural administrator, not easily ruffled, shrewd and capable. When he closed his office door at night, the problems stayed on his desk until he chose to tackle them again. George Wilson had seen his capacity in 1960 when he recommended MacLean as dean to A.E. Kerr. It was

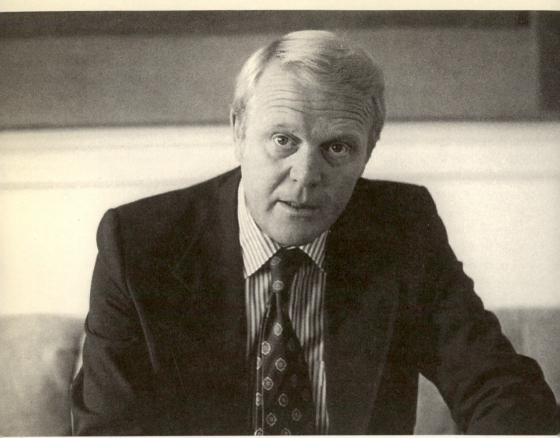

Guy MacLean, Professor of History, 1957–80; Dean of Graduate Studies, 1966–9;
Dean of Arts and Science, 1969–75; Vice-President Academic, 1974–80; President,
Mount Allison University, 1980–6.

abundant evidence of his talent that he would remain dean of arts and science until 1975, and be vice-president academic after that. Then in 1980 Mount Allison chose him as its president.

The man whom the faculty committee selected to succeed James as chairman of Psychology was a new arrival in 1963, Charles Brimer. He did not really want to be chairman; James pressed him to take it. So did the department. Brimer had a PH.D. from McMaster, was divorced, and upon arriving at Dalhousie soon married a Dalhousie student, Ann Connor. The chairmanship took too much of his life, for he liked research, his specialty being aversive stimuli in classical conditioning in animals. In 1970, with the new Life Sciences Building under way, someone had to struggle for budgets, space, and programs for Psychology. But, diabetic, unhappy with the personal decisions that a chairman must make that affected friends and colleagues, domestic problems overwhelming him, late in 1971 Brimer shot himself in the laboratory.[26]

The Life Sciences Complex

The building that Brimer was working on was a big one that Psychology shared with Biology and Oceanography. "Shared" is not the word. As it had developed by 1968 it was three large inter-connected buildings with common facilities, lecture rooms, workshops, student areas, using some of the ideas in the Dalhousie plan of the NSTC architectural students of three years earlier. The lecture rooms would be university ones, available to the whole campus, which Dalhousie badly needed. Dalhousie's lecture rooms were used to 90 per cent of capacity from 8:30 AM till late afternoon and even during the evenings. The new building's design began under C.D. Davison of Halifax, but the firm withdrew in December 1967 and the design was taken over by an exceptional Montreal firm, Affleck, Desbarats et al. It faced technical problems of some severity, the most important being that it was an infill building – that is, a complex nearly surrounded by other buildings. Not only that, but it was four to five storeys high, and had to be excavated out of Halifax ironstone, most of it lying on edge. The First Baptist Church across Oxford Street was already worried in May 1969 about the blasting that would be necessary. J.G. Sykes, university architect, was confident that all would be well. Mostly it was.[27]

The buildings around the Life Sciences – Shirreff Hall, the A. and A. Building, and King's – were all built of cut-stone exteriors. The Montreal architects came up with a building unique to Halifax, not to everyone's taste, but which won the award of excellence from the *Canadian Architectural Yearbook* in 1968. The architects ignored both cut stone and concrete slab, and went for a highly innovative building – what one biologist dared to call the most advanced building in Nova Scotia of the time – constructed of poured concrete with the finish sand-blasted to expose the aggregate underneath. The type is now familiar; thirty years ago it was not. The exterior shape of the building resolutely reflected its interior functions. Not all observers agreed that the Life Sciences complex was "a very happy escape from rectangularity," but escape it certainly was. There was an aesthetic integrity to it, no frills, no fuss, and on the inside it looked much the same as it did on the outside. Ray Affleck told Dalhousie people that at first they would be horrified at the lack of interior paint and finish, but in time they would come to like it. It proved serviceable and sensible to its users, though often a surprise to visitors.[28]

The cost was formidable, not so much because of the design but what the building had to do. There had to be salt-water tanks for marine animals, which was pumped up from the North-West Arm by a pipeline along South Street. For that the National Research Council promised $1 million. The Atlantic Development Board promised another $2 million for marine biology. Hicks and the two deans of arts and science and graduate studies went to work with the heads of Psychology and Biology and Gordon Riley, of the Institute of Oceanography, who had the difficult task of chairing that building committee.

The Institute of Oceanography had been clubbed together in 1959 by Ronald Hayes from four Dalhousie departments – Biology, Chemistry, Geology, and Physics. It was supported directly by the National Research Council and indirectly by several other federal agencies. In 1962–3 there were nine faculty members, cross-appointed from other departments, and twelve graduate students who took M.SC. degrees. Hayes left for Ottawa in 1963 to chair the Fisheries Research Board, and Hicks needed a new director of the institute. Dr Gordon Riley, oceanographer at Yale, came to give a seminar, to see and be seen, in October 1964. He was fifty-five years old, experienced and sage, and took to Hicks at once:

He [Hicks] was affable and witty and above all open and frank. He was a delight. I was used to guarded and political top-brass types … He spoke convincingly and I believed him. And I must say that in all my subsequent dealing with him, I never knew him to be less than frank and honest, even when the truth was painful.

As director of the institute Riley would report directly to the president, but his working arrangements with four departments were peculiar. Riley wanted full departmental status for Oceanography which, eventually, he got. There were, though, enemies lurking in the forest

Kraft von Maltzahn, Chairman of Biology, 1962–72, and Gordon Riley, Director of Oceanography, 1964–72, in a relaxed mood.

who thought Oceanography was just a conglomeration, much the way faculty had felt about Geography. The supreme despot was C.G.I. Friedländer, head of Geology, a crusty, austere Swiss who ran Geology with a heavy hand. But he came soon to retirement.[29]

The building program for the Life Sciences complex forced the pace of Oceanography's recognition as a full department at Dalhousie. For it was really the Oceanography money that got the building going in the first place. Hicks was able to use the two federal marine grants, and go to the province with that $3 million as evidence of solvency and good faith. As Gordon Riley put it, "Henry went scrounging and came back with a handsome pot." Handsome it was; the committee estimated the building at $13 million, but it rose steadily. In 1969 Dalhousie applied for a provincial loan of $12,750,000; it got Treasury Board in Ottawa, through Allan MacEachen, then minister of manpower, and E.J. Benson, minister of finance, to raise the Atlantic Development Board money from $2 million to $5 million, on the basis of a final estimate of $18,750,000. The loan from the Nova Scotian government was approved in July 1969. But it was subject to one certain and severe condition: if the cost were to rise further than $18,750,000, the Nova Scotian government would bail out entirely from any support. The work was started that summer of 1969, but its completion took four years. The special convocation to open the Life Sciences complex was in April 1974, with honorary degrees to Allan MacEachen and others. The one to MacEachen, at least in terms of the money he was able to direct towards the complex, was well deserved![30]

Students of the late 1960s
Behind the new buildings, the flourish of new programs, the developing role for professors in university governance, the new accountability of senior administrators, was an issue that Basil Cooke perceived but which Sir James Duff and Robert Berdahl had not so much ignored as underestimated. As *University Affairs* observed, "the dust from the walls of Jericho had hardly settled before students began to follow the faculty in demanding a greater role in university government."[31]

There have always been student protests, even riots, of one sort or another, since the town and gown clashes in mediaeval Paris and Oxford. Much of it was youthful high jinks; Dalhousie convocations at the turn of the twentieth century were sometimes unseemly affairs, paper bags of flour and peashooters being much in evidence. After a major disruption at the convocation of 1904, that in 1905 was abandoned altogether. But there was little other conflict at Dalhousie other than occasional brushes with the law.

What was different about the students' turbulence of the 1960s was that it was rooted not so much in poverty as in affluence; the instigators were middle-class students of ambitious middle-class parents. There were also a lot more of them. By 1968 the number of university students per capita in Canada was treble that of twenty years before. Many of these new students were not well prepared for university, nor did they know how best to take advantage of it. Too many expected that education could be acquired by easy osmosis; if that did not work, it was the fault of the system. Students in courses that imposed discipline and hard work by their nature – medicine, law, engineering, the natural sciences – were doing things that were important to their careers. They were, in short, working. The rebellious students tended to be in the humanities and social sciences, especially sociology, disciplines where much of the real work has to be directed from inside rather than imposed from without.[32]

Student radical leaders were most of them from comfortable middle-class backgrounds, and they were driven by an ideology that struck at the base of university life – the rejection of traditional values and mores. The philosopher that delivered this ideology in the United States, Germany, and to some extent in Canada, was Herbert Marcuse (1898–1979), a German who came to the United States in 1934. Out of Marx, Hegel, and Freud he produced the thesis of "the great refusal," that one had to reject the existing social order as inherently repressive. So student radicals argued that all society, all knowledge, was hopelessly skewed by class bias: rationality, freedom of speech, tolerance for other points of view, these were doctrines from a well already poisoned. Intolerance in such circumstances was a positive virtue. Be intolerant, of class bias, old structure, old ideas. These arguments sent elements of the student left into centrifugal distances, hallucinogenic drugs, experimentation with new experiences of all kinds, discovering the irrational subconscious, a world outside the too-structured present.[33]

Canadian radical students used American examples and precedents freely when it suited their purposes, whether from Berkeley, Chicago, Kent State, or Columbia. But such examples had only limited relevance to Canadian university experience. Canada had no Vietnam war, nor the draft that sent young soldiers to it, which did much to drive the American movement during the last years of President Lyndon Johnson and the early years of the Nixon presidency. The Canadian example closest to the strife at Columbia in April 1968 was at Sir George Williams University in Montreal in February 1969, when the computer centre was burnt and the police called in.

Not that the universities were blameless, as they sought to deal with the huge influx of students in the 1960s. Mass teaching, sometimes via closed-circuit TV monitors, or by ill-prepared instructors, was too common. Professors were apt to spend too much time on their research and not enough on students. Nor did all professors invest their power over marks with patience, conscientiousness, gentility. Some were just arbitrary. At Dalhousie one professor of biology in 1955 was ready to flunk an otherwise first-class student in pre-med because, a Cape Bretoner, he had not learned to pronounce "pharynx" properly. Appeal procedures to get out from under such actions were minimal or lacking altogether and the young Cape Bretoner managed to reverse that decision only with difficulty. By the 1960s the old heavy-handedness was going, but for the students it was not going fast enough.[34]

There was also criticism that the university curriculum was "irrelevant" to contemporary issues, which meant all too often, in the new TV age, students' sometimes naive view of what world issues really were. Radicals aimed, said Northrop Frye, at dissevering the present from its past, to minimize the history of western values. Some student criticism was valid: too few courses in the third world, in labour history, women's issues, Canadian literature. The *Dalhousie Gazette* took the view that to develop a critical faculty in students, Canadian literature was just as useful as Chaucer.[35]

Although Halifax and Dalhousie were continually being apprised of conditions in Vietnam, Paris, Berkeley, Columbia, and other flashpoints of 1968, nevertheless, the great bulk of its students were sceptical of radical rhetoric. "What has Rap Brown to do with us?" "What does Vietnam have to do with Nova Scotia?": those questions measured the gap between the 1968–9 rhetoric of the *Dalhousie Gazette* and most Dalhousie students.

The *Gazette* in the two years after 1967–8 was run by radicals who drove its editorial comment and slanted selection of news. As early as November 1967 there were complaints that there was far too much Vietnam and not enough Dalhousie. The *Gazette* conceded the point; on 22 February 1968 it admitted it did not reflect student opinion. It couldn't, it said. "The *Gazette* cannot reflect the opinion of the average student as we feel there is no such thing. One cannot editorialize by consensus." Thus the next "relevant" headline in the *Gazette* was: "Rap Brown Must Be Set Free," Rap Brown being one of the radicals, imprisoned temporarily in New York, who later helped lead the Columbia disruption and occupation in April 1968. It was all very well for the *Gazette* to say in a headline in November 1969 that "Vietnam – It's our War Too," but it wasn't. The students wouldn't have it. Their coolness led Jameel Ramahan, representative of the International Students' Association, to deplore the lack of student protests at

Dalhousie for world issues. Campus events and protests have failed, Ramahan said, because "Bookworms and other such lifeless forms that exist at Dalhousie show a complete lack of guts, self-confidence and a pitiful ... lack of individuality." Doug Hill ('70) remarked in October 1968:

When I see the Gazette is out, I immediately snatch it up in my hot little hand and hopefully look for some news about DAL, but inevitably a manhole cover is staring me in the face or there is a grape boycott somewhere in California. ARE YOU GUYS FOR REAL?

In 1969 Sifford Pearré Jr, a graduate student in oceanography, criticized it for "lazy man's journalism," and for simply being a conduit for outside editorials, outside Dalhousie, outside Nova Scotia, even outside Canada. Medical students were particularly critical of the Gazette, a "non-paper not worth wrapping garbage in" was the opinion of Vox Medica. Dalhousie students pay out $11,000 a year to keep that going? Henry Hicks was asked about the Gazette by Harris Sullivan for CJCH TV. "I do not read it," he said, "It does not speak for the university. It speaks only for itself."

The great majority of Dalhousie students also opted out of campus politics. There was a substantial core, perhaps as high as 80 per cent, who were not really touched by radical student politics. Three students were now full members of Senate; Hicks saw no reason why students should not become full members of the Board of Governors. (The Dalhousie Act had to be changed to effect that, and was in 1976.) The Faculty of Arts and Science had given some flexibility to old curriculum rigidities. Faculty generally had been willing to listen. There was still the tradition of senior faculty doing the first-year courses; and while there was some alienation in some of the very big first-year classes where accommodation was inadequate or lecturers the same, it did not reach the level of TV anonymity so noticeable elsewhere. The Halifax students, almost half of Dalhousie, came with a variety of political ideologies, but most were far from being metropolitan radicals aiming to unsettle the innate conservatism of students from the rest of Nova Scotia.[36]

Thus Hicks had some reason for confidence in the good sense of Dalhousie students. He did not believe in preparation for student unrest, which he thought might only invite action. But he told Chisholm, "I am resolved that we would move quickly to uphold the law." It was a position not unlike that of S.I. Hayakama of San Francisco State College, who believed that universities should respond by all means to the need for change, but totally resist change pushed by violence.

Universities were easy targets. They were, as one American law professor told an Osgoode Hall convocation, "helplessly vulnerable." Professors were overwhelmingly a peaceful lot, used to deciding issues by discussion and argument. Naked intimidation they were not used to; they tended to believe that there must be something in students' demands that were broached so vociferously. That was meat and drink to real radicals whose demands were never-ending. The irony was that some student demands were legitimate and some were not; academic bodies were not always well mettled to discriminate. Academics who had not been through the toughening of war or other perils, who had not encountered intimidation first-hand from communist cadres, were often in a state of puzzled pusillanimity, as if, not knowing what to do, it was best to give in.[37]

Hicks was good at defusing issues, but some issues with fuses already lit had to be dealt with less circumspectly. That happened with sociology. By 1968 the Department of Sociology had evolved a group chairmanship composed of seven staff members and seven graduate students. It aimed to create an academic community of equals, students and staff together, without distinction of power or privilege, and with power to decide on new staff, promotions, curriculum. When W.N. Stephens of Florida Atlantic University was appointed chairman of Sociology in November 1968 he ran straight into Sociology's newly formed course union. The negotiating stance of the department was unmistakable in their letter to Stephens:

There can be no question ... of private discussions with Dr. Gamberg [acting chairman] in regard to the nature and future of this Department. If you want consultation it is there for the asking, but it must be real consultation with the Department ... you must by now have realized that we take seriously our responsibility to the idea of democracy ... We have, for instance, progressively integrated the student caucus in the Department into collective decision-making. Partly, we have fostered this, partly this has been their demand ...

This means that, whereas formerly the headship was an authority position deriving its power from its place in the administrative hierarchy, the chairmanship is a position deriving its authority solely from the Department ... the chairman is a front-man representing the majority wishes of the Department as a whole.

Stephens sent that argument to the president. Hicks liked it not at all. Nor did Senate Council, whom Hicks consulted at once. The change from "head" to "chairman" made no difference in the line of responsibility. Appointments and budgets were recommended to the president by department chairmen and the faculty dean. The change of title simply meant that the appointment was made "for a term certain rather than at the pleasure of the Board of Governors." Hicks explained this to the two senior sociologists, Herb Gamberg and Graham Morgan. That led the Sociology Graduate Student Union to threaten strike action and occupation if the acting chairman and incoming chairman-designate did not accept, first, that the existing democratic structure of the Sociology Department is non-negotiable; and second, that the Student Union will oppose any attempt to impose a reactionary authority structure within the Department. Action would commence the next afternoon.

That afternoon under Hicks's chairmanship the Senate Council made its position clear: no department at Dalhousie could by its own volition change the university rules and regulations laid down by Senate. Nevertheless, members of departments might appeal decisions of departmental chairmen. Certainly departmental chairmen should continuously consult the department, "including students when appropriate," and should normally be acting on the basis of consensus of opinion in the department.

However, the Department Chairman is charged with certain responsibilities, and hence has the necessary authority to make recommendations, even when they are not concurred in by a majority of the members of his Department. It is hoped that such situations would be exceptional.

The threat of a strike by graduate students did not last long; Sociology Department meetings, however, continued to be harangues that went on and on. By Christmas 1970 Stephens was glad to go on sabbatical to Spain. A year later, however, new appointments had moved the department to the right, and there was a new chairman, Don Clairmont. What the Sociology Department needed, said John Hamer, a new staff member in 1971, was "less democracy and more Sociology." By November 1971 a new system was in place, a central committee of three faculty, two student representatives, and the chairman. That did not end the pressures in Sociology, for some of them were embedded in the staff; but the department began to be less confrontational. Jerome Barkow, another new faculty member, described the history in a dramatic sentence, "a small, highly exclusive clique of poor-to-failing sociology students had ripped off the slogans of the radical left and were masquerading as oppressed proletarians in order to make faculty members too guilty to flunk them out." That was one explanation, though only one, of the complex series of events in Sociology.[38]

The President's Office Occupied, April 1970

Hicks's one confrontation took place when he was away in Toronto making a speech claiming, ironically enough, that Dalhousie had been singularly free of the troubles that had characterized Simon Fraser, Toronto, and other universities. He and his vice-president, W.A. MacKay, former dean of law, had agreed between them that if there were ever an occupation, Hicks would go home to his stamp collection and let the courts work on the problem. MacKay phoned him at the Park Plaza in Toronto after his speech. "You'd better have a look at your Bermuda stamps!" said MacKay jocularly.[39]

Senate had been debating procedures for the appointment of presidents, vice-presidents, deans, and associate deans, which were contained in a report by the George Committee to Senate early in 1969. Student members of Senate were specifically asked for their comments (which they did not give); faculties gave their input; revisions were made and the report came to Senate on Monday, 13 April 1970.

At that meeting Senate was presented for the first time with a wholly new document by a group representing the Dalhousie New Democratic Youth (DNDY). It proposed the election of all senior administrators by students and faculty. Senators pointed out that this was incompatible with existing university statutes, but nevertheless spokesmen for DNDY were heard. They insisted that their submission must be discussed in Senate as a whole and not relegated to committee. K.T. Leffek of Chemistry grew impatient at this. "There's been five years' deliberation on this subject. Shall we go around the mulberry bush again?" When A.J. Winstanley, Student Council president-elect and senator, moved that Senate postpone consideration of the report, Senate voted against him. The DNDY students then left Senate for a "caucus," and later returned with a demand, non-negotiable, that if the Senate did not reconsider its action and postpone adoption of the report, they would occupy the president's office. Senate was not prepared to reconsider, and by the time it finished its agenda, at 6:45 PM, the president's office was already occupied by students of the DNDY. The doors had been locked but one of the windows had been left unlocked. When Vice-Presidents MacKay and McNeill arrived, there were about fifteen people in the president's office, including two students from Saint Mary's. They were all asked to leave, MacKay pointing out the unlawfulness of their occupation. They said they intended no harm. Winstanley arrived and pointed out to them that the Dalhousie Student Council could not support the DNDY tactics. MacKay gave deadlines; the students insisted that Senate reverse its decision. MacKay replied that no one could dictate to Senate, neither he nor President Hicks, nor would he expect Senate to reverse its decision in the face of unlawful acts of a few students.

The students remained overnight, promising no damage would be done, a promise almost kept.

The next day MacKay came at 8:45 AM and said that a Senate meeting had been called for 4:30 PM that day in the McInnes Room and that the occupation should now end. It didn't; MacKay then asked for, and got, from the Supreme Court of Nova Scotia, an interim three-day injunction, that prohibited those named in it from disrupting the university. The order was served by the sheriff of Halifax and his deputies dressed in plain clothes. When they arrived at 5 PM the occupiers had gone.

At the Senate meeting there was good turnout both of senators and students. The student senators moved that Senate reconsider its decision on the George Report. The discussion that followed was serious, orderly, and constructive. Senate refused to table the report, but it did agree to reconsider the form of its decision: it would recommend the George Report to the board on a year's interim basis, with Senate willing to receive representations until 30 September 1970. Only one submission came in, from the DNDY. It was duly circulated to faculties by Senate for comment but elicited little. Thus did it end. Of 5,600 students, 20 per cent of whom lived on campus, the proportion of students in this incident was very small; perhaps sixteen were actually involved in the occupation. After Hicks got back to Halifax the occupying students told him: "We knew you weren't here and we weren't upsetting anything and we wanted to make the gesture." That says much about student radicalism at Dalhousie.[40]

Another development that year began on 29 October with the disruption of a Law School panel on Trudeau's War Measures Act. Five Maoist radicals pushed into the room shouting slogans and waving placards. There was some hurly-burly in trying to contain them. One law professor, Robert Samek, a refugee who had seen much of communist techniques in Czechoslovakia and who had fought intimidation there, was not going to have it here. He was the Maoists' particular target and later in the evening was confronted and jostled, though no injuries resulted.

One Maoist was the Killam professor of mathematics, F.W. Lawvere, BA (Indiana), PH.D. (Columbia), who had an enviable reputation in a new field, category theory; with senior fellows and post-doctoral fellows added, his work became an important centre in the Mathematics Department. It started extremely well, but in his second year things changed. He became part of, probably leader of, a small Maoist group that took to physically disrupting meetings on campus they didn't like. After Lawvere was again in a disruption at King's, Dean MacLean and Arnold Tingley, chairman of Mathematics, talked to

Arnold Tingley of Mathematics, Registrar, 1973–85.

him through the whole of one evening. The conversation went in circles. At issue was not his competence, nor his Maoism, but his insistence that he would continue to disrupt "fascist" lectures or meetings whenever he felt it appropriate.

Tingley by now felt Lawvere had to go, and that was possible to arrange. When Lawvere first came he declined tenure, for there was a wrinkle in Canadian income tax law that exempted non-residents from having to pay tax. Thus Lawvere's contract was simply allowed to expire. The Department of Mathematics voted by mail ballot; eighteen voted not to recommend Lawvere's reappointment, thirteen voted to recommend it, and there were five abstentions. But Tingley's decision took courage. He had been criticized almost daily by Lawvere supporters in the department. Some departmental members were hypocrites enough to say that they had to support Lawvere publicly but assured Tingley privately they really supported Tingley. He thought that was "less than admirable." Departmental conservatives were even more of a nuisance than the radicals. As for the media, the best solution Tingley found, time and again, when there were phone calls, was simply to reply, "No comment." The affair gradually ceased to be news. In similar troubles at Acadia and Mount Allison, Tingley observed, university officials presented logical arguments against such disruptive influences. That assumed that illogical positions could be refuted by logical discussion. They couldn't. For his part Hicks left the affair mostly to his vice-president and deans, but told both Tingley and MacLean that they were wrong. In the end he reluctantly accepted their judgment that Lawvere had to go.

One result of Lawvere's disruptions was that Senate in December 1970 affirmed its obligation "to preserve freedom of speech and assembly and to ensure the orderly conduct of its academic functions." Thus, for "any deliberate disruption either by staff or students" of Dalhousie's academic business, lectures, or organized meetings, Senate reserved the right to recommend disciplinary action "which may include suspension or dismissal from the university."[41] But there were few occasions after that to apply Senate's new rules. Disruptive radicalism was consumed by its own excesses, and it had never had much student support at Dalhousie. The university had in the meantime introduced student membership in faculties and Senate, and brought in changes to the curriculum that met most student demands for more flexibility.

Transition Year Program

The idea behind the Transition Year Program was to bring disadvantaged students from visible minorities up to the standard of university entrance. What high-school dropouts, victims of years of low self-es-teem, needed was the will and the opportunity to succeed. Such at least was the basic philosophy. The program was proposed to the Fac-ulty of Arts and Science in 1969 by Dalhousie graduate students, with Senate Council approving it in February 1970. Arts and Science then invited members of the black and Micmac groups to submit propos-als. The whole process was urged on by Vice-President W.A. MacKay, the judicious and thoughtful former dean of law. Funding was awk-ward; before Dalhousie could approach appropriate agencies in Ot-tawa and Halifax it had to have some proof that the program was supported by the local communities who were to benefit; yet Dalhou-sie did not wish to arouse false hopes. The project was estimated to cost $100,000 a year. With $59,000 in hand, $16,000 from Indian Affairs, $10,000 each from the two federal departments of Man-power and Citizenship, $23,000 from the Nova Scotia University Grants Committee, with a few private donations trickling in, Dalhou-sie officially announced the program on 27 April 1970. The director was P.D. Pillay, professor of history, of South African origin and In-dian (from India) extraction.

The first year cost $90,000 in out-of-pocket expenses; Dalhousie put up 30 per cent of this but in fact contributed much more, for a significant number of instructors were Dalhousie professors whose TYP work was free-loaded on Dalhousie. In that first year, 1970–1, there were twenty-three students, seventeen blacks and six Micmacs. Eight of the twenty-three were women. About 40 per cent of all the TYP students came from Halifax/Dartmouth. By January 1971 the consensus of the instructors was that sixteen of the students were ca-pable of doing university work if they continued to progress as they had been doing. There were problems of financing, but eventually fif-teen of the twenty-three from that year attended Dalhousie, and four eventually earned bachelor's degrees.[42]

The black community organizations wanted more input into the program. Dalhousie would have welcomed that had it not been accom-panied by suggestions that Senate could not have accepted: equal share in decisions, in selection of students, and in evaluation of staff and stu-dents. Hicks was never an enthusiast for the program anyway; it was MacKay who was carrying it forward in the face of difficulties. In 1972 the decision had to be made as to whether it was worth while carrying on. Certainly some had been admitted to the program who could never have become university students. Faculty and Senate agreed that there were probably too many students in the program, and that the annual admissions should be limited to ten, selected on the basis of stricter academic criteria. So it was continued in 1972–3 and with much more success. Of the ten students admitted, nine continued to the BA program, and six got a degree. Thus the program survived.[43]

Maritime School of Social Work

Another Dalhousie outreach was its taking over the Maritime School of Social Work (MSSW). It had been established in 1941 by S.H. Prince, professor of sociology at King's. The school's directors consulted Nova Scotian university presidents and the school deliberately followed the model of the Nova Scotia Technical College, eventually affiliating with Mount Allison, St Francis Xavier, Saint Mary's, and King's.

By the 1960s, looking for accreditation, which required incorporation into a university, MSSW came to King's. King's liked the idea but lacked the base to develop it. Hicks told H.D. Smith, president of King's, that it would be purposeless for King's to attempt this, for it would have to use Dalhousie facilities. It was a complicated issue; Saint Mary's was ready and willing to take over the MSSW, and the MSSW board liked Saint Mary's. The staff did not; they feared that their school would not get accreditation via Saint Mary's. Hicks was not willing to be baited into a popularity contest. He wanted a Dalhousie takeover of MSSW discussed with a completely open mind. In May 1967 the MSSW board split equally between Dalhousie affiliation and the status quo, and the decision to join Dalhousie required a two-thirds vote. Dalhousie won out after internal wrangling at MSSW between board and staff. Amalgamation was effected as of 1 September 1969.[44] MSSW would be in Graduate Studies.

The province of New Brunswick balked at making its proper contribution to the school. Hicks pointed out that while once New Brunswick students were only 15 per cent of the school's enrolment, now in March 1970 they were 30 per cent, and Dalhousie should not have to carry the MSSW deficit of $70,000 when New Brunswick was contributing only $5,000. There was action to be taken; Hicks told the dean of graduate studies, Forbes Langstroth, that action should resemble that taken by the Medical School five years earlier:

I think we ought to start squeezing out New Brunswick students in the Maritime School [of Social Work] without actually announcing that we are doing so. Almost certainly this will be the only way we shall induce them to reconsider their grant support. As you know, it was only when New Brunswickers thought we were doing this in medicine that they re-calculated their support to the medical and dental schools on a realistic basis.[45]

A minor incident in 1972 illustrates Hicks's social and political sensitivities. Betty Dugas of Church Point applied to attend the MSSW. A borderline student, she had been accepted, then abruptly told she was not. She applied political pressure. Benoit Comeau, minister of lands and forests, wrote to Hicks about it. So did Peter Nicholson, minister of finance. By the time the admissions committee had favourably reviewed her request for reconsideration, she'd got herself accepted at the University of Ottawa. Hicks did not like it, and for several reasons:

It seems to me to show the inadequacy of our own admission procedures and the unwisdom of our forcing an Acadian girl to go to Ottawa for her MSW degree, when we, ourselves, have a substantial shortfall of students and ought to be serving our Acadian community, even if it does mean stretching things a little bit to take into account the deficiencies in background and preparation which our Acadian people all too often have.

... I think this is a fine example of how the University does itself harm in the eyes of its constituency, which, in this case, includes two members of the Provincial Cabinet, one of whom is, and will continue to be, highly influential in shaping the Government's attitude toward universities in particular.

As to accreditation of MSSW, that was coming but on prescribed terms. By 1973 accreditation was Canadian and the Canadian committee was fairly blunt. It met Hicks on 3 April and told him what in fact he feared, that there would have to be a new director before accreditation. It felt that the whole staff was fairly undistinguished and still too isolated from Dalhousie. The committee reported, in effect, said Hicks, that "you have a group of nice, mediocre people, who are trying hard but are not terribly good." L.T. Hancock, director since 1949, resigned; accreditation, Canadian and American, followed that summer.[46]

Buying Fenwick Tower

In 1968–9 Dalhousie's total enrolment, full-time and part-time, was 4,600; the next year it rose by 23 per cent to 5,600, and the following year by 18 per cent to 6,600. In 1968 Dalhousie commissioned a housing study, which concluded that the open rental market in Halifax was close to saturation and the ceiling would be reached in 1969–70. The amount of rental housing available to students would remain static; if Dalhousie was to grow, as anticipated, to some 9,000 students by the end of the 1970s, it would need places for 3,000 more students than it had currently available. Already in December 1968, according to Dean James, the need for student housing was desperate; it was worse in August 1970. Then Dalhousie bought Ardmore Hall, the Sisters of Charity former convent at Oxford and North streets, for about $300,000. It would house seventy women students. The board also leased Quinpool Hall, the former Holy Heart Seminary, from the Roman Catholic Corporation, at $17,000 a year. It housed 188 men. Shirreff Hall now had 424 students and Howe Hall 416. In addition, Dalhousie had seventeen houses, eleven for men, six for women, that housed an additional 147. Altogether there were 1,250 students in residence.

Dalhousie was considering building a new residence on what was called the Paradise lands, at Summer and College streets, and the proposal had already been approved by City Council and the CMHC; it would accommodate 480 single students with eighty-eight married students in apartments. Sister Catherine Wallace, now on the Dalhousie board as a result of the affiliation of Dalhousie and Mount St Vincent in 1969 (a five-year trial marriage), said that the Mount had discovered that the old-style dormitory residences were no longer meeting student needs.

Just at that point the Dalhousie board had a special meeting to deal with the bankruptcy of Kenney Construction of Yarmouth, contractors for the Arts Centre and the service tunnels from the Central Services Building. Both contracts were almost complete; three months' work would complete the Arts Centre, three weeks the tunnels. Both contracts were protected through contractors' performance bonds and would be completed without much difficulty, though there were legal wrinkles that made things awkward.[47]

One of the structures that Kenney Construction had been building was a tall, thirty-two-storey apartment complex on Fenwick Street, in the swale below Fort Massey hill. Hicks reported that it was almost finished and was awaiting sheriff's sale in April 1971. It could probably be bought for about $5 million, and would house some 812 single and married students. It would need another $1.3 million to finish. Hicks smelled a bargain, but the board had difficulty with it. At that point in 1971 Dalhousie already had $30 million worth of construction going on. Although the Dalhorizons campaign, launched in 1969, had been going well with $4 million already in, and with hopes of another $7 million to come, nevertheless Dalhousie had heavy financial commitments on its plate. McInnes thought Fenwick was far too dangerous financially. But in the end the building was bought for $5,255,041. At that price it was a bargain. So much so that the Construction Association complained that Dalhousie was too sharp.

Fenwick had problems. Construction was not all it might have been; hurricane Beth came through on 15–16 August 1971 with 9.4 inches (235 mm.) of rain, and it filled the elevator shafts with up to 17 feet of water. Elevators had to be corrected; for such a large building they seemed a trifle rickety. In October a window blew in. From the upper floors the view was marvellous; so was the wind. On a windy day one could see the water in the washbasins sway slowly from side to side as the building did. Halifax building rules allowed Fenwick to sway 8 inches in an 80 m.p.h. wind; the building was substantial enough that the sway was only 5 inches. There were some 10,000 joints in the hot water system; in February 1974 when one of the hot water pipes burst on the seventeenth floor, the manager of Fenwick apologized for the mess, but added that only three of ten thousand joints had burst!

Not all student parties could be kept at a decent noise level, but there were controls; and no one in authority wanted Fenwick to become the Rochdale – that notorious Toronto experiment – of Halifax. On the whole the students at Fenwick were understanding and kept their complaints low-key. After all, Halifax certainly did not have a plethora of apartments on offer; one could say that there had been a chronic housing shortage since 1749.[48]

Henry Hicks Becomes a Part-time President

Early one morning in 1972 Hicks had a phone call from an old political colleague, Paul Martin, then government leader in the Senate. Hicks had not always supported him; at the 1958 Liberal party convention Martin had asked Hicks to back him for the leadership of the party. Hicks said, sorry, he was supporting Lester Pearson. In 1968 when Pearson retired, Martin said, "Henry, you couldn't support me last time but surely you can this time." Hicks again had to demur; he would have to back Trudeau. Paul Martin carried few grudges. In 1972 he said, "I think we'd like to have a university president in the Senate." Hicks replied that he could not abandon Dalhousie, but that if Martin was interested in having "a university president who will continue his university presidency in the Senate, I'll think about it."[49]

Hicks believed in public service. He had already gone to battle for members of staff, mostly NDP or Conservatives, who wanted to run in elections. In 1972 he called the executive committee of the board together; most of them had been on the committee that had asked him to serve as Dalhousie president ten years before. What did they think? Most of them agreed with Frank Covert: "Accept by all means; just don't stop being president of Dalhousie." A.G. Archibald was not enthusiastic but later even he came round.[50]

The truth was that Hicks really wanted the senatorship but was not sure if the Dalhousie presidency could stand it. Louis Vagianos, now director of communications services, told Hicks he would be a 60 per cent president, exactly what Hicks feared. Upon his vice-president, W.A. MacKay, and his dean of arts and science, Guy MacLean, much

This cartoon appeared in Dalhousie's *University News* in 1976, when President Hicks was in his fourth year as a member of the Senate. Between 1972 and 1980, when Parliament was in session, Hicks flew to Ottawa on a Tuesday afternoon, returned on a Thursday afternoon.

depended. MacKay and MacLean were old friends; they had been students at Dalhousie together, played football together, on the Student Council together, and after post-graduate work both came back to Dalhousie in 1956 on staff. If Hicks became senator much more work would devolve upon MacKay. MacLean, who had already had three years as dean, was willing to continue, mainly to help MacKay. They thought they would be able to manage. Of course Parliament did not sit all year. When it did, Hicks said, he could take a Tuesday afternoon flight to Ottawa, get there for the Tuesday evening sitting, and take a flight back to Halifax late Thursday afternoon. Parliament would get two and a half days, and Dalhousie would get two and a half days, plus the Saturdays which he would have to inflict on his vice-presidents and deans.[51] Hicks accepted, and in April 1972 became a part-time president. There were many at Dalhousie, on the board not least, who believed that 60 per cent of Hicks was quite good enough. There may even have been a few who were glad to see some of the preternatural energy deployed elsewhere!

· II ·

Coming to the Plateau
1972–1976

Changes in residence life. Flexibility in Arts and Science. Registrar's office, 1952–73. Trouble in Classics, 1968–74. Accrediting the Library School, 1973. Graduate Studies, 1972 and after. A new Faculty of Administrative Studies, 1975. The Atlantic Institute of Education, inception and demise, 1970–82. Trying to expand Dentistry, 1966–82. The Medical Faculty, 1972–80. Expanding the Law School. The Dalplex saga, part 1, 1966–76.

By 1972 the longstanding principle of Dalhousie being *in loco parentis* to students had largely disappeared. The most telling indication of that was a Committee of Deans resolution, 28 February 1969, that examination marks would be sent to students only, and to their parents only when authorized by the student. In 1969 it was clear that, the great majority of students having reached the age of nineteen, they could and should act for themselves. This shift of responsibility was confirmed legally in the Supreme Court of Nova Scotia in a 1978 case, *G.W. Sutcliffe* v. *University Governors of Acadia*.

Since the 1930s Dalhousie fraternities had exemplified that principle. Established at Dalhousie between 1923 and 1938, they provided a home away from home, and were in effect largely self-governing. In the days when universities could not afford to build residences, fraternities provided for male students an important focus to their university life. They acquired houses and ran them near the campus. The wooden ones at Dalhousie were a far cry from the big brick ones at Toronto or McGill, and even more from the substantial stone ones on American campuses; they often needed paint; they were occasionally accused (sometimes with justification) of being noisy and rowdy. But a 1966 survey by the *Gazette* suggested a genial tolerance by neighbours: "We were all young once"; "they've got to live"; "they're nice boys. I'd be happy if they would ... not make so much noise Saturday nights." Fraternities were a useful student solution to residence problems; that was Carleton Stanley's view back in 1935. At that time some 30 per cent of Dalhousie male students were members; the advent of Howe Hall in the 1960s made fraternities as residences less important, but their membership was in 1969 still 8 per cent of the student body.

Before the 1960s women had to live in Shirreff Hall or with their parents or a near relative, and it was not just a *pro forma* rule. Thus women's sororities were social. There were two, ΑΓΔ (1932) and ΠΒΦ (1934). Both were still in place in 1969.

In 1969 new regulations were established at Howe Hall and Shirreff Hall, giving much more responsibility to residence committees to determine their own house rules. The dean of women, Christine Irvine, suggested the Shirreff Hall committee consider a new system of leaves: that they would be wholly unrestricted except for the first-year girls, many of whom were under nineteen, but that even they would have freer leaves than before. The advice of the *Gazette* of November 1968, "take the wire gratings off your windows!" was not really needed, for in effect it was already being done by the young women themselves. The *Gazette*'s 1971 poetry was also symbolic:

> love –
> as your mind
> grows to the one
> beside you
> touch her hand
> accept her gift
> and sleep.

It all suggested that the days of the NATO girl, "No Action, Talk Only," a *Gazette* complaint of 1964, was anachronistic by 1969. Under the new rules in Howe Hall women were allowed in all areas from 9 AM to 3 AM, seven days a week. In Shirreff Hall male guests were allowed in rooms from 12 noon to 3 AM on weekdays, and from 9 AM to 3 AM on weekends. After 6 PM male visitors had to be signed in by a resident who registered her name and room number; the 3 AM limit for male visitors to be out of rooms was enforced, a peremptory buzzer sounding its warning in the room. In January 1970 a Shirreff Hall referendum asked, "Are you satisfied with the present visiting hours?" Some 85 per cent of Shirreff Hall residents voted, and the result was overwhelming: 95 per cent of the young women voting preferred the new system.[1]

In April 1979 the rules were liberalized again. The board's Residence Committee, chaired by Dr J.M. Corston, recommended that except for freshettes, women at Shirreff Hall could have male guests in their rooms the whole weekend, from 6 PM Friday until 9 AM Monday. That proposal came from the Shirreff Hall residents themselves, though this time some 25 per cent opposed it, as did Christine Irvine herself. Nevertheless the board proceeded, providing designated areas for those who did not want the extension of hours, and also provision for male washrooms. Christine Irvine and Mrs D.K. Murray, president of the Women's Division of the Alumni, felt that Dalhousie "was degrading Shirreff Hall by allowing female students to accommodate male visitors in their rooms," and setting a bad example for freshettes. Hicks told the board in September 1979 that this was now a *fait accompli*, but that there would be a review. That satisfied neither lady. Zilpha Linkletter, who chaired the board's budget committee, also wanted her vote recorded as opposed. It was probably a contest difficult to win; 75 per cent support from the Shirreff Hall residents was not easy to combat. It was also a contest between new ways and old, and for better or worse, the new won.

There is some irony in the conclusions of the review that took place a year later. Christine Irvine reported that the use of the weekend visiting privilege had not been at all widespread, that on the average weekend there were as few as eleven visitors registered. The Women's Division of the Alumni continued unhappy, but the board's Residence Committee concluded that the new policy was presenting no problems, that there had been no complaints from resident girls, nor from the dons nor from parents.[2]

These residence rule changes of 1969 and 1979, and their acceptance, show how far the sexual revolution, and the pill, had changed mores in fifteen years. As late as 1964 such rules would have been unthinkable; by the 1970s they were clearly possible. Dalhousie accepted what had clearly come from the residents themselves.

Changes in Arts and Science

In 1972–3 there were 7,335 Dalhousie students, of whom 14 per cent were part-time. While the total rose only by 3 per cent in 1973–4, the big jump in the 1970s was the 12 per cent increase from 1973–4 to 1974–5, from 7,544 to 8,447. After that, registration levels evened out, rising slowly in the late 1970s, reaching 9,018 in 1980–1. By then part-time students were noticeably on the increase, some 17.5 per cent of registration. Part-timers in Arts and Science were 16 per cent, Health Professions 17 per cent, and Graduate Studies 24 per cent. There were none in Medicine. About 42 per cent of all students at Dalhousie were women, and the percentage would continue to rise through the 1970s. Part-time students were about 56 per cent women in 1975 and 60 per cent by 1980.[3]

There were also substantial changes in the Arts and Science curriculum, though not nearly as extensive as some students, and the *Dalhousie Gazette*, talked about. As of the autumn of 1969, experimental classes in any subject could be formed on the initiative of students or faculty, subject to announcement of it in the calendar if far enough in advance, or in the *Gazette* or in the new (1970) *University News*. A faculty member had to be rapporteur and submit a report on the content and work of the class to the Faculty Curriculum Committee.

As of 1 September 1969, English 100 was no longer a required subject for the BA, B.Sc. and B. COM. Professor S.E. Sprott warned faculty that levels of verbal skills in students were already declining and abolition of English 100 would be "another nail in the coffin." Nevertheless it carried, by twenty-nine to five. With that went also the abolition of the compulsory language requirement. These changes were part of a general increase in the flexibility of the BA and B.Sc. programs, not all of them necessarily for the good, created by that hydraulic pressure from students, circumstances, and *Zeitgeist* which could bend even well-established principles. By the early 1970s the compulsory side of the BA had almost vanished; what remained was that in the first year one *had* to take at least one class from three of languages, humanities, social sciences, and sciences.

In April 1969 a committee on examinations urged massive changes in the whole system. Final examinations, it said, put an "inordinate premium on unimportant attributes," that is,

the ability to organize and recall large bodies of factual material, and the ability to perform mental gymnastics under stress. One of the strongest complaints of students at all levels is that success in final examination depends to far too great an extent on the memorization and reproduction of the material presented in lectures.

The report also criticized the physical conditions under which the examinations were written; it argued that if some students responded positively to stress, if they found "in the sordid squalor of the examination room an almost masochistic stimulus," most students did not. To say that examinations were useful because they forced students to study was "not legitimate in a University, if anywhere." Most serious of all, said the committee report, examinations were unreliable as a test of performance or of achievement.

An earnest look at examination lists in the basement of the A. and A. Building.

That radical rhetoric from the Committee on Examinations did not move the Faculty of Arts and Science very far. Few faculty members could really jettison examinations in some form as tests for student skills, knowledge, and work, although take-home examinations became more widely accepted. The History Department did experiment with a first-year class in 1972 mounted by two young and talented historians, where the only condition was attendance. It offered a huge *mélange* of the history of the last hundred years which included even all of Wagner's *Der Ring des Nibelungens*. There was no examination and it attracted much attention. After three years, faculty's impression was that the historians were doing all the work and the experiment was shut down as something of an embarrassment. Many Arts and Science professors looked at the professions, Law, Medicine, Graduate Studies, where stiff written or oral examinations prevailed. That tended to prevent any great liberalization of undergraduate examinations. What did evolve was a greater emphasis on term work, on essays, research, seminars, so that examinations became less horrific in character and consequence. The general view of faculty was, one might as well learn to deal with examinations because sooner or later one was going to need to. That was the unspoken major premise in most of the academic minds that resisted radical proposals.

The most important change in Arts and Science was the increase in the number and quality of staff. Dean MacLean got Hicks's authority to look for first-class people. It required technique to initiate such appointments, for not all departments welcomed having big names parachuted in. Edgar Z. Friedenberg, famous both in Sociology and Education for *The Vanishing Adolescent* (1959) and other books, appointed in 1970, was not accepted by Sociology and stayed in Education. The technique was to persuade departments that the ideas came from them. Some stars were named McCulloch professors, such as S.D. Clark in Sociology, Wilfrid Cantwell Smith in Religion. Some were hired to build up a department. Peter Fletcher, hired in 1973 as chairman of Music, was told by MacLean that Dalhousie wanted a Music Department that "*made* music, not just talked about it." By 1975 that's what it had become. In one year alone Dean MacLean added seventy new faculty to Arts and Science, ten of them in one department.[4]

He could do that because he now had assistant deans who could look after many things that Basil Cooke had had to do himself. The shoulders of the assistant deans carried the day-to-day work of the faculty while MacLean did what he was good at, hunting for able people. In 1975 MacLean was appointed vice-president academic, and the new dean of arts and science was James Gray, a scholar in eighteenth-century English writers, especially Dr Samuel Johnson. Gray, talented, sprightly, and amiable, would be dean until 1980. Thus did Arts and Science grow in the 1970s.

The faculty, or more properly the Arts and Administration Building, had long had a worthy old retainer, Jim Stoker, one of those domestic sergeant-majors who gradually become part and parcel of an institution. He came to Canada from Tyneside in 1929; after working on railways in western Canada, he landed at Dalhousie with his northern English accent largely intact. He and his wife, Margaret Baillie of Lunenburg, did much to give continuity and coherence to the work and living around the A. and A. Building. Stoker retired in 1972, grown grey in forty years of honest and unremitting service.

The Registrar's Office and the Registrar

A still longer-serving official was Miss B.R.E. Smith, "Trixie" to her friends. Appointed registrar in 1952, she was almost the last working link with the Dalhousie of the 1920s. She had come in 1921, a willowy young woman of nineteen, as secretary, half-time in Law, half-time in Medicine, at $12 a week. She came to work eventually for President MacKenzie whom she much admired, and then to the Registrar's Office under Murray Macneill. Everyone liked her: benign, hard-working, knowledgeable, and under Kerr long-suffering, for he believed people worked best under pressure. Trixie did not work that way; she did things at her own pace. After hours or on Sundays she would often be found at Dalhousie. Few members of the clerical staff gave more of their time. As students crowded in during the 1960s, her salary fell behind those of other registrars and when she retired in May 1968, her pension after forty-seven years' work was $267 a month. To that was added the new 1966 Canada Pension and the old age pension. The board raised the university pension by 15 per cent *ex gratia*, subject to further improvements in the future. That was decent but the least they could do. In 1968 she was given an honorary LL.D., deserved in ways few LL.D.s are.[5]

Technically her successor was H.J. Uhlman, but he was also dean of student services, which was where he concentrated his attention. Peter Griffiths, the associate registrar, really ran the office. Trixie Smith spent considerable effort organizing her thoughts and her records to make Griffiths's takeover as easy as possible. Her system, inherited from Murray Macneill, was good enough to survive into her successors' time, although an IBM 360 was added. She even offered to help Griffiths for a while, but he brushed her off. "You just close the door," said he, "and I'll take over." The contrast between Trixie Smith's meticulous annotations on student records in

Miss B.R.E. Smith, Registrar of Dalhousie, 1952–68. She first came to Dalhousie in 1921 as secretary to two deans.

steel-nibbed pen and ink, and the impersonal computer print-out, sometimes garbled, was palpable.

The office work became garbled too. Griffiths plunged the Registrar's Office into a computer system without taking sufficient time to gear up for it. Other registrars were surprised to hear what Dalhousie had done; they were taking two to three years to make the conversion that Dalhousie's new registrar was attempting in as many months.

The senior women under Trixie Smith, Marion Crowell, Faith De-Wolfe, Frances Fraser, all of whom shared her views and carried her traditions, were devoted, hard-working, and underpaid. They knew Griffiths from registrars' meetings, for he had been associated with Acadia. When the news came that he was coming to Dalhousie and that they would actually have to work under him, they were stunned. One went home and burst into tears. Peter Griffiths proceeded to ignore them, indeed shut them out as much as he could from his mode of operation, relying for his principal assistant upon a lady favourite within the office. A busy and important office carries on for a while under its own inner momentum, but its strength and morale is not proof against such arbitrary favouritism. Within eighteen months the Registrar's Office was almost wholly unstrung.[6]

Not much of this was known outside the office; some departments never divined that there were problems. But morale was sufficiently bad that in the fall of 1970 a president's advisory committee was struck to investigate, driven by Louis Vagianos, then director of libraries. In December he presented a blistering report on the Registrar's Office and the Admissions Office. There had been no clear-cut reporting structure, and worse, there were serious personality problems. Vagianos urged a wholesale clean-out of the principal officers, Griffiths in particular. The matter was urgent.

Nothing happened, except that things got worse. Universities do not like firing senior officials whom they have been at some pains to hire; once in place it was decent to allow them time to find their feet. That was how Carleton Stanley survived the 1932 attack of Fred Pearson. By 1972 there were protests by faculty over the operation of the Registrar's Office. There were protests by junior staff in the office itself. There was talk of resignations. A further report by Vagianos in January 1973 finally brought action. Uhlman resigned on 31 January 1973 for "health" reasons. He recommended Griffiths be kept on as registrar, noting that circumstances had clouded Griffiths's "untiring efforts" to be useful. But Dalhousie had had enough. Griffiths was out. Vagianos, now director of communication services and general trouble-shooter, thought of a new registrar, preferably someone from within Dalhousie.[7]

One of the professors who had been uniformly helpful to Trixie Smith over many years was J.G. Adshead, head of Mathematics from 1953 to 1965, and for a long time chairman of Arts and Science's important Committee on Studies. A great teacher, a walking encyclopedia, a marvellous wit, he had been a bachelor all his life. When asked about that, he replied, "I didn't really start out to be a bachelor. It's just that as I became more particular, I grew less desirable!" He had known Trixie Smith since he had first come in 1927 and he had long acted as faculty spokesman for, and defender of, her and her office. Thus there had been a traditional connection between Mathematics and the registrar. Vagianos approached Arnold Tingley, chairman of Mathematics, nearing the end of his term as chairman. Tingley looked at the Registrar's Office, saw a challenge there, and accepted the position on two conditions: one, that the three senior ladies, upon whose loyalty and service so much had depended in the past and who had somehow preserved the office from utter chaos, would stay and work with him; the second that he have a free hand to fire and hire.[8]

Thus did A.J. Tingley become registrar on 1 March 1973, and registrar he would remain for the next twelve years, running the place with integrity, vigour, and common sense. Best of all, his staff stood by him.

The Classics Department and Dr Bruno Dombrowski

From the beginning Dalhousie had imported talent from the outside. Most of the time it had worked, sometimes brilliantly. But the disruption in the Registrar's Office was matched by one in Classics, and for analogous reasons.

In 1965 the Classics Department decided that to qualify for giving PH.D. work, it needed to develop studies of the ancient Near East. The head was then J.A. Doull, MA, one of the best-read men in Arts and Science, though not the most popular. He hired as visiting associate professor Bruno Dombrowski, MA Manitoba, PH.D. Basel, to teach Akkadian (Babylonian) history and culture. Three years later the department also hired T.E.W. Segelberg to develop the Coptic tradition.

In 1968 Doull recommended Dombrowski for tenure, but in May 1969 Dalhousie renewed his contract without tenure. Both Dean James and Hicks were opposed to tenure for Dombrowski. There had been examples of his intemperate remarks, bullying a visiting speaker, as he sometimes bullied younger members of Classics, and he could also be belligerent with students. He meant well, but he was abrasive and outspoken. He blamed Doull for his failure to get tenure, believing Doull had double-crossed him. Dombrowski was furious; he now saw his duty as ridding Classics, and Dalhousie, of James Doull.

But the department split on that issue. There were three associate professors, all with PH.D.s, including Dombrowski on one side; there were three junior members, all working toward PH.D.s, and Doull (who did not have one), on the other. Doull had published very little. That was not lost on Dombrowski's group; they demanded Doull's removal for several reasons but high on their list was what they called his scholarly deficiencies.

Not surprisingly, the work of the Classics Department, apart from meeting students and classes, stopped dead. Faculty Council investigated, and decided that the Dombrowski group did not have a case against Doull. One professor accepted that verdict and joined the Doull group. But Dombrowski and his colleague Segelberg refused point blank. So the split remained, though now five to two.

Dombrowski's case for tenure was heard in the fall of 1970 by the Faculty Tenure Committee, chaired by a respected historian, John Flint. The Tenure Committee recommended tenure in forty-three cases, including Dombrowski's. The president and Dean MacLean accepted forty-two, refusing to accept Dombrowski. There were appeal procedures which Dombrowski proceeded to invoke. In May 1971 an ad hoc committee of the Board of Governors heard his appeal. By then the nub of the issue was his collegiality. The Faculty Tenure Committee had felt that on the whole Dombrowski could work with his colleagues; Hicks and Dean MacLean, who had the right to review Tenure Committee recommendations, felt that Dombrowski could not. The board committee backed the president and dean. In April 1972 Dombrowski was given a final two-year appointment as research scholar, the second year being leave of absence with pay.

He still did not give up. Unwisely advised by a downtown lawyer, he sued Hicks and Dalhousie for his right to tenure. The trial took place in the Nova Scotia Supreme Court in November 1974. The evidence of a senior classicist from England, A.H. Armstrong, now in the Dalhousie Classics Department, who had an unassailable reputation, was decisive. Dombrowski, he said, was an impossible colleague. Justice Hart rejected Dombrowski's claim for tenure. He was out.

Bruno Dombrowski had vigour and talent but in the end they burned him and colleagues around him. But no one in Classics who lived through those five years was likely soon to forget the experience.[9]

Accrediting the Library School

Hicks was probably right in rejecting someone whose effect on a university department had been disastrous. Thus, if authority and decision had been lacking in dealing with the Registrar's Office, Hicks could use his power to good effect. He also showed his skill and panache in defending the new Dalhousie Library School in 1972–3. From the beginning Dalhousie wanted a Library School for the Atlantic provinces and it wanted its program, of course, accredited. It was also in a hurry. Many such schools waited five years before asking for accreditation. Dalhousie established its Library School in 1968–9; it asked for and got an American Library Association team of six that came to Dalhousie in March 1972. On 27 June 1972 the Committee on Accreditation (COA) decided against the Dalhousie master of library science program. The chief ground for this rejection were alleged deficiencies in the number of faculty, and an absence of a "native-born Canadian among its full-time professors." Apparently Canadians on the COA did not like the lack of Canadians nor calling the degree master of library science. Most other post-graduate degrees in the subject were called bachelor of library science.

There was a right to appeal this COA decision. Rejections had never been appealed before, but Dalhousie proposed to do it. The hearing was set for January 1973 before the American Library Association executive, with the accreditation team present. Dalhousie's ground for appeal was that the COA had exceeded American Library Association standards in considering Dalhousie. Dalhousie sent four senior officials: Hicks, W.A. MacKay (vice-president), Norman Horrocks (director of the school), and Louis Vagianos. The appeal was held in Washington on 30 January 1973. Hicks, in Washington on Canadian government business, came to the hearing in black coat and homburg. He made a short speech. "Before you start, gentlemen, let me say one thing. If you tell us our program is no good, it will be killed tomorrow. We're a good university; we don't want second-class stuff in it." Hicks won the battle there and then, as it turned out. After the hearing the Library Association executive overruled its COA, and voted to accredit the Dalhousie program as of 1970–1.[10]

That was a surprise. Pre-decision gossip was that Dalhousie did not stand a chance. "After some of the most tortured soul searching we have ever observed," said the editorial in the American *Library Journal*, "the University and school decided that their case was worthy of a hearing, despite the odds." It put the cat among the pigeons at the American Library Association too. The accreditation team were furious and refused any more work. An editorial in the *Library Journal* praised "the Dalhousie appeal" as showing that the Library Association was making progress towards establishing fairness in its procedures. Perhaps Dalhousie might have won the appeal anyway, but Hicks's intervention seems to have clinched it.[11]

Graduate Studies

A new dean was to be appointed for Graduate Studies in 1972. There were probably a dozen professors in Arts and Science who could handle the job, wrote one chemist, K.T. Leffek, "and, casting aside false modesty, I would include myself in that dozen." Hicks liked Leffek and A.M. Sinclair of Economics; but he was reluctant to pull Sinclair out of Economics where he was badly needed; J.F. Graham, the chairman of Economics, was on leave to the Nova Scotia government's Royal Commission on Education, Public Services and Provincial-Municipal Relations. Leffek was appointed dean in September 1972.

In the meantime the president and Senate Council ordered a review of the whole system of Graduate Studies. The review in December 1972, which drew heavily on the system at McMaster University, recommended that Dalhousie's Faculty of Graduate Studies be dissolved and replaced with a School, with eight committees appended to it. Dean Leffek, who resisted these McMaster innovations, used an argument from Petronius Arbiter, Roman official in the time of the Emperor Nero: "We tend to meet any new situation by reorganizing. And a wonderful method it can be for creating the illusion of progress while producing confusion, inefficiency and demoralization."

Leffek thought the Faculty of Graduate Studies was in excellent shape as it stood. He had a first-class group in his office. Only minor adjustments were needed: Leffek believed that standards in Dalhousie's PH.D. programs would be maintained, even enhanced, by having a senior academic chair a thesis defence in another department. For Dalhousie's size and scale, that was eminently sensible. The changes were mostly Leffek's doing, for he and the president had not found a single hour for "an unhurried exchange of ideas ... How can we hope to understand a problem, let alone agree on a solution, if we never talk about it?" In the end it was Leffek's good sense that prevailed, and by 1 June 1974 it was agreed between Hicks, MacKay, Stewart, and Leffek that the faculty would continue in its present form. Moreover, Leffek was right that he was dean material. He stayed on not just for that year but for a further sixteen years, through three deanship reviews, only retiring in 1990. Graduate Studies had not needed reorganizing so much as having common sense and administrative talent applied to it. Leffek devised an excellent staff in his graduate studies office; they repaid him with devoted service.[12]

A New Faculty of Administrative Studies

The confusion that attended the proposed reorganization of Graduate Studies also attended the creation of the Faculty of Administrative Studies. Here one suspects Hicks's subterranean prejudice against

K.T. Leffek of Chemistry, Dean of Graduate Studies, 1972–90.

Political Science that went back a decade or more. Creating such a faculty was based on the useful idea of bringing together Business Administration and Public Administration under one umbrella, with benefits to both. The idea came out of York University. It had recently created just such a faculty, with a core program and options towards either Business Administration or Public Administration. It was really an MBA program that with proper options could be made into a MPA one. Most Dalhousie political scientists would have seen it as a form of subordination. The difficulty was that the committee struck by the president did not take sufficient, if any, cognizance of well-established structures in public administration in the Political Science Department. The original committee was set up by Hicks in March 1972 to review the Department of Commerce, its work in business administration and "related studies." Hicks appointed as chairman C.J. Gardner, Arts and Science administrative assistant, with Michael Kirby and A.J. Tingley of Mathematics. They were to report in six months. It looked like a committee thrown off mercurially by Hicks, perhaps under pressure from Vagianos, Kirby, or both. He ought probably to have proceeded by a slower and more ponderous route, via Arts and Science and Graduate Studies, and included in its terms of reference Political Science's program of public administration.

The report's publication was the first that Political Science had heard of the idea and the department hit the roof. A sixty-one-page critique of the report landed on the desk of the secretary of Senate. J.H. Aitchison said: "I have not in my life, even in Dr. Kerr's day, witnessed a case in which such crass administrative stupidity was shown." A special sub-committee of Senate Council was set up to study the Gardner Report and report back. It did, in April 1973, largely echoing the views of the first committee. But the issue was so hot that the second report was tabled for a future meeting which took place three months later in July 1973. In the meantime the air was rent with cries of execration from political scientists who were frankly horrified at the cavalier gutting of a good program in their department, putting it under a wholly new faculty. As they saw it, they were being sold to Business Administration.[13]

It was a contest between academics wanting to conserve what was already established in public administration and university officers who believed that a new framework for change was necessary, that the status quo would hinder the development of new specialities. Political Science replied that with consultation and ingenuity it was possible to do both. But once Political Science's outrage was aroused, it was difficult to persuade it of any merit at all in having a Faculty of Administrative Studies. The professors teaching public administration, Paul Pross,

David M. Cameron, James McNiven, were an integral part of Political Science, also teaching classes in Canadian politics and government.

In July 1973 Hicks believed that Political Science was being negative and too inward-looking. A steering committee was now struck to arrange matters; Hicks did not want J.H. Aitchison on it, declaring he would probably want to sabotage its work. K.A. Heard, chairman of Political Science, protested against any such assumption; as chairman of the department, he felt that if it would serve the department's interest to nominate Aitchison, he would do so. Hicks backed off a bit. "Our views may differ on the usefulness of adding Professor Aitchison to the Steering Committee, but I agree with all you have to say about his integrity and service to Dalhousie University." In the end, Heard himself and Cameron went to the steering committee, and in the end, too, most people climbed down from outrage and went to work to fashion sensible programs in Administrative Studies. They came up with a federated faculty of several schools: Business Administration, Public Administration, Social Work, Library Sciences. A majority of the committee wanted to call it Professional Studies but the business side disliked that so thoroughly it was left as Administrative Studies.[14]

In April 1974 nominations came in for a dean. Hicks had Michael Kirby in mind, a good choice, and was trying to be patient. He told Lieutenant-Governor Victor Oland, a member of the board, that the five-year principle for deans' appointments had worked much better than expected. With a few trifling exceptions, Hicks said, "I have managed to have administrators appointed and re-appointed who were acceptable to me." But with the Faculty of Administrative Studies it did not go like that. The search committee knew Hicks had a favourite candidate; Hicks expected to get his way after a couple of months' delay. But he didn't. The search committee was disposed to explore alternatives. So they went to Hicks to find out if any other candidate would be acceptable. Hicks was furious, tore a strip off the committee, telling them that he supported Kirby because he was the best candidate. If the committee did not want Kirby, he was withdrawing the nomination. The committee's choice, and the new dean, was Peter Ruderman, Harvard PH.D. in economics, who was professor of health administration at the University of Toronto before coming to Halifax. Classes began in September 1975. The creation of the faculty had taken more than three nerve-wracking years. It might have been done in half the time, with more care, more tact, and less impatience. Inevitably the person who had to pick up the pieces, handle the negotiations, was Hicks's patient, hard-working, cool-headed vice-president, W.A. MacKay.

In this episode Hicks's weaknesses showed up perhaps more tellingly than in any other. He had always retained a certain animus against J.H. Aitchison, not so much for his 1960 resistance to Hicks's appointment as dean – that could be passed over – but more for his flat refusal to give Hicks any standing at all in the Political Science Department. Hicks was never allowed to teach a course in political science. Moreover, Political Science had taken a strong stand against Henry James as dean of arts and science, a choice that Hicks had pushed hard. James and his supporters were seen by Hicks as progressives, his opponents as conservatives who opposed change because it altered the status quo. It is altogether probable that Hicks did not set out in 1972 to mutilate Political Science, but he might not have been unhappy had that been the result. He sometimes liked to run hard his authority.[15]

If so, he sometimes knew when it was sensible to avoid doing so. An example of this is his conduct of Dalhousie through the trials and temptations offered by the Nova Scotia government's wish to establish on the Dalhousie campus a post-graduate Institute of Education.

Atlantic Institute of Education: Its Rise and Fall

The idea behind the Atlantic Institute of Education (AIE) was to focus and strengthen graduate studies in education in a degree-granting body in Halifax, which would cooperate with the other Atlantic universities. With the universities' help and with a relatively small staff, it could develop an ambitious program that would revitalize teacher education in all the universities. The idea was driven by Robert Stanfield in his double role as minister of education and premier, an idea he seems to have had almost since he took office in 1956. The Nova Scotia Department of Education took it up and in 1964 got it on the agenda of the Association of Atlantic Universities (AAU). The AAU suggested that advice should be sought from outside the province, and Stanfield duly invited Professor Basil Fletcher, of the Institute of Education at Leeds University, to come and report. Fletcher knew Dalhousie; he had been professor of education here from 1935 to 1939, when Stanfield was a student. Fletcher made a flying visit in 1966, and recommended that an Atlantic Institute of Education be established without delay, at Dalhousie's Faculty of Graduate Studies. Basil Cooke, then dean of arts and science, thought Fletcher was too precipitate by half, and the report too weak on facts and figures to justify such a departure. Nevertheless, Fletcher's recommendations were accepted by the Nova Scotia government. Stanfield wanted the institute on the Dalhousie campus, as Fletcher recommended, and he wanted it as soon as possible.[16]

One fundamental difficulty was that the enthusiasm of Stanfield and the Nova Scotia Department of Education was not shared by the other three provinces. New Brunswick's participation was important and Dalhousie tried to persuade UNB to join in, but its deans of arts and science, and graduate studies, were plainly reluctant. Memorial's Faculty of Education had the largest teacher training program in the whole region and was even more disinclined. And at every opportunity, Hicks deliberately played down any suggestion that there was anything in it for Dalhousie. In December 1967, asked by Berton Robinson, secretary of the University Grants Committee, if he would call a meeting of heads of Education Departments, Hicks said he couldn't; it would not be wise. He thought it was unreasonable to expect the Nova Scotian universities, to say nothing of Atlantic ones, to rush to support an Institute of Education at Dalhousie. If any movement was to be made, the government of Nova Scotia would have to do it. That the Nova Scotian universities had agreed to accept an institute at or near Dalhousie was all they could be expected to do. Now the government would have to do the rest.[17]

Hicks's caution reflected his experience as a former education minister who knew the sensitivities; but he also knew that both Acadia's and Mount St Vincent's departments of education were better than Dalhousie's. Dalhousie students may not have been aware of comparisons, but they did not much like what they saw of education at Dalhousie. The big explosion came on 11 January 1968; most of the *Gazette*'s front page was devoted to the iniquities of Dalhousie's Department of Education, using especially Professor B.M. Engel's Christmas examination in Education Mathematics 4:

QUESTION 3: Which of the following is "twelve thousand, thirty five": 1235, 12035, 120035, 1200035
QUESTION 31: Which of the following is one-half of 1 hour, 40 minutes: 20 minutes, 45 minutes, 50 minutes, 70 minutes.

The *Gazette* rubbed it in: both inside and outside Dalhousie its Department of Education was regarded as a farce, a school for morons, a waste of time. "The reputation enjoyed by our Department of Education is something less than enviable."

That *Gazette* issue hit the Education Department the next morning like a bombshell. The department's question, according to the *Gazette*, was not the accuracy of the facts, but who had written the article? It was said that Professor A.S. Mowat, head of Education, would soon be wiping the smirks off the faces of the students who had. Mowat considered the criticism "almost wholly undeserved and in part dishonest." He thought no student newspaper should be allowed to print an anonymous statement without being called to account for it, especially the *Gazette*'s remark that Dr Engel was "a fool admittedly." Mowat thought some effort should be made to discipline the writers concerned. Hicks was sympathetic but believed that any attempt to punish those responsible at the *Gazette* would give the students a fine opportunity to mount a crusade. Besides, he said, "a strong and competent Department is on solid ground in ignoring such student comment."[18]

But the ground was not solid. Three months later a questionnaire conducted on his own initiative by Peter Robson ('68 B.Ed.) asked some three hundred B.Ed. graduates from 1965–7 what they thought of their courses in education. Robson received sixty-six replies. The questionnaire had for answers five categories: very valuable; quite valuable; useful; slightly useful; of no value. The majority of replies agreed with the last two categories. Percentages of the replies in the two lowest categories were:

	Of no value %	Slightly useful %	Total %
History of Education	45	31	76
Philosophy of Education	42	22	64
Methods	45	40	85
Educational Psychology	23	28	51
Testing and Measurement	18	37	55
Practice Teaching	2	22	24[19]

A.S. Mowat had come from the University of Edinburgh in August 1939 at the age of thirty-three, to take the O.E. Smith chair in education at $3,800. He had largely created the Dalhousie Department of Education, set its standards, chosen its professors. He was a decent man with a pawky sense of humour, who had long served as secretary of the Faculty of Arts and Science. But for almost as long, the Department of Education had been the step-child in the faculty, its programs at best tolerated rather than respected. Dean James was less than tolerant. In July 1968 Mowat handed in his resignation as head, effective 31 May 1969. The front-page criticism of the *Gazette* had been too much.

The government believed that teacher education needed sprucing up. The *Chronicle-Herald* of 18 April 1968 noted that enough had been said in the papers to warrant a thorough review of teacher training programs. The government acted as soon as possible. After some difficulty in finding the right man as director, Dr Harold Nason, deputy minister of education, nominated a friend of his who was retiring as dean of the University of London's Institute of Education, Dr Joseph Lauwerys, a Belgian long time resident in Britain. Lauwerys was friendly, affable, full of ideas (not all of them relevant), but he knew nothing of the region and little of the situation he would be getting into. He was also old, though not, as rumour soon had it, too old for everything! He came and reported. His report seemed to have only a remote relevance to Nova Scotian and Atlantic provinces realities. It reminded one Dalhousie historian of "the dreary papers which the British Colonial officials in the more backward islands of the West Indies used to send to the Colonial Office in the 1930s, bemoaning the fact that nothing could be done." He suggested that all that Lauwerys's proposals did was to add another layer of cumbersomeness to a situation already replete with it. As Dean James pointed out, it was difficult to separate Lauwerys's ideas from the exhortatory language in which he expressed them.[20]

Despite these warning signs, the government, now with G.I. Smith as premier, plunged ahead. The Atlantic Institute of Education was duly chartered in 1970, with a board of directors. It got modest premises at 5244 South Street. Hicks did his best to soften the resistance of the Dalhousie Department of Education. He told Stuart Semple, acting chairman after Mowat's retirement, that now the AIE existed, "we must try to make as much use of it as we possibly and properly can."

Lauwerys for his part found that the Dalhousie Library in Education had "extraordinarily poor and limited resources." That might have been ascertained earlier; it was of a piece with the generally superficial appraisal the whole project had received. An Academic Council had to be set up to advise the AIE board and finally, in December 1973, the AIE began to grant degrees. Lauwerys retired in 1975 and Professor W.B. Hamilton, a Nova Scotian recruited from the University of Western Ontario, became the director. By this time, however, the AIE was in difficulty.

There had been several mistakes. One was to call it what it was not. *Atlantic* Institute of Education might well have been what the Nova Scotian government would have liked, but the other three provinces were massively uninterested. New Brunswick had already rationalized teacher education; what Nova Scotia chose to do with the departments of education in its many universities was Nova Scotia's problem. Moreover, the AIE's degree-granting powers were a threat, a tacit acknowledgment that the university departments of education needed strengthening. But the senior personnel of AIE were not reassuring, especially Lauwerys and his brilliant but abrasive assistant, Gary Anderson, a recent Harvard PH.D. As Peter McCreath ('68) remarked in the *Chronicle-Herald* on 3 June 1976, Lauwerys and Anderson had been an odd combination: "While Lauwerys confounded all with his congeniality, and his unending list of ideas, Anderson scared all with his caustic wit and rapier-like mind."

After 1975, however, strenuous efforts were made by W.B. Hamilton and his new assistant, Andrew Hughes, to redeem the original mission of the AIE. Hamilton was a good choice, but in the autumn of 1975 as he made the rounds of Maritime universities, he began to wonder if he made a mistake in taking on the AIE. One of his first visits was to Hicks, who as usual was candid to a fault. He told Hamilton that the only way Hamilton could get cooperation from the universities was to get them involved in AIE's administration. In due course that indeed was done; the Academic Council, AIE's second tier, developed representation from all provincial universities. Hicks also helped to bring AIE into the Association of Atlantic Universities in 1976. The Regan government was encouraging, not Regan himself so much as successive ministers of education such as Peter Nicholson, William Gillis, and George Mitchell. By 1978, just as things for AIE were looking more hopeful, the Regan government was defeated in the general election. John Buchanan's Conservative government was distinctly unsympathetic and in August 1982 abruptly pulled the plug on the whole institution.

The rise and fall of the AIE reminded one of the fate of the University of Halifax, one hundred years before: a useful idea, badly implemented, followed by a struggle to retrieve it, and finally caught up by politics and destroyed. The massive rationalization of Nova Scotian university education departments effected in the mid-1990s, although its motive was fiscal rather than educational, does suggest that Stanfield's dream of an Institute of Education might have been right after all.[21]

The Failure of a New Dalhousie-NSTC Initiative, 1969–75

Dalhousie and the Nova Scotia Technical College found each other irresistible, and despite impediments thrown in their way, agreed to a trial affiliation for five years, which began on 1 September 1969, with representatives on each other's boards and senates. To assuage the nervousness of other universities, Arthur Murphy of the University Grants Committee said in 1969 that no grandiose university such as the University of Halifax, or a University of Nova Scotia, was contemplated. There was even talk of an integrated engineering program for Halifax that might include Saint Mary's. The love affair continued; in November 1972 the Faculty of Engineering at NSTC recommended the integration of Dalhousie and NSTC. By 1974 it had been approved by both senates in principle and successive drafts of agreements were being discussed at Dalhousie and NSTC. Cabinet approval for the principle had been obtained, and by the late autumn 1974 it had got to the stage of legislation when bills 110 and 111 went to the Law Amendments Committee. But the *Chronicle-Herald* weighed in, opposing the idea root and branch. It claimed that the Dalhousie-Tech merger would establish one Nova Scotian university to which all the others would become just affiliated colleges. That was, indeed, the way the other colleges perceived the merger. The Law Amendments Committee promptly gave the bills the three-months' hoist and that ended their life for 1974–5. While Dalhousie expressed the hope that initiatives at Province House would resume in 1976, in fact the Dalhousie-NSTC merger was off. The Regan government could not face the political consequences. In 1996 a later Liberal government, bent on saving money, would face them more ruthlessly.[22]

Trying to Get a New Building for Dentistry
The Nova Scotian government was also resistant to putting up the substantial money to expand Dentistry, perhaps more so under G.I. Smith, Stanfield's successor, and the Liberal administration of Gerald Regan. Dentistry as faculty had always had a difficult time finding money. When Dean J.D. McLean came in 1954 the whole Dental School was five rooms in the south end of the Forrest Building. He was the faculty plus a dozen part-timers, all of whom had dental practices and were paid a pittance by Dalhousie. Dentistry was not in the public eye and never had the same transcendent importance as Medicine. For that reason it was much harder to persuade governments to support it. Yet it was also more expensive, per student, to run. Full-time professors of dentistry were not easy to acquire either; university salaries could not equal what a good dentist earned in private practice. J.D. McLean shouldered this tough burden. He brought to fruition the new Dentistry Building of 1958 costing $1,019,000, to which the government contributions were less than 25 per cent. Most of that expense was on Dalhousie's back.[23]

McLean was vigorous, trenchant, and outspoken. He did not suffer fools much, and he could be rough on students. He could be hard on staff too, and one of the difficulties in getting and keeping staff might perhaps have been Dean McLean. Nevertheless by 1967 Dentistry had fifteen full-time staff and thirty-one part-time. By then it was necessary to rethink the philosophy and scale that dictated the size of the 1958 building. The Tupper Medical Building influenced Dentistry, fostering ambitions and raising hopes.

Nova Scotia was under-supplied with dentists. As late as 1966 the three eastern counties of Guysborough, Richmond, and Victoria had no dentist at all. Four others – Cumberland, Pictou, Hants, and Shelburne –

had dentist-to-population ratios of worse than 1:10,000. Other Atlantic provinces were as bad or worse. Dalhousie, studying those figures, projected it would need to bring in sixty-four dentistry students a year and sixty-four dental hygienists. That was too ambitious, and it became an issue between Dean McLean and the Atlantic region dental associations. They did not want *that* many dentists! If Dean McLean was stubborn and intractable (as Hicks said), dental associations could be too.[24]

Dental building specialists from Detroit came in 1966 and plans were sufficiently advanced that Stanfield, who saw them and the projected cost, blanched. He protested in March 1967 that $11 million was a lot of money; was the Dental School trying to emulate the Tupper Building? By Stanfield's arithmetic, if the Tupper Building started out at $5 million and became $18 million, what would a dental building that started at $11 million become? He found McLean's figures "a little frightening." Do urge your people, he told Hicks, to be realistic, for "financial necessity will compel the province to be pretty tough."

Dean McLean made the point, rightly enough, that any comparison between Medicine and Dentistry was misleading: the teaching hospitals provided medical students with their teaching facilities, but Dentistry had to fund and operate its own clinic for teaching. The reason, moreover, for the very great increases in costs was that in the 1950s it cost Dalhousie $1,100 per dental student. It was now, in 1967, over $6,000.

Hicks told Stanfield that Dalhousie would make no move whatever without the government being fully informed. "I am a firm believer in as large a measure of independence for the universities as possible, but this [Dentistry and Medicine] is one area wherein I am totally convinced that a private university cannot move without complete cooperation of the Government of the area it is serving." Hicks was not at all sure he liked what McLean and the Detroit planners were doing. By July 1967, when the Medical Building was just being opened with all the fanfare, Hicks, discouraged about dental prospects, told Stanfield to explore "all possible alternatives, even to the extent of having someone else take over dental education from Dalhousie University, if you and your colleagues believed there is any more economical way to serve the needs of Nova Scotia and other Atlantic Provinces." The difficulty of getting four governments to agree on sponsoring Dalhousie's dental needs made for slow and rough going.[25]

The site of the new building was to be on the south side of University Avenue between Henry and Seymour Streets. J.D. McLean held to that site with tenacity. Hicks later said the new dental school would have been ready two to three years earlier if the dean of dentistry had been more flexible. Building it was still not on track when Dean

McLean resigned as dean in 1975 at the age of fifty-five, in truth because he did not get his way. He had built the Dental Faculty of the 1960s; he had also instituted the teaching of dental hygienists, the first class of three graduating in 1963. But in 1975 students were still entering Dentistry at twenty-five per year, an admission rate that only just kept pace with natural attrition of practising dentists. Since 1962 Dalhousie had only been able to accept 363 of 1,355 qualified applicants; there was no room to accept more. The *Chronicle-Herald* pointed this out in February 1976.[26] By that time proposals for a new dental building had already taken ten years. Dentist/population ratios did not improve. Dental authorities claimed the ideal ratio was 1 dentist per 1,000 population. In the United States the ratio was 1 to 1,300; in Nova Scotia it was 1 to 3,600, and in Newfoundland 1 to 5,000. It was bad arithmetic that none could take pride in.

In October 1976 Dr James McGuigan, president of the Nova Scotia Dental Board, made an appeal to the Dalhousie board executive, meeting jointly with Senate Council. To qualify for federal funding, the new dental building had to be ready by the end of 1980, but getting agreement among four Atlantic province governments and the federal minister of health had proved very difficult. It was made more so by the fact that provincial ministers of health, as McGuigan admitted ruefully, "seem to change portfolios as frequently as Elizabeth Taylor changes husbands." They still hadn't agreed at the end of February 1977. Last-ditch meetings between Dalhousie and the Nova Scotia and New Brunswick ministers of health were scheduled. Should Dalhousie launch a public appeal – "everything else having been tried"? It wore an air of desperation.

There were now hints that a new dental building might have to be added on the existing one. It was in fact on that basis that in April 1978 a new dental complex was put together, with contributions as follows:

Health Resources Fund (federal)	$13,319,222
Atlantic Provinces	6,180,778
Dalhousie (contribution of land and building)	2,465,000
	$21,965,000

The new dean of dentistry, Ian C. Bennett, was largely responsible for breaking the deadlock. The new building was designed in-house, as was construction management.[27]

The new structure took the form of a substantial addition to the existing three-storey 1958 Dental Building, and it would in fact contain four times as much space as the original. Blasting began in June 1978 and went on for some months. At last, in June 1982, the new Dental complex opened. Annual admissions would not be sixty-four dentists and sixty-four hygienists, but a more modest forty-eight of each.

Changes in the Faculty of Medicine
The Medical Faculty calendar for 1973–4 listed as professors on the roster of 1972–3 some 440 at various levels and a dozen preceptors, some 20 per cent more than all of Arts and Science. True, only one-third of the professors in the Medical Faculty were full-time; nor were they all in Halifax. There were about sixty teaching in Saint John General Hospital, another three in Moncton, with a clutch of preceptors scattered over the Atlantic provinces – doctors who taught interns out of a private practice. But even when those outside of Halifax were deducted, the Dalhousie Medical Faculty in Halifax was still a substantial professoriate of about 375.

This was the faculty that Dean Chester Stewart had developed since he had taken office in 1954. That was one of his major legacies to Dalhousie; another was a string of good appointments; and the third was the handsome Medical Building, the idea behind which was basically his. Much of the detailed work that had gone into it, however, was Dr Lloyd Macpherson's, the assistant dean in the 1960s. The medical staff at Dalhousie may have underestimated Stewart's contribution; the younger ones felt the pressure to introduce the five-year rotating deanship established in Arts and Science. Should there not be a new dean of medicine, one less authoritarian and more flexible? In 1971 Chester Stewart was only sixty-one years old; although he had been dean for seventeen years, there seemed to be lots of deaning in him yet. But he had never worn his authority lightly, and his faculty were beginning to chafe. There was no sign of his retiring; he and his colleague Dean J.D. McLean of Dentistry both sailed serenely on. The principle that when assuming an office one should contemplate the resignation of it did not seem to concern either dean. So the Faculty Council of Medicine acted; they went to Dean Stewart, some more outspoken than others, and said there was a substantial feeling that it was time for him to step down. He resigned as of 1 July 1971, and almost at once was promoted to vice-president of health sciences, a useful role for a retiring dean. Dr Lloyd Macpherson was made dean until a new one could be appointed.[28]

That was not so easy. Others outside Dalhousie thought Stewart would be extremely difficult to replace. Dean Douglas Waugh of Queen's believed Stewart had served "with dedication and ability that are not fully appreciated by all of its [the Faculty's] members." So also said Dean W.A. Cochrane of Calgary. A search committee was duly elected, chaired by John Aldous of Pharmacology. Several candidates

Honorary degree recipients, May 1974. L. to r., Sister Catherine Wallace, President, Mount St Vincent University, 1966–74; Roland Michener, Governor General of Canada, 1967–74; Dr. Kenneth Frederick Boyd; and President Hicks.

were suggested: internal ones were Richard Goldbloom, head of Pae-diatrics; John Szerb, head of Physiology; Ross Langley of the Depart-ment of Medicine, as well as some external ones. The internal ones bowed out, Goldbloom with particular grace: "Underneath the thin academic veneer, I am just a children's doctor whose greatest single satisfaction comes from the daily contact with children and their fam-ilies. I am simply too selfish to give up this extraordinary source of satisfaction."

One external candidate, Dr E.D. Wigle of Toronto, came to Halifax with his wife in March 1972, but he bowed out too; the financial sac-rifice in changing houses from Toronto to Halifax was too much. In the end the search came to nothing, and the Medical Faculty in July 1972 were well content to confirm Macpherson as dean of medicine, setting his term to 30 June 1976. That was the end of indefinite terms for medical deans, and that suited Macpherson. He was an excellent dean, his PH.D. an advantage, rather than other wise. He was humane, and he paid attention to students, something not all senior administra-tors had time for. His faculty even had an opportunity to debate the faculty budget; that was new. Nor did he glory in power; he saw the deanship as duty and self-sacrifice, not as personal aggrandizement. He also took the view, hovering inarticulately in the faculty for some time, that it had responsibility for doctors' education "*from the day he arrives in medical school until he ceases to practice.*" Continuing edu-cation was important everywhere: it was vital in Medicine.[29]

Dalhousie Medical School had one other characteristic that Macpherson noted for the accreditation team of April 1973. For many years it was the remaining bastion in North America of university-controlled internship. Dalhousie believed that when interns passed un-der the sole control of the hospital their education was largely ne-glected. That interns were to work not learn was a prevalent hospital philosophy. The Dalhousie degree was five years, the intern year still being included and controlled. As a result of changes in the 1960s in medical education across Canada, Dalhousie found itself in the van rather than odd man out. In 1974 the Maritime governments agreed to fund the intern year, and Dalhousie could join other medical schools in awarding the degree at the end of four years. June 1974 thus saw two medical classes graduating at once, those finishing the five-year pro-gram, and those finishing the four-year one, all of the latter going to university-controlled internships, but clutching their MD degree.[30]

In May 1974 Macpherson set in motion procedures for finding a successor. The search committee took its time; finally at the twenty-fifth meeting on 8 May 1975, the committee recommended G.H. Hatcher of Queen's. He agreed to come as of March 1976. His term

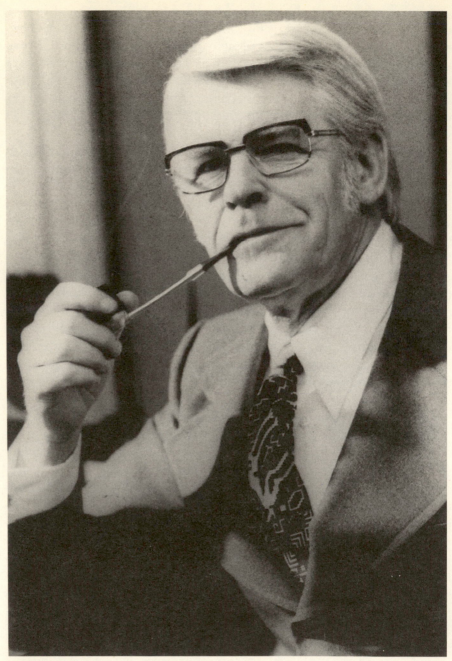

L.B. Macpherson, Dean of Medicine, 1971–6.

would be seven years; too much work had gone into his selection! The result was worth it; Hatcher was a powerful dean who took immense pains to drive forward the research of his faculty.[31]

In 1974 Robert Dickson retired. He was finding the going more difficult, getting two hip replacements, and finding his administrative work an increasing drain on his time with patients. Out of his work in 1962 for the Glassco Commission on northern health had come the impetus for Dalhousie's program of outpost nursing. Out of medicare (1969) came a Department of Medicine Research Fund using surpluses of medicare income. When he was president of the Royal College of Physicians, from 1970 to 1972, Dickson was on committees formulating the qualities of good resident training. Dickson insisted on, and got, "compassion" included in it. He explained to the Dalhousie medical graduates of 1980:

Compassion and scientific medicine ... complement one another. The first words of a doctor when he has made a diagnosis of a serious disease for which curative treatment is available – if he is a wise and compassionate man – are words of explanation and reassurance. And lo before the first medicine has been given the patient feels better. And it takes so little time to make the difference between "competent physician in a rush" and the "competent and compassionate physician" ... So take a moment and do not fear to be involved.[32]

Dickson's memorial, the Robert Clark Dickson Centre, a $12 million building for ambulatory care and for oncology, was put up by the province and named in his honour. It opened in 1983; a year later Dickson died of a stroke.

Changing the Law School

In 1963 the Law School had fewer than a hundred students. The class of 1963, for example, started in 1960 with thirty-two students in its first year and ended with twenty-two in its third. The flavour of the place was like that of the 1920s and 1930s, virtually every class a seminar. There were nine full-time professors, all but one of those a Dalhousie graduate. When the Weldon Building opened in 1966 there were ninety-four students in the first year, and they so outnumbered the third year that the old tradition of the first year taking its tone and ethos from mature students of the third was dissipated and probably lost. By 1972 there were four hundred students in all and over thirty full-time professors, the outsiders by now much out-numbering old Dalhousians.[33]

The dean of law in 1964 after Horace Read's departure to the vice-presidency, was W.A. (Andy) MacKay, son of R.A. MacKay, Dalhousie

355

political scientist from 1927 to 1946. MacKay, thirty-five years old, quiet, cool, dispassionate, thorough, was well suited to the Law School with the big changes in staff and students already in train. MacKay became vice-president himself after Read's retirement in 1969. By then the new mode of choosing a dean, by a committee of senior faculty, already in evidence in other parts of the university, was brought in. Internally, no one wanted to be dean, none at least whom the committee thought acceptable; an outside appointment split the committee. In the end a senior faculty member, R.T. Donald, was appointed caretaker dean. Donald was an expert in corporate law and two years short of retirement; he carried a big load, especially with a law curriculum with many more options than the old, virtually compulsory one.

The major innovation in Donald's time was a product of law students' initiatives, the Legal Aid Clinic. Students were concerned about the number of people who were appearing in magistrate's court without any legal advice at all, not being able to afford it. With a five-year grant from National Health and Welfare, and cooperation from the Nova Scotia Barristers' Society, the Legal Aid Clinic was opened on Gottingen Street, using third-year law students and the expertise of Mr Justice V.J. Pottier, retired Supreme Court judge and general adviser. It was Pottier who calmed the Bench, and that meant too that the Bar would not make too much objection to what was, in effect, a store-front law service, unknown at the time. For the law students it was valuable experience: "For many law students it is the first and perhaps the last opportunity they will have to be sensitized to the needs, legal and otherwise, of that very large part of the population that does not customarily enter a lawyer's office."[34]

By 1971-2 there was a substantial influx of women law students and by 1976 they were a quarter of the total. By that time the Faculty Admissions Committee were forced to decide how many Nova Scotian, Maritime, and Canadian students would be admitted. It was settled that of the 150 places available in the first year, 60 per cent would be for Nova Scotians, 15 per cent for other Atlantic provinces students, and 25 per cent from elsewhere (nearly all Canadian). That proportion was not the Law School's decision, however; it was the result of political pressure from Premier Gerald Regan. He said, in effect, "I want 60 per cent of the new students to be Nova Scotians."

It was not the last time Premier Regan threw his weight around. When Gordon Archibald's appointment to the Board of Governors was renewed for six years in 1975 it reminded Regan that he did not want to have two strong Conservatives in senior positions on the Dalhousie board, McInnes as chairman and Archibald as vice-chairman. Archibald stepped down. After Regan was defeated by Conservative

John Buchanan in September 1978, Archibald, on Hicks's initiative, was reappointed and would become chairman on McInnes's retirement in May 1980.[35]

Dean Donald died suddenly in October 1971. It so happened that an associate dean, Murray Fraser ('60), had been appointed in September; at the age of thirty-four he stepped into Donald's shoes while the search began for a new dean. Ronald St John Macdonald came in 1972. He was born in Montreal, studied at St Francis Xavier, Dalhousie, London, Harvard, and Geneva. As that provenance suggests, he became a specialist in international law and came with a wealth of experience, having taught at Osgoode Hall and Western Ontario, and was dean of law at the University of Toronto when Dalhousie persuaded him to come east again. At Dalhousie the news of his appointment created a certain xenophobic unease; who knew in what directions such an outsider might take the old Law School, especially with those credentials in international law?

They need not have worried. Macdonald insinuated himself deliberately, pleasantly, into the Law School, not masking his penchants but, like Horace Read, being willing to listen to what others might say of them. He had been editor of the *University of Toronto Law Journal* and it was not surprising that the *Dalhousie Law Journal* appeared in 1973. It was a journal by professionals for professionals, with an editorial committee of four professors, two students, and Dean Macdonald himself as editor.[36]

The Dalhousie Law Library, which in the 1950s had been appalling, had been changed out of all recognition by Dunn money and by Eunice Beeson, the Sir James Dunn law librarian. She was also one of the leading lights in the founding of the Canadian Association of Law Librarians. She died, too soon, of cancer in 1966; it took five years to find her replacement.

The Dunn scholarships had by this time been going since 1958, seven of them at $1,500 each, raised to $2,500 in 1967, and renewable for the second and third year. Lady Beaverbrook took an active personal interest in the Dunn scholars, reading the files of candidates whom the faculty recommended. She expected and received reports on post-graduate awards that her Dunn scholars won. She expected high standards all round. So much did the Law School follow them that it was not until 1968 that all seven Dunn scholarships were awarded. Suddenly in 1973 she discontinued them. She felt that the frequent non-renewals from the first to second year were a signal that the students were not quite up to the mark. Besides, she told Dean Macdonald, none of the Dunn scholars had matched the record of her husband![37]

A learnedness of lawyers, 1973. L. to r., Horace Read, Dean of Law, 1962–64; R. St J. Macdonald, Dean of Law, 1972–9; Moffat Hancock, Professor of Law, 1945–9, later at Stanford; John Willis, Professor of Law, 1933–44, 1972–5, the author of *A History of the Dalhousie Law School*.

While this was disappointing, the Law School had by that time developed a substantial outreach in publications. The new law teachers of the 1970s put old styles behind them. One old style had been teaching, not writing. Dean Read used to say that 95 per cent of what was published in the journals was a waste of time, the reader's and the writer's. That was certainly a prevalent view at Dalhousie in the 1950s. But Dean Macdonald, a prolific writer himself, soon made it known that he liked to see his faculty in print.

From Toronto Macdonald brought Douglas Johnston, active in international and in marine law. The grounding of the tanker *Arrow* on Cerberus Rock in February 1971, and the resulting oil spill, sharpened perceptions about environmental issues. Johnston acquired as assistant a young law student, Edgar Gold, who was clerk to the commission investigating the *Arrow* disaster. Gold was doing research at the University of Wales when Dean Macdonald invited him back to strengthen the Marine Environmental Law Program (MELP). This innovation was followed by the Canadian Marine Transportation Centre (CMTC) brought into existence by Vice-President Guy MacLean, and funded by CN. Within Dalhousie it was free-standing, only indirectly connected to the Law School, reporting to Guy MacLean. The CMTC was soon headed by Graham (later Sir Graham) Day. MacLean thought such institutes and centres extremely useful; they attracted research money and would do things that were not a priority of mainline departments. The Centre for Foreign Policy Studies, for example, an off-shoot of Political Science, received substantial outside funding ($750,000) from the Donner Foundation for research and new staff. Granting organizations rather like the narrow, practical focus of such centres. At Dalhousie, too, they tended to feed one another. Thus by 1977 MELP and CMTC, together with the Institute for Environmental Studies (originally founded by Ronald Hayes) put together a major research initiative that in 1979 won a $1 million research grant from the Social Science and Humanities Research Council for a five-year study of the law of the sea, marine pollution, and Georges Bank.

With Dean Macdonald's MELP initiatives came others. He made Dalhousie's international law section into one of the most important in Canada. He initiated exchanges with the civil law schools at Laval, Sherbrooke, and other Quebec universities. He began exchanges with the University of Maine. Ronald Macdonald looked outward, beyond Mauger's Beach lighthouse to the wide horizons of sea and the lands that lay beyond.[38]

The Law School's relations with the administration were relaxed and easy in these years. Dean Macdonald was an admirer of Hicks; that was not the only reason he came to Dalhousie, but it was certainly one of them. As to budgets, in those palmy days they were simple. With the current budget in hand, Dean Macdonald once a year went up to see Guy MacLean, and in forty-five minutes over coffee they had the new one mapped out. This informality over budgets could not last after the Dalhousie Faculty Association (DFA) became the professors' bargaining agent in 1978, but the attitudes behind it did. H.W. Mac-Lauchlan who came in 1983 (out of Prince Edward Island, UNB and Yale), remarked on the ethos he found:

The distinguishing features of Dalhousie Law School are still the nature of the student body, the sense of common purpose, and, I might add, decency ... But there is a civility about the place that is not to be gainsaid ... Halifax is a decent place in which to live. In fact, more and more people tell me that it is one of the most interesting and most livable places in the country.[39]

Dalplex, the Physical Education Complex, Part 1
What made Halifax a good place to live in was sea, lakes, trees, and neighbourhoods. Dalhousie had not contributed much to the last. It had pushed its way outward for a decade, swallowing up houses, making old properties into new edifices, converting others from family homes into departmental offices that operated only forty hours a week. This continued assault on south-end ways of living from 1963 to 1973 had sensitized residents. And City Hall with them. Hicks had never been particularly tender about public opinion; what Dalhousie needed, Dalhousie wanted and took. Was Dalhousie's importance as a public institution to be stunted by mere private concerns? To one lady on Larch Street Hicks wrote in March 1974:

... it is easy to blame Dalhousie, as a large landowner in the centre of the city, for a situation which is developing all over the Halifax peninsula. As the city grows, it is more and more difficult to maintain, on this peninsula, the kind of single-family dwelling and the life style accompanying it.

There may have been truth in that, but Hicks would not make many friends by emphasizing it. But then, he was never a good hypocrite.[40]

City council was also concerned with the continued conversion of taxable private property into non-taxable (or only partly taxable) university property. Under the Nova Scotia Assessment Act the property of every college and school was exempt from tax, with the exception of property used for commercial, rental, or non-educational purposes. Dalhousie official residences on campus were not taxable; the president's house was, as also were parking lots, land held for development, unsupervised student houses, and the Student Union building

There is no title to this cartoon in the Halifax *Herald*, but Chambers knew his public and knew no comment was necessary.

itself. In January 1973 the city council proposed to classify Dalhousie parking lots as commercial property and subject them to business occupancy tax. Hicks protested to the minister of municipal affairs. Halifax wanted to go further and tax all university property, but the Nova Scotia government refused to countenance that until the federal government accepted the principle that municipal taxes were a legitimate part of university expenses, and until the Nova Scotia government had received and digested the findings of the Graham Royal Commission on Municipal Government.

In 1973 Dalhousie held property with a total assessed value of $75 million. Only about 11 per cent of that was taxable: Fenwick Towers; Ardmore Hall, a women's residence at North and Oxford Streets; Peter Green Hall, the married student housing on Wellington Street; and numerous parking lots and houses. Still, Dalhousie's tax bill was already $250,000 a year. Nevertheless, from the council's point of view, to have 89 per cent of Dalhousie property wholly exempt was a fairly substantial deprivation of potential revenue. Thus the city council taxed every scrap of Dalhousie property it could construe as not used directly for educational purposes.

Naturally Hicks fought against that and naturally he had few friends at City Hall. Thus, when the massive quarrel arose in the 1970s between Dalhousie and its neighbours over what was called the Physical Education Complex, the outrage of the south-end residents found solace and support on city council, and a witches' brew of indignation began.

Dalhousie had long needed space for athletics. Since 1932, when the gymnasium was rebuilt, the only substantial addition to Dalhousie's athletic facilities was the rink in 1950. In those forty years since 1932 Dalhousie's student numbers had gone from 900 to 7,500. Behind Dalhousie's renewed interest in athletics was a president who believed in it, but also a solid push from the Nova Scotia Department of Education looking for teachers of physical education. Senate established the Bachelor of Physical Education in 1966, and from that developed the School of Physical Education under the fine work of a zesty Australian, Allen J. Coles, within the Faculty of Health Professions. By 1969–70 it had eighty students and by the following year had developed graduate work. This was some distance from the philosophy that Senate formulated in 1962, that Dalhousie athletics was "recreation not triumphs." There were also some advantages in the long delay in getting these programs going; it allowed Dalhousie to profit from others' experience.

Coles was not pleased, however, when Acadia announced in 1969 that it would start a four-year program from Grade 11, saying it had more facilities than Dalhousie. That was true; Studley field was a

Three successful female athletes in 1972 with their trophies. L. to r., Gail McFall (swimming), Carol Sparks (basketball), and Nancy Dunbrack (hockey). (Thanks to Judith Rice for identification.)

football pitch, and the gym was small and crowded. But Dalhousie had begun to acquire properties south of South Street, and by the end of the 1960s had a substantial seven acres of land, all of it zoned R2 for institutional and recreational use. With that as a base, Dalhousie began to make plans for a big new athletic centre, and on 6 August 1973 developed its ideas at a public meeting. Hicks and other Dalhousie officials were wholly taken aback by the violence of the reaction against the proposal. They withdrew their ideas, regrouped, and in the fall went on to apply for a building permit.[41]

The south end citizens regrouped too, forming the Committee of Concerned Dalhousie Area Residents (CDAR), and successfully petitioned residents of the sixteen city blocks around Dalhousie to have the lands Dalhousie proposed to use rezoned from R2 to R1, residential. That would neatly end Dalhousie's plans. But, as Eleanor Wangersky pointed out in the *Mail Star*, if the move to block Dalhousie should succeed, Dalhousie would sell the land to a developer. Then it might well be rezoned again in a juicy land assembly deal. How about, she suggested, a nice high-rise? Surely Dalhousie's athletic complex, that children could use, was much better. City council called a public meeting at St Francis School on 17 October. Five hundred residents attended and another hundred wanted to get in, with both Dalhousie and CDAR conducting a publicity war in advance of it. Hicks, who was not there, was heaped with abuse. An old lady complained of "bearded, barefoot men" in the houses Dalhousie already owned. On the other side Laura Bennet, wife of Jim Bennet, asked what would CDAR do if Dalhousie were to donate the land for low-cost housing? This was greeted with a roar of disapproval from local residents. But at that public meeting Dalhousie lost.[42]

City council had the athletic complex on their agenda on 25 October and again on 15 November. At that meeting it voted seven to three to rezone the Dalhousie land from R2 to R1. Hicks laid blame on the *Dalhousie Gazette* for an ambiguous headline from which the local newspapers extracted the wrong meaning. But privately Hicks also blamed himself. One night late that autumn Jim Sykes, the university architect, was surprised to get a 1:30 AM phone call from the president. Would he come over and talk? Now? They had always got along well. Sykes knew how to get around Hicks: never let him be in a position to give a positive refusal. Withdraw the issue before that happened. Sykes arrived to find Hicks rather distraught. "Should I resign as president?" Hicks asked bluntly, "I'm not the best Dalhousie representative." Sykes replied, "Just back off the sports complex. It's much better than changing presidents." The process of backing off became in effect a slowing down, enjoined by legal processes.

Dalhousie's lawyers got to work on how to reverse the city council decision. The precedents were not promising. Donald McInnes related how one of his lawyers brought in a whole pile of precedents – all the wrong way. McInnes flared up. Usually so careful about books, he swept the whole lot on the floor. "Go find some other law!" They did. McInnes was not upset with the petitions against Dalhousie. "You can get people to sign a petition for their own hanging!" was his dismissal of that issue. So an appeal was mounted to the Provincial Planning Appeal Board against such spot rezoning, asking for a writ of mandamus to compel council to issue a building permit. There were suggestions from Mayor Walter Fitzgerald that perhaps the city council might help Dalhousie find somewhere else, but alternative solutions were much more expensive and much less satisfactory.[43]

The Dalhousie appeal proceeded amid tremendous ill-will. According to Grant Jarvis, spokesman for the CDAR, 85 per cent of the residents in the sixteen city blocks near Dalhousie had signed the petition in favour of rezoning. But the students made amends for any earlier ambiguity. On 24 March 1974 the Student Council voted fifteen to one (with four abstentions) in favour of the athletic complex. On 23 April Mr Justice Gordon Cowan of the Supreme Court of Nova Scotia granted Dalhousie the mandamus it sought, ruling against Halifax city council. Council then appealed to the full Supreme Court, where it was argued on 24–25 June 1974. On 31 July the Supreme Court of Nova Scotia again decided in Dalhousie's favour. The city now appealed to the Supreme Court of Canada, where it was argued on 26–27 February 1976. There the city's appeal was finally dismissed without the court even calling on Dalhousie's lawyer. And with costs.

Thus did Dalhousie get the right to build its athletic complex. As the *Mail-Star* remarked, there was no use for the city council to gripe about having to issue the building permit; "Dalhousie did what it was entitled to do under the law." Still, it was a victory that came at a stiff price in public relations. George Mitchell, minister of development in the Regan government, told Hicks that any Dalhousie application for substantial funding for its athletic complex "could well run upon the shoals." Funding would be a problem, for in the three-year interval costs had risen from $5 million to $8 million. Dalhousie rethought, redesigned; that "horrible little man," Henry Hicks, was still there, but he had the good sense to retreat from the limelight. He now relied heavily on a much more deft and judicious public relations man, his vice-president, W.A. MacKay. Dalhousie had lost ground but it was not irretrievable.[44]

Professor Ernest Wilmot Guptill

When Dalhousie was enjoying its difficult and not wholly satisfactory triumph, one of its sterling professors, Ernest Guptill of Physics, died tragically. It was on the first day of spring in 1976. Guptill, who sailed a boat himself, who had been brought up in and around boats on Grand Manan, decided that day with a friend, John Vickery, to look for winter wrack missing from the Royal Nova Scotia Yacht Squadron along the North-West Arm toward Purcell's Cove. What happened no one knows, but a stormy wind and sea capsized their small rowboat a hundred feet off Point Pleasant. Vickery could not swim, but Guptill could. In that icy March water, he got Vickery lying across the upturned boat; then, exhausted, he too clung to the boat. There was no one about that dark Sunday afternoon. After forty minutes a tug came and managed to drive the boat into shallow water with the wash from its propellers. By that time both men were dead of hypothermia. Guptill was fifty-six years old.

He was born in Grand Manan, a big island in the Bay of Fundy, girt with sea and cliffs, twenty kilometres off the New Brunswick coast. There had been Guptills there since Loyalist days, and a hardy lot they were. In the mid-1930s his family moved to Wolfville so that he and his brother could go to Acadia. After they had finished and gone their separate ways, the family returned to Grand Manan. During the war Guptill did radar research at McGill leading to his invention of the slotted array microwave antenna that helped with the air defence of Britain and has since been used in ocean-going vessels. After work in nuclear physics with the National Research Council at Chalk River he returned to McGill for his PH.D., where he helped in developing Canada's first cyclotron, a complex machine for the electro-magnetic acceleration of charged atoms. In 1947 Johnstone brought him to Dalhousie. Within ten years he was full professor and after a year's research at a famous physics laboratory in Leiden, came back in 1958 to head the Physics Department. In 1968 Guptill got out of administration to return to research and teaching.

For he was that treasure, an excellent researcher and a gifted teacher. Like many senior professors at Dalhousie, he took on the teaching of first-year classes. He prepared his lectures with care, and before each tried to be relaxed and in good spirits. He would approach the class smiling, as if to say, the way old Charles Macdonald used to, "Let us enjoy ourselves." With two hundred students at 8:30 in the morning that was an achievement. Guptill believed that lectures were *ipso facto* dull; therefore schemes had to be devised to stir students up, competitions within class, votes for the right answer. He was an inveterate story-teller; once when students had difficulty understanding torque he explained it by recalling swinging on the kitchen door back in Grand Manan. It was a good place to come from for other stories as well. But the focus of his lectures was on the underlying simplicity, beauty, of physics.

There were not many professors either who, in the two or three weeks before the Christmas and the final examinations, would hold extra classes at 8 AM on a Sunday morning. Or, having made such an offer, would find a crowd of students there. He would go home for his lunch when the last student left. Curly-haired, turned-up nose, laughing eyes, Guptill introduced his lectures by "Good morning," and at the end would say, "Thank you, ladies and gentlemen." One might thank him with a 1980 poem by Margot Griffiths in the *Dalhousie Gazette*:

> when I was a little girl
> I used to wonder where the water on the beach went
> when the tide went out ...
> Have Faith They Said,
> and sure enough when I crept back that night
> with the moon and the crickets
> there it was
> lying like liquid silver in the shadows.
>
> Since then I've learned about tides,
> And looking at your face as you turn away from me,
> I feel the pull of the water
> As it rushes to some distant shoreline,
> And I know that if I creep back
> When the moon and the crickets are out,
> There you'll be,
> With a smile on your face and beach sand in your pockets.[45]

Guptill is buried on Grand Manan.

· 12 ·

Shifting Power: The End of the Hicks Regime 1976–1980

Triumphs and frictions at the Cohn. Finishing Dalplex, 1976–9. The Dalhousie Staff Association. The Dalhousie Faculty Association and the Faculty Club. The advent of collective bargaining, 1978–9. The adventures of CUPE local no. 1392. Senate strives for a more purposeful mission. The status of women and improvements in campus life. Finding a new president, 1979. The wages of the Hicks era. A retrospective.

Henry Hicks was outspoken on many subjects; he enjoyed jazz, about which he considered himself, as in so much else, something of an expert. His opinions were largely unchecked by either diffidence or hypocrisy. It was the same with art. In November 1967, opening the Second Atlantic Exhibition of Art in the Arts and Science Building, he disagreed openly with the decision of the judges in awarding the first prize. Hicks preferred Christopher Pratt's Newfoundland realism, "Woman with a Slip" to Lawren Harris's abstract "Pentagon," to which the judges had given the prize. This incident afforded the local papers a rich feast for comment and cartoons, most of which supported Hicks.[1]

By the late 1970s Dalhousie's main achievement in community relations had been the Arts Centre. It now had a masterful impresario and functioned under the president's Committee on Cultural Activities. This committee had become largely administrative and in 1968 had been taken from under the fostering wing of Senate. Senate surrendered it not only because of the committee's functions, but because it had confidence in the chairmen and in the cultural aspirations of Henry Hicks, unlike those of President Kerr, in whose regime the Senate's committee was first struck.

The Committee on Cultural Activities had a series of able chairmen in these years – C.B. Weld of Physiology, M.M. Ross of English, and in

"Woman with a slip" by Christopher Pratt, Henry Hicks's preference at the Second Atlantic Exhibition of Arts, 1967. The ladies looking at the Pratt are, l. to r., Pat Nicholls, wife of G.V.V. Nicholls; Gene Hicks, wife of Henry Hicks; and Kathy Weld, wife of C.B. Weld.

the 1970s G.V.V. Nicholls of Law. It branched out with sub-committees in theatre, music, film, the art gallery; its membership now came to include artistic representatives from around Halifax, including Saint Mary's and Mount St Vincent. The Dalhousie Arts Centre had created cultural ferment, some of it excellent, some of it raucous, some of it the result of the taste of the Cultural Activities Committee, and increasingly more of it the result of the range and vigour of the executive secretary of the committee, who ran the Cohn operation.

The first of these was John Cripton, who pioneered the style of the Arts Centre and helped to bring the Atlantic Symphony there. In 1973 the Canada Council decided it wanted Cripton as its Impresario Canada, so Dalhousie had to find a replacement. There were seventy-seven candidates, mostly American. Those in the short list were invited to Dalhousie and Hicks looked at all of them. He liked a woman candidate, Joyce Dawe, but Nicholls and the committee were most impressed with Eric Perth, who was reputed to have "flair for seeking out the new and unusual" as well as capacity as a first-class administrator. Hicks liked him, though reserving the suspicion that "he might develop into somewhat of an autocratic person in his relations with ... the Departments of Music, Theatre."[2]

Dalhousie took Perth on and a marvellous impresario he was. Born in 1934 in Denmark, he spoke Danish, Swedish, German, English, some French, and before coming to Dalhousie had been house manager of the National Arts Centre in Ottawa. He had connections innumerable. He knew Luciano Pavarotti's agent in New York and on a trip from Europe back to New York Pavarotti was persuaded off the plane in Halifax to give a concert in the Cohn to, it seemed, the whole Italian community. One important item in Pavarotti's fee of $8,500 was twenty pounds of Nova Scotia smoked salmon which he carted off to New York. By 1976 the Cohn under Perth had gone from fourteen concerts a season to sixty-five, with something close to 7 per cent of the whole population of Halifax going through the Arts Centre doors at some time during the year.

But there were frictions between Perth and the Music and Theatre departments, arising mainly from differences in philosophy over what the Dalhousie Arts Centre ought (or ought not) to be doing. Peter Fletcher, chairman of music, resigned in December 1976, on that very issue. His last act at Dalhousie was conducting a splendid *Messiah*. Fletcher's argument was that an Arts Centre ought to aim at presenting new artistic experiences, developing taste in the arts. Like one's first beer or first escargots, he said, artistic taste was not acquired spontaneously. It needed educating. He would have understood the *Gazette*'s headline of November 1967 about the Cohn, "White Elephant for

Eric Perth, the impresario at the Cohn Auditorium, 1974–85, with assistants
M. Riding and Laura Bennet.

Dal," which suggested that students needed artistic education like everyone else. Art was the communication of emotion; to Fletcher, entertainment was just that and little more. Foot-stomping programs had their place, no doubt, but in Fletcher's opinion not in the Arts Centre.[3]

Perth won that round, partly because it was a position that Hicks and the Cultural Activities Committee took. But it was made to appear sensible by the argument that popular performances would subsidize with full houses the cultural ones with occasionally thin houses. Fletcher's replacement as chairman of the Music Department was Walter Kemp, a musical historian whose temperament and taste gave him rather more ductility, much needed in dealing with Eric Perth's sweeping vigour and electric opinions.

Dalhousie's Music Department received considerable support from musicians in the Symphony Orchestra. The one was essential to the other. Hicks was flexible here, as in so much else, even persuading the Board of Governors to lend $80,000 to a promising young violinist, Philippe Djokić, a new member of the Music Department in 1975, to buy an equally promising violin. The money was repaid in full and many times over in the contribution the violinist would make to Dalhousie music in the future. Out of this came in 1975 the formation of the Dalart Trio: William Valleau, cello, William Tritt, piano, and Phillippe Djokić, violin. It gave Dalhousie and Halifax its first glorious taste of a resident classical trio. They were frankly marvellous and they carried the Dalhousie name to many places where it had never been known before.[4]

The Dalhousie Theatre Department, separated off from English, had its base in the Sir James Dunn Theatre. One of its very successful offshoots was its three-year diploma program in costume studies, approved in February 1977. The Theatre Department plays did what Peter Fletcher wanted Music to do, educate the students and public to long-neglected live theatre. The Neptune Theatre downtown, established in 1963, and the Sir James Dunn, reinforced each other, particularly during John Neville's regime as director of the Neptune from 1978 to 1983.

Dalplex, Part 2
Besides Dalplex, Hicks wanted to build a Physical Sciences Centre, between the Sir James Dunn Building and Howe Hall, facing Coburg Road. But Gerald Regan, something of an athlete himself, was not so interested in the physical sciences, and liked athletics much better. Hicks could and would use that preference for Dalhousie's purposes; thus when the smoke cleared over Dalhousie's right to a building permit, Hicks had Regan onside. It was just as well; by 1977 the cost of

The Dalart Trio in 1976. L. to r., William Valleau, cello; Philippe Djokić, violin; William Tritt, piano.

the Dalhousie Athletic Centre had risen from $5 million to $10.5 million. Dalhousie launched the Dalplex campaign in October 1977 to raise $3.5 million towards it. By September 1978 $2.3 million had come in, of which the Dalhousie Student Union gave $350,000 by extending for a further ten years their annual mortgage contribution towards the Student Union Building.[5]

Construction began in October 1976, with blasting that started at 8 AM each weekday until Christmas, at the rate of ten to twelve substantial thumps each day. It was heavy work, for in that part of Halifax the hard iron stone lay on edge, roughly 20 degrees off the vertical.

The design was now a building with a low profile, literally and metaphorically. The maximum height was to be thirty-five feet, but covering as large an area as possible without pillars. J.G. Sykes, the university architect, visited Ontario where Trent and some other universities had what were called "air structures" – that is, roofs sustained by lightly compressed air. The pressure differential was usually the equivalent of that between the top of a ten-storey building and the ground. All of the air structures had problems, however, until Sykes discovered that Atlas Steels of Toronto were making a thin, stainless steel skin which could be held up by air. Atlas were willing to give such a roof to Dalhousie at less than cost. Sykes and Hicks reported to the board that no such roof had collapsed. (The reason it hadn't was because none had yet been built!) Thus the Dalplex roof was more of an innovation than the board knew, than Hicks dared tell them, though one member of the Building Committee suspected something of a gamble. The roof was successfully inflated in March 1979, and the building ready for opening, more or less, on 19 October.[6]

The original idea was to ask the new Conservative premier, John Buchanan, to open it; but perhaps remembering the tremendous obloquy Dalhousie had incurred over the building, he backed off and Hicks was asked, on the understanding that should a major donor come along who wanted his name attached to it, the building would be so named. No major donor did materialize and the building, not inappropriately, was named by popular usage after the campaign that solicited a wealth of small contributions. So it became Dalplex. At the official opening there was a huge open house with some twelve thousand visitors inspecting the Olympic-size swimming pool, the squash and racquet courts, to say nothing of the thirty-five feet of interior height.

Three months later, in January 1980, after a big fall of wet snow followed by rain, the roof collapsed – that is, it caved inward, coming down to within twelve to fourteen feet of the floor. The person in

Dalplex in 1979. Erected despite bitter local opposition, it was soon a major community asset. The huge stainless steel roof was only one-sixteenth of an inch thick. Held up by lightly compressed air, it could be walked on.

charge of maintaining air pressure, located in the bottom of the building, did not know of the rain. But when the pressure was increased to compensate for the huge weight of the rain-soaked snow, the roof came right back to normal. For the board, to say nothing of Sykes and Hicks, that gave the "greatest satisfaction"; it was now known that the roof could be collapsed and reinflated with no damage.

But still greater satisfaction with Dalplex was to come. Within a few years of its completion, when a house in the neighbourhood was being offered for sale, to its many advertised charms there was a further one: "Close to Dalplex." And there was supreme irony in the story Hicks related about someone driving by South Street in the 1980s, who looked over to where the Dalplex was and not seeing it, said: "Isn't it lucky that Dalhousie never got authority to build that big Athletic complex there!"[7] In fact, by the mid-1980s Dalplex had become a major community asset, the way the Arts Centre already was.

Problems in Labour Relations: The Dalhousie Staff Association

Dalhousie's eight-fold expansion in physical plant and assets from 1963 to 1980, at the cost of some $120 million, came with some stress. Inflation made it worse. In the early 1970s inflation in Canada was 7 per cent per annum until 1975, roughly the same as in the United States and West Germany. But the price of oil quadrupled between 1972 and 1974, and this fuelled a much steeper inflation from 1975 to 1980 and beyond. In 1981 inflation reached 12.5 per cent per annum. Across the ten years from 1970 to 1980 the Canadian Consumer Price Index rose 137 per cent. Salaries and wages were thus continually trying to overtake prices.

Dalhousie's relations with its working clerical staff had not so far been difficult. As employer, at least under A.E. Kerr, the university was both benign and close-fisted. Salaries were low, but hours were not unsatisfactory. Staff were patient and long-suffering, their attitudes an outgrowth of the depression of the 1930s, when one was fundamentally grateful to have a job at all. At least one of the officials in the Registrar's Office could not have resigned in protest against Peter Griffiths because she could not have afforded to.

Into this came the Canadian Union of Public Employees (CUPE). CUPE was formed in 1963 from two other unions and was soon the largest in Canada. By 1980 as many as 50 per cent of its members were women. CUPE was particularly interested in unionizing the clerical staff at Dalhousie, and was not without ambitions for the professors. In November 1971 CUPE moved to unionize Dalhousie's non-academic employees, but in a heavy-handed way, assuming it had only to offer to be accepted. The Dalhousie clerical workers were not sure they wanted CUPE; in 1972 they organized their own Dalhousie Staff Association (DSA) with some 212 paid-up members from a total of some 750 clerical staff. The DSA looked to classification of staff positions, hours of work, fringe benefits, aiming at parity with Nova Scotia civil servants. In the midst of that their work week was extended from a 32.5-hour week to a 35-hour one with commensurate salary increases.

There were at least two modes by which the DSA could function as a bargaining unit. One was to become a CUPE local (no. 1275 had already been constituted) and go before the Nova Scotia Labour Relations Board (NSLRB) and apply for certification as official and exclusive bargaining agent. Another less formal mode, voluntary recognition, could be agreed between employer and employees. The two routes were mutually exclusive. Once it had been determined who was in the bargaining unit, an official vote would be held to decide which union. A majority would win. Probably the majority of the DSA were leaning towards voluntary recognition. It had not helped CUPE's cause that it used some sleight-of-hand about green sign-up cards, disguising them as offers of more information. As Hicks put it to M. McIntyre, assistant regional director for CUPE, Dalhousie would deal in good faith through whatever union the employees chose. "We are only concerned that the employees are given a fair opportunity to make this choice." By May 1974 the CUPE local had enough support to apply to the NSLRB for certification as bargaining agent for Dalhousie non-academic employees. In the meantime Dalhousie recognized the DSA as exclusive bargaining agent for Dalhousie employees under voluntary recognition. Thus was the struggle joined between CUPE and DSA. The NSLRB refused local 1275's application for certification and insisted on a vote of the employees. It was held on 5 September 1974 and confirmed the DSA as the exclusive bargaining agent for non-academic clerical staff. CUPE was out.

There was more to the DSA than salaries and fringe benefits. Most of its members were women; one attractive young woman (who later became a senior Dalhousie official) declared that between 1968 and 1975 some parts of Dalhousie began to resemble Peyton Place. The threat of sexual harassment was to her real and always uncomfortable and doubtless was for others. One or two university officers were notorious. The creation of the DSA helped by making it possible to resist unseemly blandishments and still keep one's job, or better still, transfer to another department. The DSA did not end sexual harassment but it offered a procedural refuge to those so victimized. By the end of the 1970s most of the worst offenders were out of the university. On the whole the long history of Dalhousie's relations with its

Signing the contract between the Dalhousie Staff Association and the Board of Governors, 2 May 1975. L. to r., Mrs H.A. MacDonald, Board; Mrs Enid Jimenez, President DSA; President Hicks; Suzanne Jodrey, secretary DSA.

clerical staff was fairly creditable.[8] Its business relations with its professors had become by the 1970s more complicated and difficult.

The Dalhousie Faculty Association

The Dalhousie Faculty Association (DFA) began in the 1950s as an informal association; it had motions and minutes but it was mainly an instinctive reaction against low salaries and President Kerr. In the 1960s it gradually got bigger and stronger. One of the early concessions of the Board of Governors was staff mortgages which were established in November 1962. They were taken up with enthusiasm, especially by junior staff with families, for the Dalhousie mortgage rate in those years was 6.25 per cent, less than the commercial. Originally a staff member had to have tenure to qualify, but in November 1970 the rules were broadened. In December 1979 they were broadened again; loans could be made for purchases of duplexes and condominiums, provided the mortgagor lived there. Second mortgages were also allowed. One governor, perhaps attached to a mortgage firm downtown, asked in 1979 why Dalhousie should be in the mortgage business. The answer was that after seventeen years' experience, "mortgages to staff gave the highest yield of any part of the University's investment portfolio."[9]

The DFA used a large room at the top of the A. and A. Building for its meetings, that commanded a view over the North-West Arm, right to the sea's horizon. There in the 1950s and early 1960s there used to be talk and gossip and meetings, where Jim Aitchison and George Grant played billiards and talked about Pierre Bayle or Simone Weil. It had eventually to be given over to Political Science offices, while the philosophers, mathematicians, and historians were moved out to centrifugal distances from talk of Bayle and Weil. The need for a central meeting place became more palpable as new staff, new offices, many in old houses, grew. In 1965 the DFA asked the board for help in the purchase of a house for a faculty club. The board was sympathetic but asked for concrete proposals. The DFA considered its options, but for several years nothing tangible emerged. Then in 1971 a member of the DFA Faculty Club Committee, Mirko Usmiani of Classics, went to see the president. Hicks did not want to *give* property to the DFA, but when Usmiani said that the association was thinking of renting or leasing, Hicks opened up. Usmiani returned to his committee and said, "Hicks will let us have the old Law Building." "But what rooms, what floors?" the committee wanted to know. Usmiani laughed. "All the rooms, all the floors, basement, main floor, attic, everything." The place was in fact almost empty, and the computer people in the basement were moving to other quarters. The university was providing heat and light and water and no one was using it. The board agreed to put up $20,000 (later raised) if DFA would match it, to do renovations.[10]

These renovations were a story of their own. Hicks was particularly attracted to a European interior designer, a lady, and liked what she was suggesting. The DFA committee went along with Hicks's interest. What emerged was a night-club ambience, bean-bag chairs, the building's Georgian ceilings lowered by means of large coloured tubes, a study in reds, oranges, and purples. It eventually was got rid of in favour of more conventional decoration. Thus did the Faculty Club get established in the handsomest building on the campus. The best discovery, uncovered by the Law School, was what came to be called the Great Hall, with a fine hammer-beam roof; in 1974 it was renovated to expand the Faculty Club's catering facilities.

During these years the DFA slowly gathered weight and substance. Many senior and middle-rank academics served as its president, from Law, Medicine, as well as from Arts and Science. The association was concerned with salaries, pensions, bread-and-butter issues, and its officers, while vigilant, were mostly courteous and not without appreciation for what had been accomplished already. Hicks told Dr Tarun Ghose of Pathology, president from 1975–6, that "Dalhousie has been fortunate in my time in generally having very good relations with its Faculty Association."[11] That was too rosy a view.

For there were frictions. K.T. Leffek (president, 1969–70), complained of lack of board attention to DFA's salary briefs, and his successor, R.L. Comeau of Economics, said the same. Leffek was unable to prevent the DFA from passing a motion in 1970 that since staff were already making their contributions to Dalhousie in the form of low salaries, requests from the Dalhorizons campaign would not be supported. Something of the frustrations behind the motion (which Leffek personally opposed) is reflected in a letter by R.L. Comeau to Dr R.C. Dickson, who strongly opposed the Dalhorizons motion: "We are caught between an administration that prefers to ignore us with polite gestures, and a rising student movement that threatens to run roughshod over us." The board gave a little. In December 1974, at DFA's request, it agreed to allow the association president to sit in on board meetings as observer. By 1977 its officers would discuss the forthcoming budget with the board's budget committee.[12]

By now unionization of university faculties across Canada was proceeding apace. In February 1973 Notre Dame University in Nelson, British Columbia, became the first faculty in English Canada to unionize. The University of Manitoba followed in November 1974. The Canadian Association of University Teachers (CAUT) recognized that it would have to support faculty unionization or lose out to CUPE, a more aggressive union. A major battle between the two was joined at Saint Mary's in 1974. CUPE wanted to represent the faculty; but the Saint Mary's Faculty Union preferred to work through its own affiliation with CAUT. Both organizations put major efforts into what was regarded as a decisive beachhead. A vote ordered by the Nova Scotia Labour Relations Board gave the nod to CAUT's affiliate, the Saint Mary's Faculty Union. After another failure in 1975, CUPE backed away. Between 1975 and 1980 some nineteen major Canadian universities followed Saint Mary's, Acadia, and Moncton in 1976, UNB in 1979, and NSTC in 1980.[13]

By 1977, with inflation running high, Dalhousie academic salaries were almost the lowest in Canada, lower than those of other local universities. Dr Philip Welch, DFA president in 1977–8, believed that an extra $200,000 which had somehow materialized from the government, should be used not to reduce the deficit as the board wanted, but to raise academic salaries. But the board was facing a deficit of $300,000 and was caught by rules for controlling current account deficits laid down by the new Maritime Provinces Higher Education Commission (MPHEC). It had been established in 1974 to supervise the burgeoning problems of funding fifteen universities and seven other institutions, and had ruled that any university's annual deficit had to be kept within 2 per cent of its annual operating grant. Otherwise, MPHEC would require that 2 per cent of the following year's grant go towards the elimination of the deficit. Caught between the MPHEC and the DFA, the board declared it could not manage more that a 5.5 per cent increase in salaries. MacKay warned the board that this was lower than any Nova Scotian university, that "salaries of Dalhousie professors will have slipped significantly behind those paid elsewhere." Hicks was less generous. A few weeks later he asserted that probationary appointments and others, prior to tenure, would have to be short term, from one to three years, despite a recent regulation that such new appointments would normally be for three years. "Normally" could be used at Dalhousie as a "bolt-hole" word, allowing one to get out from under a rule when it was deemed essential to do so. In mid-1977 Hicks thought it was, but he alarmed young and still untenured members of faculty, all of whom had votes in DFA.

Between November 1977 and March 1978 Dalhousie was served up with platefuls of labour problems. In November 1977 there was a two-week strike of the International Operating Engineers Union, local 968, responsible for Dalhousie heating and without a contract since February. The only way to end the strike, said Louis Vagianos, vice-president of university services, was to go back to the bargaining table; but, he added unhelpfully, the 5.5 per cent salary increase was not negotiable. The strike was settled early in December with, in effect, an 8 per cent increase (5.5 per cent with additions to come later). A long struggle with CUPE local 1392, the cleaners and caretakers union, was finally settled in February 1978, with a similar increase. The Dalhousie Staff Association broke off contract talks in March 1978 and was proceeding to conciliation. On top of everything else, the DFA came to the Board of Governors in January 1978, wanting collective bargaining by voluntary recognition, which DSA already had.

The DFA asked for it with three conditions: binding arbitration of salary and fringe benefits disputes, and of individual grievances; recognition of the association as sole bargaining agent of academic staff; and the sharing of all relevant information between board and DFA. The most important of these was binding arbitration. The whole package was modelled on one that had been established at the University of British Columbia. The board could have seen it coming. In 1977 a DFA questionnaire asked members if they would favour a legal union like those at Saint Mary's or Carleton; 44 per cent said yes, 36 per cent said no, with 20 per cent undecided. A majority, 50.4 per cent, also favoured formal consultation and arbitration procedures but without the formation of a legal union – in other words, the principle of voluntary recognition. The DFA then approached the board about having voluntary recognition granted, and in the summer and autumn of 1977 it was discussed at length between board and association representatives. It was a mode that Dr Philip Welch, DFA president in 1977–8, wanted right to the end. But the board representatives did not like it and by January 1978 it had gone nowhere.

Thus, in January 1978 the board finally turned down the DFA request. Though the reason was unclear, the board may have been confident that the proposal came from a minority of faculty, and that the majority would resist unionization on any principle. For a DFA meeting called for 16 February, the board were asked to put their refusal in writing, which they did on the 10th. A last-minute phone call to the DFA president asked that the letter of refusal be disregarded, and new counter-proposals by the board were promised. These were: arbitration on salaries but on nothing else; recognition of DFA as the primary, but not the sole, bargaining agent; and a reasonable release of information. These proposals arrived on 14 February, two days before the DFA meeting that was to begin to discuss certification.

At the meeting there was a spirited debate, in which a succession of former association presidents testified to the difficulty, if not the impossibility, of securing what DFA wanted through the Board of Governors. Welch cited the question of free tuition for dependants, which he said "had gone on for several years sliding up and down the administrative ladder without any appreciable result." To many at the meeting the board's three-fifths concession of 14 February, seemed too much like "a death-bed repentance" to be plausible. There was also some dissatisfaction with the Hicks-MacKay leadership, which seemed to be confirmed by their rejection of voluntary recognition. The DFA then voted by 119 to 29, with three abstentions, to ask its executive to seek certification under the Labour Relations Act. (A week later the board agreed to a 50 per cent reduction in university fees for dependants of faculty members!) After cards had been signed by the required 40 per cent of the bargaining unit, certification was asked for on 7 April. A week later the official NSLRB vote was held, the result held in abeyance until after NSLRB hearings.[14]

A strong core of intensely conservative opinion in the DFA opposed faculty unionization in any form, but especially the form it took – that is, a union to be certified under the Nova Scotia Labour Relations Act. Edgar Z. Friedenberg, the spectacular American import of 1970 (and president of DFA, 1980–1), commented on the " 'old boy' oligarchy of senior faculty that is impossible to distinguish from the administration and I want protection from that." Actually the conservatives were not so much an oligarchy as traditionalists, who had long since grown up with and accepted a holistic view of the university. They bridled at the confrontational delights enjoyed by ardent spirits in the DFA. The issue that worried the conservatives most and drove their anti-union passion, was fear of a university strike. The president of the DFA in 1977–8, Dr Philip Welch, was at pains in March 1978 to assure the conservatives that even if the association did become a certified union, a strike was most unlikely. To many a strike was barely conceivable, for it would be against the students, innocent third parties to such a confrontation. It was these strongly held opinions by 40 per cent of the faculty which had probably persuaded the board in January not to recognize the DFA as exclusive bargaining agent. Now it was too late to turn back. Unionization could only be defeated at the Labour Relations Board.

The Labour Board heard the DFA application in July 1978. The university's position was first, that the Trade Union Act might not apply to Dalhousie or any other university. MacKay, who led the university's negotiating team, held out little hope for that line; failing that, Dalhousie should try to make the bargaining unit as large as possible, to include both union sympathizers as well as those opposed to union. That would have the effect of weakening extreme union positions.

The NSLRB hearings were long and complicated. Who was to be included in the bargaining unit? How far and where did the chain of management go? The middle ground that emerged across Canada in the mid-1970s was to include in the bargaining unit departmental chairs, but exclude from it deans, assistant deans, directors. Professional librarians, as at Dalhousie, were usually included. Dentists, and doctors in the clinical departments of Medicine at Dalhousie were not. That was usual, too. Finally, in November 1978, certification was announced of the Dalhousie Faculty Association as the official and exclusive bargaining agent of Dalhousie professors and professional librarians. There were 636 members in the bargaining unit; 489 had voted, 265 in favour, 217 against, with seven spoiled ballots. That was a yes vote of 55 per cent. Although the outcome was determined by a mere 41.7 per cent of those eligible to vote, it was a victory for the new DFA union.[15]

The figures pointed to the divisiveness of the unionization process. Some departments were almost wholly in favour of the union; some, like Political Science, were equally opposed; most departments were split. The feelings pro and con were intense. For a time friends of many years were divided, each feeling betrayed by the other. It was not pretty. Senate entered the picture with notice of motion on 11 December 1978, that the negotiating team for the university not accede to any collective agreement that would impinge on the authority and prerogatives of Senate. That motion carried in January 1979, with the sensible observation by Madame E.C. Pielou, Killam professor of biology, that a contest between Senate and DFA was unlikely, since Senate was interested in academic questions, and the association in money.

Bargaining between the administration and the DFA began in February 1979. The management team of six were: vice-presidents MacKay and McNeill, David Cameron, Norman Horrocks, plus the university solicitor and a Hicks's designate. The DFA was represented by Michael Cross (History) as chief negotiator, Alan Kennedy (English), R.S. Rodger (Psychology), Susan Sherwin (Philosophy), plus a place for a representative from CAUT (who was present once) and one other designate. The association was anxious to get a contract in hand; within a month it was suggesting that the university was not bargaining in good faith. Language could occasionally become rhetoric, arguments manipulative, facts distorted, in such missives. MacKay replied that the DFA were being unreasonable about the length of time needed to "forge a first contract." The shortest time for establishing a first contract in Canada was seven months of intensive work, the longest thirty-five months.

The DFA team were very well prepared, coached by CAUT, and with model clauses from other agreements on what they wanted at Dalhousie. The administration team were ill prepared. They met for the first time the evening before the actual negotiations started, with the chief negotiator for the University of Ottawa. They had no specific instructions from the board. Their entire philosophy was reactive. They lacked also technical sophistication. They had great difficulty with salary negotiations because they had no computer base. The DFA team did have; R.S. Rodger had a desk-top computer program that covered each member's salary, sabbaticals, and other benefits. The vice-president finance once had to work all night with his little black book (in which he had recorded by hand all increases to each member of staff year by year), cranking out on a hand calculator a total salary base for the DFA bargaining unit. The two salary bases came to almost the same, but what a difference in method! Moreover, there was little direction from Hicks. He seemed, as one Dalhousie negotiator said, "to have no stomach" for the negotiations. Hicks left those wholly to MacKay, even the reporting of them to the Board of Governors.[16]

The summer of 1979 was long and arduous as both sides wrestled with innumerable questions. There's a world of fighting in details! The draft contract was not ready until the end of October. No one, said MacKay, was entirely happy with the final agreement, which "might not be a bad feature of it." It had 420 clauses in thirty-three articles, together with three schedules and four appendices, some sixty-eight legal-size pages of single-space type. The DFA had wanted the Rand formula, which comprehended a closed shop, but MacKay was under heavy pressure from the board and from conservative members of faculty not to concede that. It had dragged on a long time and finally the association gave up the point, accepting a variation: members of the bargaining unit who refused to join DFA would still have to pay dues, but they could ask that their money go to a scholarship or other charitable fund. Salary increases that had been shut down since 1977 were now unlocked, with an overall increase of 18.1 per cent – 9.5 per cent for 1978–9 and 8.6 per cent for 1979–80. That purpose had certainly been achieved. Few believed, even now, that any issues between Dalhousie and DFA would ever come to a strike. Many also felt that Hicks had been too cavalier in resisting the associations pleas for better salaries. The germ of the unionization of the Dalhousie faculty, said K.A. Heard, a political scientist, may have been in Hicks testing once too often the outer limits of his authority.[17]

The Strike of CUPE Local 1392
Just as the DFA was getting its certification in November 1978, a strike of CUPE local 1392, representing Dalhousie's cleaners, caretakers, drivers, and porters, started on 6 November. The CUPE contract had expired on 31 August. Negotiations over the old contract had

been difficult and bitter. Louis Vagianos, who became the vice-president administration for 1977–9, was quick, talented, and at times abrasive. He felt that Dalhousie had to save money and he would help do it. The grounds work was contracted out, with Dalhousie's crew cut in half. Another union grievance dating back to 1976 was "back-shifting" from day shift to night shift (midnight to 8 AM); an increasing number of Dalhousie buildings could no longer be cleaned properly during the day. That year, Vagianos explained, the number of cleaners had gone from 295 to 221. "We're not trying to be harsh. But there's no question some people are unhappy. They have to be. They had a much better deal before." Buffeted by Dalhousie cutbacks, and by Nova Scotia's application of federal Anti-Inflation Board rules, CUPE leaders were in a fighting mood in November 1976. "The Anti-Inflation Board is doing Dal's dirty work for them," was the opinion of one CUPE spokesman. The union was going to grievance procedures, then to arbitration, and then, said a spokesman, "we'll pull our people out on these bastards."

A contract was finally signed, but a year and a half later, with the mood little improved, the new negotiations that started in July 1978 went nowhere. The main issue was wages, the union wanting an increase of 85 cents an hour in a one-year contract, (that is, a 19 per cent raise), and would not budge. Al Cunningham, the national representative for CUPE, was leading negotiations. Many thought Cunningham's stubbornness was because he was putting CUPE's national strategy ahead of the interests of local 1392. Some Dalhousie staff who supported CUPE against the administration found him indecisive. In early December, at a conciliation meeting called by the government, Dalhousie offered 17.2 per cent. It was not apparently reported to union members. So the strike went on.

In the meantime, since November Dalhousie was kept clean by volunteers from its administrative staff, including deans. The work detail for the Law School, for example, included Vice-President W.A. MacKay, Vice-President Academic Guy MacLean, Vice-President Finance D.H. McNeill, W.H. Charles, the new dean of law, Ronald Macdonald, the former dean of law, and Arnold Tingley the registrar. The six would start at 6 AM on Sunday morning and would be finished at 9 AM. Then they would sit down for coffee, the talk being about everything except the strike. The first day Hicks came and happily cleaned the dean's office, deliberately doing the windows which were in full view of the pickets outside. The others thought that a bit provocative and persuaded him to give it up. The upshot was that they discovered that Dalhousie cleaning could be done with fewer volunteers than were in the regular cleaning force.[18]

For some time Dalhousie had been wondering if it should be in the cleaning business at all. Other universities, such as Memorial and UNB, and three hospitals in Halifax, had all contracted their cleaning out to a firm called Modern Cleaning. The union had charged Dalhousie with having too few cleaners and too many supervisors; advice from outside firms and Dalhousie's own experience since November suggested that the reverse was the case. Dalhousie found indeed that it could cope indefinitely with the strike. Valiant efforts by the administrative cleaners kept the university clean, though cleanliness was deteriorating at the edges as the strike went on. For faculty had begun to take sides; some Dalhousie professors in some departments, sympathetic to CUPE, helped to contribute to the litter. While Dalhousie was anxious to resolve differences and get its administrators away from cleaning, Hicks pointed out there was "no evidence of willingness to compromise, or even to discuss the situation realistically, on the part of Mr. Cunningham [of CUPE]." It was also very difficult to get through to the members of the union exactly what Dalhousie's offers had been. According to Louis Vagianos, Dalhousie's December offer would make Dalhousie's cleaners the highest paid in the province, but the offer was never reported to the membership.[19]

On 21 December 1978, perhaps on Vagianos's suggestion, Dalhousie closed with an offer from Modern Cleaning to take over all Dalhousie cleaning. Dalhousie made two conditions: all employees currently on strike would be offered employment; and Modern Cleaning would offer CUPE wages and benefits comparable to those offered by Dalhousie or better. Modern Cleaning would do the negotiating with the union; Dalhousie would no longer be in the cleaning business. It would save, so it was alleged, some $300,000 a year. Legal advice was that Dalhousie's sudden move did not constitute strike-breaking.

Perhaps not, but it was sharp practice nevertheless; the old contract that expired in August had a clause prohibiting contracting out. That clause was now dead: Dalhousie acted. It was shrewd, smart, smacking of the style of the vice-president administration. The Dalhousie campus did not like it. CUPE went to the Nova Scotia Labour Relations Board with a protest. Kell Antoft, head of the Institute of Public Affairs, was deeply chagrined, since his institute's Labour-Management Bureau was currently studying just such questions. He wrote an anguished Christmas Day letter to Hicks, alleging the Dalhousie action had almost no precedent in Canadian labour relations. Dalhousie professors were also upset. The Biology Department, the Philosophy Department, graduate students of English, protested. So did the Political Science Department. Dale Poel, the chairman, wrote on behalf of himself and eleven other members of Political Science, on 18 January 1979:

You are probably aware that the two main reasons why unionization [of the Faculty] succeeded at Dalhousie were the widespread concern among junior faculty about low pay and future job security, and the equally widespread concern among senior faculty about the uncertainties of the University's administrative processes, particularly at the higher levels. The way in which the decision to contract out cleaning has been handled served to reawaken and reinforce these doubts and fears, just at a time when things were beginning to settle down and some of the rifts opened by the debate over unionization had begun to close.

The DSA was upset. The DFA passed two motions on 11 January 1979, asking the Board of Governors to overrule its executive committee which had endorsed the decision, and censuring that committee, the president, and vice-presidents who were responsible for it. Some members of the board were extremely uneasy. Marilyn MacDonald ('62) thought that such an important issue should have been taken to a full meeting of the board; she much disliked being held responsible for a decision in which she had had no part.[20]

CUPE certainly bristled. Rich Dalhousie was starting a special course, CUPE said, "How to Bust a Union in the 1970s." There was talk about old and faithful members of the Dalhousie cleaning staff being handed over, body and bones, to the untender mercies of a commercial cleaning outfit. But of the 228 members of the union, only 3.5 per cent had worked for Dalhousie fifteen years or longer, and at the other end of the scale, 30 per cent had worked for Dalhousie for a year or less. Half the group had worked five years or less.

By this time Dalhousie's wage offer was no longer the main issue; rather it was flexibility in assigning cleaning staff. The union did not want management moving cleaning staff from one building to another. And the switch to Modern Cleaning loomed over everything else. After an all-day, all-night discussion under the aegis of the minister of labour on 23 January, Dalhousie made an important concession: Modern Cleaning would not be the employer, Dalhousie would; Modern would simply supervise. The union still held out, over "flexibility" in assigning work.

On the initiative of a CUPE support group on campus, the Nova Scotia Federation of Labour agreed to pitch in; it called a day of protest for Wednesday, 24 January. Busloads of steel workers from Cape Breton, students from Acadia, workers of many sorts, were moved into Halifax to close Dalhousie down. The picket lines were formidable. Dalhousie did not close officially; it said it would stay open and it did. But not by much. Many Dalhousie professors honoured the picket lines. Hicks and his secretary were jostled when they crossed;

Henry James when he crossed was struck by some wooden implement; a car trying to run picket lines at the Killam struck a Saint
Mary's professor, who was not seriously hurt. The car, driven by a
student who was trying to hand in a late essay, was damaged by irate
picketers. But by then the protest was almost redundant; a few days
later the Dalhousie offer was, at last, put to a proper union vote and
approved overwhelmingly, by a vote of 149 to 18.[21]

Thus did the CUPE strike end. As usual, no one really won. Dalhousie remained accused of sharp practice, though it had eventually
backed out of giving its workers wholly over to Modern Cleaning. It
did the administration and board no good. The union came close to
getting the money it originally asked for, though no one, said Hicks,
mentioned the "many thousands of dollars damage done to University property during this strike."[22] It might well have been settled in
early December on the basis of Dalhousie's offer then, had the union
leaders been more flexible and been willing to present Dalhousie's offer to the rank and file. Hicks did not come out of it well. One could
understand the university's frustration when there was absolutely no
give by the CUPE negotiators. But effective administration is knowing
when to be patient, as well as knowing when to act.

One inevitable major consequence of having five labour unions on
campus (the fifth after demonstrators and instructors were given a
separate union in 1978), was a great increase in litigiousness. The negotiations and renegotiations of labour contracts was enormously
time-consuming and exacting work. In the case of the DFA, probably
the laying out and codifying of rights, duties, and responsibilities was
a useful exercise, making procedures explicit and establishing criteria
for promotions and tenure. Those written rigidities had their value,
but they came with a price; there was now much less flexibility and
informality, much more bureaucracy. The Dalhousie world was becoming more ponderous and legalistic.

Senate Flexes its Muscles

Senate also exemplified this trend. The focus of power in Canadian
universities was shifting in the 1970s. J.A. Corry, principal of Queen's
from 1961 to 1968, one of the most delightful academics this country
has produced, said at UBC in 1969 that power had already passed
from the president's office to the academics. They had "constitution-
alized the president's office, clinched their control of academic matters and so got very powerful leverage in all important decisions." His
complaint was that the academics were not exercising that power, and
the result was indecision, dissension, and possibly in the distance, outside interference. A huge shift of responsibility was taking place.[23]

While Hicks was preoccupied with building, with bringing into the university new faculties, institutes, with expanding Dalhousie's horizons, the Senate was slowly but definitely moving towards establishing what could be thought of as a parallel power. The leader in this development was John Finlayson Graham (1924–90), professor of economics. He had come to Dalhousie in 1949 out of UBC and Columbia, and by 1960 was head of Economics, a post he retained for a decade. His work was careful, thorough, scrupulous, so much so that at first he was not fully appreciated by those in authority. His integrity, loyalty, and capacity won him considerable outside attention, as he was president of the Canadian Economics Association in 1970–1. The Regan government appointed him chairman of its Royal Commission on Education, Public Service and Provincial-Municipal Relations, a project and a report which took from 1971 to 1974. By the late 1970s he had become, as Guy MacLean put it, the conscience of the university.

He was especially good at defusing issues where his own intensely held personal beliefs were not at risk. In 1976 the anthropologists in the Department of Sociology/Social Anthropology wanted to have their own department, some having come to Dalhousie believing in the possibility. Asked to adjudicate, Graham earned respect from both sides, suggesting that Dalhousie could not get into the full range of physical anthropology and archaeology, that the social anthropologists be content with the status quo, as cousins of sociology.

It was not always that easy. Once Graham had his mind made up he was a determined, relentless adversary. He had a lasting distrust of the Institute of Public Affairs under Guy Henson, deploring mostly its standards, which he considered too slipshod by half. He kept his Department of Economics at stern arm's length, distrusting the institute's social science, believing it should be hived off somewhere on its own, preferably out of Dalhousie altogether. Hicks had to tell him in 1965 that the Institute of Public Affairs was going to remain a useful part of Dalhousie for the foreseeable future and he had better get used to it.[24]

Graham was normally a cooperative and hard-working member of faculty, but the idea of the DFA becoming a trade union and exclusive bargaining agent for the teaching staff he abhorred root and branch. He felt that the traditional rhetoric of trade unionism was wholly inappropriate to an academic community; the right of disassociation was as important as its opposite. His dislike, perhaps his fear of the DFA on the one hand, and his growing distrust of the ways of administrators on the other, may have been part of the driving force behind his hopes and ambitions for the Dalhousie Senate. In March 1978, he moved in Senate that it appoint an ad hoc committee "to negotiate

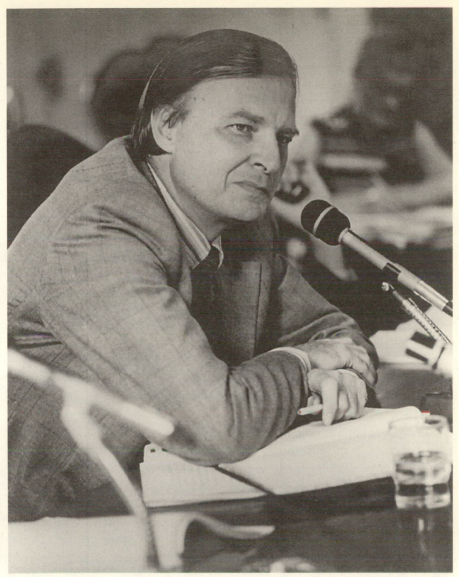

J.F. Graham, Professor of Economics, 1949–89, seen here as chairman of the Nova Scotia Royal Commission on Education, Public Services and Provincial-Municipal Relations, 1971–4.

such changes and clarifications of the present constitutional arrangements as might secure confidence among faculty and elsewhere that … academic self-government is possible and can be made to work in this university." In other words, could Senate be made into the main academic motor at Dalhousie that Graham believed it ought to be? Such a committee should consider whether Senate was getting enough financial information; should there be an understanding with DFA about appointments and tenure, and should Senate be the approving body in such matters? Two weeks later Senate met in special session, when Hicks agreed to answer Graham's questions:

Q. Are conditions of appointment, tenure and promotion under the control of Senate?

HDH: Agreed.

Q. Ought not Senate to have effective control over Dalhousie's priorities?

HDH: Agreed, but the administration must have some discretion.

Q. Ought not the procedures of Senate be modified to make it more effective?

HDH: Agreed, but how can it be done?

Q. Should not Senate be made more broadly representative of Faculty as a whole?

HDH: Senate can change itself with the consent of a majority of its members.

Q. Should not more financial information be made available both to Senate and DFA?

HDH: Agreed, but both Senate and DFA will have to work much harder than they have done in the past if they are to use it.

Aye, there was the rub. If Senate wanted to control things it had to devise means of putting the control in place. But little enthusiasm existed in Senate for the work of creative planning; Senate committees were quite busy enough. In September 1978 the secretary of Senate, Arnold Tingley, pointed out that of the many reports of faculties and institutes that came into his office, "Never, within the recollection of the present Secretary, has anyone wished to examine any report." That comment spoke volumes about the enthusiasm of senators for the kind of work that John Graham had in mind.[25]

Nevertheless, Graham's constitutional committee believed that Senate should have "a decisive place in policy making, including all aspects of physical, academic and financial planning." The Graham report's basic logic was that Dalhousie's administration should carry out policies that were determined by Senate. The consequence of its new role was, thus, the removal of the president from the chair of Senate. But it did not come at once; a straw vote in January 1979 indicated that not all of the Senate was following Graham's logic. But the separation did come in 1980, after Hicks stepped down.

Hicks thought that the general effect of the Graham committee's recommendations would be to separate Senate and administration. Graham did not mind that; power to the Senate was his aim. He wanted also to do away with the Senate Council, by now a sort of executive of Senate, heavy with deans *ex officio*. Graham especially wanted reform of the composition of Senate. There were then 278 members of Senate among whom were many full professors who never attended. To change Senate's composition required a majority vote of all the senators, 140 votes. In April 1979 a referendum gave 124 in favour of change, twenty-nine opposed, with twenty-seven spoiled ballots. Some ninety-nine did not vote at all. Thus it failed, though narrowly. The vote was close enough that in May Graham proposed, and got Senate to agree to, a second referendum in October. The second time the answer was more decidedly against change. Thus Senate and Senate Council, admittedly clumsy and awkward, stayed largely the way they were. Senate did eventually get its own elected chairman, and the president stayed on as *ex officio* member and frequent commentator. It was a curious system, but not without advantages. The Senate legislated, and the president listened and commented, administering the result with his still considerable power.[26]

One useful right the president had used, and would continue to exercise, was appointing president's committees. These had started in Hicks's time as a means of getting at administrative issues; a good example was the conversion of the Cultural Affairs Committee from a Senate Committee to a president's, once it became clear that its work was fundamentally administrative. Obvious administrative questions, such as the operation of the Registrar's Office, were solved by president's committees, though mostly academics were appointed to them. Some committees were appointed that ought to have been left to Senate, as the hassle over the Faculty of Administrative Studies showed. One of Hicks's committees, appointed in 1976, was on the Status of Women at Dalhousie, particularly directed at the position of women academics. The chair of it came to be Professor Virginia Miller of Sociology.

The Status of Women Report and Changes in Campus Life
The report's immediate concern was appointment, working conditions, and salaries of women academics. It reported late in 1978 with some striking statistics for 1977–8. For 777 cases overall, mean salary at Dalhousie was $26,598. The mean salary for 650 men was $27,924; for 127 women it was $19,808. That was a formidable gap. At the younger

levels, however, it was closing: 191 male assistant professors earned $22,680; fifty-two female ones $20,571. In the Arts and Science Faculty at the assistant professor level, there was almost no salary gap, $18,262 for the eighty-nine male assistant professors, $18,244 for the sixteen female. That in turn made the other gap, numbers, all too palpable. Of the 369 Arts and Science professors, only thirty-four were women. Of the 650 in Medicine, only thirty were women. The Status of Women Committee recommended that Dalhousie should aim firmly at equal opportunity and equal treatment to redress imbalances both in salary and in numbers. It should also consider giving maternity leaves.

When the report was published in 1979, women students were 42 per cent of all students at Dalhousie. Even more striking, in Arts and Science they almost equalled men students in numbers. They also had much more to say about things on campus that they did not like, and they recruited male students to their cause. The *Gazette* became more stern, as did the Student Council, about the kind of entertainment offered at male stag parties. At the 20 March 1979 Student Council meeting questions were raised about "exotic dancing," a well-understood euphemism at an engineers' entertainment the previous weekend. There were some two hundred protests over bringing in strippers. The male writer in the *Gazette* was articulate, but perhaps more high-minded than the majority of his fellows:

The reduction of sex, a private matter, to a show designed merely to excite its audience, is ignominious and unpleasant in any context. That it should happen in a university is incongruous in the extreme ... The spectacle of seedy stag bashes going on at the SUB will hardly help students' petitions [to the government for more funding].

The Student Council should have cancelled such an event, concluded the writer. The following year the engineers did cancel their "Stag and Stein" with similar dancing because of protests. Women still had a long way to go towards real equality, but their voices on campus were being heard; some of their complaints were acted on.

But students were students. In September 1979 there was an engineers' raid on Alexandra Hall, King's women's residence, eggs thrown, windows broken, some of the engineers encouraged, it was said, by young ladies draped Juliet-like in windows. King's sent the Engineering Society a bill for $535. That same month a party in Fenwick Tower got out of hand, with the stereo going at full blast, the party cascading out into the hall. After complaints, by some ingenious system the power in that one apartment was cut off, and the stereo mercifully fell silent. Presumably the occupants gradually did too.

Michael Power, President of the Students' Council, 1978–9.

A good deal of beer was consumed on these occasions. The *Gazette* in November 1979 dealt soberly with "Alcoholism at Dalhousie." According to Student Health, 12 per cent of any given population is prone to alcoholism. The Student Health doctor reported that he knew at least six students who had to have eight to ten beers a day. The Grawood bartender said that he would call 60 per cent of the students at the Grawood heavy drinkers, consuming some twenty to twenty-five beers a week. The assistant manager noted that some of the heaviest drinkers were alumni. One Quebec student thought Nova Scotia students were indeed apt to drink heavily, their attitude being, "I want reality to cease being real." It was a bad direction to aim at.[27]

In September 1976 the *Gazette* published a list of gay bars and discos in Halifax, noticing a movement that had developed publicly after 1969. It received anti-gay letters, the nub of which was, "we all know you exist and that is all we want to know. We really don't give a damn whether monkeys do it, or where your last or next meeting was and/or will be, so knock it off!!"

In general the students of the later 1970s were more conservative than a decade before, not only in style and manners but in attitudes and purposes. They were as good academically but distinctly more job-oriented, thinking of careers rather than bucking the establishment. The labour troubles of Dalhousie in 1977–9 were reported in the *Gazette*, and students sympathized with CUPE local 1392, but their basic concerns, not surprisingly, resembled those of students of the 1980s. If six hundred Dalhousie students joined the Atlantic Federation of Students march on the legislature in March 1977 to protest funding cuts to universities, they begged off a labour rally in September. Michael Brown ('78), editor of the *Gazette* was furious: "Colour them Yellow" was his editorial; they were "apathetic, self-centred, conceited, unimaginative, insensitive, smug." But even the organizers of the rally took issue with that remark. One student replied that he didn't have to take time off to listen to "simplistic exhortations of local labor leaders." Students were, in short, severely discriminating in the causes they would support. Government funding cuts were one thing, but other social issues had a harder time.

J.T. Low was visiting professor of English at Dalhousie for two years, from 1974 to 1976. He had come from Scotland and he found surprising resemblances between his Scottish students and those at Dalhousie, with just as many problems, just as many pleasant surprises. But, he said, there was one important difference:

Canadian students seem much more interested in their own cultural scene than Scottish students are or have been up to recently. I have been impressed with Canadian literature – its development, its promise, its availability; and I am so pleased that students have opportunities in colleges and universities here to study Canadian poetry, drama and the flourishing Canadian novel and short story.

How old Archibald MacMechan would have delighted in that![28]

Looking for a New President

On 31 March 1978, Senate was presented with a motion that at its next meeting it institute a search committee "for a full-time President." That did not rattle Hicks, in the chair; he merely suggested that he would prefer that nothing be done until the end of the year or early 1979, and the Senate, not unwilling to put down such a sharp-edged motion, agreed. In April 1979 the board and Senate struck a joint committee, with two co-chairs, Basil Cooke of Senate and Zilpha Linkletter of the board. The DFA protested that it was not formally represented on the search committee. The committee agreed that the association could participate on the distinct understanding that all proceedings be strictly confidential. The board advertised the position in Canada, the United States, and Great Britain. By June 1979 the committee was meeting weekly. They received some ninety names, sixty serious nominations, and thirty-one fully-fledged applications. By August the committee had rejected all but four, and were meeting with representative groups on campus for confidential exchanges of views. Interviews with the four short-listed candidates took place in November. Then, on 29 November 1979, the *Dalhousie Gazette* published the short list, hitherto confidential. The leak came over the phone from an unknown caller who said that the university had the right to know who were the short-listed candidates for its presidency. The vice-president of the Student Union, Graham Wells ('80), blamed the DFA. Susan Sherwin, the current president, denied it was responsible, though it had withdrawn from its membership on the search committee for the very reason that it felt the short list should be made known. But it is likely that the caller was from the DFA.

Making short lists public is not usually a good tactic, however desirable it might appear to inform the university public. It disintegrates the process. It makes life awkward for the candidate at his home base. A successful candidate on a presidential short list obviously does not mind too much; but unsuccessful candidates usually do. A recent publication of the short list at a York University search resulted in all the candidates withdrawing. At UNB, where the 1979 process was open, the result was failure to get a president at all. At Dalhousie the *Gazette* publication caused two of the four candidates on the short list to

W.A. MacKay, Dean of Law, 1965–9; Vice-President, 1969–80; President, 1980–6.

withdraw. Of the two remaining, one outside, one inside the university, there was some preference among the Senate members of the search committee for the outside candidate; a board member, however, urged the inside appointment and that managed to carry the committee. On 8 January 1980 at a special meeting of the full board, the search committee made its selection known: W.A. MacKay, Dalhousie's senior vice-president, for a six-year term, from 1980 to 1986.

At the February board meeting MacKay as the new president-elect said Hicks's contribution to Dalhousie could not be matched; he had taken Dalhousie from " 'a small college by the sea' to one of the great universities in Canada." Hicks's contribution was unique; but the rest was hyperbole and doubtless so intended. In 1963 Dalhousie was some distance beyond being a small college by the sea; it had probably ceased being that by 1925. Nor could it quite be said that it was one of the great universities in Canada; Toronto, McGill, UBC, Laval could be called that. But Dalhousie was solid middle rank in Canada and in 1980 that was good standing ground.[29]

The Hicks Era

Hicks stepped down as president on 31 August 1980. Since 1963 Dalhousie had been wholly transformed – in size, buildings, students, research, finances, debt. By any concrete test, it was almost unrecognizable from the university of two thousand students that he first came to as dean of arts and science in 1960. It was now a big, sprawling, increasingly amorphous institution of nine thousand students. In 1963–4 the operating deficit had been $107,000, the accumulated one $484,000. In 1979–80 they were $1,330,000 and $4,678,000. In 1963–4 endowment gave Dalhousie 13.3 per cent of its income, in 1979–80 only 4.4 per cent, even though the endowment's market value had reached $55.4 million. Dalhousie's physical assets in building and equipment, estimated at cost, totalled $135 million, some $25 million of which was under mortgage to the province and being paid off in annual instalments under provincial capital funding programs. Without Hicks's ingenuity, panache, passion for building, Dalhousie probably could not have kept up with the vigorous competition of universities elsewhere in Canada for physical plant.

In 1979–80 Dalhousie's total revenue was $79.4 million, about 57 per cent of which came from the Nova Scotian government, including the federal money channelled through the province. Research grants came to almost $9 million annually. Oddly enough, it was the research grants, as much as the buildings, of which Hicks was proud. Buildings were obvious; research grants were what mattered. Hicks may have been headlong, but he had many of his priorities right.[30]

Hicks was the right president for the right time, said Gordon Archibald, chairman of the board from 1980 to 1985. Hicks loved building. At home he was a good carpenter; J.G. Sykes, the university architect, who knew something about wood, admitted that Hicks knew far more than he did. Creating, developing, getting a building going, challenged him. As Gordon Riley of Oceanography once said, Hicks went scrounging and came back with a fat packet of money. The time was ripe for that kind of swashbuckling. It is doubtful if Hicks could have managed that in the 1950s, and certainly not by the 1980s.

Like any builder, he left a lot of odds and ends behind, including in Dalhousie's case substantial odds and ends of debts. Governments, federal and provincial, never quite covered Dalhousie's expenditures on most of the buildings that now decorated the campus. Perhaps the Board of Governors should have reined him in harder, but the board only met once a month; to keep track of Hicks one had to be around every day, and you could not count on finding him even then. At Christmas 1966 the *Gazette* had as gift suggestion, the Henry Hicks Doll: you wound it up and it went to Europe. That had immediate reference to Hicks's autumn sojourn in Paris as head of Canada's delegation to UNESCO, but he was an inveterate traveller. Even when in his office he was hard to keep hold of. Horace Read, his vice-president, complained that having an appointment with the president gave him little standing. He was "bumped" several times by students to whom Hicks would give higher priority. Read could be a bore, and Hicks did not take kindly at any time to being bored. Nevertheless that year, 1966, Read said he had to review pressing university business driving Hicks to the airport!

It was never easy to rein Hicks in. He frightened D.H. McNeill, his able and discerning vice-president finance, with some of his financial adventures. Then, said McNeill, depressed by the deficits, he would go into a board meeting, hear Hicks talk, and soon felt that things were not so bad after all. Donald McInnes seems to have thought that Hicks was like a powerful horse; if he got you into trouble he was strong enough to get you out of it again.[31]

Hicks liked to do things his way. In the struggle with public opinion over Dalplex in 1973, he was sure that had he done it his way – full speed ahead and damn the torpedoes – it would never have got hung up in long legal wrangles, costing the university (and the public) $2–3 million more. He believed his biggest mistake in all his seventeen years as president was agreeing to have a public meeting to explain Dalplex to Halifax citizens. According to Hicks, one leader in that neighbourhood collectivity wanted Dalhousie's land himself to carve it up into saleable lots.[32]

The presidents who are taking the money so cheerfully are, from l. to r., Dalhousie, Technical College, and St Francis Xavier.

By 1978 the age of that kind of enterprise was passing. The MPHEC had taken over the questions of funding from the University Grants Committee. No longer could Hicks draw Dr Murphy aside and explain to him crisply what Dalhousie needed. MPHEC meant long and rather dreary position papers. The main fun Hicks got out of MPHEC was dancing the rhumba with its head, Sister Catherine Wallace, when they met on various excursions in the Caribbean. They were both good at it, but she was too clever to be got around by a few dances. "You leave those gentlemen to me," she once told her nuns at Mount St Vincent about the University Grants Committee. They did and they were right.

After 1978 there were no more buildings to be planned. Dalplex and Dentistry were on track, and that was that. At the end Hicks was jocular, quoting his older contemporary Clark Kerr, president of the University of California from 1958 to 1967, that a university president had three duties: to provide football for the alumni, parking for the faculty, and sex for the students. Hicks said he had not been good at any of those! "The last two years," he said of his presidency, "I didn't enjoy as much as I did the years of rapid growth and forward-looking decision making all the time, you see." Not to put too fine a point on it, routines bored him. He wanted, he craved, he thrived, on the excitement of doing.

Government restrictions gradually closed down his opportunities. The cutbacks of the 1980s started in the late 1970s. One basic reason for Dalhousie's labour troubles after 1977 was of course inflation; but coupled with that was a government that had decided that university expenditures needed to be held down, and some of the high-flying presidents with them. The $22 million for the Dental Building was the last really big money that Hicks was able to spend. Dalhousie was caught both by inflation and by government. Of the senior personnel, the one that paid most heavily was perhaps Louis Vagianos, a talented and clever trouble-shooter, too frank for his own good; in March 1979 he had had enough and resigned.

The long 1978 negotiations with the Dalhousie Faculty Association in which Hicks took so little interest, and the CUPE troubles of 1978–9, marked the real end of the Hicks era. Until then he and his vice-presidents operated a benign dictatorship. Dean Ronald Macdonald's experience with his budget was characteristic; an outline based on the previous year got approved with minor variations, new appointments were authorized individually and informally. That went out with unionization. Now there were formulas where once there had been secrets. The easy-going ways belonged to an age when the university was an intimate, cohesive place, the days of the 1950s, and which carried over to the time of Hicks's presidency in 1963. But within a decade the conditions that had sustained that informality were largely undone. The style survived but it sometimes looked anachronistic. Perhaps, indeed, Hicks stayed too long; it was apparent, as early as 1977, that he was not adapting to new challenges in university governance. That may well have been the final price Dalhousie paid for his senatorship.[33]

The new president, W.A. MacKay, was different. Hicks claimed to read only the first and last paragraph of a letter and made up his mind from that. That was exaggeration, but suggestive. Andy MacKay would read it through. Hicks made his decisions on perhaps no more than 55 per cent of the evidence, if that; MacKay with his background in legal arbitration was concerned with both sides of a question, and wanted to master 90 per cent. MacKay had eleven years' experience as Hicks's senior vice-president.

From 1972 onward MacKay was indispensable. When Parliament was in session, Senator Hicks would bounce into town Thursday night, become President Hicks from Friday until Tuesday, make decisions and leave MacKay to implement them. It worked because each did what they were good at. MacKay was much more judicious and careful. It was fortunate for everyone that the students in April 1970 decided to occupy Hicks's office when he was away, in effect leaving MacKay to deal with them. Hicks would have used the "straightforward Hicks" route, had the police in, had the students charged with trespass, and had them carted off with a fair amount of fuss and notoriety. MacKay's injunction route was much better, quieter, more effective, with the final responsibility for the action resting on the court. Sheriff's deputies came to Dalhousie, not police. Hicks admitted that MacKay's mode was superior. But in general his appreciation of MacKay lacked substance, as if disliking routines himself, Hicks dismissed too easily the qualities in others required to master and sustain them. He was not mean-spirited or ungenerous; rather he was self-centred, its quality genial, confident, pervasive. Thus he did not fully grasp the persistence, the indefatigability that MacKay's many duties entailed; Hicks's presidency owed much more to W.A. MacKay than he realized. If the Dalhousie presidency in 1980 was the reward for eleven years of faithful, intelligent, unremitting service, then MacKay well deserved it.

The style of the Dalhousie governance changed that autumn of 1980, in some respects much for the better – serious, careful, competent, decent. Swashbuckling it was not. It remained for the new president to pick up the pieces left by Hicks's seventeen years of building, to begin to pay off the deficits accumulated, the wages of Henry Hicks's salad days when everything was possible.

From 1925 to 1980 Dalhousie, like most other universities, went through changes that none could have anticipated. The Dalhousie of 1980 would have been unrecognizable to the graduate of 1925, in manners, morals, dress, perhaps even university standards. In 1925 2 per cent of the 18–24 age group across Canada were going to university; by 1980 it was 14 per cent. The selection of students was very much broader, their aims were both shallower and more professional. The idea of liberal education on which the old BA (and B.SC.) had been built had almost disappeared. First-class students in 1925 and in 1980 would recognize each other, but the second-class ones might not, for the modern Dalhousie comprehended a much larger segment of society than in 1925.

A few traditions persisted; one was trying to keep up with the best even if at times having little more than human resources to go on. That was Nova Scotian and Scottish, trying to do well with not much, not always realizing how good, and occasionally how mediocre, the result was. In 1949 J. McGregor Stewart, laying the cornerstone of the Arts and Administration Bulding, extolled the virtues of poverty and hard work; that was from his student life forty years before, from Dalhousie's hard curriculum of classics and mathematics. Vestiges remained too of old Dalhousie's decency and of the "genial anarchy" that R.A. MacKay noted for Arthur Lower in 1938. It was an informality sometimes helpful to administrators; perhaps because their rule had always sat rather lightly, it gave them room for manoeuvre, allowed them to reward favourites. In short, as Denis Stairs observed, the same problems did not always receive the same solutions. This was apt to baffle faculty new to Dalhousie, some of whom felt they were victims of a culture they could not fathom. They were the ones who rejoiced in the new mechanisms that came with faculty certification in 1978. Nevertheless, something of the old style still held and it gave the big university, even in 1980, an ambience not without charm and intellectual vivacity.[34]

Dalhousie was lucky in finding outside support that strengthened its graduate programs as well as its cultural base. Substantial money came from three widows, none of them Canadian and all very different: a Jewish immigrant from Galicia who had once owned some not too savoury (though respectable) houses down on Jacob Street (Rebecca Cohn); a Cypriot tobacco dealer's daughter from South London who had gone to Roedean (Lady Dunn); and a rich man's daughter from St Louis, Missouri, Dorothy Johnston, who at the age of twenty-two decided she was going to marry Izaak Walton Killam.

Something of Dalhousie had always been recorded in its students' poetry, some of it certainly noisy and crude; but occasionally the

Gazette printed a poem that caught at the evanescence of life and appearances, a metamorphosis of a present passing, a triumph of the student's mind and Dalhousie's civilizing.[35] David Wegenast's "Les Feuilles" about the Student Union foyer in late October with its sale of prints:

Cézanne Japan Monet
  and the jostling crowd
gai

      pastiche of thick coats, scarves
        milling rosy-cheeked around the
          stalls

        Dehors, les feuilles s'envolent
         en pleine couleur

         A door swings open in the wind
           and all are swirled away
             like summer balloons

             Now for the white walls of winter
             we hang prints of summer art
             as these dry leaves, pressed in the
             catalogue.

Statistical Appendix

TABLE I
DALHOUSIE UNIVERSITY HISTORICAL ENROLMENT FIGURES* FOR 1925–6 TO 1959–60

Academic year	Faculty							Total	Part-time only	By Gender		
	Arts & Science	King's	Law	Medicine	Dentistry	Graduate Studies	Health Professions			Male	Female	Total
1925–26	508	48	43	113	20			730				
1926–27	512	48	40	119	29			748				
1927–28	557	67	36	133	30			823				
1928–29	603	60	42	127	37			869				
1929–30	638	68	42	147	30			925				
1930–31	632	82	58	171	27			970				
1931–32	680	73	64	176	22			1015				
1932–33	618	66	70	164	21			939				
1933–34	563	70	77	183	33			926				
1934–35	493	65	74	175	39			846				
1935–36	518	53	78	186	53			888				
1936–37	478	61	74	207	52			872				
1937–38	463	50	75	211	47			846				
1938–39	374	191	91	215	37			908	27	712	196	908
1939–40	369	205	73	221	36			904	53	694	210	904
1940–41	314	195	50	220	31			810	44	610	200	810
1941–42	260	145	40	206	25			676	25	524	152	676
1942–43	321	131	29	209	25			715	16	575	140	715
1943–44	283	153	23	173	22			654	25	489	165	654
1944–45	294	185	33	170	29			711	39	513	198	711

1945–46	625	224	106	171	27			1153	64	918	235	1153
1946–47	1022	244	173	232	38			1709	72	1446	263	1709
1947–48	1117	256	212	251	37			1873	62	1596	277	1873
1948–49	1006	254	200	269	41			1770	52	1492	278	1770
1949–50	1041	124	184	279	48			1676	52	1365	311	1676
1950–51	893	102	167	283	48	60		1553	43	1235	318	1553
1951–52	812	94	156	272	49	59		1442	35	1147	295	1442
1952–53	818	83	130	274	50	58		1413	42	1074	339	1413
1953–54	812	75	147	266	50	59		1409	24	1074	335	1409
1954–55	815	92	164	266	48	56		1441	43	1098	343	1441
1955–56	825	105	163	266	47	59		1465	51	1126	339	1465
1956–57	874	104	182	274	47	60		1541	not avail.	1177	364	1541
1957–58	894	112	153	279	53	64	53	1608	85	1217	391	1608
1958–59	962	106	131	272	55	115	59	1700	100	1285	415	1700
1959–60	1058	136	115	267	60	123	70	1829	137	1331	498	1829

Note: Medicine includes Post-graduate Medicine

Dentistry includes Dental Hygiene

Part-time enrolments are included in the enrolments by faculty

Part-time figures and breakdowns by gender are not available prior to 1938–9.

* These tables have been prepared by Lynn MacDonald, of Dalhousie's Office of the Registrar.

TABLE 2
DALHOUSIE UNIVERSITY HISTORICAL ENROLMENT FIGURES FOR 1960–1 TO 1969–70

Academic year		Faculty								By Gender		
		Arts & Science	King's	Law	Medicine	Dentistry	Graduate Studies	Health Professions	Total	Male	Female	Total
1960–1	FT	1119	182	103	320	53	71	84	1932			
	PT								143			
	Total								2075	1511	564	2075
1961–2	FT	1240	186	106	312	68	88	121	2121			
	PT								137			
	Total								2258	1632	626	2258
1962–3	FT	1375	219	110	339	85	124	129	2381			
	PT								213			
	Total								2594	1868	726	2594
1963–4	FT	1566	184	124	340	100	166	219	2699			
	PT								182			
	Total								2881	2008	873	2881
1964–5	FT	1781	251	154	395	106	235	287	3209			
	PT								186			
	Total								3395	2303	1092	3395
1965–6	FT	1885	276	175	398	117	317	317	3485			
	PT								216			
	Total								3701	2430	1271	3701

									Total			
1966–7	FT	1770	242	214	410	118	359	338	3451			
	PT								268			
	Total								3719	2444	1275	3719
1967–8	FT	1767	201	244	449	120	490	384	3655			
	PT								309			
	Total								3964	2588	1376	3964
1968–9	FT	2049	192	284	483	121	501	448	4078			
	PT								490			
	Total								4568	2953	1615	4568
1969–70	FT	2515	242	308	590	131	710	577	5073			
	PT	277	6	1	0	0	254	22	560			
	Total	2792	248	309	590	131	964	599	5633	3277	2356	5633

Note: Part-time enrolments by faculty are unavailable from 1960–1 to 1968–9.

TABLE 3
DALHOUSIE UNIVERSITY (INCLUDING KING'S) REGISTERED STUDENTS FROM 1970 TO 1980
(AT 1 DECEMBER) BY FACULTY

Academic year		Arts & Science	Law	Medicine	Dentistry	Health Professions	Graduate Studies	Admin. Studies	King's	Grand Total
						Faculty				
1970–1	FT	2984	346	635	133	673	774		269	5814
	PT	452	1	0		59	263		14	789
	Total	3436	347	635	133	732	1037		283	6603
1971–2	FT	3456	374	633	138	725	777		247	6350
	PT	554	1	0	0	101	253		11	920
	Total	4010	375	633	138	826	1030		258	7270
1972–3	FT	3409	397	676	141	730	715		236	6304
	PT	638	5	0	0	149	227		12	1031
	Total	4047	402	676	141	879	942		248	7335
1973–4	FT	3363	433	701	141	780	759		247	6424
	PT	770	3	1	1	62	272		11	1120
	Total	4133	436	702	142	842	1031		258	7544
1974–5	FT	3885	435	722	140	785	818		258	7043
	PT	967	7	1	0	98	320		11	1404
	Total	4852	442	723	140	883	1138		269	8447

Year										
1975–6	FT	3522	432	726	145	815	885	556	320	7401
	PT	812	5	1	0	80	305	61	8	1272
	Total	4334	437	727	145	895	1190	617	328	8673
1976–7	FT	3488	430	705	146	828	962	637	339	7535
	PT	839	3	1	0	92	333	100	7	1375
	Total	4327	433	706	146	920	1295	737	346	8910
1977–8	FT	3347	435	713	143	878	988	711	343	7558
	PT	776	5	0	0	70	374	163	11	1399
	Total	4123	440	713	143	948	1362	874	354	8957
1978–9	FT	3207	432	707	141	871	961	694	349	7362
	PT	732	6	2	0	84	450	298	15	1587
	Total	3939	438	709	141	955	1411	992	364	8949
1979–80	FT	3061	418	706	142	898	947	791	370	7333
	PT	662	3	1	0	72	494	283	16	1531
	Total	3723	421	707	142	970	1441	1074	386	8864
1980–1	FT	3047	425	729	138	927	921	885	371	7443
	PT	689	3	0	0	73	483	312	15	1575
	Total	3736	428	729	138	1000	1404	1197	386	9018

TABLE 4

DALHOUSIE UNIVERSITY HISTORICAL ENROLMENT
FIGURES BY GENDER FOR 1970–1 TO 1980–1
(AT 1 DECEMBER)

Academic year	Dalhousie		King's		Total		Grand Total
	Male	Female	Male	Female	Male	Female	
1970–1	4048	2272	144	139	4192	2411	6603
1971–2	4424	2588	141	117	4565	2705	7270
1972–3	3942	2126	not available				7335
	(full-time only)						
1973–4*	4474	2812	138	120	4612	2932	7544
1974–5	4888	3290	134	135	5022	3425	8447
1975–6			not available		5116	3557	8673
1976–7			not available		5216	3694	8910
1977–8	4930	3673	179	175	5109	3848	8957
1978–9	4723	3862	171	193	4894	4055	8949
1979–80	4591	3887	192	194	4783	4081	8864
1980–1	4548	4084	202	184	4750	4268	9018

* 1973–4 figures for Dalhousie are estimated using percentages from figures at year end, by gender.

TABLE 5
DALHOUSIE UNIVERSITY REGISTERED FULL-TIME STUDENTS FROM 1970 TO 1980 (AT 1 DECEMBER) BY PERMANENT RESIDENCE

Permanent Residence*	Academic Year										
	1970–1	1971–2	1972–3	1973–4	1974–5‡	1975–6	1976–7	1977–8	1978–9	1979–80	1980–1
Nova Scotia	3853	4346	4256	4656		5168	5048	4939	4671	4712	4860
New Brunswick	470	534	572	578		834	912	954	973	991	941
Prince Edward Island	157	163	182	190		241	258	259	256	249	260
Newfoundland	176	162	132	116		103	101	106	114	127	142
Quebec	125	140	122	111		115	121	164	137	124	121
Ontario	263	289	314	292		397	408	403	392	331	348
Other Canada	97	119	137	138		93	199	205	194	196	228
USA	104	113	121	110		151	117	106	97	97	97
Abroad†	300	237	232	173		274	371	422	528	506	445
Not reported				60		25	0	0	0	0	1
Total	5545	6103	6068	6424	N/A	7401	7535	7558	7362	7333	7443

* Distributions by permanent residence for 1970 to 1972 do not include King's.
† Includes all countries except United States and Canada.
‡ Distribution by permanent residence for 1974 is not available.

Bibliographic Essay

This essay describes the main sources of Dalhousie history, primary and secondary; it does not pretend to cover all the sources mentioned in the notes that follow. The main sources for Dalhousie's history, 1925–80, are in a way patent: Board of Governors' Minutes (cited as BOG Minutes), Senate Minutes, and those of the several faculties. They have disadvantages; they are as a rule the bare bones of what went on, rarely the whys and wherefores.

To get behind the scenes one needs correspondence. When President Kerr retired in 1963, his successor, Henry Hicks, got Kerr's secretary, Miss Lola Henry (1903–) to spend some months organizing the Dalhousie presidential files. Miss Henry had worked briefly for President A.S. MacKenzie, was secretary to Carleton Stanley and to A.E. Kerr. She knew more about the presidential files than anyone. She put together what is called here and in the Dalhousie University Archives (DUA) The President's Office Correspondence (POC), housed in forty-three large boxes. This correspondence is indispensable for Dalhousie history from 1911 to 1963. Citations to it are marked POC, A-101 and so to A-1070. "Acadia University, 1921–1963" is, for example, POC, A-102 and A-103.

Between 1963 to 1980 Henry Hicks kept his own set of files which are now housed in thirty-four equally large boxes at DUA. They were put together after his retirement in 1980 and are quite comprehensive. The files are in alphabetical order, and citations to them are in the form, POC, HDH, box 1, and so on to box 34. Only a few files go back beyond 1963, though for some reason Psychology does. It is cited as POC, HDH, box 21, Faculty of Arts and Science, Psychology.

Carleton Stanley kept personal papers beside his presidential ones and they are exceptional. Stanley was an excellent correspondent, wrote to colleagues on both sides of the Atlantic, his letters vivid, literary, lean and opinionated, the way he was. Lola Henry had the useful habit, before his letters went out, of checking whether there were any postscripts; if so, she would type them on the bottom of her carbon copy. Some of Stanley's most revealing asides are recorded in this way. Lola Henry much admired Carleton Stanley, but she found A.E. Kerr, his successor, a bore, and he was bad at dictation, being forever distracted by what he saw out the window. Kerr's letters were unusually flat and prosy, and Lola Henry made little effort to improve them. A.E. Kerr kept no personal papers, or apparently not. Kerr's Dalhousie papers are entirely subsumed within POC.

Henry Hicks's personal papers are not very useful, but his presidential ones are sufficiently comprehensive that there is almost no need to look elsewhere. One could say that with Hicks everything was personal. He also dictated letters with the speed of light, quick, vigorous, to the point, with rarely a look backwards.

A certain number of personal papers outside Dalhousie have significant Dalhousie material. The R.B. Bennett Papers at the University of New Brunswick have considerable Dalhousie correspondence, not surprising since Bennett was on the Dalhousie Board for almost two decades. There are Dalhousie letters in the Sidney Smith Papers at the University of Toronto Archives, and a substantial collection in the C.D. Howe Papers in the National Archives in Ottawa.

There are a number of collections of professors' papers at DUA, though none are as comprehensive as the MacMechan Papers, which run out after his death in 1933. H.L. Stewart's are preoccupied with publishing. And there are some papers that ought to be there that unfortunately are not. G.E. Wilson's papers, which must have comprehended a vast correspondence, were lost or more probably burnt after his death in 1974. His friend and colleague, J.G. Adshead, who died in 1979, seems to have left no papers. His diaries, rescued by Mrs Marion Cumming, are now at the Department of Mathematics at Dalhousie. There are a number of collections of professors' papers that are not yet open.

DUA has also extensive collections of faculty and departmental papers, most of which I have not found it possible to canvass in any detail. There are some useful departmental histories, most of which are cited in the notes, for Chemistry, Geology, Mathematics, Psychology, Medicine (department of, not faculty), Obstetrics and Gynaecology, Pharmacology. There is a good history of the Faculty of Dentistry, Oskar Sykora's *Maritime Dental College and Dalhousie Faculty of Dentistry: A History* (Halifax 1991), and a superb one of the Faculty of Law, John Willis's *A History of Dalhousie Law School* (Toronto 1979). A recent and valuable addition is R. St J. Macdonald, ed., *Dalhousie Law School, 1965–1990: An Oral History* (Halifax 1996).

A most refreshing and fruitful source has been interviews with Dalhousie colleagues, alumni, and alumnae. These are all cited as interviews and if outside of Halifax, the place where the interview was held. The word "interview," however, conceals considerable variation: some are quasi-formal hour-long interviews; many are over lunch, some just gossip over drinks or coffee. All are recorded not by tape recorder but by notes that I made either at the time or as soon as possible afterward. Tape recorders stiffen people's minds, or they did as a rule with the people that I was interviewing. They are also formal and cumbersome.

The most important source for student life is of course the *Dalhousie Gazette*. Decade by decade from 1925 it gradually becomes less stylish, less obviously literary; in the raucous days of 1968–70 the *Gazette* is a lonely voice, a bittern crying its radicalism in a wilderness of its own making. From 1925 to 1964 it is not difficult to find quotable and intelligent poetry in the *Gazette*. Then for a decade it becomes more difficult. About 1973 the literary touches are gradually picked up again. For student news and events on campus the *Gazette* can sometimes be vulgar and tasteless, but one still needs it, and some events on campus after 1973, such as the great Dalplex controversy, it covered quite well.

In 1970, simply because the *Gazette* no longer gave regular campus news, the university itself established *University News* which came to appear weekly during term time. It gave reasonably dispassionate coverage of university affairs and needs to be used in the 1970s to supplement the *Gazette*.

What historians call secondary sources – that is books or articles about Dalhousie or Dalhousie people, as opposed to those written by them – there are some important ones. For political background, Murray Beck's *Politics of Nova Scotia: Volume Two, Murray-Buchanan 1896–1988* (Tantallon 1988) is essential. David M. Cameron's *More than an Academic Question: Universities, Government, and Public Policy in Canada* (Halifax 1991) is indispensable for the history of government support, both provincial and federal, of universities in Canada from 1956 to 1990.

Of the several university histories, the most useful are John Reid's *Mount Allison University: Vol. II, 1914–1963* (Toronto 1984); Stanley Brice Frost's *McGill University: For the Advancement of Learning: Volume II, 1895–1961* (Kingston and Montreal 1983). James Cameron's new history of St Francis Xavier (Montreal 1996), came too late for me to use. One of the best of the modern university histories is A.B. McKillop's *Matters of Mind: The University in Ontario, 1791–1951* (Toronto 1994), though as the title suggests, it is only peripherally relevant to Dalhousie. Paul Axelrod's *Making a Middle Class: Student Life in English Canada during the Thirties* (Montreal 1990) is a fine example of how to make good social history of universities. It is analysis, readable and informative. John Reid's essay, "Beyond the Democratic Intellect: The Scottish Example and University Reform in Canada's Maritime Provinces, 1870–1933," is splendid, and ought to have been cited for volume 1 of Dalhousie's history as well. It is in Paul Axelrod and John G. Reid, *Youth, University and Canadian Society: Essays in the Social History of Higher Education* (Kingston and Montreal 1989), pp. 275–300.

There is no modern history of Halifax to take up where T.H. Raddall left off in *Halifax, Warden of the North* (Toronto 1949), which stops at the end of the Second World War. William March's *Red Line: The Chronicle-Herald and The Mail-Star, 1875–1954* (Halifax 1986) is useful for Halifax background.

Notes

INTRODUCTION

1 Boris Petrovich Babkin (1877–1950) left Dalhousie in 1928 to become McGill's research professor of physiology. His essay "How I came to Dalhousie" was written in 1934 and comes from the McGill University Archives. It was brought to my attention by Professor David Sutherland of Dalhousie, for whose perspicacity I am grateful.
2 The railway train story is reported in the Halifax *Morning Herald*, 2 Dec. 1878. The statistics are from M.C. Urquhart and K.A.H. Buckley, *Historical Statistics of Canada* (Toronto 1965) and from Paul Axelrod, *Making a Middle Class: Student Life in English Canada during the Thirties* (Montreal and Kingston 1990), pp. 8–9.
3 The argument is developed in Axelrod, *Making a Middle Class*, pp. 10–11.
4 A vivacious history of the changes is Frederick Lewis Allen, *Only Yesterday* (New York 1931). The issues of the Halifax *Chronicle* and *Herald* of the 1920s and 1930s are deliciously instructive. The *Chronicle* in June 1932 has the Lifebuoy advertisements.
5 For Dalhousie's isolation, see John Willis, *A History of Dalhousie Law School* (Toronto 1979), p. 103.
6 See James L. Bennet, *Jim Bennet's Verse* (Halifax 1979), "I remember – Sometimes," reprinted here with the kind permission of Jim Bennet.
7 Halifax currency had become by 1820 a working standard and it gradually spread to the other British North American colonies. £1 Halifax currency equalled $4 American. Thus a shilling (£1=20 shillings) was the same as 20 cents. The Newfoundland 20-cent piece, still prevalent in 1949, is a remnant of this old system. The pound sterling was worth $4.86.
8 Dalhousie University Archives (DUA), Archibald MacMechan Papers, Private Journals, 28 Mar. 1922; 6 Apr. 1922.

1 DALHOUSIE IN THE 1920S

1 For the Flexner Report and its effects, see P.B. Waite, *The Lives of Dalhousie University, Volume One, 1818–1925: Lord Dalhousie's College* (Montreal and Kingston 1994), pp. 202–4 (cited hereafter as *Lives of Dalhousie I*).

2 G.F. Pearson (1877–1938) graduated from Dalhousie in 1900. He was twice married, to Ethel Miller in 1900 and after her death to Agnes Crawford in 1913. See Alvin F. MacDonald, "In Memoriam," *Alumni News*, Nov. 1938.

3 There is a curious story about Mackenzie's widowerhood that ought to be recorded. When his wife was dying she is reported to have said to him as prophecy, "You will never marry again." This comes from Murray Macneill via his daughter, Janet Macneill Piers ('43), interview, Chester, NS, 17 Sept. 1992. For two retrospective views of MacKenzie, see *Alumni News*, Nov. 1938, J.H.L. Johnstone, "MacKenzie – the Teacher," and G.H. Anderson, "MacKenzie – the Scientist."

MacKenzie's chiding of MacMechan is in DUA, staff files 312, "Archibald MacMechan," A.S. MacKenzie (hereafter ASM) to MacMechan, 19 Dec. 1923.

4 MacMechan once described Macneill as "that Ferocious Registrar," staff files 312, MacMechan to ASM, 9 July 1919, from Windsor NS.

In the Macneill family papers there is a letter from Lucy Maud Montgomery in 1908 explaining how she has just begun work on the successor to *Anne of Green Gables*. Interview with Janet Macneill Piers, 17 Sept. 1992.

Macneill's account of his life at the Sorbonne in Paris is in *Dalhousie Gazette*, 3 Mar. 1899.

5 For Covert on Macneill, see Harry Bruce, "The lion in summer remembers Dal," *Dalhousie Alumni Magazine* 1, no. 1 (Fall 1984), p. 15; for John Fisher, transcript of his CBC broadcast of 11 Mar. 1951, in staff files 315, "Murray Macneill."

6 *Dalhousie Gazette*, 9 Oct. 1930, letter by T.A. Goudge ('31) on Howard Murray; see also staff files 353, "Howard Murray"; Andrew C. Hebb ('25, '28) to PBW, 14 Dec. 1990, from Toronto. Mr Hebb's reminiscences are of unusual interest since he was editor of the *Dalhousie Gazette* from 1926 to 1927.

7 On Archie MacMechan the best essay is by G.G. Sedgewick ('03), "A.M." in *Dalhousie Review* XIII, no. 4 (1933–4), pp. 451–8; also Andrew C. Hebb's letter, cited above; Eileen Burns ('22, '24) gave me the story of "perspirers," interview, 20 Aug. 1990; MacMechan's views are also noted in the *Dalhousie Gazette*, 22 Feb. 1916.

8 George Wilson gave me the description of Dawson, and also the story of Sidney Smith and the bicycle, the latter confirmed in interview with Beatrice R.E. Smith, 31 May 1988.

9 DUA, President's Office Correspondence (hereafter POC), A-489, "*Dalhousie Review*, 1920–1933," D. Macgillivray to ASM, 23 Dec. 1920; memorandum of same date; circular, Howard Murray to Dalhousie alumni and alumnae, 24 Mar. 1921.

The original incorporators of the *Review* were Macgillivray, Pearson, I.C. Stewart, and J.S. Roper. Capital was $5,000 with two hundred shares. Fifty shares were held by the board, others were bought slowly over the next decade by governors, alumni, and professors, and in due course ended in estates. The first print run of 1921 was 7,100 but that was too ambitious; in the 1920s subscribers averaged 2,500. This information is in the R.B. Bennett Papers in the University of New Brunswick Archives, vol. 908, nos. 569318–22, "History of the Dalhousie Review," dated 27 Feb. 1936.

The limerick comes from Henry D. Hicks to whom Stewart told it; interview with Henry D. Hicks, 8 July 1988.

Of Stewart's carelessness with lectures the stories are legion. The 1919 incident
is in POC, A-542 "Philosophy 1915–1955," H.L. Stewart to ASM, 4 Oct. [1919].
There was another incident in 1921 about his being late for classes, about which
Stewart wrote President MacKenzie, "The eagerness of the [Registrar's] Office to
report – or invent – charges of negligence on my part is not new to me." A-542,
H.L. Stewart to ASM, 19 Oct. 1919. George Wilson, dean of arts and science
1945–55, used to say that students in Stewart's philosophy classes claimed they
could use the notes made by their mothers or fathers, jokes and all.

10 Staff files 10, "H.B. Atlee," Atlee to ASM, 11 Apr. 1920. See Harry Oxorn, *H.B.
Atlee, M.D.* (Hantsport 1983), pp. 11–36. This biography has been criticized as
unfair to Atlee by a fine Dalhousie surgeon; interview with Dr Edwin Ross,
19 June 1989. It is at time brutally frank, that can indeed be said. Whether the
result is a balanced portrait is an open question. It is badly proofread and has no
index, but vigorous it certainly is.

11 Halifax *Mail*, 26 Sept. 1922; staff files 10, Atlee to ASM, 11 Oct. 1922; ASM to
Atlee, 7 Nov. 1922; Dr Comyns Berkeley to ASM, 27 June 1923; *Halifax Herald*,
13 Apr. 1923.

12 Oxorn, *Atlee*, pp. 40–1, 275–5; Carl Tupper, "Atlee," in *Nova Scotia Medical
Bulletin* (Dec. 1978), pp. 161–3. There is an extensive bibliography of Atlee's
writings in Oxorn, *Atlee*, pp. 345–52.

13 Oxorn, *Atlee*, pp. 276–7; H.B. Atlee, *The Gist of Obstetrics* (Springfield 1957),
p. 24.

14 POC, A-574, "Medical Faculty, 1921–1931," A.P. Colwell to ASM, 4 Nov. 1925;
also Halifax *Mail*, 25 Nov. 1925.

15 Senate Minutes, 14 Apr., 11 May 1908. A new history of dentistry at Dalhousie
has been a great help. See Oskar Sykora, *The Maritime Dental College and the
Dalhousie Faculty of Dentistry: A History* (Halifax 1991), pp. 26–39.

16 *Dalhousie Gazette*, 29 Mar. 1922; POC, A-364, "Carnegie Fund for the Advancement of Teaching, 1918–1922," ASM to Learned, 11 Feb. 1922; Board of Governors (BOG) Minutes, 28 Apr. 1922; Sykora, *Dalhousie Dentistry*, pp. 69–70.

17 *Dalhousie Gazette*, 1 Nov. 1922; for student statistics, see *Annual Report of the
President*, especially for 1911–12 and 1924–5.

18 *Dalhousie Gazette*, 8 Nov. 1922; Senate Minutes, 16 Jan. 1923.

19 *Dalhousie Gazette*, 31 Jan., 14 Feb. 1923; POC, A-968 "Student Publications,
1921–1931," ASM, "A Parting Word to the Class of 1924." On the university
year, see Senate Minutes, 20 Oct., 11 Nov., 14 Dec. 1922.

20 Senate Minutes, 9 Jan. 1923. There was a further three-hour debate on dances on
20 Jan., which ended with the rules virtually unchanged.

21 For Rex cigarettes, *Gazette*, 9 Mar. 1928; for the jokes, 18 Oct., 18 Nov. 1922.

22 Staff files, 275, "Margaret Lowe," ASM to Margaret Lowe, 29 June 1923, telegram; Margaret Lowe to ASM, 1 May 1930; *Dalhousie Gazette*, 15 Oct. 1924;
Halifax *Morning Chronicle*, 10 Aug. 1921, reporting Mrs Eddy's speech to Dalhousie students of October 1920.

23 POC, A-493, "Frank Darling, 1911–1920," ASM to Darling, 18 July 1919, telegram; A-494, "Frank Darling, 1920–1923," ASM to C. Thetford, 20 Dec. 1921;
A-148, "R.B. Bennett, 1912–1928," Bennett to ASM, 28 Apr. 1922, from Win-

nipeg; Bennett to ASM, n.d. but probably 11 Dec. 1922 from Montreal en route to England.

24 Ibid., ASM to Bennett, at Calgary, 17 Oct. 1923; *Dalhousie Gazette*, 2 Apr. 1924.

25 *Dalhousie Gazette*, 14 Jan. 1925; the comment on bobbed hair, 3 Dec. 1924.

26 POC, A-228, "President's Residence 1924–1959," Campbell to ASM, 9 Oct. 1924 from Calgary; Bennett to Campbell, 10 June 1925, letter and telegram; Campbell to ASM, 11 June 1925, telegram to Ottawa.

27 POC, A-389, "Committee of Nine, 1926–1935," Campbell's memo. The committee originated in a letter from the Alumni Association commenting on some lack of cordiality between students and staff. Campbell believed the Alumni could act as a cementing body between students and staff, hence the three Alumni members of the committee.

28 Senate Minutes, 4 May 1925; *Dalhousie Gazette*, 4 Feb. 1926. For the information of the Students' Council of 1912, see *Lives of Dalhousie*, I, p. 372.

On professors who found it difficult to stop their lectures on time, see *Dalhousie Gazette*, 25 Nov. 1925 and 28 Jan. 1926 when it was the subject of an editorial. On library hours, see ibid., 11 Mar. 1926; the hard-hitting editorial is 4 Nov. 1926. The consequences are described by A.O. Hebb, 16 Jan. 1991; his three letters of reminiscences to PBW, 14 Dec. 1990, 16 Jan. and 20 Feb. 1991 have been most useful.

29 *Dalhousie Gazette*, 4, 11 Mar. 1926; POC, A-968 "Student Publications, 1921–1931," David Soloan to ASM, 17 Mar. 1926; ASM to Soloan, 22 Mar. 1926.

30 A.O. Hebb to PBW, 16 Jan. 1991; *Dalhousie Gazette*, 13, 27 Jan. 1927; the poem is ibid., 11 Jan. 1929.

31 For obituaries of Campbell, ibid., 25 Nov. 1927.

32 BOG Minutes, 8 Oct. 1929. Dalhousie's financial statements and questionnaire answers prepared for John Price Jones give an useful perspective of Dalhousie finances in 1929. They are in UNB Archives, R.B. Bennett Papers, vol. 907, nos. 568770–7. The National Archives of Canada (NA) has microfilms of the UNB collection. R.B. Bennett was appointed to the Dalhousie board in July 1920 and attended his first meeting on 28 March 1922.

33 The proportion of mortgages in Dalhousie's portfolio was changing. In June 1929 it had been 19 per cent; the board's finance committee felt that was too high, and while no money had ever been lost on Dalhousie's mortgages, one or two big ones were renegotiated that summer and the proceeds reinvested in government bonds. BOG Minutes, 8 Oct. 1929.

2 CHANGING THE GUARD

1 For the Gowanloch affair at Dalhousie and the Symons at King's, see Henry Roper, "Two Scandals in Academe," *Collections*, Royal Nova Scotia Historical Society, vol. 43 (1991), pp. 127–45. The story of Gowanloch's lecture in full evening clothes is given by Constance McFarlane (BA '29, MSc '32), interview, 25 June 1989. The most important archival source is DUA, staff files 165, "James Nelson Gowanloch." Letters about his bills occur in 1923, 1924, and especially 1930. His essay is in *Dalhousie Gazette*, 9 Nov. 1928; the banquet, with a picture

of him, is in the *Gazette*, 23 Nov. 1928. For his sonnet, see *Dalhousie Review* 9 (1929–30), p. 100. Reference to his broadcasts is in *Dalhousie Gazette*, 18 Jan. 1929. His example was followed in 1929 by what were called university extension lectures by President MacKenzie, on Maritime provinces' scientific research, and by Archibald MacMechan on recent developments in Nova Scotian literature.

2 Staff files 165, Memo for the President, 20 Mar. 1930, by G.F. Pearson. The description of Eleanor is from Mrs Phyllis Skeen Ross, who was at Shirreff Hall at the time, interview in Halifax, 19 June 1989. "Picked chicken" was a Bermuda expression for someone who was scrawny and scraggly, perhaps with a few feathers missing.

3 Staff files 165, a long memorandum of seven pages written about 18 Mar. 1930 by Margaret Lowe. The story about Eleanor's father coming to town with a gun was told to me by Professor George Wilson in the 1950s.

4 DUA, Archibald MacMechan Papers, Journals, 24 Mar. 1930; BOG Minutes, 19 Mar. 1930; 2 May 1930. See Roper, "Two Scandals," pp. 140–2.

5 Senate Minutes, 17 Apr., 14 May 1930; MacMechan Journals, same dates; Senate Minutes, 9 Oct. 1930; Eleanor's *Sponsio Academica* is in DUA, Dalhousie graduation records, signed in Hantsport, 24 Oct. 1930.

6 MacMechan Journals, 12 May 1930. MacMechan here refers to Thomas Gray, the author of "Elegy Written in a Country Churchyard"; the poem quoted from is "Ode on a Distant Prospect of Eton College."

7 Staff files 353, "Howard Murray." Janet Murray was left with a very small income and would need the widow's pension for which MacKenzie solicited the Carnegie Corporation, 16 Sept. 1930.

8 MacMechan Journals, 2 Jan., 30 May 1930; staff files 312, "Archibald MacMechan," ASM to Walter C. Murray, 1 Dec. 1927. Murray was president of the University of Saskatchewan from 1908 to 1937 and former Munro professor of philosophy at Dalhousie.

9 MacMechan Journals, 23 Oct. 1930; staff files 312, "Archibald MacMechan," MacMechan to ASM, 29 Dec. 1930; MacMechan Papers, *c.* 1930, W.E. Thompson to MacMechan, 27 Jan. 1931; BOG Minutes, 10 Jan. 1931.

10 BOG Minutes, 8 Oct. 1929; MacMechan Journals, 8 Nov. 1929. MacMechan had three daughters, all of whom were married. For C.L. Bennet, see Helene Sandford Bennet, *Back in the Days, A Reminiscence* (privately printed 1987), lent to me through the kindness of Mrs Bennet and her son Jim.

11 MacMechan Papers, C-655, ASM to MacMechan, 29 Dec. 1930; BOG Minutes, 2 Dec. 1930; DUA, A.S. MacKenzie Papers, G.E. Wilson to ASM, 3 Dec. 1930; J.C. Tory to ASM, 4 Dec. 1930; Sidney Smith to ASM, 3 Dec. 1930.

12 MacKenzie's reply to Smith is in University of Toronto Archives, Sidney Smith Papers, vol. 13, MacKenzie to Smith, 2 Jan. 1931. Mackenzie's speech in honour of R.B. Bennett was on 9 Mar. 1929, reported in *Dalhousie Gazette*, 16 Mar. 1929.

13 POC, A-252, "Shirreff Hall," E. Margaret Lowe to the president, General Report, 30 June 1930.

14 See the *Gazette* editorial in its Christmas issue, 3 Dec. 1930, "The Social Whirl." The poem is by Florence Brewster in *Dalhousie Gazette*, 7 Dec. 1928. For exami-

nation results, see ibid., 14 Jan. 1931. Yale is noticed in ibid., 5 Nov. 1931. The Dalhousie calendar was specific, that if students failed at Christmas in more than two-thirds of their classes (i.e., four classes) that "they shall be advised and, in extreme cases, may be required to discontinue attendance at the University for the remainder of the session."

15 Ibid., 29 Oct. 1930.

16 Staff files 275, "Margaret Lowe," Lowe to ASM, 1 May 1930; ibid., 381, "Dixie Pelluet," Pelluet to ASM, 15 June 1930, from New York; ASM to Pelluet, 18, 19 June 1930, telegrams; Pelluet to ASM, 18 June 1930, telegram; ASM to W.A. Maddox, 23 June 1930; Maddox to ASM, 27 June 1930; ASM to Pelluet, 3 July 1930.

17 POC, A-707, "King's 1925–1930," A.H. Moore to ASM, 23 Dec. 1925; W.E. Thompson to Moore, 8 Jan., 5 Feb. 1926; same, 14 Oct. 1928, reply to Moore's of 12 May.

18 BOG Minutes, 4 July, 30 Oct., 2 Dec. 1930.

19 POC, A-851, "Public Archives of Nova Scotia, 1924–1930," Edgar Rhodes to J.C. Webster, 10 Jan. 1929 (copy); Webster to G.F. Pearson, 3 Feb. 1929, from Shediac; Rhodes to G.F. Pearson, 22 Feb. 1929. The reminiscence of D.C. Harvey I owe to Miss Shirley Elliott, 11 Mar. 1992.

20 BOG Minutes, 7 May, 17 July, 8 Sept. 1931. Rumour of arson was suggested by Dr Charles Armour, Dalhousie university archivist, 2 Nov. 1992.

21 BOG Minutes, 30 Jan., 3 Mar. 1931.

22 PBW Archive, Murray Macneill, "Memoirs," dated 7 Nov. 1934, p. 9. A copy is in the Dalhousie Archives. Both are owing to the kindness of Mrs Janet Macneill Piers. For Sidney Smith, see Sidney Smith Papers, vol. 13, C.J. Burchell to John W. Dafoe, 28 Apr. 1934. Burchell added, with the benefit of three years' hindsight, "Smith was a thousand times the better man [than the president Dalhousie did choose]."

23 BOG Minutes, 2 June 1931. For Stanley's reaction, and his father-in-law's, see DUA, MS-2-163, Carleton Stanley Papers, W.J. Alexander to Stanley, 23 Oct., 30 Nov. 1930; 3, 5 May 1931; McGill University Archives, RG2, C43, F. Cyril James Papers, file 315, James to B.K. Sandwell, of *Saturday Night*, 27 Feb. 1945; ibid., summary of file on Carleton Stanley as assistant to the principal, by Currie's private secretary, Mrs Dorothy MacMurray, formerly of Halifax. There is no date on this summary but it was probably compiled in March 1945, as a result of an article in *Saturday Night*, 24 Feb. 1945. The article alleged that Carleton Stanley, out of loyalty to Dalhousie, had refused the offer of the principalship of McGill in 1933, which Mrs MacMurray said was untrue.

24 For Currie, see Stanley Brice Frost, *McGill University: For the Advancement of Learning: Volume II, 1895–1971* (Kingston and Montreal 1984), pp. 131–6; A.M.J. Hyatt, *General Sir Arthur Currie* (Toronto 1987), pp. 142–3. For the advantages of living in Halifax, see DUA, Carleton Stanley Papers (CS Papers), W.J. Alexander to CS, 5 May 1931.

25 CS Papers, B-12, CS to Pearson, 1, 6 May 1931; drafts; Pearson to CS, 4 May 1931; B-15, CS to Bill [W.D. Herridge], 8 June 1931, to Washington (copy).

26 A.S. MacKenzie Papers, MacKenzie to Murray, 23 May 1931; Murray to MacKenzie, 27 May 1931, from Montreal.

27 CS Papers, B-15, CS to Herridge (copy), 8 June 1931; UNB Archives, R.B. Bennett Papers, vol. 907, no. 568828, G. Fred Pearson to Bennett, 16 June 1931, telegram; A.S. MacKenzie Papers, box 1, Murray Macneill to ASM, 19 June 1931, from Montreal; ASM to Macneill, 23 June 1931, radiogram; Macneill to ASM, 23 June 1931.

28 CS Papers, B-15, Pearson to CS, 24 July 1931.

29 Ibid., B-47, CS to Mrs Sylvia Ross, Bangor, Maine, 1 Feb. 1939. The account of Stanley's early life comes from his daughter, Mrs Laura Woolner, "Memories of My Father"; also Mrs Woolner to PBW, 8 Apr. 1992.

30 POC, A-736, "Dugald Macgillivray, 1926–1938," CS to Macgillivray, 24 Nov. 1931. Macgillivray (1862–1937) was formerly superintendent of the Maritime and Newfoundland branches of the Canadian Bank of Commerce, and after retirement became general manager of the Eastern Trust. Interviews with Lola Henry, 19 Jan. 1988; 18 Apr. 1990.

31 CS Papers, B-34, CS to H.S. Ross, Montreal, 20 Apr. 1936. The quotation is from act 1, scene 1 of Le Misanthrope (my translation). The wise friend was not identified. CS Papers, B-18, CS to A.K. Maclean (on the Exchequer Court of Canada), n.d., but c. 20 Oct. 1931.

32 Interview with Beatrice R.E. Smith, 10 June 1988.

33 Statements relating to the incumbency of Carleton W. Stanley, President of Dalhousie University, submitted to the Board of Governors by G. Fred Pearson and by President Stanley (Halifax 1932), p. 1. This pamphlet was prepared by the board. The president is mentioned once in the 1863 Dalhousie Act, in section 4, and only to the effect that the governors have the right to appoint one.

34 Ibid., p. 2; Senate Minutes, 15 Oct. 1931. The Bennett correspondence is in R.B. Bennett Papers, vol. 907, no. 568880, Bennett to W.E. Thompson, 8 Sept. 1931, indicating he would try to come. Stanley's speech is reported in the Morning Chronicle, 10 Oct. 1931; Atlee's letter is in staff files 10, "H.B. Atlee," Atlee to CS, 19 Oct. 1932, a comment on Stanley's inauguration speech. For scholarships, see BOG Minutes, 29 Oct. 1931.

35 For a succinct and well-balanced modern history, see T.D. Regehr, The Beauharnois Scandal: A Story of Canadian Entrepreneurship and Politics (Toronto 1990), especially pp. 124, 136. Stanley's description of the circumstances is in CS Papers, B-17, CS to W.D. Herridge, 18 Jan. 1932, personal. Herridge was appointed Canadian ambassador to Washington in March 1931 by R.B. Bennett, and married Bennett's sister Mildred in April 1931. For Pearson's correspondence, see R.B. Bennett Papers, vol. 907, Bennett to W.E. Thompson, secretary of the BOG, 22 Mar., 1932; vol. 908, Pearson to Bennett, 6 Apr. 1932; Bennett to Pearson, 12 Apr. 1932 (two letters).

36 Alan Wilson, born and brought up in Dartmouth/Halifax, and his wife Budge Archibald Wilson have offered reflections on Fred Pearson and his friends. Alan Wilson to author, 11 Jan. 1996. Board pamphlet, pp. 2–3; POC, A-822, "G. Fred Pearson, 1919–1932," Pearson memorandum of interview with Stanley, 25 Mar. (sic, should be 24), 1932.

Many executive committee meetings of the board, and even occasionally full meetings, are unreported in the minutes, especially when delicate or difficult personal issues are discussed. Some Senate meetings the same; certainly the meeting of 24 Mar. has no minutes, though that it took place is attested by the J.G. Adshead diaries, now at the Dalhousie Mathematics Department, for 24 Mar. 1932.

37 Board pamphlet, p. 6; BOG Minutes, 10 June 1932; Stanley's reply is in board pamphlet, pp. 7–14; Pearson's rejoinder, pp. 14–17. Halifax *Chronicle*, 7, 8 June 1932.

38 CS Papers, B-22, J.M. Macdonnell to CS, 5 Aug. 1932, private and confidential.

39 Ibid., CS to Macdonnell, 15 Aug. 1932, a draft in CS's handwriting. Luther's words are the conclusion of his speech at the Diet of Worms, 18 Apr. 1521. The translation is: "God help me; I cannot do otherwise."

40 Archibald MacMechan Journals, Wednesday, 10 May 1933. CS Papers, B-15, Pearson to CS, 3 July 1931. Pearson did not put his quotation in limerick form, which I have done, but it is otherwise the same as he wrote it. He has taken only a few liberties with "There was a young lady of Riga." H.B. Atlee, "Dalhousie Medical School, 1907–1957," *Dalhousie Medical Journal* (1958), p. 33.

41 Archibald MacMechan Journals, Thursday, 22 June, Friday, 28 July 1933.

42 Ibid., Thursday, 22 June 1933; *Dalhousie Gazette*, 28 Sept. 1933.

43 R.B. Bennett Papers, vol. 908, no. 569346, Bennett to Hector McInnes, 20 May 1936; CS Papers, B-18, CS to Leslie R. Thomason, Montreal, 12 June 1932.

3 CARLETON STANLEY'S KINGDOM

1 For Hutchins's view, see Robert Hutchins, *The Higher Learning in America* (New Haven 1936), pp. 42–3.

2 MacMechan's criticism of Arts funding is in *Morning Chronicle*, 14 Sept. 1920, with supporting editorial comment.

3 F. Ronald Hayes, "Two Presidents, Two Cultures, and Two Wars: A Portrait of Dalhousie as a Microcosm of Twentieth-Century Canada," *Dalhousie Review* 54, no. 3 (Autumn 1974), pp. 405–17. Hayes was appointed to Dalhousie in place of Gowanloch in 1930; he saw something of MacKenzie's, and all of Stanley's and Kerr's presidencies.

4 Stanley's 1941 convocation address is in *President's Report*, 1940–1, p. 80.

5 The Arnold quotation is from the preface to Arnold's *Essay in Criticism First Series* (1865).

6 POC, A-102, "Acadia 1921–1963," CS to F.W. Patterson, 24 Apr. 1933; A-281, "Campaigns 1939," CS to W.N. Wickwire, 17 Dec. 1938; DUA, Faculty of Arts Minutes, 4, 19 Apr., 29 Sept. 1931; 18 Feb. 1932.

7 Arts Minutes, 6 Mar. 1934; POC, A-774, "Mount Allison University 1923–1945," Trueman to CS, 22 Mar. 1934. John Reid, *Mount Allison: A History, to 1963, vol. II: 1914–1963* (Toronto 1984), pp. 141–2, has a pertinent elaboration of this point. Officially accredited schools for Grade 11 and Grade 12, outside of Halifax, were Kentville, New Glasgow, Glace Bay, Yarmouth, and Pictou. Some others were accredited for Grade 11 only.

8 Arts Minutes, 4 Apr. 1933; POC, A-398, "Conference of Canadian Universities, 1936–1939," CS to R.H. Coats and J. Robbins of Dominion Bureau of Statistics, 23 Mar. 1937, private and confidential.

9 POC, A-384, "Professor Fred Clarke, 1931–1945," CS to Clarke, 29 Oct. 1934. Clarke was with the Department of Education, McGill University. A-173, "Board of Governors Correspondence," CS to Governors, 27 Oct. 1934, confidential, reporting conversation with C.C. Jones, 26 Oct. 1934.

10 A.J. Tingley has a brief, useful history, *Mathematics at Dalhousie* (1992).

11 For G.V. Douglas, see DUA, staff files 108, L.C. Graton, of Harvard Laboratory of Mining Geology to CS, 4 Dec. 1931. There is an excellent departmental history of geology by G.C. Milligan, who knew Douglas well, *On the Rocks: the Training of Geologists at Dalhousie* (Dalhousie 1995), pp. 26–34. Also interview with D.H. McNeill ('33), 6 Dec. 1995.

Stanley's idea about appointments is suggested in POC, A-384, "Professor Fred Clarke, 1931–1945," CS to Clarke, 26 Apr. 1935. For comments on the graduates of his father-in-law's time, see DUA, CS Papers, B-32, CS to Sir Edward Beatty, 15 Sept. 1935; B-40, CS to Chas. A. Maxwell, Salt Springs, Pictou County, 17 Dec. 1937.

12 Titus Lucretius Carus, *De Rerum Natura*, Book iv, lines 1, 133; Dalhousie University, *President's Report for the Year July 1st, 1933-June 30th, 1934*, pp. 5–6. On sending his son to Rothesay, Stanley wrote to Allan Gillingham, a Newfoundland Rhodes scholar then at New College, Oxford: "Halifax had become completely impossible. The teachers are illiterate women struggling with classes of fifty-five and sixty, even in high school grades." POC, A-647, "Allan Gillingham 1932-1944," CS to Gillingham, 19 June 1935. Gillingham became professor of classics and German as well as secretary of the faculty of Memorial College. See photograph no. 7 in Malcolm Macleod, *A Bridge Built Halfway: A History of Memorial University College, 1925–1950* (Montreal and Kingston 1990), after p. xvi.

POC, A-281, "Campaigns, 1939," CS to R.J. Messender, Bridgetown, NS, 8 Aug. 1939; A-169, "Board of Governors Correspondence," James Bertram to CS, 18 Sept. 1934; McCurdy's note on it is 26 Sept. 1934, with Stanley's rejoinder the next day. F.B. McCurdy (1875–1952) was head of a Halifax financial firm and had been on the Dalhousie board since September 1928. He was MP for Colchester, 1911–21, and minister of public works, 1920–1.

About the Halifax Ladies College, Stanley said: "It is the only remaining friend to us among the Secondary Schools." CS Papers, B-79, CS to J. McGregor Stewart, 4 Mar. 1938. Stewart was at this point chairman of the Board of Governors.

13 See President's Reports, 1933–4 *et seq.*, especially 1938–9 which has a consolidated balance sheet as of 30 June 1939. For Bennett, see UNB Archives, R.B. Bennett Papers, vol. 908, no. 2, 569337–9, J.L. Hetherington to Bennett, 6 May 1936; Bennett to Hetherington, 9 May 1936.

14 POC, A-574, "Medical Faculty, 1921–1931," Income and Expenditures for 1929–30, dated 14 Nov. 1930, confidential.

15 Staff files 193, "William Harop Hattie," Stanley's funeral oration of 7 Dec. 1931. Pearson complained of the attendance at Hattie's funeral. Of 1,075 staff and students, there were between 125 and 150 people present. Pearson thought this was too few. Stanley suggested that every year Dalhousie would gradually grow to seem less like the compact community that Pearson had once known. (Ibid., Pearson to CS, 7 Dec. 1931; CS to Pearson, 12 Dec. 1931.) For Hattie and mental ill-

ness, see R.O. Jones, "Early Recognition of Mental Illness," *Nova Scotia Medical Bulletin* 34 (1955), p. 324.

16 POC, A-836, "Provincial Government of New Brunswick, 1935–1947," CS to A.A. Dysart (premier, 1935–40), 5 May 1939, recounting events of November 1931.

17 H.B. Atlee, C.B. Stewart, and H.L. Scammell, "Harry Goudge Grant 1889–1954," *Nova Scotia Medical Bulletin* 33 (1954), pp. 169–70; staff files 170, "H.G. Grant," Wilson G. Smillie, School of Public Health, Harvard University, to CS, 10 Mar. 1932, on Grant: "Excellent judgment, fine mind, and would make you an excellent Dean."

18 POC, A-575, "Faculty of Medicine 1931–1945," Grant to CS, 8 Dec. 1932; A-736, "Dugald MacGillivray, 1931–1938," CS to Macgillivray, 1 Apr. 1937.

19 See the speech of Premier Murray on laying the cornerstone of the Public Health Clinic in November 1922, *Halifax Echo*, 9 Nov. 1922. See also two articles: W.H. Hattie, "Public Health Clinic Correlates Preventive and Curative Practice," in *The Modern Hospital* 25, no. 2 (August 1925); and Dr Franklin Royer, "A method of teaching the public health point of view to the medical student," in *Journal of the American Medical Association*, 15 May 1926. In the Australian journal, *Health* (Sept. 1926), Dr Royer raised the question of the medical profession's antipathy to public health. These are also in POC, A-855, "Public Health Clinic, 1926–1929," and Halifax *Mail*, 25 Nov. 1926. For a modern review, see John G. Reid, "Health, Education, Economy: Philanthropic Foundations in the Atlantic Region in the 1920s and 1930s," *Acadiensis* 14, no. 1 (Autumn 1984), pp. 64–83.

20 POC, A-736, "Dugald Macgillivray, 1931–1938," Macgillivray to CS, 29 June 1933, from Annapolis Royal. There is some evidence that G.F. Pearson arranged to have the Public Health Clinic established on the Dalhousie campus. William Buxton, "Private Wealth and Public Health: Rockefeller Philanthropy, the Massachusetts Relief Commission and the Halifax Explosion," in Colin Howell and A. Ruffman, eds., *Ground Zero: Perspectives on the 1917 Explosion in Halifax Harbour* (Halifax 1994).

21 The history of this development has been admirably told in Janet F. Kitz, *Shattered City: The Halifax Explosion and the Road to Recovery* (Halifax 1989), pp. 125–212.

22 BOG Minutes, 8 Sept. 1931; POC, A-856, "Public Health Clinic, 1930–1943," CS to W.H. Hattie, 9 Sept. 1931; draft letter, CS to Hector McInnes, dated 9 Sept. 1932, probably for a submission to the Rockefeller Foundation.

23 POC, A-843, "Provincial Governments, Nova Scotia 1920–1935," G.H. Murphy to CS, 10 Feb. 1933 (two letters); CS to G.H. Murphy, 11 Feb. 1933; A-878, "Rockefeller Grant for Teaching in Public Health and Preventive Medicine, 1933–1942," Norma Thompson to CS, 12 May 1933.

24 Ibid., A-382, "City of Halifax, 1932–1964," submission by Dalhousie, Feb. 1934; Stanley's address to aldermen and the Board of Health, 23 Feb. 1937.

25 Ibid., A-876, "Rockefeller Foundation 1921–1941," CS to Dr Alan Gregg, 20 Oct. 1933.

26 For Angus L. Macdonald, see staff files 283; J. Murray Beck, *Politics of Nova Scotia, Volume Two 1896–1988* (Tantallon 1988), p. 166.

27 This interesting letter is in CS Papers, B-36, Angus L. Macdonald to CS, 22 Feb. 1937, personal and confidential.

28 The history of board appointments and their modes is given in BOG Minutes, Appendix A, 14 June 1934. POC, A-928, "Senate, 1906–1943," Report of Senate Special Committee of Senate on the University Charter, 20 Nov. 1934.

29 BOG Minutes, 10 Nov. 1934. The appointment of Dalhousie governors by governor-in-council was discussed at the committee stage of the Dalhousie bill. After being divided equally for and against, the committee decided in favour of the old system. (Those governors elected by alumni, alumnae, and appointed by King's and the United Church did not require such confirmation.) This information, retailed by Carleton Stanley, is in POC, A-167, "Board of Governors Correspondence," CS to Hon. F.C. Alderdice, 30 Apr. 1935. Alderdice was the newly appointed governor from Newfoundland.

30 The 1934 act was chap. 17, but it was repealed by the 1935 one, 25–26 Geo. V, chap. 104.

   The development of the Six-and-Six idea is seen in Senate Minutes, 3 July, 20, 27 Nov. 1934; 5, 23 Feb., 9 Mar. 1935. For Stanley's views about Pearson's influence, see POC, A-1004, "Dr. Clarence Webster, 1934–1964," CS to Webster, 20 Mar. 1935; CS Papers, B-120, CS to Webster, 7 Mar. 1945.

31 POC, A-740, "Hector McInnes 1931–1937," CS to McInnes, 31 July 1934, confidential.

32 Ibid., A-719, "Col. K.C. Laurie, 1939–1945," CS to Laurie, 3 Dec. 1940.

33 Staff files 315, Murray Macneill, Macneill to CS, 16 Oct. 1935; CS to Macneill, 19 Oct. 1935; Macneill to CS, 23 Oct. 1935; Angus L. Macdonald to CS, 30 Oct. 1935; Macneill to CS, 25 Feb. 1936; CS to Mcneill, 29 Feb. 1936.

34 POC, A-708, "King's College, 1931–1945." The feud surfaces again here. See CS to Macneill, 15 Jan. 1934; Macneill to CS, 16 Jan. 1934. For the position of President A.H. Moore, see Moore to CS, 19 Oct. 1935, 16 Mar. 1936; CS to Moore, 17 Mar. 1936. The quotation is from Moore to CS, 28 Mar. 1936.

35 Staff files 315, Murray Macneill, W.E. Thompson to Macneill, 15, 20 May 1936; BOG Minutes, 14, 18, 20 May 1936. For attitudes of Macneill's staff, see Beatrice R.E. Smith to PBW, 22 Sept. 1992. For Macneill's reply, see staff files 315, Macneill to Hector McInnes, 28 July 1936. Family reaction comes from interview with Janet Macneill Piers, 17 Sept. 1992, at Chester, NS. See also Murray Macneill, "Memoirs," p. 9.

   On the other side there is a strong anti-Macneill editorial in the Sydney *Post-Record*, 4 June 1936. The gist of it was that Macneill's dismissal was seventeen years too late. The editor/owner, H.P. Duchemin, was however on the Board of Governors and a Stanley supporter, hence his judgment that Macneill was "a chilling liability" can be assumed to be *parti pris*. In the Carleton Stanley Papers, B-110, there is a brief typed summary, "Reasons for the Instant Removal of M.M. from the University." R.B. Bennett thought the quarrel "almost a calamity." He sympathized with Stanley, believing Macneill's attitudes had been fomented by G.F. Pearson downtown. R.B. Bennett Papers, vol. 908, nos. 569346, 569348, Bennett to McInnes, 20 May 1936; McInnes to Bennett, 30 May 1936.

36 CS Papers, B-24, CS to C.F. Crandall, Montreal, July 17 1933. Much the best article on Dalhousie in this period is the analysis by Paul Axelrod, "Moulding the Middle Class: Student Life at Dalhousie University in the 1930s," in *Acadiensis* 15, no. 1 (Autumn 1985), pp. 84–122, the reference here being to p. 89. For Henry Hicks, see below, chapter 9. For law, see John Willis, *A History of Dalhousie Law School* (Toronto 1979), pp. 140–1.

37 Axelrod, "Dalhousie Students in the 1930s," pp. 90–4; the napkin ring principle was enunciated by Professor Lorne Morgan, economic historian at Toronto in the 1940s. A much more sophisticated and modern analysis of the middle class is available in Paul Axelrod, *Making a Middle Class* (Montreal and Kingston), Appendix A, pp. 167–73.

38 Axelrod, "Dalhousie Students in the 1930s," p. 88, gives this analysis, based on Dalhousie registration books. For Lucy Maud Montgomery's editorial, see *Dalhousie Gazette*, 24 Feb. 1939. The Dalhousie calendar for 1934–5 gives the origins of students. It lists the medical students for 1933–4; in the fifth year, of thirty-three students there is one American. The fourth year, with twenty-three students, has three Americans. The first year, with fifty-five students, has eighteen Americans.

39 New Glasgow *Eastern Chronicle*, 2, 11 Mar. 1937; POC, A-740, "Hector McInnes, 1931–1937," CS to McInnes, 16 Mar. 1937; McInnes to G.F. Pearson, 31 Mar. 1937, replying to Pearson's complaint of the falling off of Dalhousie registration. *Dalhousie Gazette*, 8 Feb. 1934, letter from F.B. Squire.

40 Axelrod, "Dalhousie Students in the 1930s," pp. 86–7; Senate Minutes, 13 May 1933.

41 The 1937 salaries are a personal reminiscence of the author.

42 POC, A-962, H.G. Grant to CS, 5 Feb. 1935; CS to Grant, 9 Feb. 1935.

43 Ibid., A-635, "Fraternities 1924–1961," Falconer to ASM, 21 Nov. 1924; A-561, "Faculty of Law, 1921–1934," Sidney Smith to CS, Feb. (n.d.) 1932; *Dalhousie Gazette*, 12 Oct. 1934.

44 On the badminton affair, see *Dalhousie Gazette*, 15, 22 Feb. 1934; 7 Mar. 1935; Halifax *Citizen*, 16 Feb. 1934. On the Abyssinian crisis, see *Dalhousie Gazette*, 17 Oct. 1935, 7 Feb. 1936.

45 *Dalhousie Gazette*, 1 Nov. 1935; CS Papers, B-40, CS to Chas. A. Maxwell, Salt Springs Pictou County, 17 Dec. 1937. For a slightly more positive view of students, see CS Papers, B-41, CS to Rev. Wm. T. Mercer, 6 Oct. 1938, of Dominion, Cape Breton. This was however in a special context, for Mercer had written praising Stanley's 1938 address to the students, an address not well received in other quarters.

46 POC, A-879, "Rockefeller Foundation Grant for Study in Public Administration, 1936–1944," Stacy May to CS, 12 June 1936, telegram; A-681, "Institute of Public Affairs, 1936–1939," Norma S. Thompson to CS, 18 June 1936.

47 Ibid., A-736, "Dugald Macgillivray, 1931–1938," Macgillivray to CS, 8 July 1935, reporting on a letter received from Sir Robert that day; A-681, Sir Robert Borden to CS, 4 Feb. 1937. Borden died four months later. One of Richter's studies, of a Cape Breton community, "The Effect of Health Insurance on the Demand for Medical Services," was published in *Canadian Journal of Economics and*

Political Science 10, no. 2 (1944), pp. 179–205. *Winnipeg Free Press*, 8 Apr. 1942 has an editorial praising "Dalhousie's Experiment."

48 Interview with Donald J. Morrison (nephew of J. McGregor Stewart), 3 Apr. 1990, Halifax; see also Morrison's sketch of his uncle's life, 29 Sept. 1990, PBW Archive.

49 *Dalhousie Gazette*, 14 Oct. 1938. Letters to Marjorie MacKenzie King on her father's death, are in A.S. MacKenzie Papers, Ethel Walker Smith to Marjorie MacKenzie King, 30 Jan. 1939, from Havana; Esther Nichols to Marjorie MacKenzie King, 9 Oct. 1938, from New York. The Mr Barnstead was probably A.S. Barnstead (Dal. '93), deputy provincial secretary in the 1920s and 1930s and a member of the Dalhousie Board of Governors.

50 The portrait is partly from Donald J. Morrison, cited above.

4 DALHOUSIE AND THE SECOND WORLD WAR

1 See Arthur R.M. Lower, *My First Seventy-five Years* (Toronto 1967), chap. 16, "Some impressions of Nova Scotia," pp. 214–20. There is an interesting and characteristic picture of G.V. Douglas opposite p. 163.

2 That there is an enormous literature on the subject of the Second World War goes without saying. Suffice it to mention three books, succinct and eminently readable: B.H. Liddell Hart, *History of the Second World War* (London 1973), the quotation being from p. 12; C.P. Stacey, *Canada and the Age of Conflict, Volume 2: 1921–1948, The Mackenzie King Era* (Toronto 1981); James Eayrs, *In Defence of Canada: Volume 2, Appeasement and Rearmament* (Toronto 1965).

3 The Skelton memorandum is in J.A. Munro, ed., *Documents in Canadian External Relations, Volume 6, 1936–1939* (Ottawa 1972), pp. 1247–8; Halifax *Herald*, 26, 28 Aug., 4 Sept. 1939. For the story of Bob Chambers's switch from the *Chronicle* to the *Herald*, see William March, *Red Line: The Chronicle-Herald and the Mail Star, 1875–1954* (Halifax 1986), p. 260.

4 I have ventured to suggest the two polarities in Canadian foreign policy in "The Two Foci of an Elliptical Foreign Policy: French-Canadian Isolationism and English Canada 1935–1939," in *Zeitschrift der Gesellschaft für Kanada – Studien* 1 (1981), pp. 112–28. For Senator Dandurand's speech, see Marcel Hamelin, ed., *Les Mémoires du Sénateur Raoul Dandurand 1861–1942* (Québec 1967), p. 273n.

5 The New Brunswick correspondence is cited in Dalhousie University, *President's Report, 1938–1939*, pp. 1–2, note 1. The Hardy poem is from "We are Getting to the End" in his *Winter Words*, published posthumously in 1928.

6 POC, A-359, "Carnegie Corporation," R.M. Lester to CS, 16 Dec. 1937; Dalhousie University, *President's Report, 1938–1939*, pp. 7–8.

7 *President's Report, 1938–1939*, pp. 4–5.

8 POC, A-168, "Board of Governors Correspondence," CS to Col. C.H.L. Jones, 28 Apr. 1939.

9 Ibid., A-876, "Rockefeller Foundation 1931–1941," Dr Raymond Fosdick, president, to CS, 28 Mar. 1939.

10 Ibid., A-1016, "Central Advisory Committee on Education in the Maritime Provinces and Newfoundland 1933–1937," Minutes of the Moncton meeting, 29–30 Dec. 1936. The expenses of the meeting were paid for by the Carnegie Corpo-

ration. The text on which Dalhousie set such store is on p. 15. DUA, H.L. Stewart Papers, box 1, has correspondence from Stewart's survey.

11 POC, A-844, "Provincial Government, Nova Scotia, 1936–1945," CS memorandum, 21 Mar. 1939. Stanley among his other talents could manage some shorthand, how rapidly or accurately is impossible to know. But the conversations are probably his transcription. Ibid., CS's memorandum of 22 June 1939.

12 Ibid., A-836, "Provincial Governments, New Brunswick 1938–1943," CS to Dysart, 5 May 1939; Dysart to CS, 26 May 1939; A-876, "Rockefeller Foundation, 1931–1941," "University Affiliation as it affects Public Hospitals," by Dr Allan Gregg, *c.* 1937.

13 Dalhousie's position in 1940 on whether to close its medical and dental schools is neatly summarized in POC, A-836, CS to Blakeny, 17 Jan. 1942. See also A-844, Angus L. Macdonald to CS, 19 Apr. 1940; BOG Minutes, 26 Apr. 1940; POC, A-844, CS to J. McGregor Stewart, 15 Apr. 1942; BOG Minutes, 24 Apr. 1942. For the Rockefeller grant, see POC, A-844, Norma Thompson, secretary of the Rockefeller Foundation to CS, 6 Apr. 1942. The $150,000 grant was to be expended by 31 Dec. 1944. For Psychiatry, see A-877, "Rockefeller Grant for Teaching in Psychiatry, 1933–1961," Alan Gregg to CS, 3 Apr. 1934; Norma Thompson to CS, 24 June 1941; Alan Gregg to R.O. Jones, 23 Nov. 1942.

14 DUA, staff files 220, "John Hamilton Lane Johnstone," Johnstone to ASM, 23 May 1925, from St. John's; ASM to Vincent Burke, 27 June 1925. Dalhousie's relations with Memorial are referred to in Malcolm Macleod, *A Bridge Built Halfway: A History of Memorial University College, 1925–1950* (Montreal and Kingston 1990), pp. 118, 184, 234–5.

15 POC, A-167, "Board of Governors Correspondence," CS to Hector McInnes, 16 July 1934; Alderdice to McInnes, 7 July 1934. Frederick Charles Alderdice (1872–1936) was premier of Newfoundland in 1928 and 1932–4. He was appointed to the new Commission government in 1934. See Peter Neary, *Newfoundland in the North Atlantic World 1929–1949* (Montreal and Kingston 1988), pp. 12–19.

For the 1942 trip, see POC, A-839, "Newfoundland 1932–1943," CS to Raymond Gushue, 6 May 1942; CS to Ira Wild, auditor general of Newfoundland, 26 Aug. 1942; Gushue to CS, 27 Aug. 1942; H.A. Winter to CS, 30 Oct. 1942, telegram. Some details of the Newfoundland party for Stanley and Grant were filled in through the kindness and energy of Professor Peter Neary of University of Western Ontario and Melvin Baker of Memorial University. Andrew Carnell (1877–1951), mayor of St John's, was John Crosbie's maternal grandfather and a rare old character. The judge is probably Justice William Higgins (1880–1943) and a good friend of Carnell's. See Peter Neary to PBW, 28 Jan. 1993, from London, Ontario.

16 POC, A-836, "New Brunswick, 1938–1947," CS to C.H. Blakeny, minister of education, 17 Jan. 1942; CS's report on interview with Blakeny in Ottawa, 20 Feb. 1943; memorandum to government of New Brunswick, Mar. 1943, and report of meeting with Premier McNair, 3–4 Mar. 1943. At this point there were forty-two New Brunswickers at Dalhousie in medicine and dentistry. The 1946 refusal is in ibid., Blakeny to A.E. Kerr, 31 Oct. 1946.

For Prince Edward Island, see A-848, "PEI 1938–1963," J. Walter Jones, premier, to A.E. Kerr, 14 Feb. 1948. Note the date. A-837, "New Brunswick 1947–1959," J.J.H. Doone to A.E. Kerr, 23 May 1947.

17 POC, A-951, "J. McGregor Stewart, 1934–1944," Stewart to CS, 25 Feb. 1940.

18 For some further background, see *Lives of Dalhousie, I*, pp. 424, 472.

19 For Birchdale, see POC, A-182, "BOG Committees, Finance 1912–1960," F.B. McCurdy to Board, 13 Oct. 1932; BOG Minutes, 10, 21 Nov. 1932; 17, 21 Nov., 14 Dec 1933; 13 Mar. 1934; 13, 26 July 1934; 7, 12, 20 Mar. 1935; 27 Feb., 22 May, 11, 18 Sept. 1941. The Carleton Stanley Papers, B-79 has correspondence: CS to Stewart, 3 Dec. 1937, 4 Mar. 1938; W.L. Harper to CS, 18 Sept. 1941; Theakston to R.G. Beazley, 12 Mar. 1935.

Susequently, when in late 1944 Birchdale became an issue between Stanley and the board, more correspondence ensued: CS Papers, B-79, J.C. Webster to K.C. Laurie, 19 Nov. 1944 (copy), and Stanley's comments thereon, 27 Nov. 1944. These occasioned a defence by J. McGregor Stewart to K.C. Laurie, 27 Nov. 1944 (copy). This letter turns up in PANS, MG17, Universities. It is an early xerox copy of a typed original that is not available. The Stewart letter is an accurate recitation of the facts but for one or two minor mistakes and a slight exaggeration of the money to be saved for Dalhousie by the sale of Birchdale. What is absent from the letter is any sense that there was anything wrong with the transaction, which one could attribute to the manners and morals of the time. This letter was brought to my attention by Barry Cahill, of PANS, to whom I am most grateful. His paper on J. McG. Stewart's law firm is being published. See Carol Wilton, ed., *Inside the Law: Canadian Law Firms in Historical Perspective* (Toronto 1996), Gregory Marchildon and Barry Cahill, "Corporate Entrepreneurship in Atlantic Canada: The Stewart Law Firm, 1915–1955," pp. 280–319.

There is a detailed survey of the Birchdale subdivision in CS Papers, B-81, made 6 Aug. 1941. In that same file is CS to H.P. Duchemin, 11 Nov. 1944 (copy) and other correspondence.

20 According to W.L. Harper, Dalhousie's business manager, the lots went as follows: Lot 9, Mrs Stewart; lot 2, Mrs Mary L. Cooke; lot 7, Mrs Mildred L. Doane; lot 8, Mrs Emily R. Laing; lots 1, 5, and 6, F.C. Manning; lots 3 and 4, Eastern Trust.

21 Interview with Lola Henry, 19 Jan. 1988. For Professor Beecher Weld, two interviews, with both Kathy and Beecher Weld, 12, 15 Jan. 1988.

22 POC, A-360, "Carnegie Corporation 1939–1945," CS to R.M. Lester, 20 Sept. 1943, on the occasion of Keppel's death. The assumption that Stanley was thinking of McGregor Stewart is only an educated guess. The *Winnipeg Free Press* had an editorial about Dr Keppel on 14 Sept. 1943.

23 POC, A-769, "William Inglis Morse 1936–1937," CS to Morse, 12 Nov. 1937: A-719, "K.C. Laurie, 1939–1945," CS to K.C. Laurie, 30 Apr. 1940.

24 Ibid., A-168, "Board of Governors Correspondence," CS to C.H.L. Jones, 28 Apr. 1939; A-771, "William Inglis Morse, 1939–1943," CS to Morse, 8 Aug. 1939; A-282, "Campaigns, 1939 Loyalty Fund, 1939–1949," CS to Dr R.W. Matheson, of Shawinigan Chemicals of Montreal, 18 Apr. 1940; S.R. Balcolm to CS, 20 Mar. 1940; Balcom to Stewart, 8 Oct. 1941.

25 Ibid., A-719, "K.C. Laurie 1939–1945," CS to Laurie, 3 Dec. 1940; Senate Minutes do not record the outburst, of course, but they do mention the president's departure. The meeting continued with Dean Grant of Medicine in the chair.

26 Ibid., "K.C. Laurie, 1939–1945," CS to J. McGregor Stewart, 2 Dec. 1940 (copy); Halifax *Chronicle*, 18 Feb. 1941; A-708, "King's College 1931–1945," CS to K.C. Laurie, 4 Mar. 1941, confidential; CS Papers, B-77, CS to Webster, 21 Dec. 1944 (mimeographed copy); B-81, Memorandum by CS of issues with Stewart and Laurie, n.d.

27 The recollection of C.L. Bennet I owe to Dr Louis W. Collins ('44), telephone conversation, 13 Jan. 1993.

28 For the history of the NCCU (later called the Association of Universities and Colleges of Canada, AUCC), see Gwendoline Pilkington, "A History of the National Conference of Canadian Universities, 1911–1961," (PH.D. thesis, University of Toronto 1974); POC, A-396, "NCCU, 1915–1920," ASM to Peterson, 15 Dec. 1914; J.S. Thomson noted in his memoirs the enlightened views taken by Ottawa; see *Yesteryears at the University of Saskatchewan 1937–1949* (Saskatoon 1969), p. 37. The whole issue is well described in Stanley Brice Frost, *McGill University: For the Advancement of Learning: Volume II, 1895–1971* (Kingston and Montreal 1984), pp. 219–21.

29 The meeting of 5 July 1940 is vividly described by Stanley in a speech to the third- and fourth-year medical and dental students and other male students, 6 Nov. 1941. POC, A-1024, "National Defence, 1934–1944," a four-page draft of Stanley's speech. For the Wartime Bureau of Technical Personnel, see C.P. Stacey, *Arms, Men and Governments: The War Policies of Canada, 1939–1945* (Ottawa 1970), p. 405. The whole James-Wallace episode is elegantly described in Frederick W. Gibson, *Queen's University, Volume II 1917–1961: To Serve and Yet Be Free* (Kingston and Montreal 1983), pp. 201–7.

For Stanley's reactions, see POC, A-399, "NCCU, 1939–1943," CS to Sidney Smith, 14 Nov. 1942, personal and confidential; Smith to CS, 20 Nov. 1942, personal and confidential, from Winnipeg; CS to Cyril James, 30 Apr. 1942, telegram; CS to H.J. Cody, 30 Apr. 1942.

30 POC, A-613, "Federal Government Assistance, 1941–1944," Lothar Richter to CS, 3 Feb. 1942. For Findlay, see CS Papers, B-84, a short pencil description for the board meeting of 28 Nov. 1944. John Willis mentions Findlay in *A History of the Dalhousie Law School* (Toronto 1979), p. 126. There is a vivid account of the Ottawa version of this affair in F.W. Gibson and Barbara Robertson, *Ottawa at War: The Grant Dexter Memoranda, 1939–1945* (Winnipeg 1994), based on Dexter's talks with John MacNeill, the law officer of the crown who advised the mounted police and the censors. MacNeill was opposed to prosecution but in 1940 believed that he was wrong. Dexter was Ottawa correspondent for the *Winnipeg Free Press*. The Halifax trial is in *Chronicle-Herald*, 29 Dec. 1939, the reference being given to me by Barry Cahill of the Public Archives of Nova Scotia.

31 BOG Minutes, 10 Dec. 1940; 16 June 1942; 18 Sept. 1941; CS Papers, B-77, CS to Webster, 21 Dec. 1944, mimeographed copy.

32 Stanley's estimate of November 1941 juxtaposed Dalhousie with Queen's, nearest to Dalhousie in diminution of students, Dalhousie with 25 per cent and Queen's

with 15 per cent. Stanley somewhat exaggerated the 1941 loss. See POC, A-1024, "National Defence, 1934–1944," Stanley's speech of 6 Nov. 1941. A-613, "Federal Government Assistance, 1941–1944," C.D. Howe to CS, 17 Mar. 1942; CS to C.D. Howe, 30 Mar. 1942; Gordon B. Isnor (MP for Halifax) to CS, 26 May 1943, personal. CS to Angus L. Macdonald, 5 May 1943; CS to R.B. Hanson, 10 July 1944.

The BOG stand can be seen in the minutes for 27 Oct. 1942 and 27 Apr. 1943. There were two major submissions of the board to Ottawa for compensation, also in POC, A-613, one of 23 Feb. 1942, and the one quoted here, submitted through CS to C.J. Mackenzie, president of the National Research Council, 13 Mar. 1943. Unfortuantely I have not found the letters from Ilsley that so offended Stanley.

33 Gifts to Dalhousie at that time are conveniently listed in the *1944–1945 Calendar*, pp. 4–8. The correspondence about the Bennett donation is in POC, A-151, "R.B. Bennett 1943–1948," Bennett to CS, 29 Mar. 1943, from Mickleham; CS to Bennett, 23 Apr. 1943; Alice Millar to CS, 24 Apr. 1943, from Sackville, NB; CS to Capt. Ronald Bennett, 23 Sept. 1943; Ronald Bennett to CS, 25 Sept. 1943; BOG Minutes, 27 Sept. 1943. Alice Millar's account is in UNB Archives, R.B. Bennett Papers, vol. 936, nos. 589989–92, Millar to R.B. Bennett, 29 Apr. 1943, from Montreal. She writes that President Stanley told her and Capt. Bennett of his difficulties: "I can understand what a burden he was relieved of."

34 POC, A-151, "R.B. Bennett," John Willis to Vince MacDonald, 3 Dec. 1943 (copy); Willis to CS, 4 Dec. 1943; CS to MacDonald, 25 Nov. 1943; MacDonald to CS, 28 Dec. 1943; J. McGregor Stewart to CS, 3 Jan. 1944. The question was still being discussed in February 1945, but wearing the appearance of a *fait accompli*; see K.C. Laurie to F.B. McCurdy, 24 Feb. 1945, from Oakfield.

See Willis, *Dalhousie Law School*, pp. 128–9. The only source for the statement that Stewart wanted to close all or part of Dalhousie down during the war is Stanley, and that during his 1944–5 row with Stewart. New Brunswick Museum, J.C. Webster Papers, CS to Webster, 17 Nov. 1944.

35 For other aspects of Stewart's 1943 resignation as chairman see supra, pp. 111. Stanley's comments in 1943 are in DUA, staff files, "Carleton Stanley," CS to Webster, 30 Apr. 1943; Webster to CS, 3 May 1943; CS to Webster, 5 May 1943.

5 FIRING CARLETON STANLEY

1 For an account of Halifax in wartime, see Thomas H. Raddall, *Halifax, Warden of the North* (Toronto 1948), pp. 309–15; for John Marshall's views, see Charles R. Acland and William J. Buxton, "Continentialism and Philanthropy: A Rockefeller Officer's Impressions of the Humanities in the Maritimes, 1942," *Acadiensis* 23, no. 2 (Spring 1994), p. 79.

In the notes that follow, up to and including note 6, the references are all to the *Dalhousie Gazette*, whence comes the information. On Halifax housing, 16 Oct. 1942; on Roy Atwood, 12 Jan. 1945, and the canteen's campus function, 15 Nov. 1940.

2 Rowell-Sirois Commission and Cousins juxtaposed, 15 Jan. 1941; on formals and dance bands, 9 Oct., 6 Nov. 1942; on servicemen as escorts, 20 Feb. 1942 (co-ed edition).

3 On sweaters and their queen, 24 Oct., 7 Nov. 1941; on stockings, 13 Feb. 1942.

4 On comic strip preferences, 28 Feb. 1941; 30 Jan. 1942.

5 On the library, 31 Jan., 21 Nov. 1941. Also the recollection of Dr Louis W. Collins, interview on 13 Jan. 1993.

6 On Christmas examinations, 27 Nov. 1942; 14 Jan. 1944.

7 This occasion is well known, but was given to me, with some amusement, by Dr Beecher Weld, interview on 15 Jan. 1988.

8 Col. Laurie's recollection of the troops in 1885 was given to me in the 1950s.

9 The account of Laurie's visit to J.C. Webster is based on Stanley's account, in DUA, CS Papers, B-77, CS to Webster, 21 Dec. 1944.

10 Stanley claimed to have a full record of his meeting with Colonel Laurie at Oakfield, 26 Nov. 1943. It is in CS Papers, B-109, a memorandum drafted for the board meeting of 28 Nov. 1944. It is marked, "Use only if debate forces," which, it would appear, the debate did not. Stanley was at a very anti-Laurie stage, so his account should be used with caution. On the other hand, the tone of Laurie's 1943 utterances, as reported by Stanley, is quite in character. There are two letters about the issues Stanley raised with Laurie in CS Papers, B-109, Laurie to CS, 5 Nov. 1943, and CS to Laurie, 26 Nov. 1943.

11 There is no doubt of Laurie's classroom visits. Two professors, John Willis and J.G. Adshead, gave me their recollections in the 1950s. That the intention of the visits was not a neutral inspection was suggested to me by Miss Eileen Burns (MA '24), alumnae governor, 1944–50, in a telephone interview, 23 Mar. 1993. For Laurie's disclaimer of himself as fund-raiser, see POC, A-719, "K.C. Laurie," Laurie to CS, 27 Dec. 1943.

12 For Stanley's point about practical education, see POC, A-926, "Secondary Schools, Nova Scotia, 1931–1949, N-Z," CS to H.H. Wetmore (principal of Yarmouth Academy), 26 Jan. 1940. Stanley's discussion with Senator Dennis is in A-500, "W.H. Dennis, 1924–1944," CS to Dennis, 16 Sept. 1937.

13 The Medical Society story is given by Stanley in a letter to Hardolph Wasteneys, professor of biochemistry, University of Toronto, 7 Aug. 1942. He repeated it in a draft brief, "Memorandum A.1," c. November 1944, CS Papers, B-84, p. 3. The focus of Stanley's animus against the NS Medical Society seems to have been Dr H.L. Scammell. See infra, p. 119.

The William Inglis Morse correspondence is in POC, A-769, "William Inglis Morse, 1936–1937," CS to Morse, 12 Nov. 1937. The quotation from Goethe is added as a postscript to this letter. The German is not well transcribed by Miss Lola Henry, being from Stanley's handwriting, and I have corrected the quotation from Goethe.

Torquato Tasso was an Italian poet, about whom Goethe wrote a play in 1788. The lines are from act 1, scene 2. A free English translation might be:
> Talent develops in quiet reflection,
> Character thrives on stress and action.

14 For the Underhill affair, see R. Douglas Francis, *Frank H. Underhill, Intellectual Provocateur* (Toronto 1986), pp. 115–27. On page xiv there is a 1911 photograph of Underhill and C.N. Cochrane with Carleton Stanley standing between them, a head taller than both, en route to Oxford. For the correspondence, see CS

Papers, B-56, CS to Cody, 25 Feb. 1941; Cody to CS, 3 Mar. 1941. Also Underhill to CS, 18 Sept. 1940.

15 This is based on Stanley's recollections, CS Papers, B-69, a series of specific comments put together 18–19 Nov. 1944; also ibid., B-115, under J. McG. Stewart. Note, however, Stewart's account of this incident, referred to in note 21.

16 CS Papers, B-74, p. 1 of CS's submission to the board, 23 Jan. 1945.

17 See Michael Hatton, "University Boards – A View from the Profit Sector," paper presented at the annual meeting of the Canadian Society for the Study of Higher Education, Victoria, BC, 4 June 1990.

18 For the relations of presidents or chief executive officers (CEOs) to boards, see Murray G. Ross, *Canadian Corporate Directors on the Firing Line* (Toronto 1980), p. 93.

19 The Rev. G.A.A. Beveridge (BA '36), minister emeritus of St Matthew's Church, remembers being taken on just such a walk by President Stanley, about 1934. Interview, 12 Feb. 1993.

For J.R. Mallory, see "A Year at Dalhousie," 28 Aug. 1990, PBW Archive. Mallory was professor of political science at McGill from 1946 to 1982. For Laura Katherine Stanley ('41), now Mrs L.B. Woolner, see "Memories of My Father," written in 1991, Mrs Woolner to PBW, 8 Apr. 1992.

20 The story of the lecturer in French comes from Professor John Hibbitts ('45), of King's College. Interview, 10 June 1988. Mrs Woolner pointed out how her father insisted upon truth. See her "Memories of My Father," p. 2. See also interview with W.J. Archibald (dean of arts and science 1955–60, and former professor of physics), 25 July 1988.

21 Dr Beecher Weld explained the contrast between Stanley's emphasis on truth and others' belief that he was an inveterate liar by concluding that Stanley was a highly subjective thinker. Interview, 12 Jan. 1988. For J. McGregor Stewart's gloss on the 1932 discussion with CS, see BOG Minutes, 23 Jan. 1945, p. 14.

22 The comment on the missing arts and science dean was made by George F. Curtis, Dalhousie's secretary of Senate, 1941–5. He then became UBC's dean of law, 1945–71. Interview, Vancouver, 30 May 1990. C.F. MacKenzie's comment on Stanley is in BOG Minutes, 23 Jan. 1945, p. 7.

23 Stanley's writing an anonymous column in the local papers comes from his daughter's "Memoirs of My Father," p. 4. For Principal Arthur Morgan's comment at McGill, see Stanley Brice Frost, *McGill University: For the Advancement of Learning: Volume II, 1895–1971* (Kingston and Montreal 1984), p. 19.

24 The text of CS's 1944 convocation address is in his *Annual Report 1943–1944*, pp. 23–4. Reference to it is made by his daughter, "Memories of My Father," pp. 4–5. It is quoted in J.V. McAree's column in the Toronto *Globe and Mail*, 26 Feb. 1945. Note the biting comment in the Toronto *News*, 10 Feb. 1945: "For the wealth which would have to be tapped for contributions to Dalhousie endowment is sensitive about slums, having a vested interest in them." There is also a reference to this aspect of Stanley's problems in Halifax in a *Saturday Night* editorial, 24 Feb. 1945.

That editorial may been "inspired" by Stanley, for it had more than one revealing inaccuracy. Stanley was said to have been assistant principal at McGill, when he was actually assistant *to* the principal. The wish was doubtless father to the error. More glaring was the statement that after Sir Arthur Currie's death in 1933, McGill sought CS's release from the Dalhousie presidency in order that he become principal of McGill. There is no evidence in either the CS Papers or Dalhousie ones of any such thing. Principal Cyril James wrote to *Saturday Night* that from the McGill files there was no indication that McGill sought CS as Currie's replacement. McGill University Archives, RG2, C43, F. Cyril James Papers, James to B.K. Sandwell, 25 Feb. 1945. This letter is in *Saturday Night*, 10 Mar. 1945.

25 The career of John Erskine Read is summarized in the *Halifax Echo*, 29 June 1924. More recently, in 1990, for Professor Ronald St John Macdonald's course at Dalhousie in international law, Hugh Patton produced a 34-page essay, "John Erskine Read: A Lifetime of International law." The correspondence with O.D. Skelton is in DUA, staff files 403, "John E. Read," O.D. Skelton to ASM, 7 Mar. 1929. MacKenzie replied, 22 Mar. 1929: "I owe you a grudge in having taken Dean Read away from us, and I suppose that I should accordingly be just as disagreeable as possible ... However, this is Lent ..."

26 For Read on Stanley, see John A. Yogis, "Interview with John Read: Recollections of Dalhousie Law School," *Ansul* (May 1974), p. 1; for Stanley on Read and the Allan Findlay affair, CS Papers, B-84, draft notes for the 28 Nov. 1944 board meeting. For Read's views of Stanley's Ottawa speech, B-61, Read to Laurie, 25 June 1944, from Otttawa, copy. S.R. Balcom's views are in B-65, Balcom to Laurie, 22 Aug. 1944 (copy). Miss Henry's sharp comments on Read are in B-74, Lola Henry to CS, 4 Aug. 1944, replying to CS's letter of 2 Aug. 1944. Donald McInnes's recollections of John Read are in *Ansul* (13 Jan. 1976), "In My Day at Dalhousie Law School," p. 36.

27 CS Papers, B-85, Stanley gives a summary of Laurie's moves against Miss MacKeen. The 1939 row about the Delta Gamma dance is in *Dalhousie Gazette*, 21, 28 Jan. 1939, and *Halifax Star*, 22 Jan. 1938. The 1944 criticism is in POC, A-167, "Board of Governors Correspondence," Donald A. Cameron to CS, 31 July 1944, from River John. The Shirreff Hall committee reported to the board on 28 Nov. 1944 through Mrs F.H. Pond.

28 Interview with Dr Chester B. Stewart, 9 June 1988; staff files 487, "C.B. Stewart," Stewart to Dean Grant, 19 Aug. 1944, from Toronto; Grant to CS, 22 Aug. 1944; Grant to Laurie, 12 Sept. 1944. For Fyfe's opinion on appointments, see staff files, "Carleton Stanley," Fyfe to CS, n.d. (Apr. 1938) from Aberdeen.

29 For the four-way interview on the morning of 15 Sept. 1944, the source is CS Papers, B-84, "Memorandum A.1," p. 3; BOG Minutes, 15 Sept. 1944.

30 CS Papers, B-109, Laurie to CS, personal and confidential, 24 Oct. 1944, from Oakfield (copy).

31 Ibid., B-74. This paragraph is partly based on Stanley's account of events compiled probably in January 1945. Stanley had the habit, already noted but now brought to extensive use, of writing up the substance of important conversations and interviews at the first opportunity after they ended. He would probably have as *aide-mémoire* shorthand notes. Miss Henry would then type them up. The other source is ibid., B-73, CS to Lola Henry, Sunday, 19 Nov. 1944, CS's instructions for a letter to J.C. Webster, p. 2.

32 Laurie visited Shediac on Friday, 27 Oct. and Stanley may actually have encountered him there. Stanley was accompanied by G.V. Douglas, who was no doubt visiting his daughters at Mount Allison, for Stanley met Webster alone. Webster's letter to Laurie is in ibid., B-77, Webster to Laurie, [2?] Nov. 1944, from Shediac (copy).

33 Ibid., B-99, CS to Robert P. Ludlum, association secretary, American Association of University Professors, Washington, 7 Feb. 1945 (copy).

34 Ibid., B-65, CS to R.B. Bennett, 29 Oct. 1944, cable; same date, airgraph; also 31 Oct. 1944, a four-page, single-spaced typed letter. See also J.C. Webster to CS, 29 Oct. 1944, quoted in CS to R.B. Bennett. Stanley's account of his interview with Stewart is in CS to Webster, 31 Oct. 1944, in the John Clarence Webster Papers in the New Brunswick Museum, Saint John, brought to my notice by Barry Cahill of the Public Archives of Nova Scotia.

35 CS Papers, B-81, Duchemin to CS, 9 Nov. 1944, personal, from Sydney (copy). In the same file there is a report to CS, probably by Major Logan, of the meeting of 10 Nov. It is undated, but internal evidence suggests the date.

36 Ibid., B-73, Stanley's record of the Harvey interview, transcribed in the manner referred to in note 31.

37 D.A. Cameron was the Sun Life Assurance Company's representative in Boston, whom Stanley seems to have found sympathetic. Ibid., B-66, Cameron to CS, 13 Nov. 1944; CS to Cameron, 15 Nov. 1944; Cameron to CS, 20 Nov. 1944; CS to Cameron, 23 Nov. 1944, from Montreal. See also B-119, CS to Webster, 6 Nov. 1944.

38 There is a question whether a board of directors, or of governors, can entertain proxy votes. Miss Henry consulted two Halifax lawyers and got a strong "no" from one, and a "possibly" from another. Ibid., B-119, Lola Henry to Webster, 23 Nov. 1944; CS to Webster, 24 Nov. 1944, draft telegram; Lola Henry to Webster, 21 Nov. 1944, very confidential.

Stanley's twisting the truth is worth a note. On 24 Nov. 1944, he drafted and probably sent the following telegram to Webster: "R.B. Bennett for one telegraphed his support [in 1932], and it was read. That made the Board unanimous against Pearson" (ibid., B-119). In fact there were two meetings in June 1932, and at neither of them did Bennett's name come up. In the first meeting, on 6 June, Bennett apparently asked that his name not be mentioned. Stanley wrote to him the next day, "By the way, no letter from you was read, nor was your name mentioned at the meeting." For the following meeting, on 10 June, Stanley solicited Bennett's support by telegram. But Bennett was out of town, and the day of the board meeting Bennett's secretary, A.W. Merriam, telegraphed to Stanley that Bennett was away and would not return until the following week. These latter references are in UNB Archives, R.B. Bennett Papers, vol. 908, nos. 569021 *et seq.*, CS to RBB, 7 June 1932, confidential; CS to RBB, 10 June 1932, telegram; A.W. Merriam to CS, 11 June 1932, telegram.

39 There are two sets of minutes for the 28 Nov. meeting, one that is in the regular Board of Governors series, which is remarkably comprehensive, and a second version, slightly fuller with mostly minor but sometimes important additions. I have used the second version, which is in CS Papers, B-84. For Stewart's remarks, see

pp. 14–15, 5, 7–8. The question, "to get money or get Stanley?" is not in either set of minutes but is referred to by CS as having been asked at the time. CS Papers, B-76, CS to J.A. Walker (his Halifax lawyer), 20 Apr. 1945 (copy).

As to the Pre-Campaign Committee's recommendation, that a campaign could not be put in motion as long as President Stanley remained, the fairest interpretation that can be put on it was that it was an attempt to give Stanley the easiest possible way out. That is what Stewart said, in effect, on 23 Jan. 1945. All Stanley had to do was to resign, and the matter would have been closed.

40 The scene with Colonel Laurie's spelling held up to ridicule is in the second version of the minutes, p. 21; at the bottom of the page is written, though not in Stanley's handwriting (possibly Miss Henry's), "I added: 'And in your spelling too – *speach*'." This scene is described by Miss Eileen Burns, alumnae governor, 1944–50. Interview by telephone, 22 Feb. 1993, commenting on PBW to Miss Burns, 16 Feb. 1993.

41 CS Papers, B-87, Laurie to CS, 25 Oct. 1944 (copy).

42 Ibid., B-119, CS to Webster, 29 Nov. 1944; B-77, CS to Webster, 21 Dec. 1944.

43 Ibid., B-81, G.G. Patterson to CS, 13 Jan. 1945; B-70, J.M. Macdonnell to CS, 15 Jan. 1945. For Major Logan's intercession of Stanley's behalf, interview with Miss Eileen Burns, 22 Feb. 1993. For R.B. Bennett, see CS Papers, B-65, CS to RBB, 19[?] Jan. 1945, draft cable; RBB to Laurie, 22 Jan. 1945 (copy), night cable.

44 C.F. MacKenzie, the secretary, asked Lola Henry to send him for the use of the board, all letters, correspondence, and memoranda about Stanley's appointment. Miss Henry replied that there was no trace of such correspondence. There are two possible explanations: one, that Stanley did not propose to surrender it; two, the more probable, that during the 1931–2 quarrel G.F. Pearson had it. See staff files, "Carleton Stanley," MacKenzie to Lola Henry, 13 Dec. 1944; Lola Henry to MacKenzie, 14 Dec. 1944. As chapter 2 noted, there is material on Stanley's appointment in his own papers, and in President MacKenzie's private papers.

The January 1945 resolutions are in BOG Minutes, 23 Jan. 1945. For Stewart and Farquhar's remarks, see pp. 13, 15; for Stanley's parting line, p. 18. Laurie's letter to Bennett is in R.B. Bennett Papers, vol. 908, no. 569417, Laurie to Bennett, 30 Jan. 1945, from Oakfield. Laurie reported that of the five who voted against the board resolution asking for Stanley's resignation, three felt that there was some ground for complaint against Stanley, but not to the point of asking him to resign.

45 The New York lawyer for Stanley was C.C. Ives, of Handelman and Ives. CS Papers, B-76, CS to J.A. Walker (Stanley's Halifax lawyer), 31 Jan. 1945; Donald McInnes (Dalhousie's lawyer) to J.A. Walker, 7 Feb. 1945. Stanley believed the board feared what he might do. See B-120, CS to J.C. Webster, 10 Feb. 1945.

46 Ibid., B-74, John Stevenson to CS, 31 Jan. [1945], on *Globe and Mail* letterhead.

47 Ibid., B-76, CS to J.A. Walker, 20 Apr. 1945; B-73, CS to R.C. Wallace, principal of Queen's, 7 Feb. 1945. Stanley said much the same to Viscount Bennett, B-65, CS to Bennett, B-65, CS to Bennett, 1 Feb. 1945.

As to the American Association of University Professors, see ibid., B-99, CS to R.P. Ludlum, 7 Feb. 1945, and B-105, C.C. Ives to CS, 29 Jan. 1945. There is important correspondence in POC, A-719, "K.C. Laurie, 1939–1945," Robert Ludlum to CS, 10 Jan. 1945; Laurie to Ludlum, 20 Jan. 1945, from Oakfield; Ludlum to Laurie, 22 Jan. 1945, telegram; Laurie to Ludlum, 30 Jan. 1945, from Oakfield (copy).

CS's private opinion of Angus L. Macdonald is in a letter signed "Hibbert Journal" (one of the journals Stanley read and contributed to), addressed to John Stevenson at the *Globe and Mail*, 16 Dec. 1940 (copy): "But he is *per se*, and in his own right, a cad; and though *il ment comme un Jesuit*, he has not learned the Jesuitical cleverness … Absolutely shameless and *crude* in accepting money … A sponge of flattery; a leach of pelf; a chameleon in politics; a rat and a weasel in revenge and vindictiveness; apt in perversion of History, and adroit in captivating little souls like Vincent Massey."

48 New York *Nation*, 10 Mar. 1945, "Dalhousie Drops a President," pp. 274–5. Similar views are expressed in the Toronto *News*, 10, 17 Feb. 1945. McAree's comment is in the *Globe and Mail*, 26 Feb. 1945.

49 This recollection is from Miss Eileen Burns, interview, 22 Feb. 1993.

6 A.E. KERR AND THE VETERANS

1 This chapter has been commented on by Dr Alan Wilson, until recently professor of history at Trent University, Peterborough. Dr Wilson was a student at Dalhousie from 1944 to 1949 and I am most grateful for his perceptive suggestions about Dean Wilson and the Dalhousie of the late 1940s.

DUA, Carleton Stanley Papers, B-73, Publicover to CS, 13 Jan. 1945, from New York. For Stanley's comment, see B-85, CS's submission to the board, 23 Jan. 1945 (copy).

2 Ibid., B-62, CS to W.H. Alexander, 25 Mar. 1945, his brother-in-law, then at Berkeley; B-120, CS to Webster, 25 June 1945. For United College, Winnipeg, see B-68, Principal W.C. Graham to CS, 25 Apr. 1945, personal; CS to Graham, 10 May 1945.

3 POC, A-563, "Law Faculty, 1943–1950," J. McG. Stewart to Laurie, 19 Mar. 1945. At this point Stewart said he had no further names to suggest for the presidency, and that Doull was by far the best of the candidates. See also A-720, "Col. K.C. Laurie 1945–1962," Laurie to Dr James Doull, 16 July 1945, telegram; Laurie to Doull, 11 Oct. 1945; Doull to Dr Alan Gregg of the Rockefeller Foundation, 18 Oct. 1945 (copy).

4 POC, A-150, "R.B. Bennett," A.E. Kerr (hereafter AEK) to Bennett, 28 Nov. 1946. Weld's remark was made in an interview, 15 Jan. 1988.

5 PBW Archive, "Roderick D. Kerr, 1854–1919," pp. 13, 28. This thirty-page manuscript has been copied for me by the kindness of AEK's son, Donald A. Kerr, the original of which is in his family's possession. It was written by AEK about 1967, four years after he retired from Dalhousie.

6 Ibid., pp. 13, 23, 24.

7 Ibid., p. 29; *Dalhousie Gazette*, 9 Aug. 1920, "History of the class of '20."

8 There is a further short three-page addition to the AEK manuscript by his brother, Roderick Kerr, continuing the story of AEK's life to his death in 1974. On AEK's

preaching, Dr Margaret Gosse reported that when she was in Montreal AEK was minister at the American Presbyterian Church near Windsor Station. She said he was "*extremely* popular" as a preacher. She also added she could never understand why. Interview, 26 June 1989. On AEK's attitude to libraries, Douglas Lochhead to PBW, 31 Jan. 1990, from Sackville, NB. Lochhead was Dalhousie librarian from 1952 to 1960.

9 Interview with Lola Henry, 19 Jan. 1988. Miss Henry also reported AEK's kindness to alcoholics. For the rink manager story, interview with Donald H. McNeill, 4 Apr. 1990. Donald McNeill (B.SC. 1933) was Dalhousie's business manager from 1948 to 1978. For the story of A.K. Griffin, interview with Beecher and Kathy Weld, 15 Jan. 1988.

10 DUA, staff files 21, "Stewart Bates," note by CS, 19 Sept. 1941; Bates to AEK, 6 Sept. 1945, telegram from Lunenburg. A more extensive description of this incident is given by J.R. Mallory, "A Year at Dalhousie," p. 2, from conversations with Bates. Mallory to PBW, 28 Aug. 1990. For G.V. Douglas, see McGill University Archives, RG2, C43, F. Cyril James Papers, Douglas to James, 31 May 1945.

11 DUA, Faculty of Arts and Science, Minutes, 3 Apr., 19 Sept. 1945; staff files 543, "George Earle Wilson," AEK to Wilson, 10 Sept. 1945, telegram; Wilson to AEK, 10 Sept. 1945, telegram, from Perth, and letter of same date; AEK to Wilson, 19 Sept. 1945, telegram.

12 Ibid., G.E. Wilson to A.S. Mackenzie, 2, 6 Aug. 1930, from Perth; MacKenzie to Wilson, 23 Aug. 1930. Queen's had analogous problems with morale in the Arts Faculty at the same time. See Frederick W. Gibson, *Queen's University: Volume II, 1917–1961: To Serve and Yet Be Free* (Kingston and Montreal 1983), p. 235.

13 POC, A-519, "Faculty of Arts and Science 1922–1945," Wilson to CS, 28 May 1934, from Manchester. The reference to Goethe's *Faust* is in part 1, lines 575–9. Faust: "My friend, the past is a book of seven seals, and what you call the spirit of the times, is at bottom merely the characters of those gentlemen in whom the times are mirrored." For an essay on Wilson, see Henry Roper, "The Lifelong Pilgrimage of George E. Wilson, Teacher and Historian," in Royal Nova Scotia Historical Society *Collections* 46 (1980), pp. 138–51. Wilson's own perspectives about history are admirably set out in his 1951 presidential address to the Canadian Historical Association, "Wider Horizons," CHA *Annual Report* (1951), pp. 1–19.

14 Gwendoline Pilkington, "A History of National Conference of Canadian Universities, 1911–1961" (PH.D. thesis, University of Toronto 1974). For First World War efforts, pp. 67, 76–7, 87–8, 102–3; for Second World War, pp. 306–440.

15 Charles M. Johnston, *McMaster University: Vol. 2, The Early Years in Hamilton, 1930–1957* (Toronto 1981), p. 142; John Reid, *Mount Allison University: Volume II, 1914–1963* (Toronto 1984), p. 207; P.B. Waite, *Lord of Point Grey* (Vancouver 1987), p. 120.

16 "The Law School Then and Now," interview with Dr Moffat Hancock, in *Ansul* 5, no. 4 (1973), p. 2; John Willis, *A History of Dalhousie Law School* (Toronto 1979), pp. 160–3. See also Gibson, *Queen's University Volume II*, p. 252.

17 *Dalhousie Gazette*, 13 Feb. 1948; C.L. Bennet, "What the Veteran Student Is Teaching the Universities," *Dalhousie Review* 27 (1947–8), pp. 316–17. For the poem on Milton, see "The Way of Trial Is the Way of Light," in *Dalhousie*

Gazette, 29 Nov. 1946. "City after Rain" is by Eltan Lowell, in ibid., 22 Feb. 1946. The smoker is ibid., 13 Feb. 1948.

18 Alan Wilson to PBW, 1 Feb. 1994, letter and comments; for socialism and the CCF in these years, see Leo Zakuta, *A Protest Movement Becalmed: A Study of Change in the C.C.F.* (Toronto 1964), p. 58; J. Murray Beck, *Pendulum of Power: Canada's Federal Elections* (Toronto 1968), pp. 247–57.

19 POC, A-992, "Veterans' Housing, 1945–1946," Brooke Claxton to Laurie, 7 Feb. 1946; H.R. Theakston to AEK, 20 Aug. 1946; A-700, "Senator Gordon B. Isnor, 1946–1962," AEK to Isnor, 10 Sept. 1946; 12 Mar. 1947; 2 Mar. 1949, telegram; A-991, "Veterans Housing, 1947," confidential memorandum for AEK by C.L. Bennet, 7 Mar. 1947.

20 Ibid., A-993, "Veterans' Housing 1947–1958," Bennet to AEK, 5 Mar., 9 Apr., 5 May 1947; 17 Jan., 12 Feb. 1948.

21 The story of the interview with Howe is given by Kerr in his speech at Dalhousie's memorial service for Howe, 8 Jan. 1961, in ibid., A-672, "C.D. Howe." Other references include A-993, "Veterans Housing 1947–1958," Theakston to AEK, 4 Jan. 1951; Mulgrave Park Married Students' Association to AEK, 31 Jan. 1956; AEK to Mulgrave Park Married Students' Association, 14 Feb. 1956; Robert Winters to L.A. Kitz, mayor of Halifax, 12 Apr. 1957 (copy); Murray Fraser (president of Dalhousie Student Council) to Charles Vaughan, mayor of Halifax, 11 Feb. 1958.

22 *Dalhousie Gazette*, Mar. 1946; POC, A-992, "Veterans Housing 1945–1946," T.A. Giles to AEK, 7 Feb. 1946.

23 *President's Report*, 1945–1950. From 1947 until 1963 the custom of publishing annual president's reports, which had been started in 1911–12 by President MacKenzie, was replaced by a five-year report.

24 POC, A-709, "King's, 1945–1958," AEK to J. McGregor Stewart, 14 Feb. 1949.

25 Ibid., AEK to Milton Gregg, 17 Nov. 1949; AEK to Senator Isnor, 15 Dec. 1948; AEK to R.A. Baxter, 15 Sept. 1948.

26 Ibid., A. Stanley Walker to Milton Gregg, 15 Sept. 1949 (copy); A-1040, "Terms of Association Liaison Committee, 1940–1950," CS to J. McGregor Stewart, 2 Dec. 1940; A-1044, "King's College Liaison, 1958–1963," "Considerations for Future Relations of Dalhousie & King's," a confidential statement for Donald McInnes's information, is a succinct, hard-hitting report, reviewing the whole history of Dalhousie's relations with King's, and suggesting future changes. See especially pp. 2 and 5. No name is given as author.

27 BOG Minutes, 10 Mar. 1949; 13 Jan. 1950.

28 Interview with D.H. McNeill, 4 Apr. 1990.

29 POC, A-196, "Arts & Administration Building, 1944–1950," Minutes of Joint Board-Senate Committee, 30 Oct. 1947; BOG Minutes, 12 Feb., 25 May 1948; staff files 108, "G.V. Douglas," Douglas to AEK, 27 Apr. 1949; AEK to Douglas, 30 Apr. 1949; Wilson to AEK, 11 May 1949; AEK memo, phone call to J. McGregor Stewart in Montreal re Wilson's letter, n.d., but probably 11 or 12 May 1949.

30 POC, A-718, "H.V.D. Laing, 1949–1958," Laing to AEK, 10 Nov. 1952.

31 David Farr, "A.E. Kerr: A View from a Junior Member of the Faculty, 1946–47," enclosed in Farr to PBW, 26 Jan. 1955; POC, A-520, "Faculty of Arts and Science 1945–1947," Wilson to AEK, 3 June 1947, from Perth.

32 Ibid., Wilson to AEK, 28 June, 3 Aug 1946, both from Perth.

33 Ibid., Wilson to AEK, 14 Dec. 1946 from Halifax; 16, 22 July, 17 Aug. 1947, from Perth.

34 Ibid., R.M. Dawson to Wilson, 19 Nov. 1948, copied by Wilson and enclosed in Wilson to AEK, 20 Nov. 1948.

35 H.L. Stewart's extensive publications for 1948–9 are in the *President's Report, 1945–1950*, p. 82; *Dalhousie Gazette*, 3 Dec. 1935; I have also benefited from reading two chapters of Kevin McDonald's Dalhousie MA thesis (1994) on Stewart, based on the H.L. Stewart Papers in DUA. See also staff files 168, "G.P. Grant," report of 25 Feb. 1947, probably by G.E. Wilson, on staffing the Philosophy Department.

36 BOG Minutes, 22 Apr. 1947; staff files 168, "George P. Grant," AEK to Grant, 13 Apr. 1947, cable; Grant to G.E. Wilson, 21 May 1947. A recent book on Grant presents an engaging view of him; see William Christian, *George Grant: A Biography* (Toronto 1993). For Grant's appointment to Dalhousie, see pp. 128–9.

37 POC, A-683, "Institute of Public Affairs," Richter to J. McGregor Stewart, 12 Oct. 1943; George Farquhar to AEK, 31 Jan. 1946, memorandum on the institute; AEK memorandum, 2 Nov. 1948; C.J. Rankin, John A. McDonald, J. McG. Stewart to AEK, 31 Dec. 1948, submitting resignation from the executive of the institute to assist reorganization. For a good survey of Richter's life, see Stewart Bates, "Obituary, Lothar Richter (1894–1948)," *Canadian Journal of Economics and Political Science* 16, no. 4 (1949), pp. 543–5, and Dalhousie's *Public Affairs* 12, no. 1 (Spring 1949).

38 BOG Minutes, 10 May 1946, memorandum re "Duties of a President." DUA, George Farquhar Papers, MS 2, no. 237, Farquhar to Col. Laurie, 30 May 1950 (copy); BOG Minutes, 29 May, 11 July 1950. Farquhar's letter is a good illustration of things that minutes do not say.

39 The end of campus beer and poker is described by J.G. Aldous, professor of pharmacology subsequent to M.K. McPhail, interview, 1 June 1990, Vancouver. For Pharmacology, see A.K. Reynolds, *Department of Pharmacology, Dalhousie University: A 50-Year History, 1938–1988* (Halifax 1988).

For the forlorn hope of Sunday skating, see BOG Minutes, 28 Nov. 1950. The rink was built in 1950 for $168,000. For some characteristic effusions by "Sam Peeps," see *Dalhousie Gazette*, 5, 8 Oct., 8 Nov. 1948. The story of beer via the back door of the Lord Nelson on Sunday was exaggerated but it was possible, according to "Sam Peeps," to have two poached eggs and eight quarts of beer even on Sunday. Interview with Jack D. Lusher, Ottawa, 29 Mar. 1994.

40 For Canadian football, see *Dalhousie Gazette*, 3 Oct. 1947. Lusher was from Ontario. The issue of the *Halifax Wail* (23 Oct. 1948) was withdrawn after being published, but a number of copies got out. Unfortunately it is not in DUA's file of the *Gazette*. See also *Dalhousie Gazette*, 11, 14, 18 Jan. 1949, and Senate Minutes, 18, 22 Jan. 1949 and 28 Feb. 1950; interview with Jack D. Lusher.

41 *Dalhousie Gazette*, 19 Oct., 2 Nov. 1948; 18 June 1949; BOG Minutes, 4 Nov. 1948, 10 Jan. 1949.

PANS, Angus L. Macdonald Papers, vol. 940, AEK to Angus L. Macdonald, 2 June 1949; G.E. Wilson to Angus L. Macdonald, 4 Dec. 1949, personal; Angus L.

Macdonald to Sidney Smith, 7 Mar. 1949, strictly personal and confidential; Sidney Smith to Angus L. Macdonald, 21 Mar. 1949, strictly personal and confidential.

42 Angus L. Macdonald Papers, vol. 940, memorandum, "Conditions of grant to Dalhousie Law School," marked "my views, V.C.M.," Vincent MacDonald to Angus L. Macdonald, 23 Mar., 9 Apr. 1949; AEK to Angus L. Macdonald, 11 Apr. 1949; Angus L. Macdonald to AEK, 11 May 1948 (copy); Angus L. Macdonald to Dr P.J. Nicholson, 15 Aug. 1949, personal.

See Willis, *Dalhousie Law School*, pp. 166–7; J. Murray Beck, *Politics of Nova Scotia: Volume Two, 1897–1988* (Tantallon 1988), p. 211.

7 THE WAYS OF THE FIFTIES

1 On curriculum, see *Dalhousie Gazette*, 5 Oct. 1951. For Principal W.A. Mackintosh's 1951 inauguration address, see Frederick W. Gibson, *Queen's University: Volume II 1917–1961: To Serve and Yet Be Free* (Kingston and Montreal 1983), pp. 310–13. President Kerr's designs for secretarial science and home economics were fought off by Dean G.E. Wilson and especially by his successor, Dean W.J. Archibald. Interview, 26 July 1988. For the change in classics, see Faculty of Arts and Science, Minutes, 17 Apr. 1956. It was effective the following September. For a perspective on this 1956 change and after, see Rainer Friedrich, "Classical Studies in Atlantic Canada," *Cahiers des études anciennes* 21, Université du Québec à Trois-Rivières (1995), pp. 95–100.

2 For Mary Mowat, see DUA, staff files 349, AEK to Mary Clark Mowat, 6 Mar. 1947; the alcove story was given to me in 1951 by Professor John F. Graham, a close friend of Miss Mowat's. On Christmas marks of 1958, see Faculty of Arts and Science, Minutes, 15 Jan. 1959. Helen Reynolds was warden of Shirreff Hall from 1955 to 1962.

3 The poem is by "N.B.," called "Red," *Dalhousie Gazette*, 5 Feb. 1954. Bishop Berkeley's theories of perception date from the early eighteenth century.

4 The issue of dress was raised in an anonymous letter, *Dalhousie Gazette*, 24 Jan. 1957: "One distinction between college students and laborers is in the clothes they wear." This provoked some correspondence and an editorial, 30 Jan. 1957. For a general view of Dalhousie in the 1950s, see my article, "Allan Bevan's Dalhousie," *Dalhousie Review* (Spring 1983) republished in *Dalhousie Alumni News* (Summer 1984).

5 Dr Guy R. MacLean (BA '51, MA '53), later dean of residence 1960–4, dean of graduate studies 1965–9, dean of arts and science 1969–75, vice-president academic 1974–80, has read this chapter and made suggestions on this point about the character and loyalties of Dalhousie students. H.L. Scammell's letter is in *Dalhousie Gazette*, 27 Nov. 1953, and Bennet's in 6 Nov. 1953.

6 For Sunova Beach, see ibid., 13, 20, 23, 27 Jan., 3 Feb. 1953. Also Senate Minutes, 4 Feb. 1954.

7 On initiation, see *Dalhousie Gazette*, 2, 16 Oct. 1953; 12 Oct. 1954, editorial; ibid., 5 Feb., 8 Mar. 1955; Senate Minutes, 3 Oct. 1953; 4 Feb. 1954.

8 For observations on salaries, Halifax *Mail-Star*, 29 Jan. 1957, quoted in Oskar Sykora, *Maritime Dental College and Dalhousie Faculty of Dentistry: A History*

(Halifax 1991), p. 86. For J. McG. Stewart's speech, see POC, A-196, "Buildings, A & A, 1944–1950." For Alistair Fraser's comments, A-634, "Alistair Fraser, 1947–1955," Fraser to Eric Harvie, Calgary, 30 July 1953.

9 Gibson, *Queen's*, vol. II, p. 313. On Dalhousie's Christmas examinations in 1954, see *Dalhousie Gazette*, 11 Jan. 1955. The Sam Peeps noted here was not the same as in 1948, but G. Burpee Hallett (BA '55, MA '58).

10 Interview with W.J. Archibald, 26 July 1988.

11 Walter J. Chute, *Chemistry at Dalhousie* (Halifax 1986), pp. 31–6. Note the gloss that such internal accounts are apt to render, Carl Coffin's unhappy adventure with methyl alcohol being put thus: "Unfortunately, Dr. Coffin's sight was seriously affected in 1948." For a more robust account of this incident, interview with W.J. Archibald.

12 See the excellent article by Judith Fingard, "Gender and Inequality at Dalhousie: Faculty Women before 1950," *Dalhousie Review* 64, no. 4 (Winter 1984–5), pp. 687–703, especially pp. 694–5. For Laurie's comments on Bean, see POC, A-720, "K.C. Laurie, 1945–1962," Laurie to AEK, 13 Apr. 1950, personal and private.

13 Interview with W.J. Archibald.

14 Interview with Alan Wilson, 17 Dec. 1993. When this story was told to a medical professor, he said that medical students had to have good English.

15 Fingard, "Gender and Inequality at Dalhousie," pp. 695–7; DUA, staff files 381, "Dixie Pelluet," memorandum, 23 Dec. 1949; BOG Minutes, 10 May 1946, 6 Dec. 1949.

16 POC, A-520, "Faculty of Arts and Science, 1945–1947," Wilson to AEK, 14 Aug. 1946; staff files 530, "Louise Thompson Welch." Some POC was carried over into the files of Henry Davies Hicks, president from 1963 to 1980. These are in thirty-four boxes separate from the POC boxes for 1911–63. The Psychology Department correspondence in HDH's files goes back to 1949. The references here are POC, HDH, box 21, Psychology Department, Wilson to AEK, 26 May 1953 and 10 Aug. 1953, both from Perth.

17 *President's Report, 1950–1954.*

18 See Donald Creighton, *The Forked Road: Canada 1939–1957* (Toronto 1976), p. 185; *Report, Royal Commission on National Development in the Arts, Letters and Sciences, 1949–1951* (Ottawa 1951), especially chapter 21, "Aid to Universities," pp. 352–5; J.W. Pickersgill, *My Years with Louis St Laurent* (Toronto 1975), pp. 139–41; Claude Bissell, *The Imperial Canadian: Vincent Massey in Office* (Toronto 1986), pp. 193–236.

19 Dr Rudolph Ozere, long associated with Dalhousie Medical School as professor of paediatrics, has been good enough to comment on this section. So also has the former dean, Chester Stewart. For R.O. Jones, see staff files, new series, Jones to H.G. Grant, 7 Oct. 1952; *Mail-Star*, 28 Aug. 1984; interview with Mary Allen Jones, 8 Jan. 1996. There is an article on Meyer and Jones by David Lumsden, "The Role of Adolf Meyer and his Students in Canadian and Chinese Psychiatry," in *Culture/Health: China and the Western World* 9, no. 2 (1992–3), pp. 217–52.

For Saunders, see staff files, new series, Mainland to H.G. Grant, 4 July 1937, from Edinburgh; interview with Beecher Weld, 12 Jan. 1988; R.L. de C. H.

Saunders, "The Dalhousie University Mace," *Dalhousie Review* 29, no. 1 (Apr. 1950), pp. 9-14; interview with Dr J.J. Sidorov, 6 Mar. 1994. Dr Sidorov worked for a time under Saunders.

For Jones's secretary, interview with Dr R.M. MacDonald, 7 Nov. 1992; for Atlee, Alex McCarter to PBW, 19 Jan. 1989.

20 POC, A-519, "Faculty of Medicine, 1953-1954," Grant to AEK, 15 Dec. 1953; AEK to Grant, 4 Jan. 1954. The president said he had consulted the chairman of the board about it, who agreed (according to Kerr) that Grant's travel grant would be inappropriate.

21 Members of the Medical Faculty committee were: H.B. Atlee, C.J.W. Beckwith, N.H. Gosse, R.O. Jones, J.A. McCarter, R.M. MacDonald, R.L. deC. H. Saunders. For the background in the Department of Medicine, see R.M. MacDonald and Lea C. Steeves, *A History of the Department of Medicine, Dalhousie University, 1868-1975* (Halifax 1995). The main Dalhousie sources are POC, A-579, "Faculty of Medicine, 1953-1954"; A-1035, "Faculty of Medicine, Committee on Autonomy, 1954," staff files 487, "Chester B. Stewart."

22 Staff files 206, "Dr. Clyde Holland"; H.G. Grant to AEK, 23 Jan. 1952. Grant mentioned a protest of younger members of the department in March 1951.

23 There is much detail in President Kerr's section-by-section comments on the Faculty of Medicine's protest and resolutions of 26 Jan. 1954. The president's comments, some twenty pages, are dated 15 Feb. 1954.

24 The history of the Izaak Walton Club of Dalhousie is by J.G. Aldous, "Trout Tales: Chronicles of the Izaak Walton Club of Dalhousie" (Jan. 1984). Dr Aldous's daughter, Joleen Aldous Gordon ('67) has kindly loaned me this manuscript. Comments on the club were also made by Dr John Szerb in an interview 27 Oct. 1994; Dr Chester Stewart to author, 30 Nov. 1994.

25 POC, A-867, "Research, Medical Faculty, 1947-1962." The 1953 McCarter Committee report is a nineteen-page document. See especially pp. 3, 6, 12.

26 J.A. McCarter to PBW, 19 Jan. 1989; POC, A-1035, Medical Faculty resolutions, 26 Jan. 1954.

27 BOG Minutes, 3, 24 Feb., 9 Nov. 1954. Lt.-Gov. Fraser's comments are reported by J.A. McCarter to PBW, 19 Jan. 1989. Alistair Fraser came back to Nova Scotia from Montreal in 1952, when he was appointed to the Board of Governors, and shortly after made lieutenant-governor of Nova Scotia. His priority was the former, not the latter; indeed the only reason he accepted the lieutenant-governorship was in order to do something for Dalhousie. POC, A-634, "Alistair Fraser, 1947-1955," Fraser to Eric Harvie, Calgary, 30 July 1953.

28 Staff files 487, "Chester B. Stewart," Stewart to AEK, 8 Jan. 1954; drafts of conditions, Mar. 1954, with emendations by AEK; to the suggestion that he might be assistant dean of medicine until Grant retired in 1954, Stewart replied, "I think I have sufficient administrative experience to handle the Dean's work without the apprenticeship," Stewart to AEK, 5 Aug. 1952.

Laurie's position, as chairman of the board, is contained in POC, A-2035, handwritten draft of a letter to Alistair Fraser, 15 Mar. 1954, where Laurie said he had instructed Kerr to give the Medical Faculty a free hand. Dean Stewart's role and subsequent relations with President Kerr is set out in Stewart to author, 30 Nov.

1994. The delightful reminiscence of Smallwood is in Dean Stewart's address to the dental convocation, May 1976. It is in Henry Hicks's presidential papers, POC, HDH, box 15.

29 For R.C. Dickson, see especially *A History of the Department of Medicine, Dalhousie University 1868–1975* (Halifax 1995), "The Dickson Years, 1956–1974," pp. 36–51; staff files, new series, "R.C. Dickson," C.B. Stewart to Dickson, 12 Aug. 1955; Dickson to Stewart, 25 Aug. 1955; Stewart to AEK, 12, 20 Sept. 1955; Dr Ian Macdonald, chief of service, medicine, Sunnybrook Hospital, to AEK, 24 Jan. 1956; HDH to Dickson, 17 Sept. 1974; Dickson to HDH, 16 Oct. 1974. *Mail-Star*, 12 Jan. 1970, 15 June 1974. Interviews with Dr J.J. Sidorov, 14 Apr. 1995, 3 Apr. 1996.

For Dickson's 1980 convocation address, POC, HDH, box 17, Convocation Addresses, Dickson to W.A. MacKay, 28 May 1980.

30 POC, A-184, Minutes of Six and Six, 21 Dec. 1949; ibid., 22 July 1952, taken from a resumé in the minutes. The words are as written in the minutes but the dialogue is much shortened.

31 POC, A-952, "J. McGregor Stewart," Stewart to K.C. Laurie, 29 May 1954; Senate Minutes, 29 Jan. 1953; Senate Committee Report is dated 15 Mar. 1954. The regulations were approved by the board on 2 Feb. 1956.

32 BOG Minutes, 22 Feb., 2 Apr. 1955; POC, A-719, "K.C. Laurie," Laurie to AEK, 8 Mar., 25 Aug. 1955; A-168, Board of Governors, Laurie to C.F. Mackenzie, 19 Sept. 1955; interview with D.H. McNeill, 4 Apr. 1990.

33 POC, A-1042, "King's College, Historical Review"; BOG Minutes, 10 Dec. 1953, has Brigadier Laing's memorandum on Dalhousie-King's relations. The agreement itself, signed by K.C. Laurie and A.E. Kerr for Dalhousie, and the Anglican bishop and the new president of King's, H.L. Puxley, is in A-1043.

34 John Willis, *A History of Dalhousie Law School* (Toronto 1979), p. 143. Much of this section on the Law School is based upon this delightful history.

35 Ibid., pp. 165, 172–3. President Kerr remarked to an old downtown part-time law professor, and member of the Board of Governors, "as one member of the Board to another, I do not mind saying that I have had some concern, since I became President, as to whether we were maintaining a staff [in the Law School] sufficiently strong to justify our good name." POC, A-820, "G.G. Patterson," AEK to Patterson, Mar. 1950.

36 POC, A-820, Patterson to AEK, 13 Mar. 1950, private and personal, congratulating Dalhousie on bringing Read as dean. Patterson recalled how he tried to persuade Judge Wallace not to plow young Read in torts, but the judge was adamant. Patterson told Read to soldier on, that he would make good. For Carleton Stanley's reaction in 1934, see staff files 402, "Horace Read," Read to CS, 13 June 1934, telegram; CS to Read, 18 June 1934, telegram. President Stanley wanted Read back but was forced to accept the inevitable. See also Willis, *Dalhousie Law School*, pp. 170–1.

37 Willis, *Dalhousie Law School*, p. 163.

38 See Oskar Sykora, *Maritime Dental College and Dalhousie Faculty of Dentistry: A History* (Halifax 1991), pp. 86–92; POC, A-720, "K.C. Laurie," AEK to Laurie, 13 Dec. 1951, confidential; interview with J.D. McLean, 27 Feb. 1987.

39 Staff files 309, "J.D. McLean," Walter McKenzie to H.L. Scammell, 9 Mar. 1952, telegram, from Edmonton; AEK memorandum, 16 July 1952; McLean to AEK, 20 Nov. 1952, from Edmonton; AEK to McLean, 7 Deb. 1953.

40 Sykora, *Dalhousie Faculty of Dentistry*, pp. 88–92.

41 POC, A-521, "Faculty of Arts and Science," Wilson to AEK, Apr. 1955; interview with W.J. Archibald, 26 July 1988.

42 BOG Minutes, 7 Aug. 1952, 10 Nov. 1953. There is an interesting collection of Dunn Papers in the House of Lords Record Office, London, in the Beaverbrook Papers, G/39, G/40, with some Dalhousie correspondence. Lord Beaverbrook used these papers to write *Courage: The Story of Sir James Dunn* (Fredericton 1961). Sir James's contributions to Dalhousie were listed by Dalhousie at Lady Dunn's request in 1956, in Beaverbrook Papers, G/39, and also POC, A-505, "Sir James Dunn 1948–1956." As to Dunn's marks at Dalhousie, Beaverbrook says his graduating marks were high (*Courage*, p. 54) but they were not. Dunn was spending too much time working at jobs outside Dalhousie and made only passes in his last year. (Beaverbrook Papers, G/39, has a list of marks signed by Dalhousie's registrar, Beatrice Smith, dated 20 Mar. 1956.) The 1909–10 correspondence from Murray Macneill is in G/39; there are also letters from G.S. Campbell and President MacKenzie.

43 Beaverbrook Papers, G/40, has correspondence between Irene Dunn and Christofor, Nov. 1941, some of which Beaverbrook quotes in *Courage*, pp. 156–8, with omissions. There is an extended obituary of Lady Beaverbrook in the London *Daily Telegraph*, 31 Oct. 1994.

8 IN THE FAST LANE

1 See Robert Bothwell and William Kilbourn, *C.D. Howe* (Toronto 1979), pp. 36–7, 46–8, 277, 332–4; Lord Beaverbrook, *Courage: The Story of Sir James Dunn* (Fredericton 1961), pp. 202, 268. Relations between Dunn and Howe, as well as a judicious survey of Dunn's business history, are set out in Duncan McDowall, *Steel at the Sault: Francis H. Clergue, Sir James Dunn and the Algoma Steel Corporation 1910–1956* (Toronto 1984).

Lord Beaverbrook (1879–1964) has several biographies. The best and most recent is Anne Chisholm and Michael Davie, *Beaverbrook: A Life* (London 1992). His comment on Lady Dunn in 1956 (p. 508), is taken from Richard Cockett, ed., *My Dear Max, The Letters of Brendan Bracken to Lord Beaverbrook* (London 1990), p. 50.

2 DUA, POC, A-671, "C.D. Howe, 1957–1959," AEK to Howe, 8 Aug. 1957; BOG Minutes, 22, 29 Aug. 1957. For Howe, see especially National Archives of Canada, C.D. Howe Papers, vol. 123, Edith MacMechan to Howe, 30 Aug. 1957, from Chester; Howe to Edith MacMechan, 9 Sept. 1957. Mrs MacMechan reflected how pleased Archie would have been that Howe was being made chancellor. For Professor Archibald MacMechan, see also *Lives of Dalhousie*, 1, especially pp. 159–61, 206–7.

The first mention of Howe as a possibility for the Dalhousie board is in POC, A-718, "H.V.D. Laing 1949–1958," memorandum, AEK to Laing, 28 June 1957.

This is a list of twenty-six items discussed between them. The replacement of Sir James by Howe seems to have been raised by Laing. Kerr's question was whether Howe considered himself a citizen of New Brunswick.

 The important correspondence with Lady Dunn is in the C.D. Howe Papers, vol. 199, Lady Dunn to Howe, 29 Aug. 1957, Howe to Lady Dunn, 29 Aug. 1957. Both letters originate in St Andrews and may have been delivered by hand. The use of the C.D. Howe Papers, so important for this chapter, was made possible by the kind permission of his son, William H. Howe ('40).

3 The report on the construction defects in the Arts and Administration Building is in POC, A-197, "Buildings, Arts and Administration," D.A. Gray and Co., n.d., but probably Apr. 1956. The report was especially critical of the mortar, both in its quality and application. For Mathers & Haldenby, see BOG Minutes, 12 Feb., 20 June, 19 Sept. 1957.

4 C.D. Howe Papers, vol. 119, Lady Dunn to Howe, 24 Dec. 1957, from St Andrews; Howe to Lady Dunn, 30 Dec. 1957.

5 Beaverbrook's role at UNB is described in Chisholm and Davie, *Beaverbrook*, pp. 463–5. The party for Mrs Killam is mentioned in ibid., p. 497, but it is taken without acknowledgment from Douglas How, *Canada's Mystery Man of High Finance: The Story of Isaac Walton Killam and his Glittering Wife Dorothy* (Hantsport 1986), p. 158. For Howe, see C.D. Howe Papers, vol. 120, Howe to AEK, 18 Sept. 1957, personal and confidential; vol. 119, Lady Dunn to Howe, 14 Nov. 1957.

6 *Montreal Daily Star*, 21 Dec. 1957; POC, A-175, Board of Governors, G.E. Hall to AEK, 9 Sept. 1957, from London, Ont.; Frances Ireland, secretary to Sidney Smith, to AEK, 4 Sept. 1957, from Toronto; Cyril James to AEK, 4 Sept. 1957, from Montreal. Of the three, James's letter was the clearest and most succinct. See also Frank Covert to AEK, 15 Oct. 1957.

7 Howe Papers, vol. 119, Lady Dunn to Howe, 9 Nov. 1957, personal, from St Andrews; Howe to Lady Dunn, 12 Nov. 1957, personal, from Ottawa. (There are two letters of this date in the file; the quotation is from the second.) Ibid., Lady Dunn to Howe, 14 Nov. 1957.

8 For Kerr's suggestions re a chair in divinity, see ibid., Howe to Lady Dunn, 18 Nov. 1957. Re Gaelic, ibid., vol. 120, Howe to AEK, 10 Jan. 1958, confidential. Two weeks earlier Kerr approached the Canada Council on the same subject, POC, A-328, "The Canada Council, 1957–1961," AEK to Albert Trueman, 20 Dec. 1957. It was clearly a trial balloon. For Howe's installation, Howe Papers, vol. 229, Lady Dunn to Howe, 26 Mar. 1958; Howe to Lady Dunn, 3 Apr. 1958, confidential. Howe thought his installation ceremony not that bad, "in the Edinburgh tradition, short but well done." He noted the water at lunch laconically.

9 Ibid., Howe to Lady Dunn, 22 Apr. 1958.

10 Ibid., Howe to Lady Dunn, 16 May 1958; Lady Dunn to Howe, 15 May 1958; Howe to Lady Dunn, 16 May 1958; Lady Dunn to AEK, 9 May 1958, reported in Lady Dunn to Howe, 28 May 1958. Kerr's reiteration of his position on liquor is in vol. 120, AEK to Howe, 2 July 1958.

 So far as this author is aware, there was never any specific policy or regulation on the subject of liquor at Dalhousie University funtions. After 1918, when

Halifax became dry by federal wartime regulation, until 1930 when the Nova Scotia Liquor Commission was formed, there were the inevitable outside restrictions, but not internal university ones. What was followed was social custom, what young women, chaperones at dances, student opinion, parents, would tolerate, entirely informal and extremely difficult to elucidate. There are no references in Carleton Stanley's presidency one way or the other. When Kerr came, one of the first things he did, virtually by executive fiat, was to stop faculty Saturday night beer and poker in the gym. The policy was constructed by him with Colonel Laurie's strong support. After Laurie's retirement as chairman of the board in 1955, Kerr's policy became more vulnerable, subject to whatever board and president might wish to agree on.

11 Howe Papers, W.H. Howard to Laing, 19 Aug. 1958, from Montreal, copy sent to C.D. Howe; also in POC, A-208, "Buildings, Sir James Dunn." For Howe, see Howe Papers, vol. 119, Howe to Lady Dunn, 16, 24 Sept. 1958; "Jack J." to "C.D.," 2 Oct. 1958; Howe to Johnstone, 7 Oct. 1958; Howe to Lady Dunn, 24 Aug., 30 Oct. 1959.

12 Ibid., Howe to Lady Dunn, 2 June 1958. Board of Governors meeting is reported by A. Gordon Archibald, member of the board, in *Memoirs* (Halifax 1993), p. 171; Archibald also refers to the incident in an interview on 6 June 1988, in Halifax. *Dalhousie Gazette*, 22, 29 Oct. 1958.

13 On BOG changes, see Howe Papers, vol. 119, Howe to Lady Dunn, 10 Nov. 1958. On Dalhousie Law School, this account leans heavily upon John Willis, *A History of Dalhousie Law School*, (Toronto 1979), pp. 185–91.

14 On Lederman and Lady Dunn, see DUA, staff files 258, "W.R. Lederman," Lederman to Lady Dunn, 9 July 1958, from Halifax; Lady Dunn to Lederman, 11 July 1958; Lederman to Lady Dunn, 19 July 1958, from North Sydney. For Dean Read and Lady Dunn, see Howe Papers, vol. 121, Howe to Read, 15 July 1958, and 16 Sept. 1958, confidential.

15 Howe Papers, vol. 119, Howe to Lady Dunn, 11 Dec. 1958; Lady Dunn to Howe, 13 Dec. 1958. For Archibald's 1958 resignation, see BOG Minutes, 23 Sept. 1958; *Dalhousie Gazette*, 22 Oct. 1958, "Periscope" by Murray Fraser. On salaries, Howe Papers, vol. 121, W.J. Archibald to AEK, 13 Dec. 1958 (copy); Archibald to McInnes, 14 Dedc. 1958 (copy). Archibald singled out several members of staff who ought to be paid more and promoted. It was evidence of Archibald's largeness of spirit and willingness to change his mind that one professor of economics, whom he told in 1956 that he had little future at Dalhousie, was included in the list of worthy Arts and Science staff who had to be retained.

For Lady Dunn's views of Archibald, see Howe Papers, vol. 119, Lady Dunn to Howe, 13 Dec. 1958.

16 On the failure to publish Beaverbrook's speech, see Howe Papers, vol. 119, Lady Dunn to Howe, 17 Feb. 1959, personal, from St Andrews; for other complaints about Kerr by Lady Dunn, see Lady Dunn to Howe, 2 Nov. 1959.

17 The 1959 Dalhousie-King's Convention of 25 Nov. 1959 was a revision of the 1956 agreement. The dean of arts and science was to be nominated by Dalhousie's president but in consultation with the president of King's, who might in turn discuss any matter with the dean of arts and science. The dean's authority would

extend over King's eight professors. King's would receive the income from the Carnegie endowment and supplement it. King's would remit to Dalhousie 20 per cent of all King's federal and provincial grants. King's graduating students would get a Dalhousie degree but with special reference to King's in distinctive letters and with the seals of both institutions. A liaison committee was established with the two chairmen of the board, the two presidents, and two members appointed by each board, to meet once a year. The text is in POC, MS 1/3 President's Office, Legal Counsel. See also BOG *Minutes*, 6 Jan. 1960.

18 For Howe's hopes for effecting Kerr's removal, see Howe Papers, vol. 119, Howe to Lady Dunn, 19 Feb. 1959. For Kerr's 1959 illness, Howe to Lady Dunn, 13 Apr. 1959; Lady Dunn to Howe, 24 Apr. 1959, confidential; Howe to Lady Dunn, 29 Apr. 1959.

19 Howe's ruminations about Kerr are in a letter to Lady Dunn's Saint John lawyer, Norwood Carter; Carter to Howe, 23 Apr. 1959; Howe to Carter, 24 Apr. 1959, most confidential.

On President Kerr, see Howe Papers, vol. 119, Howe to Lady Dunn, 6 Nov. 1959; his letter to Larry MacKenzie of UBC about a replacement for Kerr is in my *Lord of Point Grey* (Vancouver 1987), pp. 182, 241n. MacKenzie recommended his assistant, Geoffrey Andrew. Howe's interview with the departing A.T. Stewart is remembered by Stewart, Stewart to author, 7 June 1993, from Queen's.

On Dalhousie building program, see Howe Papers, vol. 120, Howe to AEK, 12 Mar. 1960, from Montreal. On salaries, it can be pointed out that the order of magnitude between 1908 and 1958 would be at least 500 per cent. See also Bothwell and Kilbourn, *C.D. Howe*, p. 343.

20 Howe Papers, vol. 130, Howe to AEK, 11 Nov. 1960. Another of Lady Dunn's grievances was that in Oct. 1959 President Kerr (or some other Dalhousie official) asked if they could use the Dunn building for a reception a year before it was officially open. Lady Dunn was scandalized. It was *her* building and was "quite '*out of bounds*' until I have officially opened it"; vol. 119, Lady Dunn to Howe, 12 Oct. 1959.

Howe's warning about Beaverbrook and UNB to Lady Dunn is referred to indirectly in two letters in vol. 122, Howe to McInnes, 1 Apr. 1960, private and confidential and Howe to McInnes, 31 Oct. 1960, private and confidential.

21 Lady Dunn's little blue book, *Remembrance*, is now something of a rarity, twenty-three pages and privately printed. The quotations are from pp. 8–9, 15. Howe's complaint about Kerr and Lady Dunn are in Howe Papers, vol. 119, Howe to Haldenby, 23 Oct. 1957. Howe's comment on the effect of Lady Dunn's gifts is in ibid., Howe to Norwood Carter, 24 Apr. 1959, most confidential. On Jack Johnstone, POC, A-672, "C.D. Howe," Howe to AEK, 12 Sept., 11 Nov. 1960, from Montreal. Jack Johnstone's comment was reported to me by Professor George Wilson in 1959.

22 Douglas How's book does not mention these stories about Mrs Killam, but he gives them in a letter, Douglas How to author, 6 Oct. 1994, reporting conversations with W.S. Godfrey, Donald Byers, and Watson Kirkconnell. Howe Papers, vol. 120, Howe to AEK, 4, 18 Sept. 1957, both letters personal and confidential.

23 The hypothesis is drawn from the evidence available, as always in history incomplete: Senate Minutes, 28 Feb., 4 May 1959; C.D. Howe Papers, vol. 120, Howe to Mrs Killam, 13, 22, 30 Apr. 1959; POC, A-672, "C.D. Howe," Howe to AEK, 21 Apr. 1959, personal; memorandum, C.L. Bennet to AEK, 22 Apr. 1959.

24 Howe Papers, vol. 121, Howe to McInnes, 16 Nov. 1959, confidential; vol. 120, Howe to AEK, 28 Dec. 1960.

25 Senate Minutes, 30 Apr. 1958; BOG Minutes, 27 May 1958, 24 Nov. 1959, 6 Jan. 1960.

26 POC, A-330, "CAUT, 1957–1963," Covert to AEK, 6 Dec. 1961; staff files 108, "G.V. Douglas," AEK to Douglas, 23 May 1957; Frank Covert to AEK, 12 Oct. 1957. Interview with Beecher and Kathy Weld, 12 Jan. 1988. Weld said that the old pension was known to be inadequate; one knew that and acted accordingly.

27 Howe Papers, vol. 121, Howe to McNeill, 29 Sept. 1958; POC, A-182, "Board of Governors, Finance Committee," Covert to McInnes, 29 Sept. 1960.

28 POC, A-522, "Arts and Science, 1955–1963," personal memorandum by AEK, meeting of Faculty Council, 18 Oct. 1960. Staff files 198, "D.J. Heasman," Archibald to AEK, 22 Mar. 1960; AEK to Archibald, 24 Mar. 1960. Heasman returned to Dalhousie in 1961, but went back to the University of Saskatchewan in 1963. About Professor Johnstone, see staff files 220, "J.H.L. Johnstone," 29 June 1960; AEK memorandum, 12 Sept. 1960.

29 Interview with W.J. Archibald, 17 Nov. 1994; POC, A-1029, "Faculty of Arts and Science, 1955–1960," Archibald to AEK, Howe, and McInnes, 4 Apr. 1960; Faculty of Arts and Science Minutes, 7 Apr. 1960. The minutes record that the resolution was passed "unanimously," but this probably meant without a dissenting voice, academic (and other) bodies being rather casual on this point of procedure. Arts and Science Faculty Minutes from 1959 onward are in the offices of the deans of science and of arts and social sciences.

30 On D.G. Lochhead, Lochhead to author, 31 Jan. 1990, from Mount Allison University. On A.T. Stewart, Stewart to author, 7 June 1993, from Queen's University. On Grant, POC, A-710, "Kings, 1958–1963," AEK memorandum on conversation with Puxley, 27 Oct. 1960. Grant was not an atheist, but the range of his questions, such as "Does God Exist?", the title of one of his texts, was clearly disconcerting to the church. Interview with Carol Vincent Sinclair, 5 Nov. 1994. For Kerr's views, see A-522, memorandum by AEK, items discussed with Dean Hicks, 31 Nov. 1960. For further background, see William Christian, *George Grant: A Biography* (Toronto 1993), pp. 196–204.

31 *Dalhousie Gazette*, 6, 13, 20, 27 Oct. 1960; Denis Stairs to author, 5 Nov. 1994. Dean McLean's protest is in POC, A-554, "Faculty of Dentistry, 1954–1963," McLean to AEK, 28 Oct. 1960. For Howe, interview with A.G. Archibald, 6 June 1988; Bothwell and Kilbourn, *Howe*, pp. 346–7.

32 POC, A-226, "Men's Residence, 1957–63," Theakston to AEK, 15 Jan. 1959; BOG Minutes, 10 Mar., 17 Sept. 1959. On the student union and other changes, *Dalhousie Gazette*, 18 Nov., 2 Dec. 1959; 10 Feb. 1960. On CAUT, see Howe Papers, vol. 120, Howe to AEK, 11 Nov. 1960.

33 The offer of the deanship is noted by Dr Guy MacLean, interview, 23 Jan. 1987.

34 On Henry Hicks, there is a long series of interviews conducted over some days in August 1983 by Tom Earle, for the National Archives of Canada. It is here desig-

nated HDH (E). There is a copy of this set of interviews in DUA. I also conducted three interviews with Hicks, 4, 8 July and 9 Aug. 1988.

As to the provenance of the Dalhousie offer of the deanship of arts and science, Hicks gives two different versions. In HDH (E), p. 54, he credits Kerr with the offer. In my interview with him, he attributes the offer to Frank Covert, a more likely choice. Interview, 4 July 1988,

On other aspects, see HDH (E), pp. 54–5; Howe Papers, vol. 120, Howe to AEK, 31 Oct. 1960. Stanfield described his talk with Howe in an interview on 4 Dec. 1986, in Ottawa.

35 On Hicks's background, POC, A-806, "Nova Scotia Department of Education, 1950–1963," HDH to AEK, 11 Apr. 1951. He is also mentioned several times in John Reid, *Mount Allison University Volume II: 1914–1963* (Toronto 1984), especially p. 278; Hicks's 1957 statement on standards is quoted on pp. 284–5.

President Puxley's revealing letter is in POC, A-710, "King's, 1958–1963," Puxley to AEK, 20 Oct. 1960, confidential. On Dalhousie faculty reactions, see POC, A-522, "Faculty of Arts and Science, 1955–1963," personal memorandum by AEK, 18 Oct. 1960; A.S. Mowat to AEK, 19 Oct. 1960; and personal memorandum by AEK of conversation with F.R. Hayes, 27 Oct. 1960.

On the visit to Hicks of the three professors, see HDH (E), pp. 56–7; interview with HDH, 4 July 1988; telephone conversation, Nita Sederis Graham (widow of J.F. Graham), 18 July 1994; James Doull to author, 10 Oct. 1994.

36 POC, A-522, "Arts and Science, 1955–1963," HDH to AEK, 26 Jan. 1961; Senate Minutes of 13 Feb. 1961 do not contain the president's remarks, but that is to be expected. They do contain a resolution of the Faculty of Arts and Science that staffing is becoming critical. Hicks's reply to the president is A-522, HDH to AEK, 14 Feb. 1961.

On the president's guarding of access to the board: when D.J. Heasman resigned in 1963 to go to the University of Saskatchewan, he sent a copy of his letter of resignation with its critical comments to the chairman of the board. Kerr replied to Heasman with some animus that he ought, as a political scientist, to know university procedure better than that. See staff files 198, "D.J. Heasman," Heasman to AEK, 31 Mar. 1963; AEK to Heasman, 4 June 1963.

Bronson's letter is in staff files 42; "Howard L. Bronson," Bronson to AEK, 12 Apr. 1960.

37 Senate Minutes, 8 Dec. 1960, 13 Feb., 21 Nov., 11 Dec. 1961. That Kerr's resignation was not voluntary is made clear in an interview with Donald McInnes, 2 Aug. 1988, Halifax. McLean's views of AEK are in an interview, 17 Feb. 1987. The "Limelighters" incident is described by Senator Michael Kirby, telephone interview, 22 Sept. 1995.

38 For the president's correspondence with Douglas Lochhead, university librarian, DUA, MS 1/23, B2, Librarian's correspondence, Lochhead to AEK, 27 Mar. 1957; AEK to Lochhead, 30 Apr. 1957; for more general complaints, Lochhead to AEK, 7 Apr. 1959.

"Dief the Chief Speaks at Dal" is in *Dalhousie Gazette*, 15 Nov. 1961, and is reproduced in the *Chronicle-Herald*, 29 Jan. 1962. The consequences are described in a letter from Allen Robertson to author, 12 Apr. 1990. Robertson ('63) was president of the Student Council. Michael Kirby, the editor, also gives an account in an interview, 22 Apr. 1995.

For the 1963 difficulty, see *Dalhousie Gazette*, 16 Jan. 1963; Senate Minutes, 14 May 1963; and interview with Ian MacKenzie, 23 Aug. 1994, in Halifax.

39 The military precision of Board of Governors meetings under Laing's chairmanship is suggested by A. Gordon Archibald, *Memoirs* (Halifax: privately printed 1993), p. 169. Jack Johnstone's view of Hicks's prospects as Dalhousie's president is in a letter to Alex Stewart late in 1960, but is second- hand, mentioned in A.T. Stewart to author, 7 June 1993, from Kingston, Ontario.

9 DALHOUSIE BEING TRANSFORMED

1 The Jim Bennet poem is from *Jim Bennet's Verse* (Halifax 1979), called "Just for Hicks (Henry D.)" and quoted with Jim Bennet's permission.

For personal characteristics, interview with HDH, 8 July 1988; NA, HDH (E) interviews, Ottawa 1983, p. 10.

2 Interview with Jeffrey Holmes, Montreal, 3 June 1995; "Dalhousie and the AUU," in Holmes to author, 18 July 1995, from Ottawa. Holmes was executive director of the AAU from 1971 to 1978. For Dalton Camp's opinion on HDH, see his *Gentlemen, Players and Politicians* (Toronto 1970), p. 152. Not least among Dalhousie academics who appreciated Hicks's talent and who knew him at close quarters was H.B.S. Cooke, dean of arts and science, 1963–8. Cooke to PBW, 29 Jan. 1996.

3 Dean Read reported to Senate, 14 Jan. 1963; there was then a motion that Senate express its dissatisfaction with that too soft mode of proceeding, but it was not carried; the sentiment of Senate was expressed by Read, thanking the chairman of the board for his cordiality. Also Senate Minutes, Horace Read to McInnes, 1 Feb. 1963.

4 HDH (E), p. 82; for Weldon see *Lives of Dalhousie, 1*, pp. 168–9.

5 BOG Minutes, 2 May 1963. Hicks's property was a 120' x 160' lot, and the question of what to do about his wish to continue to live there was given to a board committee, 27 June 1963. On 30 Aug. 1963, the executive committee agreed the university could buy Hicks's Coburg Road house for $40,000. There may have been further negotiations on the price, for Hicks later mentioned that he had sold his property for $45,000 early in 1964. POC, HDH, box 29, "Properties," HDH to Nicholas Destounis, 11 June 1964. R.B. Cameron's strong opposition to giving over the president's house to Psychology is noted by F.R. Hayes, then vice-president, in ibid., box 21, "Psychology," Hayes to H.B.S. Cooke, 16 Dec. 1963.

6 POC, HDH, box 29, "Provincial Governments, Nova Scotia," AEK to Stanfield, 27 June 1958; 5 May 1959; Stanfield to AEK, 1 June 1960; AEK to Stanfield, 20 June 1962.

7 E.F. Sheffield, "Canadian Universities and Colleges: Enrollment Projected to 1965," Proceedings of the NCCU [AUCC] (Ottawa 1955).

8 POC, HDH, box 34, "University Grants Committee," Hicks to Murphy, 26 Mar. 1963; University of British Columbia Archives (UBCA) Norman A. MacKenzie Papers (NAMM), box 184, Stanfield to MacKenzie, 12 Dec. 1962; interview with

Dr Arthur Murphy, 19 July 1985, Halifax. The statute that set up the University Grants Committee is 14 Eliz. II, chap. 16.

9 A short history of Larry MacKenzie's work with the University Grants Committee of Nova Scotia is given in P.B. Waite, *Lord of Point Grey: Larry MacKenzie of UBC* (Vancouver 1987), pp. 196–8.

10 POC, HDH, box 34, "University Grants Committee," Hicks to Arthur Murphy, 26 Mar. 1963, a four-page summary of their discussion of the previous day, with new information added; HDH's notes of the interview with MacKenzie, 30 Nov. 1963; HDH to the UGC, 9 Dec. 1964; UGC to HDH, 30 Nov. 1963.

11 Ibid., box 2, "Atlantic Association of Universities," McKay to HDH, 21 Jan. 1964; letters also from President Cragg of Mount Allison (3 Feb.), Mons. Somers of St Francis Xavier (5 Feb.), and Ray Gushue of Memorial (11 Feb.); Somers to HDH, 31 July 1964; minutes of meeting of deans of men and women, at Mount Allison, 17 Oct. 1966.

12 There is a succinct description of this dramatic change by Dalhousie's vice-president, Horace Read, of the 1966 AUCC meeting that had to digest the changes proposed by the federal-provincial conference of October. Hicks was away in Paris at UNESCO meetings. See box 34, "UGC," Read to HDH, 15 Nov. 1966, addressed to Prince de Galles Hotel, Paris.

13 POC, HDH, box 2, "AAU," Colin McKay to HDH, 5 Nov. 1964. For the Stanfield speech and its effects, see *Chronicle-Herald*, 13, 14 Jan., 12 Feb. 1965; *Dalhousie Gazette*, 22 Jan. 1965; POC, HDH, box 29, "Provincial Governments, Nova Scotia," HDH to Stanfield, 25 Jan. 1965, dictated from hospital.

On the proposed amalgamation of NSTC with Dalhousie, see: POC, HDH, box 20, "Nova Scotia Technical College," HDH to Rev. W.P. Fogarty, engineering, St Francis Xavier, 11 Feb., 29 Apr. 1965; St Francis Xavier statement of 8 Nov. 1965 about engineering education. Dean McLaughlin's report was done in the week of 10 Jan. 1966, and is short and to the point; ibid., C.J. Mackenzie to HDH, 14 Apr. 1966; HDH to Mackenzie, 21 Apr. 1966; Stanfield to HDH, 10 May 1966. Stanfield's reply in 1965 to the Nova Scotia university presidents is ibid., box 2, "AAU," Stanfield to the presidents, 12 Mar. 1965.

14 BOG Minutes, 6, 10 July 1964; POC, HDH, box 28, HDH to Senator Isnor, 9 July 1964; ibid., box 13, "City of Halifax, 1964–9," R.A. Cluney, Dalhousie's lawyer, commenting on the city staff report on Dalhousie's application for rezoning, n.d. but 1965. The Technical College plan by architecture students was published in the Royal Architectural Institute of Canada *Journal*, and in the Halifax *Mail-Star*, 10 Sept. 1965. The correspondence is in POC, HDH, box 28, "Marshall & Merrett," Shadbolt to HDH, 21 Sept. 1965; HDH to Shadbolt, 24 Sept. 1965. Also interview with Douglas Shadbolt, 1 June 1990, Vancouver.

15 POC, HDH, box 11, "Campus Planning," A.F. Chisholm to HDH, 11 Feb. 1965; HDH to Chisholm, 12 Feb. 1965; ibid., box 8, "Central Services Building," HDH to Chisholm, 21 Dec. 1966; Chisholm to PBW, n.d. rec'd 18 Dec. 1995, from Great Village, NS.

16 Douglas How, *Canada's Mystery Man of High Finance: The Story of Izaak Walton Killam and his Glittering Wife Dorothy* (Hantsport 1986), p. 54. The source for the story of her miscarriage is interview with Donald McInnes, 2 Aug. 1988.

17 Interview with Robert Stanfield, 4 Dec, 1986, in Ottawa.

18 "The Killam Canelco Endowment at Dalhousie, an Academic Plan," by K.T. Leffek, May 1985. K.T. Leffek was dean of graduate studies, 1972–90.

19 Interview, HDH, 9 Aug. 1988.

20 The party with the deans is described by HDH in my interview with him, without any dates. It is clear from correspondence in the HDH presidential papers that Dorothy Killam asked to meet the deans; the meeting probably took place about 15 May 1965. POC, HDH, box 26, "Mrs. I.W. Killam," HDH to Mrs Killam, 10 May 1965.

21 Interview with HDH, 9 Aug. 1988; interview with Donald McInnes, 2 Aug. 1988; How, *Killam*, pp. 163–4.

22 There is a full copy of her will in POC, HDH, box 26, "Mrs. I.W. Killam." The residue was split in a peculiar way. Two-fifths would go to the four universities named in the text, in the proportion 40:25:25:10, Dalhousie getting the 40. The other three-fifths was to be divided between the Canada Council and the named universities, the latter sharing in the same proportions. The trustees determined that of the three-fifths, the Canada Council would get 40 per cent and the named universities 60 per cent. The net effect of the residue section of the Killam will was to give Dalhousie just over 30 per cent, or about $20 million.

23 POC, HDH, box 28, "UNB," HDH to McKay, 3 Jan. 1968. In this letter Hicks gave McKay a full and accurate summary of the Killam gifts.

24 POC, HDH, box 22, "Graduate Studies," W.R. Trost to HDH, 5 June 1964; *President's Report, 1959–1963*, pp. 72–3.

25 Trost gave the history of APICS in a letter to Dr Fred Simpson, its director in the 1980s, Trost to Simpson, 10 July 1987 (copy) from Victoria, in PBW Archive; POC, HDH, box 4, "APICS," E.W.R. Steacie to Trost, 23 Nov. 1961, from Ottawa.

26 For McCarter's opinion, see staff files 278, J.A. McCarter to HDH, 27 Apr. 1965, which includes several examples of Trost's rudeness. One colleague, Mirko Usmiani of Classics, came in 1961 to congratulate Trost on his appointment as dean. Trost kept him waiting, then said, "You do *not* come into this office unannounced. You will wait until I am ready to see you." Usmiani, who prior to this used to just walk in, walked out and never returned. Interview, 31 Dec. 1991. There were also others, Allan Bevan, head of English, for one. On the other side, Devendra Varma of English, widely published, found Trost helpful and open. Interview with D.P. Varma, 19 July 1993. POC, HDH, box 22, "Faculty of Graduate Studies," Trost to HDH, 19 Mar. 1965; HDH to Trost, 29 Dec. 1965.

27 POC, HDH, Trost to H.B.S. Cooke, 29 Jan. 1965; C.B. Stewart to HDH, 14 Oct. 1964; Hicks's views are in two letters: HDH to Cooke, 29 Jan. 1965, and HDH to Cooke and Trost, 15 July 1965. To this letter Trost replied in a minatory epistle the next day, which exasperated Cooke, who disliked its tone and the intransigent attitude it represented. Cooke to HDH, 23 July 1965.

28 Ibid., Trost to HDH, n.d., but marked as received 28 Jan. 1966. Guy MacLean's views on the "Organization of Graduate Studies" is 20 Feb. 1967.

29 McCarter's comment is in DUA, staff files 278, McCarter to HDH, 27 April 1965. For Kaplan, see staff files 232, where there is extensive correspondence, among which Szerb to Kaplan, 8 Feb. 1965, and Kaplan to Szerb, 12 Feb. 1965. Both

letters are marked confidential, but by President Hicks. Dean Stewart's view of Kaplan as possible head of Physiology is abundantly clear in Stewart to AEK, 30 Jan. 1962, confidential. There is also 1966 correspondence with Hicks and two successive presidents of the Dalhousie Faculty Association, G.H. Hatcher (1965–6) and C.R. Brookbank (1966–7). For John Aldous's recollection, interview, 1 June 1990, Vancouver.

30 There is a considerable file on this vexed subject, including angry telephone calls from the president of Mount Allison and Premier Louis Robichaud. See POC, HDH, box 29, "Provincial Governments, New Brunswick," both calls logged 29 Mar. 1965. For some newspaper references see Saint John *Telegraph-Journal*, 2 Apr. 1965, and Halifax *Chronicle-Herald*, 28 June 1965. There were charges that New Brunswick students were being excluded on political grounds which Dean Stewart vigorously denied. "No student had ever been discriminated against for political reasons." *Chronicle-Herald* and *Mail-Star*, both 25 June 1965.

31 POC, HDH, box 11, "Sir Charles Tupper Building." In this file there is a reference to a letter in HDH's office, Pearson to MacKenzie 26 May 1916, without attaching Tupper's name to any building. Hicks had the habit of going through the old presidential files and pulling out letters that intrigued him. Interview with C.B. Stewart, 9 June 1988; POC, HDH, box 11, "Sir Charles Tupper Building," AEK to Alan Clarke, provisional secretary, Canadian Centenary Council, 29 Nov. 1962; Norbert Prefontaine to AEK, 12 Dec. 1962; Prefontaine was the executive director of the Centenary Council. The support of the *Chronicle-Herald* is 27 Dec. 1962.

32 POC, HDH, box 11, "Sir Charles Tupper Building," R.B. Cameron to Philip Dumaresq, 3 Sept. 1963; Stewart to HDH, 9 Sept., 2 Oct. 1963, and 17 Jan. 1964.

33 On the Tupper Medical Building, Arthur Chisholm to PBW, n.d., received 18 Dec. 1995; also 24 Feb. 1996; interview with Dr A.H. Shears, 27 Dec. 1995.

There is a strong letter in POC, A-581, Stewart to AEK, 16 May 1960, confidential, in which Stewart details struggles with Saunders.

For Hicks, see POC, HDH, box 34, "UGC," Cragg to HDH, 19 Jan. 1965; ibid., box 27, "McGrath Report," McGrath to HDH, 4 May 1967.

34 POC, HDH, box 27, Dumaresq to HDH, 7 Nov. 1966, progress report; HDH to J.S. Hodgson, principal secretary to the prime minister, 30 Sept. 1966; HDH to G.G.E. Steele, under-secretary of state, 24 Oct. 1966; HDH to Charles Beazley, clerk of the NS Executive Council, 16 Dec. 1966.

Sir James Macdonald Tupper was seventy-nine, and inherited his title from his elder brother in 1962. Old Sir Charles Tupper was a baronet, hence his knighthood was inherited, via the male line. See also *Chronicle-Herald*, 8 July 1967.

35 POC, HDH, box 11, "Sir Charles Tupper Building," H.L. Scammell to HDH, 17 July 1967, from Cape George; W.A. MacKay to HDH, 15 July 1967, from Halifax.

36 POC, A-917, "School of Nursing, 1919–1949," as well as A-918 to A-921, has correspondence and memoranda. See also Peter Twohig, "'To produce an article we are not capable at present of producing': The Evolution of the Dalhousie University School of Nursing, 1946–1956," *Nova Scotia Historical Review* 15, no. 2 (1995), p. 32; the reference to "poor girls' university" is in a Dalhousie memoran-

dum, 9 Oct. 1948. I am grateful to Dr Twohig for making an early draft of this article available to me. See also POC, A-559, "Faculty of Health Professions 1958–1962," C.B. Stewart to AEK, 5 Dec. 1960.

37 John Willis, *A History of Dalhousie Law School* (Toronto 1979), pp. 205–11. POC, HDH, box 11, "Weldon Building," M.H.F. Harrington to H.E. Read, 17 Feb. 1964; Art Chisholm to HDH, 29 Dec. 1964; same, 12 Feb. 1965; HDH to McNeill, 8 Mar. 1965; Senate Minutes, 11 May 1965.

38 POC, HDH, box 11, Lady Beaverbrook to HDH, 2 Mar. 1967, personal; R.A. Tweedie to HDH, 20 Mar. 1967, from Fredericton (two letters).

39 *Dalhousie Gazette*, 23 Feb. 1967; Senate Minutes, 12 Feb. 1968.

40 Interview with H.B.S. Cooke, 31 May 1990, White Rock, BC. As to a Department of Geography, see Faculty of Arts and Science, Minutes, 31 Jan., 3 Oct. 1967. The letters urging the establishment of Geography were from two well-known geographers, Kenneth Hare, president of UBC, to Cooke, 5 June 1967, and E.G. Pleva, head of geography at the University of Western Ontario, to A.S. Mowat (secretary of the Faculty of Arts and Science), 10 July 1967. On pure and applied mathematics, see A.J. Tingley, *Mathematics at Dalhousie* (1991), pp. 23–6; staff files 282, HDH to MacDonald, 14 Apr. 1965.

41 POC, HDH, box 20, "Faculty of Arts and Science," Cooke to HDH, 6 Feb. 1964; ibid., box 21, Cooke to HDH, 16 Jan. 1968. For information on staff, see ibid., report of 8 May 1974, on citizenship of full-time faculty; see also *Years of Growth and Change: Dalhousie University 1963–4 to 1975–6, The President's Report*, pp. 2, 18–19. For the Cooke-Trost co-signing of staff recommendations, see POC, HDH, box 20, Cooke to HDH, 25 Feb. 1964; HDH to Cooke, 26 Feb. 1964.

42 Senate Minutes, 21 Oct. 1963, 11 May 1965.

43 Halifax *Mail-Star*, 24 Nov. 1961, "Grade 12: A College Prerequisite"; POC, HDH, box 13, "Committee of Deans," AEK to HDH, 1 Dec. 1961. The failure rates are given in the *Dalhousie Gazette*, 19 Feb. 1965, with further comments on 20 Oct. 1966.

44 Leading article on Dean Cooke, *Dalhousie Gazette*, 15 Mar. 1966; on the Sorbonne, 9 Nov. 1967. Letter from Joan Hennessey is ibid., 23 Jan. 1964.

45 The Housman parody is from *A Shropshire Lad*, by Jim Hurley, in *Dalhousie Gazette* 7 Oct. 1959.

46 "Joe P."'s interview is in ibid., 12 Feb. 1964, entitled "Halifax: the Seamy Side."

47 POC, HDH, box 10, "Dalhousie Student Union," James Cowan ('62, '65) chairman of the DSU Committee, to HDH, 13 July 1964; HDH to Cowan, 15 July 1964. The matter of Miss Musgrave's property is the origin of the "L" at the back of the SUB. Dalhousie some years later acquired Miss Musgrave's lot. POC, HDH, box 29, "Properties," HDH to Miss C.G.M. Musgrave, 4 May 1966; HDH to Chisholm, 26 May 1966. The second lot was owned by Bruce Knight; Chisholm to author, 24 Feb. 1996.

48 POC, HDH, box 10, "Dalhousie Student Union," E.B. Mercer ('37) (assistant to the president) to Arthur Chisholm and J.H. Aitchison, 13 July 1965, reporting Dean Cooke's suggestion favourably. This was the origin of the McInnes Room, named for Donald McInnes's mother and father, Charlotte McNeill and Hector McInnes. In 1968 the students gave Dean Cooke a gold medal for his contribu-

tions to their building. Dalhousie put in to the University Grants Committee for a capital assistance loan covering construction costs plus land. The application was rejected because land costs were not authorized. Hicks saw the premier about that and a separate application was submitted for land costs. The students paid for the furnishings. See Ashworth to Hicks, 7 July 1967; E.B. Mercer to B.F. Macaulay, vice-president, administration, UNB, 22 Nov. 1968. Interview with J.G. Sykes, university architect, 14 Feb. 1996; *Chronicle-Herald*, 13 Nov. 1968, letter from Randall Smith.

10 TESTING LIMITS

1 It has been difficult to find information about Rebecca Cohn and I have not been able to establish firmly her maiden name, though it may have been Keshen. There is a brief obituary of her in the *Halifax Daily Star*, 24 Oct. 1942. Professor Malcolm Ross put me in touch with Dr Anne Hammerling ('34) who remembered Mrs Cohn, a friend of her parents, phone interviews, 28 Nov., 4 Dec. 1995. I am also grateful to D.H. McNeill and Dawn Owen for getting me a copy of the 1963 deed of gift. There is a useful article about the Cohn Auditorium in the *Globe and Mail*, 13 Mar. 1976, by Blaik Kirby, who seems to have gleaned his information about Rebecca Cohn from Henry Hicks.

2 Conjectures about the origin of the decision to give the bequest to Dalhousie for an auditorium were confirmed by Eileen Aldous's husband, Professor John Aldous, 9 Jan. 1996. BOG Minutes, 28 Nov. 1962, 11 Apr. 1963.

   Gilbert and Sullivan was the staple fare in student musicals, but in 1959 modernity triumphed, if temporarily; see headline in the *Gazette*, 21 Oct. 1959: "'The Boy Friend' scuttles 'Pinafore.'"

3 POC, HDH, box 8, Arts Centre and Cohn Auditorium, HDH to C.B. Weld, chairman, Senate Committee on Cultural Activities, 10 June 1965; Dalhousie University, Financial Services, Sam Goodman to HDH, 24 Apr. 1967; HDH to Goodman, 26 Apr. 1967. Goodman was the lawyer (and brother-in-law) of the Keshens.

4 POC, HDH, box 8, Arts Centre and Cohn Auditorium, HDH to Lady Beaverbrook, 17 May 1968; BOG Minutes, 20 June, 17 July 1968. POC, HDH, box 8, Arts Centre, C.A.E. Fowler to HDH, 13 June 1968, confidential memorandum.

5 POC, HDH, box 8, Arts Centre, Appendix "A," Financing; BOG Minutes, 12 June 1969.

6 The Cohn acoustics were almost too good. The audience could hear the musicians turn pages of their music, the musicians could hear every shuffle of feet. That sensitivity was ameliorated. Interview with Mirko Usmiani, 22 Dec. 1995.

7 This chapter, along with chapters 8 to 12, have been read and commented on by Dr Guy MacLean. Several specific issues in this chapter, notably Tito's visit in 1971 and Vagianos's appointment in 1966, have been much improved by Dr MacLean's detailed knowledge of men, women, and events at Dalhousie across half a century. POC, HDH, box 14, Tito's visit, Wm. M. Jones to HDH, December 1968; HDH to Jones, 12 Dec. 1968; interview with Guy MacLean, 4 Dec. 1995.

   For an account of Major Jones's exploits, see Roy MacLaren, *Canadians Behind Enemy Lines, 1939–1945* (Vancouver 1981), pp. 139–41, 143–49.

8 In POC, HDH, box 14, there is a large file on Tito's 1971 visit. A complicating factor in the date of the news release of his Dalhousie honorary degree was the Canadian state visit of Alexei Kosygin, premier of the USSR, on 17 Oct. External Affairs did not want to release news of the impending arrival of one head of state in the midst of the visit of another. There were also a number of protests, as many from the United States as from Canada. Hicks answered them, his theme being: "When a university awards an honorary degree it does not necessarily approve of everything about the person who gets the degree ... This does not mean that we approve of Communism, but it does mean that we recognize the necessity in the modern world of having to live with people whose political ideologies ... may differ from our own." This from a reply to W. Scott Hubley ('70) who had written from Charlottetown to HDH, 22 Nov. 1971, the reply being 1 Dec. 1971.

The *Globe and Mail*, 25 Oct. 1971, had a letter from G. Lazarevich, in protest, a professor at Barnard College, New York City. See also *Toronto Sun*, 5 Nov. 1971.

9 *Dalhousie Gazette*, 12 Nov. 1971. Most of this section is based on personal recollections. Eileen Burns's comment is in a letter to POC, HDH, box 14, Tito file, Sunday, 8 Nov. 1971. There is an account of Sir Fitzroy Maclean's Dalhousie degree in Frank McLynn, *Fitzroy Maclean* (London 1992), pp. 360–1. The Prince Philip story is in Fitzroy Maclean to G.R. MacLean, 6 Dec. 1971, from London, now in the Tito file, POC, HDH, box 14.

10 For HDH's 1983 reminiscences, see NA, HDH (E), p. 110.

11 POC, HDH, box 27, "Macdonald Memorial Library," Wilkinson to Cooke, 23 Nov. 1964; Cooke to Wilkinson, 4 Jan. 1965.

12 Ibid., HDH to Misses Falconer, Fullerton, and Mrs Cooke, 26 Aug. 1965; ibid., box 31, "Library School," H.P. Moffatt to AEK, 8 Feb. 1960; AEK to Moffatt, 26 Feb. 1960; Wilkinson to AEK, 10 Oct. 1962; Moffatt to AEK, 17 Jan. 1963; ibid., box 27, Library, Report of meeting, 20 Dec. 1965.

13 Interview with Louis Vagianos, 20 Apr. 1995.

14 POC, HDH, box 27, Library, Vagianos to HDH, 26 Apr. 1967; Dalhousie submission to UGC, Oct. 1967. Frank Covert claimed the board had no reservations and then proceeded to state them. Ibid., Covert to HDH, 5 June 1967, replying to HDH to executive committee of board, 16 May 1967.

15 BOG Minutes, 21 Dec. 1967.

16 W.P. Thompson, "University Government," *CAUT Bulletin* 9, no. 2 (Dec. 1960), p. 6, quoted by David M. Cameron, *More than an Academic Question: Universities, Government and Public Policy in Canada* (Halifax 1991), p. 302. Cameron's book is essential reading for the period 1960 to 1990.

17 Ibid., p. 307.

18 POC, HDH, box 20, Duff-Berdahl Report, Dr G.H. Hatcher to H.E. Read, vice-president, 16 Mar. 1966. Dr Hatcher was head of preventive medicine, and president that year of the Dalhousie Faculty Association. Covert's letter is ibid., Covert to Hicks, 26 Apr. 1966.

19 Senate Minutes, 13 Nov. 1967; Minutes, Arts and Science, 13 Nov. 1967. The Senate committee was composed of John Aldous, Murray Beck, and Roy George.

20 Minutes, Arts and Science, 11 Apr. 1966; 5, 15 Dec. 1967; 24 Feb., 25 Mar. 1968.

21 See especially the essay by Silver Donald Cameron, "In the Spiral," basically about Charles Brimer, one of the bright scholars James brought to Dalhousie, with revealing perceptions about James. Cameron was briefly in the Dalhousie English Department, 1967–8. Silver Donald Cameron, *Sterling Silver: Rants, Raves and Revelations* (Wreck Cove 1994), pp. 1–14. The essay was brought to my attention by James Clark, professor of psychology. Some of the problems of psychology departments in general and an attack on James in particular is in staff files 426, "S.A. Rudin," in Rudin's letter to HDH, 6 Oct. 1964, marked "personal, private, confidential."

22 The pertinent suggestion that talents at one level of administration do not always translate well at others comes from Louis Vagianos, interview, 25 Apr. 1995. For an example of James's outspokenness, see POC, HDH, box 21, Faculty of Arts and Science, Anthony N. Raspa to A.R. Bevan, 10 Feb. 1969, from Montreal, reporting interview with James. For James's parties, Alan Andrews to PBW, 19 July 1995; Cameron, "In the Spiral," on Psychology Department parties in general, pp. 4–5.

23 Arts and Science Minutes, 30 Jan. 1968, letter from Brookbank, Crook, Fraser, Huber, von Maltzahn, Ryan, n.d., but Jan. 1968.

24 Ibid., 11 Feb. 1969. The minutes patently don't say anything about "elation and confusion"; that's the author's recollection.

25 This report came before faculty on 5 May 1969. The committee members were E.S. Deevey, M.M. Ross, A.M. Sinclair, D.W. Stairs, and H.E. Read, chairman.

26 See Silver Donald Cameron, "In the Spiral," in *Sterling Silver*, pp. 1–14.

27 POC, HDH, box 10, Life Sciences complex, HDH to Berton Robinson (secretary of the UGC), 28 Dec. 1967; J.D. Fraser, chairman, Property Maintenance Committee of First Baptist Church, to HDH, 29 May 1969. Hicks reassured the church official that the contractors would be careful and that they had substantial insurance against eventualities.

28 M.J. Harvey, "Feedback: Dalhousie Life Sciences Centre," in *Canadian Architect* (Feb. 1974), pp. 29–36, enclosed in POC, HDH, box 20, Harvey to W.A. MacKay, 9 Apr. 1974.

29 Gordon Riley, "Recollections," unpublished manuscript, pp. 135, 141; these recollections have been loaned to me through the kindness of Dr Donald Gordon and Joleen Aldous Gordon.

30 There is extensive correspondence in POC, HDH, box 10, between HDH and Arthur Murphy, and HDH and Allan MacEachen especially; also E.J. Benson, mostly between Apr. and July 1969. The importance of MacEachen is indicated in the following, HDH to MacEachen, 8 July 1969: "Just a note to say once again how much I appreciate the efforts you have made to secure a favourable result from the Treasury Board concerning the Atlantic Development Board grant to the Dalhousie Life Sciences Centre. I am sure that without your prodding and assistance this matter would not have been brought to a successful conclusion."

31 *University Affairs* (Apr. 1968), p. 7. It was a publication of AUCC. Cited in Cameron, *More than an Academic Question*, p. 307.

32 Bruno Bettelheim was professor of educational psychology at the University of Chicago; part of his book *Children of the Dream* (New York 1969) is summarized

in his brief article, "The Anatomy of Academic Discontent," in *Change* (May-June 1969), pp. 18–26.

33 Colin Crouch, "New Militancy v. Old Liberalism," *Manchester Guardian Weekly*, 20 June 1968. Crouch was president of the Student Union at the London School of Economics, reading sociology. See also Allan Bloom, *The Closing of the American Mind* (New York 1987), p. 78.

34 Cyril Levitt, *Children of Privilege: Student Revolt in the Sixties* (Toronto 1984), p. 34. This is a comparative study of Canada, the United States, and West Germany.

The proper pronunciation of "pharynx" is "fair-inks," whereas the student pronounced it "far-nix." The professor was Ronald Hayes, and the student was a medical student who duly graduated. On the other hand, Hayes's wife, Dixie Pelluet, was kindness itself. The student believed that what might well have saved him from a zero in Zoology 2 was pillow talk between Hayes and his wife. Interview, 26 Dec. 1995, name withheld but on file.

35 Arthur Kroker, "Migration from the Disciplines," *Journal of Canadian Studies* 15, no 3 (Fall 1980), pp. 5–6; *Dalhousie Gazette*, 2 Nov. 1967.

36 *Dalhousie Gazette*, 10 Oct. 1968, letter from Doug Hill; Hicks interview with CJCH was in mid-March 1969, and is transcribed in POC, HDH, box 21, Sociology, Broadcast on CJCH, 1 Apr. 1969. The *Vox Medica* editorial also got into the *Mail-Star*. See *Dalhousie Gazette*, 11 Dec. 1970.

For the change in the Dalhousie Act to allow students as full board members, see BOG Minutes, 11 June 1976. The act passed the legislature 20 May 1976.

37 For Hicks's view, see POC, HDH, box 32, "Student Unrest," HDH to Chisholm, 26 Nov. 1968. For Hayakama, see *Christian Science Monitor*, 31 May 1969.

38 POC, HDH, box 21, Sociology, letter from seven sociologists, including H. Gamberg and Graham Morgan, to Stephens, 3 Mar. 1969; HDH to Stephens, 26 Mar. 1969; Sociology Course Graduate Student Union to W.N. Stephens, 26 Mar. 1969; HDH to Stephens and Sociology Graduate Students Union, 29 Mar. 1969; Senate Minutes, 27 Mar. 1969. See also *Dalhousie Gazette*, 17 Nov. 1971, for a long article on the developments in Sociology by two sociology students; Stephens's interview with the *Gazette*, 26 Nov. 1971; ibid., 3 Dec. 1971, Jerome Barkow letter. I am grateful to Professors James Stoltzman and Graham Morgan of Sociology for comments on this section of the chapter.

39 Interview with HDH, 8 July 1988.

40 Senate Minutes, 13, 14 Apr., 26 Oct. 1970; 11 Jan. 1971. This account is also based on W.A. MacKay's report, "Occupation of the President's Office, April 13–14," 1970, in POC, HDH, box 32, "Student Unrest." The students named as defendants were Barry McPeake, Nick Pittas, Larry Katz, Martin Langille, Kim Cameron, Neil Henderson, Will Offley, Christopher Thurrott, Simon Rosenblum, and Peter Seraganian. Cameron, Offley, and Thurrott were sociology students; McPeake was a Carleton University student who was taking one course at Dalhousie in economics; Pittas failed his year at Dalhousie 1968–9 but was a second-year BA student. Katz was a Brooklyn, NY, student who was taking one course in immunology; Langille was a graduate student in English; Serganian and Gamberg were graduate students in psychology. Rosenblum was a Saint Mary's student taking economics at Dalhousie. Pittas, Katz, Seraganian, and Thurrott all ended with

Dalhousie degrees. Hicks's recollection of what the students told him is in HDH (E), p. 69.

41 *Chronicle-Herald*, 30 Oct. 1970; POC, HDH, box 32, "Subversive Propaganda within Dalhousie," Alan Crowe to HDH, 31 Oct. 1970; HDH to Crowe, 20 Nov. 1970; interview with HDH, 8 July 1988. See especially Professor Arnold J. Tingley's account, *Mathematics at Dalhousie* (Halifax 1991), pp. 46–53.

42 POC, HDH, box 33, "Transition Year Programme," HDH to Otto Lang, minister of manpower, 25 Feb. 1971. Outside of these letters in HDH's files, documentation for the Transition Year Program (TYP) is not as ample as it should be. Files of its early days have been stolen from the TYP office. However, Professor Arnold J. Tingley, one of the teachers in the program, has written up a short history with the help of B.A. "Rocky" Jones, *The Transition Year Programme: The Early Years* (1993).

43 POC, HDH, box 33, "TYP," Black and Indian Coalition brief to Dalhousie, in MacKay to G.R. MacLean and P.D. Pillay, 6 Aug. 1971: Tingley, *The Transition Year Programme*, Appendix A.

44 Halifax *Mail*, 22 Apr. 1941. Lawrence T. Hancock, *The Story of the Maritime School of Social Work 1941–1969* (Halifax 1992); POC, HDH, box 27, "Maritime School of Social Work," HDH to H.D. Smith, 16 Jan. 1964; Fred MacKinnon to HDH, 26 Feb. 1994, personal and confidential; HDH to Walter Trost, dean of graduate studies, 2 Mar. 1964; G.R. MacLean, dean of graduate studies, to HDH, 25 May 1967.

45 POC, HDH, box 27, HDH to J.F. O'Sullivan, chairman, New Brunswick Higher Education Commission, 6 Mar. 1970; HDH to Forbes Langstroth, dean of graduate studies, 6 Mar. 1970, personal and confidential.

46 Ibid., Benoit Comeau to HDH, 29 Aug. 1972; Peter Nicholson to HDH, 29 Aug. 1972; Hancock to HDH, 20 Sept. 1972; HDH to Langstroth, 17 Oct. 1972; HDH to W.A. MacKay and K.T. Leffek, dean of graduate studies, 9 Apr. 1973, confidential; F.J. Turner, chairman, Board of Accreditation, Canadian Asociation of Schools of Social Work, to HDH, 25 June 1973, from Ottawa.

47 Faculty of Arts and Social Sciences Office, Committee of Deans Minutes, 6 Dec. 1968; BOG Minutes, 27 Aug., 17 Dec. 1970; 14 Jan., 11 Feb., 18 Mar., 1 Apr. 1971.

48 For some of the stories connected with Fenwick, see *Dalhousie Gazette*, 17 Sept., 22 Oct. 1971; 22 Feb. 1974; 20 Mar. 1980. More authoritative views were given by J.G. Sykes, university architect, in an interview on 14 Feb. 1996. BOG Minutes, 12 Nov. 1970; 14 Jan., 18 Mar., 1 Apr. 1971. Interview with Donald McInnes, 2 Aug. 1988.

49 POC, HDH (E), pp. 73–4; p. 61; interview with HDH, 4 July 1988.

50 A.G. Archibald to author, 28 Feb. 1995.

51 Interview with Louis Vagianos, 25 Apr. 1995.

II COMING TO THE PLATEAU

1 Minutes, Committee of Deans (in dean of science's office), 28 Feb. 1969.
  For fraternities, the following dates on the Dalhousie campus: ΦΚΠ, 1923; ΦΡΣ, 1925; ΦΧ, 1928; ΦΔΘ, 1931; ΤΕΦ, 1932; ΣΧ, 1933; ΖΨ, 1938. For sororities,

ΑΓΔ, 1932; ΠΒΦ, 1934. A count based on the 1938 *Pharos* suggests that of the graduating class that year some 35 per cent were fraternity or sorority members, especially strong in law and medicine. The 1969 *Pharos* gives only overall membership which was 8 per cent of the total student body. In 1969 there were five fraternities and two sororities. The 1966 survey is in the *Dalhousie Gazette*, 3 Nov. 1966, reacting to a *Mail-Star* report two weeks earlier that was critical of fraternities. For Carleton Stanley's views, see POC, A-635, Stanley to Sherwood Fox, of University of Western Ontario 9, 21 Feb. 1935. See Paul Axelrod, *Making a Middle Class: Student Life in English Canada during the Thirties* (Toronto 1990), pp. 106–8, which has an excellent discussion of their role.

For Dalhousie changes, see *Dalhousie Gazette*, 21 Nov. 1968; 9 Jan. 1969; the 1971 poem is 29 Oct. 1971; the 1964 complaint is 12 Feb. 1964. The results of the 1970 referendum are in BOG Minutes, 12 Mar. 1970.

2 The BOG Minutes record this development, via the Residence Committee of which Dr J.M. Corston was chairman. He was also professor of obstetrics and gynaecology. BOG Minutes, 3 Apr., 19 June, 28 Sept. 1979; 18 Jan. 1981.

3 For national statistics, see *Profile of Higher Education in Canada* 1991 and earlier editions (Ottawa 1992).

4 Experimental classes arose from the Curriculum Committee of Arts and Science, Arts and Science Minutes, 2 Apr., 6 May 1969. The Committee on Examinations reported 7 Apr. 1969, with a twenty-eight-page report. The last recommendation was that the present system of Christmas and final examinations be abolished and replaced with continuous assessment. Faculty could not accept such a radical change. Information about the expansion of Arts and Science in the 1970s is in G.R. MacLean to author, 24 Apr. 1996.

5 Interview with Miss B.R.E. Smith, 10 June 1998; DUA, staff files 463, D.H. McNeill to HDH, 9 Jan. 1969; HDH to Miss Smith, 24 Jan. 1969.

6 A.J. Tingley to author, 26 Jan. 1996; interview with Miss B.R.E Smith, 10 June 1988; interview with Marion Crowell, 28 Feb. 1996; Faith DeWolfe to author, 12 Mar. 1996.

7 POC, HDH, box 1, Advisory Committee on the Registrar's Admissions and Awards Office. The Awards Office got a clean bill of health. Ibid., box 29, "The Registrar, 1946–1976," H.J. Uhlman to HDH, 23 Jan. 1973. Senate Minutes, 16 Oct. 1972; 12, 15 Jan. 1973.

8 Adshead's history is from personal acquaintance; A.J. Tingley to author, 29 Jan. 1996.

9 The Board of Governors committee has an extended and judicious report on the Dombrowski affair, BOG minutes, 17 Feb. 1972. For events connected with the Supreme Court case, see *Dalhousie Gazette*, 14, 28 Nov. 1974; 25 Jan. 1975. The last gives the text of Justice Hart's decision. This section has been read by Professors Rainer Friedrich and J.P. Atherton of Classics. Comments were relayed by Professor Friedrich to author, 23 Apr. 1996. I am grateful to both colleagues.

10 POC, HDH, box 31, School of Library Science, Norman Horrocks to HDH, 28 June, 10 July 1972; interview with Louis Vagianos, 20 Apr. 1995; Robert Wedgeworth, executive director, American Library Association, to W.A. MacKay, 31 Jan. 1973, telegram.

11 American *Library Journal*, 15 Apr. 1973, p. 1225, editorial.

12 POC, HDH, box 22, Graduate Studies, Appointment of a New Dean, 1972, K.T. Leffek to W.A. MacKay, 15 June 1972; MacKay to HDH, 11 Aug. 1972, confidential; E.B. Mercer to MacKay, 17 Aug. 1972.

The report of the President's Committee on the Structure and Reorganization of Graduate Studies at Dalhousie, under F.R. Hayes as chairman, is dated 29 Dec. 1972. Leffek's letter in which he rejects the Hayes report, Leffek to HDH, 20 Mar. 1973, is followed by a crisp and decisive letter, 27 Feb. 1974.

13 POC, HDH, boxes 20 and 21, Administrative Studies, Hicks to Gardner, 9 Mar. 1972. The report of the Gardner Committee came in October 1972. Aitchison's reply is to R. Bingham, secretary of Senate, 2 Nov. 1972. Senate Council, 6 Nov. 1972, established a sub-committee to study the report, composed of Deans Leffek, MacLean, and Arthur Foote, professor of law. There are comments from the Commerce Department, J.D. Misick to W.A. MacKay, 15 Dec. 1972; MacKay to Misick, 22 Dec. 1972.

The sub-committee reported to Senate Council on 2 Apr. 1973, when its report was tabled for a future meeting. This was held on 5 July 1973 (Hicks not present), with a further one on 10 July where he was, at which the steering committee was established. There is a wealth of correspondence in the meantime, especially from political scientists: D.M. Cameron to HDH, 10 Apr. 1973; David Braybrooke to HDH, 13 Apr. 1973; J. Murray Beck to HDH, 16 Apr. 1973; Paul Pross to MacKay, 16 Apr. 1973; J.H. Aitchison to MacKay, 18 Apr. 1973.

14 On the steering committee of July 1973, see K.A. Heard (chairman of Political Science) to HDH, 11, 19 July 1973; HDH to Heard, 17 July 1973. This section on the creation of Administration Studies has been read and commented on by Professor D.M. Cameron of Political Science to whom I am most grateful.

15 In 1970 Kirby became principal assistant to Premier Regan (part-time), and in 1974 went on to be assistant principal secretary to Prime Minister Trudeau and to other Ottawa positions. He later joined Hicks in the Senate in 1984. Hicks's perceptiveness and his impatience both show up in this episode. See also K.A. Heard to author, 27 Feb., 20 Mar. 1995.

16 POC, HDH, box 25, "Institute of Education," Stanfield to HDH, 29 Sept. 1964, 24 May 1966; H.B.S. Cooke to A.S. Mowat, 24 June 1966; HDH to Cooke, MacLean, Mowat, 21 Dec. 1966; Stanfield to HDH, 17 May 1967.

17 Ibid., G.R. MacLean to Colin McKay, president of UNB, 15 Aug. 1967; HDH to Berton Robinson, 28 Dec. 1967.

18 Ibid., box 21, "Department of Education," A.S. Mowat to HDH, 19 Jan. 1968, HDH to Mowat, 29 Jan. 1968; *Dalhousie Gazette*, 18 Jan. 1968.

19 Of the three hundred, sixty-six reported back, twenty-eight were returned undeliverd. It is not clear what years of B.Ed. graduates Robson actually addressed. Numbers were as follows: 1964–5, 107; 1965–6, 119; 1966–7, 137. Robson noted that since January 1968 very little had happened in the Education Department. But it had; it forced Mowat's resignation.

20 For A.S. Mowat, see staff files, post-1969. After Mowat's resignation and the appointment of the new chairman of education, Dean James apologized to Mowat for his "bluff manner and blunt speech." See ibid., James to Mowat, 7 Mar. 1969.

For Dalhousie reaction to Dr Lauwerys and his ideas, see POC, HDH, box 25, John Flint to P.H.R. James, 18 Oct. 1968; James to Dr R.P. Carter, director, teaching education, NS Department of Education, 16 Jan. 1969; also James's notes on telephone conversation with Carter, 22 Jan. 1969.

21 POC, HDH, box 25, Stuart Semple to Lauwerys, 16 Feb. 1971 (marked "not sent on HDH's instructions"); HDH to Semple, 18 Feb. 1971 explains. On the Dalhousie Library holdings in Education, see Lauwerys to HDH, 20 Sept. 1971, personal and confidential. This section on the Atlantic Institute of Education has been commented on by Professor W.B. Hamilton of Mount Allison University. His suggestions are much appreciated. He points out that there is a substantial collection of AIE Papers at PANS. W.B. Hamilton to author, 22 Apr. 1996, enclosing his "Brief 'Ramble' on DAL/AIE relations, 1975–1980."

22 The issue surfaces in J. Murray Beck's *Politics of Nova Scotia: Volume Two, 1891–1988* (Tantallon 1988), p. 386, where he quotes the *Chronicle-Herald*, 18 Nov. 1974. Dr Arthur Murphy is reported in the *Chronicle-Herald*, 15 Feb. 1969. There are extensive refences in Dalhousie sources: BOG Minutes, 12 June 1969; 30 Nov. 1972; 25 June 1974; 27 Feb. 1975. Also Senate Minutes, 15 Oct., 3 Dec. 1973; 9 Sept. 1974.

23 Oskar Sykora, *Maritime Dental College and Dalhousie Faculty of Dentistry: A History* (Halifax 1991), pp. 131–2.

24 Ibid., pp. 106–8; interview with HDH, 9 Aug. 1988.

25 POC, HDH, box 9, "New Building, Dentistry 1966–1968," R.L. Stanfield to HDH, 10 Mar. 1967; McLean to HDH, 13 Mar. 1967; HDH to Stanfield, 15 Mar. 1967; Stanfield to HDH, 31 Mar. 1967; McLean to HDH, 17 Apr. 1967; HDH to Stanfield, 18 July 1967.

26 Sykora, *Dalhousie Dentistry*, pp. 114–23. The article in the *Herald* of 7 Feb. 1976 was written by Barbara Hinds, "Lack of teaching space blamed; Nova Scotia dentists in short supply."

27 BOG Minutes, 29 Oct. 1976; 28 Feb. 1977; 27 Apr., 14 Dec. 1978.

28 Interview with Barbara Blauvelt, 29 Jan. 1996; interview with John Szerb, 8 Feb. 1996.

29 POC, HDH, box 23, "Faculty of Medicine, Dean Selection," D. Waugh to HDH, 13 July 1971; Cochrane to HDH, 13 July 1971, confidential; Goldbloom to John Aldous, 29 Nov. 1971, confidential; E.D. Wigle to HDH, 29 Mar., 24 May 1972. Ibid., "Introduction" to Dalhousie Faculty of Medicine, for the Accreditation Team, Apr. 1973, by L.B. Macpherson, pp. 1–2.

30 Ibid., pp. 2–3; Senate Minutes, 7 Jan. 1974. It is interesting to note that two fourth-year medical students took it upon themselves, on behalf of their class, to meet with the governments of Nova Scotia and New Brunswick to broach this question of funding for the intern year. Without that funding, Dalhousie stood to lose up to $750,000. Hicks complimented the students in getting assurances that he and Vice-President Stewart had not been able to manage. It was agreed that Stewart would go back to the governments for confirmation. These were duly given and the five-year degree program ended in June 1974.

31 POC, HDH, box 23, Selection of Dean, Macpherson to Faculty Council. The committee of 1974 was selected by ballot, which turned out to be all clinicians. Two

pre-clinical members were added. The minutes of this committee give a full picture of the meetings. Hicks's complaint about its delays is HDH to Macpherson, 17 Sept. 1974, confidential.

32 Robert M. MacDonald and Lea C. Steeves, *A History of the Department of Medicine, Dalhousie University 1868–1975* (Halifax 1995), pp. 47–8. Dickson's convocation address in 1980 is in POC, HDH, box 17, Dickson to W.A. MacKay, 28 May 1980.

33 For a much fuller description of the Law School in these years, see John Willis, *A History of Dalhousie Law School* (Toronto 1979), pp. 194–205.

34 See Harvey Savage, "The Dalhousie Legal Aid Service," *Dalhousie Law Journal* 2 (1975), p. 505. There is now an important new source for Dalhousie Law School history, unavailable to Willis, compiled by R. St J. Macdonald, *The Dalhousie Law School 1965–1990: An Oral History* (Halifax 1996). This is an extensive run of interviews conducted by Dean Macdonald in 1988 and 1989 with professors who had taught in the Law Faculty. I am grateful to R. St J. Macdonald for the early loan of this work. There are a number of references to the Dalhousie Legal Aid service. My reference here is to p. 79, Hugh M. Kindred. The quotation is from Innis Christie's unpublished address, and is cited in Willis, *Dalhousie Law School*, p. 221.

35 Macdonald, *Law School*, p. 6, Clayton Hutchins. Interview with Gordon Archibald, 6 June 1988; and BOG Minutes, 28 Sept. 1979.

36 Macdonald, *Law School*, p. 58, John A. Yogis.

37 Interview with R. St J. Macdonald, 29 July 1993.

38 The development of these departures is well described by Edgar Gold, in "Law School," pp. 359–63. The argument about the value of research centres was suggested by Guy MacLean. MacLean to author, 24 Apr. 1996.

39 Macdonald, *Law School*, p. 40, Macdonald speaking during his interview with W.H. Charles; for MacLauchlan, see p. 257.

40 POC, HDH, box 8, "Physical Education Complex," HDH to Audrey E. Stuart, 20 Mar. 1974.

41 There is a considerable literature on the subject of taxation of university property, both in Halifax and elsewhere. Hicks's protest to the minister of municipal affairs, is in POC, HDH, box 33, "Taxation," HDH to Mooney, 24 Jan. 1973. Hicks claimed in 1971 that the city was taxing every bit of Dalhousie property they could; see HDH to Joseph Lauwerys, 27 Feb. 1971.

42 There is an anti-Dalhousie letter, typical of a number, by Frank V. Fryer, in *Mail-Star*, 27 Aug. 1973; The *Dalhousie Gazette* has a useful article, 28 Sept. 1973. The *Gazette* generally has good coverage of the issue as it developed in south-end Halifax. For the meeting of 17 Oct., see *Gazette*, 26 Oct. 1973.

43 *Dalhousie Gazette*, 2, 30 Nov. 1973; interview with J.G. Sykes, 14 Feb. 1996; interview with Donald McInnes, 2 Aug. 1988; POC, HDH, box 8, HDH to Walter Fitzgerald, 27 Dec. 1973.

44 *Mail-Star*, 18 Mar. 1976; POC, HDH, box 8, George Mitchell to HDH, 14 Sept. 1976.

45 *Dalhousie Gazette*, 25 Mar. 1976. I am grateful for comments by Professor Gerhard Stroink of Physics and by Mrs Miriam Guptill. The poem is by Margot Griffiths, entitled "Faith," and in the *Dalhousie Gazette*, 10 Jan. 1980.

12 SHIFTING POWER

1 *Chronicle-Herald*, 16, 22, 14 Nov. 1967; *Dalhousie Gazette*, 23 Nov. 1967.

2 POC, HDH, box 17, "Cultural Activities Committee," has correspondence and opinions. On Perth, see Hugh Davidson to G.V.V. Nicholls, 21 Mar. 1973, from Ottawa; notes by HDH on various candidates.

3 Peter Fletcher's views are in *Dalhousie Gazette*, 2 Dec. 1976.

4 For Djokić and the violin, see BOG Minutes, 5 June, 5 Dec. 1975; interview with HDH, 8 July 1988. He recollected $70,000, but Board Minutes record $80,000. The Djokić violin was made in Venice about 1740 by the family of Guarnerius. The loan (interest at 11 per cent) was repaid by Djokić in five years by giving up his whole salary to pay it off. His wife, Lynn Stodola, who taught piano at Dalhousie, paid for their joint upkeep during that time. Henry Hicks apparently invested part of the money he received from the London sale of his Bermuda stamp collection, some $40,000, in the Djokić loan. The 11 per cent interest sounds high but is not, for inflation was running about 8 per cent in 1975, and higher than that by 1980.

The Dalart Trio broke up in 1983, a victim of its own success, its members pulled apart by having to decide between concert stage and Dalhousie teaching. I am grateful to Professor Djokić for this information.

5 NA, HDH (E), p. 70; BOG Minutes, 27 Apr., 16 June 1978.

6 Interview with J.G. Sykes, 14 Feb. 1996; *University News*, 31 Jan. 1980.

7 HDH (E), p. 67.

8 POC, HDH, box 19, "Dalhousie Staff Association, HDH to M. McIntyre, 16 Feb. 1972; Dalhousie Staff Association, Minutes, 16 Dec. 1971, 2 Mar 1972; letter from a group of "local Dalhousie workers" to C. MacDougall, 30 Nov. 1971, which alleges the "very underhanded manner" in which sign-up membership cards were claimed to be only information requests.

My source for the DSA's role in improving campus problems with sexual harassment is private and must remain so. The lady is a valued official in Dalhousie adminstration.

9 BOG Minutes, 28 Nov. 1962; 12 Nov. 1970; 13 Dec. 1979.

10 Ibid., 18, 29 June 1971; interview with Mirko Usmiani, 11, 13 Dec. 1991.

11 BOG Minutes, 26 Sept. 1974; POC, HDH, box 19, "Dalhousie Faculty Association," HDH to Dr Tarum Ghose, president DFA, 1975–6, May 1976.

12 There is a run of correspondence between HDH and K.T. Leffek in POC, HDH, box 19, through 1969–70 when Leffek was DFA president. Ibid., R.L. Comeau to R.C. Dickson, 30 Apr. 1970. BOG Minutes, 20 May 1977.

13 For an excellent history of the unionization of Canadian university faculties, see David M. Cameron, *More than an Academic Question: Universities, Government, and Public Policy in Canada* (Halifax 1991), pp. 355–61.

14 Welch's suggestions are in POC, HDH, box 19, Welch to HDH, 5 June 1977, which was copied to vice-presidents MacKay and McNeill. There is a useful discussion of the formation and functioning of the MPHEC in Cameron, *More than an Academic Question*, pp. 210–12. MacKay's warning to the board is in BOG Minutes, 20 May 1977. For the Dalhousie unionization process, see *Dalhousie Gazette*,

16 Feb., 2, 9, 16, 30 Mar. 1978; see Cameron, *More than an Academic Question*, pp. 360–1; a detailed description is in *CAUT Bulletin* (Apr. 1978), p. 9. The 1977 DFA questionnaire is described by R.L. Comeau to R. Puccetti, 11 Apr. 1977 in POC, HDH, box 19, "Dalhousie Faculty Association." The relevant BOG Minutes are 26 Jan., 22 Feb. 1978. This description of unionization and other events at Dalhousie, 1977–9, has benefited much from comments by Professor Michael Cross, who was leading the DFA negotiations in 1979.

It is not a little curious that after the DFA meeting of 16 Feb. 1978, the board agreed to a 50 per cent reduction in fees for dependants of Dalhousie professors.

15 Friedenburg's views are in *Dalhousie Gazette*, 16 Mar. 1978, Welch's in 9 Mar. 1978. For an analysis of the bargaining unit, see Cameron *More than an Academic Question*, pp. 361–2. Board Minutes of 17 Apr., 23 Nov. 1978 and 3 Apr. 1979 are helpful.

16 Senate Minutes, 11 Dec. 1978; 15 Jan. 1979. For MacKay's report on negotiations with DFA on 3 Apr. 1979, see BOG Minutes, 3 Apr. 1979. This section and others have been read by Professor David Cameron, one of the administration negotiators in 1979. I am most grateful for his succinct but wide-ranging comments.

17 Mackay's report is in BOG Minutes, 22 Nov. 1979. Details of the DFA agreement are in *University News*, 15 Nov. 1979. K.A. Heard to author, 27 Feb. 1995.

18 For some of the opinions in 1976, see *Dalhousie Gazette*, 2 Dec. 1976. For 1978–9, see POC, HDH, box 12, "CUPE strike, 1978–1979," Paul Pross, Political Science, to HDH, 29 Dec. 1978; *University News*, 23 Nov. 1978. Christine Fetterly Woodbury ('79), on the Student Council in 1978–9, recalls that many CUPE members felt that Cunningham was sacrificing them in order to blazon a national victory. Interview, 2 Oct. 1996. The story of cleaning the Law School comes from Guy MacLean, letter to author, 24 Apr. 1996.

19 POC, HDH, box 12, Hicks to Brian Hall, Biology, 23 Nov. 1978; BOG Minutes, 14 Dec. 1978.

20 MacKay's explanation is in POC, HDH, box 12, memo to HDH and BOG, 4 Jan. 1979; Dalhousie protests also ibid.: Kell Antoft to HDH, 25 Dec. 1978; HDH to Antoft, 28 Dec. 1978, personal; Antoft to HDH, 5 Jan. 1979; twenty-two members of Biology Department to HDH, Jan. 1979; David Braybrooke, of Philosophy, 19 Jan. 1979 on behalf of nine professors in Philosophy; English Department Graduate Students to HDH, 23 Jan. 1979; Dale Poel to HDH, 18 Jan. 1979, on behalf of himself and eleven others; Marilyn MacDonald to HDH, 9 Jan. 1979.

21 There is a copy of the CUPE circular in ibid. The statistics about the CUPE 1392 employees are from a full-page ad in the *Chronicle-Herald*, 29 Jan. 1979, the draft material for which is in box 12. On the day of protest, see *Globe and Mail*, 25 Jan. 1979 and *Chronicle-Herald*, same date, and also 31 Jan. 1979.

22 The reference to damage to university property is in POC, HDH, box 12, Hicks to Antoft, 28 Dec. 1978, personal. See also *University News*, 16 Nov. 1978.

23 Corry's UBC lecture was "Canadian Universities: From Private Domain to Public Utility," in J.A. Corry, *Farewell the Ivory Tower: Universities in Transition* (Montreal and Kingston 1970), pp. 101–12.

24 There was considerable correspondence from 1963 to 1966 on the function and role of the Institute of Public Affairs (IPA) within Dalhousie, especially with re-

spect to the social science departments. Guy Henson, the director, felt his work was continually being vitiated by the enmity of Economics, Political Science, Commerce, and Sociology, disguised as Henson saw it, by what they called "academic excellence." Hicks tried to cut the Gordian knot with a strong statement: "It is the policy of the University to continue to support the Institute of Public Affairs, and to improve and strengthen … [its] quality and worth." HDH to Graham, 29 Nov. 1965, confidential, in POC, HDH, box 26, "Institute of Public Affairs." But it remained for Horace Read's diplomatic skills to quieten things down, in a short and sensible report, ibid., Read to Hicks, 25 Apr. 1966.

25 Graham's opposition to unionization is noted in the *Dalhousie Gazette*, 16 Mar. 1978. For the formation of the Graham committee and after, see Senate Minutes, 13, 31 Mar., 13 Apr., 10 July, 18 Sept. 1978. There was a special *University News* devoted to it in December 1978.

26 Hicks's views, *University News*, 9, 29 Jan. 1979. The two Senate referendums are conveniently described in *University News*, 25 Oct. 1979. In the second referendum in October, when Senate was 280 in all, 141 positive votes were needed for change. The October result was more decided: 119 in favour, 48 against, with 16 spoiled ballots. Not voting, 97. Thus it failed a second time, and Graham gave it up.

27 There is a special issue of *University News*, Jan. 1979, on the Status of Women Report. The *Gazette* mentions women students' enrolment on 16 Feb. 1978 and 31 Jan. 1980. On the Engineers' entertainment, see *Gazette*, 22 Mar. 1979; 6 Mar. 1980. For the raid in 1979, ibid., 27 Sept. 1979. On alcoholism, ibid., 25 Oct, 8 Nov. 1979.

28 On Halifax's gay scene, see *Dalhousie Gazette*, 23 Sept. 1976, and replies, 30 Sept., 7 Oct. 1976. Student conservatism was noted by Henry Hicks, third interview with Derek Mann, *University News*, 31 Jan. 1980. On the 1977 march, see *Dalhousie Gazette*, 31 Mar. 1977; the "yellow" editorial is 29 Sept. 1977, replies, 6 Oct. 1977. For the interview with J.T. Low, who was returning to Scotland, see ibid., 1 Apr. 1976.

29 Senate Minutes, 31 Mar. 1978; BOG Minutes, 3 Apr., 19 June, 14 Sept. 1979; *Dalhousie Gazette*, 25 Nov., 6 Dec. 1979. H.B.S. Cooke to author, 20 Apr. 1996, from White Rock, BC. MacKay's eulogy of Hicks is in BOG Minutes, 21 Feb. 1980.

30 There is a comprehensive balance sheet of Dalhousie accounts, as of 31 Mar. 1980, in BOG Minutes.

31 A.G. Archibald to author, 20 Mar. 1995; interview with J.G. Sykes, 14 Feb. 1996. Horace Read's complaints are recalled by H.B.S. Cooke to author, 21 Mar. 1996. Guy MacLean has been especially helpful in commenting on Hicks and the Hicks era. Letters to author, 24 Apr., 5 May 1996; interview, 2 May 1996. For other recollections about Hicks: interviews with D.H. McNeill, 4 Apr. 1990, and Donald McInnes, 2 Aug. 1988.

32 HDH reminisces about Dalplex, NA, HDH (E), pp. 66, 46.

33 Interview with Dr Arthur Murphy, 19 July 1985. There are nine long interviews with Hicks by Derek Mann, called "The Hicks Era, 1960–1980" in successive issues of *University News*, 17 Jan. to 13 Mar. 1980. Hicks's remarks are cited from the last issue. His reflections about his last two years as president are in HDH (E), p. 71.

The paragraph on the Hicks's presidency owes much to David Cameron, Cameron to author, 24 Apr. 1996.

34 Denis Stairs to author, 19 Sept. 1996.

35 David Wegenast's poem is in *Dalhousie Gazette*, 24 Oct. 1976. The illustration is based on the poet's suggestions and is taken from the *Gazette*.

Index

At the beginning of each chapter there is an outline table of contents. Hence the index entry under Dalhousie University is narrowly focused.

D. = Dalhousie
BoG = Member of Board of Governors